Methods of Teaching

Methods of Teaching

Applying Cognitive Science to Promote Student Learning

PRESTON D. FEDEN
La Salle University

ROBERT M. VOGEL
La Salle University

Boston   Burr Ridge, IL   Dubuque, IA   Madison, WI   New York   San Francisco   St. Louis
Bangkok   Bogotá   Caracas   Kuala Lumpur   Lisbon   London   Madrid   Mexico City
Milan   Montreal   New Delhi   Santiago   Seoul   Singapore   Sydney   Taipei   Toronto

McGraw-Hill Higher Education

A Division of The **McGraw-Hill** *Companies*

METHODS OF TEACHING:
APPLYING COGNITIVE SCIENCE TO PROMOTE STUDENT LEARNING
Published by McGraw-Hill, a business unit of The McGraw-Hill Companies, Inc., 1221 Avenue of the Americas, New York, NY, 10020. Copyright © 2003 by The McGraw-Hill Companies, Inc. All rights reserved. No part of this publication may be reproduced or distributed in any form or by any means, or stored in a database or retrieval system, without the prior written consent of The McGraw-Hill Companies, Inc., including, but not limited to, in any network or other electronic storage or transmission, or broadcast for distance learning.

Some ancillaries, including electronic and print components, may not be available to customers outside the United States.

This book is printed on acid-free paper.

1 2 3 4 5 6 7 8 9 0 QPD/QPD 0 9 8 7 6 5 4 3 2

ISBN 0-07-230514-2

Editorial director: *Jane Karpacz*
Sponsoring editor: *Beth Kaufman*
Developmental editor: *Terri Wise*
Project manager: *Diane M. Folliard*
Lead production supervisor: *Lori Koetters*
Coordinator of freelance design: *Mary E. Kazak*
Photo research coordinator: *Jeremy Cheshareck*
Photo researcher: *Jennifer Blankenship*
Supplement producer: *Kathleen Boylan*
Media producer: *Lance Gerhart*
Cover Image: © *Getty Images*
Cover design: *Larry Didona*
Interior design: *Joel Davies/Z Graphics*
Compositor: *ElectraGraphics, Inc.*
Typeface: *10/12 Times Roman*
Printer: *Quebecor World/Dubuque*

Library of Congress Cataloging-in-Publication Data

Feden, Preston D.
    Methods of teaching : applying cognitive science to promote student learning / Preston D. Feden, Robert M. Vogel.
        p. cm.
    Includes bibliographical references and index.
    ISBN 0-07-230514-2 (alk. paper)
        1. Cognitive learning. 2. Cognition in children. 3. Thought and thinking—Study and teaching. I. Vogel, Robert Mark. II. Title.
LB1590.3 .F23 2003
370.15'2—dc21

2002018854

www.mhhe.com

DEDICATION

*This book is dedicated to the teachers
who have taught us, to our students,
and to those students they will teach.*

*To our families, a loving thank you
for being patient with us for the more
than 3 years we spent writing this text.*

About the Authors

PRESTON D. FEDEN is Professor of Education in the Department of Education at La Salle University. He received the Ed.D. degree in Special Education from Temple University. A former special education teacher at both the elementary and secondary levels, he has consulted widely with school districts on applying cognitive science to instructional practice. He received the Lindback Award for Distinguished Teaching in 1984, the Provost's Distinguished Faculty Award in 2001, and was the Founding Director of the La Salle University Teaching and Learning Center. In addition, his article "The New Breed Educator: Combining Elementary and Special Education Teacher Preparation" (co-authored with Gary Clabaugh) won the 1986 Outstanding Publication Award from the Teacher Education Division of the Council for Exceptional Children (CEC). His special interests are in cognitive science, teacher education, alternative assessments, and instructional practices.

ROBERT M. VOGEL is Associate Professor of Education in the Department of Education at La Salle University. He received the Ed.D. degree in Psychoeducational Processes from Temple University. A former special education teacher at the secondary level, much of his early work was in the area of experiential education and its effects on learning. More recently, he has written, received, and directed several major grants that focus on active learning. One grant, funded by the Jim Joseph Foundation, was a four-year initiative that studied, designed, and implemented flexible scheduling models and staff development programs for Jewish Day Schools, revitalizing teaching and learning in these schools around the country. He is currently developing a travel study program to promote global understanding through cultural connections. His special interests are in cooperative learning, instructional methods, classroom management, teacher education, and block (flexible) scheduling.

About the Contributors

FRANK J. MOSCA is an Associate Professor of Education at La Salle University. He has previously held positions on the faculty at The George Washington University and as a teacher of students with emotional and behavioral disabilities for both elementary and middle school children in New York State and Wisconsin. His academic interests include teacher preparation and connecting knowledge from the field of special education to that of regular education so that all students' needs are met. He received his Ph.D. in Special Education from The University of Wisconsin-Madison. Dr. Mosca authored the "Spotlight on Behavior Management" feature for each chapter of this book.

STEVEN M. BROWN is Dean of Distance Education and Director of the Melton Research Center for Jewish Education at the Jewish Theological Seminary. He holds an MA in educational technology and instructional systems and an Ed.D. in curriculum development and teaching from Teacher's College, Columbia University. Until joining a seminary in 1996, Dr. Brown served as headmaster of the Solomon Schechter Day School of Greater Philadelphia for sixteen years. He has led numerous workshops throughout the United States and abroad, and published many articles, teacher guides, and student materials. Dr. Brown authored the "Learning and Teaching in the Age of Technology" feature for each chapter of this book.

Preface

Why We Wrote This Book

We wrote this book because we believe that "business as usual" in American classrooms will not serve our society well in the coming years. Confronted with a world characterized by rapid change, classrooms that require mostly recall of factual material will not prepare students for effective participation in twenty-first century society. We present evidence in Chapter 1 to support that claim. Schools and the teachers who work in them must consider helping learners understand big ideas and important procedures upon which they can rapidly build new knowledge and skills, now and long after they have completed formal schooling.

Abundant evidence suggests that the knowledge with which students leave our schools is fragile. Many of these students *seem* to demonstrate understanding of information at various checkpoints during their school years, at least as measured by conventional tests. Yet time and again, as they progress to higher grades and after they leave our classrooms, they revert back to naïve conceptions of fundamental concepts, or they do not think to or know how to apply what they have learned to new situations. All too often they forget what they had apparently "learned" and simply lack knowledge of important information. Teachers know that this happens, and find it to be a source of personal and professional frustration.

In our view, those teachers who cling to traditional methods based largely upon the principles of behavioral psychology that dominated American education throughout most of the twentieth century must change the ways they teach. Teachers need to broaden their instructional repertoires by using more of the methods derived from contemporary research that is based on the principles of cognitive science. In that way, they are more likely to help their students change conceptually so that students' learned knowledge is less fragile. By conceptual change we mean that students shed their erroneous beliefs and naïve concepts and replace them with deeper and less naïve understandings of important facts, concepts, and ideas. That process leads to fundamental change in the way we think about and do things. Students who can tackle difficult problems in more sophisticated ways are demonstrating true conceptual change.

Currently, few of these principles and methods are used systematically in American classrooms. We wrote *Methods of Teaching: Applying Cognitive Science to Promote Student Learning* to help prospective and currently licensed teachers learn how to apply principles of cognitive science in their classrooms in order to help their students change conceptually. Recent research from highly regarded academic centers makes clear that it is students' change from novice to more expert representations of facts, concepts, and procedures, that constitutes *real* learning. Students do not demonstrate *real* learning by parroting back what their teachers tell them, or by applying memorized rituals to solve problems.

Our Intended Audience

We wrote this book primarily for preservice teachers. Nevertheless, we believe that it can be a source of inspiration for experienced in-service teachers as well. Most of the examples we use come from practicing teachers who have used current research in cognitive science to develop powerful instruction.

Preservice teachers for whom this book is appropriate will most likely be enrolled in some type of general methods course. Typically, they will be second- or third-year students with a basic understanding of educational psychology. These general methods courses have various titles, but they all address strategies and skills for teaching in grades kindergarten through 12. We believe, for the reasons we explain in Chapter 6, that this book can also be used for those preparing to be special education teachers. Those responsible for providing in-service programs for currently practicing teachers might find this book useful in conjunction with these programs. We have presented the ideas in this book to well over one thousand teachers during staff development sessions, and they report having success using these ideas.

Overview of the Contents

A quick overview of the chapters in this book will show the importance we give to *change, deep understanding,* and *student-centered learning.*

Section I: Why Change?

In Chapter 1, Why Change the Way We Teach?, we introduce the theme of the book and set the context for all subsequent chapters. This book tells a story. The story is about the need for change, and how teachers can promote that change. In this chapter we highlight two aspects of change: the need to help students change conceptually, and the need to change traditional instructional practices in order to facilitate that conceptual change.

Section II: Changing Classroom Practices to Promote Deep Understanding

In Chapter 2, Powerful Principles from Theoretical Perspectives, we address several contemporary theories that can help us broaden our practices beyond those based on traditional behavioral theory. These contemporary theories present today's teachers with important theoretical principles that can help them bring about students' deep learning. Social cognitive, contextualist, information processing, and motivation theories all suggest that humans learn best in cooperation with one another by actively processing information that they find personally meaningful.

In Chapter 3, Practical Applications of Powerful Principles, we detail the powerful principles derived from contemporary theory that can help teachers make the shift from teacher-centered practices to more student-centered practices. We focus on cooperative learning and the importance of visualization and imagery, organization, and elaboration as general strategies for promoting deep understanding. We also discuss the importance of providing students with frequent practice opportunities and specific feedback. Finally, in this chapter we introduce the 4MAT system, focusing on its use in classroom settings to motivate learners.

Chapter 4, Using Powerful Instructional Strategies, builds on the general principles of learning presented in Chapter 3, providing specific strategies consistent with those principles to help us change practices dominated by teacher talk to practices dominated by students' active learning. We present questioning, problem-based learning, project learning, and several other strategies, and offer examples of each.

Section III: Changing Classroom Practices to Accommodate Learner Differences

In Chapter 5, Teaching and Learning Styles, we help teachers move away from "one size fits all" teaching practices by making explicit some of the ways in which individuals differ from one another. We present race, culture, gender, psychological type, mind styles, 4MAT, and multiple intelligence theory as ways to understand and accommodate some of the differences found among students.

In Chapter 6, Powerful Principles Applied to Special Education, we urge teachers to resist use of rote drill and practice techniques that too often dominate special education classrooms. We promote the use of the same powerful principles advocated for nondisabled students with students who happen to be disabled. The essential point of the chapter is that although we all differ from one another in many ways, students with learning and behavioral disabilities do not differ in any qualitatively different way from the rest of us. In that regard, they are more similar to than different from other students.

Section IV: Changes Needed to Support Powerful Classroom Practices

In Chapter 7, From Tests to Authentic Performances, we address the need to change the way we assess student learning by going well beyond traditional testing methods. In this chapter we explore ways to broaden assessment strategies so that they match the kinds of authentic tasks required in the "real" world. Further, we present the use of rubrics to evaluate student performance using alternative, authentic assessments.

In Chapter 8, Core Concepts, Generative Topics, Essential Questions, and Integrated Themes, we contend that teachers must change the way they think about "covering" the curriculum. Many years ago we might have been able to teach learners in school much of what they needed to know during their lifetimes. This is no longer possible. The unprecedented explosion of new information is unlikely to abate. The rise of technology and the media permit widespread and fast access to this information. In this chapter we address ways that teachers can use big ideas and compelling questions to help their students learn subject matter content and skills, and manage all the information that will bombard them during their lifetimes.

Section V: Putting It All Together

Chapter 9, A Blueprint for Change, serves as the culminating chapter of the book. In this chapter we offer several "tools" that may be used to think about, plan for, implement, and evaluate instruction to promote deep understanding among learners and, hence, true conceptual change.

Some Other Things You Should Know

- Our combined 60-plus years of teaching experience support what the research from cognitive science suggests—that exposing students (at any level, including higher education) to lots of material in insufficient depth has very little impact. Unless teacher education students have the time to elaborate on the material, they will most likely hold onto naïve conceptions of teaching and learning, or simply forget most of what they were supposed to learn. What they do remember they may apply in mechanical fashion. Therefore, in this book we focus on core concepts derived from research in cognitive science, and some of the practical applications of these concepts. We intend to encourage real conceptual change among those who read this textbook.

- We carefully designed the pedagogical elements of this book to encourage active learning on the part of those who read it. We strongly encourage students to use these pedagogical elements. These elements give the book a much greater impact, and free up class time for more student-initiated discussions and contributions.

- Although teaching is a very important endeavor, it need not, indeed should not, be humorless. Teachers should have fun teaching. We enjoy our students. We want to convey that to the students who read this book. So, we wrote the book in an informal and conversational style. And to set the tone, every chapter begins with a cartoon that is relevant to the content that the chapter addresses!

- Finally, *we have written the book that we had to write.* You might find it to be a bit different from traditional methods books. We have written it to appeal to a number of different learning styles. We use *real examples* from the work of *real teachers.* Only minor editing of their work has been done, and only with their permission, to make a point clearer for the reader. These examples represent the best efforts of practicing professional educators to put to use the powerful principles and strategies needed in today's classrooms.

Pedagogical Features

We have tried our best to model in this book the very principles and strategies that we advocate. One important feature is our use of a *thematic* element. The theme of *change* provides a unifying thread throughout the entire book. This theme helps students make connections among and between facts, concepts, and procedures.

A second important feature is the element of *integration.* Too often planning, behavior management, and technology appear in their own separate chapters, but the fact is that planning is done in the context of trying to teach something. It is not done in isolation, so we believe it should be presented in association with each chapter. Likewise, students' behaviors do not occur in a vacuum. Their behavior occurs in the context of classroom activity. So we address behavior management in the context of each chapter. Finally, technology is used in support of instruction, and so we have included it in each chapter.

A third important element is *interaction.* This is perhaps the most important element. We designed a number of features that encourage students to interact with the information in the text. These features are easily identified by their associated symbols. Interactive features include the following:

◎ *Core Concepts* are clearly stated at the beginning of each chapter. These core concepts provide focus on the essential point of each chapter.

⊙ᴛ Organizers, called *Getting to the Core,* provide an advance look at the key points in each chapter. Periodically, we revisit the organizers, asking students to summarize the chapter's key points in their own words. At the end of each chapter, the organizers help students review their responses for accuracy. We hope, too, that the organizers will help students make connections and see the big picture.

Scenarios present situations related to chapter content. These scenarios give students an opportunity to think about real teaching situations and how they might be handled. Students can respond to questions about the scenarios before reading the chapter, and then once again after completing the chapter. Finally, they can compare their responses to those written by experienced teachers.

 In *Voices from the Field,* experienced teachers offer their responses to the scenarios.

 Each chapter includes *Think about it* boxes designed for learner reflection on selected material.

 Planning for Instruction guides students step-by-step through the development of a unit and a lesson plan as they work through each chapter.

 In each chapter, *Spotlight on Behavior Management* focuses on behavior management in the context of the core concept for that particular chapter by addressing the question so many students ask as they plan their lessons—"But will they behave?"

 In each chapter, *Learning and Teaching in the Age of Technology* connects technology to each of the book's core concepts, and provides teaching tips and Internet sites that will be useful to current and prospective teachers.

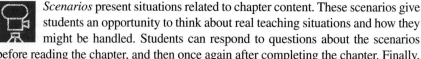 *A Person Who Helped Create Change.* We include these as our way of acknowledging a few of those people whom we feel have made extraordinary contributions to helping our schools and classrooms change for the better. As educators, we should never forget these people; nor should we underestimate the passion and commitment that led them to distinguish themselves. Including them in a prominent way in this book is our way of showing appreciation for their contributions, and our way of inspiring students to act for positive change in education.

ACKNOWLEDGMENTS

Special thanks to our wives, Carol and Marlyn, for their love, support, and assistance with this project, and to our friends and colleagues Frank Mosca and Steve Brown for their excellent contributions to each chapter in this textbook. We also offer our thanks and gratitude to our colleagues Bernice McCarthy and Susan Morris for helping us to incorporate the 4MAT System into the chapters of this textbook. We are grateful to our colleagues and friends, David Hottenstein and Richard Iano, for starting us on the path that led to this book.

We also thank the following reviewers whose comments and insights provided much appreciated guidance as we revised the pages in this textbook:

Angelo Alcala, University of Texas-Arlington; Anita Baker, Baylor University; Joseph Bondi, University of Southern Florida; Rita F. Braun, University of Maryland; Edwidge C. Bryant, University of North Florida; Sharon Y. Cowan, East Central University; Carolyn Downey, San Diego State University; Anthony J. Evangelisto, The

College of New Jersey; Roland Frank, Salisbury State University; Susan Frase, Indiana Wesleyan University; Carrie Geiger, University of Florida; Kay Gibson, Wichita State University; Mary Lynn Hamilton, University of Kansas; Pat Hays, Northern Arizona University; Howard Jones, University of Houston; Cherrie Kassem, Ramapo College of New Jersey; Catharine Knight, University of Akron; Bob Lowe, Angelo State University; Linda McKinney, University of Oklahoma; Otherine Neisler, Boston College; Karen Peterson, Governors State University; Sarah Peterson, Duquesne University; Judy Reinhartz, University of Texas-Arlington; Tamara Roberts, Grambling State University; John Roseman, University of La Verne; Patricia Ryan, Otterbein College; Judy Rymer, California State University-San Bernardino; Sharon Shrock, Southern Illinois University; Melba Spooner, University of North Carolina-Charlotte; Karen Sweeney, Wayne State College; Jeanne L. Tunks, Southern Methodist University; Nancy P. Wilder, University of Memphis; Jeanette H. Willert, Canisius College; Radine Yarbrough, University of Memphis; Barbara Young, Middle Tennessee State University

We value the special relationships we have with so many students and teachers with whom we have worked over the years. Those who graciously contributed their work and enabled us to feature authentic examples of cognitive science applied in classrooms include Laura Alampi, Jan Barbee, Ann Bell, Toba Bernstein, Anne Boagni, Leonard Buscemi, Danielle Campese, Kelly Chan, Ruth Desiderio, Kathleen DiTanna, Steve Downs, Krista Fager, Violet Feden, Katrina Girone, Genevieve Hill, Staci Horne, Roxanne Hughes, Allison Kane, Lauren Leiter, Karen Loeschner, Maria Matlack, Terri McAllister, Christopher McCool, Kristie McGovern, Kathleen McGrother, Erin McVan, Teresa Perlowski, Leslie Pugach, Steve Rebl, Sasha Roa, Linda Schaffzin, Jennifer Seery, Rachel Sohn, Jordan Sonnenblick, Linwood Stevens, Heather Tyrell, Marlyn Vogel, Donna Wake, Sara Weisman-Shein, and Staci Wenitsky.

Finally, our heartfelt thanks to the team at McGraw-Hill for their patience, guidance, and help with all phases of the development of this book:

Jane Karpacz, Editorial Director	Lori Koetters, Production Supervisor
Beth Kaufman, Sponsoring Editor	Mary Kazak, Designer
Terri Wise, Developmental Editor	Jeremy Cheshareck, Photo Research Coordinator
Diane Folliard, Project Manager	Matthew Perry, Supplement Producer

PRESTON D. FEDEN
La Salle University

ROBERT M. VOGEL
La Salle University

Contents

Why Change?

CHAPTER 1

Why Change the Way We Teach?

 ## SCENARIO

Heather was a typical student throughout her elementary, middle, and high school years. She never found school to be particularly difficult, or for that matter, particularly challenging. Earning good grades was easy because of her ability to retain large amounts of information and give to the teachers exactly what was expected. She was attentive in class, took good notes, and generally behaved in the manner expected by teachers and administrators. She graduated with a solid B average. She went on to a respected liberal arts college where she majored in English and secondary education. Heather's program prepared her well for using effective instructional strategies, understanding the developmental levels of children, and making the necessary curriculum adjustments needed to best succeed with the increasingly diverse groups found in modern-day classrooms. Heather felt well prepared to teach English.

After four weeks of student teaching in a middle school setting, she became increasingly puzzled and confused by her own reaction to the students. In many ways the school seemed similar to the middle school she had attended not more than 10 years ago. But in some ways it was *very* different. In many of the classrooms, desks were set up in rows, just as she remembered. A few classrooms had the desks grouped in fours. Just about all of the rooms were equipped with at least one computer. Computers housed in two labs, each with 35 computers, supplemented these classroom computers. Classrooms were brightly decorated with colorful bulletin boards, similar to what she remembered from when she was in the seventh grade. She also noticed that the classrooms were filled with books, dictionaries, workbooks, and stacks of worksheets. The bell schedule was the same as she remembered, 50-minute instructional periods and a 35-minute lunch period. Study halls were still being used. She recalled fondly that these study halls provided students with opportunities to sleep, pass notes, get into trouble, and (maybe) study.

Although the school's physical environment and the approaches the teachers used appeared similar to what she experienced, the students somehow seemed very different. She could see a big difference in the ways these children approached school and learning compared to how she remembered approaching school and learning. These students were not content with just listening to the teacher, doing book reports, taking multiple-choice tests, and completing worksheets. They were doing well on the tests, but demonstrated little evidence of remembering the information a week or two later. Heather was really bothered that the students had difficulty relating what they learned in class to the world outside. They wanted more activity and had difficulty just sitting at their desks. On the other hand, the students didn't appear to want to be substantially challenged in their thinking, preferring "fun" to substance.

So many of the students seemed to come from dysfunctional families. Perhaps because of this, or for some other reason, many of the children had little support at home with homework. The kids knew all the television programs that aired during the week and Heather learned that the average child was clocking in about six hours of television a day. That was a lot more than she had been allowed! These children had amazing computer skills for playing games and "surfing the Web," but had little ability to use word processing and database programs. Even using the Internet for academic research was challenging for them because they didn't know how to sort through all the information they were able to retrieve. Still, the teachers in the school were not teaching much differently than what Heather remembered from 10 years ago. It was as if the information age had passed them by.

Getting to the Core

◎ **CORE CONCEPT** Change is inevitable. Society has changed, kids have changed, and what we know about how humans learn has changed. But schools and the way teachers teach have not changed substantially in modern times. And, surprisingly, there is compelling evidence that learners themselves can proceed successfully through formal education *without* changing very much, at least conceptually!

Has Society Changed That Much?

Have Schools Changed?

Should Schools Change?
- Setting the Record Straight about Public Education
- The Context of Schooling

Should Teaching Change?
- Deep Understanding versus Surface Learning
- Promoting Conceptual Change
- The Expanding Knowledge Base about How People Learn

How Should Schools and Teaching Change?

How Can Teachers Change?

What If Schools and Teaching Changed?

How Can Planning for Instruction Change?

> **?** *If you were a teacher in this school, would you share Heather's concerns? What would concern you the most? Why? What course of action would you propose to your colleagues to address the concern? What changes might you suggest?*

INTRODUCTION

"... while it is possible to change without improving, it is impossible to improve without changing."

—Joseph Carroll
(Source: J. Carroll. 1994. The Copernican Plan Evaluated: The Evolution of a Revolution. Phi Delta Kappan *[May: 108.])*

This chapter begins our story by introducing change. In the context of this book, change refers to several things. It refers to the rather stunning change in our modern way of living. It refers to existing paradigms for teaching and learning that currently are being challenged, and leaves open the possibility that they will change. It also refers to conceptual change, or lack thereof, among learners in our classrooms. What exactly do we mean by conceptual change? When people change conceptually they not only *retain* facts, ideas, and concepts, but also are able to truly *understand* them and put these ideas, facts, and concepts to *use*. If it is true that so many learners can proceed through so much education *without* changing conceptually, then it is time to change the way we teach them.

Has Society Changed That Much?

Simply put, most everything around us has, and continues to, change. During the twentieth century so much has changed that people joke that if Rip Van Winkle woke up today, he would recognize virtually nothing around him. It's really not a joke at all. It's true! And in the last two decades the pace of change has been frenetic. In view of these changes, it just makes sense that schools, and especially the teaching that goes on inside and outside their walls, must also keep changing in order to fulfill their mission to society.

Think about it . . . If you are ill, how will a doctor's treatment differ today compared with 50 or 100 years ago?

How is a lawyer's practice different today than it was 75 years ago?

When you deposit money into a bank account, what options do you have for making that deposit today that you did not have just 10 years ago?

Now think about schools. How have they changed in your relatively brief time in them (maybe 12 years)?

Have Schools Changed?

Schools have not changed very much. To set the stage for the ensuing discussion of change, let us get a benchmark for what schools were commonly like yesterday, and what they are commonly like today. In the distant past, at the beginning of the twentieth century, lecture was the most commonly used mode of instruction. Bells rang to signal changing class periods. Students went from room to room, and subject to subject, with the occasional "special" in art, music, and physical education. Learners listened and took notes, and dutifully reviewed these notes in order to pass tests administered by their teachers. In elementary schools, the major differences were that students stayed in the same room for all subjects, and worksheets took the place of extensive note taking.

When competing for limited seats, as when applying to college, students prepared themselves to take more formal, standardized tests. These were typically of the multiple-choice variety, and compared students to one another across schools, states, and even the nation.

The schools were so similar in these procedures that one could easily feel at home in virtually any school, in any school district, in any city, in any state, and in any part of the country. This also includes postsecondary education, the very kind in which you are now engaged! Almost 40 years ago, McKeachie wrote, "college teaching and lecturing have been so long associated that when one pictures a college professor in the classroom, he almost invariably pictures him as lecturing" (cited in Gage 1963, 1125).

Are today's schools much different? In 1983, John Goodlad did an extensive study of schooling. He found that "teachers appear to teach within a very limited repertoire of pedagogical alternatives emphasizing their own talk and the monitoring of seatwork. The customary pedagogy places the teacher very much in control. Few activities call for or even permit active student planning, follow through, and evaluation" (1983, 467). Cuban (1993) studied constancy and change in American classrooms from 1880 to 1990. He found that in high schools "the basic instructional sequences and patterns in the core academic subjects have remained teacher-centered since the turn of the century"

	1900	2000
Typical Role of Teacher	Directive Lecturer	Directive Lecturer
Typical Role of Student	Passive Reactive Work alone	Passive Reactive Work alone
Typical Source of Motivation	Extrinsic	Extrinsic
Typical Learning Environment	Structured	Structured
How Knowledge Is Acquired	Through direct instruction	Through direct instruction

(273). In elementary schools, and especially in the primary grades, he found that some student-centered practices had emerged. But he also noted that these practices were restricted to just a few methods (such as learning centers, small group instruction, and the use of tables rather than desks). And he also noted that only about one-fourth of the teachers in any given school district used these "new" ideas. In concluding, Cuban pointed out that "the core of classroom practices in all grades, anchored in the teacher's authority to determine what content to teach and what methods to use, endured as it had since the turn of the century" (204). As recently as 1999 Howard Gardner wrote, after reflecting back on specific events and advances during the twentieth century, "During the same century that has seen such epochal events and scientific advances the texture of daily schooling has changed relatively little, particularly at the pre-collegiate level" (1999, 242).

We agree with him, except for the implication that college-level education has changed more than basic education. At least in terms of instruction, we believe that postsecondary classrooms distinguish themselves only by being the *most* resistant to change. In 1980, Blackburn Pellino, Bobing, and O'Connell wrote "Give a faculty almost any kind of class in any subject, large or small, upper or lower division, and they will lecture" (1980, 41). More recently, Thielens (1987) wrote that an extensive survey of U.S. university professors found lecturing to be the primary mode of instruction for most of them. As an indication that things *still* have not changed much in higher education, Guskin (1994) wrote, "The primary learning environment for undergraduate students, the fairly passive lecture-discussion format where faculty talk and most students listen, is contrary to almost every principle of optimal settings for student learning" (18).

Thielens (1987) found that lecture is the primary method of instruction used at the university level by:

- 89% of physical scientists and mathematicians.

- 81% of social scientists.

- 61% of the humanities faculty (although 81% of the art historians and 90% of the philosophers lecture).

Why do we write so much about higher education in a book that is meant to help you teach in elementary and secondary education classrooms? We have two good reasons. First, Guskin and the others we quoted above could be just as easily writing about basic, rather than higher, education. Second, if you are reading this book the chances are good that *you* are now in a higher-education setting. Think about what we write here in terms of your current experiences on your campus. Ask your parents what classrooms were like when they attended college. Ask especially about the way instruction was conducted. Compare their stories to your experiences. We would be surprised if you find that very much has changed.

We are still giving plenty of paper and pencil tests to our students. And the formal, standardized tests are as important as ever. They factor heavily into who gets into special academic programs in elementary, middle, and high school. They determine who is accepted to what college or university, law school, trade school, and the like. They often decide who gets scholarship money. They are used to judge one's suitability for entry into professions at the completion of a program of studies.

Much of what goes on in schools, and especially the teaching in those schools, is the same today as it was 100 years ago. Many teachers, believing that people learn best through direct instruction, impart lots of information to their students using lectures and very directed discussion. Students sit passively at desks, their major activity being only to copy notes or fill in worksheets and answer occasional questions on factual information. The classroom is very structured to make things efficient. Teachers motivate students mostly through the use of grades or, for the most reticent, more tangible rewards and punishments. Because these are imposed on us, they are called extrinsic motivators, in contrast to motivation that comes from within us, called intrinsic motivation. Schools, you see, have not changed much over the past century. That's a long time for things to stay the same.

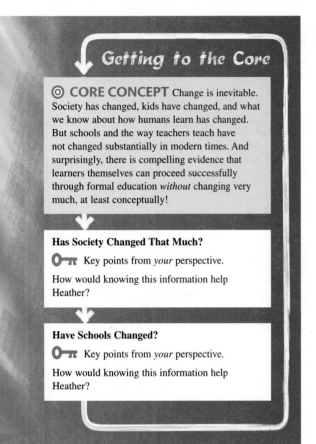

Getting to the Core

◎ **CORE CONCEPT** Change is inevitable. Society has changed, kids have changed, and what we know about how humans learn has changed. But schools and the way teachers teach have not changed substantially in modern times. And surprisingly, there is compelling evidence that learners themselves can proceed successfully through formal education *without* changing very much, at least conceptually!

Has Society Changed That Much?

🔑 Key points from *your* perspective.

How would knowing this information help Heather?

Have Schools Changed?

🔑 Key points from *your* perspective.

How would knowing this information help Heather?

Should Schools Change?

The short answer to the question "Should schools change?" is yes. But not so drastically as many people, especially politicians and the popular press, say they should. You see, the answer is not so clear cut as it first seems. That is because there are well-documented sources of evidence that schools, and the teachers who work in them, do a pretty good job for our society. This is especially true given the constraints put on them and the task they are asked to perform—to get an increasingly diverse group of learners to understand and use a great deal of knowledge (Berliner and Biddle 1995; Schneider and Houston 1993; Bracey 1995; Jennings 1996). Berliner and Biddle (1995) assert that antischool propagandists have taken advantage of Americans' longstanding inclination to criticize schools by manufacturing a crisis that simply does not exist. This manufactured crisis, they say, is fueled by a popular press that prefers bad news to good news, and a public that is generally ignorant about statistics and statistical analyses used to create the impression that schools are worse than they actually are.

Setting the Record Straight about Public Education

Will Rogers is an American icon. During his lifetime, this down-home philosopher/humorist gave us a great deal of folksy advice and offered us his valuable insights. He is credited with once having said, "The schools aren't as good as they used to be, but then they never were." Those words might well sum up the current sentiment. It seems that members of each older generation criticize the younger generation, despite the fact that they raised these youngsters. Apparently each generation remembers with great nostalgia "the good old days." Passing time, most likely, distorts the reality that members of the older generations recall. So it often seems that the good old days were much better than they really were.

Does the evidence support this nostalgic view of days gone by? Hirschberg (1999) examined how today's schools stack up against schools as they were in 1950. He asked the question, "Just how bad are our schools?" He then noted declining SAT scores, the lack of general knowledge among the populace, and a number of other contemporary problems. Finally, after asking if all of this didn't suggest that our schools are performing less well than they did 50 years ago, he said flatly "Don't you believe it!" His article continued on to document the myriad of problems with the schools back then, and especially the large number of minority students for whom education was unquestionably substandard.

The Sandia report (1993) provided what were arguably the most compelling "hard" data that suggested American education was not failing miserably. Commissioned in 1990 by Secretary of Energy James Watkins to report on the state of basic education in America, researchers from the Sandia National Laboratories studied existing data from various agencies and concluded, "To our surprise, on nearly every measure, we found steady or slightly improving trends" (Carson, Huelskamp, and Woodall 1993, 259). This report set off a flurry of offshoots. Perhaps it was Gerald Bracey who had done the best job of disseminating information that the schools were not nearly so bad as many people said they were. In an attempt to "set the record straight," Bracey (1997) responded to eighteen misconceptions about public education in the United States. He offered common criticisms that stem from these misconceptions, and then provided pertinent data and a no-nonsense reply to the criticisms based on those data. For example, in response to the common criticism, "Kids don't know as much as they used to," Bracey suggested the following responses:

1. The bulk of the evidence shows that U.S. students today read better than ever, know more math and science, and know at least as much about literature and history as their parents and grandparents did, and probably more.

2. You can remind the skeptic that most of what he or she knows has probably been learned in the many years since leaving school. You can also remind people

---

18 Misconceptions Addressed by Gerald Bracey

The following are commonly held beliefs that, when subjected to serious investigation, just do *not* hold true.

1. The United States spends more money on its public schools than any other nation in the world.

2. Money doesn't matter.

3. Spending on public schools has risen, but test scores are flat.

4. SAT scores have plummeted.

5. The proportion of students scoring very high on the SAT has plummeted.

6. Kids don't know as much as they used to.

7. In comparing what our kids know with what German and Japanese kids know, our kids don't know much.

8. The dropout rate is awful and getting worse.

9. Private schools get better results than public schools.

10. Charter schools or school choice are the only solutions to school problems.

11. Lousy schools are producing a lousy workforce that is killing us in the global marketplace.

12. Schools are not preparing students for work.

13. We have or will have a shortage of scientists, mathematicians, and engineers.

14. School productivity is being smothered by an administrative blob.

15. Teachers should be held accountable for their students' test scores.

16. Students who go into teaching are dumber than those who go into other fields.

17. Educators are spending too much time teaching kids to feel good about themselves and not enough time teaching academics.

18. Schools are spending too much money on special education.

From: Setting the Record Straight: Responses to Misconceptions About Public Education in the United States *by Gerald W. Bracey. Alexandria, VA: Association for Supervision and Curriculum Development. Copyright © 1997 ASCD. Reprinted by permission. All rights reserved.*

that those who find something easy to accomplish too often do not understand that the same accomplishments can be difficult for others. The people who have evaluated what school children know and can do are the people who find book learning the easiest thing in the world to do.

3. You can accuse the speakers of nostalgia mongering. (Bracey 1997, 67)

See the ways our lives are changing—or have changed (Courtesy of Francisco Cruz/Super Stock).

The Context of Schooling

Perhaps things are not so bad as many people think. Still, school reformer Philip Schlechty points out that Americans' dissatisfaction with their schools has a long history. He reiterates the point previously made that the problems identified by the current group of critics—low standards and poor discipline—have been identified in the past as well. Schlechty goes on to make a very crucial point for our current story about change. So far we have focused on what *has not* changed. Schlechty asserts that what *has* changed "is the context in which these problems are manifested, for the schools have changed very little—and *that* is the problem. Unless the schools can be changed to accommodate the new context in which they exist, they not only will not get better; they are almost certain to get worse" (1997, 7).

Contexts Then and Now

Society has changed. There is every reason to believe that it will continue to change even more rapidly in the future. As a society, we have moved well past our agrarian years and even our industrial revolution, to what is now called the age of technology. Schools that served us well in our agrarian years, and the structures that define them no longer adequately serve contemporary society. For example, agrarian society required labor-intensive work in fields, and just a basic knowledge of reading, writing, and arithmetic. A primarily agrarian subculture of mainstream American culture, the Amish or Plain People, even today require only an eighth-grade education of their children. Yet despite the fact that mainstream America has long since passed the agrarian age, schools still honor a throwback to those days when children were needed during the summer months to work on the farms. This throwback is called summer vacation. It is not at all clear that this tradition continues to serve contemporary society, or our children, very well.

As society moved into the postagrarian age, great factories arose to produce goods for people, and manufacturing drove much of America's economy. People needed basic skills to conduct their personal and work lives satisfactorily, and more and more people entered service fields and rose to management levels created by these businesses. These people needed even higher education. This period also saw tremendous advances in the field of medicine, beginning with the discovery of penicillin, which gave birth to antibiotics, and which began an era of medical research that has significantly lengthened life expectancies and the quality of those lives.

> **Think about it . . .**
>
> What other traditions or practices continue today that do not suit contemporary society? Make a list, and then mark those you would change, and those you would not change, and tell why.

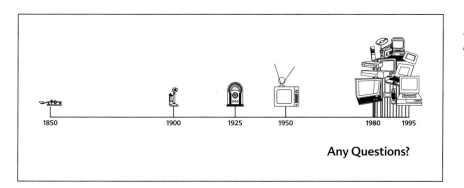

(Source: Property of AT&T Archives. Reprinted by permission of AT&T.)

Any Questions?

From this age came two important change-related events. The first was that the factory model of mass-producing goods was very successful, and American education began to use it as the model for schools (Feden, Vogel, and Clabaugh 1992). Graduates were stamped out cookie-cutter style. Of course, that may have served the times. After all, change happened more slowly then, and it could be argued that all students needed to have the same knowledge, that we could teach them the basics in a 12-year academic program, and that this knowledge would serve them during their entire life span.

But the second change that occurred because of rapid and dramatic advances in medicine managed to increase life spans to the point where many people could out-live several periods of change in a rapidly changing society. That alone has dramat-ically changed the context in which teaching occurs. For one thing, it has sparked a good deal of debate about whether or not all students should share a common *core* of knowledge (see Hirsch 1996; Sizer 1996; Gardner 1999) because they live in an age where information proliferates at a fast rate. This in turn has caused a debate about whether or not teachers can directly impart that core of knowledge, or any knowledge, in a lasting way to their learners. But there is no debate about the most critically important dimension concerning "why change." For the first time ever, it is simply not possible to teach people the knowledge and skills that they will need to serve them a lifetime. Society changes too quickly, and we live too long. Current estimates are that during the lives of today's students, total human knowledge will redouble at least four times. Human beings no longer have the possibility of learn-ing during their school years everything that they will need to prepare them for long lives as citizens in a democratic society. Teachers do not have the luxury, then, of simply imparting facts that students are supposed to retain throughout their lives.

Society is not the only thing that has changed. Children have changed, too. All of these societal changes have, in a fashion that we perhaps do not yet fully understand, changed the learners who now enter our classrooms. Stratton (1995) addressed how students have changed in a short booklet of the same title. A survey of 50 school superintendents, all finalists for the Superintendent of the Year award, asked them to identify 10 major ways students had changed since the 1960s, or major changes that have affected students. Their list follows:

- The number of dysfunctional families has grown.
- High technology has influenced school, work, and home life.
- Children are threatened by crime, violence, ignorance, and poverty.
- Communities are changing, becoming more diverse.
- Mass media grips our children, giving them more knowledge at an earlier age.

- Students question authority and shun traditional values, responsibilities.
- A hurry-up society often lacks a sense of community.
- Changing workplaces create demands for higher levels of literacy.
- Knowledge about learning styles demands new kinds of education.
- Peers exert a powerful influence on values. (Stratton 1995, 9)

Few teachers, from early childhood education to university-level educators, would argue with the claim that students have changed, although they might take issue with one or more of the above, preferring their own pet changes over those of the superintendents.

Because learners have changed in these and other ways, schools must also change. In fact, many of the items on the list above have been accorded their own places in the school curriculum. Courses related to computer literacy, AIDS education, drug and alcohol awareness, multicultural education, character education, and self-esteem have proliferated. Indeed, they have more often than not been mandated. Society has historically turned to our nation's schools not only to teach basic skills such as reading, writing, and arithmetic, but also to educate our youth about current issues as well. In this way, because of the mandates, schools have changed. But they have not changed in response to the increasingly diverse group of learners in them. They have not changed very much pedagogically to adjust for the high-tech environment in which today's children grow from their earliest years. And they have not changed much in their emphasis on facts rather than on helping learners make sense of the vast amount of information that now bombards them at a staggering rate of speed.

As an aside, at this point it might occur to you that there *have* been responses to some of the characteristics of modern-day learners. Ironically, programs established to address alcohol, drugs, and other contemporary problems have also created a dilemma for teachers and school administrators. As mandates increase, there are fewer hours available in the school day in which to help learners master the basic skills and knowledge that we have asserted they will need in this information age. Later in this book we shall argue that curriculum and instruction based upon core concepts will be needed to craft instruction and produce learning in ways that integrate the various topics about which learners must be knowledgeable.

SPOTLIGHT ON BEHAVIOR MANAGEMENT

"But will they behave?"

One of the most important concerns of new and experienced teachers is classroom management and discipline. Because this area is so important, we have decided to incorporate a special section on this topic in each chapter of this textbook. The purpose of this integration is to encourage you to regard behavior management as an integral part of every aspect of teaching.

A Change in Perspective

Shortly before our student teachers make their way to field placements they often ask, "But will they behave?" We remind them that they have been prepared to examine and meet the needs of their students. We remind them that if they challenge their students and keep them engaged, there is little time remaining for students to

⊙ **CORE CONCEPT** Change is inevitable. Society has changed, kids have changed, and what we know about how humans learn has changed. But schools and the way teachers teach have not changed substantially in modern times. And surprisingly, there is compelling evidence that learners themselves can proceed successfully through formal education without changing very much, at least conceptually!

misbehave. We suggest that the better they get to know their students, the better they will be able to fulfill their roles as developmentally oriented teachers.

Consider your own educational experience. In which classrooms did you or your classmates tend to get talkative, pass notes, or tune out? Was it in the classrooms where you were challenged and engaged? Was it in front of the teacher with whom you felt a personal connection? In the now out-of-print children's book, *The Geranium on the Window Sill Just Died but Teacher You Went Right On,* Cullum's (1971) young narrator says, "You're a good storyteller teacher, honest! And that's when I never have to be excused" (18).

Plainly stated, when your students are interested and engaged, they rarely misbehave. So teachers can solve the majority of classroom management worries simply by using the powerful strategies described in this book and by making real connections with their students. Alas, we can hear you from here: "But you just finished explaining how the world has changed. You argued that students are different now. They bring to school the baggage of a more 'dysfunctional' society! I have heard about and even witnessed problems in schools between teachers and students. What about the big problems?"

Our response is that we want to challenge the traditional perspective and weave through this text a very powerful model that will help you understand the nature of student-teacher conflict. But before we get to the actual model, we must come back to the concept of change. Do you remember specific classroom rules and school expectations from your own educational experience? Think about how those rules were enforced. What happened when students followed the rules? What happened when they didn't?

Typically, when students deviate from the teacher's or school's expectations they are sanctioned. If they

deviate too often, they are not allowed to remain in the classroom. If they accrue too many sanctions, they may be suspended from school. If the student's offense is severe enough or if too many suspensions add up, expulsion may be the final step. It seems to be a continual process of the student acting and the school staff reacting. Little time or effort is put into the development of new skills in these situations. In fact, during times of conflict, teaching and learning usually get put on hold. A prime opportunity for teaching and learning has been lost. The crisis is dealt with, then we return to the educational program—if we can. Perhaps the long-lived and powerful influence of behaviorism in American education has clouded our ability to look at the problem of managing teacher-student conflict from other perspectives.

Consider this: In Chinese the word "crisis" is made up of two distinct characters. They are "danger" and *"opportunity."* What if, rather than put teaching  and learning on hold, we changed our perspective and looked for the teaching and learning *opportunities* inherent in conflict? What if teachers were able to shift their focus from the behavior itself to *why* the behavior is occurring? Wouldn't teachers then be in a better position to teach their students new and productive ways to solve problems? What if students understood that their teachers were there to help them learn these skills? Wouldn't we then be able to build stronger, more productive relationships with our students?

Implied in the above questions is a change in the way we look at behavior and the relationship between teachers and students. This change requires a shift in theoretical orientation. The psychodynamic approach, with its roots in the work of Sigmund Freud, provides this alternate perspective. Freud's daughter, Anna Freud, and other psychologists have since expanded on Freud's original ideas and applied them to working with children. These psychologists have become known as neo-Freudians. This perspective requires a fundamental shift in the way we interpret behavior. Rather than seeing behavior as a result of stimuli in the immediate environment, psychoeducators see behavior as internal or as a result of thoughts and feelings. The difference is that whereas behaviorists focus on the behavior itself, psychoeducators see "observable behaviors, no matter how annoying or noxious, [as] the tip of the iceberg"

(Danforth and Boyle 2000, 11). Psychoeducators puzzle about *why* behaviors occur.

The resulting intervention is, of course, markedly different. The behaviorist, acting in the here and now, reinforces the desirable behavior or attempts to extinguish the undesirable. The psychoeducator intervenes by accepting and interpreting the behavior while "foster[ing] the child's individuality, security, and self-respect. Emphasis is on utilizing the child's potential to resolve his or her emotional conflicts and to support the child's movement toward emotional adjustment" (Bauer and Shea 2000, 34–35).

This seemingly small shift from seeing the "what" of behavior to looking for the "why" of behavior will lead to powerful new insights about yourself and your students and how you interact during times of conflict. However, we are certain this is easier said than done. We are human. Conflict invariably involves emotions— thoughts and feelings. Our own emotions can have a powerful effect on our actions as teachers.

When we have planned what we believe to be an effective and exciting lesson, we want it to go well. We want our students to get the most out of it. Then Juan starts behaving in a way that interrupts the class. He is making faces at Eliza. We attempt to manage his behavior with some of the surface techniques we learned in our methods class. But what we don't know at the moment is the fact that Juan and Eliza were arguing on the bus on the way to school. Eliza was teasing Juan about his unkempt appearance. Other students begin to pay more attention to them than to our beautiful manipulatives. Juan is quickly becoming more engaging than our lesson! That stirs up some emotion in us, the teachers! Naturally focusing on the perceived troublemaker, we sanction Juan, but his behavior escalates. That stirs up even more emotion! We raise our voice, hoping the volume will deescalate Juan's behavior. However, now Juan is standing and searching the room for someone or something to take his anger out on. Eliza smiles quietly to herself as the rest of the class looks to you for your next move.

"But," you say, "I do not plan to work with students who have severe behavior problems." At the 1966 New England Kindergarten Conference in Cambridge, Massachusetts, Fritz Redl, a prominent neo-Freudian psychologist and educator delivered a talk titled, "What Children Stir Up in Us." In the down-to-earth and descriptive manner that is all his own, this author of seminal works in the field of teaching troubled and troubling students implored:

> You don't have to be a teacher of disturbed or disorganized youngsters. It is a legitimate right in a free country of every person from time to time to go off his noodle. If somebody I love dies, I get into a depression and during that phase I look like anybody who is in a depression, except that I am supposed to have enough ego resilience, of course with some support from my friends, to snap out of it again. But that is the only difference. So you deal with disturbed behavior occasionally, or with temporary moods, or with curious states of mind in children even though they are not otherwise selected for special problems (Redl 1966a).

Redl delivered two messages that day: (1) troubled thinking and troubling behavior can happen to anyone at any time, and (2) in order for us to manage troubling behavior we must pay close attention to our own thoughts and feelings or "what children stir up in us." These thoughts and feelings and the way we act on them in times of crisis turn out to be an extremely important factor in determining if a crisis is escalated or deescalated (Long and Morse 1996).

Early work with troubled and troubling students led to a deep understanding about how troubled students think, how staff think, and how both act when working together and facing conflict (Redl 1966b; Redl and Weinman 1951, 1952). In the last 10 years others have built on this knowledge (Long, Fecser, and Brendtro 1998; Long and Morse 1996; Wood and Long 1991). The result is that powerful lessons have been learned about working with these most difficult students. The work of these researchers can help us easily translate these lessons into practices that can be employed in any setting with any student.

The model that we will share with you in great depth throughout this book is called the "conflict cycle" (Long 1979, 1986, 1996; Wood and Long 1991). This paradigm was developed to help staff understand the nature of student-teacher conflict. It will help us understand several important concepts: (1) school crises are often triggered by minor incidents, (2) students in conflict can manipulate staff behavior by recreating their feelings in staff, and (3) when staff act on these feelings the conflict is escalated. The conflict cycle is a powerful paradigm that helps teachers focus on the *why* of behavior. This is indeed a change from the typical classroom response of dealing primarily with the behavior itself. Throughout this book we will build on the concepts that comprise the model so that you will be prepared to look at your students in this new light and make purposeful and helpful decisions about the way you interact with them.

Should Teaching Change?

Previously we asked if schools should change. Schlechty and others answer yes, despite the fact that schools are not so bad as many believe. Naturally, school reform is a very large issue with many implications. Now we shall narrow the focus on school reform to issues surrounding instruction. We ask if teaching should change. Any discussion of teaching must also involve a discussion of learning. Another glance at the core concept for this chapter reminds us that learners can succeed in formal education without really changing their naïve levels of understanding. If that is true, we see it as a *major* problem. It means that children and adolescents can go through school being taught, but not having learned! Such a problem would suggest that, indeed, our teaching should change.

Deep Understanding versus Surface Learning

Noted researcher and cognitive psychologist Howard Gardner points to compelling research that suggests ". . . even students who have been well trained and who exhibit all the overt signs of success . . . typically do not display an adequate understanding of the materials and concepts with which they have been working" (1991, 3). In other words, learners who are doing well in our schools apparently are not learning very much. But how can this be? David Perkins offers a perspective on this apparent contradiction. He warns that we hold an overly simplistic notion of the challenges we face in helping students *really* learn. He asserts that we all too often worry only about missing knowledge—those facts and skills students should have mastered, but didn't. For example, a child in middle school who still doesn't know the difference between a subject and a verb, or an elementary-age child who doesn't know who the president of the United State is, are said to be "missing" that knowledge. Perkins cites evidence that there are many more problems of knowledge than just plain not having it.

Perkins describes three additional problems of knowledge of which we need to be aware. One problem is *inert knowledge,* which he dubs couch potato knowledge. It is there but just lies around and doesn't do anything. We simply don't think to use it unless a specific cue (like a test) brings it to the forefront. A second problem is *naïve knowledge.* Students who revert back to their earliest intuitive understandings that are partly or wholly incorrect display this knowledge. A common example of naïve knowledge is when people believe the seasons are caused by the distance of the earth from the sun. This makes intuitive sense because we learned early in our lives that things are hotter when close to a heat source, and colder when further away. But this is not the correct reason for the causes of the seasons. The third problem is with *ritualistic knowledge.* This is knowledge of the routines of solving problems and the way you are supposed to talk about things in school that students rather mindlessly perform. Learning the steps to solve a problem and routinely doing them

A Person Who Helped Create Change . . .

David Perkins has been concerned with the process of thinking throughout his adult life. After receiving his Ph.D. in mathematics and artificial intelligence from the Massachusetts Institute of Technology (1970), he codirected (until July 2000) Project Zero at Harvard University's Graduate School of Education. Project Zero is far reaching and has had a mighty influence on the way we think about teaching and learning.

Perkins's own work has focused on the "interlocking relationship" among thinking, learning, and understanding. He believes that one depends on the other two.

Among his works that have encouraged thoughtful educators to think about changing what they do in classrooms are *Smart Schools* (1992) and *Outsmarting IQ* (1995).

Source: http://pzweb.harvard.edu/Pis/DP.htm.

without understanding the reasons why you do them is ritualistic knowledge. Perkins labels this constellation of problems the "fragile knowledge syndrome" because of the very fragile, and often fleeting, grasp students have of key ideas and skills (1992, 1–27). For example, Blythe (1998) claims that research has documented student misconceptions about key ideas in math and science, their parochial views of history, and their tendency to reduce complex literary works to stereotypes (11). This happens despite years of even the best education. Why?

Surface learning causes fragile knowledge. That is to say, when we have learned something superficially it can be easily forgotten. It can be reorganized with other information in an incorrect fashion. At best it is an isolated bit of information that is virtually unusable as we go about trying to build new knowledge upon it, or when we attempt to solve a novel problem with it. In contrast, deep understandings are well connected to other things we know and we not only retain them, but are also able to understand them and apply them when appropriate. Deep understandings are indicators of conceptual change. But bringing about this conceptual change is easy neither for the teacher nor the learner. Just how difficult is it to promote conceptual change?

> Think about it . . .   How fragile is *your* knowledge?
>
> Write down on a piece of paper what causes the seasons.
>
> Check on page 24 at the end of this chapter to see if you are correct.

Promoting Conceptual Change

Watson and Konicek (1990) tell a wonderful story that makes clear how resistant children are to changing their previous conceptions. They tell of one teacher, her fourth-grade children, and her lesson on heat. Experience had led the children to believe that their clothes contained heat. After all, their parents and teachers had often told them in the dead of winter to "put on your warm clothes" before going outside. Rather than simply correcting their misconception for them by telling them correct information (the usual practice when children are wrong), their teacher decided to allow them to test their hypothesis. For three days these children tested their hypothesis that clothes were hot. They took off their hats, their coats, and their sweaters and put thermometers under them. They let them sit overnight. All the while they desperately clung to their original hypothesis—even in the face of data that they themselves collected and that consistently suggested otherwise. Finally, after the third day, their teacher asked them to take a stand on whether or not their clothes were hot. Some children had changed their minds, realizing that clothes themselves are not hot. But *even after three days of evidence to the contrary,* several children *still held to their convictions* that heat came from clothes, and two others were not certain. *To be sure, real conceptual change is difficult to accomplish.* Fourth graders are not alone in trying desperately to hold on to their existing conceptions!

Schools and teachers that continue to follow traditional methods of instruction rely almost exclusively on behavioral psychology that can perpetuate fragile knowledge. Attempts to "cover" all the material in textbooks, and to assess learner understanding of this material through conventional testing, might lead to short-term retention of information and the appearance that the material has been learned. But these attempts usually fail to promote either understanding of, or the ability to use, that information. If cognitive science tells us little else, it makes clear that cognitive change takes time and is difficult to accomplish. Humans tend to hold firm to their conceptions. It should not surprise us that helping them change these conceptions is not so simple as merely giving them information.

Working together on substantial problems promotes students' learning (Courtesy of Mary Kate Denny/Getty Images).

The Expanding Knowledge Base about How People Learn

We now know a great deal more about how people learn than we did even a few years ago, or at least we understand things better now that we did not understand so well then. This knowledge can help us help learners change conceptually. Although these new understandings do find their way into American schools and classrooms by way of curriculum and pedagogy skillfully crafted by teachers and administrators, this continues to be the exception rather than the rule. We still do not put the information we now have on how people learn to use in American classrooms in any sustained or systematic way. Unfortunately the current changes seem to be very small, and not at all widespread. David Perkins (1992) refers to "victory gardens," isolated outposts of success brought about by fundamental changes in the way we think about learning and practice pedagogy. He writes about several in his book titled *Smart Schools*. It is encouraging that these outposts exist. But if changes are isolated, they are not going to have the impact necessary to bring about significant changes in the way we go about teaching. Further, what change has occurred has been painfully slow, not systemic, sometimes uninformed, and often mandated from on high.

This fact prompted Frank Vellutino (cited in Hancock 1996) to say, "We do more educational research than anyone else in the world, and we ignore more as well." The research we have done has been quite remarkable. Much of the recent research has studied cognitive psychology as it applies to school learning. This research provides us with information that we could use to change our previously narrow view of learning and teaching that was guided almost exclusively by behavioral psychology. Nolan and Francis (1992) write that a new perspective on teaching and learning has started to gain ground. The beliefs that inform this new perspective, they say, are based on both new theories and traditional theories that have not found their ways into modern classrooms. These beliefs are:

A Person Who Helped Create Change . . .

Linda Darling-Hammond has contributed many excellent ideas to the movement to restructure our schools. In her book, *The Right to Learn,* she provides a blueprint for creating schools that work. Darling-Hammond is providing much needed leadership in helping us change schools from places where teachers *teach* to places where students *learn.* Currently she is the Charles E. Ducommun Professor of Teacher Education at Stanford University.

Photo: Courtesy of Dr. Linda Darling-Hammond
http://www.ncte.org/convention/99/speakers/
darling.shtml.

1. Knowledge is actively constructed by learners.

2. Prior knowledge greatly influences new learning.

3. Teachers must focus on how to help learners change their cognitive structures (to learn), rather than on their own teaching.

4. Learning is situated, and much of it is domain-specific.

5. Learning is a social endeavor more than an individual one. (Nolan and Francis 1992, 47–49)

These beliefs suggest powerful new principles that can be, and in some cases are now being, used to promote learning among children and adolescents, and even adults, in formal educational settings. They are wholly consistent with cognitive science. John Bruer tells us just how powerful these principles are when he asserts, "Teaching methods based upon research in cognitive science are the educational equivalents of polio vaccine and penicillin" (1993, 7–8). Bruer also points out, "There is more to medicine than biology, but basic medical science drives progress and helps doctors make decisions that promote their patients' physical well-being. Similarly, there is more to education than cognition, but cognitive science can drive progress and help teachers make decisions that promote their students' educational well-being" (1993, 8).

We have a new set of lenses through which we can view teaching and learning. They are provided by cognitive psychology. When combined with ideas from behavioral psychology, our teaching can be changed in very positive ways to match what we now know about how people learn. If we do not change the ways we teach, learners will continue to change very little as they progress through formal education.

How Should Schools and Teaching Change?

Think about it . . .

1. When have you resisted a change in your life?

2. When have you resisted learning a new idea or concept?

3. Was this resistance intentional? Unintentional?

4. How did you finally overcome your resistance to change?

Much of this book is about how schools in general, and teaching in particular, should change. Actually, schooling is beginning to change in fundamentally important ways. Some specific changes include more and more faculty members embracing some of the newer pedagogies such as cooperative learning, problem-based learning, and other active learning strategies. These pedagogies are fully explained in subsequent chapters of this book. The way student learning is assessed is slowly changing to make these assessments more performance based, another idea explained later in this book. We have even seen the birth of centers for teaching and learning in institutions of higher education. Such centers typically assist university faculty in knowing about and using a wider array of pedagogical alternatives than they typically used in the past. Does your school have one?

It is said that most people change not because they see the light, but because they feel the heat. Although schools need to continue to change, perhaps more quickly and extensively than they currently have, just to catch up to societal change and the knowledge base from cognitive science that undergirds instruction, that change should not be due to the heat.

How Can Teachers Change?

How can we, as teachers and prospective teachers, change? It will be no easier for us than it was for the fourth-grade children who struggled with the concept of heat in the story described earlier. We share with our students and teachers with whom we work a simple formula that can help us answer the question about how we can change, and in that process grow in our ability to help children, adolescents, and adults learn. That formula is:

$$\text{Knowledge} + \text{Experience} + \text{Reflection} = \text{Growth}$$

Remembering this simple formula can help you grow in your ability to teach or, for that matter, in your ability to master most anything. It suggests that we must gain knowledge, use that knowledge is some way, and think about what we know and do. Notice that the formula uses the operation of addition, which further suggests that the order of the elements may be changed with no harm done to the result. So, for example, sometimes an experience that we have may teach us something new (knowledge), which we can then think about (reflect upon). Or, sometimes as we think about (reflect on) things we get an idea for action (experience). You probably get the point. The three essential ingredients for growth can occur in any order, and can stimulate the remaining two elements.

Returning to the question of how teachers can change, in order to put some of the powerful new ideas to work in our schools and classrooms we first need to know that such ideas exist. Bruer was quoted earlier on the power of teaching methods based on research in cognitive science. In that same paragraph, he wrote, "Yet few outside the educational research community are aware of these breakthroughs or understand the research that makes them possible" (1993, 7–8). The theory-to-practice gap in education is a serious impediment to change. Teachers need to stay current with theories and research and understand them and their implications for classroom practice. Researchers and theoreticians must help teachers stay current.

Another gap that is an impediment to change is what Perkins (1992) calls a monumental "use-of-knowledge" gap. The problem, according to Perkins, is that "We are not putting to work what we know. In the school down the street, in the school across the river, students are learning and teachers are teaching in much the same way they did twenty or even fifty years ago" (3). Teachers must be willing to try out new ideas, and even conduct their own classroom research on how well those ideas work with their learners, and under what conditions they work best.

We desperately need time to think long and hard about the things we know and do. Schools mirror the rest of society in that the pace has quickened dramatically. With instant access to an overwhelming number of choices and bits of information, we are constantly "doing." Teachers need to take time to think about what they are doing. School administrators need to provide them with opportunities to do so.

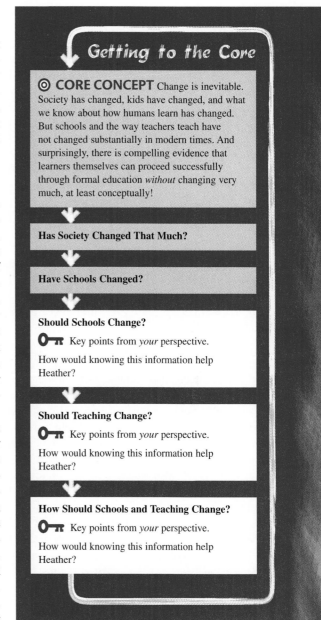

Getting to the Core

⊙ CORE CONCEPT Change is inevitable. Society has changed, kids have changed, and what we know about how humans learn has changed. But schools and the way teachers teach have not changed substantially in modern times. And surprisingly, there is compelling evidence that learners themselves can proceed successfully through formal education *without* changing very much, at least conceptually!

Has Society Changed That Much?

Have Schools Changed?

Should Schools Change?

⚷ Key points from *your* perspective.

How would knowing this information help Heather?

Should Teaching Change?

⚷ Key points from *your* perspective.

How would knowing this information help Heather?

How Should Schools and Teaching Change?

⚷ Key points from *your* perspective.

How would knowing this information help Heather?

Further, we assert that for new and experienced teachers to use contemporary instructional methods they first must know and understand the research upon which they are based. Because, typically, they have neither been taught, nor taught by, these methods, they also need to practice them. Even more, they need to practice using newer methods with guidance, to evaluate the results of using these methods, and to make modifications as necessary to promote student learning. Finally, teachers should share what they have learned with other teachers so that improved practice can progress. With improved teaching practices will come improved learning—and true conceptual change for our learners.

It may seem to those of you who have not yet taught that none of the above applies to you. After all, how can you change if you have not yet taught? But change is constant. That things will always be changing is one of the few certainties in life. So whenever you do begin to teach, you must also begin to change. The formula we offered earlier can help you do just that.

Learning and Teaching in the Age of Technology

Introduction

The use of educational technology to further the core concepts developed in this book requires that teachers engage in developing critical media literacy skills. Thoman (1999) suggests that we must help learners control the interpretation of what they see or hear, rather than let the interpretation control them. She reminds us that whatever is "constructed" by just a few people becomes "the way it is" for the rest of us, and that different people experience the same media message differently (50–51). Tapscott (1999) writes about the "Net generation," students who will manage more and more of their lives online through interpersonal communications, personal finances, shopping, checking news and sports, participating in polls and virtual parties, reviewing new movies, or listening to their latest favorite music as soon as it is published. He further suggests challenges in the form of paradigm shifts that will greatly affect what we do in classrooms and how we operationalize the core concepts you'll learn in this book.

There are untold thousands of new resources, emerging multimedia technologies, and increasingly user friendly Web-based information sources to help teachers and students. The plethora of information and resources can overwhelm us. The most comprehensive reference that is updated weekly is the *Road Map to the Web for Educators* (2001). The organization that produces this wonderful resource is called T.H.E. Institute

and strongly recognizes the role technology plays in enhancing classroom learning. T.H.E. Institute is dedicated to anytime, anywhere professional development for educators and publishes a monthly journal. Their website **www.thejournal.com** provides one-stop shopping for finding teacher resources. Though we will give only limited examples of how each of our core concepts relates to technology in the Learning and Teaching in the Age of Technology sections, we urge you to read articles in leading educational technology journals to stay abreast of developments and possibilities for the use of technologies in your classrooms.

According to Jamie McKenzie (1999) more than 60 percent of surveyed teachers felt they were not well

> ⊚ **CORE CONCEPT**   Change is inevitable. Society has changed, kids have changed, and what we know about how humans learn has changed. But schools and the way teachers teach have not changed substantially in modern times. And surprisingly, there is compelling evidence that learners themselves can proceed successfully through formal education *without* changing very much, at least conceptually!

prepared to use new technologies in their classrooms. Teachers are overwhelmed by the amount of content and range of curricular issues with which they must deal. And after huge sums have been invested in wiring schools, we have little evidence that all that much has changed in learning outcomes. If we are to use these technologies to help move a teacher's role from sage on the stage to guide on the side, schools and individual teachers must make a prolonged commitment to professional development. McKenzie cites Hank Becker's research in *Internet Use by Teachers* (1999), which shows that "traditional" teachers are three times less likely to use new technologies than "constructivist" teachers. Becker (1999) also demonstrated a strong relationship between computer use and pedagogical change toward learner-centered construction of meaning. This change was especially noted among secondary teachers in social studies, science, and noncore subjects. McKenzie's (1999) report outlines a number of essential steps that must be in place for change to occur in teachers' behavior regarding use of educational technology to enhance learning. These steps include using current research that demonstrates students' achievement, insisting on field tested software programs, implementing technology slowly and developing a comfort level for students, working in teams, and starting with what interests you the most.

Rather than get in the way, these new technological resources should make your work and your students' performance better, easier, and more powerful. The use of technology won't change you, but will change the way you approach teaching and learning. Dexter, Anderson, and Becker (1999) assert that teachers who adopted instructional practices like those outlined in this book felt that using computers helped them change their instruction to become more learner-centered, not by reason of the computers themselves, but because they had carefully reflected on their own construction of pedagogical knowledge in a supportive climate.

Teaching Tip

Have your students use both **www.thejournal.com** and **www.google.com** to locate additional content to supplement their understanding of a unit of instruction that you are currently teaching them.

Suggested Websites

http://www.proteacher.com/
Online curricular resources for teachers K–5.

http://microweb.com/pepsite
Too Cool For Grownups features Internet curricula and projects.

http://www.iste.org
The International Society for Technology in Education.

What If Schools and Teaching Changed?

Let's think of the possibilities. If schools changed, they would be responsive to the needs of a society that has emerged from one based on agriculture to one based on information. They would abandon the idea that it is possible, in 12 years, to equip children with all the information they will need to live productive lives in a democratic society. Instead, they would develop curricula on the basis of big ideas, essential concepts, things that would serve to enable these children to continue learning new things, possibly on their own, as the world around them continues to rapidly change long after they have graduated from high school and college. These big ideas would also help students solve problems that they encounter during life's journey. In short, schools would acknowledge the changing contexts in which they exist, and continue to change in ways that allow them to either better respond to the needs of these contexts, or to serve these contexts as agents of change.

And if classrooms changed? They would become hotbeds of learner activity. Real engagement of learners with substantial content would take place. Teachers would no longer just transmit information to learners who sit passively taking it all in; nor would they ask questions that have only simple answers, or provide answers too quickly for the learners. Instead, learners would work together to master BIG ideas. Teachers would base their instructional practices on the latest research rather than on trendy, but unstudied, materials.

When these changes have been made, it will no longer be possible for learners to proceed through formal schooling conceptually unaffected by it all. All too often we ask if children are ready for school. *Perhaps we should be asking if our schools are ready for children.* If things change, as we have asserted in this chapter they must, our schools will indeed be ready. And if you master the ideas in this book, *you* will be ready to teach in these schools.

How Can Planning for Instruction Change?

In chapter 9 we present a detailed Planning Template for developing instruction based on ideas that are presented throughout the entire book. However, it is not uncommon for students to have to teach lessons to peers, children, and adolescents early on in methods courses for which this book is intended. Therefore, we present here a preliminary template for going about planning lessons or units of instruction.

In order to change the way lessons are taught, indeed conceptualized, we need to consider some very basic tenets from cognitive science. This involves, first and foremost, putting students at the heart of the enterprise and focusing less on what *we* teach and more on what *they* learn. We need to engage students in learning and understanding substantial content while helping them build on what they already know. Finally, we must allow them time to put to use what they have learned under our guidance and with our expert feedback, and then allow them ample opportunity to apply their new understanding to new, authentic situations and in various contexts. Of course, this all sounds very simple and even commonplace. This is deceptive! For various reasons even this overly simplified summary of planning is not at all common practice. Despite the plethora of research on human learning, we persist in equating our teaching with student learning, and we often plow through content in a relentless fashion without allowing for significant student engagement, let alone application. We encourage you to reflect back on any plans you develop and lessons you teach as you proceed through the ideas presented in each chapter of this book. Of course, you can always visit chapter 9 to see more detail and some examples of lesson and unit planning based upon cognitive science. For now, here is the basic structure that we offer for your consideration.

Start *Planning* with a BIG Idea (Step 2 on Planning Template)

Whatever concepts or skills you intend to help students learn, try to connect them all together through some kind of big idea. This will help them, and you! If you plan to help them learn about people from various countries or even different regions of our own country, think about using *culture* or *ways of life* as the unifying idea. Then plan ways to help them learn facts and concepts through the use of the big idea. Perhaps by selecting three or four characteristics upon which to compare and contrast cultures, and then focusing on eastern, southern, northern, and western states, students can learn specific facts and ideas about regional differences.

[1] Activate Learners' Prior Knowledge Gain attention. Cue prior knowledge. Encourage personal connection and meaning.	Procedures
[2] Help Learners Understand the Content Select a BIG idea to help learners forge connections to facts, concepts, and ideas to be learned.	Procedures
[3] Allow Learners Time to Practice and Provide Them with Feedback Provide opportunities to use ideas, concepts, facts, and to assess understanding.	Procedures
[4] Let Learners Apply What They Have Learned Apply to other ideas, concepts, facts; apply in new and different ways; apply in life.	Procedures

Start *Instruction* by Cueing Prior Knowledge with a Compelling Attention Getter (Step 1 on Planning Template)

To begin your instruction, *immediately* grab the attention of your students. Get them involved in something that will interest and motivate them. Perhaps present a problem: *Your dad is getting a new job, and your family has the chance to move either to Los Angeles, Chicago, Atlanta, or Philadelphia. Where would your family be the happiest? Advise them.* Do an activity to help them recall things they already know—ask questions.

Continue by Helping Them Learn Content (Return to Step 2 on Planning Template)

Next, you may present information to the students. Better, though, is to get them actively involved by searching sources and learning all they can about the various regions, under your guidance. Have them work together in small groups. If they get stuck, help them by modeling what they might do next. Encourage them to map out their ideas, depicting them visually to facilitate sharing with their peers later on.

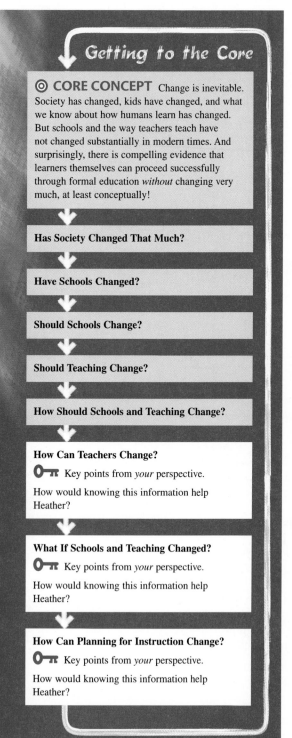

Getting to the Core

◎ **CORE CONCEPT** Change is inevitable. Society has changed, kids have changed, and what we know about how humans learn has changed. But schools and the way teachers teach have not changed substantially in modern times. And surprisingly, there is compelling evidence that learners themselves can proceed successfully through formal education *without* changing very much, at least conceptually!

Has Society Changed That Much?

Have Schools Changed?

Should Schools Change?

Should Teaching Change?

How Should Schools and Teaching Change?

How Can Teachers Change?

🔑 Key points from *your* perspective.

How would knowing this information help Heather?

What If Schools and Teaching Changed?

🔑 Key points from *your* perspective.

How would knowing this information help Heather?

How Can Planning for Instruction Change?

🔑 Key points from *your* perspective.

How would knowing this information help Heather?

Then Help Them Practice What They Learned (Step 3 on Planning Template)

Allow them to share what they learned with one another in a well-organized presentation by having them explain and defend what they have advised their families. Or have them practice what they have learned in some other way—maybe by designing a travel brochure?

Finally, Let Them Apply What They Learned to a Different Problem (Step 4 on Planning Template)

To show that they have really learned what you intended that they learn, you might have them apply what they learned to something unrelated to your lesson or unit. For example, you might have the students analyze different countries using the knowledge that they gained from your instruction. Or they might advise the president on a diplomatic approach to a given country.

You can use this sequence and the planning template we provide to begin lesson or unit planning. You will learn much more about why to use it, and methods to use with it, as you proceed through your course, and this book.

 SCENARIO REVISITED

Now is the time to review the scenario that begins on page 2 of this chapter, and the questions to which you previously responded. Answer these questions once again.

> **?** *If you were a teacher in this school, would you share Heather's concerns? What would concern you the most? Why? What course of action would you propose to your colleagues to address the concern? What changes might you suggest?*

Have your answers changed at all? If they have, in what way or ways have they changed? If not, why not? Now compare your thoughts to those from a practicing teacher who has responded to the same scenario and answered the same questions.

 A VOICE FROM THE FIELD

"You want me to do what?" I asked my department head as my stomach began to churn. Thoughts of the two sets of ungraded essays sitting on my desk at home became a brooding specter. Six unanswered and undoubtedly lengthy phone calls from parents loomed large. The impending course work for one of the courses toward my master's quickly transposed from being an anticipated intellectual challenge to a nightmarish dilemma. My family's plans for a two-week vacation at the beach during the summer evaporated.

"The board has decided that you need to integrate technology into your class-room next year so we've bought you some laptops, a master computer, and some software. Oh . . . we're also moving to a block scheduling system in September so you'll need to rewrite some curricula to fit into ninety-minute periods." She smiled. "And if I don't see you before school ends next week, have a great summer!"

Too shocked to respond, I stood rooted to the floor of my classroom, as my head exploded. In September, when students returned to school, they could be found picking up the pieces of what used to be a sane, well-organized, creative, caring, and thoughtful teacher.

For most teachers, this would be a fairly accurate picture of both the ways schools introduce change and the ways in which they are supposed to deal with it. Unless they are brain dead (and therefore, shouldn't be teaching), most educators realize that society has changed and that schools have not. After all, their own lives and those of their families are quite different than when they went to school—30, 15, or even 5 years ago. Yet accepting the fact that there needs to be change in education and doing something about transforming the ways schools meet the fluctuating needs of students and society are two vastly different notions. The two most formidable obstacles that teachers face in making necessary changes are time and the forces that drive schools (both public and private).

"Teachers work only nine months a year. That should give them plenty of time to learn new skills and write new curricula." A statement like this makes me want to strangle the speaker or at least doom him or her to watching CNN or MTV 24-7. True educational change cannot and should not ever be attempted by teachers over a summer or in isolation. In order for schools to integrate any type of modification, even the most mundane, there must be a clear plan, developed and accepted by all the parties—administration, teaching staff, parents, community—that includes a lengthy period of trial and some error and evaluation. Top-down, short-term change is doomed to failure.

In addition, because any changes in education must start with classroom teachers, the teachers must be given time—over the long term—to be able to implement successfully any types of change in a school. Because schools cannot announce a one-year sabbatical while teachers retool, learn new techniques or technologies, and revise their curricula and methodologies, administrators or educational leaders must carve out time during the school year for teachers to "revisit, rethink, revise, and reevaluate" their programs and the ways in which education is delivered to students. Furthermore, teachers need time to mentor one another as these changes are attempted. To do this, teaching loads must be reduced so that teachers have the time and energy to devote to the task of creating change. This also means that the climate of the school's internal community and administration must foster sharing, caring, and support. Teachers need the opportunity to share concerns and successes in forums that are nonjudgmental and disconnected from decisions related to job security.

"Besides, why do things need to change? We never did that when I went to school and I turned out okay." This idea is often voiced by members of the community. Educators need to accept the fact that all human beings are naturally suspicious of change, especially when it will occur in something that is such a commonly shared experience as school. Making changes requires taking risks; what if the changes don't work out as planned? Will that mean that SAT scores decline or that a school's reputation suffers? These are legitimate fears. Therefore, any proposed change in the curriculum, demands on teachers in the classroom, school programs, or the arrangement of the school day requires the acceptance, or at least the acquiescence, of the community that supports the school. One way to allay community or educators' concerns about a particular proposed change is to arrange for parents, teachers, and students from schools that have implemented the proposed change to share their experiences. Frank and honest discussions of rumors, fears, and doomsday scenarios will usually lead to a better understanding of the positive aspects of the proposed change. There is no reason for any school to "reinvent the wheel" or go through a wrenching change alone. Such cooperation will go a long way in helping the process of recreating American education to meet the needs of the twenty-first century.

Finally, we all need to remember that if one of the primary goals of education is the development of functional American citizens for our democracy, then educators must embrace change or else accept the fact that American education is quickly becoming an anachronism.

This is the voice of Leslie Pugach. Ms. Pugach is a middle and high school core studies teacher.

Answer to question on page 14:

The tilt of the earth's axis and the orbit of the earth around the sun cause the seasons. Many people think it is the distance of the earth from the sun (closer in summer, further in winter), but this is incorrect.

INTRODUCTION TO PLANNING FOR INSTRUCTION

This Planning for Instruction section of each chapter will give you an opportunity to be guided through the development of lesson plans and a unit of instruction. When completed, you will have developed a unit that is consistent with all the core concepts we present in this book, and that will incorporate the powerful instructional ideas that the book advocates. This unit of instruction will be *progressive;* that is, you will steadily build it as you complete each chapter. The information that you are learning in each chapter will be progressively incorporated into the unit to strengthen its power and potential for bringing about conceptual change among your learners.

For the purposes of this activity a *unit of study* will be considered to be part of a course or subject that involves planning your instruction around a central issue, topic, theme, idea, major questions, or set of skills. Most units last a few days and may go as long as four or five weeks, depending on how frequently they are taught and the amount of content they include. Please note that a unit includes, but is more than, a series of lesson plans. A unit is a sequenced, organized, integrated approach to helping a group of learners relate specific ideas, facts, concepts, and skills to one another. When planning a unit the teacher has not only fully researched the necessary content but also has thoroughly considered pedagogical issues related to instruction, student motivation, instructional approaches, assessment strategies, management and discipline, and materials needed to support instruction (including appropriate uses of technology).

As you develop this unit, keep in mind your overall goal(s) as well as the specific objectives for individual lessons. You will be guided in each chapter by questions you should answer. You are encouraged to build a unit of study that is thoughtful, reflective, and focused upon the core concepts from each chapter.

PLANNING FOR INSTRUCTION

Locate two units of study (found in teachers' manuals, textbooks, and curriculum guides). Find one from about 15 years ago and one published very recently. Try to find a unit that focuses on content that is familiar to you and that you would be comfortable teaching. As you examine both units, look for similarities and differences in how the content is written and the variety of instructional methods suggested and outcomes expected.

> ◎ **CORE CONCEPT** Change is inevitable. Society has changed, kids have changed, and what we know about how humans learn has changed. But schools and the way teachers teach have not changed substantially in modern times. And surprisingly, there is compelling evidence that learners themselves can proceed successfully through formal education *without* changing very much, at least conceptually!

- Are they much different from one another? How?

- Has the 15-year difference between the two units reflected any change in how the students are being taught?

- Do these units demonstrate a variety of methods to meet student needs and various ways to intellectually challenge them?

- Revisit the core concept and content of this chapter and explore the questions being asked: Have schools and teaching changed?

You are now going to begin to think about a unit of study that you will develop as you read this textbook.

1. Choose a topic that you have a genuine interest in and that would be academically sound and challenging, as well as engaging, for students. It will be most realistic if you obtain a curriculum guide from a local school. Curriculum guides typically specify topics that teachers should teach at each grade level. Choose a topic from that guide.

2. Use a source (such as a basic educational psychology book or a child development book) to identify the grade, age, and developmental levels and characteristics of the learners you will target for this unit.

3. If you decide to develop this unit for special needs children, write down specific information about individual disabilities and range of differences expected in the classroom. As you complete each chapter you will use the newly acquired information to build and enhance your unit of instruction.

Topic:

Grade/Chronological Age:

Developmental Levels and Age-Level Characteristics (Cognitive, Social, Physical, Academic):

Other Important Information:

To begin your planning you should think about and then commit to writing, the following four elements of a unit: goals, objectives, content, and organization of content. You can always revise things later on, even as you teach the unit to children. Remember, it's just a plan! We will provide examples to assist you. Our unit on *weather* could be used in grades 5 through 10. It is designed as a generic model to help you better understand the specific skills needed to design a unit of instruction. Please use our example only as a guide as you develop your own unit.

Topic: Severe Weather

Grade Level/Chronological Ages: Fifth graders, 10 to 11 years of age
Developmental Characteristics (Fifth Graders, 10 to 11 years of age):   According to Erik Erickson, (1968) fifth-grade students are in the industry versus inferiority stage of moral development. This means the students are beginning to see the relationship between perseverance and the joy of completing work. They are becoming increasingly more aware of how they interact with their peers and how others view their work. Teachers need to be cognizant of designing work that they can accomplish without public embarrassment. It is important to give these students responsibilities (according to Kohlberg (1984), they tend to like to please the teacher and their friends) in the classroom and to encourage their independence. Based on Piaget's theory of cognitive development, these learners are moving from concrete operational to formal operational. Some may be able to deal with abstractions, but most will need to generalize from concrete, real-world experiences. Students need visual and graphic organizers that help them organize and concretize factual information.

1. **Goal(s) of the unit:** In general, what are the BIG ideas and skills you want the learners to understand and master? This is your road map, so to speak.

    Example: Students will explore types of weather conditions and specifically severe storms and the impact they have on people's lives and on the environment.

2. **Objectives to be achieved:** Objectives are more specific than, but certainly related to, goals. They are statements that communicate what the teacher expects the learners to know, and to be able to do, at the completion of the unit or lesson. Objectives can be written at six different levels using Bloom's taxonomy as a guide (see chapter 4). The six levels represent the teacher's ability to design increasingly more difficult levels of questions/activities that challenge the level of cognitive thought. Objectives representing the six levels use words (verbs) that demonstrate a level of action such as:

    Knowledge: define, identify, list, write, describe, and record.

    Comprehension: distinguish, explain, paraphrase, summarize.

    Application: compute, demonstrate, modify, organize, and solve.

    Analysis: differentiate, compare and contrast, deduce, and relate.

    Synthesis: categorize, predict, create, design, and produce.

    Evaluation: validate, support, defend, criticize, and judge.

    Examples of Objectives
    Given class discussions, films, Internet research, labs, textbook and science kits the students will:

    - Identify four types of severe weather (tornadoes, thunderstorms, hurricanes, and snowstorms).

    - Describe causes of storms and precautions people can take to limit destruction to themselves and to the environment.

- Demonstrate similarities and differences of different types of severe weather.
- Categorize weather instruments by what they do.
- Formulate the relationship between severe weather and the water cycle.
- Differentiate how severe weather relates to geographic locations.

3. **Content:** What specific facts, ideas, concepts, skills will be included?

    Example

    a. Tornadoes, thunderstorms, hurricanes and snowstorms.

    b. Impact of severe weather on people and the environment.

    c. Geographic locations of severe storms.

    d. Water cycle.

    Examples of Instruments Used to Measure Severe Weather (Barometers, Anemometers, etc.)

Organization of the Content:

How are ideas, concepts, and skills usually organized? How will you organize the unit for instruction (i.e., chronologically, sequentially, graphically, major events)?

Example

We plan to sequence the teaching of the content in the following order—condensation, water cycle (which they already know), instruments to measure severe weather, severe storms, geographic locations of severe storms, types of severe storms, and impact of severe weather on people and the environment.

Your Turn

Now, you go ahead and write down your preliminary information to begin to put flesh on your unit of instruction.

Topic

Grade/Chronological Age:

Developmental Characteristics:

Other Important Information:

Goal(s):

Objective(s):

Content:

Organization of Content:

CHAPTER SUMMARY

This book is about promoting student learning through conceptual change. This chapter asks a very important question—Why change the way we teach? It focuses on a core concept, or big idea, that change has happened virtually everywhere except in schools. Even more troubling, there is evidence that too many learners can succeed in school without learning in the truest sense of the word. To illustrate that things have changed quite a bit, we described several representative ways that society has changed.

Yet schools have changed surprisingly little in the past 100 years despite all of these major societal changes. Should schools change? Even though they are doing a better job than most people give them credit for, the context in which schools now find themselves is very different from the past, and so they must change in order to prepare children and adolescents for the contemporary world in which they will live. Teaching also needs to change in order to promote the deep kinds of understandings that will be necessary for those who will participate in twenty-first–century society. We have a better understanding now of how to promote these deep understandings than we did 50, or even 20, years ago.

Schools need to change by cutting down on the sheer volume of what their teachers teach, and instead focusing students on big ideas that will serve them well in a society that will continue to be characterized by rapid change. And teaching needs to change by using the research that has been amassed in classrooms, with learners. Classrooms need to actively engage learners in tasks that promote deep understanding.

The chapter that follows will continue our story by focusing on several theories that can help us change classroom practices in order to promote deep understanding among learners. We will address theoretical perspectives from cognitive science in this next chapter of our evolving story.

Getting to the Core

> ◎ **CORE CONCEPT**   Change is inevitable. Society has changed, kids have changed, and what we know about how humans learn has changed. But schools and the way teachers teach have not changed substantially in modern times. And surprisingly, there is compelling evidence that learners themselves can proceed successfully through formal education *without* changing very much, at least conceptually!

Has Society Changed That Much?

- Rapid introduction of new technology, computers, cell phones, television, beepers, and so on, has increased amounts of information and its availability.
- Society, communities, and families are different.

Have Schools Changed?

- Lecture, large class instruction, and individual student work are the primary means of transferring information to students.
- Extrinsic motivation is the key source of motivating students.
- Teachers employ limited use of alternative teaching strategies—most teachers still rely too heavily on direct instruction and pencil and paper worksheets, and traditional tests as major forms of assessment.

Should Schools Change?

- Yes, but not as drastically as some people think. Schools are not as bad as misconceptions make them out to be. Given the constraints and the demands on schools theses days, they are actually doing a pretty good job. However, the context in which schools operate has changed. Therefore, because schools are no longer serving agrarian or industrial societies, they must change.

Should Teaching Change?

- Students are currently being taught—they are not learning. There is relatively little change in the level of student understanding—there is a lack of conceptual change. We now know a lot more about how people learn, and we should use that information and current research.

How Should Schools and Teaching Change?

- Focus on core concepts and big ideas. Embrace the newer pedagogies of instruction, engage students in active learning with relevant and substantial tasks, and structure lessons to emphasize prior knowledge, connections, and personal meaning. Assess students in meaningful and authentic ways and through performance-based activities, and stress social and cooperative learning.

How Can Teachers Change?

- Use effective, powerful strategies based on current research to lessen the theory-to-practice gap.
- Implement model that utilizes Knowledge + Experience + Reflection = Growth. Encourage faculty to work cooperatively with other teachers to share ideas, teach each other and learn.

What If Schools and Teaching Changed?

- Children would be better equipped with the information they need to be productive members of society. They would be engaged in active learning designed to promote deep, meaningful understanding. The curriculum would be based on big ideas and essential concepts to provide students with the tools needed to continue learning once they have left school.

How Can Planning for Instruction Change?

- Put students at the heart of the enterprise.
- Focus instruction on big ideas.
- Engage students in learning content and allow them time to practice and apply what they learn.

Changing Classroom Practices to Promote Deep Understanding

CHAPTER 2

Powerful Principles from Theoretical Perspectives

"Daddy, are your glasses up there so you can see your ideas better?"

FAMILY CIRCUS *(Source: Reprinted with special permission of King Features Syndicate.)*

 SCENARIO

Ms. Moore teaches history in a high school located in an affluent suburban community. She is an experienced teacher and is active in her local historical society. She knows her subject very well. She begins her classes in September by introducing students to early explorers of the Western Hemisphere. In early October they read about the colonial settlements of the 1600s. By December they have covered the French and Indian War, the Revolutionary War, and the Declaration of Independence. The winter months are spent studying the nineteenth century (e.g., the Industrial Revolution and the Civil War), and the spring is spent studying the twentieth century (including both world wars, the Korean War, the Vietnam War, the Persian Gulf crisis, and the Kosovo conflict).

Ms. Moore has high expectations for her students. In her daily class lectures she describes historical events in detail, hoping to give her students a sense of how complex many of these events really were. In addition to having students read the usual high school textbook, she also assigns articles in the historical journals she herself reads.

Occasionally Ms. Moore stops a lecture for a few minutes before the bell rings to ask questions that check her students' recall of the day's topics. Although her students can usually remember the main gist of her lecture, they have difficulty with the details, either mixing them up or forgetting them altogether. A few students remember so little that she can hardly believe they were in class that day, even though she knows for a fact that they were. Her students perform even more poorly on monthly essay exams—it's obvious from their written responses that they can remember little of what Ms. Moore has taught them.

As she leaves class after a particularly frustrating day on which she reviewed exams with the students, Ms. Moore thinks to herself, "I explained things so clearly to them, perhaps these kids just don't want to learn this stuff."

> **?** *Why do you think Ms. Moore's students are having problems remembering things she is teaching them? What do you think Ms. Moore's philosophy of teaching might be? Why?*

INTRODUCTION

Important connections between theory and practice often go unrecognized. Experienced teachers and other practitioners sometimes dismiss theories as not especially relevant or useful for solving "real-world" problems that they encounter on a daily basis. Of course, experience is of tremendous practical value in decision making. But theories *are* useful, too, and they are very practical. Theories, at least in the scientific sense, connect concepts to one another in a way that permits those who

Getting to the Core

◉ CORE CONCEPT Human beings learn best in cooperation with other human beings by actively processing information that they find personally meaningful.

How Do Theories Work?

How Do Traditional and Contemporary Theories Differ?

How Do Humans Learn?

What Is Social Cognitive Theory?
- Modeling Effects
- Modeling Processes

How Does Contextualist Theory Help Us Understand Learning?
- Constructed Knowledge
- Language, Learning, and Development
- The Social Context of Learning

What Is Information Processing Theory?
- Attention, Recognition, and Human Memory
- Getting Information to Long-Term Memory
- Declarative and Procedural Knowledge

What Motivates Humans to Learn?
- Intrinsic versus Extrinsic Motivation
- Theory Meets Practice
- What Motivation Theory Suggests

understand them to interpret facts and make predictions and decisions. They guide our practice by presenting one or several general statements that can be used to explain particular facts. In this way they help us make sense out of facts. They also help us discard misleading or dated information. In short, theories help us inform our teaching practice and change it when new information becomes available that can benefit us in our endeavor to better help our students retain, understand, and use what they learn.

How Do Theories Work?

Whenever human beings perceive information, they do so through a set of personal beliefs or theories. Change your beliefs and your perceptions of information will also change. The human mind seems innately structured to make sense of the data that it perceives. Therefore, the notion that facts exist in isolation from our beliefs and perceptions can be seriously questioned. Unfortunately, our personal beliefs and theories are often implicitly held and largely unexamined. They are not necessarily based upon interrelated and accurate concepts.

A number of facts have emerged from cognitive science over the past ten to twenty years that now form patterns. Theories that help us understand these facts have also emerged and become increasingly sophisticated. These theories provide us with very practical ways to understand many facts, to explain things that we see or hear, to predict future events, and to generate specific strategies for use in our practice.

Teachers have a special responsibility as professionals to make explicit and continually examine their theories in light of the most current research. Theories that they use to guide their practice should, naturally, be based on professional experience. They should also be based on rich information and well-grounded scientific research. Some major concepts that come out of research in cognitive science include *cooperation, active processing, and meaningfulness.* These concepts can guide much of our practice. The concepts of cooperation, active processing, and meaningfulness are critically important for you to understand if you want to know how people learn. We shall now examine them closely in the context of several powerful theories. The theories we have chosen are based upon behavioral *and* cognitive psychology.

How Do Traditional Theories and Contemporary Theories Differ?

Let us say right up front that cognitive science, and the views of learning that derive from it, stands in sharp contrast to traditional views of learning based upon behavioral science. Traditional views reflect the factory model of production in American society. The factory model "provided fertile soil for the behavioral approach to learning, which has dominated educational practices for the past fifty years" (Caine and Caine 1991, 15). Among the assumptions underlying the traditional, behavioral approach are:

- Learning is the process of accumulating bits of information and isolated skills.
- The teacher's primary responsibility is to transfer knowledge directly to students.
- The process of learning and teaching focuses primarily on the interactions between the teacher and individual students. (Nolan and Francis 1992, 45).

The focus of traditional theory is clearly on providing instruction.

In contrast, a more contemporary view, informed by research from cognitive science, posits:

- All learning, except for simple rote memorization, requires the learner to actively construct meaning.

- Students' prior understandings and thoughts about a topic or concept before instruction exert a tremendous influence on what they learn during instruction.

- The teacher's primary goal is to generate a change in the learner's cognitive structure or way of viewing and organizing the world.

- Learning in cooperation with others is an important source of motivation, support, modeling, and coaching. (Nolan and Francis, 47–48)

The focus of most contemporary theory is on bringing about learning, rather than on providing instruction.

Traditional Behavioral Theory	Contemporary Cognitive Theory
Learning is the accumulation of bits of information and skills.	Learning is holistic and much more than an additive process of accumulating information.
Teacher can transfer knowledge directly to learners.	Learners actively construct their own understandings.
Learning takes place as teacher and individual learner interact.	Learning is social and involves cooperation with others.
Emphasis is on providing instruction.	Emphasis is on bringing about learning.

How Do Humans Learn?

A host of researchers has called for teachers to reconsider their theories of teaching and learning on the basis of new information generated from cognitive science. Recall from Chapter 1 that John Bruer said, "Teaching methods based upon research in cognitive science are the educational equivalents of polio vaccine and penicillin" (1993, 7–8). This dramatic claim is supported by research. For example, in a synthesis of research on teaching, Joyce, Showers, and Rolheiser-Bennett list cooperative learning and information processing as among the most effective models in promoting student achievement (1987). Both models are derived largely from cognitive science. More recent studies, many emanating from Harvard University's well-respected Project Zero, substantiate the power of teaching strategies derived from cognitive science.

Bruer also wrote, directly following the polio vaccine and penicillin statement, "Yet few outside the educational research community are aware of these breakthroughs or understand the research that makes them possible" (1993, 7–8). Whether they are simply unaware of these breakthroughs or there is some other reason or reasons, teachers have been slow to embrace these newer theories. So classroom practice has remained relatively unchanged. Over 15 years after Goodlad's (1983) study of schooling found that teachers used mainly their own talk and seatwork as pedagogical strategies, researchers Howard Gardner (1991), David

> To learn more about Project Zero, **follow the link** http://pzweb.harvard.edu/ **or type Project Zero into a search engine.**

Perkins (1992), Linda Darling-Hammond (1997), and many others lament that what we know about learning *still* is not reflected in current teaching practice.

There is some indication that practices are beginning to change. Barr and Tagg (1995) note that subtly, but profoundly, a new paradigm is emerging for education—one that replaces "providing instruction" with "producing learning." If they are correct, this shift will make it necessary for teachers to understand cognitive theories that guide them in the direction of that new paradigm. The focus will be on providing what Guskin (1994) describes as optimal learning environments: those that move students from passive to active roles in their own learning; those that deemphasize extrinsic and increase intrinsic motivation; and those that reduce large group instruction while enhancing smaller, intimate groupings (18). The story we presented in Chapter 1 by Watson and Konicek (1990) about children who thought their clothes were "hot" is an example of such a learning environment. And we shall turn once again to that very same story a bit later in this chapter.

Prudence would dictate that we need to take care to not throw out aspects of traditional behavioral theory that prove useful in promoting certain types of learning. For example, certain skills might best be trained by using methods derived from behavioral psychology. Keyboarding is one of those skills. Teachers facing students who present behaviors that are very difficult to manage in classroom environments might need to use some form of behavior modification to instill order in the classroom. Behavior modification comes directly from behavioral theory. Students who lack significant cognitive ability, such as those with severe or profound mental retardation, might not be able to benefit from contemporary cognitive theory as much as they can from traditional behavioral theory. At least, that is, within the parameters of our current knowledge of such severe anomalies.

Ideally, teachers would take the best from both cognitive and behavioral science and synthesize the key ideas into a unified, coherent theory that they can then use to guide the development of instruction that promotes student learning. Presently, however, and perhaps ironically, traditional behavioral theory underlies the majority of the instruction used in contemporary classrooms with almost all students. The irony—although there are very few students for whom more contemporary cognitive theories are inappropriate, we treat most all of our students as if they have limited cognitive functioning or need specific training for which behavioral theory has the most merit!

Let us return now to the core concept presented earlier in this chapter to create a link between its essential components and the theories that pertain to them. We shall first address the element of the core concept that asserts human beings learn best *in cooperation with other human beings*. There are two major theories that help us understand the underpinnings of this assertion—social cognitive theory and contextualist theory.

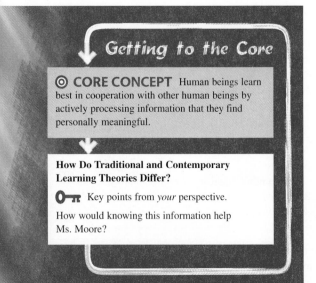

Getting to the Core

⊚ **CORE CONCEPT** Human beings learn best in cooperation with other human beings by actively processing information that they find personally meaningful.

How Do Traditional and Contemporary Learning Theories Differ?

⊶ Key points from *your* perspective.

How would knowing this information help Ms. Moore?

What Is Social Cognitive Theory?

In their attempt to make psychology a truly scientific discipline, behaviorists ruled out the study of consciousness that was espoused by the very early theorists who used introspection as a means of studying conscious behavior. Introspection is the process we use to reflect on our own feelings and thoughts. Observable behavior was the only subject matter behaviorists deemed appropriate to the study of behavior. In reaction to behaviorists' disregard of cognition, or thought, social learning theories arose to study the role that cognitive processes play in the way human beings acquire and regulate their behaviors. In a sense, these theories serve as a bridge between behavioral theories and cognitive theories. They emphasize the social nature of learning while incorporating behaviorist ideas of reinforcement.

In the mid-1980s, Albert Bandura renamed social learning theory, preferring instead to call it social cognitive theory because it had evolved to incorporate so many of the ideas from cognitive science. He is the most prominent among social cognitive theorists. According to Bigge and Shermis (1999), Bandura's theory brings together purposive cognitive psychology with elements of reinforcement theory. However, they point out that it is not reinforcement in the traditional behaviorist sense. Rather, it is shaped by the learner's expectations and insights gained on past occasions similar to the current one. At its core, Bandura's version of social cognitive theory posits that *much human behavior is learned by observing the behavior of others.*

In this theory, three elements come together to influence learning: the behavior, the person, and the environment. It is in this social milieu that people acquire cognitive representations of behavior by observing models performed by others (Bandura 1978, 1982, 1989).

We shall now focus on two key ideas from Bandura's theory of social cognition:

1. The *effects* of modeling on behavior.
2. The *processes* people use to learn from models.

A Person Who Helped Create Change . . .

Albert Bandura was born December 4, 1925, in northern Canada. After receiving his bachelor's degree in psychology from the University of British Columbia (1949) and his Ph.D. from the University of Iowa (1952), he moved to Stanford University. At Stanford he began working on pioneering research into the ways behavior influences learning.

Bandura focused on aggression in adolescents. He defined the concept of reciprocal determinism as the idea that the environment affects behavior just as one's behavior affects the environment. Bandura later developed what has become known as social cognitive theory. Through his own studies, he found that children learn many behaviors by watching others and then imitating them. His hands-on approach to research and his theories have influenced many psychologists and educators. Albert Bandura helped us change from a focus only on observable behavior to a focus on the role of cognition (thought) in understanding human behavior.

Source: http://www.ship.edu/~cgboeree/bandura.html

Modeling Effects

Bandura identifies three effects of the process of modeling other's behaviors (see Fig. 2.1). New skills or behaviors learned by observing others Bandura calls the *observational learning effect.* A second modeling effect is the *inhibitory effect.* A behavior that is previously learned is inhibited, or reduced, if one person observes another person receiving a negative consequence for having performed that particular behavior. Related to the inhibitory effect is the *disinhibitory effect,* which works in the opposite way. A person will increase a previously learned behavior if she observes no negative consequence for having performed it. To illustrate, if a child who calls out in class loses recess privileges, children observing this will be less likely to call out themselves (calling out behavior is inhibited). However, if calling out is typically followed by a negative consequence and, perhaps in the presence of a substitute teacher, a child calls out with no subsequent negative consequence, then the other children are likely to begin to call out (a formerly inhibited behavior is now disinhibited). Finally, a third modeling effect is called *response facilitation.* In this effect, a model behavior serves as a cue for observers to perform the same behavior that they previously learned or acquired. In this way,

FIGURE 2.1

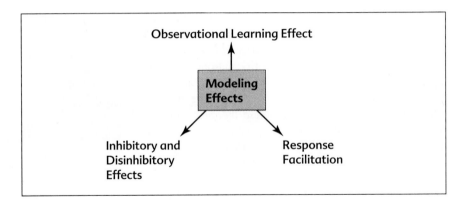

a specific response is elicited from the observer (Bandura 1986). An example of response facilitation is when one person begins to clap after watching a performance of some kind. Others typically follow suit.

The importance of others in the learning process should now be apparent. *Humans learn much from observing one another.* Parents model behaviors for their children; teachers model behaviors for their students; children model behaviors for other children; experts model behaviors for novices. Of course, models do not have to be live. They can also be symbolic. Books, television, and newer technologies can all serve as models for human learners. And they can be purely verbal instructions about how to behave without any human being even present (Ormrod 1999). However, in school settings humans, especially teachers and peers, are the most compelling models. And in classroom settings teachers must carefully select and monitor the types of symbolic activities that serve as models, or potential models, for their students.

Modeling Processes

According to Bandura (1986), in order for a person to learn from observation of models, there are certain processes that must take place. First and foremost a learner must *pay attention* to the modeled behavior. If no attention is paid, then there will be no observational learning effect taking place for that particular behavior. Second, the learner must *retain* the knowledge about the modeled behavior. This involves cognitive activity on the part of the learner, who must actively convert the modeled behavior into some type of representation that is stored in long-term memory. Third, the learner must be able to *produce* the modeled behavior by retrieving the cognitive representation from long-term memory (explained later in this chapter)

Processes in Modeling
To Teach the Study Skill of Creating an Organizer called *Spider Map*

Attention	Retention	Production	Motivation
Draw attention to material from a book. Show how to do a spider map. Put information onto map.	Student rehearses steps—material, map, match material to map.	Student produces a map of an assigned reading, gets feedback.	Teacher helps student see how organizers force connections that help the student remember the information.

Source: After the work of Hamilton and Ghatala, 1994.

and actually performing an appropriate action based upon that representation. Finally, a person must be *motivated* to either enact or suppress a behavior that he or she learned through observation. The fact that one has observed a behavior, represented it cognitively, and is capable of reproducing it does not necessarily mean that she will do so. Each of these processes—attention, retention, production, and motivation—hold important implications for what teachers must do in classroom settings to make full use of the power of social cognitive theory. And don't forget that teachers are not our only models. Other adults, our peers, and nonhuman models also bring about modeling effects. The implications of social cognitive theory for teachers will be addressed in the next chapter of this book. For now, we will focus on its relevance to the core concept of *humans learning in cooperation with other humans*.

Social cognitive theory forms a nice bridge between traditional behavioral theory and newer cognitive theory. We shall now explore another theory that addresses social interaction and its role in learning, and that moves even further from traditional views derived from behaviorism and embraces more contemporary cognitive views. This next theory provides a view of learning that articulates the primacy of the social and cultural contexts in which human learners construct their own understandings of things.

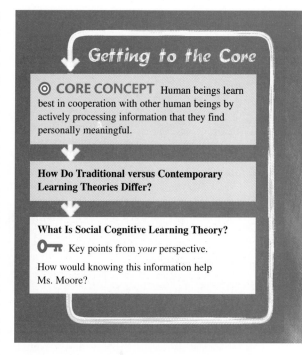

Getting to the Core

◎ **CORE CONCEPT** Human beings learn best in cooperation with other human beings by actively processing information that they find personally meaningful.

How Do Traditional versus Contemporary Learning Theories Differ?

What Is Social Cognitive Learning Theory?

○━┓ Key points from *your* perspective.

How would knowing this information help Ms. Moore?

How Does Contextualist Theory Help Us Understand Learning?

According to Miller (1993), contextualist theory asserts that "behavior has meaning (and can be 'explained') only in terms of its social-historical context" (19). In other words, we cannot understand human behavior without knowing something about the context within which it occurs. This context consists of the culture in which the person acts. People sharing common beliefs, values, customs, traditions, and languages, among other things, define cultures. The work of Lev Vygotsky, a Russian psychologist who was heavily influenced by the Marxist philosophy that sprang up in the new Soviet state after the revolution in 1917, is currently among the most influential of the contextualist theories in the field of education.

Vygotsky's theory included four major ideas that we will address in this section of the chapter. They are very important for teachers and prospective teachers to understand:

1. Children construct their own knowledge.
2. Language plays a central role in cognitive development.
3. Learning can lead development.
4. Development cannot be separated from the social context in which it occurs.

Constructed Knowledge

Vygotsky was what we now call a constructivist. Constructivism is a theory about learning and knowledge with a much different perspective than other cognitive theories, even those to which it is closely akin. In the constructivist view, human

> **Think about it . . .**
>
> Try to recall one particular time when you learned something by observing another person.
>
> 1. What was it that you learned?
> 2. Can you identify which modeling processes were involved as you went about learning the skill or concept?

A Person Who Helped Create Change . . .

Lev Semyonovich Vygotsky was born in 1896 in Orsha, Belarus. He studied at First State University of Moscow between 1913 and 1917. After completing his education at the university level, he taught literature and psychology at a school in Gomel. He was very interested in the problems of literature and science. He also founded the literary journal *Verask* at this time.

In 1924, Vygotsky moved to Moscow and founded the Institute of Defectology. He also became the director of the department for the education of physically defective children in Narcompros (Peoples Committee on Education). In 1925 he and a group of young scientists began research in the areas of psychology, defectology, and mental abnormality. At his untimely death in 1934, he was head of the department of psychology in the All-Union Institute of Experimental Medicine.

Vygotsky was a real pioneer. He was one of the first to recognize the importance of the social aspect of a child's psychological development. His work encouraged other psychologists to focus on the role of social development in children, a role that is still seen as crucial in a child's development process. His ideas have greatly influenced contemporary educational practice and changed the way we view the importance of social aspects of learning.

Photo: Courtesy of Davidson Films @ www.davidsonfilms.com
Source: http://home.pacbell.net/frendon/vygotsky.htm

beings do not gain knowledge by creating mental representations of realities that exist independent of their own experiences. Rather than attempt to know some real world, in the constructivist view humans create their own version of reality in order to adapt to the world in which they live. Humans create their own meaning in very idiosyncratic ways, based upon their experiences and prior knowledge. Therefore, teachers who view knowledge as being constructed by learners would abandon the view that there are things to be known independent of students' experiences. They would also understand that knowledge constructed by learners cannot be directly imparted to them by another person. Instead, they would operate on the assumption that students might, and do, perceive their environment in ways much different from those teachers intend. In order to help students learn, therefore, teachers must first understand how the students are representing a given concept or procedure. Then, and only then, can teachers reasonably hope to help students change their current conceptions and understandings so that they might better adapt to their environment (Fosnot, 1996).

In Chapter 1 we referred to a fourth-grade lesson on heat. We pointed out how strongly the children in that classroom held to their incorrect convictions that their clothes were "hot." The story of that classroom is the story of a classroom managed by a teacher with a constructivist attitude. The teacher would never have known the children's misconceptions had she not allowed them to first explain their current understanding of heat. When she discovered their misconceptions, she resisted the temptation to just correct them by telling about heat. Rather, in the spirit of constructivism she allowed them to test their hypotheses in order to reach a new understanding of the concept of heat. The children worked with one another, designing and carrying out their experiments. This story clearly depicts a constructivist approach to teaching. Vygotsky would have approved of this classroom!

Language, Learning, and Development

Vygotsky believed that speech is a very powerful psychological tool that lays the foundation for basic structures of thinking later in one's development. Central to the notion that humans learn best in cooperation with other humans, Vygotsky believed that speech initially arises out of the need for a child to communicate with others that share his environment. Early verbalizations such as "mine toy" or "mommy bye-bye" are examples of ways that children use speech to communicate. It is through speech and language that higher mental functions develop and are transmitted. Learning, according to Vygotsky, always involves some type of external experience being transformed into internal processes through the use of language. At the classroom level, teachers must use, and allow children to use, speech and language as primary tools for learning.

Much of the rest of Vygotsky's theory, at least as it relates to our core concept of learning as social interaction, is derived from his views on thought and language. One major idea proposed by his theory is the *zone of proximal development* (see Fig. 2.2). Teachers often have to maintain a delicate balance between providing learning opportunities that, on the one hand, a child can already accomplish without assistance on her own (called the level of independent performance), and on the other hand are entirely too advanced for a child to benefit from. One extreme can lead to boredom, the other to frustration. The zone of proximal (next or nearest) development is the area between a child's level of actual development, and the level at which a child can potentially develop in collaboration with a more capable person (called the level of assisted performance). This idea is crucial to an understanding of the

FIGURE 2.2

Visual depiction of the zone of proximal development

(Source: http://hale.pepperdine. edu/~scorcora/zpd_illustration2. html.)

When Are You In The Zone

"the zone of proximal development... the distance between the actual development level as determined by independent problem solving and the level of potential development as determined through problem solving under adult guidance or in collaboration with more capable peers. (page 86, Mind in Society, L. S. Vygotsky)

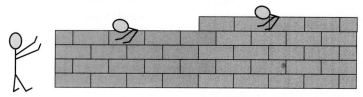

Where will the participant most likely get the assistance he/she needs to successfully get over the wall, in the gray section or in the blue section? The section where the participant can achieve success with guidance would represent the ZPD for the participant. After working in this section with guidance from adults and peers the participant could eventually get over the wall unassisted.

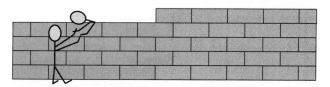

Next question: Once the participant was successful in the gray section could he/she attempt the blue section?

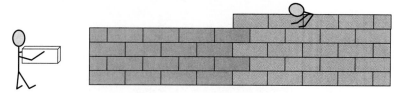

With the skills and knowledge the participant learned in the gray section he/she can now work on being successful in the blue section. Again, he/she will be assisted by adults and/or peers in climbing over the wall, thus the participant is again in a ZPD.

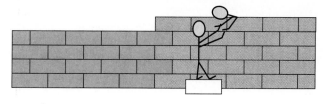

Think about it . . . **Can you think of
something you
cannot yet do or understand, but you probably
could with the help of a friend or teacher who
has already mastered the skill or concept?**

- **What is it?**

- **How do you know that you could do or
understand it with assistance?**

- **What could that more capable person
do to help you master the new skill or
understanding?**

power of social interaction in promoting learning. Hamilton
and Ghatala (citing Wertsch and Rogoff 1984) summarized
Vygotsky's view of learning "as involving social interactions
that push the child forward into his zone of proximal development where new developmental processes are triggered . . .
[and] practiced until they are internalized and become part of
the child's repertoire of independent abilities. Thus, the zone
of proximal development can be thought of as the developmental level just beyond the child's current level of functioning. There, the child encounters new cultural tools, which are
practiced *in social interaction with more experienced members of society* until they become part of the child's independent functioning" (1994, 266, emphasis ours).

This zone of proximal development is not static. It shifts
upward as learning occurs. In this manner, learning can actually lead development,
rather than being dependent on the child's level of development. Consistent with this
idea, rather than wait until a child is "ready" to learn something, teachers should find
tasks that the child cannot do alone, but can do with the assistance of a teacher or a
more capable partner. It is in this zone of proximal development that teachers must
concentrate their efforts in order to help children, or any age learner, develop cognitively. Teachers will have to assess the child's level of independent performance
and the level of assisted performance. Vygotsky was not a fan of standardized tests
because they are not appropriate for determining these levels. The assessments that
need to be used to determine levels of independent and assisted performance must
be informal and conducted in the context of the act of teaching (or, to put it more
correctly, in the context of helping children learn). Further, teachers must constantly
make decisions about what to do next to support a child's task performance. These
decisions are best made during the actual teaching and learning process.

Students learn with assistance from a more capable person (Courtesy of Charles Gupton/Getty Images).

The Social Context of Learning

Much of what constitutes learning from this contextualist view involves social discourse. Some very specific techniques have been developed that help guide the teaching and learning process in a social context. Techniques such as *cooperative learning* (Johnson, Johnson, and Smith 1991; Johnson and Johnson 1994; Kagan 1992), *scaffolding* (Bruner 1978; Wood, Bruner, and Ross 1976), and *reciprocal teaching* (Palincsar 1986) have helped teachers understand ways to systematize instruction on the basis of dialogue and conversation. For example, researchers have agreed that cooperative learning is not just group work. Rather, Millis (1995) defined cooperative learning as a *structured form of group work* where students, *who are individually assessed,* work toward common group goals (127). The exact forms of structure may vary, but cooperative learning generally requires the following:

- Each group member's success depends upon all other members' success (positive interdependence).

- Group members help, assist, support, and encourage one another in their efforts to learn (face-to-face interaction).

- Ultimately each group member is assessed individually and given feedback on his or her performance (individual accountability). (Johnson, Johnson, and Smith 1991)

We will address cooperative learning in greater depth in Chapter 3, but it is important to note here that face-to-face interaction is essential in this form of learning.

Scaffolding is a technique that, like cooperative learning, helps the learner master information or a task that is initially beyond his or her capabilities (see Fig. 2.3). To understand scaffolding, just think of the scaffold with which you are already familiar—a structure, usually a raised platform, that provides support for workers. Wood, Bruner, and Ross (1976) identify six functions of scaffolding that a teacher or adult may use to help the learner. These functions are listed as steps in the scaffolding process:

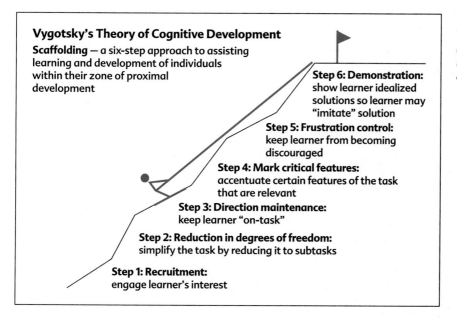

FIGURE 2.3

Visual depiction of scaffolding.

(Source: This visual was created by Donna Wake, graduate student at La Salle University.)

1. **Recruitment** occurs when the teacher first engages the learner in the task.

2. **Reduction in degrees of freedom** requires the adult to simplify the task by breaking it into subtasks that the learner can manage.

3. **Direction maintenance** involves keeping the learner on-task and motivated.

4. **Marking critical features** takes place when the teacher calls the learner's attention to relevant features of the task.

5. **Frustration control** occurs where the teacher helps the learner overcome frustration when errors are made.

6. **Demonstration** involves the teacher engaging in model solutions to problems that the learner may imitate.

> **Reciprocal teaching is a very structured way to teach reading. If you would like to learn more about this technique, visit the following website:** http://www.psy.gla.ac.uk/~steve/mant/altj.html. **If this link does not work, just go to your favorite search engine and type in Reciprocal Teaching.**

The use of language and shared experience is critical to successful use of scaffolding as an educational technique.

Finally, reciprocal teaching is an example of an instructional procedure that is, according to Hamilton and Ghatala (1994), "explicitly based upon Vygotsky's socioinstructional approach" (271). It is specifically targeted at helping learners read and comprehend, and makes extensive use of collaborative dialogue to do so. Palincsar (1986) and her colleagues have incorporated four major strategies into the dialogue that takes place. These include predicting, questioning, summarizing, and clarifying. The goal is to have learners regulate their own reading comprehension using metacognitive strategies. Metacognition is the process whereby learners think about how they go about learning or, in this case, reading text. Teachers engaged in this method of teaching provide the range of activities that are consistent with contextualist theory. They serve as models for the learners, they provide support to learners through scaffolding, they provide feedback to the learners on their performance, and they clarify by providing explanations when necessary.

Although there are many more techniques that flow from social cognitive and contextualist theories, the main point is that learners can learn much in cooperation with others. Research evidence suggests that they learn even better in this manner. Much more will be written about the applications of these theories in the following chapters. For now, however, we will turn to the next part of the core concept presented earlier in the chapter: Human beings learn best in cooperation with other human beings by *actively processing information* that they find personally meaningful.

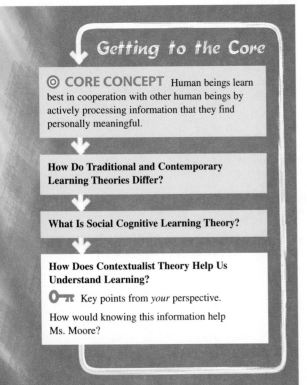

Getting to the Core

◎ CORE CONCEPT Human beings learn best in cooperation with other human beings by actively processing information that they find personally meaningful.

How Do Traditional and Contemporary Learning Theories Differ?

What Is Social Cognitive Learning Theory?

How Does Contextualist Theory Help Us Understand Learning?

⚷ Key points from *your* perspective.

How would knowing this information help Ms. Moore?

What Is Information Processing Theory?

How people learn is, of course, the most central question with which teachers must struggle. We know they learn in cooperation with other human beings. Information Processing Theory (IPT) provides yet another part of the answer to this critical question. IPT is really organized in several different models. Nonetheless, all of the models resemble flowcharts and are based upon, to one degree or another, analogies to computers. They focus on how human beings transform information from input to output (Gagne, Yekovich, and Yekovich 1993). In that sense, they are models of how humans actively process information.

Basically, information processing theory applies research on memory to how we learn. The biggest ideas can be characterized as follows:

- Stimuli from the environment impinge upon our senses, and our sensory registers in particular.
- What we recognize and pay attention to moves on to working memory.
- What we neither recognize nor pay attention to decays.
- Once in working memory, we rehearse information to maintain it long enough to decide whether or not we want to process it further, or more deeply.
- That which we process further is encoded into long-term memory through various forms of elaborative rehearsal and practice with feedback.
- That which we do not process further is often sooner or later forgotten.
- Information in long-term memory is then available to be retrieved, when necessary, in order for us to make a cognitive response (see Fig. 2.4).

In short, those are the big ideas. And the biggest idea of all is that, in this model, *nothing is learned unless it is encoded (gathered and represented) into long-term memory.* Of course, such a brief summary grossly oversimplifies the entire process. A closer look at the big ideas reveals the richness and power of Information Processing Theory.

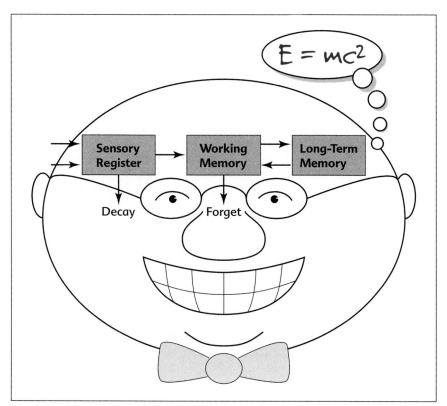

FIGURE 2.4

Information Processing Theory (IPT) as applied to memory.

Note that IPT is a hypothetical construct that depicts what goes on inside the human mind, between our ears.

SPOTLIGHT ON BEHAVIOR MANAGEMENT:

"But will they behave?"

Insight and Trusting Relationships

You have just spent the last several pages discovering that students learn best in cooperation with others. You have also been reading about motivation. Not surprisingly, these concepts are also important when trying to understand the behavior of your students. A teacher using the psychodynamic model, which we introduced in the last spotlight on behavior management, must scrutinize the "inner lives of children" (Danforth and Boyle 2000, 11). The role of the teacher becomes one of helping the student see connections among thoughts, feelings, actions, and interactions with others. At the heart of this approach is the development of an understanding of what motivates students' behavior. Two concepts that we will now introduce that can help teachers understand what motivates student behavior are *gaining insight* and *developing trusting relationships* (Danforth and Boyle 2000).

Let's go back to the example in the last chapter where Juan, who was teased by Eliza on the bus, interrupted the lesson. If you will recall, the teacher was unaware that Eliza had been teasing Juan about his unkempt appearance. The teacher reacted to Juan's behavior and emotions ran high. Clearly, she did not have insight into the thinking and acting of these two students. Could the teacher have approached the situation differently?

Because teachers using a psychodynamic perspective understand *insight* and *relationships,* they keep a keen eye on their students as they arrive and throughout the day. Because of their relationships with each student, they are able to make predictions about them on the basis of their knowledge and observations. They have developed the ability to gain *insight* about students' lives by watching and questioning.

The teacher may have noticed something about Juan's appearance, facial expression, or attitude, and then spent a few seconds talking with him to find out what he was thinking and feeling. Perhaps Eliza entered the class looking a little more smug than usual or right on the heels of Juan. Maybe she was unusually late. The insightful teacher questions Eliza. To gain *insight* we look for clues. We listen to our intuition. We ask questions and search for answers.

> ◎ **CORE CONCEPT** Human beings learn best in cooperation with other human beings by actively processing information that they find personally meaningful.

Insight is also what we want to develop in Juan and Eliza. However, insight "involves a rationality and reflective capacity that are often unavailable to a student feeling overwhelmed and driven by intense emotions" (Danforth and Boyle 2000, 12). Students in troubling situations will need the support of a trusted adult to help them. The role of the teacher, first and foremost, is to stabilize the current situation. Acting in a nonjudgmental, calm, and supportive manner, the teacher provides a physical and emotional environment for the student to pull himself or herself together and calm down. In later chapters we will give you specific suggestions that will help you do this.

Keep *insight* and *trusting relationships* in mind. These concepts will continue to be important as we introduce the conflict cycle and how to use the model effectively. What we hope will become clear to you as we proceed is that insight and trusting relationships are important both as tools for teachers to use *and* as tools for students to use.

Right now, let's search for some insight into why students misbehave. In part, we began to answer this question in the last chapter when we asked you to recall classrooms where you or your peers misbehaved. We reminded you that you probably did not misbehave in the classrooms where you were engaged, challenged, or had a personal connection with the teacher.

So what motivates behavior? Allen Mendler (1992) suggests that basic needs play the greatest role. He asks teachers to help children meet these basic needs by providing them opportunities to (1) feel successful, (2) experience a sense of belonging, (3) have control, (4) experience generosity, and (5) have fun. When these needs are met, students respond positively. Think about the classrooms that you enjoyed as a student. How were these needs met for you in those classrooms? How can you arrange for these needs to be met in your classroom?

Interestingly, Native Americans have known and practiced a similar philosophy for over 15,000 years (Brendtro, Brokenleg, and Van Bockern 1990). The "circle of courage" stresses that children need a (1) spirit of belonging, (2) spirit of mastery, (3) spirit of independence, and (4) spirit of generosity in order to develop. It seems that no matter which philosophy of developing positive behavior in children we examine, they all require one common ingredient: a significant adult-child relationship. Brendtro, Brokenleg, and Van Bockern (1990) emphasize this point:

> Adults who work with youth have long been aware of the awesome power of relationships. This was a dominant theme of the early writings in education, counseling and youth work. However, as professional literature became more scientifically oriented, relationships were increasingly ignored. . . . Research shows that the quality of human relationships in schools and youth service programs may be more influential than the specific interventions employed. (58)

Building these relationships with troubling children is not easy. As we mentioned previously, conflict in schools is also stressful for adults. So it will now be important for you turn your attention inward as we investigate relationships from another perspective, that is your relationship to yourself. What does it feel like *to you* when you are angry, stressed, confused, or tense? What do you do with these feelings? Only you can answer these questions, because these feelings are physically manifested differently in each of us. Take stress for example, do you feel it in your stomach, your lower back, or do you semiconsciously clench your teeth? Is it possible to use these physical sensations as cues to remind yourself what you are feeling? Once we recognize and own our feelings we can act on the basis of rational thought. Remember: During a school or classroom conflict it is your responsibility, as the professional, to be mature, thoughtful, rational, and helpful so that you can best meet the needs of your students.

If we don't take the time to examine how *we* think and feel in these situations, we may simply react on the basis of our own emotional response and irrational thinking. This reaction will most likely produce more stress for the troubled student. We will not be in a position to provide the kind of calm, supportive physical and emotional environment our students need during these times. In fact, we are likely to escalate the situation.

This response to a student's action, with much the same emotion that he or she is hurling at us, is known as counteraggression. Here is a simple example of counteraggressive behavior:

Teacher: Juan, stop making faces and pay attention to my lesson.

Juan: (Ignores the teacher and continues to make faces.)

Teacher: (A little louder.) Juan, I am talking to you, look at me!

Juan: No!

Teacher: (Raising voice.) Juan . . . Look at me when I am talking!

Juan: (Stands and turns back to teacher.)

Teacher: (Loudly.) That does it! Go to the office!

You can feel the escalating emotion as the teacher's voice gets louder. Counteraggressive responses are harmful. They erode the relationships we have been building. They force us to focus on emotion, power, and control, clouding our ability to gain insight. They escalate student behavior. A power struggle ensues. No one wins. Oh, it may feel like you have won. You may be thinking, "The student is out of the room and the class knows I mean business!" But have you really won? Was your response helpful for the well-being of the student or the rest of the class? Has anyone learned a productive way to deal with thoughts and feelings?

We are getting closer to an explanation of the conflict cycle, the model that we have been leading up to. The conflict cycle will help you understand where counteraggression comes from and how to handle it. For now, we would like to leave you with two points. First, the relationships you develop with your students will provide opportunities for you to gain insight into their behavior. Become a keen observer, questioner, and listener. Second, it is crucial to pay attention to your own thoughts and feelings. A good way to practice is to keep a log of emotions and the corresponding physical sensations you feel. Try to pay attention to those physical sensations. See if you can use them as cues to become more reflective, thoughtful, and insightful.

In addition, as you work in classrooms, try to identify those events that trigger a response in you. It is important not only to know what sets your students off, but also what sets you off (Muscott 1995). Make a list. After you have identified your own stressors you can "modify, eliminate, or learn to live with [them]" (Muscott 1995, 43). We hope we have made clear the importance of monitoring and reflecting on your own behavior. You will soon see why this is so crucial in helping students deal with crises.

Attention, Recognition, and Human Memory

Human learners are bombarded constantly by environmental stimuli. This bombardment occurs everywhere. The classroom is but one environment in which it occurs, and perhaps the only one under the control of the teacher. As stimuli impinge upon our senses, these sensations, all of them, enter, or are encoded in, the memory system. The first component of the memory system, according to information processing theorists, is the sensory register. This memory holds an enormous amount of information; it records virtually everything that we see, hear, touch, and so on. But it holds this information for only a very brief period of time. Although information processing theorists disagree on the exact duration, the estimates range from much less than a second to approximately three seconds. Even though the information is fleeting, it is available to us for a brief period even after the stimulus has gone. The stimuli leave a sensory "trace."

Because so many stimuli impinge upon our senses, it is a blessing for humans that the sensory memory is so limited in duration. It would not be possible to function cognitively if all of the stimuli to which we were exposed remained in our memory system for long periods of time. We would be overwhelmed and confused by such a wide range of overlapping and contradictory stimuli. Stimuli may indeed overwhelm people for whom the sensory memory fails to function properly. It is possible that responses to this failure to sort out stimuli result in hyperactivity (increased activity) or hypoactivity (decreased activity) on the part of the learner. We will expand on this idea in Chapter 6.

What determines whether stimuli are allowed to decay or to move on to working memory? Of course, a person must first *recognize* the stimuli. If stimuli are recognized, the most crucial factor that determines what moves forward to working memory is *attention*. The simple truth is, what is not attended to will be lost, and what is attended to by the learner will be processed further. Attention is so important to human learning that it deserves teachers' special treatment. Learners can learn to direct their own attention to important stimuli, and teachers can develop activities that gain their learners' attention. Although many people know intuitively that paying attention is important, information processing theory suggests why—nothing moves to working memory unless attention is paid to it.

If the learner, usually with the teacher's help, has recognized and attended to the appropriate and relevant information, that information is now in working memory. Whatever we are conscious of at the moment is in our working memory. It is where we do our thinking, or our cognitive work. Information is there long enough to permit us to make a decision about what we want to do with it. We can choose to further process it by connecting it with information in long-term memory, or we can just forget it. Working memory is a sort of bottleneck in the human learning system. It is designed only for the short term, and only for a small amount of information, at least when compared to long-term memory. Specifically, cognitive researchers estimate that information can be held in working memory for only about 15 to 30 seconds. They also estimate that working memory can hold only five to nine bits of information. Human beings are required to do something with information in working memory, or the information will soon be forgotten (see Fig. 2.5.)

Actually, humans have gotten quite good at figuring out ways to keep information in working memory for longer than 15 to 30 seconds. Using a process called maintenance rehearsal, people can repeat over and over to themselves the information in their working memories. This allows information to be held much longer. It permits people to think more about whether or not they want to retain the

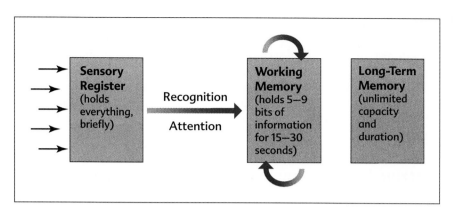

FIGURE 2.5
Recognition, attention, and maintenance rehearsal in the Human IP system.

information by connecting it to something in the long-term memory or let it drop out of the memory system. Unfortunately, and uniquely in school settings, it is often abused. For example, prior to an exam learners may engage in a concerted period of maintenance rehearsal for the express purpose of passing a test. This practice, commonly called "cramming," may often work in the short run by allowing the learner to memorize large amounts of information long enough to "spit it all back" on a test. Teachers who make tests that tap primarily lower levels of knowledge such as factual recall may inadvertently encourage this practice among learners. But alas, much of what has been memorized is either soon forgotten, or if it is retained somehow in long-term memory it is relatively disconnected from all other knowledge and therefore less likely to be retrieved when needed to perform higher-level cognitive tasks.

In addition, by not making connections learners tend to see information as isolated bits of facts and procedures. Because working memory can hold only five to nine bits of information, learners who do not look for connections quickly run out of memory space. More efficient learners try to see how pieces of information relate to one another. This process, called "chunking," can permit much more information to be held in working memory. If bits become chunks, then working memory can hold five to nine chunks of information, greatly increasing the amount of information that can be held in working memory to work on cognitive tasks.

Remember that working memory is where humans perform their conscious mental work, their thinking. They can do this work much more efficiently, and effectively, if they can easily retrieve appropriate information from long-term memory that is connected clearly and correctly to other, relevant pieces of information. One difference between novices and experts in any given domain is that experts can hold much more information in long-term memory because they have chunked this information. Thus, five to nine chunks greatly enhance the amount of information that can be manipulated in working memory. In addition, experts have organized this information very tightly, so all of the information in a chunk is connected. Think about a map that you might use to find your way to a place where you have never been. The more detailed that map, the easier it will be to find your way. This is similar to the detailed knowledge that an expert commands. Now, think about the roads on that map that show how to get from place to place. If there are no roads connecting one place to another, then these places are isolated and not easy to get to. Places with many roads leading to them are easily accessed. This is similar to the idea of organized and retrievable knowledge. Experts have lots of connections among and between similar ideas that are grouped together.

> **Think about it . . .**
>
> When have you "crammed" for a test by pulling an "all-nighter"? How did you do on that test? Can you now recall most of the material and use it when you need to?

We said earlier that, in this model of learning, nothing is learned unless it enters long-term memory. At least theoretically, long-term memory does not have limitations of space or size. That is, it can hold an infinite amount of information forever. Although some theorists argue over "forever," there is little disagreement that long-term memory holds information for a very long time, and we do not know of any human being that has exceeded the amount of space available in long-term memory. In order to understand and use information, it must first be retained in long-term memory.

Getting Information into Long-Term Memory

Information processing (IP) theorists and other cognitivist theorists widely agree that teachers cannot simply transfer information directly from their own to their students' long-term memories. The information processing model describes what goes on in the learner's cognitive world. So how can *learners* transfer information received from the environment from working to long-term memory? And how can teachers *help* them do so? From a theoretical perspective, learners can use metacognitive strategies to help them move information into their long-term memories. These strategies serve an executive function that monitors the processing of information. We earlier defined metacognition as occurring when people think about how they are thinking (see page 44). There are several strategies for accomplishing the active processing of information necessary to retain, understand, and be able to use concepts and ideas. Information processing theory suggests that elaboration, imagery, organization, and mnemonics are among those strategies that characterize active processing on the part of the learner.

Elaboration (or elaborative rehearsal as it is sometimes referred to in order to distinguish it from maintenance rehearsal) is the process by which learners add something that they already know to new information that they confront (see Fig. 2.6). For example, when learners understand addition they can build upon (elaborate) their schema for computation by connecting multiplication (adding on) to it later on. By making the connection between new information and prior knowledge, no matter how (initially) naïve, learners form networks of concepts that are linked together and that provide a rich array of related connections. These connections allow for more differentiated and, eventually, more expert mental maps (schema) of the cognitive world. These mental maps that we humans develop are what allow us to think about the world in which we live. Studies show that elaboration is a very powerful way to develop more lasting memories of facts, and deeper understandings of concepts and ideas.

Closely related to elaboration are images and other visual representations of facts, concepts, and ideas. These enable learners to represent knowledge more efficiently in working memory. Recall that working memory has limited space (five to nine chunks of information).

Human beings learn best through cooperating with others by actively processing information that they find personally meaningful (Courtesy of Ron Chapple/Getty Images).

Because pictures, visuals, and images are continuous representations of some type of idea, concept, or fact, they take up much less space in working memory. Continuous representations are holistic, as opposed to discrete, entities. For example, when considering the word "house," we all have some idea of the concept. A house provides us shelter, families live in houses, and so on. We also know that a house has a roof, a chimney, windows, doors, rooms, and so forth. Most of us represent "house" as an image that is conjured up at the sound of the word. We do not think of its discrete parts, but rather we have an image that incorporates all of those parts into a whole, or one single unit. This single unit represents a "chunk" of information. That saves a lot of space in working memory that we can use to think about other things. We might think about how a house might differ from a boat. Or we might take in new information about, or related to, house.

Images also allow us to see relationships among and between parts of concepts, ideas, and facts. By nature they put things into perspective. This perspective is often missing when we attempt to process information without using imagery. The activity involved in creating images (such as artistic representations of ideas in metaphorical terms) actively involves the learner in processing information in much the same way as does elaborative rehearsal. Because activity and passivity are incompatible, elaboration and imagery ensure active processing among learners.

Encouraging learners to organize information also helps them learn more efficiently. Once again recall the limitations of space in working memory. If material is "carefully divided into subsets, and the relations within and between subsets are noted," learners can process much information quickly and simultaneously increase their knowledge and understanding of that material (Hamilton and Ghatala 1994, 119). Teachers can help this process by organizing lectures, discussions, and learning activities in logical and discernible (to their learners) ways.

There are some things that people must learn but that have no conceptual basis. For example, the names of the Great Lakes are what we refer to as arbitrary associations. They were named as they were for no underlying, conceptually compelling reason. As such, their names are merely labels. Lacking inherent meaning, these arbitrary associations would be rather difficult for learners to connect to other, meaningful concepts and ideas they have learned. In order to be able to retain this information, mnemonics may be used. Mnemonic devices help learners take something that is less meaningful and connect it with something more meaningful. For example, the acronym HOMES can help us to remember the names of the Great Lakes (*H*uron, *O*ntario, *M*ichigan, *E*rie, and *S*uperior) by connecting a single word that we find meaningful with five separate words with less meaning. Similarly, telephone numbers are very difficult to remember because arbitrary strings of numbers are less meaningful to human learners than are words (because words are strings of

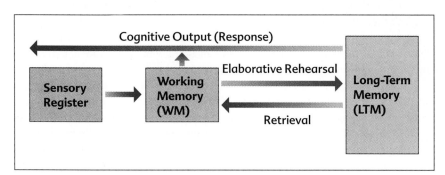

FIGURE 2.6

Elaborative rehearsal (images, organizers) and retrieval in the Human IP system. (Procedural knowledge that is automatized can come right out of LTM. We need not think about it. Declarative knowledge and some procedural knowledge come out of WM because we must first think about them before making a response.)

letters that are connected to one another to form some meaning). Therefore, entrepreneurs will use letters that make words to represent their phone numbers in order to help customers recall that number. Who can forget 1-800-PLUMBER?

Declarative and Procedural Knowledge

Information processing theory distinguishes among several different types of knowledge. Two of these types are declarative knowledge and procedural knowledge. So far the discussion of information processing theory has been mainly about declarative knowledge. Declarative knowledge is knowledge of facts, concepts, and ideas. Propositions, according to Gagne, Yekovich, and Yekovich (1993), are the basic units of declarative knowledge in the human information processing system in that they propose relationships among concepts. A propositional unit, they say, is roughly equivalent to a fact or an idea. Knowing that the American Civil War began at 4:30 A.M. on April 12, 1861, is a propositional unit. So, too, is knowing that General Pierre Gustave Toutant Beauregard was the person who gave the order to the Confederate gunners to fire on Fort Sumter on that day, and at that hour. Propositions are arranged in networks of ideas, facts, and concepts that are linked together (see Fig. 2.7). Therefore ideas, facts, and concepts related to the Civil War, for example that Abraham Lincoln was the president and that Ulysses Grant was a general in the Union army, form networks that combine with other networks to define our declarative knowledge. Understanding the concept that the Civil War was, at the beginning, a battle over state's rights, but ended as struggle over the meaning of freedom in America, is an important piece of declarative knowledge. When linked or networked with other pieces, the whole of what we know, of our declarative knowledge, becomes more than just the sum of its parts.

Procedural knowledge, on the other hand, is represented as productions because it produces a behavior. Whereas declarative knowledge is knowing "what," procedural knowledge is knowing "how." Continuing with our Civil War example, suppose you were asked to write a persuasive speech supporting the rights of states. You would have to know the facts in order to include them in your speech. You would have to know the main ideas and concepts related to the Civil War. Suppose you did not have all of these in your network of propositions. You would have to know how to go about finding this information. This would require you to know how to use the library, the Internet and its search engines, and in general how to conduct research. You would also need to know how to write a speech, and you would need to be able to actually deliver it to an audience. In addition to knowing something, you would have to *do* something. The behavior of researching, writing, and delivering a speech is produced by procedural knowledge. Procedural knowledge is a very important type of knowledge. Yet it seems as if schools do not devote as much time to helping learners develop procedural knowledge as they do to helping learners develop declarative knowledge (Feden 1994). We need to teach students more of the strategies for, say, comprehending what they read, communicating clearly, or working together productively in a group.

Earlier, some general strategies for moving declarative knowledge to long-term memory were addressed. Cognitive psychologists have made it clear that the way we learn procedural knowledge is through practice and feedback. And the more specific the feedback, the better. This is because procedural knowledge is represented as productions. Gagne, Yekovich, and Yekovich (1993) define a production as a condition-action rule. Certain actions take place only when specified conditions are present. By practicing these actions under these conditions, and receiving

Think about it . . .

What is something you recently learned (declarative knowledge) that you wish you could have had the opportunity to do something with (procedural knowledge)? What would you have liked to do?

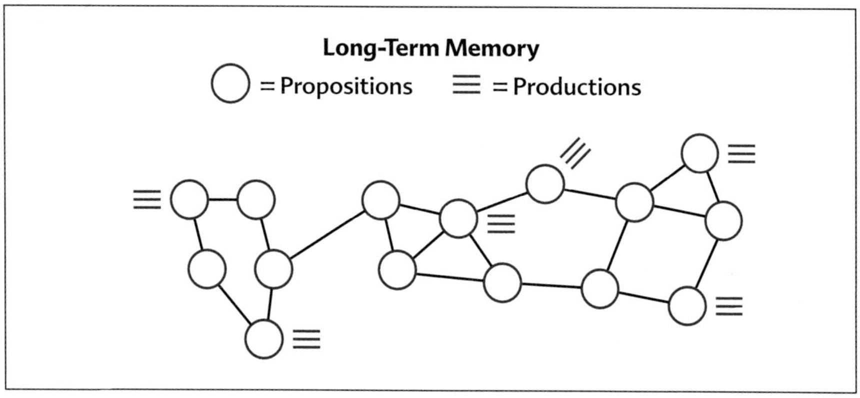

Long-Term Memory

◯ = Propositions   ≡ = Productions

FIGURE 2.7
Propositions (ideas, facts and concepts) and productions (knowing how to do things) represented in the long-term memory.

feedback on the appropriateness and effectiveness of these actions, the learner develops procedural knowledge. After these procedures are well practiced, the behaviors become proceduralized, or automatic. The learner no longer has to consciously think about them.

First, let's consider a nonacademic example of conditions-actions that represents procedural knowledge. Think about driving a car with a manual transmission. If it is not too painful, think about how you learned to drive this car. You might have represented the task something like this (assuming the engine is already running):

> If it is a car and
>
> If it has a stick shift and
>
> If I want to get to the store,
>
> Then depress the clutch, shift the stick into first gear, let up slowly on the clutch while gently depressing the accelerator.

Note the condition-action sequences above (*If these, Then these*). And it certainly was useful to have an experienced person provide feedback as you practiced (i.e., in addition to the feedback provided by the movement of the car itself!). After a while, perhaps a long while, you no longer had to think each step through. Driving a car with a manual transmission became automatic for you. You could even talk or listen to the radio and monitor traffic and road conditions while you were driving. That would have been impossible when you were first learning to drive this car. Also note that you can know the name of every part of that car (e.g., steering wheel, clutch, accelerator pedal). That is declarative knowledge. But you still might not be able to actually drive the car. Driving it requires procedural knowledge. We need both kinds of knowledge.

Now let us consider an academic example. Think about the way you solve simple computational problems (i.e., 3 + 5 = __). Or think about writing your name or reading words from a book. At this point, we trust, you do not need to think very much about these procedures. But you did at one time in your life. Experts in any domain have a great deal of procedural knowledge. Because this knowledge is often accessed automatically, on a kind of automatic pilot, it takes up very little if any space in working memory. This frees up space to think. And that, in turn, allows people to solve difficult problems because by automating basic skills they can keep more complex problems in working memory.

Information processing theory makes it clear that basic skills should be practiced to the point of being automatic. But they should not be based upon information that is not understood, or that is incorrectly understood. Therefore, what is

Think about it . . .

If you were asked to design a visual that would best depict your understanding of IPT, what would it look like? Go ahead, design it!

Now, compare your visual with one designed by a classmate. Combine the two to create a new visual that captures both of your ideas.

practiced should first be understood. Number facts should be automated to enable one to become proficient in solving complex mathematical problems. But the processes of addition, subtraction, multiplication, and division should also be understood. In addition, things that are likely to change should not be automated. For example, it might be best to *not* automate a heuristic (strategy) for solving a multistep problem. These kinds of productions can often interfere with the learner's ability to find other, better, more powerful, and even more accurate solutions to complex problems.

Note in the above discussion that, once again, the learner is actively processing information. In this case through practice, and then feedback from self and others, the learner acquires a type of knowledge that produces behavior. From an information processing perspective, both declarative and procedural knowledge are critically important for learners to acquire. And they cannot do it only by sitting and listening and copying down the words of the teacher. They must actively process the information in ways mentioned above. Because the processing of information occurs in each learner's IP system, it is the learner who must do the hard work, or produce the cognitive sweat, necessary to retain, understand, and use knowledge. The teacher cannot, from this theoretical perspective, do it for the learner. To be sure, the teacher can help students learn strategies for processing information, and can model these strategies. The teacher can establish an environment conducive to active learning, and can provide feedback to the learners. But the teacher cannot simply impart knowledge to learners. After all, if teaching were this easy we would be a lot more successful at getting our students to learn.

Information Processing Theory is not alone in positing that human beings learn best by actively processing information. A host of other theories, and corroborating evidence from educational research, suggest that active learning is crucial for learners to be able to retain, understand, and use knowledge. An increasing array of pedagogical practices has been developed to support teachers in their attempts to encourage learners to actively process information. We will write about these in the chapters that follow. For now, let us return to the core concept presented at the beginning of this chapter and address the final component of that statement: Human beings learn best in cooperation with other human beings by actively processing information that *they find personally meaningful.*

Getting to the Core

◎ CORE CONCEPT Human beings learn best in cooperation with other human beings by actively processing information that they find personally meaningful.

How Do Traditional and Contemporary Theories Differ?

What Is Social Cognitive Theory?

How Does Contextualist Theory Help US Understand Learning?

What Is Information Processing Theory?

O⚏ Key points from *your* perspective.

How would knowing this information help Ms. Moore?

What Motivates Humans to Learn?

According to Miller (1993), motivation has been relatively ignored by information processing theorists and even some other cognitive theorists. Bandura's social cognitive theory has at least one major advantage in this regard. It takes into account what Zajonc (1980) dubbed "hot" cognition. Hot cognition includes the motivational aspect of cognition, whereas cold cognition looks at just the nature of thinking without considering emotions. Social learning theory helps us understand how modeling and reinforcement work in a social context. Important sources of motivation for social learning theorists include learner expectations and personal goals (Bandura 1986). Expectations are based upon consequences of our previous actions, or the consequences of the actions of others whom we have observed. These expectations influence a learner's level of motivation for performing any given behavior. Goal setting also influences level of motivation to perform a specific behavior. It focuses on a learner's activities and, if the goals are realistic and attainable, they increase the learner's persistence in trying to reach the goals.

Learning and Teaching in the Age of Technology

In *Virtual Architecture: Designing and Directing Curriculum-Based Telecomputing* (1998), Judi Harris outlines the growing capability of telecollaboration and teleresearch (using the Internet to communicate, collaborate, and engage in research projects with people at remote locations anywhere in the world) to motivate and develop cooperative, active learning while helping learners comprehend personal meaning. She says telecommunications tools such as electronic mail, electronic bulletin boards, real-time text chat, audio/video conferencing, World Wide Web browsers, simulations, and remotely operated robotic devices allow learners to message and locate information and work with partners at widely separated geographic locations at any time of day or night (Harris 1998, 17). Group ware (products that permit groups of learners to work on the same document simultaneously) can foster cooperation and peer learning even outside the classroom. Internet "keypals" (Harris, 19) may allow teachers to create cooperative learning groups among students outside the immediate classroom. This could indeed be a boon for a child whose emotional and social needs are not well matched or met by current classmates.

The Cognition and Technology Group at Vanderbilt (Goldman, et al. 1999) has also suggested use of the power of educational technology to promote the social arrangements of instruction and to promote collaboration and distributed expertise as well as independent learning (p. 9). The ability to log on from home or school and continue group work at mutually convenient times outside regular classroom hours is itself a high motivator. When multimedia resources are used to organize instruction around the solution of meaningful problems, the ability to engage students in personally meaningful cooperative ways is powerful. "Unlike problems that occur in the real world [that happen once and are over], problems that are created with graphics, video, and animation can be explored again and again."

Development of group-produced hypermedia (multimedia) projects, shared compilation, analysis and application of databases, and group research projects are all easily facilitated with increasingly learner-centered software programs. In a school where several sixth-grade students had been working cooperatively on a National Geographic acid rain project linking their research with schools along the east coast, and working in teams to develop computerized robotics programs using Lego-Logo, students suggested creating a database to register daily recess injuries and complaints. They then proceeded to analyze it for patterns to see if certain days seemed to be worse than others as a way to develop group-based solutions to outdoor recess behavior problems. What more could a proponent of collaborative, personally meaningful learning based on the solution of real world, messy problems want? It's important to remember, however, that all of the accumulated wisdom

◎ CORE CONCEPT Human beings learn best in cooperation with other human beings by actively processing information that they find personally meaningful.

and procedures which have been developed in the last decades on well-structured, managed, and supervised cooperative learning groups (see Millis and Cottell 1998) be employed by teachers when setting up multimedia computer-based collaborations.

Teaching Tips

1. Have students communicate using e-mail, instant messenger, and chatrooms to encourage working together and using each other's expertise to brainstorm class projects, check homework and prepare for tests.

2. Provide computer time during school hours to groups of students to enable communication with students at other schools to discuss similar projects. Allow for use of listserv (a giant conversation among many people with the same interests).

3. Use software programs that are content specific to encourage social interaction, computer skills, and problem solving. For example, Tenth Planet

Explores Math (K–5 Geometry, Sunburst Communications), Multicultural Poets on Identity (7–12, Sunburst Communications), and Ocean Expedition: El Nimo (8–12, Tom Snyder Productions).

Suggested Websites

http://www-ed.fnal.gov/help/index.html
A handbook of engaged learning projects: elementary–middle–high school cooperative learning projects in all subject areas.

http://www.iearn.org/handbook/
International Education and Resource Network: enables young people to undertake projects designed to make a meaningful contribution to the health and welfare of the planet and its people.

http://www.kidlink.org/KIDPROJ/index.html
KIDPROJ, a part of KIDLINK, where teachers and youth group leaders from around the world plan activities and projects for students and other kids age 5 to 15.

Intrinsic versus Extrinsic Motivation

Teachers can apply theory to help motivate learners to want to learn. For example, teachers can help learners think about consequences of past actions (such as not studying for an exam) and then change the behavior that caused the problem (low grade on the exam). Teachers can assist learners in identifying and setting realistic, attainable goals. They can even model such behaviors. It is important to note that, in terms of theory, expectations and personal goals have two very different sources. Expectations based upon consequences have extrinsic sources. That is, the source of motivation lies outside the individual learner, and is under the control of an outside source. Punishment, rewards, and social pressure are examples of extrinsic forms of motivation. Personal goals, on the other hand, have intrinsic sources. They are under the intentional control of the individual learner. Raffini (1996) defines intrinsic motivation succinctly when he writes that it is "what motivates us to do something when we *don't have* to do anything" (3). The activity is itself rewarding when we are intrinsically motivated.

These two sources of motivation are very important to distinguish from one another. However, one cannot tell just by observation whether a behavior is extrinsically or intrinsically motivated. It is what Woolfolk (2001) calls the locus of causality (location of the cause) of the action that is crucial to understanding motivation. If the location is within the learner (personal interest) motivation is intrinsic; if the location is outside the learner (please the teacher) motivation is extrinsic. Many of what we earlier called traditional theories, especially those based upon behavioral psychology, espoused extrinsic motivation and encouraged teachers to systematically apply negative and positive reinforcers to motivate learners. Reinforcers make it more likely that a behavior will be repeated. When teachers give something to learners for engaging in appropriate activity or reaching a certain

Intrinsically motivated students see learning as interesting, challenging, and personally meaningful (Courtesy of Ian Shaw/Getty Images).

level, they are administering positive reinforcement. When teachers allow students to escape from something unpleasant by making appropriate responses, they are administering negative reinforcement. Techniques such as behavior modification (now commonly referred to as applied behavior analysis) were developed, refined, and applied in classroom settings. That such techniques are powerful is clear. Many studies of behavior change serve to document the success of properly implemented techniques of promoting motivation through extrinsic means. Few people dispute that extrinsic motivation is part of everyday life. People work for paychecks, seek the praise of others, and so on.

However, there is a person who argued, very persuasively, that extrinsic rewards, any and all such rewards, actually serve to punish us! Rewards, like punishments, are just a means of controlling others' behaviors. Taking an extreme position on this matter, Kohn (1993) argues in his book *Punished by Rewards* that the facts speak for themselves. He presents the following evidence:

Fact 1: Young children don't need to be rewarded to learn.

Fact 2: At any age, rewards are less effective than intrinsic motivation for promoting effective learning.

Fact 3: Rewards for learning undermine intrinsic motivation (Kohn 1993, 144–148).

Think about it . . .

What motivates you to:

- Attend college?

- Study?

- Pursue a teaching career?

- Play a sport or a musical instrument?

- Join a club or group?

Are you primarily motivated by intrinsic or extrinsic factors?

What do you think will motivate the students you will teach? What will you do to help these students work for intrinsic rewards?

Kohn goes on to argue that extrinsic rewards actually interfere with doing our best work, and that attempts to change people's behaviors with rewards are in vain because they do not have lasting effects. Now, what distinguishes Kohn from other writers who espouse similar ideas is that he shepherds his points with ample research studies. His is not a purely romantic view of what should be. Rather, it is a well-researched and reasoned piece on what is powerful in promoting true learning.

Theory Meets Practice

Nevertheless, when reality and practicality meet theory, compromises typically must be reached. Many theories, except for the most constructivist, include both extrinsic and intrinsic motivation. They attempt to balance the two. Social learning theorists, presented earlier, include both types of motivation—consequences (extrinsic) and personal goals (intrinsic). Perhaps it was Jerome Bruner who best blended the two sources of motivation by recognizing that both exist, but suggesting that intrinsic rewards in promoting learning are the more important of the two. In summarizing his position, Bigge and Shermis (1999) characterize Bruner as believing that external reinforcement may get a behavior going, but intrinsic reinforcement keeps it going.

Perkins (1992) addresses motivation and affirms what Kohn, Bruner, and others purport. He points out that "performances motivated by such extrinsic rewards as grades, lollipops, or dollar bills, tend not to persist once the reward structure is dropped" (65). He goes on to write, "In contrast, efforts to cultivate children's intrinsic interest in a rich activity, such as the reading of literature, are more likely to lead to sustained, self-motivated involvement" (65).

Perkins, like Kohn, asserts that extrinsic rewards undercut intrinsic interest. Further, he claims that intrinsic interest is related to creativity. So where do the theories mentioned in this chapter fit? We mentioned earlier on that information processing theory devotes little attention to motivation. It does seem to assume the importance of intrinsic motivation, however, because it portrays the learner as possessing an internal need to make sense of the world in which he or she lives. This is similar to Piaget's notion of equilibration. Human learners strive to reach a state of equilibrium, or peace, with their cognitive worlds. They do this through organization and adaptation. That is, humans impose order on information that they receive from the environment. When they take in new information, humans, by nature, attempt to incorporate it with their existing information, which Piaget called assimilation. If they cannot incorporate it into what they already know then humans change what they already know through a process of accommodation, which allows the new information to "fit" their existing information. Having done that, they can now assimilate the new information and reach a state of equilibrium (where they are at peace with their cognitive world). An analogy might help to clarify these processes. Think of a file cabinet with several folders. One is labeled *household appliances* and another is labeled *insurance policies.* If you buy a new toaster, the receipt and operating instruction can be immediately placed in the appliance folder. You can also file that new car insurance policy you just received in the mail. In

A Person Who Helped Create Change . . .

Jean Piaget was perhaps the most influential developmental psychologist of all time. Born in 1896 in Neuchâtel, Switzerland, he was contributing to professional literature when he was only 11 years old. During his lifetime his research had one major goal—to help us understand how knowledge grows. He wrote over 60 books and hundreds of articles to share what he learned from his study of the development of knowledge. He died in 1980 at the age of 84. This man was truly a giant in the field of psychology, and forever changed the way we understand how humans "come to know."

Photo: Courtesy of Jean Piaget Society.
Source: The Piaget Society, www.piaget.org.

other words, your filing system permits you to assimilate this new information. But just today you received information from the music club that you recently joined. Alas, your file cabinet has no folder for club memberships. You cannot assimilate that information into your system. So, being resourceful as you are, you create a new file folder and label it *memberships*. Now you have changed your filing system to accommodate the new information that you received, and that new information can now be filed, or assimilated, into your file cabinet. See how it works?

These tendencies to organize and adapt to our environment, according to Piaget, are natural. Human beings share these tendencies with all other animals—to reach a harmonious state with their environment. It is entirely innate. We are intrinsically motivated, perhaps even biologically programmed, to do so. Robbie Case is a neo-Piagetian. That is to say, he has taken Piaget's ideas and added to them in terms of new understandings we have reached since Piaget's death. He agrees with Piaget's basic view of motivation as intrinsic. More precisely, he believes that people are naturally motivated to solve problems. They organize their worlds into problem situations, identify objectives, and then devise strategies for solving these problems.

Vygotsky, introduced earlier in this chapter, sees learners as primarily motivated by wanting to increase their control over their environments, and increase their feelings of competence. This is decidedly intrinsic, deriving from very personal needs and goals.

What Motivation Theories Suggest

Now, to synthesize all of this thinking about motivation, theory suggests that we balance extrinsic and intrinsic motivation in order to help learners learn. If we err on one side or another, research suggests that we err on the intrinsic side of the equation. But once again, with apologies for using a cliché, we must be careful to not throw out the baby with the bathwater. Perkins (1992) points out that traditional/behavioral theory encompasses a number of important learning principles, such as providing information, arranging practice, and offering specific feedback. Note that information processing theory also includes these principles. But beyond these principles, we must think about the source of the motivation for engaging in behaviors. If we can manage to involve learners in performances that they find intrinsically motivating, we will move in the direction of providing the basis for powerful learning experiences for them. Chapters 3 and 4 will help you develop learning activities that are both powerful and motivating for learners.

 SCENARIO REVISITED

It is time to revisit the scenario described at the beginning of this chapter. Answer these questions yet again.

> **?** *Why do you think Ms. Moore's students are having problems remembering things she is teaching them? What do you think Ms. Moore's philosophy of teaching might be? Why?*

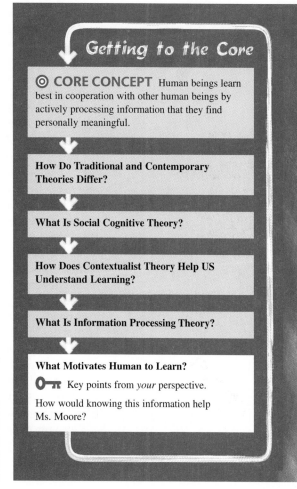

Getting to the Core

◎ **CORE CONCEPT** Human beings learn best in cooperation with other human beings by actively processing information that they find personally meaningful.

How Do Traditional and Contemporary Theories Differ?

What Is Social Cognitive Theory?

How Does Contextualist Theory Help US Understand Learning?

What Is Information Processing Theory?

What Motivates Human to Learn?

🔑 Key points from *your* perspective.

How would knowing this information help Ms. Moore?

As you respond once again to this question, think back on the core concept that has been the focus of this chapter: Use the ideas from social cognitive and contextualist, information processing, and motivation theories. In addition, think back to the idea about assumptions we hold and the ways they affect our philosophies. When you have completed your revised responses to these questions, examine your answers and reflect on how they have, or have not, changed. Then, read A Voice from the Field to see how an experienced teacher reacted to the Ms. Moore case. Compare your response to the teacher's response.

 # A VOICE FROM THE FIELD

There are quite a few reasons for the lack of recall experienced by Ms. Moore's students. I would also chance a guess that the problem stems from her philosophy of education. Ms. Moore spends her class periods talking at her students. Her philosophy of education would center on herself just as her class does. It seems she views herself as the center of the students' learning. In her view, it is her job to impart knowledge to her students. They are the equivalent of sponges waiting to absorb the ideas and concepts coming from their teacher. This idea is the root of the problem. Ms. Moore spends her classes describing, reading, and plowing through massive amounts of information. The information processing view of education would alter her classes in marvelous ways.

According to IP theory, her students can only effectively process five to nine bits of information at a time. It seems that Ms. Moore is presenting them with much more than they can handle. A large chunk of the information is rehearsed in their short-term memory and then discarded when it is no longer needed. The first thing Ms. Moore may wish to do with her content is to narrow the massive amount of information down to a smaller number of core ideas. These core concepts can then be broken into smaller manageable lessons for her students. These ideas should become the focus of her class. For example, if she were teaching about the early American colonies, she may want to pick three aspects about the colonies on which to focus. After developing an advanced organizer with the early American colonies as her main idea, she may want to have economics, geography, and politics as her core concepts. Her focus may then be on why these aspects were important to consider when making the move from Europe to the Americas.

This organizer will also serve to cue the students' prior knowledge about what they are going to study. Ms. Moore can question her students about their understanding of the three concepts before continuing with the lesson. If she finds gaps in their knowledge in these areas she can attempt to fill them. She may have her class discuss current events in politics or economics to help build a knowledge base for the students regarding these ideas. Also by introducing these ideas before her main idea she may cause the students' curiosity to be aroused regarding where the topic is headed. What do these ideas have to do with colonial America? Last, this organizer will give the students something to which the new information may be connected, thus making it easier to retrieve from their long-term memory down the road and well into the future.

Once the main idea and core concepts have been introduced it is time to turn the class over to the students. Give them activities where they are going after the information and not the other way around. An example to apply to our lesson on the early colonies would be to let the students find out about the economy, geography, and politics of a given colony or colonies. At this point it is also a powerful idea to break the class into small groups of two to four students. Three students would be the ideal number for this lesson. Give them a grading sheet outlining what you the teacher may be looking for when they are finished and then set them loose in the library or online.

Breaking your class into groups is no small task. It takes time and teacher insight. According to social cognitive theory, the members of the group, if grouped properly, will influence each other's behavior. Those who may be unmotivated during certain activities should be placed with those who work diligently in groups. Albert Bandura says that the response facilitation effect will cause all in the group to perform at the higher level being demonstrated by those students who are highly motivated to work. The other theory that works in an educator's favor when developing groups is Vygotsky's zone of proximal development. When developing your groups it is wise to group those students who are high achievers with those who are hard workers but seem to fall behind in class. Those who are higher achievers will tend to pull the others along with them to a higher level of understanding. Students learn as effectively from each other as they do from a teacher. Often students whose processing is blocked by nerves will loosen up with their peers. This allows them to process information that normally would have been lost.

Depending on the skill of your students you may want to add a bit of structure to ensure success. Go to the library beforehand and pull some of the books needed to achieve their goals or go online and bookmark the sites you know will help the students. This scaffolding, as Vygotsky calls it, will help keep the motivation level of those students who need it at a desired level. As the students build their knowledge of the colonies higher and higher, they may need the teacher to steady the information just as scaffolding my help steady a new structure being built. The teacher provides reassurance when the learner is feeling overwhelmed. This reassurance could come in many forms; verbal hints, organizers, or bookmarks on a computer.

Act as a facilitator and assist them when needed. That is the key point—when needed. It is very difficult for a teacher, especially one who is used to teaching at their students to sit back and watch without saying much of anything. It is however, a powerful tool. You are not only letting the students construct the knowledge for themselves, but also instilling confidence in them.

Now that the lower-order learning is complete, students can move on to the more complicated higher-order tasks. You will want to have them take the information they have accumulated and evaluate, analyze, and synthesize the new information. This is where Ms. Moore's class would have ended. This is where a truly powerful classroom moves into high gear. Now that the teams have the declarative knowledge, they will need to make connections and do something meaningful with it in order to get it processed into their long-term memory effectively. In our example lesson Ms. Moore may want to show the class examples of famous TV commercials, the travel section from the Sunday newspaper, or brochures of exotic destinations she has collected from a travel agent. Once again she is arousing their curiosity and triggering familiar ideas to which to make more valuable connections. Have students look for the type of layout the ads and brochures use to get the reader's attention. Once they are familiar with the format, have them develop a brochure or advertisement of their own. Its purpose is to try to sell their other classmates on coming to their chosen colony. The brochure should include a section on the economy, geography, and politics. The group members will have to ask each other which information collected is important and needed to fulfill the purpose of the ad or brochure.

The students will then share their final products. These should consist of TV-type commercials, newspaper advertisements, or a simple brochure. Their presentations should be original and lively with everyone from the group participating. When the presentations are complete, Ms. Moore could then ask her students to share with each other the importance of economy, geography, and politics in the evolution of a colonial colony. How did each impact growth? With such a lively and unique experience to connect the new knowledge with other pieces of information, Ms. Moore's students should have much less of a problem recalling the important facts regarding the core concepts of economics, geography, and politics when needed.

In the end, Ms. Moore's class still learned about the early American colonies. Rather than looking at the topics as distant bits of information that serve no real importance to them, they can now share a sense of ownership to their colonies and the information. They took the facts and constructed a definition of the importance they held for each new colony's survival. They were not overburdened with massive amounts of information and most of all they were active participants in the class rather than passive receivers.

This is the voice of Steven Rebl. Mr. Rebl is a former high school teacher. He currently teaches students with special needs in a middle school setting.

PLANNING FOR INSTRUCTION

◎ CORE CONCEPT Human beings learn best in cooperation with other human beings by actively processing information that they find personally meaningful.

You began the process of planning your unit of instruction at the end of Chapter 1. Now we are going to have you think more about your unit in light of the core concept for Chapter 2 and the information you learned in this chapter.

This chapter addresses theory; more practical applications will follow in ensuing chapters. So this is a good time to reexamine your personal beliefs about teaching and learning. Remember a good theory can be very powerful. Theories guide our actions and direct us in purposeful ways. Your personal theory of teaching and learning will guide your unit and lesson plans.

Your Turn

Now is the time to articulate your personal theory by putting it in writing. Here is the prompt:

> Suppose a parent of one of your students said to you, "Jake is not happy in your class. You do not tell him what he needs to do in order to get good marks on his worksheets, and he is disappointing us with his low grades. Anyway, he brings home so few papers that we can't see how he is possibly learning anything at all!" What is it you do with the children all day long? Why do you do what you do with them?

Think about this and write down a response by making clear your personal theory of education.

Your Response

Can you defend what you wrote? On what basis can you support your own theory? Would you use personal experiences, research, or both?

> Now, compare what you wrote to the core concept above. How does it match the theories and research presented in this chapter? What are the points of agreement? What are the points of disagreement?

In future chapters we are going to encourage you to use the research and ideas we present to craft a unit and a series of lessons that we believe will assist you in helping your learners *really* learn. However, your personal beliefs and what we present in the book might clash at places. Some of what we present might be so different from what you have experienced and believed that you are uncomfortable using these ideas to plan instruction. We ask you to try your best to use the ideas we present in each chapter. In that way you will have an opportunity to rethink your personal beliefs. If you can actually teach this unit, in whole or in part, to learners as you proceed through this book, all the better!

CHAPTER SUMMARY

This chapter tells the story of theory and its place in promoting conceptual change through powerful instruction. Theory can be very useful as a guide for our practice as educators. It provides us with a context in which to place our ideas about, and experiences with, providing learning environments and activities for students. We all operate on assumptions based upon personal theories anyway. Teachers, because of the very important nature of their work with children and adolescents, have a special responsibility to make explicit their assumptions and then continually test these assumptions against emerging, contemporary theoretical understandings of how people learn.

Traditional theories based on behavioral psychology have long dominated American education and driven its practice. Newer, contemporary theories, based on the emerging cognitive sciences, can help further our understanding about teaching and learning. Social cognitive theory blends behavioral and cognitive theory and helps us understand the role that observation plays in the learning process. It suggests ways that teachers can use the power of modeling to promote student learning.

Contextualist theory asserts that humans construct their own knowledge rather than just try to copy an objective reality. They do this as they attempt to adapt to the world in which they live. This notion of constructivism is not compatible with strict behaviorism. Teachers who use contextualist theory and constructivist practices operate from a completely different set of assumptions than those of behaviorally oriented teachers.

Somewhere in between behaviorism and contextualism/constructivism is a set of theories based upon cognitive science, called information processing theories. One such model of information processing suggests that there are three kinds of human memory, and the goal is to have learners get information into their long-term memories where it can be retained and eventually understood and used. The key to getting information into long-term memory is elaborative rehearsal, when a learner adds something she already knows to something she is just now learning.

Finally, the important element of motivation is discussed in terms of its locus, or source. Extrinsic motivation comes from an outside source. It is under the control of someone else. Intrinsic motivation, on the other hand, comes from within. We control this source of motivation, because it is driven by very personal and meaningful goals. It is possible that teachers overuse extrinsic forms of motivation, and do too little to encourage learners to be intrinsically motivated. This can be a problem because, all things being equal, research demonstrates that intrinsic motivation is far more powerful than extrinsic motivation in promoting learning.

Chapter 3 will help you understand some ways to change traditional classroom practice to promote deep understanding among learners that comes out of these theories. We will introduce you to some very powerful principles of learning, and show you how they can be applied in classrooms with the students you teach.

Getting to the Core

> **◉ CORE CONCEPT** Human beings learn best in cooperation with other human beings by actively processing information that they find personally meaningful.

How Do Traditional and Contemporary Learning Theories Differ?

- Learning is accumulating bits of information and isolated skills. Contemporary learning requires the learner to actively construct meaning.

- In contemporary learning teachers use students' prior knowledge about a topic or concept to influence what they will learn during instruction and to help the learners change their cognitive structure or way they view and organize the world.

- Contemporary learning provides an active learning process that supports motivation, modeling, coaching, and learning in cooperation with others.

What Is Social Cognitive Theory?

- Much of human behavior is learned by observing others. The person, the behavior, and the environment all come together to influence learning (triadic reciprocality). The modeling process, attention–retention–production, and motivation increase the potential for learning.

- Effects of modeling: *Observational learning* (new skills and behaviors are learned by watching others); *inhibitory effect* (a previously learned

behavior is lessened by watching someone else receive negative consequences for it); *disinhibitory effect* (a previously learned behavior will increase if no negative consequences are observed); and *response facilitation* (a model behavior will serve as a cue for others to perform the same behavior).

How Does Contextualist Theory Help Us Understand Learning?

- We learn best when information is learned in a context in which it occurs. Context means the culture in which a person acts. Children construct their own knowledge and their language and speech play an important and central role in cognitive development.

- Development cannot be separated from the social context in which it occurs. The *zone of proximal development* is the area between a child's actual level of development and the level at which he or she could potentially develop in collaboration with a more capable person.

- Cooperative learning, scaffolding, and reciprocal teaching help teachers systematize instruction on the basis of dialogue and conversation.

What Is Information Processing Theory?

- Nothing is learned unless it is encoded into long-term memory. The process begins with stimuli hitting the *sensory register*. Once information is recognized and attended to, it moves to *working memory*. Here we do our thinking and decide what to do with it. Working memory is what we are conscious of at the moment. It is where we do our thinking. What is no longer needed is forgotten, what we choose to process further can be encoded into long-term memory. *Maintenance rehearsal* helps keep information in working memory for longer periods of time.

- There are two types of knowledge: *declarative* (facts, concepts, and ideas) and *procedural* (knowing how to do something). In order for information to be encoded into long-term memory for future use it must be actively processed. Strategies such as connection, elaboration, imagery, chunking, organization, and mnemonics help the learner actively process declarative knowledge.

- Practice with specific feedback is the way we learn procedural knowledge. The more skills become proceduralized, the less space they take up in working memory and the more space can be devoted to solving complex problems.

What Motivates Humans to Learn?

- Knowing the *locus of causality* (or location of the cause) helps us understand the difference between the two types of motivation. In *extrinsic motivation* the source of motivation lies outside the individual learner. In *intrinsic motivation* the source of the motivation is under the control of the individual learner.

CHAPTER 3

Practical Applications of Powerful Principles

FOR BETTER OR FOR WORSE *(Source: © UFS. Reprinted with permission.)*

 ## SCENARIO

Mr. Mock teaches fifth graders. He is an experienced teacher. His no-nonsense approach to teaching and learning is very well received by the parents of the children assigned to his room. Mr. Mock has been teaching life sciences this year, and has focused on classification of living things. He began a recent science lesson by asking his pupils to open their textbooks to page 105, "where they left off last time." The lesson was on photosynthesis, and was meant to help the children understand the process plants use to make food. He began by having the pupils take turns, round-robin style, reading paragraphs from the textbook. After several paragraphs had been read, he would call on various students to answer questions such as "Who remembers the two end products of photosynthesis?' or "What substance do many plants change sugar into before storing it?"

After the lesson was completed, Mr. Mock distributed worksheets that each pupil worked on at his or her own desk. On this particular worksheet students were asked to define photosynthesis and several other terms from the chapter. Next, they were asked to list the steps in photosynthesis. Finally, they were allowed to share their answers with Mr. Mock, who stood in front of the class writing down correct answers for all the children to see. The children were asked to study their worksheets for homework, and told that there would be a quiz on this material tomorrow.

Mr. Mock administered the quiz, and the majority of students did very well on it. The quiz, much like the worksheet, asked them to define terms and to list steps in the food-making process. Mr. Mock, satisfied with the results, had the children return to their science textbooks to learn about the next topic in the chapter.

Much later in the year and quite by accident, the ideas of plants and food once again emerged. The children were on a field trip to Longwood Gardens in conjunction with a social studies unit on how cultures express themselves through art forms, such as flower arranging. A question was asked about how plants get food. The children were in general agreement that "the plants get food from the ground through their roots." Although this is a widely held, naïve understanding, Mr. Mock's lesson on photosynthesis was meant to help the children understand the correct scientific conception of how plants make food. And they had done so well on the photosynthesis quiz and on the end-of-chapter test on plants that Mr. Mock gave them. What happened?

> **?** *Why do you think the children held onto a naïve conception of how plants get food? How would you improve Mr. Mock's lesson so that the children have a better chance of retaining and really understanding and being able to use the concept of photosynthesis? Be very specific about what you would do differently, and how you would do it.*

INTRODUCTION

Many people do not understand what a complex undertaking it is to teach others or, more correctly, how difficult it is to help others learn. The challenge is not getting any easier as

"Everyone believes that
to be a good teacher
all you need is to love
to teach, but no one
believes that to be a
good surgeon all you
need is to love to cut."

—Adam Urbanski
*(Source: Quoted in Burke,
Hagan, and Grossen,
1998, p. 34.)*

time progresses. We are trying to get an increasingly diverse group of learners to understand and use a great deal more knowledge than in any other time in our history.

Researchers have estimated that the average teacher makes well over 150 conscious instructional decisions—every day! However, Labaree (1999) points out that, to outsiders, teaching looks awfully easy. He writes, "Its work is so visible, the skills required to do it seem so ordinary, and the knowledge it seeks to transmit is so generic" (38). For example, Labaree cites an interesting statistic; a typical high school graduate will have watched teachers "do their thing" for roughly 13,000 hours. No other profession is that visible. Of course, as Labaree notes, we cannot ignore the fact that particular subjects must be taught to *particular* learners. So the ability to know something oneself does not guarantee that one can teach that thing to another person. And experience watching others is not always the best teacher. There are many teacher "moves" that seem quite *obvious* but actually run counter to what most of us would do intuitively.

What Assumptions Do Teachers Often Make?

Assumptions that we make are based upon our personal experiences. Personal experiences are, of necessity, limited when compared with all possible experiences that we could have or with the collective experiences of a much larger group of people. Once we begin to form opinions on the basis of our assumptions, we wonder why anyone would see things in a different way from the way we see them. Things become obvious, at least to us. We know that what is apparently "obvious" does not always hold up under closer scrutiny. Let us now take a look at some of the assumptions that, at least in our experiences, teachers make quite frequently. Remember that assumptions are powerful and serve to drive actions, and all assumptions have competing assumptions that run counter to them.

Assumption 1: *If teachers don't teach, then students won't learn.* This implies that teachers can, and must, directly impart their knowledge to their learners. It also suggests that teachers must carefully control instruction.

Assumption 2: *Learners learn best by working alone.* Much of what goes on in classrooms, and in education in general, is competitive and individualistic. After all, not everyone can get an "A."

Assumption 3: *Learners need feedback on everything they do—from the teacher.* After all, what's the point of doing something if the teacher doesn't grade or comment on it? And certainly students are not knowledgeable enough to offer instructive comments to one another.

Assumption 4: *If they do well on our tests, then they understand the material.* Teacher-made tests are based upon what has been taught in the classroom. Therefore they are excellent indicators of student understanding of subject matter.

Assumption 5: *Intelligence is a fixed capacity.* IQ tests yield scores that are neurologically fixed and genetically determined, and there is not much any of us can do about this.

Assumption 6: *People learn pretty much in the same way.* We are all humans with the same basic physiological mechanisms.

Assumption 7: *Learners are pretty much the same as they used to be.* Again, people don't change very much, at least over several generations.

Experience is a powerful teacher, and you have had a great deal of experience as a student, watching teachers practice their craft and listening to them discuss their views. In Chapter 2 we attempted to challenge the most commonly held *general* assumption about how people learn. That assumption often casts teachers in commanding roles as information dispensers, and students in passive roles as information recipients who work alone to learn the information prescribed by the curriculum. In this chapter we shall challenge assumptions related to classroom practices that are based upon traditional theory. We will help you link the theories presented in the previous chapter to practice. In this way we will encourage you to rethink your own assumptions and provide powerful learning experiences for children, adolescents, and adults. Before we turn to the subject of linking theories to practice, let us address the seven assumptions we put forth by offering counterassumptions for each of them.

> Think about it . . . We have listed seven assumptions that teachers commonly hold.
>
> 1. Which of these seven have you witnessed "in action" in your own experience as a student?
> 2. Write one of these assumptions down on a piece of paper, and expand on it by telling a short story that highlights the assumption in use in a classroom.
> 3. Do you agree with the assumption being made? Would you operate on a different assumption? What would it be? How would it have made the classroom experience different for *you?*

Assumption 1: *If teachers don't teach, then students won't learn.* Cognitive science has mounted a considerable challenge to this assumption. Because we presented this challenge in Chapter 2, we shall not recount it here.

Assumption 2: *Learners learn best by working alone.* Research on cooperative and collaborative learning has demonstrated their power in promoting higher achievement. This suggests that learners learn best by working together.

Assumption 3: *Learners need feedback on everything they do—from the teacher.* This assumption can work against helping students develop expertise by limiting the amount of practice they get to what a teacher has time to evaluate. We get better at writing by writing, at reading by reading, and so on. Limiting practice unnecessarily is unwise. And research demonstrates that both peer feedback and self-assessment are powerful in promoting learning.

Assumption 4: *If they do well on our tests, then they understand the material.* This assumes that our tests are both reliable and valid. Teachers rarely have those types of data on their tests. It also assumes that the tests tap higher-order thinking. Questions must be beyond the recall level to determine whether or not a student understands, and can use, knowledge.

Assumption 5: *Intelligence is a fixed capacity.* This assumption is based upon an early twentieth-century conception of intelligence. It discounts new information on the nature of intelligence, the many forms of intelligence (Gardner 1983, 1999), and the importance of reflective intelligence (Perkins 1995).

Assumption 6: *People learn pretty much in the same way.* Whereas it is certainly true that human learners share some fundamental similarities in the ways they learn (as evidenced by the theories presented in Chapter 2), it is also true that they learn differently from one another in some ways. Some of these differences are simply preferred ways of learning information. These preferences are commonly referred to as learning styles, and researchers have identified many different styles.

Assumption 7: *Learners are pretty much the same as they used to be.* We addressed this assumption in Chapter 1. The "business as usual" approach fostered by this assumption is questionable.

How Can We Apply Theory to Practice?

Good teachers understand theory, and they keep abreast of the latest research about learning and teaching. The theories presented in Chapter 2 are among those that serve teachers well as a foundation for their practice. That good teachers use theory as well as experience to guide their practice is not at all obvious to outsiders. Nor do most of these outsiders understand theories of learning or know the research on practice. Basing practice on a sound theoretical base is fundamentally important for the practice of any profession—and teaching is certainly no exception. Theory suggests that teachers can do a number of things to encourage and promote "real" learning among their learners. By real learning we mean not only remembering information, but also understanding it and being able to use it when appropriate to solve problems, to gain additional insights, or simply to enjoy life.

Real learning means that students must take a "deep approach," rather than a "surface approach," to learning. We distinguished these two approaches from one another in Chapter 2. Rhem (1995) cited results of many experiments conducted over a long time period that found, for example, students often look for facts rather than meaning when approaching text. This, he concluded, was because "the meaning of the text stood in direct relation to the way they expected to be assessed" (1). This leads to surface learning in which students can recall just unconnected facts. Rhem also cited Australian studies suggesting that as students move to higher levels of education they progressively drop a deep approach to learning. He concludes that, at least in some ways, "traditional teaching pushes students toward superficial levels of engagement with material, even as it hopes to do the opposite" (1). Dowd (1996), citing Gibbs (1992), characterizes deep learning as when "the student works hard to make sense of what was learned by integrating and analyzing information, leading to the formation of internalized constructs" (5). Using the theories we know about how humans learn can help us develop classroom practices that promote deep learning while combating surface learning among our learners.

Some very powerful ideas have emerged from recent theory that can lead to classroom practices that promote deep understanding of facts, ideas, and concepts (declarative knowledge) and the ability to use that understanding (procedural knowledge). A core concept that captures these ideas succinctly is: The ability to retain and understand *declarative* knowledge is greatly enhanced when human learners make connections to what they already know by organizing, visualizing, and elaborating upon facts, ideas, and concepts. The ability to correctly use *procedural* knowledge is enhanced by practice and specific feedback. Recall from Chapter 2 and information processing theory that facts, ideas, and concepts are forms of declarative knowledge, whereas the ability to do something with facts, concepts, and ideas is a form of procedural knowledge.

> ". . . nothing—absolutely nothing—has happened in education until it happens to a student."
>
> **—Joseph Carroll**
> *(Source: J. Carroll. [1994, May]. The Copernican Plan Evaluated: The Evolution of a Revolution. Phi Delta Kappan, p. 108.)*

This core concept can lead us to help learners deeply process information because it defines some very powerful, general principles of human learning that teachers can readily apply in their classrooms. These principles have one thing in common—they all involve *the active creation of meaning based upon the prior knowledge that the learner brings to the task.* And they all enhance the probability that information will make it into long-term memory, where it can be understood and used.

How Can We Create Powerful Instruction to Promote Deep Learning?

As a teacher, what should you do to create powerful instruction for your learners, instruction that will promote their deep learning and ability to put to use that which they have learned? To answer this question you should revisit the theory you learned about in Chapter 2.

Here is an example. One major idea from theory is that learners trying to make connections among facts, concepts, and ideas benefit from learning in cooperation with other learners. They learn from models, and they learn in a culture that is supportive, contextually rich, and developmentally appropriate. Yet if you are typical, much of your experience as a learner might well have been working alone, under the strict control of the teacher, to master declarative and procedural knowledge. And your teacher might have been the sole source of the feedback that you received. That is why many people make the assumption that learning is a very individual endeavor that requires teachers to be at the center of the enterprise. If they become teachers, they act on this assumption that has been so consistently modeled for them. This, despite the fact that years of research have led us to know that a technique that has come to be called *cooperative learning* is one of the most powerful, if not *the* most powerful, in our instructional arsenal. In order to create powerful instruction we must hold our current beliefs up to close scrutiny, and we must use theory to guide our efforts. We shall now take a closer look at the first of several applications of powerful principles suggested by theory and research.

How Can We Use Cooperative Learning to Promote Deep Learning?

We introduced cooperative learning very briefly in Chapter 2. Even if you use none of the other strategies we shall address later on, cooperative learning alone will increase your learners' achievement. But let us make it clear up front that *there are times when learners prefer to work alone and need to work alone, and when it is appropriate to have them do so.* Teachers must provide opportunities for solitary work, too. As a teacher, you should make judicious use of the powerful cooperative learning strategy (or, for that matter any strategy) to help your learners make connections among ideas and practice what they learn.

The research base on cooperative learning is substantial. According to Slavin (1989–1990), it is "one of the most thoroughly researched of all instructional methods" (52). Johnson and Johnson surveyed the literature on cooperative learning and concluded:

> During the past 90 years, more than 600 studies have been conducted by a wide
> variety of researchers in different decades with different age subjects, in different

Think about it . . .

Think back to an experience you had working in a group with others on an assigned project.

- How did the teacher form the groups?
- What was the experience like for you?
- If it went well, why?
- If it did not go well, why not?

subject areas, and in different environments. We know far more about the efficacy
of cooperative learning than we know about lecturing . . . or almost any other
facet of education. (1994, 38)

Joyce, Showers, and Rolheiser-Bennett (1987) conducted a survey of the research
on innovative teaching practices that lead to higher student achievement. They listed
the practices in the order of their power. Cooperative learning was listed first, just
ahead of information processing models and nondirective teaching approaches, as
representing a social model where the more complex the intended outcomes of
instruction (higher-order thinking, problem solving), the greater the effects on
achievement. Marzano, Gaddy, and Dean (2000) listed cooperative learning sixth on
a list of nine powerful instructional strategies for promoting student achievement.

Given the substantial and very positive research base, grounded as solidly as it
is in theory, it is not surprising that many teachers are finally beginning to use
cooperative learning with their learners. It *is* surprising, however, how many teachers are still *not* using it, and how many more use it incorrectly and, when it does
not work, abandon it completely. Often teachers put students into groups to do
work. But cooperative learning is not merely group work. Millis (1995) defined
cooperative learning as "a *structured form of group work* where students, *who are
individually assessed,* work toward common group goals" (127, emphasis ours). It
is made up of a set of five essential elements, clearly identified by Johnson, Johnson, and Smith (1991). (See Fig. 3.1.)

- **Positive interdependence:** This is a climate where students learn that they "sink
  or swim" together. Interdependence is encouraged by, first and foremost, having
  learners work together on structured tasks that are meaningful and authentic.
  Sharing mutual goals, having assigned roles, sharing information and materials,
  and receiving mutual rewards can create this climate of interdependence. For
  example, you can set a goal for all of the learners, such as reaching consensus
  on the solution to a problem. You can structure groups so that each person has a
  role. The roles can be rotated periodically. Then you can offer mutual rewards
  such as additional points on a test if each member of the group reaches a certain
  criterion (maybe 85 percent correct) or if the group shows overall improvement.
  The BIG idea here is that all group members are linked together such that each
  member's success depends upon the success of all other group members.

- **Face-to-Face interaction:** This is an environment in which learners help,
  assist, encourage, and support one another as they attempt to learn new
  information. In this element of cooperative learning, learners will explain

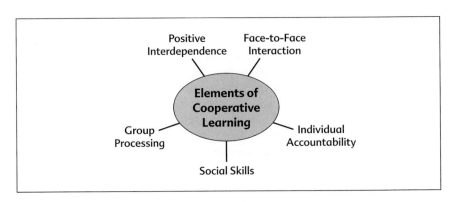

FIGURE 3.1

Spider map depicting five essential
elements of cooperative learning.

Integrating cooperative learning and complex problem-solving activities encourages student engagement, motivation and achievement. (Courtesy of Andy Sotiriou/Photo Disc.)

information to each other, clarify points, discuss concepts and ideas, and most important, help one another make connections among and between pieces of declarative knowledge. Learners do this while interacting with each other in small groups of roughly four members each.

- **Individual accountability:** In this element, it is clear that although the group members help each other learn the material, each learner is held individually responsible for actually learning it. Teachers can assess students traditionally (on quizzes and tests), or on papers done by individual members. On group projects, peer and individual self-assessment can help teachers determine the quality and value of each group member's contribution, or group projects can be weighted less than individual performances when a summative evaluation takes place.

- **Social skills:** Millis (1995) makes clear that social skills must include "listening actively, paraphrasing accurately, questioning skillfully, and providing feedback constructively" (135). In Chapter 2, Bandura made clear the power of modeling, and this is a good place for teachers to model such behaviors for the learners. When conflicts arise, as they inevitably will, conflict management skills can be taught to the learners. This element is an important part of cooperative learning, and should be seen by the teacher as a legitimate opportunity to promote student learning in an important nonacademic area. The ability to work effectively with others as part of a team is ranked very highly by business leaders and others who hire students for jobs when they graduate from school.

- **Group processing:** At the end of an assignment, the members of the group can get feedback from the teacher about how well they worked together at successfully mastering the information to be learned. Just as important, however, is that the group members give one another feedback, and engage in self-assessment about their interactions. One way this can be done is to simply ask each learner to answer two questions during a group meeting: (1) What were some ways in which I helped the group? and (2) How can I help the group even more next time?

Of all the elements, Cooper (1990) concluded that the most important are *positive interdependence* and *individual accountability*. If teachers fail to skillfully employ these elements, cooperative learning activities will often not work well. For example, some teachers simply sit learners in close proximity to one another and tell them to work on some problems together. Each student has her own materials with which to work. The result is usually that the learners, while sitting together, merely work independently on the problems (or whatever material is to be learned). The conditions requiring interdependence have not been established. One condition might be limited resources, where learners would have to share materials. Otherwise there is little reason for the learners to work together.

Another improper use of cooperative learning leads to a very frequent complaint from learners and their parents. The teacher assigns a group project, and all of the learners are told that they will receive the same grade on it. What often happens is that one or two learners do all of the work. Or, if the learners are heterogeneously grouped, the more capable among them do the bulk of the work so that their grades are not jeopardized. The practice of some students riding along on the coattails of others is typically referred to as "hitchhiking." Giving the same grade to every member of the group is not usually a wise practice, because it is impossible to know how well each student has mastered the material. In this scenario, the element of individual accountability is not being used.

So how might you garner the power of cooperative learning on behalf of your learners? We shall elaborate upon a few commonly used techniques, but caution you now that there are many, many more than we can address here. Cooperative learning encourages learners to be active. Active learning strategies, of which cooperative learning is but one, range from simple to complex. In the following sections we shall give examples that range along that continuum. Please understand, however, that what is important is not the complexity of the strategy. The biggest difference in terms of deep processing of information is not on the simple to complex continuum. Rather, it is on the inactive to active continuum. Put another way, active learning strategies are always superior to strategies that cast students in passive roles (at least in terms of promoting deep understanding). Traditional lectures (or sustained teacher talk) typically cast learners into passive roles. Middendorf and Kalish (1996) cite studies that indicate even adults can attend to a lecture

Two People Who Helped Create Change . . .

David W. Johnson and Roger T. Johnson are brothers who codirect the Cooperative Learning Center located at the University of Minnesota. David is a professor of educational psychology at the University of Minnesota. He received his master's and doctoral degrees from Columbia University. David has also served as editor of the *American Educational Research Journal.*

Roger received his master's degree from Ball State University and his doctoral degree from the University of California at Berkeley. Today he is professor of curriculum and instruction with an emphasis in science education at the University of Minnesota.

These two professors have coauthored over 30 books, but they are probably best known for their pioneering work in the area of cooperative learning. Cooperative learning benefits students by addressing multiple learners and allowing all students to participate in learning activities. The goal of the Cooperative Learning Center is to promote classrooms that meet the criteria established by the Johnsons. These two men and their staff are continuously researching and implementing new ideas and theories that can further enhance the learning environment.

Sources: http://www.clcrc.com/pages/dwj.html; http://www2.emc.maricopa.edu/innovation/Bios/rjohnson.html; and http://www.clcrc.com/index.html.

for no more than 15 to 20 minutes at a time. But simple and complex active learning strategies are not so very different from one another in terms of producing understanding.

Some Specific Cooperative Learning Strategies

First, there are a number of ways to group students. Informal groupings can be constructed "on the fly," and can be reconstituted at any time. Base groups can be formed at the beginning of the year and kept intact permanently, or changed only infrequently. They serve as a home base. Formal groups can be constituted for the purpose of completing some type of project, and then disbanded once the project is completed. Different groupings serve different purposes, and these are decisions you make as a teacher to help the students accomplish learning goals. For instance, if you want your learners to have a long-term relationship with a few others for ongoing support and assistance to promote academic progress, then base groups might be the best form of grouping. If, on the other hand, you are using direct instruction (such as lectures) but want to encourage the learners to actively process the information, then informal groups might be best. Should you decide to assign a project with specific content focus and a definite point of completion, then a formal grouping might be the best way to use cooperative learning. Below is a chart that compares the types of cooperative learning groups described by Johnson, Johnson, and Smith (1991).

Type of Group	Base groups	Informal groups	Formal groups
Typical Duration	Year or semester	Class session	To completion of project
Possible Uses	Ongoing support; good for study groups	Promote interaction and processing of information (especially during direct instruction)	Good for undertaking complex projects with multidimensions
Suggested Number of Members	Three to five members	Two to four members	Four members

Cooperative learning operates on the assumption that success in mastering information is enhanced when students interact with one another in groupings that are carefully monitored by the teacher. But how does it work daily in the classroom? Millis (1995) gives us a way to understand this:

> Day-to-day classroom functions . . . are carried out or operationalized by specific *structures*. Structures are essentially content-free procedures, such as a brainstorming technique called *Roundtable,* which can be used in virtually any discipline for a variety of purposes. When content is added to a structure it becomes a specific classroom activity. For example, the Roundtable structure can be used in a composition class to generate possible topics for a classification paper or in a political science class to challenge students to identify the ethical issues facing Congress. When a series of activities are linked, they become a lesson or unit plan." (136)

The *roundtable* technique that Millis describes has the learners brainstorm by working in their cooperative groups where each learner, in turn, writes his ideas on a tablet of paper as he expresses them aloud. As the tablet circulates, more and more information is added until a number of different aspects of a topic are explored. This is a fairly simple structure to use with any type of grouping.

There are many additional structures that you might use to actively engage learners in powerful learning activity. One of them is *think-pair-share* (McTighe and Lyman, 1988). In the think-pair-share (TPS) structure, learners typically listen to a presentation and then are asked a question about some information from it. They are given time to *think* alone, they are asked to *pair* with another learner to discuss their thoughts, and finally they are asked to *share* their responses to the initial question with the larger group. The teacher controls the length of each phase of TPS by cueing students when to change activities. This is a fairly simple structure to use, and it is adaptable to most every subject. It is especially suitable for encouraging learners to actively process direct instruction in informal groupings (two students per group). A teacher can stop a formal presentation after 10 or 20 minutes (recall the typical attention span is 10 to 20 minutes or so) and engage the learners in TPS. An additional benefit of TPS is the way it employs "wait time." McTighe and Lyman (1988) assert that "over 20 years of research on 'wait time' has confirmed numerous benefits from allowing three or more seconds of silent thinking time after a question has been posed (Wait Time I) as well as after a student's response (Wait Time II)" (19). Using TPS assures that wait time is incorporated into your lessons.

Another common cooperative learning structure is *student teams achievement division* (STAD). In STAD, learners receive information and then are asked to complete some sort of worksheet in heterogeneously grouped teams of four. The worksheets require the learners to complete a task that shows mastery of the information as assessed by the worksheet. When completed, the teacher may verbally quiz individual team members about the information. Usually the team is not disbanded until all members have been quizzed and have shown mastery of the information (Cooper, Robinson, and McKinney 1994). Sometimes a bonus is given to a team on which every member meets or exceeds a predetermined standard of mastery.

One last example of a widely used cooperative learning structure is *jigsaw* (Aronson et al. 1978). This is the most complex of the techniques listed here. In this structure, a topic or assignment is broken into parts and each member of a group or team receives one of the parts. Team members leave the original (home) group to learn their parts, usually in cooperation with representatives from other home teams that have the same part. In this manner, each member of a home team leaves to temporarily join another (expert) team to learn the information. Eventually, the expert teams disband and the experts now return to the home team, where they become peer teachers. All members of the home team, now experts in the various parts of the topic or assignment, teach one another what is needed for the team to successfully learn all of the information or to complete the assignment.

This is not meant to be an exhaustive list of cooperative learning structures that can be used by classroom teachers to help learners actively engage with other learners in deeply processing information. There are so many variations on the technique that it would not be possible to list each of them here in any detail. According to Kagan (1992), there are more than 50 forms that cooperative learning can take. But that you should use cooperative learning is clearly supported by years of research. It is consistent with the theories of human learning that call for active processing of information in cooperation with others. If you use cooperative learning structures to develop content-rich learning activities for your learners, you are taking full advantage of one of the most powerful strategies about which we currently know.

A Practical Example of a Cooperative Learning Activity

Let's just suppose you are introducing your students to the epic tradition in literature. You ask them to think about what they already know about epics. Then you have them pair up and share what they already know with one another. Finally, you have some of the pairs share with the entire class what they already know, while you list these ideas on the dry-erase board. At this point you have used think-pair-share to get the students actively engaged. You also can ascertain their current level of knowledge about epics from this activity.

Next you explain to them that there are folk and literary epics. Folk epic poems are really windows to understanding ancient cultures. After helping the students know some of the typical elements of a folk epic poem (there is usually a hero, a journey, a quest for something valuable), you then assign a project that requires them to compare and contrast four epic poems on these and several other elements. You have selected the following epics for them to read and understand: *Gilgamesh, Beowulf, Ramayana,* and the *Song of Roland.* You put them into groups consisting of four members and allow them to work on the assignment together (positive interdependence). Each person in a group takes responsibility for one of the epic poems. In order to learn that poem, she is allowed to work with those from other groups who have taken responsibility for that same poem. These new groups are called expert groups (jigsaw method). Once all students are knowledgeable about the epic for which they took responsibility, they return to their originally assigned (home) group to teach the others all about it, and learn about the other epics from their peers (face-to-face interaction). Then, the assignment is completed and handed in for your feedback. Later, you give a quiz, test, paper, or some other form of assessment that each student must complete individually so that you know the depth of understanding of all class members (individual accountability).

It is quite possible after the process is completed that you will find it does not always go as smoothly as we have described. For example, one of the problems you might encounter is that students did not work very well together. This is a problem—and an opportunity. The problem is that there might be hard feelings or lower grades among those in less functional groups. The opportunity lies in helping them work better as group members by developing appropriate social skills. To help them, you might have the groups sit together and have each member answer two simple but important questions: (1) What is one thing that I did to help the group? and (2) What is one thing I can do better the next time? By having students self-assess their performances, you can keep conflicts from developing while focusing group members on furthering their social skills (group processing and social skills).

This example is not meant to address all possible aspects of cooperative learning. It does show how a number of elements can be used to create powerful instruction that actively engages a large number of students and encourages deep understanding of content. It also allows for the fact that not all activities will go smoothly. When problems arise, teachers should seek solutions to the specific problems rather than abandoning such a powerful technique and reverting back to full teacher control of the learning activity.

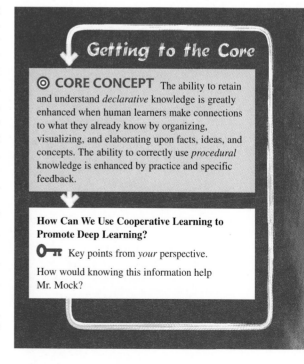

Getting to the Core

◎ CORE CONCEPT The ability to retain and understand *declarative* knowledge is greatly enhanced when human learners make connections to what they already know by organizing, visualizing, and elaborating upon facts, ideas, and concepts. The ability to correctly use *procedural* knowledge is enhanced by practice and specific feedback.

How Can We Use Cooperative Learning to Promote Deep Learning?

⊶ Key points from *your* perspective.

How would knowing this information help Mr. Mock?

How Can Information Processing Theory Help Us COVER Information?

We are now going to give a completely different spin on what it means to *cover* information. Did you know that dictionary definitions of this word include "to hide" and "to conceal"? Yet how often have we heard this word in conjunction with classroom learning? We discussed Information Processing Theory in the previous chapter. This theory, or at least one of the models that derives from it, suggests several very general but powerful principles of learning that can lead to potent classroom practices, and a *new way of thinking about covering information!* These principles were mentioned briefly in Chapter 2. They encourage active processing of information to help root it firmly in long-term memory. We shall now return to them in some detail. What follows are powerful strategies for learning declarative knowledge—the facts, ideas, and concepts that we learn and use in our lives.

The first of these is also the least powerful, but powerful nonetheless. We call it *connect* [C]. There are times when things must be learned that are simply arbitrary in nature. That is, they have no inherent meaning. You might, for example, want your learners to know the order of service of some of the presidents of the United States. You might want them to know the names of the Great Lakes or the order of the planets in terms of distance from the sun. You might want them to learn vocabulary words and how to spell the common "word demons." Because there is no major underlying, meaningful concept involved with these, we call them *arbitrary associations.* That is, they just happened by chance (names of presidents in order) or by general agreement (Great Lakes). One could argue that even this kind of information is best learned in a context or situation in which it would naturally emerge. For example, writing a story as one learns to spell words, or preparing a documentary on the presidents of the 1800s, could easily lead to knowing these arbitrary associations. Nevertheless, there are techniques for remembering information that has no inherent meaning when that is either desirable or necessary. These can be used by teachers to help their learners remember facts, and by learners to help themselves remember information. *Mnemonic devices* are among the most common techniques. They can help learners remember things that have no inherent meaning by substituting more meaningful for less meaningful items, or by relating unknown information to information already well learned. Joyce, Showers, and Rolheiser-Bennett examined research on mnemonics. They concluded that the findings are consistent—that such a method can be beneficial for most students. They mention one in particular, the "link-word" method where, for example, learners are encouraged to make associations between pronunciations of foreign words and the pronunciations of known English words. Addressing the power of this particular mnemonic, they write "Using a link word system in Spanish vocabulary, second- and fifth-grade children learned about twice the words learned by children using rote and rehearsal methods" (1987, 19).

Powerful Strategies to COVER Material

Connect: Mnemonics can help people remember things that have no inherent meaning by connecting less meaningful to more meaningful information.

Organize: People who see or hear many unrelated things at one time can remember only about seven of them—unless these things are organized in a very meaningful way.

Visualize: One picture *is* worth a thousand (or at least many) words. Things that we can see or picture in our minds are generally easier to learn than things we cannot see.

Elaborate: The process of generating new ideas related to the ideas being received from external sources is called elaboration.

Rehearse: *Maintenance* rehearsal allows us to keep information in short-term memory by repeating it over and over again. *Elaborative* rehearsal is encoding new information into long-term memory by consciously relating it to already stored knowledge, rather than just repeating or memorizing it.

Mnemonics come in many other forms as well. Some use acronyms, such as HOMES for the names of the Great Lakes (Huron, Ontario, Michigan, Erie, Superior), or FACE for the musical whole notes on the treble scale. Other mnemonics use acrostics, where the first letter of each word in a sentence relates to declarative knowledge that the learner must remember. An example of this type of mnemonic is **M**y **D**ear **A**unt **S**ally. The beginning letter of each word stands for the order of operations in mathematics; first **m**ultiply, then **d**ivide, then **a**dd, and finally **s**ubtract. Learners can also remember the order of the planets from furthest to closest to the sun. **M**y **V**ery **E**lderly **M**other **J**ust **S**erved **U**s **N**ine **P**izzas reminds us that the order is Mars, Venus, Earth, Mercury, Jupiter, Saturn, Uranus, Neptune, and Pluto. Still another type of mnemonic involves rhyming. A very helpful one for those trying to remember word spellings is *"i" before "e" except after "c" or when sounded like "a" as in neighbor and weigh.* Who can forget *thirty days hath September, April, June, and November, all the rest have thirty-one, except February which has twenty-eight.* As you can see, mnemonics can get rather complex. And, of course, we sometimes remember the mnemonic but forget what the letters or words actually stand for in the concept, fact, or idea. That could happen in the order of the planets—we could forget which planet the "M" stands for, Mars or Mercury.

There are several other forms of mnemonics, but again, they all share the same characteristic—they connect difficult-to-learn, arbitrary pieces of information to previously learned or more meaningful information. They are a sort of gimmick. Nevertheless, they are useful and they will help you help learners remember information. They enhance the chances of information moving from working memory to long-term memory, and they also assist us in recalling information that we need, when we need it. In fact, we have used one ourselves, right here in this chapter! Look again at the boxed information labeled Powerful Strategies to COVER Information. Do you see the mnemonic there? Note that COVER stands for the first letters of each powerful strategy that we are encouraging you to use with learners. Naturally, they can lead to easy recall of the words that stand for each strategy. However, understanding each strategy is quite different from just recalling its name. So again, mnemonics are not as powerful as the strategies we shall discuss next. But perhaps they can serve as a starting point to hold some of these ideas in memory until you have the chance to deeply process and understand them.

> ⌐Think about it . . .
>
> **Think of something that you are currently learning that fits the** *arbitrary association* **category and that you might need to know for an exam. Devise a mnemonic to help you remember the information.**

Information Processing Theory Helps Us COVER Information

We know from theory that human beings have limited space in working memory (five to nine chunks of information). We also know that humans possess a natural inclination to organize information in order to make sense of their (cognitive) worlds. Organizing information in long-term memory is very important. Connecting new information to prior knowledge leads to retention and understanding of facts, ideas, and concepts; it also enables the learner to retrieve these facts, ideas, and concepts and put them to use at the appropriate times. Similar kinds of information (related ideas, topics, content) should be connected to one another, and the more intricate the connections the more one knows about the information. Rich connections (called *propositional networks* by some IP theories, *schemata* by others) also lead to quicker retrieval of relevant information when it is needed to answer a question or to solve a problem.

When one proposition (idea) is activated it can lead to the activation of related propositions until, at least in a well-organized network, the most appropriate knowledge is activated and put into conscious thought (working memory). This is called *spread of activation* (see Fig. 3.2). The knowledge can be held with incoming stimuli such as a question that was asked, or a problem needing to be solved. The person can then make appropriate responses. It is important to activate only the appropriate knowledge because of the space limitations of our working (conscious) memories mentioned earlier. Too much superfluous information in working memory at one time runs the risk of crowding out information needed to make a correct response. In order to think about and formulate responses, we must make efficient use of the limited space we have available to us. Often this means writing down our thoughts on paper to make room for new thoughts and ideas in working memory without losing the previous thoughts. What we write down can be organized in various ways so that we not only record our ideas, but we also connect them to one another to show how they interrelate.

There are many different ways that information can be, and is, organized. Typically, different disciplines favor different ways to organize the knowledge that is at their core. History, for example, is often organized chronologically, whereas mathematics is often organized hierarchically. As teachers, we need to think about the organization of the content that we plan for our students to learn. We should be prepared to alter that organization if we believe that another organizational scheme would be more effective. We will argue later in this book for organizing content around big ideas such as generative topics, core concepts, and essential questions. Learners, too, have available to them many different ways to organize information, and they should be quite diligent about doing so on a regular basis. This is accomplished by thinking about how new information fits in with information already known.

What can teachers and learners do to make practical use of this powerful strategy of organization? One thing that teachers can do is to use *advance organizers* when appropriate. Simply put, advance organizers serve to shed light on what is about to be studied during a day's lesson. More specifically, advance organizers come out of the work of David Ausubel (1963), who seemed to favor direct instruction by teachers that served to organize information for learners, and present it to

FIGURE 3.2

Example of spread of activation. Active propositions, those that we are thinking about at any given time, are represented by dotted lines. Note that propositions active at Time 1 are no longer active at Time 2. This is because of the limited capacity of working memory.

(Source: After the work of Gagne, Yekovich, and Yekovich [1993]. Full citation on reference page.)

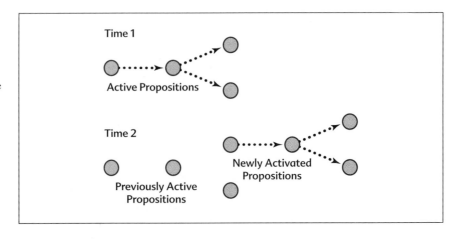

them in a clear and precise fashion. He also hypothesized that a learner possesses an existing cognitive structure that represents her "organization, stability, and clarity of knowledge in a particular subject-matter field" (26). The advance organizer is meant to "delineate clearly, precisely, and explicitly the principal similarities and differences between the ideas in a new learning passage, on the one hand, and existing related concepts in cognitive structure on the other" (83). Arends (1998) summarizes by writing that "advance organizers become the hooks, the anchors, the 'intellectual scaffolding' for subsequent learning materials" (238).

An information processing perspective makes clear in another way the power of the advance organizer—it helps learners locate themselves in the proper area of long-term memory (where ideas related to the new ones about to be presented are stored). In workshops we present, we have often likened this to "stretching" just before rigorous exercise. A good stretch prepares the body for an effective workout in much the same way that a good advance organizer prepares the mind for effective learning.

What would a proper advance organizer sound like? It is *not,* as Arends warns us, the same as other ways to begin a lesson. These other ways might include providing an overview of the lesson, motivating the learners, or even reviewing yesterday's work. Here is an advance organizer that one of us has used with our students in conjunction with a lesson on cultures:

> Today I am going to help you understand how cultures can be compared to one another. But before we begin, I want to give you something to think about for a moment. That is, *any culture can be understood if we know something about the values, customs, traditions, and technology practiced or shared by its participants.* As I discuss with you two very different cultures, I want you to note the similarities and differences between the two on these dimensions.

Research studies have generally been very positive about the effectiveness of advance organizers. Joyce, Showers, and Rolheiser-Bennett (1987) cite a number of studies that led them to conclude that "the average student studying with the aid of organizers learns about as much as the 90th percentile student studying the same material without the assistance of the organizing ideas" (13). That is *very* powerful! An average student is at the fiftieth percentile, where he does as well as or better than 50 percent of everyone in the comparison group. Using organizers helps that same student do as well as, *or better than,* 90 percent of everyone in the comparison group. If you use a simple strategy like an advance organizer prior to direct instruction you can have a truly powerful effect on student learning. Probably because of his emphasis on verbal learning, Ausubel believed that advance organizers should be both verbal and more abstract than the material about to be presented. However, more recent research has indicated that advance organizers containing concrete examples (such as drawings and diagrams) are better than abstract organizers (Hamilton and Ghatala 1994). Figure 3.3 is an example of the advance organizer on cultures presented as a spider map.

In addition to advance organizers, there are also organizers that do not necessarily precede a lesson. These organizers need not be associated only with direct instruction and they don't need to always be verbal and abstract. Commonly used organizers in today's classroom are often referred to variously as semantic maps, graphic organizers, spider maps, webs, concept maps, and mindmaps. All of these are really *visual tools* that help learners represent facts, ideas, and concepts, and the connections between and among them. Hyerle (1996) tells us, "Visual tools offer a

Think about it . . .

How can you make use of the powerful strategy of organization in your own schooling? Try using one of the visual tools to organize your notes. See if it helps you understand ideas better.

FIGURE 3.3

Spider map.

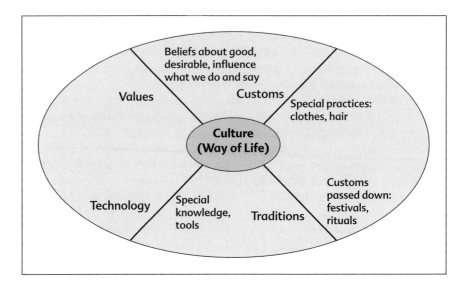

To see more examples of visual tools, also called graphic organizers, follow the link http://www.graphic.org./goindex.html or type Graphic Organizers in a search engine.

bird's-eye view of patterns, interrelationships, and interdependencies. They provide guides for making our way in books full of text or among downloaded materials from the Information Superhighway" (10). Figure 3.4 is a visual tool (a tree map) that presents the various types of visual tools.

We offer a number of examples of visual tools such as those listed in Figure 3.4 in this book. The spider map above is one example. In Chapter 4 we include several examples of visual maps made by learners and teachers. Certainly you recognize the Getting to the Core boxes that appear near the beginning of each chapter as a type of visual tool meant to help you organize your thoughts before you read the chapter.

Naturally, these tools must be used in an appropriate manner. Teachers should decide on the purpose the tools will serve to match the content to be learned, and then assist the learners (especially on their initial exposure) in understanding how

FIGURE 3.4

Visual tools.

(From: Visual Tools for Constructing Knowledge by David Hyerle. Alexandria, VA: Association for Supervision and Curriculum Development, 1996. Reprinted with permission of David Hyerle.)

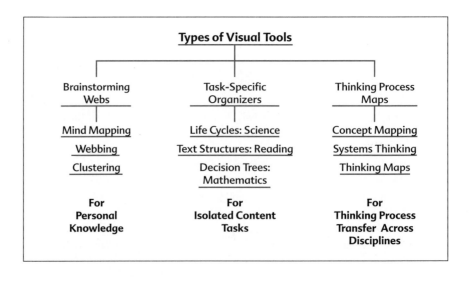

to use the tool. But all of these tools have one thing in common: They make use of the powerful strategy of organization. They help learners make connections between prior knowledge and new knowledge, and make order by organizing items in some fashion. This enhances the likelihood that, in information processing terms, declarative knowledge will be retained in long-term memory in a form that is understandable and retrievable.

SPOTLIGHT ON BEHAVIOR MANAGEMENT

"But will they behave?"

⊚ **CORE CONCEPT**   The ability to retain and understand *declarative* knowledge is greatly enhanced when human learners make connections to what they already know by organizing, visualizing, and elaborating upon facts, ideas, and concepts. The ability to correctly use *procedural* knowledge is enhanced by practice and specific feedback.

The Power of the Conflict Cycle Paradigm

By now you have spent some time reflecting on your own thoughts and feelings. Have you identified those events in the classroom that set you off? Have you identified your stressors? Now we will help you to see how your own thoughts and feelings interact with the thoughts and feelings of your students.

In this section we will introduce Nicholas Long's conflict cycle paradigm (Long 1979, 1986, 1996; Wood and Long 1991). This model explains how conflict in the classroom can be escalated by the way teachers and other adults react to troubled students. We will only be able to make a brief presentation in the space here. For a comprehensive explanation see the references cited, but particularly Long (1996).

The model has five interacting parts, (1) the student's self-concept, (2) a stressful incident, (3) feelings, (4) some observable behavior, and (5) the reaction of an adult, or peer. As we explain the conflict cycle we will highlight these five interacting parts in bold type so that you can follow along with the picture of Long's model below.

A child's beliefs about him or herself are developed early in life through feedback received from significant adults and experiences. These beliefs form the **self-concept** and are significant factors in determining how a child will act when faced with a stressful situation (see Fig. 3.5). Take Eliza and Juan, the students we have been following. Let's assume that we have tested Juan and found that he is a pretty bright student, but some clues about his physical appearance, what he does and says, and the way he and other students interact lead us to ask some questions about his self-concept. So, we investigate further. By keenly observing and talking with Juan, we learn that he doesn't think very highly of himself. In fact, Juan believes he is not a very good person. By looking at school records and talking to his parents and various professionals, we learn that Juan is in a rather difficult position at home. For many months now Juan has been in charge of getting his younger brother ready for school. Juan finds it hard enough to get himself ready for school, so he is often chastised for not doing a good job. As we investigate further, we find that Juan has never really lived up to the expectations of the significant adults in his life, and they have typically made it a point to tell him. So, even though we know Juan is a bright student, we are beginning to see that his self-image is keeping him from realizing his potential. He believes strongly, albeit irrationally, that he is not a good person.

The child's *self-concept* is one of the keys to understanding the conflict cycle. As Long (1996) states, "how a child learns to think about himself is more important in determining his feelings and behavior than any other objective professional evaluation" (247). Juan's thinking about himself has lead to *irrational beliefs* that then drive his thoughts and actions.

FIGURE 3.5

The student's conflict cycle.

[Source: Long, N., and Morse, W., (1996). Conflict in the classroom: The education of at-risk and troubled students. Austin, TX: ProEd. Reprinted with permission.]

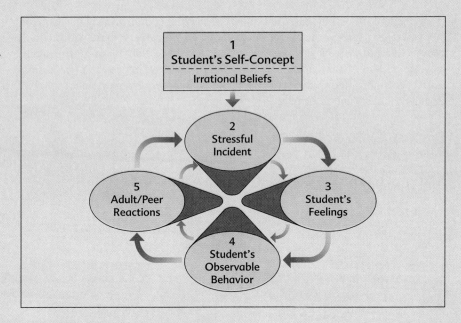

Juan's irrational belief is, "I am not a good person." Irrational beliefs are typically characterized by "all or nothing" logic. For example, "I am always wrong" or "I don't have to listen to anyone" are irrational beliefs. People maintain irrational beliefs because they are safe and predictable. They "bring order to an unstable and chaotic world" (Long 1996, 248). To maintain this order, people with irrational beliefs must think and behave in ways that validate these beliefs.

Juan, who believes he is a terrible person, behaves in the classroom in a manner that gets a reaction from his teacher. This reaction, in the form of several commands that increased in volume followed by a directive to "get out," simply validated to Juan that he was indeed terrible. For Juan, order is maintained! All is right in the world! In fact, he may even be thinking, "No need to change my behavior, I'm terrible!"

We all operate on the basis of beliefs we have of ourselves. Then along comes an event that is particularly stressful. This stress creates thought, which then ignites a particular feeling. To complete the circle these feelings create further thoughts. We often act according to our feelings. Long (1996) adds, "All feelings are real, powerful and give excitement to life, but they are not always an accurate assessment of the situation. Emotions are not facts, they are feelings that are triggered by rational and irrational thoughts" (255).

So, when Juan's teacher asked him to pay attention a **stressful incident** was created for Juan. Irrational thoughts of being a terrible person flooded his head. He felt **real feelings.** However, because they were based on his irrational thinking the next choice he made was self-defeating. He chose to turn his back and defy the teacher in order to maintain his belief that he is a terrible person. This defiance was his **observable behavior.**

Juan could have accepted and owned these feelings. However, he is clearly not able to respond in this most healthy manner. He could have defended against these feelings, burying them in his psyche and probably creating additional problems for himself. The only other possible course of action was for Juan to act out these feelings, which he did by turning his back on the teacher (Long 1979, 1996; Wood and Long 1991).

Your **reaction** to these preceding events determines if the conflict cycle is escalated and the situation gets worse or if you can act in a helpful manner, calming the student. As Long (1996) states, "While staff do not have control over the student's thinking, feelings and behaviors, they do have complete control over how they react to the student's behavior" (259). This is where your self-reflection pays off. If you can avoid acting counteraggressively, you can probably (1) help the student, (2) maintain a helpful and healthy climate in your classroom, and (3) quickly return to teaching and engaging the rest of the class.

If you do react to the student by raising the stakes, you create a new *stressful incident.* More thoughts and *feelings* are generated. The student responds with an escalated form of *behavior.* The adult *reacts* again, and usually with an escalated response. In our example above, this goes around and around until Juan eventually is told to get out. We are sure you can recall or observe conflict cycles in schools. Consider you own peer interactions or even interactions with your parents. This model works equally well for adults!

We are confident that you can understand how the conflict cycle paradigm works. In the next section we will help you understand (1) how to avoid the conflict cycle and (2) how to quickly identify and exit a conflict cycle you have entered. In the meantime you can practice. See if you can directly observe a conflict cycle in your field placement. Create a drawing of the conflict cycle to represent your observations. Compare notes with your classmates.

Information Processing Theory Helps Us COVER Information

You have probably already noticed overlap between the strategies of connecting and organizing information. Visual tools do not perform only connecting and organizing functions; they help us visualize ideas and concepts as well. But not all visual tools use pictures or images. As strategies, visualization and its cousin, imagery, are powerful in their own rights. You may recall from Chapter 2 that, according to Information Processing Theory, humans can keep only five to nine unrelated pieces of information in their working memories at one time. This is one of the limitations of working memory. You may also recall that by organizing information into related "chunks," much more information can be held in working memory. This is important because working memory is our conscious memory. It is where we do our cognitive work. It is very inefficient to have, on average, room for only seven pieces of information. So much room is taken up by these individual pieces that a person would quickly run out of space and not be able to work on complex cognitive tasks. For example, if a learner is asked to read a short essay by Mark Twain and then analyze some aspect of it (let's say for its relevance to a modern-day event), it would be almost impossible to do if the learner could not sound out letters to make words. It would also be very difficult to do if the learner could not group words into phrases, and sentences, and even paragraphs. Analysis requires first decoding written words, and then comprehending them. If most or all of the space in working memory is taken up in lower-level skills, higher-level thought such as analysis cannot take place. So being able to organize information efficiently (letters make words, words make phrases, phrases make sentences, sentences have meaning, and so on) is absolutely critical to being able to perform more complex cognitive tasks.

Visualization and imagery are also important in this regard. You have often heard that "a picture is worth a thousand words." Perhaps an overstatement, but nonetheless that saying articulates an important point. Pictures and images can represent a great deal of information in a very efficient way. Gagne, Yekovich, and Yekovich (1993) explain that "An image is a form of declarative knowledge that preserves as continuous dimensions some of the physical attributes of that which it represents" (70). In this way, images are very economical; that is, they take up less space in working memory than ideas expressed as words (propositions). We shall use a very simple example. Think, for a moment, about the concept of "school." A school is housed in a building comprised of many parts—doors, windows, stairs, various rooms, levels, pieces of furniture, and so forth. If you need to think about each of these parts, it is very difficult to form the whole. As you now know, after five to nine parts are in your working memory, anything new will push out one of the current parts (much like a glass that is full will overflow if any more liquid is added). But, if you represent the school building as an image, it now forms one large chunk of continuous information in your working memory, freeing up many "spaces" for new information to enter.

Beyond just visual images, Perkins (1992) asserts that mental images of all types are crucial to building what he calls "understanding performances." Blythe and associates (1998) explain that understanding performances "require students to go beyond the information given to create something new by reshaping, expanding, extrapolating from, applying, and building on what they already know" (56). These mental images would include not just images of things easily visualized, like physical entities such as a school building, but also of things such as, using his example, stories and what they should be like. Perkins defines a mental image as "any unified, overarching mental representation that helps us work with a topic or subject" (1992, 80). Much like the visual tools described earlier, they are tools for thinking. If you are asked to solve a problem, let's say in science class, having mental images of some of the necessary concepts will help you do so. The power of visualization and imagery is undeniable.

> Think about it . . . Ask somebody to give you *written* *directions* in paragraph form to a place in town A several miles from where you are located. Study them for three minutes. Then have the same person give you a *map* to help you find a place in town B, also several miles from where you are now. Study this map for three minutes. Which place do you have more confidence in your ability to find easily, the one in town A or the one in town B? Why?

Information Processing Theory Helps Us COVER Information

The last of the powerful strategies for promoting the deep understanding of declarative knowledge is elaboration. Elaboration is a form of rehearsal. Most of us are already very familiar with (and have probably put to extensive use) another form of rehearsal called "maintenance rehearsal." We did not call it that, of course. We called it "cramming." It is that time-honored activity in which we have all engaged so many times. Typically it happens like this—a test is fast approaching, and we have diligently taken copious notes. Now it is time to "learn" these notes. So, a night or two (maybe three) before the test date we sit down and start to memorize these notes. If we have not planned well, we end up doing this the night before the test (often called "pulling an all-nighter") to accomplish the task. Now, if we have been blessed with good memories and if the test requires only regurgitating facts from the notes and readings, and if we are not overly anxious, we have a reasonable chance of doing well on that test. Doing well will be taken as evidence that we have *learned* the information.

But deep down most of us recognize the fallacy in this reasoning. First, our goal was to pass a test, not to (really) learn the material. Second, we know that much of what we studied, especially the details, we will have forgotten sooner rather than later. Third, that which we do retain for a long period of time, even though technically in our long-term memories, is very difficult to retrieve because it is disconnected from related ideas. An important tenet of information processing theory that you should recall is that *nothing is learned unless it is in long-term memory.* Related to that tenet is that we must be able to retrieve it in order to put it to use. Memorized information is not in any sense of the word deeply processed; nor is it likely to be understood. Some argue that basic facts and ideas need to be memorized in order to serve as foundational information for higher-order ideas or operations. A counterargument is that these basic facts can be learned first in a meaningful context, then understood, and finally made automatic through sustained practice. Whatever side you take on this issue, memorized information is often shallow and fragile, and so it should constitute a minimal part of any serious learning activity.

The proper role of maintenance rehearsal is to allow us to hold information in conscious working memory just long enough to decide what to do with it. It is not suited for long-term storage. Teachers should encourage learners to use elaborative rehearsal, rather than maintenance rehearsal, to learn information. Elaboration is very different from maintenance. Maintenance involves rote rehearsal. In contrast, when we elaborate upon something we *add to it*. This involves conscious and deliberate thought during which we relate the new information to something we already know and understand. Then, when we put it back into long-term memory the new information has been actively transformed by us. It is connected and it has staying power.

What can teachers do to encourage their learners to elaborate? One biology teacher that we know had, for years, required her learners to keep notebooks. Periodically, she collected these notebooks and graded them. She looked for such things as neatness and completeness (all lecture notes and labs included). As she learned more about the power of elaboration and reflected upon this notebook requirement, it occurred to her that by changing the rubric (grading criteria) she could encourage her learners to elaborate by doing the assignment. So she began to count more heavily not whether what *she* gave the learners was complete and present, but what the learners *added* to the information and included in their notebooks. Things like drawings, diagrams, articles related to topics taught in class but not introduced by the teacher, were all heavily weighted in this reconstituted requirement. This is an example of a teacher encouraging her learners to elaborate; happily, this particular teacher noticed many positive results from changing the notebook assignment.

There are many ways that learners can elaborate on information. Teachers should encourage them to do so. Among these are some strategies mentioned above. Drawings, metaphors, analogies, and summarizing in one's own words can all be forms of elaboration. Teachers often ask questions as part of their instruction. By asking questions that require elaboration rather than simple, short answers, teachers can add power to that instruction and enhance the probability that their learners will process more deeply the information to be learned. An excellent tool for constructing questions and strategies that require elaboration is provided by McTighe and Lyman (1988). They call it a "cueing bookmark."

This tool is easy to use. Teachers can keep it folded up in a book and then construct questions "on the fly" during classroom discussions. It is an excellent way to differentiate instruction, a method we will write about in Chapter 6. Teachers can also use the bookmark to construct test questions of varying levels of difficulty. The various categories of questions that appear on the bookmark are derived from the work of Benjamin Bloom. We address Bloom's work in Chapter 4.

Elaboration encompasses many elements of the general strategies mentioned earlier. In that regard it is, in our minds, the most powerful of all the strategies. When you teach, you can make great headway in helping your learners deeply process information by using just this one powerful strategy alone. Each of the general strategies mentioned so far (COVER) provides a way for learners to truly understand declarative knowledge; taken together they suggest moves that teachers can make to encourage learners to use these strategies. Our intention here is clear; we are trying to cast the coverage of material in a completely new light. Rather than

> Think about it . . .
>
> **Elaborative rehearsal is very powerful. How will you use it in your academic life? How will you use it to help students learn when you become a classroom teacher?**

Cueing Bookmark

Front **Questioning for Quality Thinking**	Back **Strategies to Extend Student Thinking**

Knowledge—Identification and recall of information
  Who, what, when, where, how _____?
  Describe _____.
 	
Comprehension—Organization and selection of facts and ideas
  Retell _____ in your own words.
  What is the main idea of _____?
 	
Application—Use of facts, rules, principles
  How is _____ an example of _____?
  How is _____ related to _____?
  Why is _____ significant?
 	
Analysis—Separation of a whole into component parts
  What are the parts or features of _____?
  Classify _____ according to _____.
  Outline/diagram/web _____
  How does _____ compare/contrast with _____?
  What evidence can you list for _____?
 	
Synthesis—Combination of ideas to form a new whole
  What would you predict/infer from _____?
  What ideas can you add to _____?
  How would you create/design a new _____?
  What might happen if you combined _____ with _____?
  What solutions would you suggest for _____?
 	
Evaluation—Development of opinions, judgments, or decisions
  Do you agree _____?
  What do you think about _____?
  What is the most important _____?
  Prioritize _____.
  How would you decide about _____?
  What criteria would you use to assess _____?
	• **Remember "wait time I and II"**
	  Provide at least three seconds of thinking time after a question and after a response.
	• **Utilize "think-pair-share"**
	  Allow individual thinking time, discussion with a partner, and then open up the class discussion.
	• **Ask "follow-ups"**
	  Why? Do you agree? Can you elaborate? Tell me more. Can you give an example?
	• **Withhold judgment**
	  Respond to student answers in a nonevaluative fashion.
	• **Ask for summary (to promote active listening)**
	  "Could you please summarize John's point?"
	• **Survey the class**
	  "How many people agree with the author's point of view?" ("thumbs up, thumbs down")
	• **Allow for student calling**
	  "Richard, will you please call on someone else to respond?"
	• **Play devil's advocate**
	  Require students to defend their reasoning against different points of view.
	• **Ask students to "unpack their thinking"**
	  "Describe how you arrived at your answer." ("think aloud")
	• **Call on students randomly**
	  Not just those with raised hands.
	• **Student questioning**
	  Let the students develop their own questions.
	• **Cue student responses**
	  "There is not a single correct answer for this question. I want you to consider alternatives."

Source: Language and Learning Improvement Branch, Division of Instruction, Maryland State Department of Education. Developed by Jay McTighe for the Maryland Department of Education. Reprinted with permission.

"cover" material in the usual sense of the word, which can lead to superficial treatment of content, we encourage you to recast the notion of coverage. By thinking of the word *cover* as **c**onnect, **o**rganize, **v**isualize, **e**laborate, and **r**ehearse, you can, paradoxically, help your learners *uncover* the content in the disciplines.

A Classroom Example of COVER

In a middle school general science class, students were studying the cell, its parts, and the various functions of each part. They were asked by their teacher to pick a theme, and then relate each part of the cell to that theme. One group of students picked soccer. Their collage is pictured on page 89. This collage includes elements that relate directly to the cell. For example, these students made the following connections:

Using soccer to understand the cell (Reprinted with permission of the students in Michael Dooley's class at Klinger Middle School).

- The cell's nucleus is represented by the referee because he controls the game like the nucleus controls the cell and its activities.
- The nucleolus is represented by the referee's hand because the nucleolus is part of the nucleus.
- Ribosomes are the yellow and red cards given out by referees for infractions.
- The cell wall is represented by the goalkeeper because it "doesn't let things in."
- The cell membrane is represented by the defensive players because they either keep bad things out or let some things through, as when they pass the ball back to the goalkeeper.
- The cytoplasm represents the field where everything takes place.
- The mitochondria are like a sports drink because they give energy to the players just like the mitochondria give energy to the cell.
- The vacuole is represented by soccer moms who store snacks and take care of trash.

These students made several other connections between the cell and soccer. What is important here is that the teacher had the students make connections (cell to soccer) by way of visuals and images. To do all of this the students needed to elaborate on the basic information related to the cell. In contrast to straight lecture and simple worksheets, this example demonstrates empowering students and allowing them to COVER information in a deeper, richer way that is more likely to make

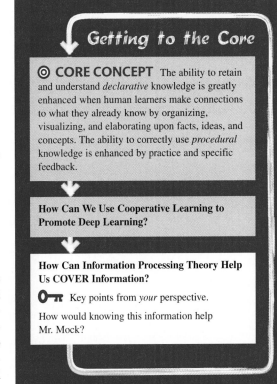

Getting to the Core

⊙ **CORE CONCEPT** The ability to retain and understand *declarative* knowledge is greatly enhanced when human learners make connections to what they already know by organizing, visualizing, and elaborating upon facts, ideas, and concepts. The ability to correctly use *procedural* knowledge is enhanced by practice and specific feedback.

How Can We Use Cooperative Learning to Promote Deep Learning?

How Can Information Processing Theory Help Us COVER Information?

⊶ Key points from *your* perspective.

How would knowing this information help Mr. Mock?

its way into long-term memory. It worked! One of our daughters was a member of the group that constructed this organizer. Months later she can explain the cell, its parts, and how they function.

Why Are Practice and Feedback Important?

Our focus so far has been on declarative knowledge, the facts, ideas, and concepts that we learn in and out of school. But remember that Information Processing Theory also identifies another type of knowledge, procedural knowledge, as being important in the learning process. Earlier we defined procedural knowledge as the knowledge of how to do something. It is to promoting that type of knowledge that we shall now turn.

Contemporary research tells us that it is vitally important that teachers allow their learners many opportunities to practice information that they are learning. It is our firm belief that schools and teachers spend lots of time trying to help learners develop declarative knowledge; they typically do not devote sufficient time to helping learners develop procedural knowledge (Feden 1994). Knowing, for example, that some piece of literary work is called a poem, and knowing the characteristics of various poetic forms, are demonstrations of declarative knowledge. Being able to find examples of poems among various genres and being able to construct a poem require a behavior or action. These require learners to demonstrate procedural knowledge. One can know what something is without knowing how to do it; an example is when a child knows her home address but can't find her house. Likewise, one can do something without understanding it (at least at some level). Many of us can solve mathematical problems by plugging numbers into formulas without an understanding of the mathematical principles at work. Perhaps procedural knowledge is shortchanged because of the sheer bulk of declarative knowledge typically required by the curriculum. But both forms of knowledge are important for a learned individual.

Some experienced teachers object to our contention that schools typically do not devote sufficient time to the development of procedural knowledge. They are satisfied that worksheets and homework require the learners to practice. Unfortunately, much of this practice requires only rote, maintenance rehearsal. That is, 20 practice problems might be assigned for the night's homework. Or fill-in-the-blank worksheets might be distributed for the learners to complete. Although some of this type of practice is warranted, teachers should not use it exclusively. Rather, they should use activities that are substantial and that engage learners in actually *doing* the subject.

Suppose you learn all about a specific form of poetic expression, and even the names of some of the poets most accomplished in that form. If you learned that information well (did you use COVER?) you now have some new declarative knowledge. Stopping there, however, is a mistake. Further suppose your teacher requires you to practice what you have learned by composing your own poem, to express a personal thought or feeling, using that same poetic form. Do you see the difference between that form of practice and rote practice?

Think about it . . . You have received lots of feedback from your teachers over the years. Think about the following:

1. You receive a B on a paper with no other comment.

2. You receive a B on a paper with the comment "This was a pretty good effort."

3. You receive a B on a paper with several comments such as "You need to support assertions you make. For example, on page 3. . . ."

You have probably seen instances of all of these examples. Which do you think will be most helpful as you try to improve your performance?

Now suppose that the teacher gave you *very specific feedback* on the quality and correctness (at least in terms of form) of the poem you wrote. Now you have the feedback you need to improve that poem, or the next one that you write. And, one last time, suppose that your teacher gave you at least one, and maybe several, additional opportunities to write poems. Can you imagine how much you would improve at writing poems (procedural knowledge)? At the same time, you would also gain, or at least refine, the declarative knowledge you have that relates to poetic form. Teachers often fail to provide feedback that is specific enough to assist a student to improve her work. The teacher might give no feedback (except for a grade, which is not really feedback at all because it tells you absolutely nothing about why you received a B). The teacher might offer nonspecific feedback, usually with a general comment such as "You did a pretty good job with this paper" or "You need to try harder and write more." The most effective feedback, however, focuses on specific areas of strength and weakness. The following comments offer specific feedback on performance, and can lead to the development of procedural knowledge:

1. "You argue effectively by presenting both sides of an issue and then supporting your position with facts and personal experience."

2. "You did not include all of the sources you cited in the text of your paper on the reference page, as required by the style manual of the American Psychological Association."

In the same way that COVER relates to declarative knowledge, *practice* and *specific feedback* relate to procedural knowledge. They are, together, very powerful general strategies that promote student learning. Unfortunately, while we pay lip service to the old adages that "it is all right to make mistakes" and "we all learn from our mistakes," the truth is, as often as not, we punish our learners for making these mistakes. Neil Postman (1995) writes, "Human beings learn and progress by making—and correcting—mistakes. Why, then, do schools teach students to avoid and fear them?" (32) Certainly what he suggests about how humans learn is supported by information processing theory. Yet we have instilled in learners, as it has been inculcated in us, that mistakes are to be avoided. Perhaps because of the rush of the school day, learners are not often given multiple opportunities to demonstrate what they have learned; teachers often do not have the luxury of time necessary to allow them these multiple opportunities. If we are to use the powerful strategies suggested by information processing theory, we must reconsider the ways we think about learners' mistakes, the kinds of practice activities we devise, and the kind of practice and feedback we employ in our classrooms, with our learners.

What Context Is Necessary for Promoting Learning?

The final thing we would like to do in this chapter is to help you pull this entire story of changing classroom practices together into a cohesive whole. All of the powerful strategies we mention—cooperative learning, COVER, and practice/feedback—should take place in a context in which the learner

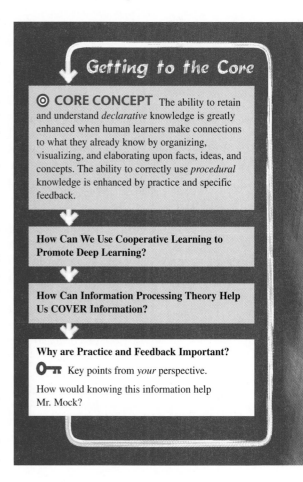

Getting to the Core

⊙ **CORE CONCEPT** The ability to retain and understand *declarative* knowledge is greatly enhanced when human learners make connections to what they already know by organizing, visualizing, and elaborating upon facts, ideas, and concepts. The ability to correctly use *procedural* knowledge is enhanced by practice and specific feedback.

How Can We Use Cooperative Learning to Promote Deep Learning?

How Can Information Processing Theory Help Us COVER Information?

Why are Practice and Feedback Important?

⊶ Key points from *your* perspective.

How would knowing this information help Mr. Mock?

A Person Who Helped Create Change...

Bernice McCarthy is the president of About Learning, Incorporated, a company that she founded as Excel, Inc., in 1979. She earned her doctorate degree in education and learning theory from Northwestern University in Chicago in 1979. She has made an impact on the field of education not only through her company, but also through the system she created, known as the 4MAT® System. About Learning, Incorporated, functions as a national consulting firm to teach others about learning. By understanding the concepts of 4MAT, leaders in business, industry, and education can teach more effectively and better reach their target audiences.

Source: http://www.aboutlearning.com/aboutlearning/bmccarthyvita.html.

Photo: Courtesy of About Learning, Inc. http://www.aboutlearning.com/images/bernice.jpg.

is *motivated* to learn, and where the flow of activities is natural for the learner and is focused on substantial content. In our minds, although lecture is a viable strategy to promote learning, it is overused and often poorly used. So we also want to help you understand a way to use these powerful strategies that may include, but that goes well beyond, traditional lecture. Here we have selected a system of planning and teaching that is highly regarded by practitioners and researchers, and that is widely used by classroom teachers (including us). We have introduced many experienced teachers to this system, and they find it quite useful in planning and carrying out lessons that are consistent with the powerful principles we present in this chapter. The system we will now help you understand and connect to the powerful strategies mentioned in this chapter is called the 4MAT system.

Motivation and the Natural Cycle of Learning

We recognize the possible problems with presenting what could be construed as a recipe-like, cookie cutter approach to planning and implementing lessons. Indeed, it is possible to use any system in such a way. However, it is helpful to provide structures for teachers that they can use to think about, and develop, instruction for learners. This is similar to the idea of mental images addressed earlier in the previous section of this chapter. So we encourage you to think of the 4MAT system as a tool that will help you plan. In fact, according to Bernice McCarthy, the person who developed the 4MAT system, it was simply meant to help teachers teach in new and different ways (1987), and to increase the chances for all students to learn (1996). It is both a visual and conceptual tool for you to use to help you promote powerful learning among your learners—*all of them.*

The 4MAT system grew out of McCarthy's concern for the fact that children learn in a variety of ways (see Fig. 3.6). These styles of learning require teachers to vary their instruction so that all students may, at some point during an instructional cycle, have the needs of their preferred style met. In addition to styles of learning, McCarthy was also intrigued by the concept of brain hemisphericity, and the differences in the manner in which the left and right modes of the brain function. Blending a model of learning styles heavily influenced by the work of David Kolb (1976) with research on brain hemisphericity, McCarthy developed a unique model she depicts as a circle that incorporates four quadrants according to how we perceive and process information (similar to Kolb's model). Each quadrant further incorporates both the left and right sides of the brain (1987). The model is depicted in Figure 3.6.

As McCarthy (1996) sees it, her model embodies a natural cycle; natural because it "contains the essential elements of human learning," and a cycle "because it begins with us and returns to us" (vii). You can understand the model more clearly by reading the information in the box that follows.

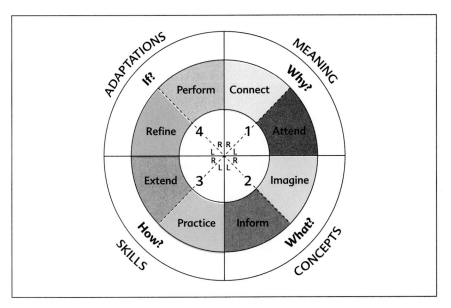

FIGURE 3.6
The 4-MAT system.

*(Source: About Learning
Incorporated, 1999. Reproduced
with permission.)*

1. **Connect:** co (with) + nectere (to bind)
   Establish a relationship between your learners and the content connecting the
   content to their lives, not telling them how it *connects,* but having something
   actually happen in the classroom that will bring them to make the connection
   themselves. The experience must encompass the heart of the content.

2. **Attend:** ad (to, toward) + tend (to stretch)
   Have your students analyze what just happened, have them *attend* to their own
   experience and to the perceptions of their fellow students; how it went, what
   really happened. Note another form of the word "attention."

3. **Imagine:** imaginen (to form a mental picture)
   You need your students to *imagine,* to picture the concept as they understand it
   (Einstein seeing light curving), have experienced it, before you take them to the
   experts.

4. **Inform:** in (in, into) + form (form, shape, mold)
   Now they are ready for the left-mode step of quadrant 2, receiving and examining
   the expert knowledge. Now you *inform* them of the content they need to understand.

5. **Practice:** praktikos (capable of being used)
   Stay first with the left mode. Your students must *practice* the learning as the
   experts have found it. It is not yet time for innovation or adaptation. They need
   to learn by practicing, they need to become sufficiently skilled before they can
   innovate. Create work practice that is fun, yet demanding. Facilitate moving
   through the activities through the centers you create to help them achieve mastery.

6. **Extend:** ex (out of) + tend (to stretch)
   This is where innovation begins. Students know enough, have enough skills to
   begin the tinkering and playing with the content, the skills, the materials, the
   ideas, the wholes and the parts, the details, the data, and the big picture, to make
   something of this learning for themselves, to be interpretive.

7. **Refine:** re (again) + fin (the end, limit, boundary)
   Stay first with the left mode again. The students have proposed an extension of
   the learning into their lives. They need to evaluate that extension.

8. Perform: per (through) + form (form, shape, mold)
Last, have your students perform: Here the content takes a new shape, as it is formed through the learners. Look for originality, relevance, new questions, connections to larger ideas, skills that are immediately useful, values confirmed or questioned anew.

(Source: About Learning, Incorporated, Newsletter, May 5, 2000. Used with permission. http://www.aboutlearning.com/enewslettersenews5_5.html.)

In Chapter 5 the learning styles component of the 4MAT system will be explained further. In terms of instruction and the natural learning cycle, as movement through the 4MAT cycle progresses, learning becomes less teacher directed and more learner centered. Teachers are encouraged to create an experience for the learners in quadrant 1, then to teach the content "conceptually, in frameworks that contain the essence" in quadrant 2. Next, teachers are to allow learners to practice the content and "tinker with it" in quadrant 3. The cycle is completed with quadrant 4, where teachers should encourage learners to "make use of the learning . . . by examining its place in their lives, its transferability" (McCarthy 1996, 251–255). Teachers may guide their planning efforts by answering the same questions posed by each learner type: *Why* should my students learn this? *What* should they learn? *How* will I have them practice it? *If* they know it, what else can they do with it? We should start planning on the basis of what the students need to know. Our primary job as teachers is to help our students master the curriculum agreed upon by the school district or entity in which we are employed. The challenge, once we identify what they need to know, is to help them establish a personal connection to the information so that they know why they need to learn the information.

Within each of the quadrants, learners are engaged in both left-mode and right-mode activities. According to research cited by McCarthy (1996, 1987), the left mode of the brain processes information differently than does the right mode. The left mode prefers to process verbally, in linear and sequential fashion, and is very analytical.

FIGURE 3.7

Visual depiction of the differences between right and left hemispheres in the way they process information.

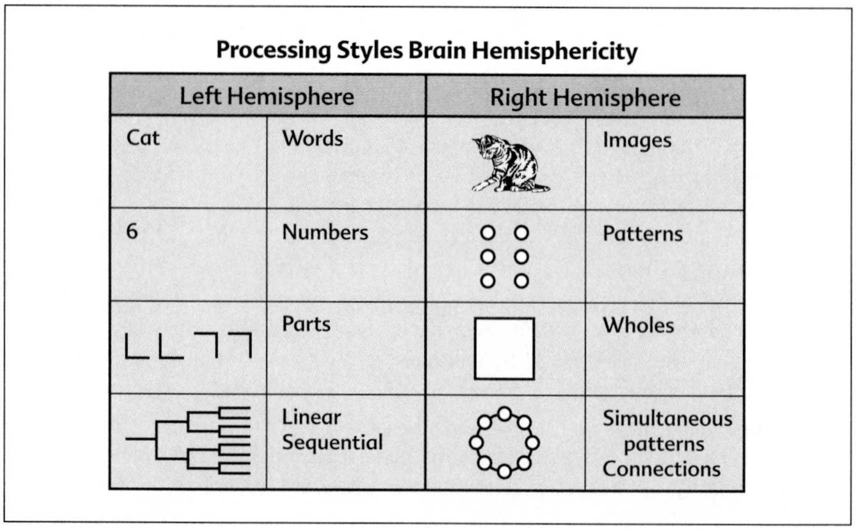

Processing Styles Brain Hemisphericity

Left Hemisphere		Right Hemisphere	
Cat	Words		Images
6	Numbers		Patterns
	Parts		Wholes
	Linear Sequential		Simultaneous patterns Connections

Teachers planning left-mode compatible activities can think of the typical school activities with which we are all most familiar—lecture, discussion, and looking at parts of the whole, for example. The right mode prefers to process visually, spatially, and simultaneously. It seeks to put things together. An analogy might be as follows: The left mode is to a computer as the right mode is to a kaleidoscope. Activities involving fine arts (dance, movement, drawing), activity (role-play, building, experiments), and imagery (visualization, metaphors) are examples of right-mode activities that teachers might plan for learners (see Fig. 3.7). On page 97 we share with you an overview of a 4MAT unit plan. Our experience is that teachers use 4MAT to plan *units of instruction* that last for a week or more, rather than for planning individual lessons (although it can be used to plan lessons, and even the entire curriculum).

Learning and Teaching in the Age of Technology

A program called Inspiration 6.0 and kidsinspiration (2001) can help learners visualize the connections and relationships so necessary to master declarative knowledge. At the click of a mouse, a student-generated outline of facts or information gleaned from reading or notes can be turned into a diagram with boxes and arrows showing links, hierarchical relationships, and correct or incorrect learner-made connections. Students can easily manipulate these concept maps, honing their understanding of relationships, and visually showing what they may or may not understand. Teachers are able to visually highlight misunderstandings of connections, allowing the learner to reorganize and refine the connections necessary for understanding. This type of visual imagery, or the use of a hyperlink record, shows how a student moved from connection to connection to arrive at a conclusion. Additionally, the culling of

computer-generated visuals and their use to show an understanding of both declarative and procedural knowledge are all alternative ways of helping learners practice, master, and apply declarative and procedural knowledge.

The Vanderbilt group has been helpful in stressing the technological tools that help shape instruction, which provides opportunities for practice with feedback, revision, and reflection (Goldman, Williams, Sherwood, and Hasselbring, 1999, 7). These are all skills involving metacognition, the ability to regulate one's own learning. They emphasize the important difference between acquisition of skills involved in *initial learning* and *fluency*, which involves quick and effortless access to the skill. Current technology is good at reinforcing previously acquired skills and facilitating learner fluency. Individualized tutorials that present new skills and help individual learners develop connections and deep understanding on their own are only in their infancy.

Bemoaning the information explosion and the inability of schools and curriculum planners to keep up with the knowledge and information explosion Lois Stanciak (Willis, 1999) opines: "Information is growing so dramatically . . . we can't continue to pile on content, because it's going to be humanly impossible. We're going to have to teach kids how to *use* information rather than collect it" (4a). His suggestion is to organize instruction by broad concepts that bridge subject areas. Thus the technology tools we have already discussed

> ◎ **CORE CONCEPT** The ability to retain and understand *declarative* knowledge is greatly enhanced when human learners make connections to what they already know by organizing, visualizing, and elaborating upon facts, ideas, and concepts. The ability to correctly use *procedural* knowledge is enhanced by practice and specific feedback.

are all cross-disciplinary in nature. The very essence of hyperlink technology that jumps the viewer from connection point to connection point is a powerful tool in helping learners see the interrelationship of disciplines. It would be very valuable for students to keep logs (online or in a notebook) of their hyperlink leaps, a record of their journeys in cyberspace as a way of reinforcing how things connect, spin off, go into tangents, become unrelated, or return you to your starting point.

Mastery of declarative and procedural knowledge can be assisted by technology in one more important area. The use of presentation software (current favorites being PowerPoint or Corel Presentations) by both teachers and students can be enormously helpful in visualizing, organizing, and showing the interrelationships of concepts. According to Lafond (1999), PowerPoint and Corel Presentations are good tools for presenting information in linear sequence and focusing on the skeleton (topic, list of details) and making or proving a point. Hyperstudio or Hypercard (a kind of computerized flash card system) allows presentations to be explored by author or audience in any sequence, uses lots of sound and graphics, and includes a built-in test or assessment for viewers (4).

It is essential that in helping students process declarative and procedural knowledge, gathering and making connections through use of many different sources of information, we stress ethical behavior when making use of that information. It is almost impossible for an instructor to know whether a student has written his or her own ideas, or copied them from some obscure website. Challenging your students to restate in their own words what they have gathered is a way of holding them accountable.

There is nothing wrong, and everything right, about bringing proof of argument from other sources, using quotes to bolster your thesis, or citing the work of others to enlarge or support your own theories or expository writing. But it must be done ethically, that is, by quoting or acknowledging the *source* (Carnevale 1999).

Teaching Tips

1. Use an overhead projector and make ample use of words and pictures that depict main points to help students get information visually.

2. Use computer software that involves solving problems, such as software put out by Tom Snyder Productions, to engage students in procedural knowledge.

3. When you use videotaped programs, be certain to introduce the tape and consider giving the students a viewing guide with questions that require them to look and listen for specific information.

Suggested Websites

http://www.kie.berkeley.edu/KIE.html
   Homework assistance—free! A place to go when students have questions: get real answers and advice via the Web.

http://www.worksheetfactory.com
   Mathematics Worksheet Factory.

http://www.engagingminds.com.
   Site for Inspiration and kidsinspiration.

A Classroom Example of 4MAT

The sample unit (page 97) we share with you would typically have daily plans to accompany it. Morris and McCarthy (1999) have collected lesson plans from primary, intermediate, middle school, high school, and postsecondary levels of education. These sample plans can be very useful to those of you who wish to develop instruction using the 4MAT system.

4MAT and the Connection to Powerful Instruction

We would like to review for a moment some of the major ideas we have presented so far in this book in order to help you connect 4MAT to powerful instruction. In the introduction to the book we explain that the theme, or "story line," is about change. Chapter 1 answers the question *Why change?* We know that despite changes in virtually everything else—society, children, what we know about learning—schools

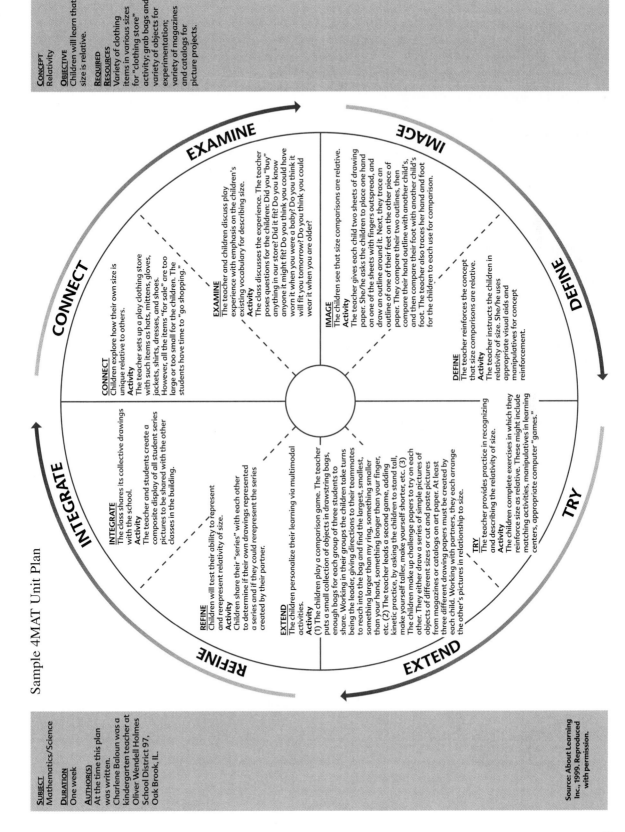

Sample 4MAT Unit Plan

SUBJECT
Mathematics/Science

DURATION
One week

AUTHOR(S)
At the time this plan was written, Charlene Baloun was a kindergarten teacher at Oliver Wendell Holmes School District 97, Oak Brook, IL.

CONCEPT
Relativity

OBJECTIVE
Children will learn that size is relative.

REQUIRED RESOURCES
Variety of clothing items in various sizes for "clothing store" activity; grab bags and variety of objects for experimentation; variety of magazines and catalogs for picture projects.

EXAMINE

IMAGE

CONNECT

DEFINE

INTEGRATE

TRY

REFINE

EXTEND

CONNECT
Children explore how their own size is unique relative to others.
Activity
The teacher sets up a play clothing store with such items as hats, mittens, gloves, jackets, shirts, dresses, and shoes. However, all the items "for sale" are too large or too small for the children. The students have time to "go shopping."

EXAMINE
The teacher and children discuss play experience with emphasis on the children's existing vocabulary for describing size.
Activity
The class discusses the experience. The teacher poses questions for the children: Did you "buy" anything in our store? Did it fit? Do you know anyone it might fit? Do you think you could have worn it when you were a baby? Do you think it will fit you tomorrow? Do you think you could wear it when you are older?

IMAGE
The children see that size comparisons are relative.
Activity
The teacher gives each child two sheets of drawing paper. She/he asks the children to place one hand on one of the sheets with fingers outspread, and draw an outline around it. Next, they trace an outline of one of their feet on the other piece of paper. They compare their two outlines, then compare their hand outline with another child's, and then compare their foot with another child's foot. The teacher also traces her hand and foot for the children to each use for comparison.

DEFINE
The teacher reinforces the concept that size comparisons are relative.
Activity
The teacher instructs the children in relativity of size. She/he uses appropriate visual aids and manipulatives for concept reinforcement.

INTEGRATE
The class shares its collective drawings with the school.
Activity
The teacher and students create a composite display of all student series pictures to be shared with the other classes in the building.

REFINE
Children will test their ability to represent and rerepresent relativity of size.
Activity
Children share their "series" with each other to determine if their own drawings represented a series and if they could rerepresent the series created by their partner.

EXTEND
The children personalize their learning via multimodal activities.
Activity
(1) The children play a comparison game. The teacher puts a small collection of objects in drawstring bags, enough bags for each group of three students to share. Working in their groups the children take turns being the leader, giving directions to their teammates to reach into the bag and find the largest, smallest, something larger than my ring, something smaller than your hand, something longer than your finger, etc. (2) The teacher leads a second game, adding kinetic practice, by asking the children to stand tall, make yourself taller, make yourself shorter, etc. (3) The children make up challenge papers to try on each other. They either draw a series of simple pictures of objects of different sizes or cut and paste pictures from magazines or catalogs on art paper. At least three different drawing papers must be created by each child. Working with partners, they each arrange the other's pictures in relationship to size.

TRY
The teacher provides practice in recognizing and describing the relativity of size.
Activity
The children complete exercises in which they reinforce size as relative. These might include matching activities, manipulatives in learning centers, appropriate computer "games."

Source: About Learning Inc., 1999. Reproduced with permission.

Would you like to try to develop your own 4MAT unit? Here is a recipe that Susan Morris, director of education at About Learning (formerly Excel) suggested might be of help.

Step 1: Mindmap the content.

Step 2: Define the concept.

Step 3: Define the essential question.

Step 4: List the learner outcomes.

Step 5: List activities and mindmap skills.

Step 6: Connect content to learners.

Step 7: Categorize the activities.

Step 8: Fill in the 4MAT wheel.

We recognize that there may not be enough detail here for you to fully understand the process. You can find that detail, along with an example, by visiting the About Learning website at www.aboutlearning.com **and clicking on and exploring the archival copies of newsletters that they publish.**

have not changed very much in this past century. The lecture-worksheet-test method prevails. Selection of content is textbook driven. Covering material is emphasized. In Chapter 2 we presented a few theories, selected for their richness and sophistication, that challenge the predominant current practices. A synthesis of these theories yields the importance of humans learning with other humans by actively processing information that they find personally meaningful. In this chapter, we attempted to help you understand some general principles upon which to base classroom practice. These principles are consistent with the theories in Chapter 2 and are empirically supported by research for their power in promoting deep learning. Cooperative learning, COVER, and practice with specific feedback were all discussed in some detail. Finally, we identified a system that, because of its sensitivity to style differences and personal connections to meaning, and its use of the natural cycle of learning (often ignored in traditional practice), enhances the likelihood that learners will be motivated to learn.

But why choose just one specific system or method out of so many that exist? We have two reasons. First, it is not productive to give you a shallow introduction to a large number of systems. That would violate some of the fundamental premises upon which our book is based. At this point, given what you have already read about how humans learn, you can probably understand why shallow treatment of many ideas would not be as productive as in-depth treatment of fewer ideas. Second, 4MAT is general enough to allow for flexibility and teacher judgment, unlike systems that are overly structured. It permits, even encourages, the use of many of the powerful principles about which we have written. We would now like to make our own connection to 4MAT by helping you understand more specifically its connection to the powerful strategies addressed in this chapter.

In our estimation the contribution of 4MAT is not just as a learning styles model. 4MAT contributes mightily as a model that provides a way to think about why and how to use the powerful strategies that we have suggested in this chapter. Let us take a look at 4MAT in light of these strategies and the theories upon which they are based. As you can see in Figure 3.8, by beginning with a strong quadrant

FIGURE 3.8

4MAT and IPT.

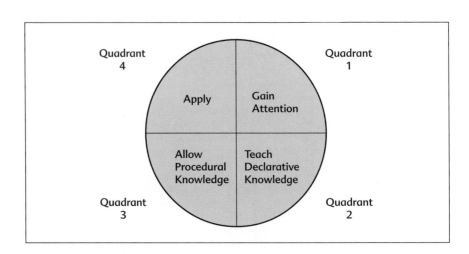

1 activity, you will help the learner make a personal connection to the content. This is very important. Quadrant 1 activities, when well planned for the learners you teach, can serve to grab the learner's attention and to activate their prior knowledge. Before anything can reach working memory, the learner must be attending to it. And prior knowledge is critical to making connections among new and already learned information. Quadrant 1 can accomplish much by way of preparing your learners for important declarative knowledge that is to come later.

Quadrant 2 activities focus on understanding the concepts to be taught. Here is the obvious place for declarative knowledge to come into play. Therefore, it is entirely appropriate to use COVER strategies here. You can have learners brainstorm using one of the visual tools presented earlier, or you can have learners listen to a well-developed lecture and have them interact by using one of the cooperative learning strategies (such as think-pair-share).

Quadrant 3 is the place where learners have a chance to practice with information taught in quadrant 2. In that regard, here is where procedural knowledge is developed. So it is now appropriate to have the learners engage in a number of practice activities, followed by specific feedback on their performances. In this way they will not only retain and understand facts, ideas, and concepts, but they will be able to use these concepts in some fashion.

Finally, in quadrant 4 the learners show how they can use what they have learned in new and different ways. Here is where you can tell if the learners *really* understand what they learned in the unit of instruction. If they can generalize beyond the context in which they learned the information and solve problems or otherwise engage in new performances, then they "own" the information, so to speak.

Cooperative learning can be used at many places in this cycle. Learners can engage cooperatively in a quadrant 1 experience, or they might be grouped in a "jigsaw" arrangement to learn declarative knowledge in quadrant 2. You might allow them to practice together in quadrant 3, to take advantage of peer coaching opportunities, or to work together on a big culminating project for quadrant 4. Of course, you need to keep in mind that all learners need opportunities to work alone, too. And you also need to remember that individual accountability is an important part of cooperative learning.

So, beyond learning styles, 4MAT is entirely compatible with the powerful strategies described in this chapter, and with the principles of the theories in which these strategies are grounded. Naturally, there are many other models or ways to teach. They range widely from very unstructured problem-based learning to very structured traditional lectures. As a middle-of-the-ground model, 4MAT has much to offer you. It gives you a way to put the powerful strategies to work, and yet it is not so much of a stretch from what many teachers already do in their classrooms. It requires a different way of thinking, and insists that you open up instruction well past "teacher talks and student responds" strategies. Quadrant 2, left mode, and quadrant 3, left mode, characterize today's instructional practices, and have for the past century. 4MAT encourages all of us to go well beyond these two modes in helping learners, *all learners,* succeed.

You should know that recent research suggests that left-mode and right-mode distinctions in brain functioning oversimplify the complexities of how our brains really work. Neuroscientific research has much to offer brain-based education, but Bruer (1998) warns that we must be careful not to apply this research incorrectly. Further, he seems to feel that we are not yet ready to apply this research in education. Because we, too, worry that educators might be too quick to use methods that are not empirically supported, we think that prudence is in order. Therefore, you

To learn more about neuroscience, visit the user friendly site http://faculty.washington .edu/chudler/neurok.html **or type Neuroscience in your favorite search engine.**

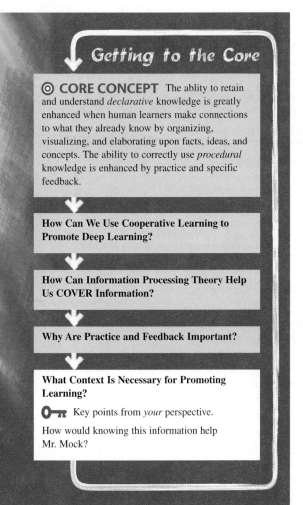

Getting to the Core

◎ CORE CONCEPT The ability to retain and understand *declarative* knowledge is greatly enhanced when human learners make connections to what they already know by organizing, visualizing, and elaborating upon facts, ideas, and concepts. The ability to correctly use *procedural* knowledge is enhanced by practice and specific feedback.

How Can We Use Cooperative Learning to Promote Deep Learning?

How Can Information Processing Theory Help Us COVER Information?

Why Are Practice and Feedback Important?

What Context Is Necessary for Promoting Learning?

Oⲧⲧ Key points from *your* perspective.

How would knowing this information help Mr. Mock?

should be alert to new developments in the area of brain-based learning, but careful not to apply them too quickly. Still, the 4MAT system that we shared with you in this chapter is much more than a simple right-mode, left-mode theory. It goes well beyond brain-based learning. It is comprehensive, rich, and well grounded in cognitive science.

SCENARIO REVISITED

It is time to look back at the scenario presented at the beginning of this chapter. As you answer the questions once again, look at the core concept for this chapter to capture the essence of the chapter's information.

> **?** *Why do you think the children held onto a naïve conception of how plants get food? How would you improve Mr. Mock's lesson so that the children have a better chance of retaining and really understanding and being able to use the concept of photosynthesis? Be very specific about what you would do differently, and how you would do it.*

Then, read A Voice from the Field to see how an experienced teacher reacted to the Mr. Mock case. Compare your response to the teacher's response.

A VOICE FROM THE FIELD

The children in Mr. Mock's classroom held onto a naïve conception of how plants get food because Mr. Mock did not provide opportunities for the students to make connections between the concept of photosynthesis and what they already knew. Although the material was maintained in the short-term memory/working memory for enough time for the students to pass the quiz and test, the concept of photosynthesis was not transferred to long-term memory; therefore, when questioned later in the year, the students were unable to explain the correct scientific conception of how plants make food.

According to the information processing theory, new information can be transferred from working memory to long-term memory when connections are made to prior knowledge contained in the long-term memory. In the beginning of the lesson, Mr. Mock should have evaluated the students' prior knowledge and assumptions about photosynthesis by asking the students to complete a before/after chart. If the students did not have prior knowledge, Mr. Mock could create a common experience for the class. This common experience would provide the students with some background information and would serve as a point of reference for the remainder of the lesson. To create a common experience for the class, Mr. Mock could have guided the students through an experiment where the students were required to observe and record some effects of photosynthesis.

By creating a common experience, whether through an activity or experiment, Mr. Mock would gain the attention of the students in the class; gaining the students' attention is the first step in helping them retain the information. In order to strengthen further the retention of information presented in this lesson, Mr. Mock could have provided opportunity for the students to organize the information through the use of concept maps. Information processing theory holds that it is easier to remember information that is organized neatly into chunks; graphs and maps provide a means for the students to organize the information. To help the students organize the information, Mr. Mock could have them complete an OWL (observe, know, learn) chart. The students would fill in the O section of the chart with what they observed from the experiment. The W section would be filled in with what the students want to know about photosynthesis and the experiment. At the end of the lesson, the students complete the L section of the chart with the information they learned.

In addition to reading the chapter and answering the questions on photosynthesis, Mr. Mock could have required the students to expand or elaborate on the information; this practice opportunity could be presented in the form of a student-planned/teacher-guided experiment. Through requiring the students to put the information into practice and think about what they have learned, the information becomes more meaningful and useful to the students. When information has a purpose and is connected to a visual or hands-on activity, it is more likely that the students will remember the concept in the future.

In his lesson on photosynthesis, Mr. Mock presented the students with declarative knowledge. The students were able to retain this declarative knowledge for a short period of time and they were able to retrieve the information for the test a few weeks later; however, the lesson did not challenge the students' misconceptions regarding how plants make food. The lesson did not require the students to practice the information which would require them to think about the information, do something with it, and proceduralize the new knowledge; therefore, the students held onto their original misconceptions about how plants get food.

Planning a lesson using the 4MAT system would address many of the concerns raised above.

This is the voice of Allison Kane. Ms. Kane teaches children with cognitive and physical disabilities.

PLANNING FOR INSTRUCTION

This chapter examines practical applications of powerful principles that promote deep processing of information. Specifically, cooperative learning, information processing theory, and motivation are used as examples to illustrate best practices based on current research on teaching and learning.

We want you to now begin the instructional planning of *your* unit using specific principles learned in this chapter to help you address the spirit of this chapter's core concept. This is not the same thing as a lesson plan; a unit plan takes place over an extended period of time. Your unit should be thought of as a block of

◎ **CORE CONCEPT** The ability to retain and understand *declarative* knowledge is greatly enhanced when human learners make connections to what they already know by organizing, visualizing, and elaborating upon facts, ideas, and concepts. The ability to correctly use *procedural* knowledge is enhanced by practice and specific feedback.

instructional planning. Use the core concept for Chapter 2 *(Human beings learn best in cooperation with other human beings by actively processing information that they find personally meaningful.)* along with the core concept for Chapter 3 to design a unit plan that describes how you would plan the following:

- Create an experience that will serve to motivate your learners throughout the rest of the unit.
- Have them learn the content deeply by using COVER.
- Have them practice what they learned, and provide them with specific feedback.
- Encourage them to make use of the learning in their lives outside the classroom.
- All the while, allow them to work in a cooperative fashion with one another.

The goal for our sample unit is that "students will explore different types of severe weather conditions, specifically severe storms and the impact they have on people's lives and the environment." Refer to unit objectives given in Planning for Instruction in Chapter 1.

Think about It . . .

To assist you, we will build a sample unit on severe weather as you design your unit. We will infuse throughout the example the core concepts from each chapter, critical elements of teaching for conceptual change, and the use of powerful instructional strategies. Our activities will appear first and then you will design your own. The word "consider" will appear before each activity to serve as a metacognitive tool. The purpose of this tool is twofold: (1) to present our thinking and rationale for using specific strategies, and (2) to ask questions that will promote thinking and encourage you to *consider* specific instructional strategies. Please keep in mind that our example has been designed generically to serve the purpose of reaching a wide range of ages, grade and developmental levels, and skill levels.

Consider
Create an Experience: This is an important step that both helps to get information past your learners' sensory registers and assists your learners to understand why what you are about to help them learn is worth their time and effort. A motivational start will encourage continued participation and will serve as a place to revisit throughout the unit. Now design an activity that creates a powerful experience upon which learners can build by using our example.

Our Example

Create an Experience
In small groups, students discuss different positions individuals might play on teams such as football, baseball, basketball, hockey, and soccer. For example, quarterbacks, centers, goalies, and pitchers all represent different positions with different responsibilities on a team. A discussion illustrating how teams work together, cooperate, and utilize each other's skills in order to perform well will lead to teamwork or "systems." Students identify how parts of a system (players) can have effects on each other, both positive and negative. When one player makes a mistake or error, it has an impact on the rest of the team. This discussion will help students see later how the unit on weather is like a system.

Students will be led through a visualization exercise (a story) that will bring to mind personal experiences or images from TV, movies, or books of various types of severe storms (tornadoes, thunderstorms, hurricanes, and snowstorms). Grouped by threes, students will share experiences and produce a chart describing each type of severe storm. Each student will describe in his or her journal how a specific severe storm affected his or her personal life and had an impact on the environment.

Consider

Encourage Students to Learn the Content: Rather than thinking about how you will teach these learners, think about how you will encourage them to learn the information. This will focus you on *them* rather than on yourself. Even though you are not yet planning lessons, think about some *key activities* that might take place during some of your lessons. How will you help them make connections to what they already know? How will you get them to organize the information, visualize it, and elaborate on it? Plan carefully; it is this type of cognitive activity that really helps learners understand information.

Our Example

Learn the Content

Using the information generated in the first activity, the teacher will lead the class through the creation of an advance organizer (AO). This AO will visually organize the new content to be learned in the unit. It will include how the topic of severe weather is connected to the water cycle, tornadoes, thunderstorms, hurricanes, and snowstorms; how these severe storms are measured; and the impact of severe storms on the environment.

Students will learn new information by watching films, lectures, and class discussions and working in research teams. The AO will gradually develop into a working graphic organizer into which students can place additional information and examples. For example, while learning more about thunderstorms, facts about electricity, temperature, sound, and air can be added to the organizer. Students will now have an organized way of collecting information.

While conducting research, students will work in learning groups of four and each group will be assigned one type of severe storm to thoroughly investigate. When watching films and during discussions, students will be paired to help each other collect information or answer questions (think-pair).

Through the use of journal writing, students will be periodically asked to develop relationships between content learned and personal experiences. For example, some students might have observed that the sound of thunder occurs at varying intervals after they see the flash of lightning (depending upon the distance of the storm). Students can now elaborate on such ideas as the speeds at which light and sound travel and have the opportunity to exchange knowledge and experiences with others.

Using the jigsaw method, students will learn about all the severe storms that were researched by the teams. Through sharing information and notes, each group will design a new visual organizer (refer to Chapter 4 for examples of visual organizers) that describes the characteristics of each severe storm. Organizers will list similarities and differences, develop a relationship to the water cycle, illustrate one measuring device, and identify three ways the severe storm impacts the environment. Each group will critique another group's organizer and check for accuracy. The teacher will give feedback and make suggestions throughout the process. Each group will add some new content or an example to each graphic organizer.

A variety of small experiments will be conducted both in and out of school to collect additional information. For example, students will monitor weather forecasts from different parts of the country and collect data on rainfall, frequency of severe storms, types of storm, and so forth.

Each group will design 10 questions based on what they learned to be used in a game called "How to Weather a Storm." All questions will be based on students' written work.

Consider

Ask Students to Practice What They Learned, and Provide Them with Specific Feedback: It is time to have the student practice the information learned. Worksheets and drill exercises are good practice; however, there are more elaborate forms of practice. Think about practice opportunities that encourage students to take the information learned and do something with it—design, create, or produce something of their own. Is the practice meaningful to the learner? What types of feedback can you give students? Can you turn students' mistakes into powerful learning experiences? Plan to lead to deeper understanding of the content.

Our Example

Practice What They Learned

Students working in pairs or alone are given a few options to demonstrate what they have learned in new and different ways. For example, students can design a new and improved visual with a written summary that connects the major ideas of the unit. They can create a severe weather book with illustrations and pictures. They can design a severe weather station for a town, write a research paper, design and carry out an experiment, or propose an idea of their own.

Consider

Encourage Students to Make Use of the Learning in Their Lives Outside the Classroom: Now is the time for students to demonstrate how they can use what they have learned in new and different ways by generalizing the content beyond what they have already learned. Encourage students to demonstrate what they have learned in an innovative way that demonstrates mastery and ownership.

Our Example

Use Information

Students will design a severe weather safety manual for the community. Safety manuals will be designed by computer to include written safety procedures, informational charts pictures/photographs, and emergency phone numbers. Students will have choices for dissemination that include presenting at school assemblies, health fairs, and community meetings.

Your Turn

Begin planning your unit of instruction using our example as a model. As you plan your unit of instruction keep in mind the use of technology. The following are some *considerations*.

Effective use of technology will require teachers to have a genuine understanding of child development, instructional and assessment strategies, and individual differences to better reach the changing learning needs of students in our classrooms. Using the information on technology from this chapter and your own personal experiences make sure you enhance your unit by adding the pedagogical power of technology.

Consider

How do I know my students are using reputable Internet sites? Can I help them with criteria to properly identify good sites and information?

Students will use the Internet to conduct research and collect data on the water cycle, weather, severe storms, and environmental issues. In order to make sure they are using reliable websites, we have designed an exercise to help them evaluate the quality of information they find on the Internet. We have chosen five sites on weather for them to evaluate. Three of them are excellent and two of them are below average. Students will be asked to evaluate the five sites on the basis of the following criteria:

- Author's or organization's name.
- Professional title of author.
- Professional organization affiliation.
- Date of publication.
- Author's contact information.
- Demonstration that information is not biased.
- Enough detail in article to make conclusions.
- Any evidence of quality control or peer review.
- Uses references to other articles or organizations.
- Provides link to other sites that appear reliable.

Consider

Where can I send students to conduct independent work or projects, to view weather conditions, and to collect data?

Storm Prediction Center: *http://www.spc.noaa.gov*
   Provides updated forecasts and images of weather conditions.

Storm-Spotter Guide: *http://www.srh.noaa.gov/oun/skywarm/spotterguide.html*
   Locates information, visual, and data on storms in progress.

http://www.lightningsafety.com
   National Lightning Safety Institute.

Consider

How do I design a weather assignment using the Internet? Working in groups of two or three, the students will:

- Conduct research to determine weather patterns and severe storms most likely to occur in their geographic region.
- Compare information on two different regions in the country or world.
- Using weather maps, chart severe weather patterns in each region noting geographic differences.
- Compare and contrast visual images of severe storms.
- Indicate safety information and precautions posted in each region.

Consider

What about other forms of multimedia?

- Videotape severe weather forecasts.
- View commercially produced videotapes such as *Savage Skies* (PBS), and Nova's *Lightning* (PBS),
- Use 35-mm cameras and video cameras to record storms and environmental damage from storm.
- Design visual displays and bulletin boards and broadcast weather forecasts via closed-circuit TV.

CHAPTER SUMMARY

On the surface, teaching looks easy to many people and much of what teachers learn and do seems obvious. But many seemingly obvious or intuitive aspects of teaching and learning are based on assumptions that can be called into question when we look at facts. Theories provide us with a way to transcend these assumptions which are typically based on our limited personal experiences. From theory, several powerful principles of learning have emerged that have been substantiated by research. These general principles help us promote deep learning and understanding among our students. We should know these powerful principles and put them to use.

Cooperative learning is one of these powerful principles. Much more than just group work, cooperative learning provides the social context and support that allow the other powerful principles to take hold. Information processing theory suggests that we rethink the idea of covering material with our students. Rather, the powerful principles that derive from IP theory encourage us to help students connect, organize, visualize, and elaborate upon the facts, concepts, and ideas that constitute declarative knowledge. In addition, IP theory makes clear that practice and specific feedback are necessary for students to develop procedural knowledge. Again, these principles are general and can be applied in virtually any classroom or learning environment.

These principles are applied in a context, usually (but not always) a classroom. The 4MAT system helps us put these principles together with unit and lesson planning by offering a model, or way of thinking about teaching, that conforms to the natural learning cycle that humans share. It is not yet clear whether, or under what conditions, the use of 4MAT leads to significantly higher achievement gains among students; it *is* clear that students who are taught by teachers using 4MAT are more motivated to learn than those being taught using more traditional methods. 4MAT also helps us view instruction through a wider lens. That is, it gives us a way to broaden the instructional activities that we use beyond the traditional "teacher teaches, students practice what teacher teaches" system that pervades American classrooms.

This chapter has offered very *general* principles upon which practice can be based. In the next chapter of the textbook we will help you understand some very *specific* strategies that will help you develop powerful instruction likely to promote deep learning among your students. Because many of these strategies take time, we will also address a movement in education that is examining, indeed changing, the way we use time, kindergarten through grade 12, during the school day and the school year.

Getting to the Core

> ⊚ **CORE CONCEPT** The ability to retain
> and understand *declarative* knowledge is greatly
> enhanced when human learners make connections
> to what they already know by organizing,
> visualizing, and elaborating upon facts, ideas, and
> concepts. The ability to correctly use *procedural*
> knowledge is enhanced by practice and specific
> feedback.

How Can We Use Cooperative Learning to Promote Deep Learning?

- Human beings learn best in cooperation with each other by actively processing information they find personally meaningful. Cooperative learning is one of the most powerful teaching techniques teachers use. Cooperative learning consists of five essential elements: positive interdependence, group processing, social skills, individual accountability, and face-to-face interaction.

- There are different ways to group students including base groups, informal groups, and formal groups depending on the method of instruction, outcomes desired, the purpose of the activity, and the length of the project or activity. Keep in mind that it is not the complexity of the cooperative learning strategy used that is important, but rather how active and engaged the students are in deeply processing the information.

How Can Information Processing Theory Help Us COVER Information?

- As a teacher, you can use powerful strategies to COVER material that encourage active processing of information and help move it into long-term memory. COVER stands for (1) **C**onnect (using mnemonic devices to help learners remember things that have no inherent meaning); (2) **O**rganize (tools to help the learner represent facts, ideas, and concepts and the connections between and among them; encourage connections between prior knowledge and new knowledge in a structured fashion; (3) **V**isualize (pictures or images that help learners chunk information in a very efficient way which frees up space in working memory; images, ideas or concepts that we can visualize are easier to learn and recall than things we cannot see); and (4) **E**laborative **R**ehearsal (When we elaborate on something, we *add to it*. This involves deliberate and conscious thought during which we relate the new

information to something we already know and understand. Then, when we put it back into long-term memory, we have actively transformed the new information. It is connected and it has staying power. This is very different from maintenance rehearsal, which allows the learner to keep information in working memory simply by repeating it over and over—rote memorization.)

Why Are Practice and Feedback So Important?

- In the same way COVER relates to declarative knowledge, *practice* and *specific feedback* relate to procedural knowledge. Students develop procedural knowledge by actually doing what it is teachers want them to know how to do (practice) and then by receiving specific feedback on their performance. It helps teachers reconsider the ways we think about learners' mistakes, the kinds of practice activities we devise, and the kind of practice and feedback we employ in our classrooms.

What Context Is Necessary for Promoting Learning?

- 4MAT is a planning system that takes into account the various learning styles students bring to a classroom as well as the differences in the way the left and right modes of the brain work. In the interest of meeting the needs of students with various learning styles, it focuses on making personal connections to create meaning and takes into consideration the essential elements of human learning.

- Using 4MAT as a planning system or tool can help increase the likelihood that learners will be motivated to learn. 4MAT incorporates all of the powerful strategies addressed earlier in the chapter—COVER, practice and feedback, and cooperative learning. The 4MAT cycle is divided into four quadrants. It begins in quadrant 1 with an experience, presents content in quadrant 2, allows for practice in quadrant 3, and finally, comes full circle in quadrant 4 by encouraging learners to make use of their learning. In each quadrant, students are actively engaged in left- and right-brain activities.

CHAPTER 4

Using Powerful Instructional Strategies

▶ **SPEED BUMP** (*Source: Reprinted with permission of Dave Coverly and Creators Syndicate.*)

 S C E N A R I O

Ralph, a teacher with over 10 years of experience teaching science at both the middle and high school levels, has been having difficulty adjusting to his school's newly implemented intensive scheduling model. Ralph is used to teaching in typical 50-minute class periods and now has 90-minute periods. He was excited to be given an opportunity to have more sustained time with his students so he could cover content more thoroughly. Ralph's teaching methods in the 90-minute periods are essentially the same as they were in the 50-minute periods. One exception is that he asks more questions of the students, occasionally grouping them to respond to end-of-chapter questions and allowing the students to begin some homework near the end of the period.

Ralph's longer lectures permit him to cover more information than he could before. However, he notices that his students now seem less motivated, and they don't seem to be retaining the same amount of information they had in the past. The students seem less prepared for in-class experiments and the quality of their lab work has been less detailed. Additionally, Ralph has noticed that his students' written responses on quizzes and tests demonstrate little depth of knowledge. These observations baffle him, because the one-day workshop he attended and the research on intensive scheduling suggests that the students should be learning more, not less.

> **?** *Why do you think Ralph's students are now learning less rather than more? What might be the biggest problem with which Ralph will now have to struggle? Can you think of what other teaching strategies Ralph might use since his lecture/question/homework approach is not working?*

INTRODUCTION

To really, and we mean *really,* understand something requires artful instruction on the part of the teacher and active learning on the part of the learner. So far we have written about *theories* and *general principles* derived from those theories that you can apply to classroom practice. Now we are going to help you understand some *specific strategies* that can actively engage students in learning and lead to deep understanding of subject matter. These, in turn, lead to a high probability of promoting real learning among your students.

Before we go any further, we feel we must confront a major issue that rears its head whenever strategies such as those we will suggest are employed. One of the discussions that frequently emerges is that of curriculum coverage. Active learning and the use of powerful strategies take time. Teachers believe that they need more time to cover an increasing amount of content, and that they do not have the time to use these strategies.

Getting to the Core

 CORE CONCEPT Deep (rather than surface) processing of information promotes retention, understanding, and the ability to use knowledge. The use of powerful instructional strategies encourages deep processing of information. Both deep processing and the use of powerful instructional strategies take time.

What Specific, Powerful Instructional Strategies Can Teachers Employ?
- Research-Based Strategies
- Interactive Direct Instruction
- Powerful Questions
- Using Problems to Promote Learning
- Case Study Method
- Project Learning as a Powerful Strategy
- Learning Centers in Your Classroom
- Graphic and Visual Organizers

What Other Instructional Methods Can Teachers Use in Classrooms?

How Can Instructional Methods Be Aligned with Standards?
- Standards-Based Education
- Standards and Powerful Instructional Strategies

Think about it . . .

Think about something
that you know well.
Perhaps you would be
considered an expert in
this area. How did you
learn it?

Did someone tell you
about it? Did you learn
it any other way(s)?

Eventually, teachers (and others) will need to make some critical decisions about what is essential and what is not essential in the curriculum. Along with these decisions, the instructional strategies used will become another critical decision point. Chapters 2 and 3 placed emphasis on powerful principles of learning that engage the student, use cooperative methods, create problem-solving and critical-thinking situations, use classroom discussions and higher-order questions, and encourage performance and project-based demonstrations of student learning. These all take more time than delivering traditional lectures and asking simple questions that require brief responses from students.

So the challenge becomes, how do we *cover* less while still helping the learner master the critical concepts in a discipline (or, for elementary education and special education teachers, helping learners master basic skills). At the heart of this challenge is identifying core concepts, generative topics, and essential questions around which to build curriculum and instruction. In Chapter 8 we will address these topics in depth. For now we shall turn to some methods that are powerful and consistent with the ways people learn, and that provide opportunities for students to uncover and deeply understand knowledge. They are more specific than the general methods presented in earlier chapters.

What Specific, Powerful Instructional Strategies Can Teachers Employ?

The instructional strategies we discuss in this chapter have emerged from the research literature and have been proven successful in both engaging learners and in leading them to greater achievement. These strategies encourage teachers to broaden the instructional strategies they use beyond lecturing, note taking, occasional questioning, and worksheets, all of which cast learners in relatively passive roles.

In previous chapters, we emphasized the importance of some powerful ideas such as cooperative learning, information processing, motivation, critical thinking, connecting learning to the student's world, and creating a positive learning environment. The following strategies will provide you with additional ideas for adding *power* to your lessons, and for enhancing the likelihood that what you do for students will help them really learn and reach new and more expert understandings—that is, you will help them change conceptually.

Research-Based Strategies

Marzano, Gaddy, and Dean (2000) authored a comprehensive study of what works in classroom instruction. This study was intended "to identify those instructional strategies that have the highest probability of enhancing student achievement for all students in all subject areas at all grade levels" (4). The researchers used a technique called *meta-analysis* to conduct their study. This technique requires that researchers summarize a large number of research studies, and then combine the results to determine the strategy's "net effect" on student achievement (2). This approach is widely accepted in the social sciences as one way to produce research-based practice.

As a result of their findings, Marzano, Gaddy, and Dean (2000, 4) list nine categories of instructional strategies that they found strongly affect student achievement. These categories are:

1. Identifying similarities and differences.
2. Summarizing and note taking.
3. Reinforcing effort and providing recognition.
4. Homework and practice.
5. Nonlinguistic representations.
6. Cooperative learning.
7. Setting goals and providing feedback.
8. Generating and testing hypotheses.
9. Activating prior knowledge.

Although the categories are, for the most part, self-explanatory, the researchers devote a chapter in their manuscript to each one of them. These chapters are well worth reading. For our purposes in this textbook, we want you to make connections to what we have already written, and what is yet to come. Really, these categories should not be all that new to you! First and foremost, you should note that many of these categories insist that the learner become actively engaged, which takes time. *Summarizing and activating prior knowledge* can be connected to information processing theory, which we wrote about in Chapters 2 and 3. Summarizing in your own words is an excellent form of elaborative rehearsal. Activating prior knowledge is essential to making connections that can be stored in long-term memory. *Homework and practice* help develop procedural knowledge, especially if the homework is substantial and the practice is followed by specific feedback. *Reinforcing effort and providing recognition* are good strategies for motivating learners. Although they are typically extrinsic ways to motivate others, if done skillfully they can help learners become intrinsically motivated. We discussed *cooperative learning* at some length in Chapters 2 and 3. Cooperative learning strategies have been well documented as effective promoters of student achievement. We will address nonlinguistic representations and identifying similarities and differences a bit later in this chapter.

Much of what you have already read in this text relates to research-based practice. Beyond just knowing strategies, however, you need to know the theories and the big ideas upon which these strategies are based. If you think about it, now you do! Knowing the theories and the big ideas that underlie any given strategy helps you use that strategy wisely—at the proper time, to accomplish specific goals with your learners—and modify it as necessary with particular learners in particular situations. In addition to (and in some cases to build upon) these categories of strategies, we offer seven additional strategies to add to your instructional repertoire.

Interactive Direct Instruction

Perhaps the most traditional form of instruction is direct instruction. It is a teacher-centered and controlled, step-by-step process that is widely considered an efficient method of covering content, new skills, and concepts. Direct instruction is an appropriate method for teaching both declarative and procedural knowledge and is based on behavioral learning principles. The name itself, direct instruction, brings to mind the words *lecture, drill and practice,* and *structure.* Gunter, Estes, and Schwab (1995) have described the direct instructional approach using six specific steps. We have summarized the model as follows:

1. **Review previously learned material:** This first step provides the student with a review of previously learned content and skills and helps the teacher assess if reteaching is necessary. Additionally, the teacher assists in connecting prior knowledge to what the student will learn next. Typically, a teacher begins the lesson with a quick review of previously learned material and answers questions so students can make connections to the new learning to follow.

2. **State objectives for the lesson:** The second step helps the student understand the purpose and relevance of the lesson by clearly communicating the objectives at the beginning of the lesson. This provides the student with a framework for organizing the information to be learned. By providing direction for the lesson, the teacher ensures that the student can better focus on the specific content he or she will teach and that the student will not be distracted by extraneous information. The teacher provides focus by stating the objectives and giving a step-by-step description of what will be learned.

3. **Present the new material:** The third step is the actual presentation of new content and skills. The teacher arranges the content and skills in a logical order and in smaller segments to help the learner grasp the new information. Providing an advance organizer is critical so that the student can connect previously learned material to new learning and to give the student a conceptual preview of the new content. The advance organizer sets the stage for the lesson and provides the learner with an anchor or a point of reference that can be used throughout the lesson. During the presentation of the new material the teacher provides examples for each of the main points and connects each point to previously learned points. It is a good idea to constantly refer back to the advance organizer throughout the lesson to help students see how the new material is unfolding and following a logical sequence.

4. **Provide guided practice with corrected feedback:** The fourth step gives the student the opportunity to practice the newly acquired content and skills under the teacher's guidance. Here the teacher demonstrates correct procedures and skills to help the student better accomplish the task. By demonstrating each step of solving a problem, writing an essay, dissecting a frog, and so forth, the teacher shows the correct procedures and relieves the student from having to guess what he or she expects. The teacher provides the student with practice situations to accomplish while he or she monitors the learning and provides corrective feedback when necessary. Throughout this guided practice, the teacher asks general and specific questions to help guide the learning experience. Using prompts and probes during the questioning allows for further exploration and greater understanding of the content. It is critical to provide corrective feedback throughout the lesson. When students make mistakes, the teacher must not hesitate to correct them by providing specific information, examples, and illustrations to clarify material. The teacher should design a personal strategy to respond to incorrect responses that is efficient and sensitive to students' learning needs.

5. **Assign independent practice with corrective feedback:** The fifth step in direct instruction provides the opportunity for the student to continue to work without the teacher's guidance. If the teacher has been successful in the first four steps, the student is now ready to independently practice the newly

learned information. Independent practice allows for additional review and reinforcement of key content and skills just learned. The teacher should answer all student questions before independent practice begins. The teacher monitors independent practice and provides corrective feedback throughout this activity.

6. **Review periodically and provide corrective feedback if necessary:** The sixth and final step of direct instruction involves reviewing the critical elements of the lesson periodically to ensure that the content and skills were covered and learned. This element of direct instruction is critical because of the swift delivery of the information. Reviewing content throughout the lesson provides constant reinforcement and a sense of closure. Periodic reviewing allows those students who might not have grasped the information the first time or were absent one day to catch up. The teacher, student, or a combination of both can conduct the reviewing process.

Many models of direct instruction similar to the one just provided have been popular over the years. Rosenshine's (1987) explicit teaching model follows the same six steps in a similar fashion. He feels the direct instructional approach is most effective in the "teaching of mathematical procedures and computation, reading, decoding, explicit reading procedures (such as distinguishing fact from opinion), science facts and concepts and rules, and foreign language vocabulary and grammar" (p. 75).

Hunter (1981) designed a model called Instructional Theory Into Practice (ITIP). ITIP is a lesson design process that is similar in structure and depth to both of the earlier mentioned models. Hunter's use of *anticipatory set* focuses student's attention on the content to be learned and helps students make connections to their prior knowledge, thereby getting them ready to learn. It helps teachers to introduce lessons in engaging ways, much like 4MAT, Quadrant 1. Hunter's model has been used by many school districts to provide teachers with a consistent and structured approach to instruction.

Mastery learning, heavily influenced by traditional behavioral theory and similar in many ways to direct instruction, provides the student with a logical, sequenced, and progressive method to learn new information. In mastery learning, each student "masters" certain concepts and skills before moving to the next set of content and skills. The model achieves student mastery because it individualizes the content and provides practice, feedback and corrections, and flexible time to complete tasks. Mastery learning can also involve traditional group-based and enrichment activities, but is highly teacher centered and controlled. It is highly structured and requires tedious planning. This approach requires the student to focus on very specific information and therefore the student might lose perspective on the purpose of the whole lesson.

The following is a summary of criticisms of direct instruction (Woolfolk 2001):

> Critics say that direct instruction is limited to lower-level objectives, and that it is based on traditional teaching methods, ignores innovative models, and discourages students' independent thinking. Some educational psychologists claim that the direct instruction model tells teachers to "do what works" without grounding the suggestions in a theory of student learning. Other critics disagree, saying that direct instruction is based on a theory of student learning—but it is the *wrong* theory. Teachers break material into small segments, present each segment clearly, and reinforce or correct, thus *transmitting* accurate understandings from teacher to student. The student is seen as an "empty vessel" waiting to be

filled with knowledge, rather than an active constructor of knowledge. These criticisms of direct instruction echo the criticisms of behavioral learning theories. (498–99)

Although this book thus far has focused on active learning strategies, we are not saying that direct instruction has no place in a teacher's repertoire. In fact, we believe that direct instruction is a valuable tool if used wisely. You should broaden your perspective of direct instruction to include more than just straight lecture. We agree that direct instruction is considered an approach to instruction that requires lower-level thinking skills on the part of the learner, but that is not necessarily bad. Students need to learn facts, content, and skills. So let's look at how we might make direct instruction more interactive by considering a lesson on "light" using the graphic organizer in Figure 4.1 (p. 141). We'll follow the six steps of the direct instruction model while actively engaging learners in the lesson.

Topic: Light (photography class)   **Grade/age level:** 10th and 11th grades

Review previously learned material: Because this is a new unit of study, there is no review of material learned from the previous day. However, the teacher will focus on making connections to prior knowledge. The teacher, using a large flashlight, will shine light on a variety of objects to create different effects. Students will record what impact the light has on different objects. The teacher will provide the students with at least two experiences that demonstrate the four variables to be studied (value, illumination, transition, and shadow). The teacher will use the response of the students to lead to the four elements of light.

State objectives for the lesson: After the above activity the teacher will communicate the objective of the lesson to the students: "Today we are going to identify, illustrate, and differentiate among the four critical elements of light (value, illumination, transition, and shadow)."

Present the new material: Using the advance organizer, the teacher will lead a group discussion on the concept of light. Each element will be defined, examples given through lecture, pictures, and videos, and relationships drawn among the four elements. The teacher will ask students questions throughout the presentation and students will be given ample time to ask questions of peers and the teacher.

Provide guided practice with corrected feedback: Working in groups of four, the students will be given a packet of pictures that demonstrate the four elements of light. They will be asked to classify them based on which element of light the picture represents. Through class discussion and questioning, the teacher will check for understanding. If mistakes are made, the teacher will make immediate corrections and clarify any misconceptions.

Assign independent practice with corrective feedback: For homework, students will search magazines to find one picture for each element of light. They will write a short description of how each meets the criteria on a 3×5 card. During the next class period the teacher will use this assignment as a review and to further check student understanding. Students will be paired to share pictures and descriptions and to check for accuracy. The teacher will monitor the process as well. Students will present the picture in class and be prepared to defend why the picture meets the criteria.

Review periodically and provide corrective feedback if necessary: Using the advance organizer the teacher will review the major elements using teacher and student examples. If you choose to use direct instruction, you should do as much as you can to bring the students into the lesson through engaging activity. Simple cooperative learning techniques, such as think-pair-share, can work well in this regard.

Powerful Questions

Did you ever think of what it would be like to live in a space colony? How has the sport of football changed in the past 20 years? People who invent new medicines need to know a lot about . . .? When teachers pose these questions to students they stimulate conversations, discussions, thinking, and exploration. These questions engage learners in the thinking process and encourage them to respond, not necessarily with *the* correct answer, but with thoughts and questions of their own. This, as you might have already realized, is a form of elaboration on the part of the students. To get students to think and understand their thoughts, teachers need to stimulate students' thinking through effective questioning techniques. The ability of teachers to ask good questions is essential for these interactions to be powerful and successful. As schools provide extended time for instruction and teachers become more comfortable with using these larger blocks of instructional time, they will have the opportunity to engage students in more thought-provoking learning activities. The teacher's ability to design questions and activities at increasingly higher levels of complexity that are developmentally appropriate will become most critical. Additionally, the teacher's ability to follow up on the student responses and nonresponses, use effective voice inflection and body language, use wait-time and probe for details, are some of the most critical teaching skills for encouraging deeper learning among students. However, none of this is effective unless we teach our *students* to question as well. Encouraging students to listen intently, and to learn to ask thoughtful questions of themselves and others, enhances their deep understanding of information.

What kinds of questions do teachers usually ask? First, we distinguish between two major types of questions: those that require *convergent* thought and those that require *divergent* thought. Questions that require convergent thought are usually narrow and limit students to single responses, or possibly a series of short responses. Typically there is one correct, or best, response. These questions focus students on a central idea or point. Responses are easily assessed as either correct or incorrect. Examples of such questions include, "Who are the six main characters on the TV show *Friends*?" or "What are the five major components of a computer?"

Divergent questions, on the other hand, usually require students to give more general or open responses to questions that may have more than one appropriate answer. These kinds of questions elicit diverse responses, and teachers have to be more vigilant in the types of responses to these

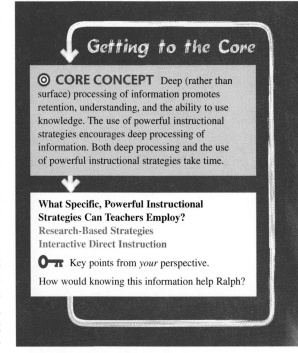

Getting to the Core

◎ **CORE CONCEPT** Deep (rather than surface) processing of information promotes retention, understanding, and the ability to use knowledge. The use of powerful instructional strategies encourages deep processing of information. Both deep processing and the use of powerful instructional strategies take time.

What Specific, Powerful Instructional Strategies Can Teachers Employ?
Research-Based Strategies
Interactive Direct Instruction

⊶ Key points from *your* perspective.

How would knowing this information help Ralph?

Think about it . . . **What kinds of questions do teachers ask during a lesson?**

Are they recall questions or do they make you really think about the content?

Do you prefer responding to "yes" and "no" questions, or do you prefer opportunities to explain your reasoning?

A Person Who Helped Create Change . . .

Benjamin Bloom has been involved in education throughout his life. After graduating from Pennsylvania State University in 1935 with bachelor of arts and master of science degrees, he went on to earn his Ph.D. from the University of Chicago in 1942.

Bloom is best known in the field of education for his development of *Bloom's taxonomy* and for the notion of *mastery learning.* Bloom created his taxonomy in 1956 as a way to categorize test questions. His goal was for educators to cover all six levels so students could receive the best education. The six levels of Bloom's taxonomy are, from lowest to highest: knowledge, comprehension, application, analysis, synthesis, and evaluation.

Source: http://www.funderstanding.com/messages/ 1137.html.
(Credit: Department of Special Collections, University of Chicago Library.)

questions they accept. Teachers should strategically sequence the questions so that they get progressively more difficult. Students need more time to think about their answers to these questions before they respond. Examples of divergent questions include, "What would be a good title for this poem, and why?" or "What is the relationship between these geometric shapes and our school building?"

Now, back to the question we posed earlier about the kinds of questions teachers usually ask. In some of the earlier studies conducted on questioning strategies, Corey (in Borich 2000) stated that 70 to 80 percent of all questions asked required just basic recall of facts. Only 20 to 30 percent of the questions required higher levels of thought such as generalizing, analyzing, and making inferences. More recent studies reveal that 20 percent of questions asked are organizational, 60 percent require recall of information, and only 20 percent challenge students to think at higher levels (Wilen 1991). The types of questions most commonly asked, then, are convergent questions that require little higher-level thought. Although such questions serve an important educational purpose, they do not engage students in deep learning.

Although teachers should be asking lower-order questions, they should also be asking questions that challenge students to think more critically and at higher levels. They should be asking lots of them, and working with students to develop such questions as well. Even most textbooks do not encourage higher-level questioning. Risner, Skeel, and Nicolson (1992) (in Orlich, Harder, Callahan, and Gibson 2001) looked at fifth-grade elementary science textbooks published by the three largest textbook publishers in the United States between the years 1983 and 1989. In some cases the newer editions had a larger percentage of knowledge-based questions than did the earlier editions. Still, only about 10 percent of over six hundred questions asked in these textbooks were at the *application level* or above. What exactly does that mean?

Benjamin Bloom devised a system to classify questions. He called it *Bloom's Taxonomy of Educational Objectives: Cognitive Domain.* It helps teachers write educational objectives at different cognitive levels, and also differentiate lower- from higher-level questions. Bloom (1984) felt that questions should be asked that not only check a student's recall and basic comprehension of facts, but that also challenge the student to analyze, synthesize, and evaluate information. These last three require higher levels of thinking, according to his taxonomy. It is much more time efficient to ask lower-level questions because they do not create much discussion and they help the teacher move through the lesson more quickly. But teachers must develop a questioning plan that uses *all* levels of questions, and that also teaches the learners how to respond better to these questions and even to develop such questions on their own.

Dillon (1982) points out that, according to his research, there is a 50 percent chance that a student will use a lower-level response when asked a higher-level question. This could be because we have not helped our students think, and reflect, at the higher levels. Teachers with a solid grounding in questioning strategies will be able to engage the learners more actively in their learning, and provide them with opportunities to use critical and creative thought processes. To help you better utilize questioning strategies, we have developed a Questioning Strategies Guide. We based this guide on Bloom's work. It will illustrate six levels of Bloom's *Taxonomy of Educational Objectives Handbook 1: Cognitive Domain* (1984). The guide provides information to help you implement these questioning strategies using powerful techniques such as framing, prompting, probing, scaffolding, wait-time, and reinforcement (feedback). Keep in mind that the goal of questioning is to engage students in critical thinking that leads to deep understanding. We encourage you to use the following questioning guide to help you, as a teacher, to ask good questions and actively involve your students in the learning process. Also, keep in mind the importance of helping your students ask good questions as well. When students ask questions of the teacher or their peers, they are actively processing information. We will first look at lower-order questioning.

QUESTIONING STRATEGIES GUIDE

Levels of Questions/Activities/ Objectives (Based on Bloom's Taxonomy)

Lower-Level Questioning

Knowledge

Students are able to recognize and recall information such as facts, terminology, and simple observations. This information has been learned previously and is readily available for recall by the learner. Words often found in knowledge questions are *recall, recognize, recite, name, list, what, when,* and *remember.*

Examples
Who is the vice president of the United States? Who wrote *The Great Gatsby?* At what point does water freeze?

Comprehension

Students are able to demonstrate an understanding of material by translating and/or rephrasing the information into their own words. They can go beyond recall and demonstrate a personal understanding of the material. Simple comparisons can be expected. Words often found in comprehension questions are *rephrase, describe, illustrate, summarize,* and *put into your own words.*

Examples
How would you describe in your own words three reasons for World War II? What defines a terrorist organization?

Application

The student is asked to apply previously learned material to solve a problem or answer a question and/or to apply information or content learned to a context different from the one in which it was learned. Words often found in application questions are *solve, choose, translate, employ,* and *write an example.*

Examples

Write an example of how the human brain processes information. Given the definition of a compound sentence, identify which of the following sentences meet the criteria. Give a scientific example of how an airplane gets off the ground.

The above examples indicate lower-level questions in that they require *less* cognitive work on the part of the student than do higher-level questions. They also require less engagement, less elaboration, and less emotional commitment among students than do the next set of questions. Now, let's look at descriptions and examples of higher-level questions.

Higher-Level Questioning

Analysis

The analysis level begins to ask students higher-order questions that require them to break a problem into smaller parts and draw relationships among them. These questions require students to think more critically by identifying logical errors, differentiating among different facts and ideas, and making inferences and generalizations. Words found in analysis questions are *compare/contrast, draw conclusions, support, determine evidence, point out, distinguish,* and *investigate.*

Examples

Compare and contrast the economic development between the United States and Great Britain between 1940 and 1990. Which one of the president's remarks best supports his program on social security? How has the Internet changed the way automobiles are bought and sold in the United States?

Synthesis

The synthesis-level question challenges students to produce something unique, new, and original. Students are asked to use their creativity to design original communications. Making predictions and solving problems are also considered synthesis level. These questions assume students understand the information (content) and are now ready to use it in a creative and inventive way. Words often found in synthesis questions are *create, predict, produce, design, construct, imagine, estimate,* and *invent.*

Examples

How would life be different if terrorist groups did not exist? Design a mode of transportation that is unlike anything that exists today.

Evaluation

The last and highest level of questioning requires students to make judgments, form opinions, and evaluate the soundness and validity of an idea, problem, or solution. Words often used in evaluation questions are *defend, assess, justify, argue, verify, recommend, do you agree,* and *would it be better.*

Examples

Justify this statement: The behavior of children in schools today is related to the amount and type of television they watch. How has the president of the United States been effective in his domestic and foreign programs? Give examples and explain why.

Note that these higher-order questions require *more* cognitive work on the part of the student. They also require more engagement, more elaboration, and more emotional commitment among students than did the earlier set of lower-order questions.

We have now introduced you to two general types of questions, convergent and divergent, and to a more elaborate guide based upon the work of Benjamin Bloom. The next step is to focus on how you, the teacher, ask a question and handle student responses. Remember, the purpose of asking questions is to engage students in the learning process. If you truly want to encourage higher-order thinking that requires deep processing of information, the questioning techniques that follow will help.

Questioning Techniques

Framing the Question

The most important role a teacher can play when asking questions is to understand the *timing* and the *pacing* of the question. The following general strategy will encourage the student to think about the question asked and to respond in a thoughtful fashion.

1. Ask the question.

2. Pause (allow thinking time).

3. Then call on student.

Prompting

Many times when teachers ask a question they get no response or an incorrect answer. What teachers want to avoid is giving the answer, because that sends a signal to the students that they do not need to think about the question. Implementing a single prompt or a series of prompts will encourage student engagement in the activity. Prompting questions are *hints* or *clues* to help students respond to teachers' questions. Sometimes teachers may need to reword the question to help students better understand the original question. By using prompts, teachers let students know that they are part of the learning process and they have a responsibility to participate.

> **Example:** Question: What is the name of the ocean on the west coast of the United States?
>
> **Answer:** No response.
>
> **Prompt:** The ocean is on the coast of California.
>
> **Answer:** Atlantic.
>
> **Prompt:** It is the name of a TV show and the cast plays police officers. The name has a color in it. The first word of the program starts with a P, it sounds like _____, surfers love to surf there.

Probing

A probe is used after a response from a student to seek clarification and to lead the student to a more complete and thoughtful answer. Probes also seek new information and redirect a response to the desired outcome. Through proper probing, students will develop the *quality* of the original response and expand their thinking on the topic. Probing questions can be used on any level of Bloom's taxonomy and with convergent and divergent questions. Using probing techniques helps combat shallow thinking and encourages more thoughtful and articulated responses.

Example: Question: Why do we have the Social Security system in the United States?

Answer: It's a retirement program.

Probe: Who benefits?

Response: Old people.

Probe: Why is Social Security so important for older people?

Response: It helps them pay their expenses.

Probe: Describe some of the expenses that retired people have. Give some examples.

Scaffolding

Sometimes probing will not work because there are gaps in students' knowledge. When a teacher realizes the student is not equipped with the ability (content matter/skill) to properly answer the question, teacher intervention is needed. The teacher will then proceed to teach or design an experience to provide the missing information. The power of questioning provides a window for the teacher to see the student's thinking. The teacher actually builds the student's knowledge through carefully constructed questions. This informal assessment strategy allows the teacher to see gaps in content knowledge and then to provide, through scaffolding techniques, the information for the student to effectively learn the material. If the teacher is successful in implementing the scaffolding strategy, students will begin to ask quality questions. Teachers should strive to encourage student-initiated questions rather than to have students just respond to questions initiated by the teacher. The more the student takes a responsible role, the more the student is invested in the learning experience.

Wait-Time

The purpose of wait-time is to allow enough time for a student to respond to a question. The general rule of thumb is to wait at least three seconds and no more than six seconds, depending on the cognitive level of the question for a response or to give a prompt. One critical factor in using wait-time is to consider the differences in students' learning styles. Many students are spontaneous and respond to questions very quickly, whereas others are more reflective and need to take more time before responding. In either case, no matter how long a student needs to process information, all should be afforded the same amount of time. Wait-time does just that; it levels the playing field by giving equal time to respond to questions. Giving too much wait-time can cause some students to get frustrated and others to possibly misbehave. The length of wait-time should be determined by student needs and level of question.

Example:

The best example to implement wait-time is to practice using a mental or visual strategy. Once the question is asked, slowly count from three to six depending on the complexity of the question before calling on the student. While you are waiting (it will be uncomfortable at first), look at the students and try to make as much eye contact as possible. Let them know you are observing them while they think about the answer. Try not to call on the first person with a hand raised. This will signal to the rest of the class to discontinue thinking about the question. Once you see a few hands raised, then call on a student—not necessarily the one whose hand went up first. As you become more skilled using this strategy you will begin to notice an increase in the number of students who raise their hands when you ask a question. Students will soon realize that they have time to *think* about their responses and the first person with a hand up might not be called on immediately. The strategy of *wait-time 2* can also be implemented and refers to the amount of time after the students' initial response until the teacher or possibly a student responds. This gives the student additional think time to modify or expand his or her original answer. Not quickly responding to the student's first answer encourages the student to probe independently and provide his or her own prompts.

Reinforcement

Reinforcing students for participation and correct responses is critical to successful questioning. Praising students and recognizing student performance encourages motivation and participation in the activity. It is important to recognize the importance of both verbal and nonverbal teacher feedback and reinforcement. Verbal reinforcement includes saying "OK," "That's correct," "Nice job," "Sounds good to me," and so forth. Voice inflection is another powerful communicator and can easily influence a student's behavior. When students make mistakes and prompting and probing strategies have been exhausted, it is acceptable to give specific feedback and make corrections—that's OK. You must avoid allowing students to complete a lesson with incorrect information—this is unacceptable. Nonverbal communication such as body movement and gestures, eye contact, and physical positioning (in the classroom) of the teacher contributes greatly to how students respond to your teaching. Students read nonverbal messages clearly and will take them personally, especially if negative. Negative nonverbal cues from teachers can turn off learners and cause them to withdraw from activities. Just think back to your own school days when teachers gave you negative nonverbal messages. How did you feel? In summary, praising students is very important. Giving specific feedback is critical and should be done in a positive and sincere way.

Although questioning strategies are useful and powerful, they can be used ineffectively and in inappropriate ways. The following misapplications are to be avoided (Cooper 1999):

1. To "control misbehavior": Teacher should avoid using the question to cause embarrassment and prevent or stop a misbehavior. Questions should be used to teach everyone—not just to manage a few.

2. To help "needy" students: Although, questions can be used to help needy students to gain a better understanding of specific content, you must be careful not to be too patronizing. Giving easy hints can look like charity and cause peer embarrassment.

3. To "put down" a student: Never use a difficult question to try to humiliate a learner. Sarcasm is also not suggested. Do not use questions as weapons.

4. To "manipulate" answers: Try not to restate an answer if response is incorrect to fit the need for students to hear the correct response. This type of paraphrasing devalues student's ideas and thoughts.

5. To offer the infamous "yes, but" teacher response: These types of responses tend to discredit student contributions. (99)

> **Think about it . . .** How can you develop the skill of probing? Can you think of a strategy?
>
> Do you see a connection between probing and elaboration?
>
> How does the think-pair-share cooperative learning strategy discussed in Chapter 3 relate to the concept of wait-time?
>
> How could wait-time personally benefit you as a learner?

Wilen's (1991) review of the literature summarizes critical elements leading to implementing effective questioning strategies:

1. Design key questions to provide lesson structure and direction and be prepared to ask spontaneous questions.

2. Phrase questions clearly, specifically, and adapted to student's ability level.

3. Ask questions logically and sequentially and at a variety of cognitive levels.

4. Always follow up all student responses, both verbal and nonverbal, and give students time to think (wait-time) before they respond.

5. Use questions that encourage participation for many of the students.

6. Encourage students to respond with their own questions. (10–11)

Formulating good questions is a skill that all teachers can learn and use to more actively engage students in the learning process. If used properly questioning is a powerful instructional strategy. Questioning is a tool for both the teacher and the student. Just as teachers can use questions strategically, so can students. Understanding and applying the different levels of questioning enhances the potential for both the teacher and student to more deeply process information, promote retention and understanding, and use knowledge. Effective use of questioning strategies provides a vehicle of communication to enhance this process. As you continue reading this chapter, the success of the five remaining powerful instructional strategies will depend on your ability, as well as that of your students, to master and best utilize effective questioning strategies to encourage critical and creative thinking.

Finally, let's take a look at one teacher's approach to using questions with her inner-city students.

Powerful Questioning: A Classroom Example

Topic: School violence   **Grade/age level:** Ninth/14 to 15 years of age

Objective of Lesson:
The student will identify, illustrate, and differentiate among the five critical elements of school violence based on personal experiences and the article "One Month after Littleton, 6 Are Shot at Georgia School" (1999).

Questioning Key

C (convergent question): narrows or limits the students to single or series of short responses.

D (divergent question): requires students to give more general or open responses that may have more then one appropriate answer.

K, COM, AP, AN, SY, E (levels of Bloom's taxonomy).

P (prompt); **PR** (probe); **WT** (wait-time); **SC** (scaffolding); and **R** (reinforcement).

The lesson begins with the teacher allowing students 30 seconds (WT) to think about what they already know about school violence. They will be asked to remember any school shootings that have been in the news lately or something that occurred at school or in their community (C/K). The teacher will remind them of the Columbine High School incident to cue up their prior knowledge (P). The students will be given five minutes to write in their journals the initial thoughts and feelings they experienced when first hearing about the shooting at Columbine High School (WT). After five minutes, students will be asked to share their thoughts and ideas with the whole class.

At this point in the lesson, the teacher introduces the advance organizer (see Fig. 4.2, p. 142, top) to illustrate the five categories of school violence to be studied that includes why it occurs, the media's influence, warning signs, punishment, and solutions. *This organizer will first be presented <u>without</u> the five categories written in the small boxes.* Using school violence as the central idea/concept with five boxes to be completed representing the categories, the students will participate in a brainstorming activity to discuss what they think are the categories of school violence. The teacher will give the following written questions to pairs of students:

- What is the first thing you think of when talking about school violence?
- How do you think the movies affect school violence?
- What are the critical elements of school violence in schools? (C/COM)

First, the students briefly brainstorm ideas in think-pair groups (WT). The teacher then conducts a class discussion eliciting students' responses and organizes them (Fig. 4.2, page 142, bottom) (C, K, COM, WT). Throughout this discussion the teacher asks each student who volunteers a response to give an example and further elaborate (PR). At the end of this exercise each student is given one to two minutes to write down a question on a 3 × 5 card about school violence. These questions will be used later to further expand understanding of content knowledge. The students are placed in small groups and given an article to read accompanied by five questions (C) that respond to the information in the article (who, what, where, when, and why). The responses are recorded on paper and the group needs to reach consensus. The teacher leads a discussion asking the following convergent questions:

- Who is the shooter?
- What happened in the article?
- What do we know about how the student had access to the guns?

The responses to all the questions will be qualified by calling on random students to agree or disagree. One purpose of this activity is to provide the necessary content information that might be missing—refer to *scaffolding* (page 122). After this discussion, each group will be provided with one *divergent question* (AN/SY). The questions given each group will relate to the advance organizer. Examples of these questions are:

- Why does school violence occur?
- How does the media affect school violence?
- What are some of the warning signs that indicate violent thoughts and tendencies?
- What are the possible punishments when an individual acts violently in cases such as these?
- What are possible solutions to school violence?

After the students discuss these questions they will design a medium in which to present to the class (picture/organizer, poem, story, skit, or simply talking to the class). This *synthesis*-level activity encourages students to use the newly acquired

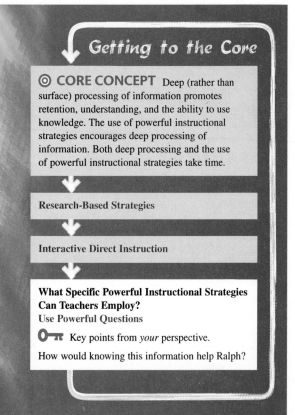

How would knowing this information help Ralph?

information in a more personal way to produce a unique or novel representation of the content. After each group presentation, the class will be given one minute to think of a question to ask the group to help clarify the content (WT). After the minute, a student will be called on randomly to ask a question and a discussion will ensue. The teacher will ask *probing* questions to encourage deeper processing of the information. The lesson will close with the teacher referring back to the advance organizer (fishbone) and summarizing the five main elements. For homework, the students will complete the organizer (see Fig. 4.2, p. 142) with specific content and personal examples of the five critical elements demonstrating understanding of school violence. Additionally, for homework each student must submit one thought-provoking question on a 3×5 card that will challenge the class to think more about school violence (D). During the next class, the teacher will distribute the students' questions and have the students respond to them. The lesson will culminate with an individual project that challenges the student to design a prevention program for school violence for the school (D, SY, E).

Contributed by: *Krista Fager (Graduate Student—La Salle University).*

Of course, the skillful use of questions is but one way to add power to your instructional methods. Another method that has the potential to bring about deep learning, and that has recently gained in popularity, is problem-based learning. That method, and several other methods that follow it, are very closely aligned with the *inquiry and discovery* methods of teaching.

Using Problems to Promote Learning

Problem-based learning (PBL), sometimes called authentic learning or problem-based teaching, is centered on posing a problem and leading students through an investigative procedure to solve it. By carefully structuring the experience with well-thought-out questions, the teacher encourages critical thought and provides learners with an opportunity to solve a complex problem. Students learn substantial content in the process.

Essentially, PBL provides students with the opportunity to understand and *resolve ill-structured problems* under the guidance, rather than the direction, of the teacher. Ill-structured problems are those for which necessary solution procedures are not readily apparent, and for which necessary solution information is not given up front. The problems may actually change course and become more complex as pupils tackle them (Kowalski, Weaver, and Henson 1990). Students work in small groups and take an active role in their own learning. They must use knowledge and skills from the disciplines to work on the problems presented to them. In this way, they are learning content and skills in the context of the types of problems encountered in the "real world" (O'Neil 1992). An example of the first page of a case written by McGininty, Gordon, and Webb appears below. The case proceeds page by page to accomplish the following objectives:

1. The students will be able to describe "addiction" in their own words.

2. The student should be able to state that nicotine is the addictive agent in tobacco.

3. The student should be able to describe the short-term and long-term consequences of smoking.

4. The students should be able to describe the common methods used to stop smoking.

Otis "Basketball" Jones

Otis is a 19-year-old freshman at Old State University. As the *Philadelphia Inquirer* wrote, "This star point guard has defensive reflexes like a cobra and can shoot like a God." These athletic abilities got him a full scholarship at Old State U.

When Otis showed up for practice, the coach saw all the talent that he expected, but Otis was really slow during the physical conditioning part of the workout. He had to stop a couple of times to catch his breath. When his coach asked about it, Otis replied that he was out of shape, but would be in shape soon.

After a few weeks, Otis still has to catch his breath in practice. The coach also noticed that Otis coughs a lot. He asks Otis to see him in his office. "Otis, you seem to be working hard in practice, but I am still concerned that you haven't developed your wind. Are you all right?" Otis replies, "I'm fine, coach. You know I can shoot better than anyone out there, so what if I can't run as many sprints? I'm also wicked at defense." The coach tells Otis, "Look, we play a fast game here at Old State U. You are going to have to run much better to make the team. Your great shooting and defense aren't going to be much good if you are always half a court behind. This is college ball and you better get used to it.

(Source: This case was written by James McGinity, Philip R. Gordon, Ph.D., and Carmen Webb, M.D., Medical College of Pennsylvania and Hahnemann University. Supported by the Howard Hughes Medical Institute. The authors grant permission to use the case freely.)

After having read this first page of Otis "Basketball" Jones, learners consider what the problem may be. They discuss what they know, what they need to know, and form tentative hypotheses about the problem. Then they develop learning issues and each learner takes responsibility to find out the answer to an issue or two. For example, one of us facilitated a session using this case. This particular group of high school learners listed what they knew: good at basketball, 19 years old, has trouble breathing, coughs a lot. They wanted to know more about Otis's heart rate, medical history, and lung sounds. They hypothesized that he might have asthma or some kind of lung condition, or pneumonia, or cardiomyopathy, or that he smoked. They identified several learning issues, including: "How oxygen is consumed by the body?" "What is meant by 'getting in shape'?" and "What might nicotine do to the body?" As the case unfolded over several days, page by page, learners shared what they learned with one another. As it became apparent that Otis smoked cigarettes, they began to explore addiction, the effect of nicotine on respiration and breathing, and finally, how one could help another person quit smoking. Exactly the objectives originally set forth by the teacher! Of course, in the process of studying the case they learned much more; they learned how to go about solving problems, finding materials, using resources, and so on.

To implement PBL in your own classroom, you need only follow these basic steps.

1. Make certain that you have a clear rationale for using it. As is true with virtually every method, you need to be certain of what you want to accomplish with your learners.

2. If you believe that PBL will help you help students accomplish the goals and objectives you have established, then look for a model you can use to

"Give students a problem that really connects with their world, empower them to generate solutions and watch the serious thinking that follows."

(Source: Savoie and Hughs 1994, 54.)

develop a problem. Problems are all around us, so you should have little difficulty with this step.

3. Design a scenario and setting that relates to the problem. Remember Otis and cigarette smoking? Look again at the scenario and setting.

4. Coach the learners as they tackle the problem and content. Provide guidance but do not give them information that you think they can find on their own.

5. Construct authentic assessments to determine what each learner knows at the end of the problem.

This relates to the individual accountability that, earlier, we insisted is an essential component of true cooperative learning.

PBL does not permit covering as much information as (apparently) efficiently as does lecture or more direct instructional methods. It does allow learners to use powerful strategies mentioned in earlier chapters. Learners work together, using visual representations (graphic and visual organizers) by mapping out concepts, organizing information, and elaborating upon that information. Torp and Sage (1998) emphasize the importance of mapping when using problem-based learning: "It allows the students working with a bank of possibilities to visualize each topic in some way and map out the terrain of problem ideas and connections. Mapping allows for multiple responses. Once you can see and examine the terrain of these possibilities, they look for areas of conflict and dissonance" (49). Maps and organizers, which will be further elaborated on later in this chapter, are important visual and thinking tools to use when trying to solve a problem.

Students are actively engaged throughout the problem-based learning approach and the role of a teacher is that of a coach who provides resources and facilitates the learning process. The students are dependent upon one another for seeking information and helping each other solve the problem. The teacher (coach) must scaffold by assisting the students with the necessary critical thinking skills that they must employ. In addition to providing resources for the students, the ability to work well together (cooperative learning) and the use of effective questioning strategies by both the teacher and student are critical. Specifically, Torp and Sage (1998, 72) have outlined the following guidelines for questioning during a PBL session:

1. Actively listen to what students are and are not saying.

2. Ask questions that require a rich response.

3. Use all levels of cognitive questioning.

4. Avoid questions requiring yes-or-no and one-word answers.

5. Pause to allow thoughtful responses.

6. Encourage and allow the conversation to reside among students as much as possible.

7. Avoid the temptation to correct immediately or interrupt.

8. Encourage support and justification of ideas—probe to extend student thinking.

9. Challenge data, assumptions, and sources.

10. Avoid feedback that cues students to the "rightness" of their statements; probe students frequently so probing is not viewed only as a cue for "wrongness."

> **Think about it . . .**
>
> **Think about a real-life problem, and write up an initial scenario that leads the learner into the problem.**

Problem-based learning is a powerful approach in promoting true, deep understanding of real-life problems. It is authentic because it places the student in situations that are real and provides problems that need to be solved. Yes, it takes "time," and lots of it. Because not as much can be covered, the process of uncovering information is very important in this method. Larger blocks of time permit PBL to be used to its fullest potential. More time permits group work and research that would be very hurried (but certainly possible) in shorter time blocks. Research suggests that PBL is efficacious in a wide range of instructional settings and for a wide variety of learners. For example, Aspy, Aspy, and Quinby (1993) examined the use of PBL in the education of physicians, and found that those students in PBL "exceeded their traditionally trained colleagues in their ability to integrate the basic sciences with clinical assignments" (24). Gordon, Rogers, Comfort, Gavula, and McGee (2001) found that PBL "improved behavior and increased science performance of low-income minority middle school students" (173).

SPOTLIGHT ON BEHAVIOR MANAGEMENT

"But will they behave?"

Managing to Create Time

Earlier we pointed out that conflict in the classroom usually stops instruction in its tracks. The teacher stops, deals with the problem, and occasionally has to continue to deal with it as the situation escalates. Time is lost. Momentum is lost. Teaching and learning are put on hold. In this section, we will show you how to get some of that time back by (1) avoiding conflict cycles and (2) quickly identifying and exiting developing conflict cycles.

As we demonstrated in the last chapter, conflict cycles are fueled by the reaction of an adult or peer. Long (1996) found that this reaction is often driven by

◉ **CORE CONCEPT** Deep (rather than surface) processing of information promotes retention, understanding, and the ability to use knowledge. The use of powerful instructional strategies encourages deep processing of information. Both deep processing and the use of powerful instructional strategies take time.

four factors: (1) counteraggressive behavior, (2) bad moods, (3) unrealistic expectations, and (4) prejudice. Let's examine each of these types of reaction.

Counteraggression was explained in the last chapter. However, its significance in perpetuating conflict cycles requires that we revisit the concept. Remember: Creating situations in which adults will mirror their behavior is one way students naturally maintain or validate their irrational beliefs. So, if a student is behaving aggressively, you will likely feel and want to behave aggressively yourself. Alternatively, think about the feelings evoked when you observe or attempt to work with a child who is withdrawn or depressed. You probably felt helpless or sad. It is crucial that you understand this concept!

Earlier we asked you to focus on your own thoughts and feelings. Practicing this personal decoding of your thoughts will help you avoid conflict cycles. You can do this by using self-talk (Muscott 1995). For example, "I can feel my teeth beginning to clench. I am getting angry. I need to relax so that I can respond thoughtfully." This process of personal decoding allows you to recognize *your* feelings so that *you* can act on the basis of rational thought. As Nicholas Long (personal communication, March 15, 2000) recently told us, "You know, all management begins with us, not the kids."

What are some things you can do once you are thinking rationally? Let's go back to our developing situation involving Juan and Eliza. If you will recall, we were just getting into the lesson when we found Juan making faces at Eliza. What if, right at that moment, we redirected Juan by asking him to come up to the front of the room to be the teacher's helper? Similarly, you can *redirect* a related student. Let us explain with an example from the journal of one of our student teachers:

> Shawn, a student in my class, has been reluctant to participate in class activities. He is a disruptive force, talking to peers, calling out inappropriate comments, and disregarding adult directions. In science class today I asked the student to move his seat to another location. He refused. I decided rather than get into a battle of wills, I would ask the student who he was bothering (who was more compliant) to move instead. I thanked him for his cooperation. Shawn continued to be a lesser disruption, eventually settling down as peers began to deride his behavior.

Clearly this student teacher understands the concept of the conflict cycle. He tried once for compliance from the disruptive student. Then he moved on to the student who was being bothered. It took a very short amount of time and the lesson proceeded. The rest of the class became interested in the lesson and the disruptive student had no choice but to join in.

It is possible to successfully redirect a child and avoid trouble for the time being. Perhaps later, when students are engaged in independent work you would decide to speak privately with the student to learn more about his thoughts and behavior.

You may decide that you just need to gain the student's attention and remind him or her of the expectations. You might try a three-step statement that goes something like this: "(1) Juan, (2) you are making faces and not attending to me, (3) look at me and listen for my next instruction." We often hear beginning teachers make the mistake of continually repeating a student's name in an effort to gain attention and communicate disapproval. Something like, "Juan . . . Juan . . . Juan . . . Juan. . . ." This is often followed by frustration on the part of the teacher because the student doesn't seem to respond. We can imagine the student thinking, "I hear my name . . . but my teacher will say it a few more times before there is any real consequence, so I will just keep on behaving this way for a while longer." So there needs to be more. Say the student's name once. Step 2 is to tell the student what he or she is doing. Sometimes the

student doesn't know. The student is acting impulsively. Additionally, clarifying the behavior for both you and the student will allow you to calmly and matter-of-factly offer an alternative. Step 3 is that alternative, communicated as an I-statement or as something the teacher and/or the class needs to have happen.

What if, as our student teacher described it above, you sense a "battle of will" beginning? What about that student who just "gets on your nerves"? You begin to feel counteraggression growing in you as soon as you see him or her enter the room. How does the teacher avoid counteraggression now?

Rita Ives, George Washington University professor emeritus, was speaking to a gathering of graduate students and teachers in the spring of 1998. The topic of her lecture was teaching troubled and troubling students. During the question and answer period that followed her prepared speech, a student teacher stood and said something like, "One of my students escalates his behavior every day! He is aggressive, raises his voice, and swears . . . I just get so angry. I *do* understand the conflict cycle. I am just getting frustrated and I really don't know how to stop myself."

Dr. Ives proceeded to create a mental image that caused the entire room to pause and think. She said, "Imagine that child carrying a tray of fine crystal glassware. It is heavily loaded and, God forbid, the child trips and falls. Glass shatters. The child is hurt. How might you respond to the child in that awful circumstance?"

The point is that the children who evoke these feelings in you are vulnerable. The thoughts and feelings carried around in their minds are like overloaded trays of delicate glass. As teachers, we have to understand that these students are not attacking us personally. By thinking of them as vulnerable and in need of our empathetic support, we can often avoid counteraggressive responses.

In Long's (1996) research, responding counteraggressively was by far the most frequent action that perpetuated the conflict cycle. Clearly, avoiding counteraggression will help you avoid the conflict cycle.

Sometimes we come to school and our "head is not in it." Perhaps car problems caused us to be late. Maybe we had a disagreement with a significant other or we were up late and didn't get enough sleep. For myriad reasons we are just not ourselves. We are not mentally available to give our students complete attention.

In his 1966 lecture, Fritz Redl reminded the kindergarten teachers he was speaking to:

. . . no matter how much you know about the importance of carrying with you a professional self detached from your personal problems and geared to the weight of your work whatever your charge may be, things happen which fill you heavily and with which you have to cope. But sometimes, my coping with what is going on within me takes so much effort that little is left for the kids, or sometimes I am not quite skillful enough in coping with what is within me, so that I usually use the youngsters as crumbs to dunk up the soup of my own confusion. And that is a normal enough temptation (1966).

As you know by now, teaching and interacting with students as we have described it in this book takes immense concentration. The most effective teachers believe that *everything* they do throughout the day must be purposeful. When we are in a bad mood or when something from outside the classroom is requiring some of our mental capacity we lose the ability to concentrate completely. When this occurs we lose sight of our rational thinking. Irrational thought and behavior creeps in. There is an increased likelihood that we will fuel a conflict cycle. It will be important to strive for total concentration every day so that you will be able to give your students the complete attention that they need.

We have been demonstrating all along that working with your students from a psychodynamic perspective requires a deep understanding of their needs. Each of your students has different needs. They differ developmentally and differ depending on activity, time of day, academic area, social situations, and more. As you zero in on these needs it will help you to create realistic expectations for your students. As Long (1996) discovered, sometimes teachers behave too rigidly. Coloroso (1994) described these professionals as "brick wall" teachers. Their expectations are simply unrealistic for a particular student at a particular time. Rather than making an adjustment, the teacher keeps pushing. The frustrated student has no way out. A conflict cycle ensues and goes around and around because the teacher was too rigid and was unable to make an adjustment.

The final type of adult reaction is prejudice. Think for a minute about your last visit to a teacher's lounge or workroom. Frequently, conversations center on students. Unfortunately, most statements are gross generalizations that don't provide for a real understanding of a situation or student. We have often heard breeches of confidentiality as teachers discuss children with others who don't have a "need to know." For example, one might hear: "Tyrone is a nightmare. I have never had a

student challenge my authority like he does. He is just a mean-spirited kid." The result of this statement is that it immediately paints a picture of Tyrone in each adult's head, probably a *different* picture for each person. After several days of a teacher talking this way about Tyrone, he gains a reputation. This reputation follows him until he is suspected of some terrible behavior that he actually was *not* a part of. Tyrone gets blamed for something he did not do. That is fuel for the conflict cycle. The two lessons here are that teachers must (1) maintain professional standards of confidentiality and (2) avoid prejudging students.

Concentrating our efforts on helping students regain their rational thought is another way to avoid conflict cycles. To begin, communicate to the student that you see his emotion. For example, "Juan, I can see by the look on your face that you are getting angry." I-statements like this, communicated in a calm manner, provide the student an opportunity to respond without feeling threatened. This kind of statement from the adult is like water on the flame of the conflict. It eliminates the fuel that might escalate the cycle. Many times this is enough. Juan might respond, "Eliza was making fun of me on the bus!" There you have it!—the missing information that you can now use to (1) talk with Eliza, (2) separate the students for the time being, and/or (3) redirect the students. This information is priceless in both avoiding conflict and helping your students learn how to solve their own problems!

Teachers can go a long way toward avoiding conflict cycles simply by becoming aware of how they function, considering the four ways adults fuel them, and helping their students regain rational thought. However, even with all of the preceding strategies in mind we sometimes find ourselves caught in a conflict cycle. How do you exit a conflict cycle that has already begun?

The best way is to remove the fuel. Take a break. Send everyone to a "neutral corner." For example, you could ask another adult for help so that you can leave the situation and regain your rational thinking. Alternatively, you and the student could agree to separate for a few minutes and come back to the discussion later. What will the student think? Well, what if you said something like, "Juan, I am getting very angry right now and it is keeping me from thinking straight. Mr. Robertson is going to talk with you for a minute while I go in the other room so that I can think straight." The message to the student is that adults can think irrationally too. When they do, they can engage in a strategy that will help them change their thoughts and actions. By calmly disengaging for the time being you provide time and space for both you and the student to regain your rational thought. Of course, you must come back to the situation when all parties are thinking rationally. Then you can have a calm discussion about the facts.

As you reflect on this section, we hope that you can see how you might use these ideas in the course of your daily interactions with your students. If you think about all the lost time you have observed in your field placements because of teacher-student conflict, you can see how some of these seemingly simple ideas might work to maintain the momentum of the classroom. You will have more time to teach, a more comfortable and safe classroom environment, and more meaningful relationships with your students.

Case Study Method

The case method, although not as new in education as is PBL, is consistent with recent research and cognitivist approaches. Like PBL, the case method requires active participation on the part of the learner and a more facilitative role on the part of the teacher. The case method is an instructional strategy that employs case studies (intensive study of one person or situation) to engage the learner in a problem-solving activity. Case studies describe a decision or problem, and they are typically written from the perspective of the person who must make the decision. Cases are presented and end with a problem or dilemma that needs to be resolved. The case method differs from PBL in that cases tend to be more clearly structured. Case problems are usually of shorter duration and cases allow pupils to practice knowledge that they have attained, rather than to actually learn new content (Kowalski, Weaver, and Henson 1990).

Using a specific case or situation, learners are challenged to tear apart the information for the purpose of drawing a meaningful conclusion or possibly supporting their personal opinions. In either situation, the learner is called on to carefully observe data, problem solve, make inferences, and eventually discuss generalizations and conclusions. Students typically receive the entire case study (content) all at once, and use their own experiences to solve the case. The case study that follows places three individuals in a situation that has no correct answer but challenges the learner to make critical personal decisions, to examine elements of personal responsibility and independence, and to look at alternative solutions and consequences.

Sample Case Study: Dennis and Mr. T

Mr. T has been a mentor/father figure for a young man named Dennis since he was 12 years old. Dennis's father left him, his two brothers, and his mother when he was about 10 years old, leaving them little money and no idea where to find him. Dennis's mother was well intentioned and helped Dennis as much as possible as she did the other two brothers. Dennis got involved with a group of friends at school who did not exert a positive influence on him. He was constantly getting into trouble in and out of school and experimenting with a variety of drugs. Eventually, Dennis was hospitalized for depression and drug abuse. After many months of counseling and rehabilitation, Dennis was ready to return back to school and try to lead a more normal life. Mr. T. assumed the mentor/father role for Dennis and kept in contact with him on a regular basis. Mr. T. encouraged Dennis to enroll in a private school that would pay more attention to his individual needs, challenge him more academically, and be more sensitive to his family issues. Mr. T. secured financial support from one of his personal friends and Dennis was able to attend this school throughout his high school years. Dennis was successful in high school, played sports, and got involved in many school activities. Dennis learned to be very independent and to fend for himself. He held part-time jobs to pay for all his personal expenses, including a car and insurance. The car was a necessary purchase because of all the part-time jobs he held.

Dennis graduated from high school on time and attended his first year of college where he did extremely well. He used money set aside from his grandparents to pay for his first year of college. At the end of his first year of college, he realized he did not have enough money or financial aid to continue school full time the next academic year. Getting money from his mother and grandparents was not feasible. Dennis went to Mr. T. and asked him to ask the person who supported him through high school to help him again, either through a gift or securing a bank loan. Both Mr. T and the anonymous financier agreed that Dennis was old enough to work out the solution to the problem himself. They felt he was given a gift of a high school education at a private school and additional financial support. It was now time for Dennis to go it alone and solve his problems without adult intervention. Dennis had a few options. He could get a loan from the university, take out private loans, go part-time for a year and establish residency in the state to qualify for reduced tuition, or take on many more part-time jobs. All of these options required that Dennis take full responsibility for the problem. What would you do if you were Dennis in this situation? What options would work best for you? Did Mr. T. and his friend make the best decision? What would you have done if you were Dennis or Mr. T? What do you think Dennis learned from this situation?

The sample case study is a compelling narrative that will provide the learner with enough factual information to begin to solve the problem. Through teacher and student questioning, an in-depth investigation of the case can ensue. The teacher can first encourage the learner to quickly decide on a solution, and then allow for small-group discussions. This allows the students to hear other opinions and personal experiences of others, as well as share their own.

Teacher-led questions can be presented to provide a structure for learners. In the sample case, questions relating to personal experiences might be most appropriate. It is important to provide debriefing sessions to allow learners to share as much information with peers as possible. The role of the teacher is most critical because the teacher structures the case and designs the important questions that encourage thoughtful discussions. Students will be required to defend their analysis and solutions as well as to challenge each other. Students can take these cases further by connecting them to situations in their own lives, by interviewing families to learn alternative methods to resolve the issue, and by possibly designing their own case studies based on the theme of the assignment.

The case study is just another powerful instructional strategy that allows teachers to challenge learners' thinking and help them use outside resources to reach more thoughtful solutions that are relevant to their lives. But again, this strategy takes time to use. The time, however, is well spent.

Think about it . . .

What do we know about learning theories (Chap. 2) that would make case studies appealing to the student? Have your teachers used the case method with you? If yes, did this method appeal to you?

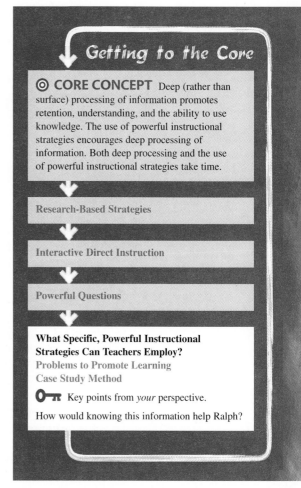

Getting to the Core

◎ **CORE CONCEPT** Deep (rather than surface) processing of information promotes retention, understanding, and the ability to use knowledge. The use of powerful instructional strategies encourages deep processing of information. Both deep processing and the use of powerful instructional strategies take time.

Research-Based Strategies

Interactive Direct Instruction

Powerful Questions

What Specific, Powerful Instructional Strategies Can Teachers Employ?
Problems to Promote Learning
Case Study Method

⦿━ Key points from *your* perspective.

How would knowing this information help Ralph?

Project Learning as a Powerful Strategy

In-depth projects, if structured properly, allow the learner or groups of learners to be immersed in one big idea, or to work toward one common goal. The project challenges learners to use a variety of skills and intelligences, and allows them to be involved in meaningful activity. Giving the learner meaningful projects allows the learning to be more connected to the real world. Projects tend to be multidimensional, and they encourage learners to extend their understanding of the content beyond the classroom and into the real world. Projects such as designing an autobiography using a minimum of three different mediums (such as the written word, audiotapes, visuals, film clips, and realia) call on the student not only to collect and assemble the necessary information, but also to integrate that information. Skills needed to accomplish the project will usually include problem solving, critical and creative thought, and the ability to present information to others. These types of assignments challenge learners to organize their time well and to plan in advance.

According to Chapman and Freeman (1996), there are two factors that need to be considered: (1) the student's ability to process information and (2) the way in which the project will be used to extend the learning experience in any particular content area. It is important for the teacher to consider students' developmental levels when designing projects. Many projects require specific levels of thinking, organizational strategies, and tactile ability. Fogarty and Bellanca (1989) designed a chart that describes skills developed through projects that include critical thinking skills, creative thinking skills, and social skills.

Skills Developed through Projects

Critical Thinking Skills	Creative Thinking Skills	Social Skills
1. Attributing	1. Brainstorming	1. Respecting others
2. Compare/contrast	2. Visualizing	2. Working independently
3. Classifying	3. Personifying	3. Managing time
4. Sequencing	4. Inventing	4. Cooperating
5. Prioritizing	5. Associating	5. Sharing
6. Drawing conclusions	6. Inferring	6. Using resources effectively
7. Determining cause/effect	7. Generalizing	7. Making choices/decisions
8. Analyzing for bias	8. Predicting	
9. Analyzing for assumptions	9. Hypothesizing	
10. Solving analogies	10. Making analogies	
11. Evaluating	11. Dealing with ambiguity and paradox	
12. Decision making	12. Problem solving	

From: Catch Them Thinking: A Handbook of Classroom Strategies *by James Bellanca and Robin Fogarty,* © *1986, 1993 IRI/Skylight Training and Publishing, Inc. Reprinted with permission of Skylight Professional Development, a Pearson Education company, Arlington Heights, Illinois.*

The following two examples represent project learning as a powerful strategy. The first example requires the student to design a multilevel project that illustrates the many aspects of Israel's geography. It encourages critical and creative thought as well as the ability to work well with others.

Example of a Classroom Project

This teacher-produced activity requires the learner to design a project that best illustrates the many aspects of Israel's geography. The purpose is to demonstrate how the geography of Israel is important to its existence and survival. The project will challenge the student to gather information on the physical, economic, and geographic aspects of Israeli society. Resources used must include books, newspaper articles, magazines, maps, news clips, Web-based Internet sites, and a minimum of two interviews with people from that country via telephone, Internet, or personal communication. The student will answer the essential question of the relationship of geography to Israel's existence. Presentation will be written, oral, and visual (with audiovisual aids). The student will set up a time line and an update of progress on the project to be submitted each week throughout the five-week project. Upon completion of the actual presentation (could be done in groups of two), each student will submit the final written project that includes goals and objective, methods of collecting data, review of content studied, results of data collection and conclusions. The conclusion section will be done by each individual student (in the case of those who worked in groups) and weighted heavily for grading purposes to better evaluate individual accountability. The final written conclusions will include students' generalizations and implications of the project findings. Also included will be personal connections of the research to the student's own life. The teacher will provide an assessment rubric to help guide the students in meeting expected criteria.

The second example challenges the student in a similar way by requiring her to conduct research and present information on social cognitive theory. This poster session project, completed by a college student studying learning theories, requires her to present the information to her peers. Does the theorist look familiar? See the two circles on the right side panel of the poster? This student connected Bandura to the 4MAT system.

Using project learning provides the learner with the opportunity to pursue individual interests, conduct extensive research, and present findings in a meaningful way. Reprinted with permission of Laura Alampi.

Think about it . . .

What projects do you remember from your elementary school days?

Why do you still remember that project?

What made it powerful?

To learn more about project learning, visit the Buck Institute of Education website at www.bie.org/pbl.

It is important that teachers allow time for meeting with students to discuss project criteria. These "miniconferences" should take place, in person, as often as possible. Because these students will be working independently, e-mail communication should be encouraged, if available. Projects provide perfect opportunities for teachers to plan miniconferences that allow students to display their projects for others to see. This is an opportunity for structured sharing of students' work. Classmates and students from other classrooms could be invited to view student presentations, as well as to evaluate them. Carefully constructed questions (lower and higher order) could provide valuable learning opportunities for students attending the "conference."

Learning Centers in Your Classroom

The use of learning centers has long been a staple of elementary school teachers, but has been used less in middle and high schools. However, learning centers can be powerful learning vehicles for students of all ages and abilities. These self-contained environments, stocked with all the necessary materials needed to complete an assignment, permit learners to work at their own pace. Learning centers can be designed to meet a wide range of academic levels, provide individualization, and meet and challenge learners' various learning styles. Learners are usually encouraged to work alone to complete assignments, but cooperative groups can be used during different phases of the work to encourage social skills development and the sharing of ideas. Centers must be well organized with clear and concise directions, procedures, rules, and objectives that make the expectations clear. Because students are working independently, organization is critical. It is also important for the teacher to carefully monitor students' progress.

Learning centers provide learners with a chance to explore selected content through a variety of mediums. Centers usually contain written material, audio- and videotapes, computers, and manipulatives. Centers are used by teachers to further their learners' content knowledge of a specific topic, and to provide extended experiences for those students needing remediation or enrichment. Centers can also provide places for students to go when they finish class assignments, and quiet spaces for those learners who like to work by themselves. These centers can take many forms, such as *structured,* with specific directions to follow; *exploratory,* where learners can design their own experiences; or some type of *combination* of these two types. There are three general steps in developing learning centers: (1) Define skills and concepts to be learned or reinforced, (2) design learning activities or tasks that will help students reach goals, and (3) provide for extension activities (Davidson et al. 1976, 6). The following are two examples of centers that could be designed and put to use at all grade levels.

Listening or Viewing Centers

Listening or viewing centers include a collection of audio- and videotapes that enhance and enrich lesson content. This type of center is appropriate for all grade levels because it allows students to work at their own pace and to choose the content they wish to explore. Teachers can provide commercially produced materials or teacher-made materials that are accompanied by written directions and exercises. For younger students, poems and stories on audiotape are popular and with older student's videotapes help bring the content alive, such as clips from World War II, real footage of earthquakes, and segments of acts of a play being studied. The use of videodiscs and the Internet (specific assignments) are wonderful additions to centers.

Learning and Teaching in the Age of Technology

The Vanderbilt group reminds us that quality instruction provides scaffolds for achieving meaningful learning (Goldman et al. 1999, 6–7). The ability of technology to provide many levels of exposure to a subject area or topic that allows students to observe complex processes in action, visualize relationships, view trends and complexities through the use or construction of graphs, databases, spreadsheets, maps, or diagrams can greatly amplify traditional classroom and teacher resources in teaching for deep understanding. Electronic references such as online dictionaries, math problem-solving hints, short biographies of characters in history or in a novel, maps, and glossaries can "unstick" a learner at the moment of greatest need, freeing her or him to make the otherwise illusive connection that earlier might have had to wait for a teacher's attention, or another day's lesson. Increasingly sophisticated feedback cycles scaffolded by teachers help move learners from novice to expert. As tutorial programs grow in sophistication and artificial intelligence programs allow them to more accurately respond to a particular learner's style and needs, branching programs for reinforcement, deeper, more personalized learning may be the norm, rather then the exception. To a large extent, teaching for understanding is not at all dependent on the use or nonuse of educational technology. Rather, it is a function of the way you organize and approach instruction and learning in your classroom. When you teach for deep understanding, the power of multimedia resources will be self-evident. Combining deep understanding with the time needed to process new learning will indeed mean less is more, especially if students employ a variety of technological tools. And although you must always maintain that delicate balance between allowing for acquisition of declarative knowledge to prepare for more sophisticated understanding and use of procedural knowledge, allowing learners to use technology for independent, lifelong learning is an important mission of teaching for conceptual change.

Teaching Tips

1. Rather than provide information through lecture, ask students to use webquests to find information.

2. Teachers and students can design questions using different levels of Bloom's taxonomy in response to videotapes, featured films, and television programs assigned for study. This encourages higher-level thinking and processing of information by both teacher and student.

3. Use interactive learning centers and project-based assignments that incorporate audiotapes and other multimedia to encourage students to synthesize content from chapters, classroom activities, specific skills, and reading materials.

Suggested Websites

http://www.covis.nwu.edu/info/
   Learning through Collaborative Visualization (CoVis): Through the use of advanced technologies, the CoVis project is attempting to transform science learning to better resemble the authentic practice of science.

http://www.math.ucalgary.ca/~laf/colorful/colorful. html
   IS THIS REALLY MATHEMATICS? These games are not about arithmetic or numbers. They are about problem solving, search, and discovery of patterns, which are all at the very heart of mathematics.

http://www.thinkingmaps.com
   Great site to help design visual organizers

http://www.mcrel.org
   Practical and research-based organization for "best practices"

> ◉ **CORE CONCEPT** Deep (rather than surface) processing of information promotes retention, understanding, and the ability to use knowledge. The use of powerful instructional strategies encourages deep processing of information. Both deep processing and the use of powerful instructional strategies take time.

Experimental and Discovery Centers

Experimental and discovery centers include a collection of calculators, tools, building materials, science materials, household items, paper, cardboard, and so forth, that are used to design projects that coordinate with content being taught in class. The center could be focused on one topic or used to work on a variety of different projects. Rules should be posted and supervision is critical to ensure safety precautions. These centers provide students with a meaningful project to work on when they complete assignments early.

Learning centers usually stand alone as self-contained exhibits. We have provided a picture of a learning center below. This particular learning center is aimed, developmentally speaking, at elementary-age children.

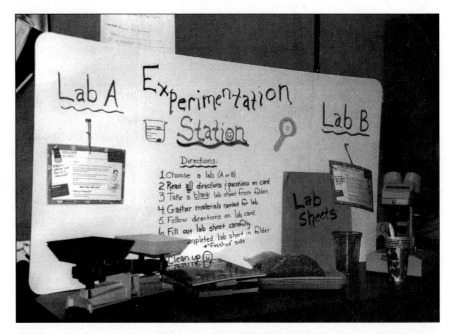

This 5th grade science learning center allows students to work independently or in small groups to learn new material, extend understanding, or to gain additional practice.

Think about it . . .

How can learning centers be used to help students teach other students?

How would the teachers' knowledge of questioning strategies be helpful in designing learning centers?

Learning centers provide a rich and rewarding avenue for critical and creative thinking. Centers are excellent mechanisms for student input. Designing their own learning centers can be excellent projects for students to demonstrate knowledge of content. Having students create learning centers for future classes and topics is an excellent way to motivate the more adventurous learners and help support the learners who need remedial work.

Centers can challenge the many intelligences of learners and provide opportunities to allow students to exert their individual differences. We discuss multiple intelligences and individual differences in the next chapter. Discovery and inquiry centers can be set up in any classroom, K through 12.

Graphic and Visual Organizers

Graphic and visual organizers are powerful tools that help learners master both declarative and procedural knowledge. Working with organizers helps make the learner's thinking visible. Whether learners work alone or in small groups, these organizers encourage them to draw visual representations, make connections among facts, ideas, and concepts, and make better sense of information. Through a process of constructing visual representations, learners organize information in a deep and meaningful way.

Bellanca and Fogarty (1991) discuss the value of visual representations. They write:

> These visual tools are referred to as cognitive maps, visual displays and advance organizers. There is a saying that "thinking is invisible talk." These cognitive tools can be used to see what students are thinking and how they are thinking. The cognitive organizers provide visual representations that make the invisible talk visible. They help students organize, reorganize, revise, and modify the connections they are making as they process information. Using graphic organizers, students learn how the concepts fit with their prior knowledge or background experience and how they will be used, applied and transferred in novel situations. (Bellanca and Fogarty 1991, 106)

The cognitive emphasis in education has caused us to look again at how we learn. This change has encouraged teachers to place more emphasis on helping learners to see patterns and relationships among ideas and facts, and not just to learn isolated pieces of information. Brooks and Brooks (1993) make this point well when they write:

> Much of traditional education breaks wholes into parts, and then focuses separately on each part. But many students are unable to build concepts and skills from parts to wholes. These students often stop trying to see the wholes before all the parts are presented to them and focus on the small, memorizable aspects of broad units without ever creating the big picture. . . . We need to see the "whole" before we are able to make sense of the parts. (98)

Graphic and visual organizers encourage learners to take particular ideas and concepts, those that are often learned in isolation from one another, and make them into a sensible "whole."

David Hyerle (1996) discusses a wide variety of applications of visual organizers. He asserts the importance that they play in helping students organize their learning, in encouraging these students to think at higher levels, and in providing opportunities for student-to-student and student-to-teacher communication. He states:

> . . . visual tools of many kinds are used to build and then more explicitly express relationships, interdependencies, and forms of knowledge. Verbalizing and writing out ideas are only one way of representing thinking, and often this is a thin, linear veneer of students' thinking about content. With visual tools, students begin to visually integrate their own holistic forms with the tightly wound structures of information and thus interpret text. They begin to identify and then integrate their forms with the text as they naturally link information. Visual brainstorming webs, task specific organizers, and thinking-process maps thus bridge between their own forms and the structures that are embodied in the text but hidden in the guise of linear strings of words. (15)

The use of graphic and visual organizers is time consuming because it encourages students to manipulate information at various levels of thinking. Some lower-level thinking organizers place information into organized frameworks that encourage students to use charts, graphs, sequence patterns, time lines, and matrix charts. These

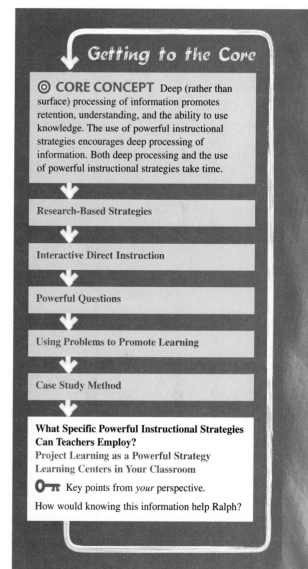

Getting to the Core

◎ **CORE CONCEPT** Deep (rather than surface) processing of information promotes retention, understanding, and the ability to use knowledge. The use of powerful instructional strategies encourages deep processing of information. Both deep processing and the use of powerful instructional strategies take time.

Research-Based Strategies

Interactive Direct Instruction

Powerful Questions

Using Problems to Promote Learning

Case Study Method

What Specific Powerful Instructional Strategies Can Teachers Employ?
Project Learning as a Powerful Strategy
Learning Centers in Your Classroom

⚷ Key points from *your* perspective.

How would knowing this information help Ralph?

visual organizers help students think and better manage large quantities of information. These lower-level thinking tools are powerful strategies for learning facts, ideas, and basic concepts. Other types of organizers require students to analyze, synthesize, and evaluate information. Some of the more popular organizers that challenge students to think at higher levels are skinny/juicy questions that ask students to think of questions that require either short or simple (skinny) responses, or questions that require discussion and further exploration (juicy). The Open Compare and Contrast chart encourages higher-order thinking.

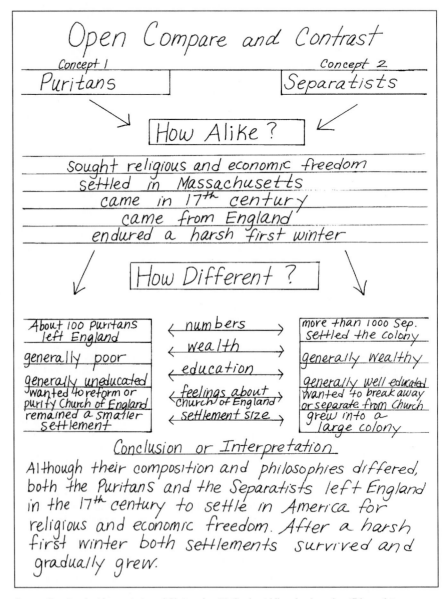

Source: Reprinted with permission of Christopher McCool, middle school teacher (7th grade).

Organizers can be used in a variety of ways, including teacher directed, student centered, or a combination of both. They can be used as advance organizers to show the larger conceptual picture or show a lesson or unit, to help develop relationships between and among variables, to show a process or order, or to extend thinking.

The following are examples of graphic and visual organizers designed and used by practicing teachers. Carefully read the descriptions to better understand how the organizers approach both declarative and procedural knowledge.

The organizer in Figure 4.1 serves as an advance organizer. It was designed by a high school art teacher to introduce the concept of light in a photography course. During a workshop for teachers, we challenged the teachers to examine a concept that they routinely taught and to develop an advance organizer that would communicate the message in as few words as possible. As you can see, this organizer uses few words to describe the power of light (illumination, shadow, transition, and form). What was interesting in this exercise was how long (30 minutes) it took this experienced teacher to conceptualize the concept of *light.* He commented, "I can't believe I had to struggle so much to design this organizer. I have been teaching photography for many years. I really wasn't sure what components needed to be included. I can just imagine how difficult this concept must be for my students." The teacher used this organizer as a way of introducing the unit and came back to it periodically during the lesson to reinforce the concept. At the end of the unit, the teacher had the students draw their own organizers depicting their perspective of light, and then had them develop relationships among the four variables.

The "fishbone" organizer in Figure 4.2 assists the teacher and student in effectively manipulating critical attributes of an idea, object, or concept. It helps categorize and manage data and visually structures different thinking processes. The fishbone serves the teacher and student as both an advance and a graphic organizer. This organizer was used in the questioning example earlier in the chapter as an advance organizer to help students see the major elements of the lesson on school

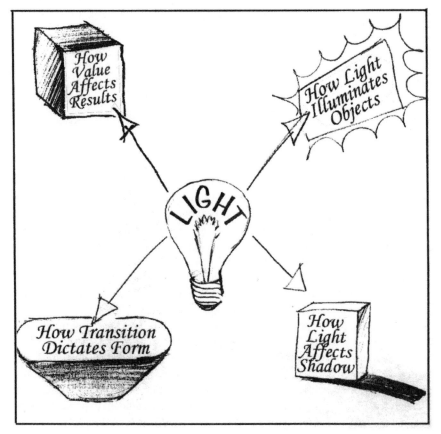

FIGURE 4.1

Graphic organizer.

(Reprinted by permission of Leonard Buscemi, Jr., Fine Arts Teacher, Nazareth High School)

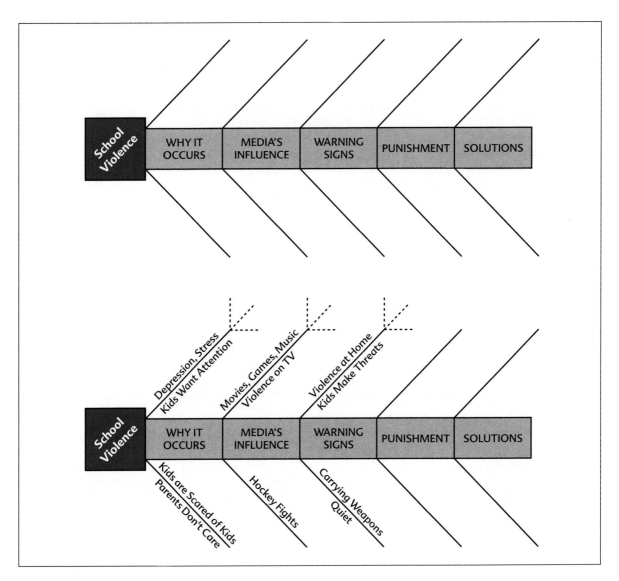

FIGURE 4.2

Fishbone organizer.

(Source: Reprinted with permission of Krista Fager.)

violence. The teacher could just provide the top organizer, to the students as a road map or design a questioning strategy that helps the students construct five core ideas related to school violence. In the bottom organizer, the students, through class discussion or think-pair groups, begin to construct more detailed information pertaining to school violence. This organizer can be expanded as indicated by the dotted lines. Here, the student could be given a newspaper or magazine article to find more information about the given topic. The fishbone is a powerful tool because it provides a structure for the content and the opportunity for the student to elaborate and collect detailed information.

The example in Figure 4.3 is from a high school biology class studying the five layers of the epidermis. The teacher required each student to construct a visual interpretation of the epidermis that represented the five layers of the epidermis. The purpose of the activity was to encourage further elaboration of content knowledge, critical thought, and creativity as a method of assessing student understanding of the concept. This activity provided an opportunity for the student to personalize the content by designing an image that represents many parts (chunking).

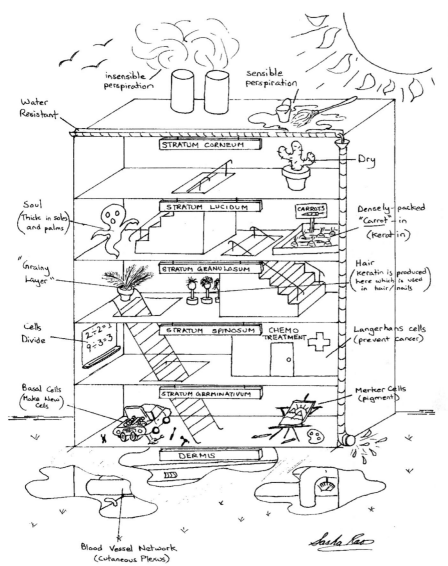

FIGURE 4.3

Five layers of the epidermis.

*(Reprinted with permission of
Sasha Rao, high school student.)*

As these examples demonstrate, graphic and visual organizers are powerful instructional strategies that provide teachers and learners with tools to explore content, concepts, and skills more meaningfully. But remember, these tools must be used with care. Students should learn how to use these tools properly if they are to help them learn. As the teacher and student struggle to learn increasingly more information, the organizer will play an important role in managing that information. Hyerle (1996) writes in reference to using visual tools:

> It is today's student's who will construct new knowledge. As we come more and more to believe that knowledge is not only interconnected but also interdependent, then we will see how much we need to provide students with dynamic new mental tools. These tools will help them unlearn and relearn what we have taught them so that they may build theories of knowledge and also have the experience and capacity to create new tools for making their world. (127)

How we use graphic and visual organizers is critical to how powerful they can be for our students. Our knowledge of questioning and cooperative learning strategies

Think about it . . . Develop an organizer that focuses on information you are currently learning in one of your classes. It need not be extremely elaborate. It might involve making an organizer on one day's notes.

Do you think this organizer might help you see the BIG picture?

Getting to the Core

⊙ CORE CONCEPT Deep (rather than surface) processing of information promotes retention, understanding, and the ability to use knowledge. The use of powerful instructional strategies encourages deep processing of information. Both deep processing and the use of powerful instructional strategies take time.

Research-Based Strategies

Interactive Direct Instruction

Powerful Questions

Using Problems to Promote Learning

Case Study Method

Project Learning as a Powerful Strategy

Learning Centers in the Classroom

What Specific Powerful Instructional Strategies Can Teachers Employ?
Graphic and Visual Organizers to Promote Learning

O🔑 Key points from *your* perspective.

How would knowing this information help Ralph?

will influence student involvement and engagement. Learning how to use effective organizers in problem-based learning, case studies, project learning, and learning centers can be critical to the success of these strategies. Organizers help students better manipulate the information they are supposed to learn. It's as simple as that. Again, it takes time for students to complete these organizers, precisely because they have to think critically about the information and make connections, draw relationships, and examine conclusions. All the powerful instructional strategies discussed in this chapter take time to engage students in meaningful learning. Therefore, it is imperative that we not lose sight of the relationship between instructional practices and the amount of time we have to accomplish our goals.

What Other Instructional Methods Can Teachers Use in Classrooms?

Naturally, there are many other instructional methods that can be, and are being, used every day by classroom teachers in their work with students. It is better to have a bit of depth with a few methods, rather than a brief exposure to many methods. After all, our core concept for Chapter 8 is *less is more*. Therefore, we present, in depth and with many examples, a few select methods that hold promise for their power to promote deep learning. They represent contemporary variations of direct instruction, discovery, inquiry, concept development, and advance organizer models. In Chapters 2 and 3 we addressed cooperative learning strategies. Some additional methods that are worth your consideration and that we will describe very briefly include:

Socratic seminars: Ball (in Canady and Rettig 1996) touts the value of Socratic seminars as an alternative to traditional discussions. According to her, during these seminars students speak 97 percent of the class time (29). As she describes it, students sit in a circle and, with the skillful guidance of a teacher, engage one another in thoughtful dialogue about a shared reading. The success of this technique is very dependent on the ability of the teacher to ask good, open-ended, higher-order questions. Three types of seminar questions are the *opening question,* the *core questions,* and the *closing question.* Whereas the opening question is broad and serves to get the students into the material that they have read, the core questions are meant to focus ensuing discussion on specific elements of the reading or material under discussion. Finally, the closing question encourages students to make a very personal connection to the material (Ball, in Canady and Rettig 1996). The Socratic seminar is generally used for text-based reading materials. It includes, as do so many other powerful strategies, the use of skillful questioning and the establishment of personal meaning. Both questioning and personal meaning have been, and will continue to be, stressed in the chapters of this textbook.

Simulations: According to Smith and Ragan (1999), "a simulation is an activity that attempts to mimic the most essential features of a reality but allows learners to make decisions within this reality without suffering the consequences of their decisions" (143). Although good simulations can be very difficult to create, the advent of computers has made it much easier to access commercially produced simulations. Companies such as Tom Snyder Productions (http://www.tomsnyder.com) and Mattel (http://www.mattelinteractive.com) produce some excellent, reasonably priced simulations that are computer based and that involve students in solving real problems. For example, *The Oregon Trail* (originally developed by MECC) puts learners into the role of the leader of a wagon party on a westward journey from Independence, Missouri, to the Willamette Valley in Oregon Territory. It is a rugged trip of approximately 2,000 miles. Many decisions must be made along the way in order to successfully make the journey. There are many authentic maps, journals, and so forth, from the 1840s to help, and the leader can even ask questions of people! Simulations have high motivational value; students typically enjoy working on real-life problems. While doing so, they learn a great deal of subject matter content. Simulations get students actively involved in their learning and increase engagement time, which in turn increases achievement. Finally, simulations can be very useful in subjects such as math and science, in contrast to Socratic seminars and synectics, which emphasize verbal subjects.

Synectics: A teaching method used to facilitate creative problem solving or stimulate creative thinking on the part of groups or individuals, synectics help students learn new material by encouraging them to make their own personal connections to it through the use of analogies. Couch (1993) identifies three types of analogies used in synectics. *Using direct analogies,* students compare two ideas or concepts. *Personal analogies* challenge students to think of themselves as objects, and then tell how they feel as those objects. *Compressed conflict* requires students to pair words or concepts that seem to contradict one another (i.e., open secret, deafening silence).

To use synectics, the teacher:

1. Chooses a topic to explore with the class, for example, pollution.

2. Asks students to generate descriptions of the topic in writing, orally, or through drawing.

3. Asks students to make a direct analogy between the topic and an object with which they are already familiar. For example, "Pollution is like a. . . ."

4. Using one of the direct analogies, the students create personal analogies. For example, "How would it feel to be pollution?"

5. Students then share their personal analogies and examine the list to look for compressed conflicts. For example, "clean pollution."

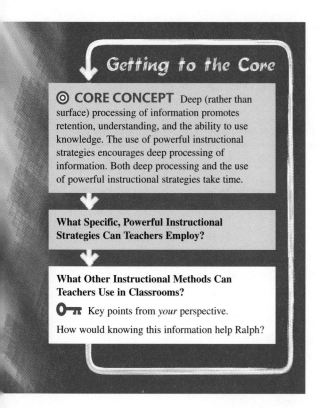

Getting to the Core

◎ **CORE CONCEPT** Deep (rather than surface) processing of information promotes retention, understanding, and the ability to use knowledge. The use of powerful instructional strategies encourages deep processing of information. Both deep processing and the use of powerful instructional strategies take time.

What Specific, Powerful Instructional Strategies Can Teachers Employ?

What Other Instructional Methods Can Teachers Use in Classrooms?

⚬╍ Key points from *your* perspective.

How would knowing this information help Ralph?

6. Students then create a new direct analogy by thinking of things such as plants, animals, or food that have the same compressed conflict.

7. Finally, the students use the new direct analogy and compare it to the original topic.

Using these steps, students should be able to examine the original topic with more insight by using rich imagery. These steps should lead to a clearer and deeper understanding of the topic (Couch 1993). Studies have demonstrated the effectiveness of synectics in grades kindergarten through 12. Note that the use of imagery and metaphor, along with forging personal connections, are aspects of the general principles of powerful learning we wrote about earlier.

You might have noticed that the three additional methods we briefly describe above all use, as an integral part of the methods themselves, some element or elements of the methods we shared with you in detail. Mastering the art of questioning, the use of organizers and imagery, the structuring of cooperative groups, the use of problems and cases, and interactive direct instruction will help you use virtually any other methods that you will come across during your teaching career.

How Can Instructional Methods Be Aligned with Standards?

We have just devoted a lot of space to helping you learn about instructional strategies. Teachers have both the right and the professional responsibility to decide *how* to teach subject matter to learners. They must do this in a way that includes what they know about their learners' developmental levels, prior understandings, and learning styles. Teachers must also keep their own teaching styles in mind as they craft instruction. They need to consider the resources that are available to them and that may help them as they provide learning experiences for their learners. Of course, the specific subject matter must also be considered, because academic disciplines often have their own, unique organizational structures. But we would be remiss if we did not address the standards-based movement that began at the end of the last century.

Standards-Based Education

Although teachers decide how to teach, one problem with American schools, at least in the eyes of some, is that teachers often make independent, idiosyncratic decisions about *what* to teach. It is true that schools have curriculum guides that specify what is to be taught at a given grade level. These guides, though, are often merely topical outlines or extended lists of expected outcomes that are overcrowded with too much material or too many outcomes; so, too, are textbooks. Schmoker and Marzano (1999) conclude, "In a system that does little or nothing to help them coordinate priorities, [teachers] are forced to select or to omit different topics haphazardly" (19). In worst case examples, we know of teachers who include only one social studies unit a year in their classroom instruction. We also know of teachers who *never* teach science.

It is against this backdrop and to address this problem that *standards-based education* has become perhaps the hottest topic in American education. The idea, at least at some level, is simple to understand. Standards make explicit that which students will know and be able to do, and then teachers work toward this achievement with the students they teach. *Content standards* express, in clear and understandable terms, what students will be taught and what they should know. *Performance standards* express what students should be able to demonstrate that they can do. Both are meant to establish priorities that focus teachers' instructional efforts on the same goals.

Standards and Powerful Instructional Strategies

Although it is too early to know for certain, let us assume that standards do not suffer the same problem they are meant to correct. So much has crept into the school curriculum that it is very difficult to bring order to the priorities. If local school districts promulgate one set of standards, the states another set, and the federal government yet another, then it is obvious that standards will not assist teachers in setting priorities; there will be too many of them! Assuming an orderly development of critically important content and performance standards, you will best serve your learners if you align your instruction to these standards. This makes it even more important that you use the most powerful instructional strategies that you can. If the standards identify core knowledge and skills that have been agreed upon by a large number of stakeholders, then it behooves you as the teacher to help your students *really* master this knowledge and these skills.

Let us use as an example the following standards from a school district (eighth grade):

> **Content standard:** Students will know that the components of a standard essay include an introduction, body, and conclusion.

> **Performance standard:** Students will be able to write a persuasive essay with a stated opinion and supporting detail.

These standards have been agreed upon, so they establish a priority for you and your students. Presumably they will also be assessed by you as well as by the school district in which you teach. So this is *what* you must teach. *How* you help the students master these standards is another matter. As a teacher, it is one of the key aspects of your job to decide the best manner in which to teach a given standard. You might decide to use a graphic organizer to help your students visualize the components of a good essay. You might even have them use imagery by creating a metaphor for an essay. Then you might engage the students in a letter writing campaign in which they attempt to convince government officials to take (or not to take) some action that has recently been highlighted in the local news. In this way you are focusing powerful instructional strategies on agreed-upon standards; this is what educators refer to as aligning instruction with standards.

Think about it . . . Locate some of the standards that have been written by the following:

- National groups such as the National Council of Teachers of Mathematics (NCTM).
- Your state department of education (often available on the World Wide Web).
- A local school district (ask the director of curriculum and instruction).

How would you use some of the strategies addressed in this chapter to help learners meet these standards?

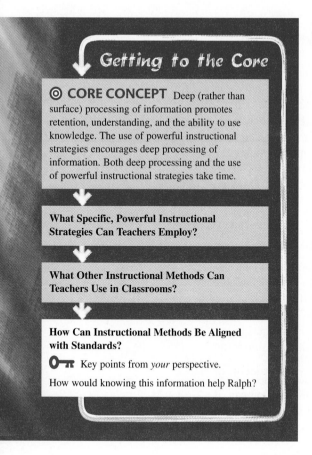

Getting to the Core

⊚ CORE CONCEPT Deep (rather than surface) processing of information promotes retention, understanding, and the ability to use knowledge. The use of powerful instructional strategies encourages deep processing of information. Both deep processing and the use of powerful instructional strategies take time.

What Specific, Powerful Instructional Strategies Can Teachers Employ?

What Other Instructional Methods Can Teachers Use in Classrooms?

How Can Instructional Methods Be Aligned with Standards?

🔑 Key points from *your* perspective.

How would knowing this information help Ralph?

SCENARIO REVISITED

Let's look back at Ralph, the teacher presented in the opening scenario. It is now time to answer the questions we posed earlier. Keep in mind the core concept for the chapter: Deep (rather than surface) processing of information promotes retention, understanding, and the ability to use knowledge. The use of powerful instructional strategies encourages deep processing of information. Both deep processing and the use of powerful instructional strategies take time.

> **?** *Why do you think Ralph's students are now learning less rather than more? What might be the biggest problem with which Ralph will now have to struggle? Can you think of what other teaching strategies Ralph might use since his lecture/question/homework approach is not working that well?*

Then, read A Voice from the Field to see how an experienced teacher responded to these very same questions. Compare your answers to the teacher's responses.

A VOICE FROM THE FIELD

Although enthusiastic about the newly afforded class time of intensive scheduling, Ralph has not changed his teaching style to promote meaningful learning. Instead, he has continued to employ instructional strategies that passively share declarative knowledge of the subject matter. Information processing theory tells us that learners can only process a limited amount of information in a fixed period of time. Ralph's students are likely supersaturated with facts during these extended class periods and not forging sufficient cognitive connections with the extra material now included in his lessons.

Many educators new to intensive scheduling are not very comfortable using, or are not correctly implementing constructivist best practices that are conducive to an increase in class time. Rather, they often find themselves looking to "fill" the time with worksheets, seat work, and videos. In addition, many teachers just continue to lecture for the full 90 minutes. These practices do not promote constructive learning—they expose students to facts that they have no real opportunity to explore for themselves. In addition, students who are not actively engaged in learning activities become restless and bored, especially with an extended 90-minute period. As a result, for some students, this inactivity lends itself to discipline problems and an overall decrease in achievement.

Another problem that Ralph may be facing is that his school, like many schools, may emphasize pedagogy that is discipline centered rather than student centered. Discipline-centered courses are content driven rather than structured around the learning needs and requirements of the student. Under this scenario, students are presented with a series of facts and formulas to be memorized as part of the curriculum requirement—and the content is divided into distinct and seemingly unrelated fragments (usually sequential chapters as presented in the text). This pedagogical focus lends itself to a classroom that is teacher centered rather than a facilitative, student-centered classroom.

To help Ralph avoid some of the issues he is facing, it would be beneficial to implement a curriculum that focuses on interrelated generative topics and active learning strategies. By providing learners with a core base of topics, as well as a sense of how they are connected, students will be better prepared to engage in active learning and problem-solving activities. A course that regularly implements successful constructive strategies and builds a program of learning around generative concepts could serve to foster student-centered learning and, therefore, involve more learning styles. By eliminating superfluous subject matter (and unnecessary filler activities), more time could be allocated to conducting learning units that allow students to actively construct knowledge via inquiry and cooperative learning groups.

The use of constructive techniques (e.g., problem-based learning, cooperative learning, inquiry, and graphic organizers) in the course honors the various learning needs and styles of students. Units and individual lessons should be structured to bridge between learning styles and modalities. If successfully implemented, these approaches to teaching should engage and motivate students of varying academic strengths, backgrounds, and capabilities for the full 90-minute period.

In reality, changing teaching styles to incorporate cognitively powerful instructional strategies requires a significant amount of planning, practice, and refining. However, intensive scheduling affords educators the opportunity to experiment and construct learner-centered, interactive, and meaningful lessons that would have been difficult to achieve in a traditional 50-minute period. Constructive learning methods prepare students to be inquisitive, interested, and active in learning. The application of such techniques may have additional positive effects in the school environment and beyond; they encourage students to learn to respect one another and to develop problem-solving skills proactively. Both qualities are applicable to real-life situations and the working environment.

A common generative theme in the biological and life sciences is the relationship between the structure and function of living organisms. This theme can be woven from the atomic level throughout the ecosystem level of biological organization. The following unit exploring eukaryotic cell structure and function was developed using active learning approaches drawn from McCarthy's 4MAT, Gregorc's learning styles, and Gardner's multiple intelligences.

Day 1

- Be able to identify each of the organelles of the cytoplasm and describe the function of each.
- Know the structures of different types of cell parts (e.g., cell wall; cell membrane; cytoplasm; cell organelles such as nucleus, chloroplast, mitochondrion, Golgi apparatus, vacuole) and the functions they perform (e.g., transport of materials, storage of genetic information, photosynthesis and respiration, synthesis of new molecules, waste disposal).

Materials

- Video: *The Magic of Cells,* tape and tape player, box, foil, and markers.

Procedures

- Cell advanced organizer: Decorate box (tape player inside) with foil, and so on, so it appears "cosmic." Have students guess what this piece of space technology is—play around with it to spark curiosity. Explain that it is a communication capsule from the future. Play a tape that describes futuristic, self-contained society (analogy for cell). Students listen once. Then play it again and ask them to draw a picture of what they are visualizing. Ask students to share results. Explain that this was an analogy for a cell and how a cell manufactures and exports proteins with its organelles.

- Have students work in groups to make a table of predictions about what structures would likely be found inside a unicellular organism—What specific functions would a one-celled organism need to carry out in order to live? (Set induction for function of organelles.) Prompting questions will be needed to get started.

- Show Magic of Cells (or laser disk segment). While viewing, ask students to determine which organelle takes care of specific functions on their list.

Days 2 to 4

- Be able to identify each of the organelles of the cytoplasm and describe the function of each.

- Know the structures of different types of cell parts (e.g., cell wall; cell membrane; cytoplasm; cell organelles such as nucleus, chloroplast, mitochondrion, Golgi apparatus, vacuole) and the functions they perform (e.g., transport of materials, storage of genetic information, photosynthesis and respiration, synthesis of new molecules, waste disposal).

- Discuss the composition of the cell nucleus and describe the function.

- Know that DNA is located in the cell nucleus and that chromosomes are composed of double-stranded DNA.

Materials

- Colored pencils and large white paper
- Laserdisc
- Overheads and pens
- Poster paper and markers
- Text books and supplementary textbooks, guides, or Internet access
- Cell project handout
- Cell organelle table
- Peer evaluation rubric

Procedures

- Draw plant and animal eukaryotic cells with students. Draw plant cell on half of the board and animal cell on other half using colored chalk. Have students draw with you at their desks using colored pencils and larger paper. As you draw organelles that are in both plant and animal cells, list them in the space in-between the cells. For organelles specific only to one

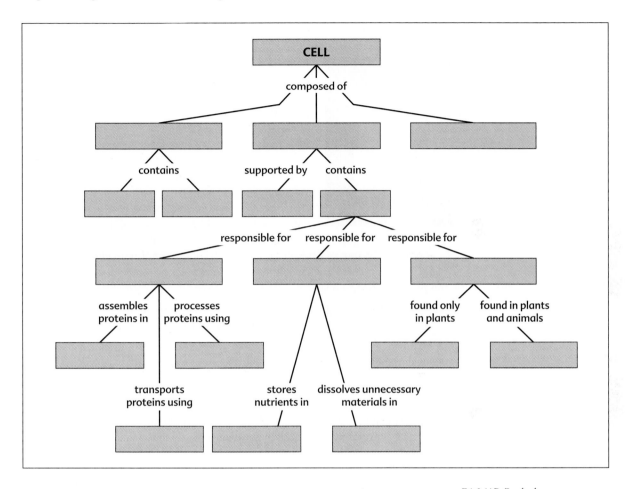

FIGURE 4.4
Cell function flow chart

cell type, label on the outer side of cell. The result is an adapted Venn diagram comparing organelles in plant and animal cells. (See Fig. 4.4.)

- Hand out project assignment.
- Student groups (two to three people) research organelle assigned to them.
- Be sure materials above are provided. Circulate to check for understanding and on-task behavior. Be sure those individuals with organelles involved in protein synthesis know that they should emphasize that information in their presentations.
- Student groups present their organelles, end with nucleus. All students must complete the cell organelle table and organizer and submit them; therefore, you will need to ask questions of other groups if information presented is not clear or information is missing.

To conclude this unit, the students do a project on cellular organelle that consists of both group and individual work (Schraer and Stoltze 1993; Organelle Project 1999).

This is the voice of Jennifer Seery. Ms. Seery is a high school biology teacher.

PLANNING FOR INSTRUCTION

◎ CORE CONCEPT Deep (rather than surface) processing of information promotes retention, understanding, and the ability to use knowledge. The use of powerful instructional strategies encourages deep processing of information. Both deep processing and the use of powerful instructional strategies take time.

In the last chapter you considered powerful learning principles and sketched out a unit of instruction. In this chapter you have learned about specific instructional strategies. As schools restructure daily schedules and number of classes students take and teachers teach each day, we must prepare to use varying lengths of instructional time to better engage our learners. Restructuring learners' time allows opportunities to explore, examine, reflect, and provide critical feedback. The powerful instructional strategies discussed in this chapter increase the potential to engage students in deep processing of declarative knowledge and in practice to promote procedural knowledge.

Remember, a unit of instruction is comprised of several individual lessons. As you continue to develop your unit of study, please focus on the design of *one lesson plan* that incorporates the following:

1. Questioning strategies that engage your learners both in lower- and higher-order thinking and that encourage deeper processing of information.

2. Graphic and visual organizers to help your learners better organize content and manipulate information in new and more expert ways.

3. One or two of the other powerful instructional strategies that allow for the learners to engage in more individualized instructional approaches.

The amount of time to teach this lesson is entirely up to you. It could take 45 to 90 minutes, several hours, or a day or more. It is always smaller than the unit of instruction.

The following lesson takes place after the section of the unit plan described in Chapter 3 that *creates an experience.* The students have connected to prior personal experiences of the four types of severe storms, discussed them, and written in their journals. Students have been presented with an advance organizer for the unit that visually illustrates how the topic of severe weather is connected to tornadoes, thunderstorms, hurricanes, and snow storms as well as how storms are measured and how severe storms impact the environment.

The following lesson is an introduction to thunderstorms. Students will have the opportunity later on in the unit to further develop the content in smaller group settings. Similar lessons will be taught for tornadoes, hurricanes, and snowstorms. Use our sample lesson to help you design your own and pay close attention to the key word "consider."

Sample Lesson

Theme: Severe Weather
Lesson Topic: Thunderstorms

Objectives

Consider
Will objectives lead you to expected outcomes?

- Identify and describe the attributes of a thunderstorm.
- Distinguish between lightning and thunder.

- Develop relationship between thunderstorms and air temperature.
- Know what weather conditions contribute to the formation of thunderstorms.
- Analyze the impact of thunderstorms on the environment.
- Create a thunderstorm safety manual for your family.

Connecting Prior Knowledge and Experience to New Learning

Consider
Have you considered students' prior experiences and knowledge of content? Students
have an understanding of what causes changes in weather. This includes the facts that
earth receives almost all its heat energy from the sun and that this energy causes
atmospheric motion, warmer air rises because it is lighter, the higher the air goes the
colder it gets, and cold air cannot hold evaporated water (water vapor) as well as
warm air. So, as the air chills the evaporated water condenses into liquid water forming clouds and eventually storms. Students, when engaged in the "creating the experience" activity, can connect personal experiences to the overall goal of the unit.

Developmental Characteristics

Consider
Are you using developmentally appropriate content and activities for this particular lesson? Tenth graders are capable of more formal thought than are younger students and have the cognitive abilities to accomplish mental manipulations and
understand abstractions. They are in the psychosocial stage of identity verses role
confusion, therefore they are concerned with identity status, sex roles, and career
choices. Peer groups and friends are important and need to be considered when
grouping. Activities need to be career oriented to show relevance.

Fifth graders are concrete operational thinkers. They think logically but will
need to generalize from concrete experiences (provide lots of hands-on activities
and manipulatives). They are much better with speech than writing, so provide
opportunities for presentations. They usually follow rules and obey authority, however reminders are needed constantly. They are in the industry-inferiority stage of
psychosocial development, which means they need to keep busy with engaging
activities that are concrete and show final outcomes and products.
Instructional Strategies (Cross Reference to Instructional Procedures):
Advance and graphic organizers, questioning strategies, cooperative learning/
group activities, learning centers, project learning, and use of technology.

Consider
Have you considered these instructional strategies in your lesson?
Instructional Procedures: Detailed description of the lesson that includes an
introduction, body of presentation, closure and assessment strategy

Consider
Did you review previously learned content and show big ideas? Review advance
organizer and communicate the goals of the unit.

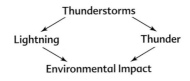

Displaying the advance organizer (AO) on an overhead projector (give written copy to student), begin lesson with a short verbal introduction to thunderstorms focusing on lightning and thunder.

Consider

Did you build new content on prior experience, personalize, encourage working together, ask good questions, and use a multisensory approach? View thunderstorm videotape (10 minutes) that shows thunderstorms and examples of origination of the lightning and where it strikes and gives a demonstration of thunder sounds at different intervals depending on location and intensity of the storm. Students record observations as they watch the video (not on advance organizer).

Following the videotape students individually record observations and then work in think-pairs to compare responses. This will activate prior knowledge, provide visual and auditory cues, and help students make specific content connections. Use the following questions to generate initial discussion:

1. What comes first, the thunder or lightning?

2. Where did most of the thunderstorms occur?

What experiences have you had that are similar to what you saw on the video?

Consider

Are you providing rich materials, continuing to encourage working together, and asking questions at lower- and higher-cognitive levels?

Following the short questioning period each student will receive a thunderstorm study pack that includes written questions, spaces for answers, and specific directions for completion. Working in think-pairs or triads, students read the information and prepare written responses. Questions are designed to challenge students at different cognitive levels and, working in small groups, to allow students to assist each other, share tasks, and teach each other.

1. What are thunderstorms? Describe lightning and thunder.

2. Does the temperature of air affect thunderstorms?

3. Can you tell how far away a storm is from where you are standing?

4. Where does lightning usually strike?

5. Is lightning really dangerous? Why? Why Not?

6. What causes the sound of thunder?

7. Why do we see lightning before we hear thunder?

8. How much electricity can a lightning bolt carry?

9. What does it feel like to be hit by lightning?

10. When you are caught in a thunderstorm, what should you do?

11. Should I be worried about thunderstorms when I am in my own house?

12. Now, create two questions about thunderstorms that were not asked. Know the answer.

Consider

Are you providing flexibility in using time to accomplish work? Give enough time to read materials and to answer questions. Use "time" wisely both in class and as homework assignments. Encourage students to work together and also complete individual work.

Consider

Are you using questioning strategies and organizers to encourage critical thinking? How are you helping students organize their thinking?

Using the advance organizer to record important information (use the overhead transparency while the student records information on AO), the teacher leads discussion to answer questions. Remember, frame the questions (ask question-pause, then call on student). Also, do not answer any of the questions yourself. Use prompting and probing techniques discussed in this chapter to elicit responses. Remember wait-time—count to three once questions are asked before calling on a student. Think time is needed. If students demonstrate difficulty with the answers, design another activity or go to original materials to fill in the missing links (scaffolding). It is critical that the correct information is recorded on the organizer. An advance organizer (Fig. A) helps students focus on key elements of the lesson. A graphic organizer that provides more detailed content with examples (Fig. B) can also be used to further develop the key points.

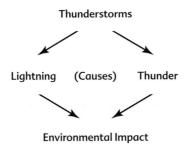

FIGURE A
Advance organizer

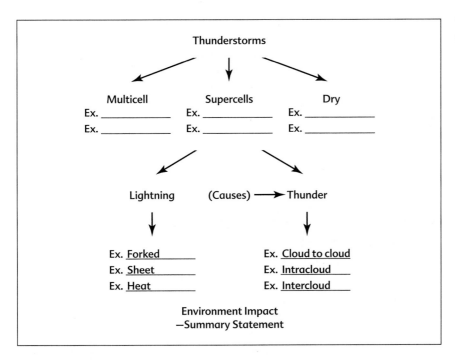

FIGURE B
Graphic organizer

Learning centers will be set up around the room to allow students to access additional reformation, materials, and Internet sites.

Consider

How will learning be demonstrated? The final stage of this lesson on thunderstorms will be project oriented. Each student will create a thunderstorm manual for the family.

Your Turn

Don't forget to *consider* the chapter's core concept and how our example structures you through the teaching process. Remember you are designing a lesson that includes powerful instructional strategies in order to engage and challenge the learner to think critically.

CHAPTER SUMMARY

In previous chapters we addressed general theories and powerful principles of learning that are rooted in theory. In this chapter we got more specific. We introduced you to some specific strategies that are rooted in both theory and the general principles we discussed earlier. These specific strategies included interactive direct instruction, questioning, problem-based learning, case studies, project learning, learning centers, and visual organizers. In less detail, we shared Socratic seminars, simulations, and synectics. All of these strategies have one thing in common. They have the potential to engage students in deep processing of declarative knowledge and practice to promote procedural knowledge. By doing so they invigorate classrooms, students, and teachers. They enliven the learning environment. They are not the only strategies that help us actually put to use the powerful principles that promote deep learning. At this point you might be able to read about other strategies not mentioned here and judge whether they will do as well in promoting true learning among students.

Providing students and teachers with opportunities to have more time for each class and, more important, more time each day to explore each subject, can help them take maximum advantage of the general and specific powerful strategies that we have championed in this and earlier chapters. If enough instructional time is provided to allow teachers to use more effectively the specific methods we have addressed in this chapter, there is a far greater chance that these teachers can promote true conceptual change among their learners. Even in traditional settings and with the usual time constraints, powerful strategies that we write about in this chapter can, and *should,* be used with learners when possible. A creative teacher can find ways to make the use of these strategies possible.

Getting to the Core

What Specific Powerful Instructional Strategies Can Teachers Employ?

Research-Based Strategies

- Research shows that instructional strategies such as identifying similarities and differences, summarizing and note taking, reinforcing effort and providing recognition, homework and

◎ CORE CONCEPT Deep (rather than surface) processing of information promotes retention, understanding, and the ability to use knowledge. The use of powerful instructional strategies encourages deep processing of information. Both deep processing and the use of powerful instructional strategies take time.

practice, nonlinguistic representations, cooperative learning, setting goals and providing feedback, generating and testing hypotheses, and activating prior knowledge most strongly affect student achievement. This research can be easily connected to some of the powerful instructional strategies mentioned in earlier chapters (prior knowledge, declarative and procedural knowledge, and cooperative learning).

Interactive Direct Instruction

- Direct instruction, one of the most traditional forms of instruction, is a teacher-centered and controlled, step-by-step process for teaching both declarative and procedural knowledge. This model uses six specific strategies (review previously learned material, state objectives, present the new material, provide guided practice with specific feedback, assign independent practice with corrective feedback, and review periodically and provide corrective feedback, if necessary). Despite the criticisms of direct instruction, it can be a valuable tool if used wisely and made interactive through simple cooperative learning techniques.

Powerful Questions

- The ability of teachers to ask higher-level thinking questions can help stimulate conversations, discussions, thinking, and exploration. High-level questions engage learners in the learning process and encourage them to respond with answers, questions, and thoughts of their own. This is a form of elaboration and is a very powerful tool that helps promote deep understanding of information. There are two major types of questions: convergent and divergent. Convergent questions are usually narrow and limit students to a single response or possibly a series of short responses. Divergent questions require a student to give more general or open responses to questions that may have more than one appropriate answer.

- Bloom's book *Taxonomy of Educational Objectives: Cognitive Domain* discusses a six-level taxonomy to help differentiate between lower- and higher-level thinking. Questions on the lower level consist of knowledge, comprehension, and application. The next three are higher level—analysis, synthesis, and finally evaluation. The higher-order thinking questions require more cognitive work, engagement, and elaboration on the part of the students. The use of framing, prompting, probing, scaffolding, wait-time, and reinforcement helps make questioning more powerful.

Using Problems to Promote Learning

- Problem-based learning gives students the opportunity to solve a complex problem while engaging in critical thinking and learning substantial content in the process. Students work together under the guidance, rather than the direction, of the teacher to solve "ill-structured" problems. They must use knowledge and skills from the various disciplines. Through this process, students learn content and skills in the context of real-world problems and situations. PBL uses powerful strategies such as cooperative learning, visual and graphic organizers, mapping out concepts and organizing information, and elaborating on that information so students are actively engaged in an authentic, real-world situation.

Case Study Method

- The case study method is an instructional strategy that employs the use of case studies (intensive study of a person or situation) to actively engage the learner in a problem-solving activity. Students are challenged to work through the presented information to draw conclusions or support personal opinions. Learners are called on to carefully observe data, problem solve, make inferences, and discuss generalizations and conclusions that are personally relevant.

Project Learning as a Powerful Strategy

- Project-centered activities, if structured properly, allow the student or group of students to be immersed in one big idea or to work toward a common goal. These projects challenge the learner to use a wide variety of skills, knowledge, and intelligences while they are involved in a meaningful activity. Projects are very often multidimensional and encourage learners to extend their understanding of content to a real-world experience.

Learning Centers in Your Classroom

- Learning centers provide learners with a place to explore selected content through a variety of different mediums (written, audio, visual, computer, and manipulatives). In addition, centers can be designed so that learners can work at their own pace, thus meeting a wide range of academic levels that challenge many of learners' intelligences and provide ample opportunities for students to exert their individual differences.

Graphic and Visual Organizers to Promote Learning

- Using graphic and visual organizers is a powerful way to help students master declarative and procedural knowledge. They encourage learners to draw visual representations and make connections among facts, ideas, and concepts. By creating these graphic and visual organizers, students actually organize content and information in a way that best fits their individual learning styles. Organizers help learners see patterns, relationships, and whole pictures in their learning, not just isolated bits and pieces of information.

What Other Instructional Methods Can Teachers Use in Classrooms?

- Socractic seminars can serve as a valuable alternative to traditional discussions about a shared reading. Their success depends on the teacher's use of skillful questioning and the student's establishment of personal meaning connected to the material. Simulations are highly motivational learning tools that involve students working on real-life problems. Through synectics, students learn new material by making personal connections to it through the use of analogies, imaging, and metaphor.

How Can Instructional Methods Be Aligned with Standards?

- Standards-based education was developed to establish priorities that focus teachers' instructional efforts on common goals. It provides teachers with a specific outline of what students will learn and be able to accomplish. Content standards express what students will be taught and what they should know and performance standards express what students should be able to demonstrate that they can do.

Changing Classroom Practices to Accommodate Learner Differences

CHAPTER 5

Teaching and Learning Styles

"Daddy, why do you have your cap on backwards?"

FAMILY CIRCUS *(Source: Reprinted with special permission of King Features Syndicate.)*

 SCENARIO

Ms. Beidler decides to assign a major project to her seventh graders. Under her guidance and with her instruction, her learners just finished learning about research and the elements of a research paper. They completed a short project for practice. Now she plans to assign an open-ended project with only three stipulations. First, the research has to stem from something that her pupils always wanted to know more about or understand better. Second, following the statement of the major question there must be several subquestions that will help lead to answers to the major questions. Third, at the end of their quest there must be a final paper and a presentation to the rest of the class members that shares what was learned.

Ms. Beidler presents this assignment to her learners on a Monday morning. Then she asks for questions. Immediately Sammy's hand shoots up. He wants to know how long the paper has to be, and also what form the presentation can take. Sally pursues this line of questions with "How many sources must we have?" As Ms. Beidler listens, Jill offers that maybe they can make these decisions on their own with the teacher's help since the directions were not very specific. John agrees, saying that he likes to have some "space" and that in the past there were just "too many pages of directions to follow." Linda asks if she can work with somebody else on this project. But Lou says he would rather work on something this big by himself. Ms. Beidler, meanwhile, is struck by the conversation that is taking place. She normally gives specific directions for projects, but decided to experiment with a more open-ended approach this once. Now she realizes for the first time the diverse preferences in what she assumed was a rather homogeneous group of talented preteens. She is not quite certain about what to do next—give more explicit directions or stay the course with a more open-ended project.

> **?** *Why do you think Sammy and Sally are more focused on the need for specific information than are Jill and John? And why might Linda want to work with another classmate whereas Lou prefers to work alone? What might others be thinking but not articulating during this discussion? If you were Ms. Beidler, what would you do now, and why?*

INTRODUCTION

Indeed, all of us do have our little ways, somewhat like the young athletes who appear on ball fields ready to play baseball. They come with different kinds of bats, gloves, uniforms, shoes, glasses, levels of experience, and attitudes toward winning and losing. Their approaches to the game differ, sometimes in little ways and sometimes in big ways. Is this much different than the ways these young athletes might approach

> *"A trifling matter, and fussy of me, but we all have our ways."*
>
> **—Eeyore to Pooh in A. A. Milne's *The House at Pooh Corner***

everyday tasks and, for that matter, the way they learn? Each of us is equipped differently and these differences in our students must be carefully examined and understood if we are to maximize the chances of success we have in helping each individual student to learn. In fact, these differences can actually *enhance* the learning environment in ways we will discuss later on.

In the chapters that preceded this one, we addressed learning as if all human beings are the same, and as if we all learn in exactly the same manner. Now, it is true that by virtue of being human we all share many similarities. That also applies to the ways in which we learn. The theories and powerful strategies that we presented earlier generally apply to all of us. They are sufficiently sound to allow you to use them as a basis upon which to build your teaching practices. Still, it is undeniably true and biologically proven that indeed we are not all exact clones of one another. What a boring world it would be if we were all exact copies of one another. Differences among people are what make the planet such an interesting place to live, and differences among learners can make our classrooms that much more interesting as places to learn. These differences can, if used to their fullest advantage, enrich the learning environment and benefit everyone in it.

It is not just learners who are unique and bring their own gifts to the classroom setting. Teachers, too, are human beings! They bring important individual differences to the classroom setting. The combinations of individual differences that learners and teachers bring to the classroom can be understood in light of social categories and theories grouped together under the common category of learning and teaching styles. It is to these categories and styles that we shall now turn our attention.

Before we turn to social and learning style differences, however, it is important that you think about your own background and style preferences.

1. Do you perceive things as they are, or as they might be?
2. Do you use logic, or gut feelings, to think about problems and their solutions?
3. Do you prefer to work alone, or in the company of others?
4. Do you like closure in your life, or do you constantly seek new experiences?
5. Do you prefer ideas, or do you prefer facts?
6. Would someone characterize your room as orderly or messy?
7. How has your family's socioeconomic level affected your experiences in life?
8. How has your ethnic heritage affected your educational experiences?
9. How has your gender been a liberating or restricting influence on your experiences in our mainstream culture?

Please put your answers to these questions aside for the moment. We shall return to them later on.

How Do the Social Categories of Culture, Class, and Gender Differences Affect Our Classrooms?

In this chapter, and in the two that follow it, we would like you to consider teaching and learning through a *social justice perspective.* Oakes and Lipton (1999) define this perspective as doing three things: (1) "It considers the values and politics that pervade education, as well as the more technical issues of teaching and organizing the schools; (2) it asks critical questions about how conventional thinking and practice came to be, and who in society benefits from them; and (3) it pays particular attention to inequalities associated with race, social class, language, gender, and other social categories, and looks for alternatives to the inequalities." To narrow the focus in line with the core concepts and intent of this textbook, we shall address only number 3.

Social categories of culture (ethnicity and race), social class, and gender are especially important to the kind of teaching and learning that we have advocated in earlier chapters. That is so because learners build upon what they already know, their prior knowledge, in order to learn new things. In addition, they do this learning best in interaction with other learners and with their teachers. Therefore, what learners bring to school with them is absolutely crucial to consider when we try to help them learn new information and skills. It is also important to consider these social categories when we assess what learners have actually learned, or when we decide to make educational decisions for them based upon assessment data.

Regarding teaching and learning, the differences that learners bring into our schools and classrooms first must be understood, and then used, to benefit all learners and maximize their opportunities to learn. What is it, then, that we should understand? And how might we use that information in our classrooms?

Social class is determined by socioeconomic status. Socioeconomic status, most commonly known as (SES), refers to the relationship between family income, occupation, and formal education of parents. Research has consistently demonstrated that SES is directly correlated with school performance. Specifically, SES predicts intelligence (as measured by IQ tests), student grades and scores on achievement tests, and attendance (including dropping out of school and suspensions) (McLoyd 1998; Macionis 1997; and Miller 1995). Consider the following statistics on SES from The National Center for Children in Poverty (1999) and Young and Smith (1999), reported by Eggen and Kauchak (2001), and what influence they might have on the classroom and the teacher's ability to provide effective instruction.

A Person Who Helped Create Change . . .

Jeannie Oakes is Presidential Professor of Education in the Graduate School of Education and Information Studies at the University of California, Los Angeles, where she directs IDEA, UCLA's Institute for Democracy in Education, and Access.

Formerly a senior social scientist at RAND, Oakes received her Ph.D. in Education from UCLA in 1980 after a seven-year career as a public school English teacher. She has studied the very important issue of how tracking and ability grouping affect the school experiences of low-income students and students of color, most of whom are identified as "low" ability or as slow learners. This work is the subject of her widely read book, *Keeping Track: How Schools Structure Inequality* (1985), and *Multiplying Inequalities* (1990). Her most recent books are *Teaching to Change the World* (1999) and *Becoming Good American Schools: The Struggle for Civic Virtue in Educational Reform* (2000). *Becoming Good American Schools* won the AERA Outstanding Book Award in 2001. It focuses on promoting socially just classrooms and schools.

Source: Professor UCLA.
http:www.gseis.ucla.edu/faculty/pages/oakes.html

- Children living in poverty under the age of six increased from 3.5 million to 5.2 million between the years 1979 to 1997.

- The poverty rate in 1995 for children was 20 percent but varied depending upon different populations. For Whites it was 16 percent, for Hispanics it was 39 percent, and for Afro-Americans it was 42 percent.

- The percentage of children living in single-parent homes has more than doubled since 1970, averaging 25 percent for all families, with higher rates for Afro-American (60 percent) and 29 percent for Hispanic families.

- The poverty rate for parents who didn't graduate high school was 62.5 percent.

Impoverished families often suffer poor health and nutrition. Over half of impoverished young mothers receive no prenatal care and are more likely to have premature babies. Children in poverty are more likely to have been exposed to drugs and alcohol before birth. They are more likely to have suffered the effects of lead poisoning. All of these may lead to neurological impairments and lower school achievement (McLoyd 1998).

What are teachers to do to help children and adolescents from low SES homes? Among many other things, they can:

- Encourage students and their families to take advantage of community resources that provide for such things as free or subsidized breakfasts and lunches, and that provide emotional support for them.

- Make use of any home resources, such as parents, grandparents, and local recreational and cultural facilities to promote involvement of the learner in appropriate activities.

- Establish nurturing, caring, and safe in-school environments so that learners feel a sense of belonging and safety.

- Communicate the same levels of expectation to low SES learners as they do to all other learners, with appropriate support mechanisms to make achievement attainable.

Culture is a larger concept than is SES and includes values, customs, religious preferences, physical characteristics and traits, attitudes, and beliefs. All these variables are a reflection of the learner's social group. *Ethnicity* and *race* are part of a learner's culture. Ethnicity refers to a way a family, group of people, or individuals identify with their ancestors and where they are from. Groups reflect ethnicity in the holidays they celebrate, the foods they eat, and the religions they practice. Race refers to specific traits such as skin, hair, and eye coloring. Here we will focus on ethnicity and race in the larger context of culture, keeping in mind that the major goal is to help all children achieve to their greatest ability. The following population trends indicate how the culture of our schools will change as our general culture changes.

- 14 million people immigrated to the United States between 1970 and 1990. Between 1980 and 1994, Asian American students increased by 100 percent, Hispanic students increased by 46 percent, African American students by 25 percent and Caucasian students by only 10 percent. Between 1980 and 1990, 80 percent of all immigrants came from nations in Latin America and Asia and only 9 percent from Europe. By 2050, 47.5 percent of the nation's population will be made up of people of color (U.S. Bureau of Census 1996).

- In 1997, 12 percent of all Americans were African American, 11 percent were Hispanic, 3.5 percent were Asian, and 0.77 percent were Native American (U.S. Bureau of Census 1997).

- Experts predict that by the year 2020 the Caucasian student population will decrease by 11 percent. The Asian American student population will increase 100 percent. The Hispanic student population will increase between 47 and 61 percent. African American students will increase between 15 and 20 percent, and the Asian/Pacific Islander/American Indian/Alaskan Native student population will increase between 67 and 73 percent (Young and Smith 1999).

- Ormrod (2000) summarized research on the many ways the cultures of some ethnic minority students may be very different from the culture of the typical North American classroom. Ormrod noted differences in language and dialect, sociolinguistic conventions (use of silence and wait-time when speaking or speaking only when spoken to), cooperation versus competition, private versus public performance, eye contact, conceptions of time (punctual), types of acceptable questions asked, and family relationships and expectations.

Given these data, teachers will need to build classroom environments that are inclusive in the truest sense of the word. These classrooms will have to invite all learners into the teaching and learning process. To do this, teachers will have to:

- Be more sensitive to peer differences in languages, holidays, religions, physical characteristics, values, and beliefs.

- Adapt to the predominant culture without losing their own cultural identity.

- Celebrate the differences and commonalties among ethnic groups.

- Celebrate and recognize different holidays and why and how they are celebrated.

- Understand how community leaders of ethnic groups are role models and ways they have achieved their status.

- Identify how people of different ethnic groups have made contributions to society and how they represent their ethnic group to the community.

- Have learners trace the historical routes of their ethnic groups through interviews, readings, and Internet activities.

- Help learners work with others who come from backgrounds different from their own on classroom projects and extracurricular school activities.

- Build lessons and units related to their learners' and other people's cultural backgrounds.

- Use curriculum materials that are culturally sensitive and show positive attributes of different cultures.

Gender differences have been studied with great interest in the past several decades. The research that has been amassed leads to conclusions that have important implications for teachers. That research suggests that:

- Boys are allowed to roam farther from home at earlier ages than girls, and are given more independence to handle personal problems on their own. Girls are less likely to be able to play more dangerous games, cross the street by themselves, and are more often helped by their parents when problems arise. Both initiative and independence are more encouraged in boys than girls (Fagot et al. 1985).

- Young children, especially preschoolers, often talk about gender roles in school. Preschoolers are inclined to stereotype gender roles and have traditional ideas about what boys can do and what girls can do. Older children appear to have more rigid interpretations of male occupations than of female occupations (Martin 1989). Furthermore, parents encourage many of these behaviors that lead to stereotyping.

- Television, movies, video games, children books, and many elementary reading primers promote gender stereotyping. Often these media show males as aggressive, problem solvers, and leaders, whereas females are depicted as followers, helpers, and as generally less aggressive (Sadker and Sadker 1994).

- Peers more often react positively to friends that play in gender-appropriate roles and negatively to those who do not. (Eisenberg, Martin, and Fabes 1996). Furthermore, many children will ridicule or avoid peers who are good in gender-inappropriate roles (such as boys who like to dance or write poetry and girls who excel in math and science) (Sadker and Sadker 1994).

- Gender bias has traditionally been prevalent in the mathematics and sciences where women are greatly underrepresented. The National Science Foundation has been making a major effort to recruit woman as well as minorities into math- and science-related fields of study. Recent studies indicate that girls are being encouraged to enroll in mathematics-related courses, and that test scores in mathematical proficiency are closer among boys and girls, especially in the later grades. In science, the studies showed boys slightly ahead of girls in grades 4 to 12 with very little difference in grade 12. This would indicate that gender differences are subsiding (O'Sullivan, Reese, and Mazzeo 1997; Reese, Miller, and Doose 1997; Rop 1998).

- Boys outnumber girls in math and remedial English classes, are more often held back a grade, and are placed in special education two to three times more often than girls. In measures of writing abilities, boys consistently receive lower grades than do girls (Willingham and Cole 1997).

- Single-gender classrooms and schools have found that girls are more likely to ask and answer questions in middle school mathematics classes as compared to girls in coeducational classes. These girls view themselves more as mathematicians. Research has demonstrated that in single-gender schools girls adopt more leadership roles, enroll in more science and math courses, and feel they are in more control of their learning (Streitmatter 1997).

- Research on single-gender classes and schools has shown their positive effects in achievement in areas such as mathematics and science but also that they encourage stereotypical attitudes toward the opposite sex. Additionally, separating boys and girls does not prepare these students for coexistence in the workplace (Datnow, Hubbard, and Conchas 1999).

- In elementary classrooms, boys receive more praise, criticism, and rewards from teachers than do girls. Boys generally ask more questions and present more discipline problems. Teachers interact more with the higher-achieving boys than they do with the higher-achieving girls (Sadker and Sadker 1994). Teachers tend not to answer all of boys' questions, but rather help them think through the solution to obtain the right answers. With girls, teachers tend to just tell them the right answer (Sadker and Sadker 1985). Additionally, boys are usually encouraged to try harder when they are having difficulty getting correct answers, whereas girls are praised for just trying to work toward correct responses. Teachers generally expect less from girls (Eccles and Jacobs 1986).

What can teachers do to diminish gender biases in their classrooms? The following suggestions can help in this regard:

- Be sensitive to and aware of unconscious gender bias—videotape classes to observe on whom you call, and the level of questions and types of feedback you give to male and female students.

- Be conscious of roles you give students in cooperative learning groups, role-plays, and classroom assignment responsibilities.

- Pay close attention to instructional materials, including magazines and books, videos, and computer materials and choose those that do not feed into stereotypical conceptions of gender or race.

- Do not hesitate to allow girls and boys to work in single-gender groups. This will allow both genders to assume roles sometimes designated only to the opposite gender.

- Allow time in class for students to discuss gender bias and roles they assume.

- Use gender-free language as much as possible. Try not to generalize careers/jobs that tend to lead the student to think that only one gender fits the role. For example, use firefighter instead of fireman, mail carrier instead of mailman, and chairperson instead of chairman.

- Provide written material, books, and films written and produced by both men and women. Provide examples of how both men and women are important in what is being studied or investigated.

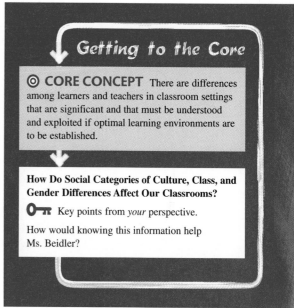

Getting to the Core

◎ **CORE CONCEPT** There are differences among learners and teachers in classroom settings that are significant and that must be understood and exploited if optimal learning environments are to be established.

How Do Social Categories of Culture, Class, and Gender Differences Affect Our Classrooms?

⊶ Key points from *your* perspective.

How would knowing this information help Ms. Beidler?

What Do We Mean by "Styles"?

Social categories are not the only ways that people differ from one another. Even within social categories, learners differ in their preferred ways of learning. Just as schools favor learners of certain social categories, they also seem to favor learners who have certain styles. It seems as if schools favor some learners over others.

Styles are simply *typical preferences that we have and that cause us to behave in predictable ways.* You have probably had someone, perhaps a good friend, say to you, "You are just not yourself today." Sound familiar? You might well have said the same thing to others. Well, of course you are still yourself. Who else would you be? But you are not acting in the same ways that others who know you have come to expect. That is, you are acting out of character, or out of style. When we come to know someone well we become familiar with his or her style. We can then predict how a person will react or respond under particular circumstances. It works the same way with learners in our classrooms.

Many people give lip service to the fact that we are all individuals and, as such, differ from one another in some ways. At job interviews teacher candidates can often be heard to express this very point. Responding to questions about teaching methods, these candidates typically make some vague comment to the effect that they would "treat each child as an individual" and try to "meet each child's needs." When pressed, they can often mumble something about social class and

> Think about it . . .
>
> **Suppose you were asked to be specific about ways that children differ from one another in terms of their learning styles and preferences. What would you say?**

racial differences. When further pressed, they are hard put to go beyond these slogans and generalities. This is true of experienced teachers as well. It is possible to understand styles well enough to operationalize individual differences, and to be able to elaborate on the general answers usually offered during interviews and discussions.

What Do Learning Styles Have to Do with Active Processing of Information?

When examined closely, many of today's most influential learning style theories share a common theoretical framework. They are built on two major dimensions in which humans differ, often independent of the specific social categories to which we belong:

1. The manner in which we *take in,* or *perceive,* stimuli.

2. The manner in which we *process, order,* or *make decisions about using* the stimuli.

Understanding these two dimensions helps you understand much about learning (and teaching) styles. These dimensions are important to understand because human beings spend their waking hours actively exploring the world around them, seeking to understand it and live in it comfortably. We tend to seek stimuli, and then to organize them to make sense of the environment in which we live. These tendencies come naturally to us, and that we differ in how we exercise them makes the world an interesting place in which to live, and the classroom an interesting place in which to learn.

A very common way of understanding different styles, with a long tradition in education, is to consider the sensory channels, or modalities, through which we prefer to learn information. The most common modalities used in school are visual, auditory, kinesthetic (large-muscle movement), and tactile (touch). These are often referred to as VAKT. It is important to know about these basic modalities, and the importance of varying instructional activities to accommodate them. In Chapter 3 we addressed the importance of active learning (AKT) and the power of visuals (V) in helping learners deeply process information.

Interestingly, two people can look at, and listen to, the very same stimulus and perceive it quite differently. Some of us, for example, will focus on the physical attributes of the stimulus. We will look carefully at the way the lines are configured, the shades of each section if it is a complex picture, and so on. Others among us will take in the entire stimulus, or the "big picture." They will look at, for example, relationships among items in the picture. The ways we perceive or take in stimuli from our environment differ among people along a continuum. These differences have been used to formulate learning style theories.

We not only differ in the way we take in stimuli, but in what we do with the information once we take it in. Some of us put the things we perceive into neat

> Think about it . . . Look at any picture or photograph of people engaged in an activity that you have on hand. When you look at it, are you drawn to the items of clothing the people are wearing? Do you notice the details in the picture? Or are you drawn to what the people might be doing, or why they are doing it, or what they might do next?
>
> Show the picture to a friend. Is he or she drawn to the same things?

categories in a logical fashion, in an attempt to impose a structure or order on them. Others are more likely to care less about order and structure of information they have perceived; rather, they tend to want to continue perceiving even more information and they organize these perceptions much more loosely than others do.

Well, that is the general way in which we operate in regard to actively processing information that presents itself in our environments. Let's recall for a moment what we learned earlier about information processing theory (IPT). Stimuli from the environment impinge upon our senses, including among others, our auditory, visual, tactile, and kinesthetic senses. Many of the stimuli simply decay because they are not recognized or attended to. But those we attend to move forward to working memory, where we begin to actively process information. And although IPT does not address the different ways people perceive and use information, that is exactly what we shall turn to now. Understanding these differences will help *you* elaborate on IPT and all the powerful strategies that emanate from it by taking a general model of human learning and informing it with learning style theories.

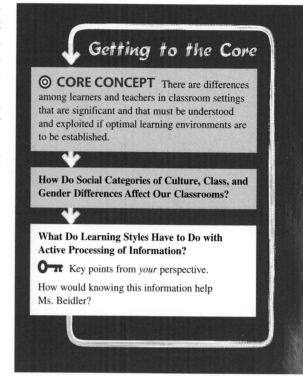

Getting to the Core

◉ **CORE CONCEPT** There are differences among learners and teachers in classroom settings that are significant and that must be understood and exploited if optimal learning environments are to be established.

How Do Social Categories of Culture, Class, and Gender Differences Affect Our Classrooms?

What Do Learning Styles Have to Do with Active Processing of Information?

🔑 Key points from *your* perspective.

How would knowing this information help Ms. Beidler?

What Is Psychological Type?

Think for a moment about ways that you and one of your very good friends are similar and different. Think about going to a restaurant with this friend. Does one of you greet the waiter easily and engage in animated conversation with him, while the other sits quietly by, barely saying anything? When it comes time to order your food, maybe one of you knows right away what you want to order (because that person always orders the same thing?), whereas the other can't decide because "everything looks so good." When the food arrives, does one of you eat the main entrée first, then the side dishes, in some type of order, and the other just digs in sampling everything seemingly at once? Does any of this sound familiar to you? If not, just think about being with a different friend! Eventually you will be able to relate to this scenario. We have all had experiences similar to this one. When people differ from us, there is the potential to get angry with them. We are, after all, certain that they were put on this earth to make our lives absolutely miserable. But if we know that people differ from one another and, most important, if we have a way of understanding these differences, then we are in a position to at least tolerate, and maybe even value, these differences.

When two or more people differ, there is the potential for each to enrich the other in ways we cannot even imagine. In a classroom setting, we can strive to actually *celebrate* these differences, a point well made by Myers (1990) in her book *Gifts Differing.* Carl Jung's (1971) theory of psychological type, and Myers's (1980) and Mamchur's (1996) connection to educational practice, have given us ways to understand these differences in terms of classrooms and the learners in them. Psychological type has to do with our preferences much in the same way that learning styles do.

The Different Psychological Types

Jung helped us understand the preferences that human beings have for behaving in the environment. Essentially, there are four mental functions that we humans use daily. They are sensing (S), intuition (N), thinking (T), and feeling (F). We differ only in the priority we give to each function, and in the attitudes, introversion (I) or extroversion (E), in which we use the function (Myers and McCaulley 1985).

Specifically, Jung, Myers, McCaulley, and others explain that one difference among us is the way we prefer to acquire information. Some people prefer to focus on realities, work with what is given, and focus on the physical aspects of a stimulus. They prefer facts and details. These people are *sensors* (S). They prefer to get information directly from their senses (auditory, visual, tactile, etc.). In contrast are people who prefer to take in meanings and relationships, who make sense of their worlds by creating patterns, and who prefer to see the big picture. They are *intuitors* (N). They prefer to use intuition as they acquire information from environmental stimuli. Everyone falls somewhere along a continuum between sensing and intuition. Some of us have a very strong preference for one way of acquiring information over another, and some of us have less strong preferences. It is very important to understand, however, that we take in information using *both* our senses and intuitions—it is just that we often have a preference for one way over another. Do you prefer sensing, or intuition? Look back at your answer to question 1 on page 162. If you perceive things as they are you might prefer sensing. If you perceive things as they might be, you may well prefer intuition.

Another difference among human beings is the way we prefer to make decisions once we have taken in information. Some people make decisions using dispassionate logic. They analyze information and strive for objectivity in decision making. They are called *thinkers* (T). Contrast them with people who prefer to make decisions on the basis of how these decisions feel to them. This preference is very subjective and empathetic, and is often centered on personal values. People with this preference for making decisions are called *feelers* (F). Again, we make decisions using both thinking and feeling, but usually we have a preference for one over the other. How about you? Look back at your answer to question 2 on page 162. If you use logic you are most likely a thinking type, and if you use gut feelings you might be a feeling type.

In addition to priorities given to these functions, we also differ in the attitudes in which we use each function. Basically, these attitudes have to do with where we prefer to focus our attention. Some people prefer to focus on the outer world of people and things. They prefer action and variety. They tend to be very talkative. They are called *extraverts* (E) and are characteristically outgoing. Other people focus their energies or attention on the inner world of personal thoughts and ideas. They prefer having time to reflect before they act. These people are called *introverts* (I) and are typically quiet and reserved. These attitudes are probably not new to you. They have made it into the vernacular and are quite often used by people in everyday conversation. These attitudes are especially important to understand in social settings—and classrooms are social settings. We shall return to this point later. But first, think once again about yourself. Return to page 162 and look at your answer to question 3. If you prefer working alone or with only one other person, perhaps a close friend, you might be an introverted type. If you prefer the company of others, and the more the merrier, you probably are an extroverted type.

So far we have discussed the four functions of S, N, T, and F, and the two attitudes of E and I. That's about as far as Jung took it. But implicit in Jung's work, according to Myers and McCaulley (1985), was the *overall* preference individuals have for either perception (acquiring or taking in information, the S and N functions) or judgment (doing something or making decisions based on information, the T and F functions). When Isabel Myers and Katharine Briggs developed the Myers-Briggs type indicator (MBTI), they made these explicit. The overall preferences we have for the perception function or the judgment function are ways we use to orient ourselves *to the outer world*. People who prefer judging to perceiving like order, regulation, and control. They strive for organization and closure in their world. They are judgers (J). People who prefer perceiving to judging like flexibility and spontaneity. They like to keep options open, and they seek to understand and follow their own curiosity rather than predict and control. They are perceivers (P). Again, Myers and McCaulley remind us that for every type of person, *the J-P scale describes the orientation to the extraverted, or outer, world.* They say that because these dimensions show in the outer world, they are among the earliest recognized. And they further point out that perceivers, while they use both S and N functions to perceive and T and F functions to judge, typically linger in the perceiving function. Judgers, on the other hand, move more quickly through perception in order to reach conclusions. What about you? Return one last time to page 162 and look at your answer to question 4. If you prefer closure, you are probably a judging type. If you prefer to seek new experiences, then it is likely that you are a perceiving type.

Extraverts (E)	Focus on outer world of people and things, talkative, action oriented.
Introverts (I)	Focus on inner world of thoughts and ideas, quiet, reflective.
Sensors (S)	Reality oriented, practical, prefer facts and details.
Intuitors (N)	Possibilities oriented, look for BIG picture, imagination, and inspiration.
Thinkers (T)	Objective, analytical, logical.
Feelers (F)	Person-centered values, sympathetic, tactful, value harmony.
Judgers (J)	Planned, orderly, organized, seek closure.
Perceivers (P)	Flexible, spontaneous, adaptable, keep options open.

Source: Summarized from the work of McCaulley (1976).

So there you have it. A way to really understand individual differences! As you can surmise from what has been explained thus far, by putting together the four preferences of any given person we come up with 16 possible psychological types. For example, a person who prefers to direct his or her energy to the outside world (E), to perceive using sensing (S), to judge using feeling (F), and to seek organization in the outer world (J), has the psychological type of ESFJ. By convention, the attitude of E or I always comes first in the type, followed by the perceiving function of either S or N, followed by the judging function of T or F, and ending with the orientation to the outer world of J or P. Knowing this, we can at least understand another person.

Think about it . . .

Now, we would like you to try to understand Roger. He was a child in one of the author's classes a few years back. The author kept anecdotal notes on observations of children in the classroom over a period of several weeks to try to understand their personalities. The author made these observations not only in class, but also during assemblies, recess, and so forth. Here is how the author summarized his observations of Roger:

> Roger communicates well and greets people easily. He has a relatively short attention span, possibly because he is so enthusiastic about activities that involve action. In fact, he often initiates and promotes new ideas and activities, and he has a decided distate for work that needs to be precise and that includes many details. This very personable young man loves to work in groups, but he is easily upset if there is conflict among group members. Actually, he seems more interested in people than in ideas. His parents report that Roger is a real adventurer. He is very curious and is constantly searching for new experiences. He starts so many new projects that he has difficulty finishing them all.

First, write down the four-letter type that you think might best describe *your* type.

Write down the four letters that you think describe Roger's style preferences, and why. Then, turn to page 199 to see if you are correct.

Now, suppose that Roger is in your class. Psychological type is interesting, you might be thinking, but how is it related to what goes on in classrooms? We will turn to this question next. Note first, however, that we came to know Roger's style by observing him in the learning environment, *not* by testing him. Just *watch* your learners, and *listen* to them, and then apply type theory as you just did with Roger.

SPOTLIGHT ON BEHAVIOR MANAGEMENT

"But will they behave?"

Managing Individual Differences

This chapter asked you to focus on the importance of accommodating your students' individual differences. Clearly this fits comfortably with the concepts we have been developing in this behavior management strand. If we are to keep conflicts from escalating in our classrooms and schools, we truly need to understand the individual needs of our students. We need to make connections with them. We need to care. Our students must feel like they belong in our classrooms and schools. In the book, *I See a Child,* Cindy Herbert (1974) writes:

> The relationship that develops between the teacher and student forms a foundation for what is taught and learned in the classroom. . . . A positive relationship takes conscious work to see the other person as he truly is. At first, most of the work must come from me, the teacher. My responsibility is not as easy as it seems: I must become interested in another human being. (3)

⊚ **CORE CONCEPT**   There are differences among learners and teachers in classroom settings that are significant and that must be understood and exploited if optimal learning environments are to be established.

Becoming interested in our students, as Herbert (1974) sees it, goes much deeper than developing a casual interest. If you have followed the explanation of the conflict cycle, you will have gathered that the more deeply you understand your students' needs, the easier it is to avoid escalating a conflict. With this deeper understanding you will be able to explain and work with your own counteraggression. Additionally, you will be more effective in teaching your students how to solve their own problems.

More recently, Hewitt (1998) stated, "One of the factors that I have found very important in determining how much students care about their behavior is *how valued they feel by the people around them*" (155) [italics in original]. Our students must feel like they are wanted and cared for in our schools. Unfortunately, for many students this is not happening:

- In 1997, Luke Woodham, a high school student in Pearl, Mississippi, stabbed his mother to death then went to school and murdered his girlfriend. Before he was apprehended he had killed another girl and wounded seven more. When recently interviewed by a secret service psychologist he stated, "In my life things have never been okay. . . . It never seemed like anybody cared" (CBS News 2000).

- A sobering letter to the editor of a college newspaper, sparked by the Columbine High School shooting, described the life of a high school student as painful and frustrating because of the constant bullying he suffered. Painting a vivid picture, he describes the rage that built up in him over the course of several years. One day the last straw was cast and he put his hands around the neck of another student, choking him. Although the description of how this bullying and teasing fueled his anger and frustration is a powerful insight, even more disturbing is his observation that the adults never stepped in. Not when he was the victim. Not even when he was the victimizer. In fact, he points out that the choking incident took place in a classroom and *in front of a teacher* (Fransen 1999)!

- The Massachusetts Governor's Commission on Gay and Lesbian Youth (1993) found that 97 percent of students in public high schools report regularly hearing homophobic remarks from peers. Astonishingly, the commission also found that 53 percent of students report hearing homophobic comments made by school staff.

As we grapple with trying to understand these horrendous acts, several patterns emerge. These students talk of (1) having no significant connection to one or more caring adults, (2) suffering constant, intense bullying, and (3) being unable to rely on adults to step in and stop the words or actions.

Research is bearing out that teachers do very little to stop bullying (Froschl and Gropper 1999; Olweus 1993). The following journal entry by one of our freshmen, who was recently completing a fieldwork component of our teacher preparation program, confirms the research:

> While walking to the next class a fight broke out in the hall. At the end of the hallway two adults were sitting at the sign-in desk. They did absolutely nothing to end the fight. I got in the middle and told the two girls who were fighting to go back to the class. They continued calling each other names and then they left. No other teachers or administrators did anything!

Yet, Froschl and Gropper's (1999) findings demonstrate that children, "yearn for adults to intervene" (72). The question is: "How?"

We constantly hear about the increasing numbers of metal detectors, security personnel, and expulsions in our nation's schools. We wonder how these items and policies impact the school's ability to create a community and demonstrate caring, particularly for the students who don't see school as a place where they belong. These "act out and get kicked out" policies fail to take individual student needs into account. In fact, they clearly demonstrate to some of our most needy students that they *do not* belong! If they cannot find belonging in our schools, then where will they seek it?

The lack of personal connections between teachers and students leads to feelings of powerlessness for adults as they find themselves in situations where they must intervene. When adults *do* intervene they are flooded with frustration and helplessness. Their counteraggression takes over. The conflict cycle begins and goes around and around! All of this speaks to the absolute necessity of getting to know your students as individuals and creating a school environment that fosters belonging.

Chodzinski and Burke (1998) remind us that "there are some students who need to learn somehow what they have not learned; that is, that they are loved, wanted and most important, capable" (9). Once more we will ask you to reconsider your own educational experiences. In which classrooms did you feel like you belonged? Who were the teachers that cared about you?

How did you know? Who made you feel capable? How did they accomplish this?

In her research, Hewitt (1998) asked students how they knew they belonged to a group. She arrived at a list of 20 items. All of the items are important, but here are a few of their responses: (1) they know my name, (2) they take time to talk to me, (3) they smile at me, (4) they include me, and (5) they trust me. These are really some very simple things we can do as teachers to help our students feel valued in our schools.

How can you create an atmosphere of caring and belonging in your schools and classrooms? Here are some suggestions:

- Learn the names of students, even students who are not in your classes.

- Make a particular effort to learn about and interact with marginalized students. Help these students feel valued in your classroom and school.

- Become interested in the unique qualities of all students.

- Work to eliminate simple name calling, put-downs, and epitaphs.

- Intervene when bullying occurs. Demonstrate to your students that it is not going to be tolerated by the adults in your schools and classrooms.

Cindy Herbert (1974) reminded us that, at first, most of the work in the teacher-student relationship comes from the teacher. In the spirit of changing the status quo we are asking you to (1) create real connections between you and *all* students, (2) eliminate bullying and intolerance, and (3) step in when bullying and intolerance occur. The only authentic way to accomplish this is to develop an understanding of the individual characteristics of each of your students.

With this increased attention to individual differences you will enhance your relationships with your students. You can use these relationships to foster a sense of belonging. This knowledge will help you deal with your own counteraggression during times of stressful interactions with students. You will be able to pause and avoid the conflict cycle. Finally, rather than get involved in a "no-win" situation, you will be able to use the interaction to make the student feel more capable and cared about.

Using Type Theory in Our Classrooms

To use type theory in our classrooms, we first need to be absolutely clear about three very fundamental facts:

1. In the context of type as we are using it here, Jung was talking about psychologically healthy human beings, not those with any form of psychopathology.

2. Jung placed no value on a particular style, so that one style is not better than another, only different.

3. The 16 types are not evenly distributed in the general population.

Some learners might have significant learning, emotional, or behavior problems. In that case, it is important to make sure those learners receive appropriate help, both from you and from others who are in a position to assist you or the learner directly. Style theory as we are discussing it here is not meant to address learners with psychological problems. Suppose there is a learner in your classroom who sits back and rarely participates. You might believe that this learner is simply introverted. But you also note that the learner has few friends, often looks sad, occasionally breaks into tears for no apparent reason, and seems distant and withdrawn. These behaviors are not indicative of a healthy person, especially if they persist. This learner might be depressed or distressed. Behaviors that call attention to themselves because they are extreme are usually not signs of healthy behavior. Dismissing this particular learner as introverted could be a big mistake. When in doubt about such behavior, seek the counsel of an experienced, trained professional in your school.

Think about it . . .

From what you have already done, you have some idea about your personality type. And you have an idea about Roger's type. Now think about this question: *How would Roger make out in your classroom?*

With the caveat that we are dealing with psychologically healthy learners, the important implication for classroom teachers is that, no matter how we feel about it, differences will exist in our classrooms. Because each type or style is characterized by its own strengths and weaknesses, it might be well for teachers to build upon the unique strengths that each style offers and to see these as potential benefits that can be brought to the classroom. In this way each learner can enrich the classroom environment. For example, an extravert might be very quick to jump into an activity, which might encourage an introvert to get more involved. On the other hand, an introvert might exert a positive influence on an extravert by encouraging more reflection prior to activity. In another example, when presented with a problem to solve, a sensor might be excellent at doing library research to uncover information, whereas an intuitor might be best at seeing the big picture and uncovering important questions that go beyond the apparent and about which information should be gathered.

It is also important to recognize that you and every other teacher bring your own type and preferences to the classroom as well. This fact brings with it a very special responsibility to be aware of your personal type and recognize that not everybody shares it. Because teachers are in the "power" position in a classroom (that is to say, they do the planning, run the activities, establish reward systems, and determine the learners' grades), they must be quite sensitive about type differences and the various styles that learners bring to the classroom. In this way teachers can be fairer in wielding this considerable power, and can promote more effective learning among children in classrooms that will contain those who exhibit a variety of types and styles, some at odds with their teacher's preferences. Can you imagine how an extraverted teacher might react to an introverted learner? That teacher might mistake introverted behavior for disinterest on the learner's part. Or a teacher with a preference for thinking might be overly critical of a learner with a preference for feeling, believing that the learner's logic is soft and fuzzy. Just being aware that style differences exist, and what each constitutes, will help you be more sensitive to individual differences among your learners (and among your colleagues, friends, and family members, for that matter).

An interesting fact is that, in the general population, all styles are not evenly distributed. Depending upon the specific sample, it appears that extraverted-sensor (ES) types are far greater than introverted-intuitive (IN) types, with the other preferences more or less evenly distributed. This is very interesting in light of Lawrence's (1993, 48–49) observation that traditional instruction seems to fit some types better than others. Let's think about this for a moment. Remember back to Chapter 1. Traditional teaching involves lots of listening on the part of the learners to the ideas and to concepts that the teacher is imparting (verbally) to them. Usually learners are sitting at their desks while this goes on, and occasionally one or two learners respond to the teacher's questions. In addition, learners will often be asked to do some in-class work, again usually at their own seats and by themselves. This is the way that Goodlad (1983) and Cuban (1993) characterized most classrooms. If this characterization is accurate, then traditional teaching is best suited for introverted-intuitors (IN). These learners prefer to think and work alone, and they enjoy the world of ideas, possibilities, and meanings. But don't let the implications of the data escape you. In the general population, IN learners account for the *smallest* percentage of all learners. Interestingly, then, *many if not most of the current methods being used to teach meet the needs, or at least the preferences, of the smallest number of learners!*

What does this mean for teachers wishing to teach in ways that accommodate style? Lawrence (1993) suggests several steps to use as you approach lesson planning, given the data on the distribution of types in our classrooms:

1. Start planning with your own natural teaching style in mind.

2. Next consider the needs of ES learners.

3. Develop alternative activities for IS, EN, and IN learners.

4. Adjust for TF and JP dimensions that are important to *your* learners. (57–58)

What, exactly, does it mean to start with the needs of ES learners? Let's return to what we know about what each of these letters signifies. Extraverted learners focus their energy outward. They are social, and they like action. Sensing learners are detail and fact oriented, and they like practical work. So ES learners do best when provided with opportunities for hands-on, practical activities that involve learning declarative knowledge (facts) in the company of other learners. Perhaps using a jigsaw cooperative learning activity (explained in Chapter 3) might meet the extraverted attitude of the ES learner. This technique would permit the E type to work with others in both expert and home groups, and to talk aloud about what he or she has learned. Type E students typically like to share ideas and tasks. If the learning activity involves content that is realistic (as opposed to theoretical) and of practical value, so much the better. Going to resources to find information to solve a problem (such as what is killing the fish in the local river?) will help meet the S preference of an ES learner. S types like facts and detail. Using the jigsaw method, roles might be given to each learner (one is a biologist, one is a geologist, etc.) and they can then gather information from that perspective and bring it back to the group. As you can see, if you understand the big ideas from type theory, you can devise an infinite number of pedagogically sound, content-rich learning activities for various types of learners. In this way you can devise style-sensitive instruction.

Another way to use type theory is to use it to adjust learning activities so that they work better with one, several, or a whole room full of students. Suppose you used the activity suggested for the ES learner above. How might an IN learner fare during this activity? Remember that introverts usually prefer to work alone or with one other person, and they prefer conceptual activities that involve the big picture. Actually, their preferences are the exact opposite of ES learners. We can change that ES activity described above to meet the IN preferences without changing the content of the lesson. We can allow the IN learners to work alone, and allow them some input as to how they would like to learn the information. Perhaps exploring concepts such as what living things need in order to live, and then what fish might need in order to live, would suit their needs better.

This is not to say that *everything* we do in a classroom should meet every child's preferences. That would be very

---

Some Teacher Preferences for Instructional Alternatives

Sensing: Emphasizes facts, skills, concrete outcomes. Prefers controlled activities.

Intuitive: Wide-ranging presentations of ideas. Emphasizes concepts over facts. Encourages interrelationships among concepts.

Thinking: Emphasizes logical structure of ideas and activities. Focuses on content. More lecture, less individual interaction.

Feeling: Priority to individualization of instruction and assessment. Prefers to use small-group learning activities.

[Source: R. Barger and R. Hoover. (1984). Psychological type and the matching of cognitive styles. Theory into Practice, 23(1), 61.]

Summary of Learner Preferences

ES: Learns best through hands-on activities in cooperation with others.

IS: Learns best through hands-on activities that can be done alone or with one other person.

EN: Learns best with others, through conceptual activities.

IN: Learns best alone or with one other person, through conceptual activities.

[Source: (Fall 1985). The Type Reporter 2(2).]

difficult to accomplish, and perhaps even unwise. There is nothing wrong with requiring learners to stretch a bit by doing things in ways other than the ways they prefer to do them. This helps those learners develop their other functions. Just remember that, currently, classroom activities might be consistently favoring a particular style over all others. Lawrence feels that they favor IN learners.

Even if you disagree, there is considerable evidence that we teach in ways that are consistent with our own type preferences. That would mean that learners who happen to be in our classrooms, and who happen to share our preferences, are fortunate indeed. But those who differ from us will be out of luck if we stick with only *our* preferred way of teaching. Knowing about styles will certainly help us be aware of the dynamics that take place in our classrooms and that might be related to different psychological types.

For a moment, let us just consider that the ES and the IN types described above were allowed to work together on a learning activity, each in her or his own way. While the ES type is out and about happily gathering facts and details, an IN type might be just as happy reflecting quietly on the problem and reading about what might cause fish to die. When they put their heads together to complete the assignment, their strengths will complement one another. The IN will typically slow down the exuberance of the ES a bit, and encourage some thought about possible causes of the problem. The ES will be excellent at digging out some of the facts, will be more likely to use other people as resources, and will keep the project moving along. We have often told our own students that if you want (or need) to get something done *quickly,* work with others who are like you. If you want to get something done *thoroughly,* work with those who are unlike you. There is a good deal of power in garnering the strengths from learners whose types differ. And it is a wise teacher who garners this power and uses it to enhance and enrich his or her classroom.

Psychological type, then, can be useful to you in a number of ways. You can:

- Meet learners' preferences and needs by creating instructional activities that match their styles.

- Encourage learners to develop their preferences by creating activities that do not meet their styles, but rather force them to stretch.

- Adjust any one instructional activity so that it meets the styles or needs of a variety of learners with different styles.

- Group learners so that they are working either in homogeneous or heterogeneous style groups.

Excerpt from a Teacher's Journal

"The first problem was having a large group discussion that lasted for a long period of time. The discussion was an IN activity, and we found that the majority of our students preferred ES activities better. [To make this an ES task] we could have broken the class up into pairs and placed all items in the center of the floor [and then] told each pair to find (for example) one vegetable that grows from the soil, or something that comes from a cow. Students would have to work together to retrieve an item. This activity would be geared more toward ES learners since the students would be working with others at a hands-on task."

—**Staci Wenitsky**

Think about it . . .   Now you can practice using this information by considering Missy. As you read the teacher's summary of Missy's behaviors, try to figure out her preferences (using the conventional four-letter format). Check page 199 to see how well you did. Then,

1. Construct a learning activity that will meet Missy's needs.
2. Adjust that activity so that it will also meet Roger's needs (remember Roger from earlier in the chapter?).

Missy

Missy is a learner in your classroom. She is a quiet, shy girl, and often chooses to work alone when given the opportunity. Missy is a very observant young lady, and keeps accurate track of details. She is particularly good at memorizing facts. Missy often goes along with the others in her group during a discussion, and is very concerned about the feelings of others. Though not particularly curious about things, she likes to be "right" and prefers assignments to be clear and definite.

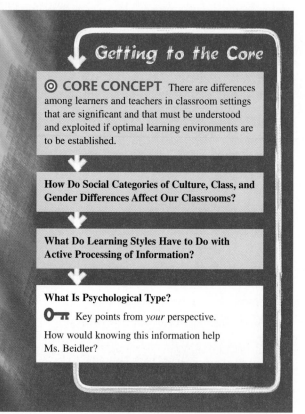

Getting to the Core

◎ CORE CONCEPT   There are differences among learners and teachers in classroom settings that are significant and that must be understood and exploited if optimal learning environments are to be established.

How Do Social Categories of Culture, Class, and Gender Differences Affect Our Classrooms?

What Do Learning Styles Have to Do with Active Processing of Information?

What Is Psychological Type?

O—π   Key points from *your* perspective.

How would knowing this information help Ms. Beidler?

What Are "Mindstyles"?

Jung focused on the basic *functions* that human beings perform in their lives. In contrast, Anthony Gregorc's reflections on his personal and professional experiences led him to see styles as indicators of the *qualities* of our minds. He decided to look at the various styles of the mind, or what he calls mindstyles. He looked closely at people's behavior as an indication of the qualities of their minds. From this work, he identifies style patterns in the context of a person's life, and calls this the "organon system."

> The organon deals with the phenomenological study of two mediation abilities of the mind: perception and ordering. A study of these mind qualities offers practical, economical, and effective ways of addressing how you, as an individual, function and relate in your outer world. (Gregorc 1982, V)

Gregorc focuses his model on looking at the implications of the two ways we have of *perceiving* and *ordering* as they relate to getting and making sense of new information. This is not so different from Jung's functions. The first way, perceiving, refers to how a learner prefers to get or obtain new information. This has two qualities, concreteness and abstractness. The concrete-type learner prefers to get information through physical senses (sight, smell, hearing, taste, and touch). The abstract learner prefers more symbolic, feeling, or emotional and intuitive methods of getting information.

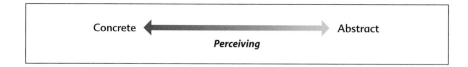

The second way, ordering, refers to how the mind grasps and arranges new information and ideas. This way has two qualities as well, sequence and randomness. Sequential learners are more methodical and prefer a logical order for the new

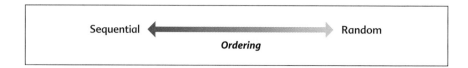

information. They prefer to develop an order to follow and like to work on one task at a time. They naturally put information together in a predetermined order and prefer organization. Random-type learners place information in a more nonlinear order and are less concerned with order and arrangement. They tend to find their own order for information and are good at working with lots of different information at one time (Gregorc 1982, 5).

The Four Mindstyles

On the basis of these two dimensions, Gregorc identified four patterns of mindstyles:

1. *Concrete sequential (CS),* where learners (and teachers) prefer to perceive in a concrete way and order sequentially. Personal characteristics of this style are practical, predictable, organized, and structured.

2. *Abstract sequential (AS),* where learners perceive abstractly and order sequentially. Personal characteristics of this style are studious, analytical, conceptual, and critical.

3. *Concrete random (CR),* where learners perceive concretely and order randomly. Personal characteristics of this style are investigative, intuitive, and the ability to solve problems

4. *Abstract random (AR),* where learners perceive abstractly and order randomly. Personal characteristics of this style are sociable, imaginative, and expressive.

Using these four learning style descriptions, Gregorc developed a self-reporting instrument that is helpful in classifying learners' styles. This instrument is called the style delineator (Gregorc 1985). This instrument is user friendly and can be administered easily to a group of individuals within a five-minute time period. But again, we believe that only a properly trained professional who is also knowledgeable about how to help others interpret the results should administer psychological instruments. The style delineator asks learners to describe themselves in terms of a number of descriptors that are rank ordered. There are 10 questions, each with four words to rank. People are asked to choose the word that best describes them *as a person* (rather than as a teacher, a student, etc.). They are asked to move quickly through the instrument and not to get hung up on words that are unfamiliar to them. Learners score the style delineator with guidance from the instructor and receive a learning style profile. Learners will usually show a preference in one style and have a strong secondary preference. We have given this instrument to more than 1,500 undergraduate and graduate students, practicing teachers, and administrators in our classes and staff development sessions. Usually, about 2 percent of those taking the delineator will not follow directions correctly and therefore get results very different from their expectations. Ten to twelve percent of the participants will disagree with the scores for a wide variety of reasons. However, the purpose of using this instrument is not to validate it but to show the wide variety of learning style differences in any given class or group of people. We usually ask participants to volunteer their scores and record them on an overhead transparency to be viewed by the whole group. An average group size is 25 people. The typical distribution will usually look like the following.

CS = 9	AS = 3	CR = 7	AR = 6

We ask these teachers to describe how they would teach a classroom full of learners with this same profile. We ask:

- What are the challenges you would face?

- Do these distributions seem similar to, or different from, how you have been taught?

> **Think about it . . .**
>
> What do you think your mindstyle is? Look at questions 5 and 6 on page 162. How did you answer them?
>
> Facts (C) vs. ideas (A)
>
> Orderly (S) vs. messy (R)

- Why is there such a distribution? Is this normal? Why are there so few abstract sequential learners?
- How does your style match those of the learners? What happens when your style differs from the majority of the learners in you class?

Lively discussion usually follows when we pose these questions. Teachers are surprised by the differences among them, and the realization that even though there are fewer AS than other styles, most of what goes on in classrooms addresses AS learners' needs. And another thing—it dawns on these teachers that the identification of specific learning styles is really not that important after all. What *is* important is that these style differences exist and no matter how many times you give this instrument, you will always get a slightly different distribution. No two groups are exactly the same. Ever! So no two classes that you teach will ever be exactly the same, either.

Think about it . . .

Now that you have an explanation of Gregorc's model, we shall let you peek into a classroom where we interview four learners about their preferred ways to learn. Also, we ask the classroom teacher and a few of the learners' friends their impressions of how these particular learners learn.

> The first learner we interview is Rachel. She likes hands-on approaches, computers, measuring exercises, building models, and working with time lines. She doesn't typically like to try new ideas and she gets somewhat uncomfortable around brand-new situations. Her teacher says she likes to be correct all the time and will get angry and walk away when she's incorrect or told she is wrong. The second learner, Trevor, just loves to sit back and listen to the teacher lecture, and read books and magazines, do library research, debate with other learners on just about everything, and thoroughly enjoys writing research reports. In discussions with his teacher we found out that Trevor doesn't like low grades and will get very upset when he receives anything less than an A. He expects to be the best in the class and lets his peers know his expectations. Trevor can become critical of those around him because he expects perfection. As we continue the interviewing process, the third learner, Donna, tells us how she works best in small groups, likes to work on complicated, unstructured webbing activities, needs to write personal things in her journal, likes to conduct interviews of other people, and really likes personalized examples when being taught. Her teacher and peers are quick to tell us she doesn't like to follow specific directions and is not very detail oriented. She prefers to work with others, and will always ask if she can work with a partner. Donna gets quickly frustrated and will give up working when things are not going her way. The last person to be interviewed, Danny, tells us he likes when the teacher designs simulations and allows him to learn through games. He likes to brainstorm ideas with others, explore new places, be involved in two or three things at the same time, and to invent things. We find out that he is very independent and likes to take risks in and out of the classroom. However, the teacher claims he doesn't always finish his projects and when asked to explain what he has done, tends to give short explanations. He is not great with recording details that are important to his tasks.

With the interviews concluded, you should now realize these learners are very different in many ways from one another. Now, do you think you can identify their preferred learning styles using Gregorc's mindstyles theory? Let's see how well you can do. Using the information in this section identify and explain the predominant learning style of each of our four learners. The correct answers can be found on page 199.

Using Mindstyles in the Classroom

Like Anthony Gregorc, Kathleen Butler is also a learning styles pioneer who is making connections between learning style theory and classroom practice. Butler (1996, 1993, 1987) has developed extensive practical applications for teachers, and she advocates that teachers understand the dominant strengths that underlie each learning style so that they can create learning activities for students that build on those strengths. For example, learners who are highly personal and enjoy talking and reflecting seem to work best by sharing, interpreting, and visualizing. Activities such as group work, role-play, and interpreting through writing or drawing all utilize their strengths.

Butler (1987) developed a lesson design model called style differentiated instruction (SDI) that allows the teacher to create instructional activities that challenge students at all of Bloom's levels of thinking (knowledge, comprehension, application, analysis, synthesis, and evaluation) and are, at the same time, sensitive to style differences. We presented information about Bloom's taxonomy in Chapter 4.

Butler's model helps teachers organize instruction that maximizes the opportunity for students to learn through all four of the predominant learning styles. Using what Butler calls the SDI action plan, the teacher plans a lesson using one of three different approaches. The first approach is called *bridging*. It encourages the teacher to focus a learning activity on just one learning style. All students complete a given activity together and the teacher provides bridges, or assisting techniques, for those students who did not learn well in that specific style. For example, if students were asked to meet as a group and create a presentation on the benefits of the Social Security system, the teacher would need to help accommodate different learner types. The activity is a good match for learners with a personal style who like to work in groups and create a product together (AR). Learners who need step-by-step sequence and specific

The diverse backgrounds and learning differences can be used to enrich and enhance the learning of all students (Courtesy of © Mug Shots/Corbis Stock Market).

directions would benefit from a list of expectations, ways to organize information, and specific time requirements (CS). Learners who need to analyze and think about concepts would find it helpful to have written resources and a practice session to make sure the information is correct (AS). Learners who need to think in open-ended and unique ways would benefit from brainstorming activities and freedom to be creative (CR). In this way, all students receive the *same* materials for their use throughout every segment of the lesson. This is a popular approach among teachers because it allows them to use a predominant style (usually their own) and still meet the needs of many types of learners.

The second approach is called *variation*. Using the variation approach, the teacher rotates learning activities throughout the lesson. Each rotation meets the needs of one of the learning styles. This ensures that all learners' needs are met or challenged during any given instructional cycle. All of the students will complete all of the activities. Variation can be effectively used in conducting a day's lesson as well as a month-long unit. It provides a great deal of flexibility for the teacher in using different style strategies.

The last approach is called *choice* and is usually used for homework, end-of-unit projects, and out-of-school experiences. The choice approach gives students the opportunity to choose an activity with which they feel most comfortable and gives them the freedom to complete the assignment on their own. The activity choices available to students represent the preferences that students have from each of the four predominant styles.

With all these approaches, however, it is essential that students understand the expected outcome and that the activities directly address the outcome. Otherwise, teachers run the risk of using a variety of style-sensitive strategies without ensuring accomplishment. In summary, you can use mindstyles to:

1. Guide your understanding of similarities and differences in your classroom. Remember, students and teachers have a combination of learning styles but usually work from the strengths of one or two of them.

2. Understand that your teaching style will match some students' styles and will conflict with others. You are the one responsible for being sensitive to learning differences. It is up to you to make accommodations, both for students and for yourself. Use bridging, variation, and choice to help you do this.

3. Learn about your students' styles through observation during activities rather than by testing them, for reasons we mentioned earlier.

4. Be careful to develop lessons and activities using *your* least favorite learning style. Remember that it will be some of your students' strongest style.

5. Challenge students to learn in their least favorite style. They probably need to stretch their styles of learning.

6. *Don't use the style descriptions as labels.* You do not want to be known as a CS or AR. You especially don't want your students labeling themselves and others.

Planning your lessons and activities to accommodate for mindstyles is most challenging, especially as you begin to include powerful instructional strategies in your lessons. You will no doubt find interesting the ways in which teachers think about and plan lessons using the ideas from Gregorc's mindstyles. Here are two examples for you to consider:

Example 1: Terri McAllister (1st/2nd grade teacher)

Grade/age level: Multiage 1 to 2 (ages 6 to 8).   **Subject:** Science

Objective:

Given an advance and graphic organizer, fictional story, and hands-on materials, the student will cooperatively discriminate between two types of water (fresh and salt), hypothesize possible causes of death of the fish, know why salt caused the death of the fish and design a warning poster for fish entering salt water.

> I planned the lesson keeping in mind two dominant styles. The design of the lesson emphasized investigation and exploration and brainstorming of possible solutions to a problem. I wanted to challenge the students with divergent questions, and encourage them to think for themselves. These aspects of the lesson are consistent with a CR style of teaching. Other parts of the lesson indicate an AR style. I designed the lesson around working cooperatively to share strategies to solve a problem: I developed the problem-solving activity around a story to engage and stimulate imagination; and I provided opportunity for the students to use personal, creative abilities to design a warning poster to demonstrate concept learning.

> Although two teaching styles seem to be dominant, during the planning process I explored ways to vary techniques to connect with various learning styles in my class. The lesson was organized and structured using both advance and graphic organizers. Because some of my students are just beginning to read, I used picture/sketches to accompany words in the organizers. These strategies along with hands-on materials will accommodate the CS learner. Expecting the students to summarize information and report their investigations encouraged AS-type learning. In addition to the above, oral directions were provided for the cooperative learning activity, wait-time to give opportunity for the more reflective students to think and develop their ideas, and the use of prompts and probes to guide student thinking. Also many visual cues were provided while reading the story, to assist with comprehension of the story.

Example 2: Danielle Campese (High School Teacher)

Grade/age level: Ninth (ages 14–15)   **Subject:** English (short story/
symbolism/prewriting)

Objective:

Given an advance organizer on symbolism and the short story, "Sweet Potato Pie," students will be able to discuss, examine, and evaluate a series of questions in cooperative learning groups.

> This lesson was planned to use all the learning styles in the lesson. However, the majority of the lesson is directed toward AR learners. Accommodations and matches will be made for the CS-, CR-, and AS-type learner.

> The task-oriented CS learning style will be matched when asked to prepare the graphic organizer on the descriptive writing project. The chart will allow those students to chunk, label, and sort information on the basis of a realistic situation that would allow them to choose their own symbol. In the next couple of lessons, the CS learner will be able to exhibit the finished product in the presentation portion of the symbolism project. Moreover, although the CS learner may be weary of the cooperative learning groups, specific detailed instructions will help bridge what might be an "out of comfort zone" strategy.

The discussion/questioning handout and graphic organizer will provide the AR learner with opportunities to critically think and debate among peers on a convergent path. The use of convergent questions will provide time for deliberation and formation of ideas. In addition, research will be expected from students to find out the origin of objects they will use as symbols.

The bulk of the lesson will be centered around techniques of the AR learner profile such as arts and visuals, group work, mapping, personalized examples, peer teaching, communication, emotions, and interviews. I will use a drawing of a pink rose as my advance organizer to help them visually see the rose and what specific aspects a rose might represent or symbolize. The students will create their own symbol in groups using the "teammates consult" approach that encourages effective communication and fosters peer teaching. During the activity I will give specific convergent open-ended questions that will allow for interpretation. The graphic organizer will allow students to map out ideas and give personal examples. This will allow the students to use prior knowledge and make connections from their personal lives. The symbols will have an emotional attraction and motivation for the students.

The closing brainstorming activity with the graphic organizer will target the CS learner. Moreover, the symbolism project that will take place during the next few lessons is an independent assignment where the CR will flourish. Students will explore and consider possible answers during the entire lesson through the introduction, group work, and closure. One question will involve creation of a symbol for the major concepts of the story. The CR learners will enjoy making something new on the basis of the information they already knew.

How Do Learning Styles Relate to Social Categories?

A sample of recent research on cultural learning styles involving personality types as measured by the Myers-Briggs type inventory (MBTI), and mindstyles as measured by the style delineator, indicates the following:

- Summarizing current issues in education, DiTiberio (1996) believes that type theory and research contribute much to the education of disadvantaged students. He writes, "What has in the past been classified as pertaining to culture or gender differences may be re-framed in light of type concepts in order to highlight the virtues of all learners and to avoid stereotyping of members of ethnic or gender groupings" (155).

- In a study of relational styles (people-oriented versus analytical), Melear and Alcock (1998) found that African American children showed significant *feeling* preference in sixth grade when compared with white children. This difference declined by 11th grade.

- Picou, Gatlin-Watts, and Packer (1998) found that Mexican American children whose primary language was Spanish were proportionally more concrete random than the general U.S. population. Female Hispanic children were more abstract sequential than the general U.S. female population.

- Park (1997) found significant differences in learning style preferences for visual learning among Korean, Mexican, Armenian American when compared with Anglo populations in 10 southern California high schools. She also found a preference for group learning in the Mexican American group of students.

- Johnson and Johnson (1996) found that teachers with more abstract thinking styles were better able to adjust teaching practices in multiethnic educational settings.

All of these studies concluded that teachers must recognize differences in culture along with differences in learning style to truly help minority students succeed in the classroom.

How Is the 4MAT® System Also a Learning Style Theory?

We have attempted to help you understand two very powerful models for understanding individual differences against the backdrop of social categories. Now you should be able to go well beyond generalities when asked about the ways in which people—students and teachers—differ from one another. Earlier, in Chapter 3, we introduced you to the 4MAT system. In that chapter we explained to you how the 4MAT system could be used to plan lessons that made use of social learning theory (Bandura), contextualist theory (Vygotsky), and information processing theory, and the powerful strategies that derive from these theories. Now we are going to revisit 4MAT as it was *originally* conceived—as a learning style model. Because we addressed it earlier in some detail, this treatment will be brief.

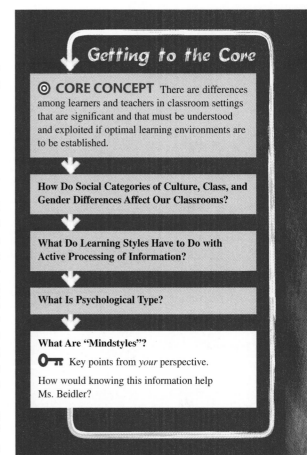

To reiterate what we wrote earlier in Chapter 3, 4MAT is a system of instruction or "a constructivist model of pedagogy" (www.aboutlearning.com) that champions an eight-step sequence of learning activities based upon two other major theories: David Kolb's model of learning styles and the research on brain hemisphericity (Scott 1994). In a manner similar to Jung and Gregorc, it bases the notion of learning styles on two major dimensions upon which humans differ: on the way they perceive experience and information, and on the way they process this experience and information. The combination of how we perceive and how we process form our unique styles of learning, according to 4MAT (see Fig. 5.1).

4MAT postulates that some people perceive or take in information through concrete experience—sensations, emotions, physical memories, whereas others take in information through abstract conceptualization—ideas, language, and hierarchical structures. These are at opposite ends of a continuum of human preferences. 4MAT further postulates that when processing or doing something with new information, people prefer to engage in either reflective observation—by structuring it, ordering it, or intellectualizing about it, and others prefer to engage in active experimentation—applying the information in the real world, testing it, manipulating it. The interactions between the "feeling" of experience and the "thinking" of conceptualization, and the "watching" of reflection and the "doing" of action, incorporate the entire range of the learning experience, according to the 4MAT system (McCarthy 1996). However, and similar to the Jung and Gregorc theories, learners seem to favor one particular type of learning.

McCarthy (1987) identified four different learning styles. These styles are described in the accompanying chart. Each type corresponds to a quadrant in the 4MAT system. Type 1 learners are most comfortable in quadrant 1, type 2 learners

FIGURE 5.1

4MAT system.

(Source: About Learning, Inc. Reprinted by permission.)

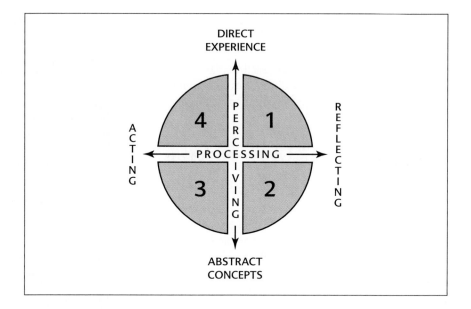

Type One

Imaginative Learning-Feeling and watching, seeking personal associations, meaning, involvement. Making connections.

Key question: Why?

Type Two

Analytic Learning-Listening to and thinking about information; seeking facts, thinking through ideas; learning what the experts think. Formulating ideas.

Key question: What?

Type Three

Common Sense Learning-Thinking and doing. Experimenting, building, creating, usability. Tinkering. Applying ideas.

Key question: How?

Type Four

Dynamic Learning-Doing and feeling. Seeking hidden possibilities, exploring, learning by trial and error, self-discovery. Creating original adaptations.

Key question: If?

(Source: http://www.aboutlearning.com/aboutlearning/4MATsys.html.) Reprinted with permission.

in quadrant 2, and so on. Like the other style theories, 4MAT looks at individual differences in terms of how learners take in, and what they do with, information. We referred to this research and its connection to 4MAT in Chapter 3, so if you need to review it, go back to that discussion.

Perhaps 4MAT's greatest contribution, at least in our minds, is that it provides a system of instruction (and assessment, which we will discuss in Chapter 7) that teachers can use to plan, implement, and evaluate lessons. Even though McCarthy and her associates developed an instrument to measure a person's style, called the learning type measure (LTM), the system clearly calls for teaching "around the circle." That is, we should teach by beginning with quadrant 1, and then move in a sequential fashion through quadrants 2, 3, and 4, all the while incorporating left- and right-mode learning activities. This, McCarthy (1996) says, is the natural progression of learning. There is really no need for teachers to determine the style of each student, because the 4MAT plan will meet all learner styles at some point during an instructional sequence.

According to Ault (1986), type 1 learners respond best to group discussions, movies, and audiovisual presentations. Type 2 learners prefer reading assignments, lectures, and "think" sessions. Quadrant 3 learners like workbooks, manuals, demonstrations, and hands-on activities. And quadrant 4 learners like games, simulations, independent study, problem solving, and contract-activity assignments. The important point is that all learners will be comfortable at some point in the sequence because their most preferred style will be met; in other parts of the sequence they will be challenged to develop their other learning abilities. In the hands of a sensitive teacher who understands and appreciates individual differences, this can be a very positive growth experience.

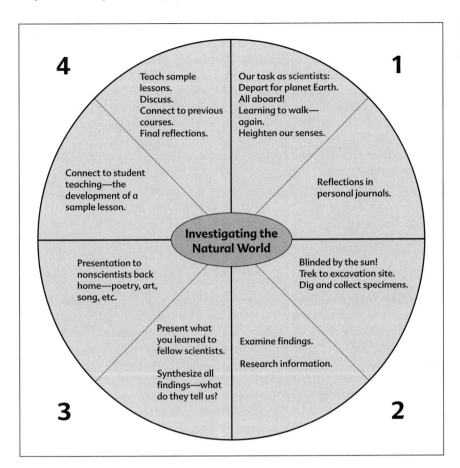

FIGURE 5.2
Unit plan for La Anna,
Education 475.

We have developed many instructional units in the spirit of 4MAT that we use with our own undergraduate and graduate students. To illustrate how such a unit might work, we offer one unit plan for you to think about. First, let us establish the context. Just prior to beginning a 15-week student teaching experience (the first of two—our students practice teaching for an entire year), we take our students away from campus for two days. We travel to a youth hostel located in a rural area of the Pocono Mountain region of Pennsylvania in a small town named La Anna. It is a two-hour drive from our Philadelphia campus. During the ensuing 26 hours (six of which are used for sleeping) we engage them in a unit of instruction to model (á la Bandura) what we would like them to do with their own students. The core concept or generative topic (both of which we will discuss in Chapter 8) of the unit is *investigating the natural world.* Through this unit we tell a story while the students learn about the outdoors. The story line goes like this:

1.   We live on the planet La Anna.

2.   We are scientists charged by our superiors with visiting and exploring planet Earth.

3.   We travel to Earth to collect artifacts, and return to La Anna to learn about these artifacts through reading and research.

4.   We share artifacts and synthesize all that we have learned, and then make individual presentations of our findings to our fellow La Annians.

Well, that's it in a nutshell. Figure 5.2 shows how it looks as a 4MAT unit of instruction.

Think about it . . .

How would you feel if you were one of our students engaged in the 4MAT unit that we describe in the text? Which activity or activities might you like best? Least? Why?

Each year we modify the unit to reflect what we learned from the previous year's student evaluations of it. Our students are very positive about the experience and what they learn about themselves as learners. They often comment on how important each step and each quadrant was in the total learning experience. We often hear our own students say things like, "The first activity made me feel more comfortable . . . ," or "The second activity was my favorite because I never knew a salamander was. . . ." And then we encourage them to remember what the experience was like for them as learners, so that when they arrive at their classroom assignments they are careful to develop instruction that actively engages their children "around the circle."

Are There Connections among Jung's Types, Gregorc's Mindstyles, and McCarthy's 4MAT System?

At this juncture, you might be asking yourself what the differences are among these theories. They sound so much the same. Good question! These theories share some very similar ideas. Perhaps it is validation of the concept of learning style that three people look at the same thing and see it slightly differently. Let's look at the similarities.

These theories all look at the ways *people take in information,* and the ways people *make use of this information.* They do so with only minor variations. Then, using different words, they all describe various styles of learners. To show the relationships among and between the styles from the various theories we have included a visual in Figure 5.3. In Quadrant 1, we find type 1 imaginative learners (McCarthy), abstract random learners (Gregorc), and feeling-type learners (Jung). This is the quadrant where learners are making personal connections, making meaning of information and experience, and having an emotional response to the material. In quadrant 2 we find type 2 analytic learners (McCarthy), abstract sequential learners (Gregorc), and thinking-type learners (Jung). These learners prefer traditional methods that are usually sequential and designed to impart knowledge, usually through language. In quadrant 3 are type 3 commonsense learners (McCarthy), concrete sequential learners (Gregorc), and sensing-type learners (Jung). These learners like hands-on, concrete practice and application of information and ideas.

Last but not least, quadrant 4 learners are type 4 dynamic learners (McCarthy), concrete random learners (Gregorc), and intuitive-type learners (Jung). They like to discover things on their own, and go beyond the information that was given to create new ideas and applications. McCarthy (1987, 34–35) made connections to Jung and Gregorc in her own work. Although she uses slightly different descriptors, our connections are substantially the same. Extraverted and introverted types would be represented in each of the quadrants; it would be their preference for working alone or with others that would distinguish them in each one. And as for the judging and perceiving types, they, too, would be in all quadrants and distinguished mostly by whether they need order and closure in any given instructional activity, or are content with openness and exploration.

Using 4MAT as an instructional design tool does three things for you and for your learners. First, and partly because it was influenced by them when originally developed by McCarthy, 4MAT is very closely related to the theories of Jung and

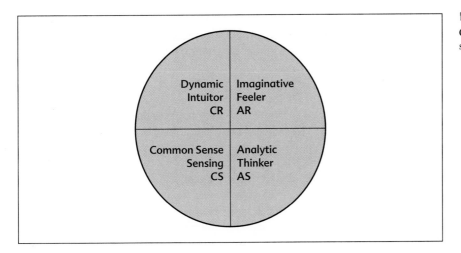

FIGURE 5.3
Connection among three learning style theories.

Gregorc. Therefore, by using 4MAT you are also using some of the major ideas from those two theories. Second, because 4MAT encourages the application of some of the seminal theories of sound pedagogy (see Chapter 2), by using it you will be basing your instruction on solid theoretical ground. Third, 4MAT allows the use of very powerful pedagogical principles (COVER, practice, and feedback—see Chapter 3), and so using it will also allow you to make use of some very potent techniques from teachers' current pedagogical arsenal. 4MAT is *a learning style theory, and more!* It can help you to be an effective teacher.

Learning and Teaching in the Age of Technology

Educational technology can be helpful in meeting differences in three spheres: management, individualized instruction plans, and individualized learner response options. Though most teachers would willingly individualize assignments, instructional formats, pace, and response modes to meet the needs of differing learning styles, managing these tasks in a class of 20 to 30 students is often daunting. Several tools are currently available to help you in your task. The 4MAT system, which attempts to meet a variety of individual learning styles through whole-class lesson and unit planning, conveniently provides a computerized version of its planning circle and a data bank of previously developed and tested lesson plans. 4MATION (McCarthy, D., 1994, 1999, 2000) software can help you carefully plan, record, and store your 4MAT units, as well as access on disk or online the work of countless other teachers who have adopted the 4MAT approach. Increasingly, software companies are creating electronic grade books which help you store, calculate, and analyze grades, test scores, and even do item analysis to better understand individual progress and needs. Robyler, Edwards, and Havriluk (1997) remind us to look for the capacity to track many

> ◎ **CORE CONCEPT** There are differences among learners and teachers in classroom settings that are significant and that must be understood and exploited if optimal learning environments are to be established.

assignments and flexibility in report formats (sort by name, group, individual), to interface with a wide range of peripherals (various printers and networks), and to note the ease of set up and use on multiple computer platforms (163). The growing popularity of PDAs (personal digital assistants) may also be a boon to managing instruction for individual differences. Teachers will be free to walk around the classroom recording observations and checking mastery of declarative knowledge. Wireless models may enable students to more easily transfer assignments directly to their teacher's computer, and handwriting and voice recognition software may help those with motor or speech difficulties.

Individualizing instruction is at the heart of multimedia technology. The increasing democratization of information access allows individuals to pursue their own interests and paths of discovery. Surfing the Web using the guidelines outlined in earlier chapters can allow an individual student to pursue a realistic plan of discovery, research, and analysis of problem-based learning heretofore impossible in the regular classroom. Individually tailored skill plans also become much easier because teachers can review, highlight, and make lists of frequent student response errors or writing problems, developing personal plans for self-improvement (Roblyer, Edwards, and Havriluk 1999, 81–126.)

The new technologies allow learners to respond in many idiosyncratic and personalized ways to their learning. The ease with which students can develop multimedia presentations to demonstrate their mastery of declarative or procedural knowledge and their ability to overcome small motor disabilities and construct a beautiful brochure or include computer-generated visuals in a report can greatly increase self-esteem. A commitment to multiple intelligences is powerfully enhanced by allowing students to use a wide range of combined sound and sight resources available to them in constructing their knowledge through multimedia formats.

In a powerful example of differentiated learning at its best, Tomlinson (1999) describes a third-grade teacher engaging her students in the study of ancient Rome. After students first select an individual role such as teacher, soldier, healer, farmer, or slave, Ms. Cassell works hard to individualize each student's activity based on readiness, ability, and skill mastery. "Learning-profile differentiation is reflected in the different media that students use to express their findings: journal entries, an oral monologue, or a videotape presentation. Guidelines for each type of product ensures quality and focus on essential understandings and skills established for the

unit. Students may work alone or with a "parallel partner" who is working with the same role, although each student must ultimately produce his or her own product" (16).

Teaching Tips

1. As resources permit, use PDAs to provide individual opportunities for students to work alone or in small groups to collect data for projects. Using computer access, data charts, written reports, online news reporting portals, and research documents, students can collect important information to be shared with class members. This allows for individual work as well as sharing information with fellow students.

2. Using short clips from feature films, videotapes and CD-ROMs, television dramas and sit-coms, and radio and television commercials, students can observe how people communicate in different ways.

3. Subscribe to recognized free *online* newsletters by commercial companies (aboutlearning.com— 4MAT) and professional organizations (ASCD.org) to stay current on instructional practices. About Learning offers a weekly newsletter that provides learning style–sensitive lesson plans and ideas for the classroom teacher.

Suggested Websites

http://peabody.vanderbilt.edu/projects/CTRS/LTC/Research/Jasperoverview.html
The Jasper Series: The Adventures of Jasper Woodbury consists of 12 videodisc-based CD-ROM adventures (plus video-based analogs, extensions, and teaching tips) that focus on mathematical problem finding and problem solving. Each adventure provides multiple opportunities for problem solving, reasoning, communication, and making connections to other areas such as science, social studies, literature, and history. The program is designed to meet current standards recommended by the National Council of Teachers of Mathematics.

http://www.lessonbank.com/cgi-local/hazel.cgi
Lessonbank.com captures the student's attention and promotes real-world problem solving and stimulates new ideas and beliefs.

http/www.aboutlearning.com
Website for 4MAT and 4MATION.

What Is Meant by Multiple Intelligences?

Another way of thinking about individual differences is through the concept of multiple intelligences. First proposed by Howard Gardner in 1983, this notion that there is more than one way to be smart caught on in schools and among teachers. It is very different from the three theories of individual differences that we have already addressed in this chapter. In the theory of multiple intelligences, the question becomes not how smart are we, but how are we smart (Kagan and Kagan 1998)? Let us help you understand the main idea of multiple intelligences by using a scenario.

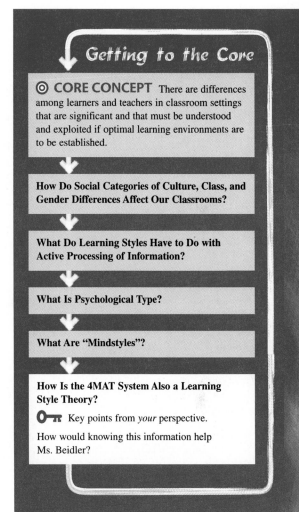

Getting to the Core

◎ **CORE CONCEPT**   There are differences among learners and teachers in classroom settings that are significant and that must be understood and exploited if optimal learning environments are to be established.

How Do Social Categories of Culture, Class, and Gender Differences Affect Our Classrooms?

What Do Learning Styles Have to Do with Active Processing of Information?

What Is Psychological Type?

What Are "Mindstyles"?

How Is the 4MAT System Also a Learning Style Theory?

⌐━ Key points from *your* perspective.

How would knowing this information help Ms. Beidler?

> Three children just arrived at Disney World for a two-day fun-filled vacation. As they enter the park on the first day, they are all attracted to different things. Sam immediately hears the different musical themes playing over the loud speakers in the background. He begins to mouth the words of some of the songs and uses his fingers to match the beat on his belt. He sometimes plays the beat on Grant's head. It is not long before he begins to make up new words to the music and encourages his less than enthusiastic friends to join him as he sings. As Sam travels through the different exhibits from the countries around the world he quickly uses some of the foreign vocabulary words to make up short poems and sayings. He really begins to get Juanita annoyed when he makes up a story about his new imaginary friend "Luis" and describes his relationship with him. Sam also shows great interest in the various cartoon characters and dancers strolling in the park. He is taken by how they use their costumes and bodies to communicate. One of the characters actually comes up to him when he is singing a song and dances to the beat of his song.

Grant, on the other hand, begins his journey in the park much differently. He sees the prices illuminated on the electronic chart describing all of the different ticket combinations and their prices. He immediately begins to calculate the best deal for his group. He considers the number of days they want to be at the park and how many times they plan to leave and come back on the same day. There are some special attractions he really wants to see and some he has no interest in at all. As he begins to walk around the park he surveys the restaurant menus and quickly figures out where he and his friends should eat their meals. He plans to eat an assortment of foods at a variety of establishments, all at the best prices. Grant pays careful attention to the physical environment of the park. He can't help but notice how clean and neat the park is kept. He is amazed by the environmental transitions from one part of the park to another. He keeps on pointing out to Juanita the various rock formations and plant life as they travel from exhibit to exhibit. He begins to annoy Sam when he keeps showing him the different cleaning vehicles and instruments at different locations throughout the park.

Juanita loves the various sculptures on display as she enters the park. She is equally impressed with the variety of colorful and animated exhibits. She is ecstatic with the relationships among the different themes and colors used to help set the mood of the different countries at EPCOT, especially those in France. Juanita can't stop talking about the creativity and detail of the map they were given to navigate through the park. The colorful images and pictures that persuade the visitors to rush to the next exhibit really intrigue her. Juanita spends much time during the day talking to the gatekeepers at the amusement rides and theme exhibits. She is really curious how they managed to get such a fun job. She even spent some time going to the teacher's center at EPCOT to find out about possible summer internships. On her way back she found a little boy who was lost and helped him find his parents. She told the boy she got lost once herself when she was his age while attending a baseball game. She eventually found her parents after about 15 minutes. Juanita also kept a journal of her two days at Disney World where she wrote down descriptions of her favorite exhibits, made observations about her reactions to exhibits, and even drew pictures of her favorite places, especially the Japan exhibit.

As you think about the three children described above, think about how different they are from one another. They approach the same environment in many different ways related to their personal interests, comfort levels, curiosity, knowledge, skills, and intellect. Each of them connects quite differently to the environment, yet they each bring a unique perspective to it. These approaches to the amusement park are more than just learning style differences. They represent different patterns of intelligence. This section of the chapter will explore the many different ways of being intelligent, not just the verbal, logical, and mathematical ways measured by traditional IQ tests. Now let us look more carefully at the work of Howard Gardner and this challenge to the prevailing notion of intelligence in his theory of multiple intelligences (MI).

Frames of Mind: The Theory of Multiple Intelligences (1983) and *Multiple Intelligences: The Theory in Practice* (1993) are two of Howard Gardner's major works in which he articulates and explores his theory and ideas of multiple perspectives of intelligence. He claims that intelligence is narrowly defined and the measuring of intelligence using IQ scores is very limiting. He feels strongly that the culture of society mirrors intelligence in ways that limit human potential and the ways that we can demonstrate our intelligence. He further concludes that intelligence can change from the time we are born, that it is not stagnant or totally fixed at birth. Intelligence is a dynamic and fluid process that we as parents, teachers, and mentors can nurture and have influence upon. We can help it grow in the children we teach and parent. He also sees intelligence as multidimensional and believes that we can be intelligent in many different ways.

A Person Who Helped Create Change . . .

Howard Gardner is a remarkable man. His contributions to the field of education have revolutionized the way we think about teaching and learning. From his theory of multiple intelligences to his study of extraordinary minds, Gardner challenges us to develop deep understandings of ideas and concepts, and he helps us broaden our typically restricted views of what it means to be smart. His latest work, *The Disciplined Mind* (1999), serves to synthesize much of his earlier writing.

Gardner is currently professor of cognition and education and adjunct professor of psychology at Harvard University; adjunct professor of neurology at the Boston School of Medicine; and former codirector (with David Perkins) of Project Zero at Harvard University.

Source: Photo by Jay Gardner (© 1993 and © 1998/99).

This all makes intuitive sense when we think about the strengths, weaknesses, talent, and skills of our friends and family members, athletes, artists, and our three new friends we just met at Disney World.

According to the work of Gardner (1983, in Campbell 1994) human intelligence consists of three components:

1. A set of skills that enables an individual to resolve genuine problems encountered in one's own life.

2. The ability to create an effective product or offer a service that is of value in one's culture.

3. The potential for finding or creating problems which enables an individual to acquire new knowledge. (3)

From this perspective, Gardner developed his theory of multiple intelligences in which he identified seven different intelligences. Gardner writes:

> I do not insist that the list of intelligences presented here be exhaustive. I would be astonished if it were. Yet, at the same time, there is something awry about a list that leaves glaring and obvious gaps, or one that fails to generate the vast majority of roles and skills valued by human cultures. Thus, a prerequisite for a theory of multiple intelligences, as a whole, is that it captures a reasonably complete gamut of the kinds of abilities valued by human cultures. We must account for the skills of a shaman and a psychoanalyst as well as of a yogi and a saint. (1983, 62)

In fact, about 14 years later in 1997, Gardner added his eighth intelligence, which he named *naturalist,* which further demonstrates the fluidity of his theories. The following eight intelligences are described below. We have added some learning and activity preferences for each of these intelligences.

Verbal-Linguistic

This intelligence is mainly concerned with language and the use of words. These individuals have a highly developed vocabulary and a strong sensitivity to the meaning of words. They communicate extremely well in both oral and written communications. They have excellent listening and speaking skills and communicate in clear and interesting ways.

> They like to read; debate; and write journals, reports, plays, and poetry.

Logical-Mathematical

The logical-mathematical person has the capacity to use numbers effectively and is especially competent in discerning quantitative relationships and connections, particularly related to calculations and scientific areas. These people are extremely good at mathematical processes such as classifications, generalization, calculations, and hypothesis testing.

> They like to classify and analyze lots of data, evaluate and hypothesize different ideas, use visual tools like organizers, calculate problems, use computers, and work with mathematical formulas.

Visual-Spatial

These people can skillfully manipulate images, and recognize and create visual forms mentally as well as on paper. Their intelligence involves sensitivity to color, line, shape, form, and space and the relationships among them. They have vivid imaginations and can create new images quickly.

> They like to create visuals such as posters, advertisements, book covers, and cartoons; create brainstorming maps, visual events, and objects; watch films and TV; use maps to find places of interest; and use and construct objects of different dimensions to make sense of information.

Bodily Kinesthetic

Bodily kinesthetic people have special expertise in using the whole body to express ideas and feelings. They have graceful body movements and an awareness of their own and others' positions in space. They have physical agility such as represented by dancers, actors, skilled workers, surgeons, and athletes. They are well coordinated and have a great sense of balance, dexterity, and flexibility.

> They like to use movement to express themselves (dance and act; build projects, models; conduct real science experiments; use tools to build things; play sports or involve themselves in physical activities).

Musical

Musical individuals exhibit strong sensitivity to sound and an ability to create and communicate through tones and rhythmic patterns. They can perceive, discriminate, transform, and express in musical forms. They gain much meaning from music and use it as a communication tool with others.

> They like to create songs and poems, play musical instruments, sing, listen to music, and interpret and analyze songs and poems.

Interpersonal

These people perceptively understand the perspective of another person, and they relate to others easily. They are skilled at working cooperatively. They have the ability to perceive and make distinctions in the moods, intentions, motivations, and feelings of other people. They are sensitive to facial expressions, voice, and gestures.

> They like to work in groups to solve problems and work on class projects, share learning and ideas with classmates, solve simulations that are problem based, role-play, take the lead in projects, and volunteer initiatives.

Intrapersonal

Intrapersonal individuals have the ability to reflect thoughtfully about themselves, are perceptive about personal abilities, and are attuned to personal history. They can key into their own strengths and weaknesses such as inner moods, intentions, desires, and temperaments. They are also self-disciplined and have good self-concepts.

> They like to write in journals and reflect on what they have experienced and learned, describe personal feelings, work independently on projects, defend actions of themselves and others, and express positions and opinions.

Naturalist

Naturalists have a strong understanding of the ecosystem. They are interested in and knowledgeable about the natural world. They effectively discriminate among sensory things.

> They like to be involved in outdoor natural environments like farms, woods, oceans, and environmental preserves; observe and record characteristics of different objects, animals, changes in the environment; care for animals; and collect examples from the naturalist world to classify, evaluate, and study the impact on the environment.

The eight intelligences mentioned above give us a good overview of Gardner's MI theory. Similar to our discussions about learning styles and personality types, individuals do not just have one intelligence, or two, but many, with varying degrees of competence. We are not just musically or mathematically smart. Most individuals have superior intelligences in a few areas. For example, Leonardo da Vinci was a painter, sculptor, architect, and scientist and Thomas Jefferson was a scientist, inventor, musician, statesman, and author. Think about some of your friends or teachers who have different kinds of intelligences. You can probably think of some that are excellent students, great athletes, fine artists, wonderful musicians, and gifted actors. However, they might be weak in another area or two, such as interpersonal or intrapersonal intelligence. Armstrong (1994) writes, "MI theory is not a 'type theory' for determining one intelligence that fits. It is a theory of cognitive functioning, and it proposes that each person has capacities in all eight intelligences. Of course, the eight intelligences function together in ways unique to each person" (11). It is important to realize that there are many ways to be smart, not just one or two. And few if any of us are gifted in all eight intelligences.

Since *Frames of Mind* was published in 1983, Gardner has continued to explore the powerful idea of intelligence. Gardner (1991) has made major connections between education and multiple intelligence. He argues that inside every learner or, for that matter, every person there is a five-year-old "unschooled mind" struggling to express itself. He is referring to the fragile grasp learners actually have on what they have been taught in school. Much information has been memorized and applied in narrow ways. He asserts that schools in many instances do not challenge learners to *really* think and are too book and test driven. He challenges us to move the learner beyond rote learning so that the learner will achieve a genuine understanding and richness of what is being taught. He advocates more apprenticeships, action-oriented projects outside the school (in museums, for instance), and service learning so that learning takes place in a rich and meaningful context. Recently, Gardner (1999) has synthesized his 30 years of research in education. He now argues that the purpose of K–12 education should be to enhance learners' deep understanding of truth (and falsity), beauty (and ugliness), and goodness (and evil) as defined by their culture. This deep understanding will be accomplished only if we are careful to allow learners to use the many forms that intelligence takes.

In summary, Howard Gardner encouraged the education community to step back and reexamine the way we are teaching our students. His recommendations challenged many educators to widen and lengthen the playing field to accommodate different intelligences. These challenges have led teachers, school districts, and even the very influential Education Testing Service (ETS) to expand their concept of assessment and the ways they measure understanding. We conclude our discussion of multiple intelligences by emphasizing how important it is for all teachers, and you, to recognize the unique characteristics of the students we teach. All of us must put forth great effort to celebrate students' differences by providing rich and diverse opportunities for students to learn.

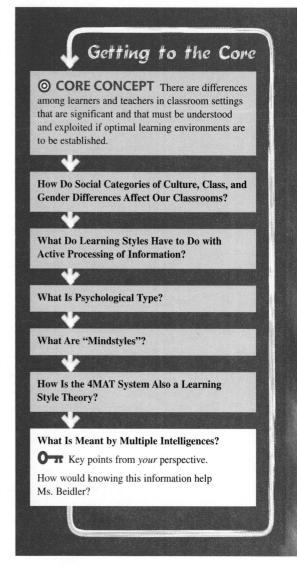

Think about it . . . **Return to the children who were exploring Disney World (page 191). What intelligences are each child exhibiting as he or she explores the park?**

Go to page 199 to see if your answers match ours.

If these children were people *you* know, who would they be?

Getting to the Core

◎ **CORE CONCEPT** There are differences among learners and teachers in classroom settings that are significant and that must be understood and exploited if optimal learning environments are to be established.

How Do Social Categories of Culture, Class, and Gender Differences Affect Our Classrooms?

What Do Learning Styles Have to Do with Active Processing of Information?

What Is Psychological Type?

What Are "Mindstyles"?

How Is the 4MAT System Also a Learning Style Theory?

What Is Meant by Multiple Intelligences?

�🗝 Key points from *your* perspective.

How would knowing this information help Ms. Beidler?

SCENARIO REVISITED

Once again it is time for you to consider the opening scenario, and your answer to the questions that we posed. Think back to the core concept for the chapter: There are differences among learners and teachers in classroom settings that are significant and that must be understood and exploited if optimal learning environments are to be established.

> **?** *Why do you think Sammy and Sally are more focused on the need for specific information than are Jill and John? And why might Linda want to work with another classmate whereas Lou prefers to work alone? What might others be thinking but not articulating during this discussion? If you were Ms. Beidler, what would you do now, and why?*

Use what you have learned from reading this chapter as you answer the questions. Then, read A Voice from the Field to see how an experienced teacher, knowledgeable about style differences, reacted to the Ms. Beidler case. Compare your responses to the teacher's responses.

 # A VOICE FROM THE FIELD

Many of the questions the students asked provide clues about the types of learners they are and give clues about ways to bridge the lesson for their needs. For the concrete sequential learners, I would provide more structure and direction by giving them guidelines on approximately how many subquestions and sources they should include in their papers. The abstract sequential learners like Jill will enjoy coming up with their own ideas, but they should be given a chance to brainstorm ideas with others or have teacher conferences. As each step of the project is completed, a conference would be helpful to give these learners a chance to record details in smaller chunks. This will allow the abstract sequential learners to stay on task. I would also supply some resources for these students to give them a place to start. The abstract random learners should be given the option to complete the project with a partner. However, these small groups will also need to have teacher conferences to keep them on-task and detail oriented. Any children working in groups would be required to write a reflective journal piece for individual accountability. They would need to reflect on the specific tasks they completed and how the group worked together as a whole.

Because the children have always had specific directions for projects, I would try to devise a style-sensitive project with more explicit directions. Going on the assumption that the whole lesson was developed using 4MAT, this project would fit in quadrant 4 and would best meet the needs of dynamic learners, concrete random learners, and intuitive-type learners. These students like to discover things on their own, and go beyond the information that was given to create new ideas and applications.

Ms. Beidler should design her project according to Kathleen Butler's *Style Differentiated Instruction* (1996). All of the students will complete the project as originally planned. However, I would use the bridging approach because the project itself is already directed toward one learning style. These assisting techniques will bridge the project to help all students use their own styles.

SDI action plan

Specific outcome: The students will understand the value of research.

Specific objective: Given the elements of a research paper, the students will report information learned through a paper and a presentation.

Materials: Encyclopedias, periodicals, computers with Internet access, and access to a library for any other materials that may be needed (abstract sequential). An advanced organizer identifying the elements of a research paper (concrete/abstract sequential).

Time frame: 1 month

Introduction:

1. Brainstorm with students some questions about major topics they would like to research.
2. Have them choose two questions and brainstorm several subquestions that would help lead to the answer to the major questions. Students may come up with their own individual major questions to be approved by the teacher (abstract/concrete random).
3. If students have common questions, they may work as a team. However, they may choose to work alone (abstract sequential).
4. Student/teacher conference at the end of the first week to choose the best topic question and subquestions for research (concrete/abstract sequential).

Procedure:

1. Review advanced organizer identifying the elements of a research paper.
2. Length of research paper is up to individual questions. When question is answered, the research is complete (concrete random).
3. A minimum of five sources is required (concrete/abstract sequential—given structure, concrete/abstract random—given open-ended number of sources).
4. Sources can include any typical reference materials or verbal sources from specialists in the field (abstract random).
5. References are due at the end of the second week.
6. Rough draft of research paper due at the end of the third week (concrete/abstract sequential).
7. Brainstorm different types of presentations to share information researched (abstract/concrete sequential).
8. Student/teacher conference to discuss the type of presentation to be used by the group or individual to share information researched (abstract/concrete random).
9. Some ideas for presentations using Howard Gardner's theory of multiple intelligences could include but not be limited to:

   • A completed original organizer of information with oral presentation (logical-mathematical intelligence)

- A videotape of interview of living resource (interpersonal intelligence)
- An audiotape of information (verbal-linguistic)
- A slide show presentation on the computer (visual-spatial intelligence)
- A play (bodily kinesthetic intelligence)
- A poem (verbal-linguistic intelligence)
- A song (musical intelligence)
- A form of artwork with an oral presentation (visual-spatial intelligence)
- Individual idea

Closure:
1. Final paper should be handed in at the end of the fourth week.
2. Presentations should be scheduled using a sign-up sheet of day and time.
3. Journals of reflection for individual accountability are due the day of the presentation (intrapersonal intelligence).

Reflections on Individual Students

Sammy and Sally's psychological type preferences seem to be sensing, thinking, and judging. They prefer to get information directly from their senses. They want the directions for the project written down on an assignment sheet or answers given orally directly from Ms. Beidler. Sammy and Sally need to make their decisions about their projects directly from the information given. They prefer the judgment function of order, regulation, and control. They prefer that the project outline already be organized for them with a specific closing activity. Their learning styles are more concrete sequential.

Jill and John's psychological type preferences seem to be intuition, feeling, and perception. They make sense of their worlds by creating patterns and prefer to see the big picture. As feelers, they prefer to make decisions on the basis of how these decisions feel to them. Being judgers, Jill and John want to keep options open. They prefer to seek to understand and follow their own curiosity. Jill and John would prefer the original way Ms. Beidler set up the project. They are more random-type learners.

Linda's interests flow to the outer world of actions, objects, and persons. As an extravert with a tendency toward an interpersonal intelligence, Linda relates to others easily. She would like to work in a group to complete the class project because she prefers to share learning and ideas with classmates. Lou states that he would prefer to reflect on something this big by himself. As an introvert with a tendency toward an intrapersonal intelligence, Lou's preference is to work independently on the class project. He probably has the ability to be self-disciplined and have a good self-concept in order to accomplish the project independently.

Other students in the class may be thinking but not articulating their thoughts during this discussion. Some abstract sequential learners might prefer more structure and direction such as a brainstorming session exploring some ideas about what others are researching. They may also think that they should have a choice between a final paper and the presentation. This new type of open-ended research may make the concrete sequential learners feel uncomfortable about this project. These students may want to know how many sub-questions they need. The concrete random learners may want to know how much each part of the project is worth for the final grade. They may ask for a rubric to meet all of the teacher's expectations for the project in order to receive the highest possible grade. The abstract random learners may want to know if they work in groups, how will Ms. Beidler know if they all did their part. They may want to keep a journal of how effectively they participated in the group.

I would keep the final paper and the presentation as a requirement even though it may take many children out of their "comfort zone." As stated in this chapter, "There is nothing wrong with requiring learners to stretch a bit by doing things in ways other than the ways they prefer to do them. This helps those learners develop their other functions." However, when considering Howard Gardner's theory of *multiple intelligences,* I would give a variety of options to the students for their final presentations. This would allow the students to be able to present their information in a way that is comfortable to them. It would also enable me as a teacher to see the different ways my students are smart. Once again, the students would need to conference with the teacher in order to propose their idea of a final presentation.

As always, my class makeup is different each year. Some classes require more detailed information, others more flexibility and spontaneity. As a teacher, it is my job to step back and reflect on the types of learners that are in my class. I then need to stretch my teaching style to meet students' individual strengths and weaknesses.

This is the voice of Kathleen McGrother. Ms. McGrother is a second-grade teacher.

Answer to Roger case (p. 172):

Roger's type is ENFP. He is outgoing (Extravert). He prefers activity and possibilities to precise details (iNtuitor). Roger does not like group conflict (Feeler), and in his outer world he seeks new experiences rather than closure (Perceiver).

Answer to Missy case (p. 177):

Missy's type is ISFJ. She is quiet and shy (Introvert). She prefers precise details to activity and possibilities (Sensor). Missy, like Roger, does not like group conflict (Feeler), and in her outer world she seeks closure rather than new experiences (Judger).

Answers to Gregorc Learning Style Scenario (p. 180).

Rachel—concrete sequential
Trevor—abstract sequential
Donna—abstract random
Danny—concrete random
(Remember, these are only predominant styles—all learners share characteristics of the other styles—no individual learner is just one style.)

Answers to Question in Think about it box (p. 195).

Sam—visual-spatial
     bodily-kinesthetic
     visual-linguistic
Grant—logical-mathematical
     visual-spatial
     naturistic
Juanita—visual-spatial
     interpersonal
     intrapersonal

PLANNING FOR INSTRUCTION

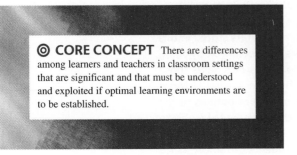

◎ CORE CONCEPT There are differences among learners and teachers in classroom settings that are significant and that must be understood and exploited if optimal learning environments are to be established.

Your unit of study now includes a comprehensive lesson plan that incorporates core concepts and many of the powerful principles and strategies discussed in Chapters 1 through 4. Now we ask you to turn your attention to *adjusting* that instruction to meet the needs of individual learners. Throughout Chapter 5, you have examined how humans actively process information—through style preferences. Individuals differ in how they take in and perceive information and what they do with the information. The combination of individual differences that learners and teachers bring to the classroom fall under the category of learning and teaching styles. Also critical to meeting the needs of learners are the considerations related to how you can adjust instruction to include elements of socioeconomic status, culture (ethnicity and race), and gender differences. All these differences are important when designing instruction for diverse learners.

These differences must be reflected in our lesson and unit planning if we are going to strive to reach a larger percentage of our students. So, keeping in mind the core concept written above, we ask you to reexamine your unit and lesson plan. What adjustments can you make to better address learners' individual differences? How can an understanding of the four learning styles enhance your instructional strategies and promote your learners' active processing of information? Specifically, look at both your unit and lesson plan and make adjustments based on (1) psychological type, (2) mindstyles, (3) 4MAT types, and (4) multiple intelligences.

1. Social Categories of Culture, Class, and Gender Differences

Consider

These are our adjustments to our lesson and unit plans for social categories of culture, class, and gender differences.

- Communicate the same level of expectations for all students with the understanding that different students will need differing levels and types of support.

- Use examples of role models such as scientists and weather forecasters from the community that represent both genders.

- Be conscious of the roles you give students in group projects. Make sure role responsibilities are not gender stereotyped and over time are geared to areas of strength and areas to be strengthened.

- Provide materials, books, and media that are produced by both men and women and that feature representations of all types of diversity.

2. Psychological Type

Consider

These are our adjustments for personality types. In our weather unit, we meet the needs of *extraverted* learners by allowing them to work in groups and by using such strategies as jigsaw. For *introverts,* we include options for working alone or in very small groupings (such as pairs, by using think-pair-share). *Intuitive* types like the "what-if" questions and the opportunity to design, for example, their own weather stations. *Sensing* types benefit from the videotape and making severe observations, recording information, and doing research that goes into writing a report. *Thinking* types like information. They enjoy learning about the facts related to weather phenomena. Preparing a thunderstorm safety manual delights the *feeling* types. They like to see the personal relevance related to their work. Perhaps we could increase the opportunities for students to link weather facts to the thunderstorms' impact on our lives, or the lives of other living organisms.

3. Mindstyles

Activity

The lesson plan in Chapter 4 has the students view a thunderstorm videotape (10 minutes) which shows thunderstorms occurring in various parts of the country. Students view examples of origination of lightning, sounds of thunder, and intervals depending on location and intensity of the storm and record their observations.

Consider

What are our adjustments for learning styles? What are we doing to accommodate for different styles?

This activity is well suited for *concrete random (CR)* and *abstract random (AR)* learners. *Abstract sequential (AS)* learners will do fine with this activity, too, but might prefer something more sequential. However, *concrete sequential (CS)* learners would be least comfortable with this type of activity and would need a graphic organizer to classify information. The organizer would help the CS learner look for specifics—types of lightning, places lightning strikes, and sounds of lightning and thunder. This would help CR and AR learners who probably need organizational strategies. Now, as you accommodate for one learning style you are always stretching another. When you plan to meet students' individual learning needs, you also grow professionally as you stretch your own teaching style.

Consider

Did we try to include other powerful instructional strategies? We set up learning centers with computer capabilities where students can access additional information about thunderstorms. They provide an environment for the AS to work independently, investigate, and read additional materials. The CR learner enjoys the opportunity to explore, the search for alternatives to issues, and the open-ended environment. The final stage of this lesson on thunderstorms is project oriented (refer to project learning in Chapter 4). Each student creates a thunderstorm safety manual for his or her family. We asked ourselves what type of learner would like this activity? How could we design the project to accommodate a wider range of learners while stretching others?

Special Consideration

How do levels of thinking and learning styles relate? Can you blend these ideas in your lesson? (Revisit "Create an Experience" in Chapter 3.)

Create an Experience: Students are led through a visualization exercise (a story) that brings to mind personal experiences or images from TV, movies, or books of various types of storms (tornadoes, thunderstorms, hurricanes, and snowstorms). Grouped by three's, students share experiences and produce a chart describing each type of severe storm. Individually, the students describe in their journal how a specific severe storm affected their personal lives and had an impact on the environment.

This activity is attractive to the random-type learner who likes imaginative, open-ended, group-oriented, journal writing, and divergent activities. It allows for producing a chart that would be attractive for the sequential learner, making the lesson style sensitive. Now let's consider levels of thinking (lower- and higher-ordering questioning/activities) discussed in Chapter 4. Using Bloom's taxonomy as a guide, you can design instruction that is also style sensitive at varying levels of complexity. The visualization requires basic recall (knowledge), and describing each type of storm puts information into the learner's own words (comprehension). Charting the information based on different types of storms requires categorization or classifying (application and or analysis based on the content and prior learning) and writing how a storm affected their personal lives and the environment is either application or a lower level of interpretation or connecting (analysis). If you wanted to challenge students at a higher level (synthesis or evaluation) for this specific activity you could construct the following kinds of activities based on style preferences:

CS: Develop a questionnaire asking adults to describe personal experiences with thunderstorms.

AR: Predict the dangers for animals, plant life, and playgrounds during thunderstorms.

AS: Develop a policy of procedures for your family to follow during thunderstorms.

CR: Based on a story about being stuck in a dangerous thunderstorm, figure out what to do.

Consider

Have we blended the lower- and higher-order questioning strategies and activities to accommodate for style differences?

4. 4MAT (a Learning Style Theory)

In Chapter 3 you were introduced to the 4MAT system. The chapter explained how this system could be used to plan lessons that make use of social learning, contextualist, and information processing theory. 4MAT encourages us to plan instruction based upon learning style and individual differences, and adds the dimensions of brain research (right- and left-brain learning) and assessment strategies. It is now time to place your unit or lesson plan into the eight steps of 4MAT. Below is our example from the weather unit for you to use as a guide. Or, you can go back to page 187 and review the unit "Investigating the Natural World" that uses the 4MAT system.

Quadrant 1—Why?

Step 1: Create an experience activity designed to demonstrate the power of teamwork and how it relates to the concept of "systems." A teacher-led visualization exercise helps bring to mind the sights, sounds, and experiences of storms.

Step 2: Analyze the experience; in groups discuss and chart the experience.

Quadrant 2—What?

Step 3: Integrate the experience. Describe in a journal how storms have impacted your life and the environment.

Step 4: Learn the content—use an advance organizer, conduct teacher-led activities about weather, severe storms, water cycle, and their impact on the environment. Form research groups.

Quadrant 3—How?

Step 5: Practice—jigsaw activity, design new graphic organizer, list similarities and differences between storms, and set up practice and feedback mechanism.

Step 6: Personal adaptation—experiments conducted in and out of school, design questions for game "How to Weather a Storm."

Quadrant 4—What-If?

Step 7: Analysis of results—review class notes, journals, experiments, group organizers, Internet sites, and learning center content in preparation for final project.

Step 8: Create more complex understanding.

- Design a new and improved visual with a written summary that connects the major ideas.
- Create a severe weather book with illustrations and pictures.
- Design a weather station for a town, write a research paper, design and carry out an experiment, or propose an idea.
- Develop severe weather manual for your community.

5. Multiple Intelligences

The last model we present comes from Howard Gardner, who sees intelligence as multidimensional and believes that we can be smart in many ways. This relates to how we design and adjust instruction based on learners' strengths, weaknesses, talents, skills, preferences, and personality types. Gardner adds to the challenge by saying learners vary in the ways they are intelligent and speculates that if students were to approach learning from an intellectual strength, then maybe they would be more motivated and have a greater chance of understanding and being successful. Gardner (1991, 1993) has illustrated his model using *entry points* to address varying intelligences which can be a successful way to access students' prior experience or knowledge. This strategy encourages learner exploration of a topic through as many as five of the intelligences. The five include narrational (presenting a story); logical-quantitative (using numbers or deduction); foundational (examining philosophy and vocabulary); aesthetic (focusing on sensory features); and experiential (hands-on). Using an alternative approach to the Creating an Experience activity in the unit plan from Chapter 3, we've taken Gardner's information and developed five examples of how to begin the weather unit that would give the students their own choice of entry point.

Consider

How can we motivate, connect to prior knowledge, involve in a meaningful activity, and consider students' multiple intelligences? We let students decide how to begin learning about the content. They can pick from the following options:

Narrational—presenting a story (verbal-linguistic intelligence): Student can research information, use personal experience, or talk to friends and families about storms. Then, the student could write a story or poem, create a skit, or produce a short audio- or videotape about severe storms.

Logical-quantitative—using numbers or deduction (logical-mathematical intelligence): Student collects storm data from Internet sources and charts results, observes severe storms or videos of severe storms and classifies results, or designs a question about severe storms, answers questions and generalizes or classifies results.

Foundational—examining philosophy and vocabulary (combination of verbal-linguistic-logical intelligence): Student might want to examine the question, "Why do we need severe storms?" and produce a statement based on personal beliefs and information collected, or, collect assorted kinds of information, pictures, and statistics and make some type of conclusion about severe storms.

Aesthetic—focusing on sensory features (combination of musical, visual, spatial intelligence): Student might watch a movie about severe storms and pick a scene to draw or write about, collect famous photographs of severe storms, listen to various sounds of storm conditions, or draw a storm theme.

Experiential—hands-on (bodily kinesthetic, interpersonal, intrapersonal, or naturalistic intelligence): Student might explore damaged areas after a severe storm, care for an animal who was injured in a severe storm, build a small dam to help protect wildlife, conduct a storm experiment, or build a storm protector for a dog house.

Special Note

Consider

Are entry points teacher or student driven? In our example, the students are given choices of ways to "enter" the learning experience. They choose a specific method of entry and pursue it either individually or in a small group. Even though the teacher designs the options, the student pursues his or her own interest. An alternative method would be to have the teacher design all the entry points and present them in class for all the students to experience. This would allow students to *stretch* the way they enter into the new information (i.e., to accommodate an entry point that does not match their preference). This would be consistent with our understanding of meeting and challenging the learning styles of all students.

Your Turn

Continue developing your lesson and turn your attention to adjusting that instruction to meet the needs of individual learners.

CHAPTER SUMMARY

In previous chapters, we treated human learning as if we are all the same. In this chapter we talk about individual differences—those that exist among students and their teachers, and really among all human beings. We suggest taking a social justice perspective, one that strives to make our schools and classrooms truly inclusive. That means understanding, appreciating, and putting to use the social and cultural differences learners bring to school. Further, we explained in this chapter that learners have different styles, or characteristic ways of behaving and learning, that are not necessarily the same as everyone else's preferred way of doing things. Even though schools often act as if these style differences do not exist by developing "one size fits all" instruction, we have evidence that this is not the best way to help all learners succeed in our classrooms. When we actively process information, we usually do so through our style preferences. We humans differ in how we take in, or perceive, information; we also differ on what we then do with that information.

In order to be able to intelligently address these individual differences, we need to turn to people who have spent their careers studying them and helping us make practical use of them. Carl Jung developed the notion of personality types, and Isabel Myers and others built upon his work to help us understand how we can use type theory as we develop powerful instruction for our learners. The ideas of introversion, extraversion, sensing, intuition, thinking, feeling, judging, and perceiving, and how they play out in our classrooms, were all derived from the works of these people.

Another way to look at differences is through Anthony Gregorc's concept of mindstyles. Mindstyles differentiate between those of us who perceive information either concretely or abstractly and those who order that information either sequentially or randomly. Learners bring these differences into our classrooms, and Kathleen Butler has helped us identify them and know some ways to address them through instruction.

The 4MAT system connects these two learning style theories together and gives us an instructional system that we can use in a very practical manner to plan and conduct lessons for our students. This system helps us broaden our typical instruction well beyond just presenting information and then requiring students to practice it in traditional paper-pencil format. If we follow the system, we ensure that we are addressing students' different learning styles. The bonus of using this system, in addition to the fact that it brings together both personality-type theory and mindstyles, is that it relates beautifully to information processing theory as well. And for that matter, using 4MAT gives us a structure within which we can also use major ideas from social learning and contextualist theories.

Another approach to the idea of individual differences is the notion of multiple intelligences (MI). In this view we are all smart in some ways. Unfortunately, traditional education values certain intelligences (verbal, logical, mathematical) more highly than others. But the key idea here is to allow learners multiple entry points to deep understanding of ideas and concepts. In that regard, MI theory can be of great help to teachers as they promote student learning through powerful instruction.

Chapter 6 will continue our discussion of teaching for conceptual change by helping you understand a very important, but often poorly understood, point. There are some individuals whose differences are so great that their education requires special considerations. But successfully educating these students is not so simple as just placing them in a special class segregated from most other children in the school.

Getting to the Core

How Do the Social Categories of Culture, Class, and Gender Differences Affect Our Classrooms?

◎ **CORE CONCEPT**   There are differences among learners and teachers in classroom settings that are significant and that must be understood and exploited if optimal learning environments are to be established.

- These differences are crucial to help learners acquire new information and skills. Social categories help teachers make educational decisions and assess what learners have actually learned.

- Social class is determined by socioeconomic status (SES) which is directly correlated with school performance and predicts intelligence (as measured by IQ tests), student grades, and performance on achievement tests.

- Culture is a larger concept than SES and includes values, customs, religious preferences, physical characteristics and traits, attitudes, beliefs, *ethnicity and race.*

- Gender differences and bias must be considered when designing instruction.

What Do We Mean by "Styles"?

- Styles are typical preferences that we have that cause us to behave in predictable ways and help the teacher better predict how students will react in the classroom.

What Do Learning Styles Have to Do with Active Processing of Information?

- Styles are simply typical preferences that cause us to behave in predictable ways. Style theories look at how human beings differ in the manner we take in or perceive stimuli and the manner in which we process, order, or make decisions about the stimuli.

What Is Psychological Type?

- Jung's theory helps us understand the preferences we have for behaving in our environment. There are four mental functions that we use each day: sensing, intuition, thinking, and feeling.

- Sensors and intuitors differ in the way they prefer to acquire information. Sensors look at realities, work with givens and focus on the physical aspects of stimuli. Intuitors focus on ideas as they acquire information. They create patterns and prefer to see the big picture. Thinkers and feelers differ on the way they prefer to make decisions once they've taken in information. Thinkers analyze information, strive for objectivity and use dispassionate logic. Feelers make decisions based on personal values.

- Humans differ on where we focus our attention when we use each function. Extroverts prefer to focus on the outer world of people and things; they prefer action and variety. Introverts prefer to focus their energies on the inner world of thoughts and ideas. They prefer to reflect before they act.

- Myers and McCaulley expanded Jung's work by adding Perceiving (perceivers like flexibility and spontaneity and like to keep their options open and follow their curiosity), and Judging (judgers like order, regulation, and control and strive for organization and closure).

- When planning to accommodate different learners, start planning with the ES learner in mind. Develop alternative activities for IS, EN, and IN learners and then adjust for TF and JP dimensions that are important to your learners.

What Are Mindstyles?

- Gregorc looks at the two functions of perceiving and ordering as they relate to getting and making sense of new information. The perceiving function, concerned with getting or obtaining new information, has two qualities: concreteness or abstractness. Concrete learners prefer getting information through the physical senses. Abstract learners prefer more symbolic, feeling, or emotional and intuitive methods for getting information. The ordering function deals with the way the mind grasps and arranges new information and ideas. This function has two qualities as well: sequence and randomness. Sequential learners are more methodical and prefer a logical order for new information. They like to develop an order to follow and like to work on one task at a time. Random learners place information in a less linear order. They are not so concerned with order and arrangement. They tend to find their own order and are good at working on more than one thing at a time.

- Four patterns of mindstyles emerge from these two dimensions: concrete sequential, abstract sequential, concrete random, and abstract random.

How Do Learning Styles Relate to Social Categories?

- Research on cultural learning styles, personality types, and mindstyles indicates that teachers must recognize differences in culture *and* differences in learning styles to truly support and help minority students so that they succeed in school.

How is the 4MAT System Also a Learning Style Theory?

- According to the 4MAT system, interactions among the feeling of experience, the thinking of conceptualization, the watching of reflection, and the doing of action incorporate the entire range of the learning experience. Because the 4MAT plan teaches using a natural cycle of learning, there is no real need for teachers to determine each student's style, since all learners' styles will be met at some point during the instructional sequence. By using 4MAT, you are using some ideas from the work of Jung and Gregorc and designing instruction using powerful strategies such as COVER and practice and feedback.

Are There Connections among Jung's Types, Gregorc's Mindstyles, and McCarthy's 4MAT System?

- These theories all look at the ways people take in information, and the ways people make use of this information. They vary slightly and use different words to describe how people learn.

What Is Meant by Multiple Intelligences?

- Developed by Howard Gardner, the theory of multiple intelligences states that there is more than one way to be smart. Gardner sees intelligence as a dynamic and fluid entity that is multidimensional and that we can be intelligent in many different ways.

- Human intelligence consists of three things: (1) a set of skills that enable a person to resolve genuine problems, (2) the ability to create an effective product or offer a service that is of value in one's culture, and (3) the potential for finding or creating problems which enable an individual to acquire new knowledge.

- Gardner has identified eight intelligences thus far: verbal-linguistic, logical-mathematical, visual-spatial, bodily kinesthetic, musical, interpersonal, intrapersonal, and naturalist.

Powerful Principles Applied to Special Education

Frank & Ernest / Bob Thaves
(Source: Frank & Ernest © NEA. Reprinted by permission.)

 SCENARIO

Ms. Bailey was a student teacher at a public school in Philadelphia. As a college senior, she did her student teaching at a school for learners with physical disabilities. The 10 fourth graders she worked with all faced physical challenges such as cerebral palsy, spina bifida, and traumatic brain injuries. Their cognitive abilities varied widely, with reading skills ranging from primer to seventh-grade level. Their math levels also varied greatly. Perceptual difficulties further challenged them. They had trouble refocusing from the board or chart in the front of the room to their desks, and had difficulty with number and letter reversals. Many of the learners had scattered cognitive abilities. For example, they might be able to read but unable to answer comprehension questions related to what they read. They might be adept at computation but unable to independently solve math problems. Finally, the learners possessed a variety of hand skills. Some had full use of their hands, whereas others had very limited hand movement. One learner could use only one finger and had extremely limited verbal skills.

The classroom theme at the time of Ms. Bailey's lesson was colonial America. The objective of the lesson was for students to explore the concepts of problem solving, basic geometry, and patterns. To accomplish this goal, Ms. Bailey asked students to build a colonial postage stamp. The colonial postage stamp was a traditional design sewn on quilts during colonial times. The students' task was to build a 16-patch postage stamp design using eight colors of textiles with no color touching the same color on a side or a corner. They would then record the design on grid paper.

At the time that Ms. Bailey conducted her lesson, the learners had been studying colonial America for approximately three weeks. She introduced the lesson by reading them a short paragraph on the historical background of the postage stamp design and how it was used as a pattern on a colonial quilt. Her effect was flat and disinterested as she read the paragraph. The students did not seem to be engaged or to understand exactly what she was talking about. This may have been the first exposure the learners had to the idea of a colonial quilt.

Ms. Bailey then proceeded to tell the learners that they were going to use textiles to create the postage stamp quilt design using eight colors and that no two patches of the same color could touch each color on a side or a corner. The students worked individually at their desks after receiving their instructions. She gave them 10 minutes to work on the task. As she walked around the room, she told the learners whether their work was right or wrong. She used verbal praise when the learners were on-task and working correctly. She also used verbal prompts to redirect students who were not on-task. For example, she said, "Remember, textiles are not toys." Several learners were "playing" with the textiles. Ms. Bailey used a verbal reprimand, "Nate, stop playing with the textiles!" Although there was a classroom behavior plan in place at this time, Ms. Bailey did not use it consistently.

After 10 minutes, one learner had completed the design successfully. It seemed the others were confused and having difficulty completing the task. After a few more minutes, Ms. Bailey displayed a large poster of the postage stamp design. The poster was stationed in the front of the room. She then told the students to stop using the textiles and to copy the design onto the graph paper using the poster in the front of the room as a model. Seven learners displayed confusion when trying to transfer the design to graph paper. Two were on the road to

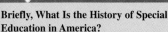

Getting to the Core

 CORE CONCEPT Learners with special needs are *not* so different from other learners. Therefore, when instruction is properly adjusted, powerful techniques can and should be used with these learners.

Briefly, What Is the History of Special Education in America?

How Do We Group Learners for Instruction in America's Schools?

How Homogeneous Are Our Classrooms, Really?
- Grade Designations in Regular Education
- Labels in Special Education

How Should We Use General and Specific Information?
- The Emergence of Developmental Theory
- Some Significant Developmental Differences

How Do Powerful Principles Relate to Learners with Special Needs?
- IEPs and Traditional Learning Theory
- Using Powerful Principles in Special Education Classrooms
- Adopting a Growth Paradigm

How Can We Teach Groups of Learners with Diverse Abilities and Needs?
- Social Dimensions and Special Education
- Differentiated Instruction

What Are Some Specific Techniques to Use with Learners with Disabilities?

How Can Powerful Principles Accommodate Learners with Special Needs in Regular Classrooms?
- Teach Students Learning Strategies
- Use Specific Techniques to Accommodate Learners

completing this task without difficulty. One learner completed this task success-fully and then sat with nothing to do. Shortly after the students had begun this transfer assignment, it was time to leave for lunch. Ms. Bailey ended the lesson by telling the students to stop what they were doing and to line up for lunch. The learn-ers seemed puzzled as they were getting in line.

> **?** *Why do you think the learners were puzzled as they left the room to go to lunch? Do you agree with Ms. Bailey's approach to discipline? Do you think Ms. Bailey individualized her lesson appropriately to accommodate her students' various physical and cognitive abilities? Do you think requiring the learners to complete the activity individually was a good idea?*

INTRODUCTION

There is a serious misunderstanding of special education among many teachers, and certainly among members of the general public. In this chapter we hope to provide an educationally sound and morally defensible perspective. We are certain that this will be the most controversial chapter in the book. That is because the core concept asserts a notion that few people either can or are willing to entertain—that learners with disabilities are not as different from nondisabled learners as many have been led to believe. (We also insist that nondisabled learners are not so simi-lar to one another as schools pretend they are, a point we shall expand upon later.) As the cartoon that leads off this chapter and the quote that appears in the margin suggest, none of us is perfect. We all have strengths, and we all have weaknesses. That idea, at its most superficial level, is a slogan with which few would argue. Because of the importance of grades and achievement in school, however, those learners who do not succeed are often singled out from others for special treatment. This, too, sounds like a good thing. But in practice it takes on an often vicious form that has unintended consequences for the learner. A brief look at the history of spe-cial education will provide a context for issues that teachers must understand before they can truly change classroom instruction to make it more powerful for learners with special needs.

"Because all humans are subtle variations on a theme—each person's genome is slightly different—none can be considered perfect. And none can be considered flawed. The new lens of genetics teaches that human beings are, at once, all different and all the same."

(Source: McFarling and Boyd, 1999.)

Briefly, What Is the History of Special Education in America?

In their article that calls for reforming elementary and special education teacher preparation, Feden and Clabaugh (1986) provide a historical perspective that can help put special education into a larger context related to some ideas presented in Chapter 1 of this book. Very early American education in the late colonial and early national period was characterized by teachers listening to individual learners recite answers to questions that they were asked. Based upon these answers, teachers made decisions about what to do next to help that learner progress.

But a confluence of factors eventually changed the individualized nature of this type of instruction. America saw the dawning of the Industrial Age, where facto-ries, specialization, and mass production replaced cottage industries and private artisans. At about the same time, compulsory attendance laws required bigger classes and schools to accommodate increasing numbers of learners. Reflecting the factory model of efficiency, schools organized themselves for group rather than individual instruction. A popular way of doing this was to place learners into grades according to their chronological ages (Feden and Clabaugh 1986, 180). Despite isolated and largely failed attempts at innovation, this is the system we have in today's schools.

To be sure, the most severely disabled among learners were always excluded from formal schooling during these periods of American history. As chronological age groupings became more systematized, other learners who had previously been able to at least cling to the fringes of the system began to fall between the cracks. This gave way to the rise of special education classes for learners who, in those days, were called exceptional learners. Two different kinds of teachers were trained; there were those who would work with "regular" education learners, and those who would work with "special" education, or *exceptional* learners. Because chronological groupings did not work as well for learners with serious learning and behavior problems, assignments to special education classes were made as much upon the basis of disability labels as upon the basis of age. Learners were grouped by categories such as mentally retarded, emotionally disturbed, and physically handicapped.

The field of special education grew as more and more learners were identified as having learning and behavior problems. A new label for those with learning problems emerged in full force—*learning disabilities.* Students with learning disabilities displayed a number of learning problems that could not be explained by low intelligence or other kinds of sensory or behavioral disabilities. Often they had specific problems processing language. Students with learning disabilities commonly exhibited reading problems and frequently reversed, omitted, or added letters in words, and words in sentences. The word *dyslexia* was often used to refer to these learners, and it became a household term even though many people failed to realize that rather than a single disorder, the term itself refers to any number of disorders in the lexical (verbal) system.

Now an interesting and very unfortunate chain of events was established that led to tremendous growth in the number of learners enrolled in special education classes. Federal and state money poured into local school district budgets to subsidize the education of those with *handicaps.* Because students with learning disabilities exhibited subtle but nonetheless apparent learning problems, many who otherwise would have remained in regular education were referred to special education. Why? Schools were handsomely subsidized to educate these learners, and it was relatively easy to refer learners for special education services. Regular education teachers did so with great frequency, and in increasing numbers these teachers lost their tolerance for deviance from the norm. The cycle was then established—learners with increasingly milder learning differences were referred to special education classes, thereby further reducing the range of abilities among learners in regular education classes, leading to additional referrals of learners with even milder differences, and so on.

This is the way learners and adolescents *were* educated until the human rights movement in the mid- to late 1960s began to have a mighty influence on our culture. At the same time, some people were beginning to question the effectiveness of full-time placement of learners, at least those with mild disabilities, into special education classes. This led Dunn (1968) to ask in the title of his seminal article on the efficacy of self-contained classes, "Special Education for the Mildly Retarded—Is

> *Think about it . . .*
>
> In Boston schools, 37% of all students are identified for special education, bilingual education, or chapter 1 compensatory programs (Miles 1995).
>
> In New York State, spending for students with disabilities was 5% of total budgets in 1980, and increased to 13% of total budgets in 1992 (Lankford and Wyckoff 1995).
>
> Should these trends continue, what do you predict will be the consequences for regular education?

Some Interesting Facts

- In 1996, learners with disabilities receiving services in federally supported programs constituted 12% of all students enrolled in public schools (grades K–12), up from 8% in 1977.

- The number of students who participated in federal programs for learners with disabilities increased 51% between 1977 and 1996.

- Between 1977 and 1996 the percentage of learners identified as having specific learning disabilities rose from 2% to 6%.

- In 1995, 73% of public school learners with disabilities were served in regular classrooms or in resource rooms in a regular school building, while 23% were served in separate classes in regular school buildings.

(Source: U.S. Department of Education, Office of Special Education and Rehabilitative Services: http://nces.ed.gov/pubs98/condition98/c9845a01.html.)

A More Contemporary Look at Efficacy

In a recent monograph, Kavale and Forness examined the *special* techniques used in special education, including stimulant medication, psycholinguistic training, psychotropic medications, social skills training, modality instruction, the Feingold diet, and perceptual-motor training. They also examined the *education* part of special education, including mnemonic strategies, reading comprehension, behavior modification, direct instruction, early intervention, peer tutoring, and computer-assisted instruction. The *special* techniques, the special part of *special* education, produced only about a 10% advantage for students who received them. They wrote, "As a group, special *education* is almost four times as effective as *special* education, and is likely to move the average special education student from the 50th percentile to the 82nd percentile" (80–81). So it is education, not special education, that should be stressed with learners with disabilities, a point made by Lloyd Dunn over 30 years ago!

[Source: K. Kavale, S. Forness, and G. Siperstein (1998). Efficacy of special education and related services. *Monograph of the American Association on Mental Deficiency 19.]*

Much of It Justifiable?" He reported research that found students with mild learning problems fared better when left in regular education classes than they did when they were removed from such classes and placed in special education classes. By the early 1970s, legislation was passed that had a huge impact on special education. It was meant both to curtail unnecessary special education placements, and to ensure appropriate services for those learners who genuinely needed them. This legislation changed the fundamental relationship between regular and special education.

The most influential piece of legislation was Public Law 94-142, also called the Education for All Handicapped Children Act. Passed in 1975, this law protected the due process rights of learners so that they were not unfairly labeled as handicapped and segregated from other learners into full-time special education classrooms, even as it encouraged the identification of learners who needed special education. Just as important, it required that all learners, regardless of handicap or disability, be allowed access to a free, appropriate public education. Learners with the most severe disabilities could no longer be excluded from school. Finally, this law mandated that learners identified as needing special education services be educated in the least restrictive environment possible. In other words, those learners not needing full-time special education placements were to be placed into regular education classes for that part of the school day for which special services were not required. This practice came to be known as *mainstreaming.* Although the word itself never appeared on paper in the legislation, P.L. 94-142 became known as the *mainstreaming law.*

That is the historical perspective. Some of the political context has changed since then. Nowadays schools are not so handsomely reimbursed by federal and state governments for educating learners with disabilities, even though the mandates continue and even grow in number. Laws have also become more complex, and school districts spend more time and money in the courts defending their special education practices while teachers spend more time and energy writing individualized education programs that now run to 12 pages in length. These legal and bureaucratic mandates distract professionals from their instructional roles and actually discourage the growth of special education services that have now become a drain on schools with finite resources.

One thing that has *not* changed is the lack of tolerance among regular educators for more than just slight deviance from the norm among their learners. This lack of tolerance is further exacerbated by the current movement in education for teacher accountability as indicated by students' performance on standardized tests. Regular class teachers fear, with good reason, that their competence will be called into question if their students do not perform well on these tests. Therefore, they are tempted to solve this problem by referring these students for special education services. No doubt you can discern a real tension here between a system that tries to include as many learners as possible in regular education, and regular education teachers who actively seek special services for the many students who do not do well in school, especially on traditional tests.

P.L. 94-142 has undergone many revisions since its original enactment. Now known as the Individuals With Disabilities Education Act (IDEA), many of its original mandates have been amended. There are two major concepts that emerge from this historical context that are most directly relevant to this chapter on changing classroom practices and its core concept. The first has to do with the information on which we base instructional decisions; the second has to do with the very nature of that instruction.

How Do We Group Learners for Instruction in America's Schools?

We mentioned earlier the roots of a system that has endured to this day in American education. That system is the way we group learners for instruction. Learners are placed in classrooms based on their chronological ages. Most learners begin school in kindergarten at around age five. They then move in sequence from grade 1 to grade 12. Unless they encounter problems, they proceed through basic education until they graduate from secondary school at the age of 17 or 18. Therefore, to know where a learner is in school, you need only subtract 5 from the chronological age (CA). A learner with a CA of eight is usually in, or close to entering, third grade (8 − 5 = 3). Or you can add 5 to the learner's current grade placement to estimate the CA. A 10th grader is usually 15 years old (10 + 5 = 15), and will probably turn 16 sometime during the 10th grade. The system is quite neatly organized. Presumably, then, teachers can teach to a large group of students because they are all the same age. This is a presumption that will be challenged a bit later on.

As mentioned earlier, there are learners who have serious learning or behavior problems and for whom this system of grouping does not work well. Even though they share the same chronological ages as their peers, they simply cannot keep up in the classroom (and perhaps even outside of it). These are the learners who end up in special education classrooms. Chronological age is not adequate for grouping them because of the wide variety of problems they display. Learners who find their way into special education classes must, by law, have a disability label placed upon them in order to be eligible for these special services. McCoy (1995) identifies the basic disability categories as mentally retarded (MR), emotionally disturbed (ED),

---

Current Special Education Law

Special Education: The term "special education" means specially designed instruction, at no cost to parents, to meet the unique needs of a child with a disability, including instruction conducted in the classroom, in the home, in hospitals and institutions, and in other settings; and instruction in physical education.

Child with a Disability: The term "child with a disability" generally means a child:

1. With mental retardation, hearing impairments (including deafness), speech or language impairments, visual impairments (including blindness), serious emotional disturbance, orthopedic impairments, autism, traumatic brain injury, other health impairments, or specific learning disabilities.

2. Who, by reason thereof, needs special education and related services.

The term "child with a disability" for a child aged 3 through 9 may include a child:

1. Experiencing developmental delays, as defined by the state and measured by appropriate diagnostic instruments and procedures, in one or more of the following areas: physical development, cognitive development, communication development, social or emotional development, or adaptive development.

2. Who, by reason thereof, needs special education and related services.

(Source: Individuals With Disabilities Education Act Amendments of 1997, Section 602.)

Think about it . . .

Imagine, just imagine, that you were a student recommended for, and then placed into, a special education classroom. Maybe it was because of a minor problem with math.

How might your life be different today?

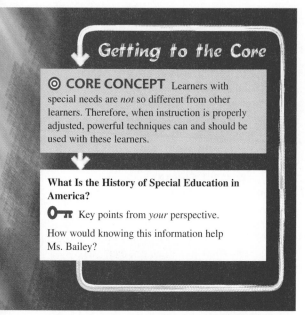

Getting to the Core

◎ **CORE CONCEPT** Learners with special needs are *not* so different from other learners. Therefore, when instruction is properly adjusted, powerful techniques can and should be used with these learners.

What Is the History of Special Education in America?

⚷ Key points from *your* perspective.

How would knowing this information help Ms. Bailey?

learning disabled (LD), visually impaired (VI), hearing impaired (HI), crippled and other health impaired (COHI), speech and language disordered, severely multiply handicapped (SMH), and gifted (26). So it is that one of these categories often substitutes for grade levels as the way to group learners into special education classrooms. Although CA is a factor in placing a learner into any given special education classroom, the CA ranges in special education classes are much greater than in regular classrooms and the category or label of disability is the primary grouping consideration.

How Homogeneous Are Our Classrooms, Really?

Disability labels have been, and still are, used in special education in the same manner, and for the same reasons, that grade levels are used in regular education. They provide a basis for designing instruction. Curriculum can be designed at the local, state, and national levels that specify topics that should be taught to, for example, 5th graders or 12th graders. Modifications of this curriculum by way of adapted courses of study can be used with learners who have various disabilities, especially disabilities that are cognitive (MR, LD) and behavioral (ED) in nature. This served well the school-as-factory model (which we discussed in Chapter 1) that grew out of the Industrial Revolution and that used behavioral science as its theoretical framework for understanding learning and developing instruction. Much like an assembly line, American schools could mass-produce learners who proceeded through a linear, sequential education program in one of two basic tracks—regular education or special education.

There is, however, a serious problem inherent in these groupings and the way they are used to make instructional decisions. They share a logic that is more apparent than real. It seems logical that grouping learners by either CA or by type of disability will result in more homogeneous classrooms, and will allow teachers to make appropriate instructional decisions on the basis of learners' needs. The problem? Learners of the same chronological age are not as similar to one another as we might assume they are. Nor are learners with disabilities so different from their chronological age peers as many might assume they are. The presumed homogeneity is misleading. Let us examine these assertions in more detail. To do so will require a crash review of basic statistics.

First, what we wrote in Chapter 5 about individual differences should make clear that we humans differ in a number of important ways on the basis of our preferred ways, or styles, of taking in and then doing something with information. Rather than appeal to what

Physically challenged students can more easily find success in today's schools (Courtesy of Ian Shaw/Getty Images).

some might see as "soft" theory, though, we shall use a statistical concept to look at the assertion that not all learners with the same CA are as similar to one another as we might assume. Central to this argument is the notion that we all possess two "ages." One is our *chronological age,* determined at birth. The other is our *mental age,* or the age at which we function on cognitive tasks similar to those required in school. To the uninformed, intelligence (IQ) tests seem to hold rather mystical power because they can determine how "intelligent" we are. They even result in a "quotient," a number that gives us a way to put a value on intelligence. Here's how it works. You have probably learned about the bell-shaped curve in your high school math courses. Remember that it represents a theoretical *distribution* of scores of a given variable or trait, and assumes that sufficient measurements of that trait have been gathered.

At the height of this bell-shaped curve is the *mean,* or average, score. Going out from the mean in both directions of the curve are scores that fall one or more standard deviations above (positive) or below (negative) the mean. The mean is really a measure of central tendency because it sums up any given distribution by giving us one score. The standard deviation, on the other hand, is a measure of *variability.* That is, it gives meaning to any particular score by telling us where that score falls in terms of the mean. We know what percentage of scores fall in any given area under the curve (see Fig. 6.1).

What's the point here? Well, we said earlier that learners at the same CAs are not so similar to one another as you might think they are. We also pointed out that we all have mental ages as well as chronological ages. To demystify the IQ test, let us make clear that what these tests do is ask questions that most people at a given CA answer correctly. Then they test individuals and see how well they stack up against people at various CAs. Suppose you are 12 years old and you correctly answer questions that most 15-year-olds answer. These tests certainly cannot change your CA. So instead, you would be given a mental age. In this case it would be 15. Then, by using either a ratio or proportion, your IQ would be determined and expressed as a quotient. A

> Think about it . . .   **You might have taken the SATs. The mean score for the verbal part is 500. The mean score for the quantitative part is also 500. The mean for the combined parts is 1,000. ETS sets the standard deviation for each part at 100.**
>
> **If you get a 600 on the verbal section, you have scored one standard deviation (SD) above the mean (+1SD).**
>
> **Suppose your friend scored 300 on the same section. What is the corresponding SD?**
>
> **[Answer is on page 249.]**

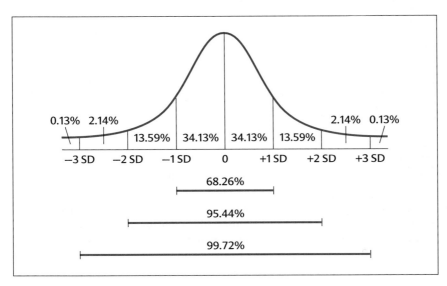

FIGURE 6.1

The normal probability curve.

(Source: Biehler, Robert F., and Jack Snowman, Psychology Applied to Teaching, *Sixth Edition. Copyright © 1986 by Houghton Mifflin Company. Reprinted with permission.)*

FIGURE 6.2

IQ score and standard deviation.

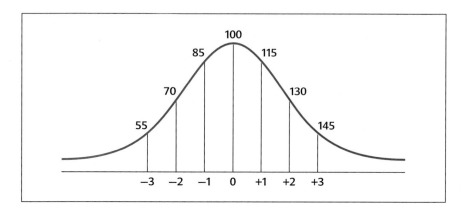

ratio formula would be: IQ = MA/CA × 100. Notice that the CA is given from the birth date, so in order to solve for IQ in this equation we need the MA. An IQ test yields an MA. Now we can calculate IQ.

$$IQ = MA/CA \times 100$$
$$= 15/12 \times 100$$
$$= 1.25 \times 100$$
$$= 125$$

Therefore, a person with a CA of 12 and an MA of 15 would have an IQ of 125. Since the mean IQ is equal to 100, and the standard deviation is 15, the score of 125 is almost two standard deviations (SD) above the mean (see Fig. 6.2). This score is quite favorable on this particular test. By definition, giftedness is determined by an IQ of 130 (exactly 2 SD above the mean).

Grade Designations in Regular Education

Now, let's look again at the assumption that learners with the same CAs are similar to one another. Using the concepts addressed above, let us take a very average fifth-grade classroom. Learners will typically have CAs of 10 years (5 + 5 = 10), using the formula for finding CAs we described earlier. Now, while the normal curve has an exact mean (average), it also defines an average *range*. Any score that falls between –1 SD (low average) and +1 SD (high average) is said to be in the average range. This is an important concept for you to remember—*average is really a range, not just one score.* In our "average" fifth-grade class, then, we shall use the normal curve and the concept of IQ to test for homogeneity. Remember that the mean IQ is 100 and the standard deviation is 15. Therefore, the average range is 85 to 115 (subtract 15 to get –1 SD and add 15 to get +1 SD). If we convert these low and high ends of average to MAs using the ratio formula, we get an MA range of 8.5 to 11.5 years (see Fig. 6.3). That is a three-year span among learners with identical CAs! And that is in a perfectly average class. Most people agree that there is a developmental difference between 8- and 11-year-olds. Yet the presumption is that they are very similar and can be grouped in the same classroom. This classroom does not seem so homogeneous as many people believe it to be. Even if common sense and the notion of style differences are not sufficiently compelling, the normal curve provides some statistical evidence that learners in regular education classrooms are not so similar to one another as many people think they are.

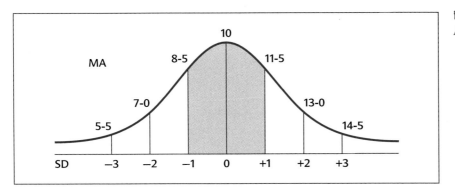

FIGURE 6.3
Average MA range, fifth grade.

Labels in Special Education

In special education classrooms, disability labels have typically been used to group learners. Again, presumably at least, this homogeneity helps teachers plan and carry out instruction. But again, this homogeneity is more apparent than real. In basic subjects such as reading, writing, and arithmetic, learners who have the same label (mental retardation, for example) certainly all share some kind of learning problem or problems. But the kinds of problems can differ widely. Some of these learners may have difficulty with hearing sounds, others with seeing letters, others with gross motor movements, and still others with fine motor movements. Some learners will have multiple problems, and others might have multiple disabilities (for example, mental retardation and behavior disorder). In some subject areas, such as music and art, some learners who are cognitively disabled can do well and actually excel. Students with learning disabilities often have wide fluctuations in abilities. They can be truly gifted in some areas and quite disabled in other areas.

In terms of social skills, learners with disabilities often are much more like their nondisabled peers than unlike them. As these learners grow into adolescence and adulthood, and after they leave school, their social skills differences may greatly diminish. Years ago, learners with mild mental retardation were referred to as the "six-hour retarded" learners. That was meant to signify that during the school day these learners were "mentally retarded," but when school ended and they returned home they were not readily distinguishable from their "nonretarded" peers. When academics were factored out, these learners did quite well in their neighborhoods. Even in school, as the efficacy studies we previously referred to found, learners who were labeled mildly retarded often fared better when left in regular education classrooms than did their similarly labeled peers who were placed in special education classrooms.

Let us add one caveat here. What we write above holds true for the majority of special education students who, fortunately, have mild to moderate learning or behavior impairments. There is a group of individuals classified as severely and profoundly disabled. These individuals often have multiple problems and are extremely cognitively and socially impaired. They most likely will never be able to function independently. They will always be dependent upon caretakers during their lifetimes. Fortunately, this group is small in number. It is for such students that special education can provide the most appropriate services—services that will help them lead lives as close to "normal" as possible, and during which they can find personal fulfillment. For reasons we explained earlier, special education services expanded well beyond providing services for those absolutely needing them. Addressing the

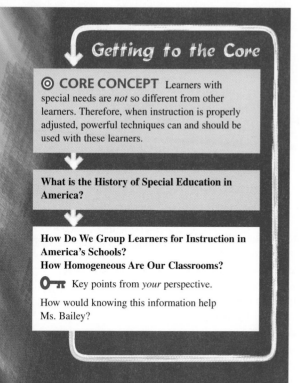

Getting to the Core

◎ **CORE CONCEPT** Learners with special needs are *not* so different from other learners. Therefore, when instruction is properly adjusted, powerful techniques can and should be used with these learners.

What is the History of Special Education in America?

How Do We Group Learners for Instruction in America's Schools?
How Homogeneous Are Our Classrooms?

⚷ Key points from *your* perspective.

How would knowing this information help Ms. Bailey?

education of learners with severe and profound disabilities is well beyond the scope of what is possible to address in this book. Teachers who work with these learners need to possess very specific skills and techniques. In this book, when we refer to learners with disabilities or special needs we mean those who fall in the mild to moderate ranges of disability. Further, we concentrate on cognitive and behavioral disabilities rather than physical, sensory, or communication disorders.

How Should We Use General and Specific Information?

When all is said and done, both regular educators and special educators use labels to group and teach learners. After all, regular education uses grade-level designations (3rd, 11th) in much the same ways that special educators use categorical labels (MR, LD). How *do* teachers use these labels? All too often they are used as if they yield the *specific* information that is needed to teach these youngsters. Feden and Clabaugh (1986) discuss the difference between specific information and general information and their usefulness for classroom teachers.

Suppose you are hired during the summer to teach a third-grade class. Immediately you have some *general* information that you can draw upon to help you prepare for the beginning of school in the fall. You know, for example, that most of the learners will be (chronologically) eight years old. You know that many will be reading from a beginning third-grade reader. They will be ready to start cursive writing. They will be able to work productively, in groups, with lots of guidance from you. This information is certainly helpful. You will have graded textbooks to use with these learners (third-grade math, spelling, reading, etc.).

What the grade-level classification does *not* tell you is anything about the individual learners who will arrive in your classroom. You will not know about personality types or learning styles, or even academic strengths and weaknesses, until the learners actually arrive and you have a chance to get to know them. Even last year's teacher's notes will only be of limited use. Learners, especially young learners, change a great deal from year to year. And individual learners respond to different teachers quite idiosyncratically. All too often we pretend that we can prepare for these learners before we actually get to know them. We develop units of instruction well ahead of time, or use the same units each year. We allow textbooks to determine both the content and pace of our instruction. After all, experts write these books for learners at particular grade levels.

This use of general information as if it were specific information is a mistake that *keeps classroom instruction from changing to accommodate the needs of learners, even those in regular education and at every grade level.* If we truly believe that it is our job not to teach, but to help learners learn, then we need to focus on specific information. Much of Chapter 5 addressed specific information about how learners are different from one another in educationally relevant ways.

Information about academic levels such as reading and math and student work samples gathered during formative and summative assessments (which we will address in the next chapter) also yield very specific information about how best to go about helping any given learner learn and improve his or her performance. Grade-level groupings simply do not provide sufficient appropriate information to help us plan and carry out effective instruction to promote deep learning.

How do special educators use the labels that serve as their grouping mechanisms? The answer is that they all too often use labels in much the same way that regular educators use grade-level designations—as sources of specific information upon which to base instruction. To make an argument parallel to the one that we made for regular education, let us assume that you have been hired to teach learners who are moderately mentally retarded. These learners are often called trainable mentally retarded, or TMR. Knowing this gives you some general information.

You know, for example that these learners will not be on grade level. Their mental ages will, by definition, be lower than those of their chronological age peers. Thus, their academic levels will also be lower. It is likely that these learners will have impaired adaptive behavior. That means that they will not be as independent or socially responsible as are their CA peers (Kirk and Gallagher 1986). So you know that these learners will be developing more slowly than their CA peers. In fact, if you know their MAs you can use these to judge approximate grade levels. Suppose these learners have CAs that range from 8 to 11 years. Further suppose that their developmental levels are more like 4- to 6-year-olds. Academically, this will put these learners at anywhere from readiness level to first-grade level of academic functioning.

Once again, however, this information tells us very little about any one of these individual learners who will enter the classroom in the fall. After all, TMR learners differ from one another in the same way that all other learners differ from one another. The categorical label TMR tells us little about what we should do to teach these learners as a group, let alone how we should teach any single one of these learners.

The Emergence of Developmental Theories

A myth has grown that perpetuates the notion that there is something mysterious about learners who are disabled. So mysterious are the labels *mental retardation, emotional disturbance,* and *learning disabilities* that most regular classroom teachers truly believe that they cannot teach such learners. So many learners with even mild to moderate learning and behavior problems have been taken out of regular education and put into special education classes that fewer and fewer teachers with elementary or secondary certification even encountered them during student teaching. It should not surprise us that these very same teachers, who have been led to believe that learners with disabilities are fundamentally different from their nondisabled peers and that it takes very technical skills to respond to their needs, now protest having these learners in their classrooms. Added

> **Think about it . . .**
>
> You are asked to plan and teach a lesson. Which information will you find most helpful, and why?
>
> The learners are in eighth grade.
>
> Or
>
> The learners read at the sixth-grade level, just finished a unit on space travel, know how to add, subtract, multiply, and divide, and are very extraverted.

A Person Who Helped Create Change . . .

Samuel A. Kirk began his career in the field of special education in 1929. He worked with delinquent and mentally retarded boys. His research on remedial methods for students with mental retardation and his contributions to the field of learning disabilities are legendary. His introductory textbook, *Educating Exceptional Learners,* is still used today by teacher educators.

Sam Kirk contributed in so many ways to the field of special education and won numerous distinctions during his long and productive career. He died in 1996 at the age of 92.

Source: R. Thomas (1996, July 28). Samuel A. Kirk, 92, pioneer of special education field. The New York Times, *32. Photo courtesy of UA News Services.*

to the problem is that these regular classroom teachers have precious little experience with learners who fall more than a just a little below the average range. It need not continue to be this way.

Suppose we think of learners in terms of *developmental* theory. That is, all people develop in essentially the same way, but at differing rates and with varying strengths and weaknesses. We presented some of the theory underlying this idea in Chapter 2. All learners share similar general characteristics by virtue of their being human. In this regard, general information *can* help us plan and develop instruction. *But no two learners are exactly the same.* We all differ qualitatively from one another, whether or not we happen to be singled out as having learning problems and therefore needing special education services. The major difference between learners in special education and those in regular education is typically a *quantitative* one rather than a qualitative one. In other words, some learners happen to be developing more slowly academically and socially (i.e., mentally retarded) than others. Some are developing more quickly than others (i.e., gifted). Still others are developing more quickly or similarly to most others in some areas, but much more slowly in other areas (i.e., learning disabled). If you understand this idea, there really is no deep mystery in special education. Learners properly identified and labeled typically exhibit the same behaviors as all other learners, but the behavior (whether academic or social) is usually more extreme. It calls attention to itself and causes these learners some type of problem or advantage in school.

Here is an example of how this might work in practice. You are teaching second grade. Most of the learners are seven years old. In a very average class, where MA = CA (and IQ = 100), they are seven, both mentally and chronologically (although we know that there will actually be an MA spread even in an average class, as explained earlier). These learners, then, fit our conception of what a typical seven-year-old will be able to do. They will be able to print, read from a second-grade reader, understand basic addition and subtraction, and so forth. Now suppose these seven-year-olds are gifted. Their MAs might be 10 (which would make their IQs approximately 142). IQ, of course, tells us nothing about how to go about teaching learners, or what to teach them. Yet MAs do give us general information that we might find useful. In this case we have 7-year-olds who are functioning, at least mentally, more like 10-year olds. They probably can read from higher-level readers, do more complicated math, and so on. Notice, though, that the differences among these learners cannot be known until we meet and get to know them. The general information certainly is not so hard for us to understand and use.

Now let us suppose that we are teaching learners who are classified as trainable mentally retarded. They have CAs of 14, but with IQs of roughly 50 their MAs are closer to 7. Notice that we have teenagers who are functioning (cognitively) more like second graders. Because we know something about second graders, we know something about the academic levels of these teens. These teens are certainly well below their CA peers (most of whom would be in ninth grade and functioning at or close to that level). Note that the difference is quantitative more than it is qualitative. These teens have the same human spirit as their CA peers—they want to make sense of the world in which they live, they have similar hopes, fears, dreams. They need meaningful and challenging work to help them learn to the best of their abilities. If we put these teens into a developmental context, we can think of them as 14-year-olds who are academically at the second-grade level. But be careful. This general information may not stand the test when we get to know these youngsters as individuals.

We have written all of this to make the point that learners with learning and behavior disabilities are not so different from all other learners. The difference is mostly quantitative. And yet, all learners are not as similar to one another as we would like to think they are. There are qualitative differences among us all.

Still, it is not quite so simple that we can merely think of these 14-year-olds as 7-year-olds in big bodies. In terms of educational programming, we need to realize that having these teens read from second-grade readers and work from second-grade math books is not appropriate. (Of course, it is not appropriate for all seven-year-olds either!) After all, by this age if their skills are still so low it is unlikely that they will catch up to their CA peers. It would also be demeaning, or at least embarrassing, to these youngsters to be reading from second-grade readers. They are 14, and socially they have matured well beyond 7-year-olds. Their interests are much different from these younger learners. So the special education teacher would have to select more age-appropriate materials from which they would work. The teacher should begin helping them prepare for life in the outside world through some prevocational and vocational training and academic work that has direct applicability to that world. Is this really so different from what some "average" students should be getting in school? Perhaps these average students will get a more practical program a year or so later, but for some whose plans do not include college such educational programming is both realistic and prudent.

Why have we taken so many pages and such great pain to outline these ideas? It is because we want you to realize that, as teachers, you have the responsibility to help *all* students learn to the best of their abilities. Your responsibility is not just to certain learners who fit some type of stereotypical notion of "average." The assumptions that special needs learners are so different from other learners and that regular education learners are so similar to one another are so widely held that we simply could not let them go unchallenged. If you focus on learners and not labels by getting to really know your students, you can be a much more effective teacher.

A Person Who Helped Create Change . . .

Although we have not cited his work in this chapter, we do want you to know about Burton Blatt. He was a pioneer in the disability rights movement. After a distinguished teaching career in special education and higher education, Blatt served as the dean of the School of Education at Syracuse University. There he formed the Center on Human Policy, devoted to the study and promotion of open settings for people with mental retardation and other disabilities. An inspirational humanism and ingenious ability to understand the essence of the human condition characterized his work. To experience the power of his thoughts, we recommend that you read *Christmas in Purgatory* (1974). This book exposes the horrors of institutional life that many people with mental disabilities had to endure for all too long.

Source: Herr, S. (1995). A humanist's legacy: Burton Blatt and the origins of the disability rights movement. Mental Retardation, 33 *(5), 328–331 (Reprinted with permission. Center on Human Policy, School of Education, Syracuse University).*

Some Significant Developmental Differences

Having said all of that, we will now present an idea that seems to contradict our contention that "kids is kids." Although we firmly believe that learners with special needs are not so different from other learners, some researchers suggest that a small portion of these learners may indeed be very different in some specific ways. For instance, research from the neurosciences has demonstrated that some learners process information differently from the general population. Their underlying brain functions appear to be different based upon findings from MRIs and postmortem examination (Hynd and Semrud-Clikeman 1989). Further, Moats (in Torgeson, Wagner, and Rashotte 1997) contends that many of the teacher education programs do not provide their graduates with effective skills and knowledge that are essential to adapting instruction for learners who do not learn "normally." For example, learners with dyslexia process auditory and/or visual stimuli in different parts of their brains than do learners with no reading problem (Hynd and Semrud-Clikeman 1989). They may need some very specific instructional interventions to help them compensate for phonological processing deficits that are the underlying reasons for many reading problems (Torgeson, Wagner, and Rashotte 1997; Lyon 1995). An example of such an intervention would be a multisensory language-based program with direct instruction of the alphabetic code and phonetic awareness skills. These programs teach sound-symbol associations very directly and in a highly structured and sequenced manner. Lyon (1995) writes, "For most individuals with learning disabilities, the primary learning difficulty is one that involves reading. In fact, at least 80 to 85 percent of learners and adults diagnosed with LD have most severe difficulties in learning to read" (123). He concludes in his research that these specialized strategies can be combined with other powerful strategies that we previously addressed to provide a rich and balanced educational program for learners.

Another example of a learner who might need some very specific interventions is one with pervasive developmental disorder, or autism. There is research evidence that such learners respond quite well to an intervention called applied behavior analysis (Matson et al. 1996). Most students with autism cannot interpret and respond to multiple stimuli and cues that are part of a typical classroom environment. Such an environment provokes self-stimulating behaviors as a reaction to stress. The powerful strategies and active learning we recommend in this book might overstimulate these learners.

You should be aware, then, that in some very specific ways some learners do indeed differ from others. *Their numbers are small.* They may need very specific instructional strategies. But even these learners differ widely in the scope of their disabilities. The mistake we must guard against is generalizing from a small population with very specific needs to the entire population of learners with special needs. That leads to the *deficit paradigm* that we shall present a bit later on in this chapter. Indeed, some learners with autism *might* be able to benefit from the rich environments that we suggest in this book. They certainly deserve the chance, or multiple chances, to successfully participate in these environments before we conclude they cannot do so. All learners deserve that opportunity.

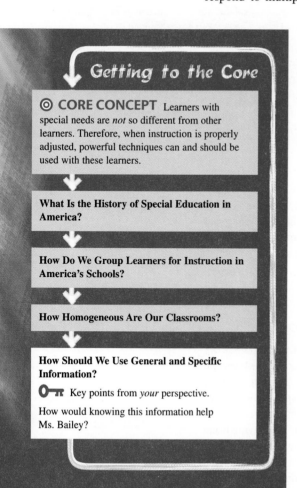

Getting to the Core

◎ **CORE CONCEPT** Learners with special needs are *not* so different from other learners. Therefore, when instruction is properly adjusted, powerful techniques can and should be used with these learners.

What Is the History of Special Education in America?

How Do We Group Learners for Instruction in America's Schools?

How Homogeneous Are Our Classrooms?

How Should We Use General and Specific Information?

⊙━🗝 Key points from *your* perspective.

How would knowing this information help Ms. Bailey?

How Do Powerful Principles Relate to Learners with Special Needs?

The general principles of learning hold true for learners with special needs just as they do for all other learners. Unfortunately, few teachers use these powerful principles with students who have learning and behavior problems. To understand why is to understand a real paradox. Although we contend in this book that things have not changed very much in American education for well over a century, they *have* changed more in special education than perhaps in any other area. That is because of the legislation relating to human rights that we discussed earlier in the chapter. The change that relates most to classroom instruction was the mandate, as a part of P.L. 94-142, that an individualized education program (IEP) be developed for all learners who need special education and related services. At first blush, this sounds like an excellent idea—not just for special needs learners, but for *all* learners. An IEP establishes an education program on the basis of the needs of an individual learner. In theory, if not always in practice, it is developed cooperatively by the parents, the teacher, and others who are deemed potentially helpful or involved in the program. A learner may also be involved in the development of his or her own IEP. The IEP specifies, among other things, academic and behavior goals and objectives for the learner.

IEPs and Traditional Learning Theory

The basic premise of an IEP is sound; develop a specific plan for each learner to help that learner learn. The problem with IEPs is the way they have been implemented. More fundamentally, the problem is with the orientation of the entire field of special education.

Throughout the entire past century, education has been heavily influenced by behavioral psychology. The instructional tradition that comes from that theory emphasizes direct instruction, accumulation of isolated skills and bits of knowledge, and interactions between the teacher and individual learners (Nolan and Francis 1992), rather than a more balanced approach to teaching. If general education has been influenced by behavioral theory, then special education has been *even more* greatly influenced by it! Most of us who received degrees in special education in all but the last decade were trained as behaviorists. The thinking seemed logical. Most of the learners we serve are learning more slowly than are other learners. They have some type of problem. We need to fix the problem and get them caught up as quickly as possible so that they can return to the regular grades. If we don't think we can do that, then we need to teach them the skills they need to survive in the real world. Whichever the case, there is a sense of urgency and precious little time to waste. Because, at least on the surface, behavioral theory seems most efficient, and the skills it produces are readily measured, special education took naturally to behavioral science as its driving force.

It is quite natural that IEPs reflect this orientation. In fact, they are the quintessential behavioral document. IEPs allow teachers to break down large tasks into smaller tasks, identify the steps required to perform these tasks, and then teach those steps to the learners. This process is called *task analysis.* Goals are analyzed further into objectives, and instruction is directed at attaining these objectives. Objectives are written behaviorally—for example, "Given 20 counting blocks as manipulatives, the learner will add single-digit numbers with sums to 9 with 85 percent accuracy." IEPs are part of federal law. They are mandated. So long as they are in force, special education seems locked into the behavioral tradition even as more contemporary research has suggested the use of very powerful principles and strategies derived from cognitive science.

This behavioral approach assumes that learners with special needs are fundamentally different from other learners. It implies that much of what we have written in the first chapters of this book does not apply to them. It denies all the points we made in the first part of this chapter. Despite recent movements like *inclusion* (the practice of including learners with disabilities in regular education classrooms and

Sample Individualized Education Program (IEP)

Student: Birth date: 10/25/89, age 10 years 2 months, grade 4

IEP Team: Regular and special education teachers, local educational agency representative, school psychologist, and parent.

Special Considerations the IEP Team Must Address before Developing the IEP Include the Following

Is the student blind, visually impaired, deaf, hearing impaired? Does the student exhibit behaviors that impede his/her learning or that of others? Does the student have limited English proficiency? Does the student have communication needs? Does the student require assertive technology devices and services? Does the student need transition services? Is the student within three years of graduation?

Summary—Current Educational Levels (Edited from Original Document)

Reading

- Ability to discriminate and produce rhymes with 90% accuracy.
- Identifies sounds of 20 to 21 consonants, 9 of 10 vowels.
- Reads closed syllable, nonsense words with 80% accuracy.
- Difficulty with multisyllabic words.
- Sight vocabulary at mid-second grade.
- Lacks automaticity in decoding and fluency.
- Unable to read with fluency materials beyond the first-grade level.
- Instructional needs in reading beginning at a second-grade level.
- Slower rate of acquisition and rate of retention as compared to the peer group.

Spelling/Writing

- Second-grade instructional level in spelling.
- Strengths in basic sight words.
- Weaknesses with vowels, silent e, vowel combinations, and homophones.
- Demonstrated slower rate of acquisition and rate of retention as compared to the peer group.

Math: Functioning adequately in fourth-grade curriculum

Summary of General Functioning

Strengths

- Average to high average ability.
- Cooperative, pleasant, sensitive, and caring.
- Average to above-average skills with verbal tasks, nonverbal reasoning, thinking in visual images, and visual processing.

Need to Improve

- Encoding and decoding skills.
- Because of disability in the area of encoding and decoding, the student's general curriculum will need modifications. Student will need additional supports as well as modifications in instructional strategies, curriculum materials, and assessments, as documented by IEP.

(continues)

Sample Individualized Education Program (IEP) *(concluded)*

Short-Term Instructional Objectives or Benchmarks

Encoding and Decoding: Student will consistently apply sound-symbol associations, decode one syllable words following the consonant-vowel-consonant (cvc) pattern, decode and encode multisyllabic words following the cvc pattern, decode and encode multisyllabic words with consonant blends and consonant digraphs, encode and decode one-syllable words with vowel-consonant-ending "e" (vce) pattern, and decode multi-syllabic words combining two syllable types. Expected level of achievement is 80%.

Reading Fluency and Automaticity: Student will read controlled text using cvc syllable types in single and multisyllabic words and vce syllable types in single and multisyllabic words. Expected level of achievement is increasing rates of fluency over baseline. Methods of assessment will be curriculum-based assessment.

Special Modification and Specially Designed Instruction

- Instruction in an environment with necessary adaptations.
- Instruction with multisensory language approaches.
- Instruction in the alphabetic code.
- Instruction should move from the concrete to the more abstract.
- Skills taught to automaticity and fluency.
- Instruction in encoding and decoding skills in coordination.
- Use of controlled texts.
- Adaptations to content area materials.
- Provision of shorter assignments and easier texts.
- Materials read when necessary.
- Exposure to higher-level materials.
- Provision of additional time for completion of assignments.
- Key concepts highlighted.
- Provision of cooperative activities with peers.
- Tests read aloud.
- Additional time for tests.
- Hands-on manipulative activities.
- Use of diagnostic/prescriptive teaching in mathematics.
- May need a modified quantity of work.
- May need project outcomes.

Related Service: Regular bus transportation, physical education as per district requirements. Extended school year to be determined.

Recommendations

Because of the functioning described in the present educational levels of this IEP, the student will be instructed in the special education classroom for phonemic support. Therefore, the student would derive the most educational benefit from an itinerant level of special education supports.

Placement
Appropriate group: learning support
Level of intervention: supplemental intervention—itinerant
Location of intervention: regular school student would attend if nonexceptional

Supports for School Personnel

Consultation to staff from reading specialists, parents, school psychologists, learning support staff, etc.

instruction), special education practice has not changed much in its fundamental conception. *We need not buy into this long-standing conception.* Indeed, special educators who have seen beyond the rigid interpretation of how to accomplish the goals and objectives set forth in IEPs do incorporate powerful principles and strategies into the specially designed instruction portion of the IEP. Particularly skillful teachers who work with learners needing special interventions manage to incorporate powerful strategies *and* remedial strategies into lessons and units of instruction to help learners meet goals and objectives within a meaningful context.

Using Powerful Principles in Special Education Classrooms

In earlier chapters we encouraged you to do the following:

1. Understand the alternatives to behavioral theory, including social-cognitive, contextualist, and information processing theories.

2. Know the difference between declarative and procedural knowledge, and the general but powerful principles represented by COVER and practice/feedback that promote them.

3. Use specific instructional strategies like questioning, problems, case method, projects, learning centers, and organizers to promote learning.

4. Understand the nature of individual differences and ways to identify them.

The Deficit Paradigm versus the Growth Paradigm in Special Education

Deficit Paradigm	Growth Paradigm
• Labels the individual in terms of specific impairment(s) (e.g., ED, BD, EMR, LD).	• Avoids labels; views the individual as an intact person who happens to have a special need.
• Diagnoses specific impairment(s) using a battery of standardized tests; focuses on errors, low scores, and weaknesses in general.	• Assesses the needs of an individual using authentic assessment approaches within a naturalistic context; focuses on strengths.
• Remediates impairment(s) using a number of specialized treatment strategies often removed from any real-life context.	• Assists the person in learning and growing through a rich and varied set of interactions with real-life activities and events.
• Separates the individual from the mainstream for specialized treatment in a segregated class, group, or program.	• Maintains the individual's connections with peers in pursuing as normal a life pattern as possible.
• Uses an esoteric collection of terms, tests, programs, kits, materials, and workbooks that are different from those found in a regular classroom.	• Uses materials, strategies, and activities that are good for *all* kids.
• Segments the individual's life into specific behavioral/educational objectives that are regularly monitored, measured, and modified.	• Maintains the individual's integrity as a whole human being when assessing progress toward goals.
• Creates special education programs that run on a track parallel with regular education programs; teachers from the two tracks rarely meeting except in IEP meetings.	• Establishes collaborative models that enable specialists and regular classroom teachers to work hand in hand.

Source: From Multiple Intelligences in the Classroom *by Thomas Armstrong, Alexandria, VA: Association for Supervision and Curriculum Development, p. 135. Copyright © 1994 ASCD. Reprinted by permission. All rights reserved.*

These same ideas can be used in special education classrooms much more frequently than they are currently being used. Teachers who have learners with special needs included in their classrooms and, therefore, must adjust their instruction to accommodate these learners, can also use these ideas.

Special education classrooms can be characterized as emphasizing lots of skills and drills. Instruction is very direct, from teacher to learner or learners. The focus, more often than not, is on teaching discrete, unconnected facts, rote memorization, and paper and pencil practice. According to Perkins (1992), the kinds of programs into which slow learners are placed "assume they need to focus almost exclusively on routine basics." He goes on, "In such classrooms, rote learning and drill-and-practice dominate even more than in ordinary classrooms" (14). Such an approach, Perkins contends, bores these slow learners. Much of what goes on in these classrooms, based upon assumptions listed earlier, runs counter to contemporary theories and practices. The "fix it" mentality that permeates special education is driven by a *deficit* view of learners that assumes they are somehow broken. It further assumes that what is broken is significant and that drill and practice can actually fix it. Both assumptions can be called into serious question. The first can be questioned because of the rather narrow range of mostly verbal and mathematical knowledge demanded by schools. The second can be questioned because of all that we now know about how people learn. For example, many people who have been successful in life have artistic, interpersonal or other strengths not valued much in traditional school settings. Even though regular education is changing ever so slightly in light of research findings from cognitive science, the change in special education is imperceptible. We suggest you adopt a *growth* view of learners with special needs in order to help them reach their full potential.

Adopting a Growth Paradigm

Let us first examine where learning problems may be encountered, and then consider how traditional classroom practices can be brought into line with the growth view by changing instruction to incorporate more of the powerful ideas that emerge from cognitive science. We shall begin with the IEP. That is the document that is written by teachers, parents, and school administrators and adhered to by special education teachers. Most of the learners in the special education classroom will have a goal and several short-term objectives that focus on the development of mathematical concepts and skills. Even though students' objectives might not be exactly the same, they will probably be similar. Let's say the general goal for the students in math is to get them to the fifth-grade level of mathematics. An objective for one learner might be to have him learn to multiply and divide fractions. Another learner might be working on measuring angles. A third might be mastering the metric system.

Here is one special education classroom scenario. Try to picture it. It is what often passes for *individualized* instruction. Learners are sitting at their desks working on worksheets and learning packets, and getting individual instruction from the teacher who circulates among the learners as they work. The learners might even be placed into small groups with others who share their objective. This makes direct instruction much more efficient. Occasionally, or in some kind of rotation, the teacher gives a lesson to a group of learners. The lesson is very direct and emphasizes the specific concept or skill to be learned. To make certain that all the students behave while they are working, the teacher could use a behavior modification plan that rewards students in some way for behaving, staying on task, and completing their work. The rewards could be stickers or points or candy.

SPOTLIGHT ON BEHAVIOR MANAGEMENT

"But will they behave?"

Managing Students with Disabilities

We often set out to solve problems on the basis of how we frame them in our minds. This is no different in education, particularly when we are confronted with learners who are perceived as being different. Allow us to illustrate. What follows are two different descriptions of a group of students who need special education services. They have emotional or behavioral disabilities. We suggest that you read the first description and then, before reading the second description, write down any thoughts that have come to mind about the children being described. What if you were told a student with emotional or behavioral disabilities was going to be placed in your classroom? Perhaps even discuss your thoughts with your classmates or colleagues.

> Many emotionally disturbed children have long-standing patterns of defiant and disruptive behavior. These children are particularly upsetting to teachers because they challenge the teacher's role and threaten the order and composure of the classroom. Some of these children exhibit the feelings needed to get what they want (i.e., to manipulate others), but they don't experience the feelings. These children are often able to identify weaknesses in the teacher and exploit them. . . . These children may be at a high risk for delinquency later in life . . . and seem to have little sense of right or wrong. (Paul and Epanchin 1991, 19–20)

Remember, before continuing, record your thoughts and feelings. Find a friend to talk about what you have just read. Now read Hayden's (1980) perspective on the same kinds of children:

> They are simply children, frustrating at times as all children are. But they are gratifyingly compassionate and hauntingly perceptive. . . . They are courageous. . . . Some of these children live with haunted nightmares in their heads that every move is fraught with unknown terror. Some live with such violence and perversity that it cannot be captured in words. Some live without dignity accorded animals. Some live without love. Some live without hope. Yet, they endure. (8)

Again, record and/or share your thoughts. How does this new perspective impact your thoughts about children with emotional or behavioral disabilities?

This chapter makes a point of steering you away from relying on the labels that are often associated with students who learn differently. Why? And what does that have to do with their behavior? Quite simply, labels do not solve problems. Labels do not provide us with precise instructional strategies or interventions that will help students become successful.

From a classroom management standpoint, we have often heard labels used to *explain* behavior. Clearly, this is not helpful to students, parents, or teachers. Have you ever heard a conversation that goes something like this?

"Why is Jason so explosive? It seems like he becomes extremely upset at the drop of a hat," remarked the student teacher.

"Oh, Jason? He's emotionally disturbed," replied the teacher.

Using labels in this manner explains absolutely nothing. What has the student teacher learned about Jason or the reasons behind his explosive behavior?

The only path toward making educationally sound decisions for children is to have precise information upon which to base those decisions. When you communicate or document the behavior of students you must be descriptive. Avoid loaded words or terms that can be interpreted differently by different people. Focus on describing your observations. Develop the habit of answering the following questions:

◎ **CORE CONCEPT** Learners with special needs are *not* so different from other learners. Therefore, when instruction is properly adjusted, powerful techniques can and should be used with these learners.

- Specifically, what did you see?
- How long did the behavior last (duration)?
- When did it occur (time or during what activity)?
- How often does it occur (frequency)?
- Was this episode more or less intense than usual for this student? In what way?

Put off your interpretation of the events or what the child may have been thinking until *after* you have clearly described the observable behavior. Then, base your interpretation on what you saw and what you know. Connect your guesses to actual, observable events. This will inevitably lead to further questions. This is good. It means you are reflecting. Don't stop there. Find the answers that lead you to the child's thinking. You are looking for patterns. People behave predictably. If you find the pattern, you have a reasonable chance of predicting future behavior. This will allow you to intervene sooner and in a more rational manner.

If you have been following our discussion about managing students' behavior, you are getting used to our mantra of "focus on the individual needs of the student." Early in our teacher preparation program, when we introduce students to this seemingly simple concept, we often get reactions that make us think we are stating the obvious. We hear comments like, "Of course I am going to know my students. I will care about my students and help them feel good about themselves. I chose this field because I love kids!"

Yet the same preservice teachers are often perplexed by the actions of teachers (both new and seasoned) as they observe and interact in their field placements. Although we do hear stories of success and truly dedicated and special teachers, we hear a fair share of poor examples of teacher behavior. Recently, one third-year student wrote the following:

> My co-op was a good teacher who tried her best to provide a supportive learning environment for her students. She usually had strong, yet encouraging control . . . but there was one student who was a major discipline problem. . . . The students were meant to take a math test, so while the teacher was explaining the directions this particular student tore up her copy of the test. The teacher was shocked and appalled that a student would show her so little respect. She sternly asked the child, "What do you think you are doing?" The student responded saying, "I am not taking the test." The teacher then became very angry and began yelling and saying things like: "I am sick and tired of you

acting like this. Everyone else is ready to take the test. Why aren't you? I have never seen a seventh-grader with as little respect for authority as you have. Why don't you ever listen?"

The episode escalated into a shouting match until the principal was called and the student was removed from the classroom.

The student above clearly had the reputation of being a "major discipline problem." Whether or not he or she had special education needs is irrelevant. A label has been attached to this student. Did this label influence the teacher's response? We would need more information to be sure; however, this is a perfect example of how counteraggression can lead a teacher into the conflict cycle. As we explained earlier, there are reasons teachers behave counteraggressively. As you develop your professionalism, you will have to come to terms with your own counteraggression. We all experience it. However, if we become reflective enough to recognize when we are experiencing counteraggression, we can do something about it, think rationally, and make educationally beneficial decisions.

So what would have been a more therapeutic response? Here is where the depth of the interpersonal relationship between teacher and student is critical. This journal entry was written in April. Could this have been the first time during the school year that this student refused to do work? Why would any student refuse to take a test? Perhaps they are frustrated because they have not learned the material. Perhaps a significant event in their lives has upset them. Could something have happened in the hallway on the way to math class? The only way you will know is to question and support the student.

If this student's reaction reflected the signs of a long-term pattern of behavior, then we might want to investigate test anxiety, understanding of the material, or our relationship with the student. If it was an unusual event for the child, we might want to shorten the time span of our investigation. In other words, what happened on the way to class, on the way to school, on the way to the bus stop, or at home that morning?

Above all, take a look at yourself. Use your counteraggression as a signal to pause and think so that you can act calmly and rationally. The teacher in our example could have continued to pass out and explain the test, then once the others were working, she might have taken the upset student aside for a private conversation.

The point that has been made in this chapter is that special needs learners are not so different from other learners. Unfortunately, special education and other labels are emotionally loaded terms that cause some to develop preconceived notions about children.

The reality is, students' needs in our classrooms are more diverse than ever. Some of your students will have disabilities. As the fabric of our society changes, you will find more and more students who, for whatever reason, from time to time (recall Redl's (1966a) words in Chapter 1) and for a relatively short time, behave *like* students who have disabilities. You will be faced with an intriguing challenge. How will you meet all of their needs? The response, "I don't have the training to work with students who have _____" will simply be unacceptable.

The answer lies in the powerful strategies you have been reading about in this text. They force you to look at the needs of individual students. They help you engage your students and keep them excited about their learning. They prepare you to make all students feel better about themselves and their learning. When you adjust instruction appropriately and apply these powerful strategies you will meet the needs of all students.

How you define a problem makes all the difference. It can open up new possibilities or deny all hope. Our preconceived notions about particular students can stop education dead in its tracks. The professional response is to use your preconceived notions, your hunches, and your questions to lead you to seek further information that will help you make better educational decisions for students. We are confident that you can employ the many strategies you are learning to do just that!

But wait. What might be happening to cause these learners to have learning problems in the first place? We can use information processing theory (IPT) to help us understand at least some of the possible problems. Perhaps a few learners simply lack any prior knowledge upon which to build new knowledge that the teacher wants them to learn. Because humans cannot learn anything new unless they already know something about it (no connections can be formed in long-term memory), no real learning can take place unless the teacher goes back to more fundamental concepts that the learners already know and understand. Not doing so is like building on sand. Or maybe the learners do have prior knowledge, but it is either incorrect or the learners are simply not retrieving it. Again, either incorrect or no connections can be made between new and previously learned information.

Suppose that some of the learners have attention disorders. If attention is not paid to the new information to be learned, IPT holds that this information cannot get past the sensory register. It has no chance of being learned. If the learners are attending to the lesson and the new information, it will be in their working memories (WM). Here it might well be that the learners do not know how to engage in maintenance rehearsal. That is, they cannot keep the information in WM long enough to decide how to connect it to other things that they know. Even if they can engage in maintenance rehearsal, they might have no way to *encode* (place) information into their long-term memories (LTM). They may lack the learning strategies (COVER) to encode the information, or they may lack the *metacognitive* (thinking about how they think) strategies to encode this information. They may have a number of these problems.

Will the scenario described above address these problems? Probably not. Let's envision a different scenario. Suppose the teacher develops a project on which the learners will work. Perhaps it requires the learners to design one of the walls in the classroom that will represent a finished product and connect to the specific objectives of the lesson plan. The teacher gives the task assignment to the learners. She has carefully designed the assignment so that, in order to complete it, learners have to multiply and divide fractions, measure angles, and use the metric system. She allows them to work together on this project. They organize the work set before them—not only by dividing tasks, but also by listing what they already know and what they still need to know in order to do the task. They also draw the wall and do a graph to plan out their design. When they run into problems that they themselves cannot solve, the teacher provides some direct instruction if it is needed. More often, though, the instruction is carefully designed not to solve the problem for them, but to provide just enough assistance so that they can solve it for themselves. At the end of the project the learners evaluate their work with the teacher. Finally, the learners each decide upon a project that they will carry out, independently, at home.

Do you recognize the elements of cognitive theory in the above scenario? The learners work with one another (social-cognitive and contextualist theories). The teacher models through direct instruction if needed (traditional and social-cognitivist), and provides scaffolding in the zone of proximal development (contextualist) by helping the learners solve their own problems. Using ideas from IPT, she most likely gained their attention by posing a novel, authentic task on which they could work. To ensure that the learners process the information deeply into LTM, she has them organize (O) and visualize (V) the work, and then engage in several forms of elaborative rehearsal (ER). They self-assess their own work as she assesses it (feedback), and they then carry out another project in a different venue (practice). In addition to theory, specific powerful strategies that are (or easily could be) employed by the teacher include cooperative learning, project learning, higher-order questioning, and graphic organizers. All the while, of course, these learners are working on concepts and skills included in their IEPs. Rather than learning and practicing these as isolated facts and skills out of context, they are now engaged in contextualized learning that enhances the likelihood that they will retain, understand, and be able to use this knowledge.

And that's not all! By allowing these learners to be actively engaged in this type of learning, the teacher gains a wealth of information by observing and interacting with them. She can then use this information to judge learning preferences and styles, strengths and weaknesses, and so forth. That will permit her to plan even more effectively for future lessons.

How Can We Teach Groups of Learners with Diverse Abilities and Needs?

Providing a variety of instructional strategies to a group of diverse learners is not such a new idea. One of us had a grandmother who was a teacher in the early 1900s and taught in a little one-room schoolhouse with as many as 25 children, ages 5 to 17. She used a variety of instructional techniques to meet the diverse learning needs and levels of the students. Today, as they did back then, classrooms represent a community of diverse learners that consists of students with different developmental levels, learning and personality styles, cognitive abilities, cultural differences, and motivational needs.

So what have contemporary schools done to deal with these differences among students' learning abilities? Most likely they

Think about it . . .

What makes this approach potentially more powerful than the typical approach described earlier?

What specific strategies are being used, and how?

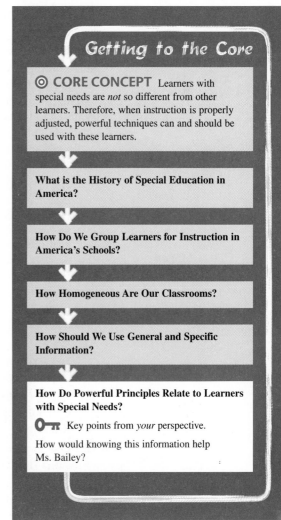

Getting to the Core

◎ CORE CONCEPT Learners with special needs are *not* so different from other learners. Therefore, when instruction is properly adjusted, powerful techniques can and should be used with these learners.

What is the History of Special Education in America?

How Do We Group Learners for Instruction in America's Schools?

How Homogeneous Are Our Classrooms?

How Should We Use General and Specific Information?

How Do Powerful Principles Relate to Learners with Special Needs?

🔑 Key points from *your* perspective.

How would knowing this information help Ms. Bailey?

employ what we call ability grouping. That means that they group learners on the basis of ability and attempt to match instructional strategies to the specific needs of the particular groups. We tend to see different approaches to ability grouping when we look at elementary, middle, and high schools. In elementary schools we are likely to see students grouped by ability levels, especially in math and reading. Schools and teachers look at a grade level (let's use fourth grade as an example) and group children by low, middle, and high levels for math or reading. Then one of the fourth-grade teachers takes all of the low achievers, another takes all of the middle achievers, and yet another takes all of the high achievers. Another approach is for one teacher to have three different groups within one classroom. It is also possible for schools to place students from many different grades into homogeneous groupings. This is becoming more popular because of the wide differences of ability across grade levels.

In middle or high schools, the approach is quite different. Whole classes and even entire curricula are designated for specific purposes such as advanced placement, honors, college preparatory, academic, and vocational training. This is a system of *tracking*. Some schools even refer to the different tracks by letters (10A or 12C) or numbers (10-1 or 12-3). The efficacy and fairness of ability grouping and tracking have become hotly debated among researchers in recent years.

Much research has been conducted on ability grouping and tracking over the years. This research has given us cause to rethink these ways of organizing the delivery of curriculum and instruction. Alexander, Entwisle, and Dauber (1994) say that tracking has been used primarily to match instruction with the specific needs of students. Cotton and Savard (1981) claim that by grouping learners by ability or putting them into tracks, teachers are better able to deliver instruction that is adjusted to learners' rates of learning and to make better use of more appropriate methods and materials.

But some in the educational community have mounted a serious challenge to the use of ability grouping and tracking. Zemelman, Daniels, and Hyde (1998) state:

> One of the single contributions of recent educational research has been the explicit rejection of tracking and the affirmation of heterogeneous grouping. One of the most shameful and unnecessary practices in American schools has been the routine division of children into separate classrooms or instructional groups on the basis of "ability." Indeed, one of the earliest common experiences of most American children (which many remember clearly and painfully as adults) is being disguised with cutesy and, to the children, entirely transparent, euphemistic names like "Bluebirds," "Robins," and "Owls." (258)

Eggen and Kauchak (2001) summarized the research findings that have identified a number of problems with all forms of ability grouping such as:

1. Within class grouping creates logistical problems, because different lessons and assignments are required and monitoring students in different tasks is difficult (Good and Brophy 1997; Oakes 1992).

2. Improper placements occur, and placement tends to become permanent. Cultural minorities are underrepresented in high-ability classes (Grant and Rothenberg 1986; Oakes 1992).

3. Low groups are stigmatized. The self-esteem and motivation of low groups suffer (Hallinan 1984).

4. Homogeneously grouped low-ability students achieve less than heterogeneously grouped students of similar ability (Good and Brophy 1997, p. 133).

As we examine the implications of this research, it helps us better understand the need to reexamine our methods of teaching learners with varying or differing abilities. Zemelman, Daniels, and Hyde (1998) write, "we now have conclusive evidence that such ability grouping is academically harmful to kids labeled low and middle—their measured achievement is depressed when they are segregated by levels. The evidence of tracking's benefits for "high" kids is slight, ambiguous, and still under hot debate among academic researchers" (258).

It is not the purpose here to debate ability grouping or tracking. We simply want to make you aware of the issues involved in these practices. Obviously, special education is a form of *both* ability grouping and tracking.

Social Dimensions and Special Education

Related to the issue of ability grouping is the fact that a disproportionately large number of learners who are placed in special education classrooms for all or part of their school day represent minority groups. Hardman, Drew, and Egan (1999) suggest that the fact that this issue continues to surface may mean that "special education has been used as a tool of discrimination, a means of separating racial and ethnic minorities from the majority" (51). According to Drew, Hardman, and Logan (1996), African Americans, Latin Americans, and Native Americans are overrepresented among those who have been identified as having learning disabilities, mental retardation, and behavior disorders. On the other hand, VanTassel-Baska, Patton, and Prillaman (1991) point out that disproportionately few members of these cultural groups have been identified as gifted and talented. There is a clear link between social categories and special education. Naturally, these data raise some very complex issues and concerns. From the social justice perspective, we need to find alternative ways to meet the needs of learners who are members of minority groups.

Differentiated Instruction

There is a worthy alternative that provides instructional opportunities for teachers to better meet the needs of *all,* or at least a greater number, of their students. It can certainly help in every classroom, thereby reducing unnecessary referrals of learners to special education. In addition, it can help in inclusive settings. This alternative is called *differentiated instruction.*

Although some teachers approach diverse classrooms by aiming instruction at the average students in the classroom, or "teaching to the middle," many teachers are beginning to explore the potential of differentiating their instruction to meet the needs of individual students. They are making efforts to design instruction that challenges the learning needs of slower, average, and gifted students, all of whom are in the same classroom.

Carol Ann Tomlinson has done the most comprehensive work on differentiated instruction to date. The table on page 234 illustrates a model for thinking about how to differentiate

A Person Who Helped Create Change . . .

Carol Ann Tomlinson is associate professor of educational leadership, foundations, and policy at the Curry School of Education, University of Virginia. Tomlinson works with teachers throughout the United States and Canada toward establishing more differentiated classrooms. Her experience includes 21 years as a public school teacher at the preschool, middle, and high school levels. Tomlinson's research interests include differentiated instruction in the middle school, use of multiple intelligences with high-risk and high-potential primary grade learners, and practices of preservice teachers related to academic diversity. Her book and videotape series, *The Differentiated Classroom: Responding to the Needs of All Learners,* are popular with classroom teachers because they blend research and classroom application.

Photo: Courtesy of Professor of Educational Leadership, Foundations and Policy, Curry School of Education, University of Virginia (http://curry.edschool.virginia.edu/curry/dept/edlf/gifteded/faculty/cat/).

instruction. It strongly suggests that curriculum can be differentiated by closely examining its content, process, and product as it relates to students' learning needs. Prior knowledge, experiences, and readiness need to be considered before instruction begins. All students should be given access to the same core information, content, or concepts but should be challenged at different levels according to their abilities. Those students with less extensive knowledge in reading or math, for example, may need to use materials most suitable to their ability level. This will require the teacher to be very clear about the content, process, and product (outcomes) of the curriculum.

As outlined in the table below, many strategies can be employed to differentiate instruction. We highlight the following strategies, condensed from Tomlinson's (1999) work:

1. **Flexible grouping:** Students work in many different groups as well as independently on individual learning profiles.Teachers create skills or interest-based groups that are heterogeneous or homogeneous to maximize success. Provides a variety of working groups that allows the student to showcase strengths and interests.
2. **Tiered activities:** The teacher provides the same concepts and skills for all students but allows them to access the information at varying levels of complexity and abstractness. Working in heterogeneous classrooms, students' prior knowledge is considered as they explore new ideas through varied instructional approaches.

Flexible Grouping

(Left side: Active Orientation; right side: Escalating Expectation)

Content	Process	Product
Concept and generalization based High relevance Coherent Transferable Powerful Authentic	Concept and generalization driven Focused High level Purposeful Balancing critical and creative thought Promoting cognition and metacognition	Concept or issue centered Skills of planning taught Skills of production taught Requires application of all key skills and understandings Uses skills of the discipline Real problems and audiences Multiple modes of expression
Differentiation through Multiple texts and supplementary print resources Varied computer programs Varied audiovisuals Varied support mechanisms Varied time allotments Interest centers Contracts Compacting Triarchic-based orientation Complex instruction Group investigation	**Differentiation through** Tiered assignments Learning centers Triarchic model assignments Multiple intelligences assignments Graphic organizers Simulation Learning logs Concept attainment Concept development Synectics Complex instruction Group investigation	**Differentiation through** Tiered product assignments Independent study Community-based products Negotiated criteria Graduated rubrics Triarchic-based orientations Multiple intelligences-based orientations Complex instruction Group investigation

Source: From The Differentiated Classroom: Responding to the Needs of All Learners *by Carol Tomlinson, Alexandria, VA: Association for Supervision and Curriculum Development, pp. 121–122.*

3. **Interest centers or interest groups:** These centers are designed for the enrichment of those students who have completed assignments and are motivated by special or other interests. These centers can be differentiated by complexity, interest, and ability to work independently.

4. **Learning centers or stations:** These provide an opportunity for students to explore topics of interest and to practice skills independently. Additional resources for projects can be made available as well as a place for independent reading.

5. **Compacting:** This three-step process includes assessing students prior knowledge and skill levels, deciding what activities to excuse the student from participating in, and plans for the saved time to be spent in enrichment and accelerated study.

6. **Independent study:** Method where the student and teacher identify problems or topics to be studied. Process of investigation and method of demonstrating outcome are mutually agreed upon before the study begins. This allows for maximum flexibility, attention to student interest, and opportunity for the student to demonstrate research and personal independence.

7. **Adjusting questions:** The teacher designs varying levels of questions for class discussions, tests, homework, and research projects based on student readiness, interests, and learning abilities.

8. **Entry points:** This strategy is based on Howard Gardner's multiple intelligence work in which he encourages student exploration of a topic through as many as five avenues. The five include narrational—presenting a story, logical-quantitative—using numbers or deduction, foundational—examining philosophy and vocabulary, aesthetic—focusing on sensory features, and experiential—hands on.

Examples of how differentiated instruction works in specific classroom situations may help you to understand it better. Our first example is from an 11th-grade history class and the second example is from an elementary-age reading class.

Example One: Compacting and Learning Contracts (High School)

An 11th-grade history teacher is about to teach a unit on the automobile and how it has influenced America's economy and culture. The teacher begins the class with a visualization exercise asking the students to think about a favorite car they have seen or driven. The students are asked to concentrate on the car's size, color, shape, interior and exterior, comfort and safety accessories, tires, engines, and so on. They are asked to think about places they have traveled and visited in cars. The students will have a few moments to share this information with peers and to write down what the cars have in common. The teacher will lead a discussion to construct a visual organizer that demonstrates how students' responses reflect either America's economy or social structure. For example, relationships will be drawn between the automobile and America's culture (personal and business travel, urban, suburban and rural living, personal taste, etc.). This exercise provides a motivational activity, a method to activate prior knowledge and for the teacher to observe the student's level of interest and knowledge, and an opportunity for many students to participate.

Think about it . . .

Have many of your teachers "taught to the middle"? Describe how it affected you by giving an example.

Give an example of a setting in which you participated in differentiated instruction.

Given the above activity, the teacher can now provide an opportunity for the students to begin in-depth investigation on the automobile, through varying differentiated instructional approaches. The following are just a few examples of some of the differentiation strategies listed above.

Compacting: If the teacher finds that some of the students have content knowledge of economic and cultural connections to the automobile, then these students can spend their time doing independent work that allows for acceleration and enrichment. Those students who still need the basic information will work more with the teacher.

Learning contracts: Depending on the skill and content level of the student, written contracts between student and teacher can be designed specifying what activities need to be accomplished. By eliminating unnecessary time spent on skills and content already known, the student can proceed at an individual pace. In this situation, a talented and motivated student might want to investigate the economies of producing automobiles (assembly line/mass production) and how these economies impacted jobs and working conditions during the 1930s to the 1980s (this could also be completed in groups of two or three, each student having specific individual accountability).

Example Two: Flexible Grouping First through Fifth Grade, Schoolwide (Elementary Level)

One school is providing for the individual needs of students in reading through flexible grouping and differentiated instruction. This takes place during large-group instructional periods. Reading is taught through the framework of the four-block structure (Cunningham, Hall and Sigmon 1999). *The Teacher's Guide to the Four Blocks* provides a multi-method, multi-level framework for teaching reading which includes guided reading, self-selected reading, writing, and working with words. Students are heterogeneously grouped in grades one through five. The classroom teacher is responsible for providing reading instruction for all students during some time of the two-hour reading period that is divided among these four blocks. The reading teacher works collaboratively with the classroom teacher to identify individual student patterns of strengths and needs and to work with select groups of students in flexible groups. Classroom aides are another source of support for students. Flexible groups are used to provide both remediation and acceleration. Students' remedial needs have been identified in the following areas: decoding skills, including phonemic awareness; automaticity and fluency of reading connected text; and comprehension. The reading teacher groups students according to these needs and meets with these flexible groups two to five times a week for 30 to 60 minutes. Some students may participate in several groups; other students may join groups for brief periods of time for short-term supports. The reading teacher may work with these students during the guided reading block when the classroom teacher is providing direct instruction at the students' instructional level. During this same time or during the self-selected reading block, other students may work with the teacher or classroom aide on novels, which provide acceleration and enrichment to the regular reading program.

Differentiated instruction is also provided during reading instruction to meet individual learning styles and levels. The classroom teacher provides this differentiated instruction in

> *Think about it . . .* **Where to find some great resources on** differentiated instruction.
>
> Tomlinson, C. A. (1999). *The differentiated classroom: Responding to the needs of all learners.* Alexandria, VA: ASCD.
>
> Tomlinson, C. A. (1997). *Differentiated instruction: Facilitator's guide.* Alexandria, VA: ASCD. (Great classroom videotape examples.)
>
> www.ascd.org. Go to reading room and search for *differentiated instruction.*

the classroom on a daily basis, but the reading teacher also may work in the classroom to provide support to both remedial students and students who may need support with particular skills. During the self-selected reading block students have the opportunity to select and read books at their instructional level. The teacher confers with students to assure that they are selecting books at their instructional level. All students also benefit from listening to the teacher read good literature during instruction. Students may work at centers during this time period. When the writing block takes place, the students work on their pieces according to their individual needs and have opportunities to choose their own topics. Journal writing can take place at this time. During the working with words block, the teacher may present a skill and then vary the words and activities according to individual needs. The teacher also individualizes spelling words to be coordinated with the child's reading words.

With this model both the classroom teacher and the reading teacher have reported that they feel satisfied with the approach and see students making progress. The classroom teacher has benefited from having the regular consultation by, and support of, the reading teacher. The reading teacher has had the opportunity to work with a wider range of students because the classroom teacher is responsible for providing instruction to all students for some period of time. The students have benefited because those who need remediation or acceleration receive it, but they also have the opportunity to participate with their classmates in instructional activities according to their needs.

(Contributed by Dr. Marlyn Vogel, school psychologist.)

Differentiating instruction challenges teachers to be flexible with time and space, to develop instruction based on prior knowledge and interests of learners, to use a variety of instructional strategies based on student needs, to develop multilevel assessments, and to monitor the progress of many levels of student work. The challenge is loud and clear—we cannot package our instruction with the expectation that "one size fits all." Our classrooms are changing—and so must we.

What Are Some Specific Techniques to Use with Learners with Disabilities?

Historically, special education students have been relegated to second-class citizenship by a school system that assumed if they knew *less, more* rote drill and practice would solve the problem. Enlightened educators are now finding ways, even within the constraints often foisted upon them by regulations and political agendas, to incorporate more engaging, cognitively oriented strategies for all but the most severely and profoundly disabled learners. There are a plethora of general strategies suggested by researchers and practitioners that are worth your consideration. We will address a few here.

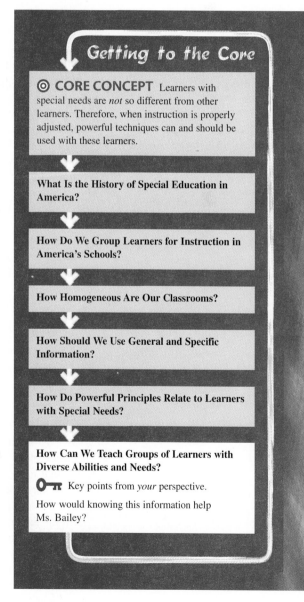

Getting to the Core

⦿ CORE CONCEPT Learners with special needs are *not* so different from other learners. Therefore, when instruction is properly adjusted, powerful techniques can and should be used with these learners.

What Is the History of Special Education in America?

How Do We Group Learners for Instruction in America's Schools?

How Homogeneous Are Our Classrooms?

How Should We Use General and Specific Information?

How Do Powerful Principles Relate to Learners with Special Needs?

How Can We Teach Groups of Learners with Diverse Abilities and Needs?

O━ㅠ Key points from *your* perspective.

How would knowing this information help Ms. Bailey?

Outlining the current thinking on best practice in special education, Sikorski, Niemiec, and Wahlberg (1996) propose a four-step process for teaching exceptional learners. These steps include:

1. Introducing the lesson by identifying key concepts to be learned and motivating the students to learn them.

2. Presenting the lesson by teaching small, connected chunks of information that logically build upon one another. They suggest that teachers also demonstrate metacognitive strategies to aid their students' memories.

3. Student participation that promotes group cohesion and group work to increase engagement.

4. Corrective feedback as part of the evaluation process and that identifies what, if anything, must be retaught.

The sequence they suggest is very similar to implications from IPT. Attention is gained and prior knowledge is cued by way of an advance organizer. Declarative knowledge is presented and ways to encode it into LTM (by way of metacognitive strategies) are demonstrated. Students are actively engaged in the lesson. Procedural knowledge is developed through corrective feedback and further practice. The match between what these authors describe as best practice in special education and cognitive science is close indeed.

Collopy and Green (1995) address motivational theory with at-risk learners. They call for a learner-focused environment that uses peer tutoring, cooperative learning, and interage cooperation as critical motivators for special needs learners. The emphasis on social learning is a far cry from the "sit at your own desk and be quiet strategies" that too often characterize special education classrooms.

Grossen and Carnine (1996) identify features of what they term "considerate instruction" and provide evidence that considerate instruction increases achievement of special needs learners. They define considerate instruction as instruction that "combines effective teaching practices with effective teaching tools" (77). The characteristics of considerate instruction include:

*   Focusing on big ideas, preteaching background knowledge.

*   Integrating new knowledge with old knowledge.

*   Using mediated scaffolding (personal guidance, assistance, and support).

*   Teaching conspicuous strategies (specific steps that lead to solving complex problems).

*   Judicious review that requires students to frequently revisit and apply previously learned knowledge. (78)

Once again, these ideas have little in common with traditional (or as they call it "inconsiderate") instruction. Such instruction bombards learners with facts and details that have obscure relationships, discounts the importance of prior knowledge, includes poorly integrated concepts, does not use scaffolding, seldom teaches strategies, and includes review that is neither systematic nor frequent.

Several authors suggest the use of some specific strategies to teach special needs learners. These strategies provide support for the idea that COVER and practice and feedback are just as useful for learners with disabilities as they are for nondisabled learners. Heaton and O'Shea (1995) and Day and Hackett (1996) discuss the use of mnemonic devices with special needs learners. These devices help students remember declarative knowledge by making arbitrary facts more meaningful. We gave examples of mnemonic devices in Chapter 3. One strategy that Heaton and O'Shea share with us is the *NEAT strategy*. It is a strategy for helping students turn in neat, legible papers. It is as follows:

NEAT

Never hand in messy work.

Every paper should be readable.

Always keep your paper clean.

Try to remember to put your name and date on every paper. (1995, 34)

Day and Hackett (70) share a mnemonic that can help learners with disabilities address their biggest nemesis—taking tests. They call it LEARN.

Listen for hints, clues, and important information.

Examine your notes, books, and papers.

Apply study and memory strategies.

Review every night.

Nail the test!

Admittedly these are lower-level encoding strategies. Still, these strategies are often developed to help learners with disabilities learn strategies that help them retain information. Without this retention, there is no hope of understanding and being able to use what they are learning in school. Learning will be short term, at best. There is evidence that at least some students with learning problems have problems mostly with short-term (working) memory. When helped to learn how to retain information in their working memories, these students can learn much more easily. The movement in special education toward teaching students with special needs to use learning strategies is a welcome one.

Werts and Associates (1996) describe the technique of instructive feedback for special needs learners. Feedback, as you now know, is critical to the development of procedural knowledge. Instructive feedback, they say, "involves systematically and consistently presenting extra information when students respond to direct instructional questions" (71). The additional benefit of this type of feedback is that it encourages learners to elaborate on information (the ER in COVER).

Blum and Yocum (1996) suggest using instructional games to provide practice for special needs learners. One game they suggest is speech BINGO. This game uses the bingo board format with parts of speech on it (i.e., noun, preposition, adverb). Players identify parts of speech from their boards, select sentence cards from a pile, and identify the part of speech in the sentences selected. If correct, players get to cover that spot on their boards. The first player to get BINGO by covering words is the winner (63). Any standard game can be adapted for use as a practice exercise. While acknowledging that there are few research studies that address the effectiveness of games as a way to practice what is learned, they point out that the few studies that do exist often have special needs students as subjects. They cite three specific studies that yielded positive results. It certainly makes sense that students would find games a fun way to practice.

> **Think about it . . .** You learned about the 4MAT system in Chapter 3. Earlier in this chapter we presented a learner's IEP. Try sketching out a 4MAT unit that could be used in a classroom with learners who would have IEPs similar to the one presented earlier. Be sure to help the learners meet their goals and objectives in the context of the unit's big ideas. Try to make use of as many powerful principles and strategies as you can.

It is encouraging to see instructional strategies for special needs students begin to reflect principles derived from cognitive science. There is no reason that these same strategies cannot be used with learners in regular education classes! All the articles cited above come from one of the journals published by the Council for Exceptional Children (CEC). CEC is the major organization that advocates for learners with disabilities and supports the instructional efforts of teachers dedicated to helping these students.

Unfortunately, as has been the case in all of American education, practice changes very slowly. One reason we mentioned earlier in the book is that in education, researchers and practitioners simply do not have enough opportunities to share information. Research often ends up on shelves, whereas practice continues as usual. Neither informs the other very effectively, or efficiently. Even those strategies that we elucidate above do not go far enough toward making special education classroom environments exciting and vibrant learning places. For the most part they still assume that direct instruction (by this we mean teachers attempting to impart knowledge directly to learners) is the most effective way to teach. They fall short of promoting the "thoughtful" learning that Perkins (1992) alludes to when he writes, "We need *thoughtful learning.* We need schools that are full of thought, schools that focus not just on schooling memories but on schooling minds" (7). We need these schools for all learners. Though Perkins wrote those words in 1992, we still do not have these schools for even most, let alone all, learners.

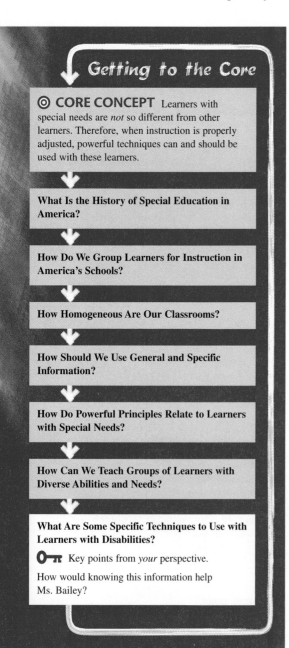

Getting to the Core

◎ CORE CONCEPT Learners with special needs are *not* so different from other learners. Therefore, when instruction is properly adjusted, powerful techniques can and should be used with these learners.

What Is the History of Special Education in America?

How Do We Group Learners for Instruction in America's Schools?

How Homogeneous Are Our Classrooms?

How Should We Use General and Specific Information?

How Do Powerful Principles Relate to Learners with Special Needs?

How Can We Teach Groups of Learners with Diverse Abilities and Needs?

What Are Some Specific Techniques to Use with Learners with Disabilities?

⚷ Key points from *your* perspective.

How would knowing this information help Ms. Bailey?

How Can Powerful Principles Accommodate Learners with Special Needs in Regular Classrooms?

Before we help you understand how you might use some specific principles and strategies in your regular education classroom, you need to consider the context in which you will likely be teaching special needs learners. We have emphasized time and again that they are much more like the other learners you will teach than they are different from them. Unless you are a special educator, you will not have to abide by the IEP rules and regulations, because IEPs are written only for the education that takes place in special education settings. The learners with special needs that arrive in your classroom will do so by way of the practice called *mainstreaming.*

We referred earlier to the concept of mainstreaming and the law that initiated it. According to Rogers (1993), *mainstreaming* is closely linked to traditional forms of delivering special education services. Special education students are placed into one or more regular education classes when they demonstrate their ability to keep up with the work assigned to the nondisabled students in the class (1). In contrast, Rogers writes that *inclusion* is a "term used to refer to the commitment to educate each learner, to the maximum extent possible, in the school and classroom he or she would otherwise attend" (1). In this case, support services are brought to the student rather than the student being brought to the support services. Even more fundamentally important, the requirement is not that the student must keep up with other students, but only that the student will benefit from being in the class.

The learners most likely to be mainstreamed into your classroom, therefore, will have been selected because it has been determined that they can benefit from your classroom and the learning environment that you have established. You will have the opportunity to collaborate with special education teachers, and by so doing enhance your own professional development. Of course, the student or students who have been mainstreamed into your classroom will arrive with certain challenges. These can be real opportunities for you to think about your teaching and your students' learning. Accommodations that you make for students with learning problems just might help some of the other students in your classroom! In fact, Klingner and Vaughn (1999) synthesized 20 studies of students' perceptions of instruction in inclusive classrooms. They found that students with disabilities wanted to be treated the same way as their classmates were treated with regard to homework, grading, activities, and the like. Their nondisabled peers agreed that this was fair. Interestingly, the researchers also found that "students *with and without disabilities* value teachers who slow down instruction when needed, explain concepts and assignments clearly, teach learning strategies, and teach the same material in different ways so that everyone can learn" (23, emphasis ours).

Truth be told, you can use much of what we wrote about in the previous section of this chapter with your regular education students. In addition, differentiated instruction can be a great help in accommodating students who are included in your classroom. By using these principles and practices, you are already going a long way toward accommodating learners with special needs. After all, some of these learners are disadvantaged by virtue of the kind of teaching that pervades American classrooms. Remember that in Chapter 1 we cited Goodlad (1983), Cuban (1993), and others who point out the rather restricted range of pedagogical alternatives used by teachers. Some learners just do not learn well by these methods. Other learners simply do not have the learning strategies they need to study and remember information imparted during traditional instruction. Still other learners are simply not motivated by the traditional teaching methods that focus more on what the teacher does than on what learners do. These students often end up with learning and behavior problems, at least in school, and subsequently end up in special education classes for all or part of the day. Just imagine what it might be like to have a language problem in schools that put a much higher value on verbal ability than they do on, let's say, artistic ability. Or imagine what frustration a learner for whom analytical and sequential thought poses problems might suffer in a school system that values this type of thinking much more highly than, for example, holistic and random thinking. What about the learner who prefers cooperation to competitiveness? Do you see how *some* students end up in special education classes? The current system simply does not value their strengths.

In addition to just plain teaching well using the powerful principles and practices we have discussed in this and previous chapters, what else can you do to accommodate special needs learners? Plenty!

Think about it . . .

Suppose schools valued artistic ability over verbal ability. How might that affect who is identified as being in need of special education services?

What does that suggest to you? What are the implications?

Think about it . . . There are many learning strategies that have been formally developed for inclusive classrooms. Find information on *one* of the programs listed below. Then decide how you might use it in your classroom.

- Success for all
- Reading recovery
- Classwide peer tutoring
- Reciprocal teaching
- Adaptive learning environments model
- Cooperative learning
- Circle of friends

Teach Students Learning Strategies

One realm of cognition often neglected by teachers—those in special education, regular education, and even higher education—is learning strategies. Earlier we mentioned the problems that some learners have with metacognition, or thinking about how they think and learn. Learning strategies are closely related to the concept of metacognition. All teachers can help their students practice and improve their learning strategies. Much of the research in the area of learning strategies has come out of the University of Kansas Center for Research on Learning during the past several decades. They write:

> A learning strategy is a person's approach to a learning task. It includes how a person thinks and acts when planning, executing, and evaluating performance of a task and its outcomes. Learning strategies instruction focuses on making the student a more active learner by teaching students how to learn and how to effectively use what has been learned. (University of Kansas, Center for Research on Learning 1997–1999)

Learning and Teaching in the Age of Technology

Everything we have suggested so far is applicable to special needs learners. Exciting new tools available through technology to help students with serious learning challenges communicate, create, write, and creatively respond are a blessing for many, from the paraplegic who can now use a mouth-held wand to control any function of a computer to a blind student who can pass a handheld reader over any standard text and hear it electronically synthesized into speech. Online e-mail and fax projects allow students with severe learning differences to create books and pictures with fellow students around the world, thereby allowing educational technology to enhance the powerful models of instruction outlined throughout this book (Burtch 1999). Access to virtual museums and the use of virtual reality software for physically challenged students allows them an emotional and physical experience in cyberspace denied them in real life. Though some of the newer approaches developed for students with learning or mental disabilities may promise more than they can deliver (Roblyer, Edwards, and Havriluk 1997, 310–311), technology's ability to enhance communication and personal response, espe-

cially for individuals with physical handicaps, is enormously promising. Deaf students, for example, can be liberated from the costly need for interpreters through the use of Internet-based distance learning, where all instruction is available visually and learner processing and reasoning can be undertaken using e-mail bulletin boards via keyboard input.

So important is the use of technology for learners with special needs that the reauthorization of the federal Individuals with Disability Education Act (IDEA) in 1997 emphasized the importance of technology. The

> ◎ **CORE CONCEPT** Learners with special needs are *not* so different from other learners. Therefore, when instruction is properly adjusted, powerful techniques can and should be used with these learners.

In this particular learning strategies curriculum there are three strands. The first is the *acquisition strand.* It provides strategy instruction in reading; in particular, it teaches word identification, paraphrasing, self-questioning, and visual imagery strategies. The second strand, *storage,* is designed to help students encode information into their long-term memories (Reid 1988). It includes *first-letter* mnemonics, paired-associates, vocabulary, and practicing the storage strand strategies. The third strand, *expression and demonstration of competence,* teaches strategies for participating in class discussions; writing simple, compound, complex, and compound-complex sentences; writing paragraphs; monitoring their own writing and detect/correct errors; completing assignments; and taking tests. This curriculum also teaches cooperative strategies, motivation strategies, math strategies, and teaming strategies. According to the researchers, direct, explicit instruction is essential when teaching students a new strategy (University of Kansas, Center for Research on Learning 1997–1999) or a metacognitive strategy (Palincsar and Brown 1987).

Think about it . . .

1. Sketch out a 4MAT unit that you might use in your own classroom.

2. Next, suppose that the learner whose IEP appears earlier in this chapter is included in your classroom. Disregard the age of the learner, and just focus on the learner's needs. How might you modify some of the activities so that:

   - The learner will be able to work toward the individual objectives written in the IEP.

   - The learner will be fully included in the unit's activities, thereby benefiting both academically and socially.

sharing of cutting-edge advances in the field requires that assistive technology (AT) devices and services be considered for all children who have exceptional needs. *Research Connections in Special Education* (1998, 3) provides excellent guidelines for educators seeking AT for their students. (http://www.cec.sped.org/osep/recon3.html)

Teaching Tips

1. When teaching writing in inclusive settings, the use of specific computer-based writing programs can be extremely beneficial. Try using Inspiration or other graphic organizer programs to develop concept maps (brainstorm ideas); Writing Away 2000 to help find words, provide speech output and spell check (assist in beginning drafts); and Desktop Publishing for final editing (provides methods of formatting and organization).

2. Using think-pairs and small groups, encourage students of different abilities to become study buddies and to communicate about assignments and tests via telephone, on e-mail, and in person.

3. Design learning centers that include computers with appropriate software, print materials, and frequently asked questions to support learners

who need extra help. Centers may consist of special materials for the hearing and vision impaired. They provide a safe haven for those who need more individualized instruction.

Suggested Websites

http://www.set.gov.bc.ca/
SET-BC: A provincial resource program designed to assist school districts in British Columbia, Canada, in meeting the technology needs of students with physical disabilities and visual impairments.

http://www.rit.edu/~easi/
EASIs K to 12 Education Technology Centre: Offers access to resources on adaptive technology and special education. Features links to newsletters, journals, and memos.

http://www.closingthegap.com/
Computer Technology in Special Education and Rehabilitation: Provides information to professionals, parents, and others interested in how technology can help school programs for children with disabilities.

htttp:www.cec.sped.org
Council for Exceptional Children

This curriculum was developed for at-risk learners. However, all learners can benefit from this kind of instruction. Providing instruction in learning strategies for students with special needs included in your classroom, whether you use a published curriculum like the one above or an informal version that you incorporate into your ongoing instruction, will help you to accommodate their needs by helping them to be more self-sufficient. It will likely help all of your other students as well. Too often strategy instruction is not included in the curriculum; nor is it included in instruction.

Likewise, research-based strategies that you might normally use with your nondisabled learners will often help learners with disabilities included in your classroom. For example, Lenz, Alley, and Schumaker (1987) found that the use of advance organizers (described in earlier chapters) in secondary classrooms can have a significantly positive effect on the capacity of students with disabilities to retain content material, provided that the these students are taught to attend to and use the organizers.

Use Specific Techniques to Accommodate Learners

Again, you should think about teaching in terms of units of instruction that are centered on big ideas and that bring in facts, skills, and concepts in the context of pursuing those big ideas. In the process of teaching these units, whether at the elementary or secondary education level, there will likely be adaptations that you can make to help included students benefit from the unit. These same adaptations may well assist other learners in your classroom, too. What follows on page 245 is a table of some adaptations that can accommodate learners who exhibit specific difficulties. This list is in no way comprehensive. The number and types of possible adaptations is endless. Note, though, that these adaptations are not based upon a specific grade or disability label. Rather, they are based upon problems the student actually exhibits. In that regard, they are your response to what you actually observed the student do, rather than some stereotypical notion of what that student can do based upon a label.

Many of these strategies are just plain good for *all* learners. Above all, you should hold high standards for all learners while accommodating their needs. Adaptations and accommodations should not be seen as dumbing down the standards; rather, they should be used as a way to help students attain higher standards.

 SCENARIO REVISITED

We now ask that you revisit the scenario that we presented at the beginning of this chapter. Answer the questions yet again, using what you learned from reading this and previous chapters. Focus

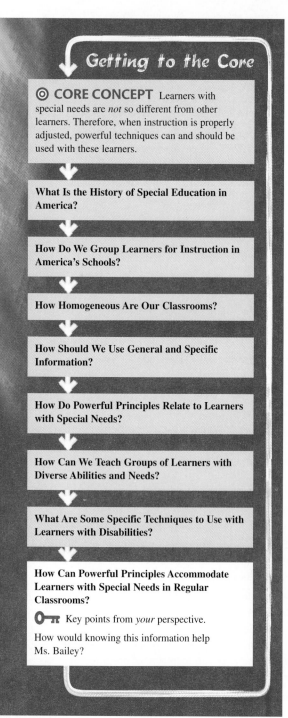

Getting to the Core

◎ **CORE CONCEPT** Learners with special needs are *not* so different from other learners. Therefore, when instruction is properly adjusted, powerful techniques can and should be used with these learners.

What Is the History of Special Education in America?

How Do We Group Learners for Instruction in America's Schools?

How Homogeneous Are Our Classrooms?

How Should We Use General and Specific Information?

How Do Powerful Principles Relate to Learners with Special Needs?

How Can We Teach Groups of Learners with Diverse Abilities and Needs?

What Are Some Specific Techniques to Use with Learners with Disabilities?

How Can Powerful Principles Accommodate Learners with Special Needs in Regular Classrooms?

🔑 Key points from *your* perspective.

How would knowing this information help Ms. Bailey?

Learner's Problem	Possible Adaptation to Accommodate Learner
Taking Notes	Provide outline of lecture. Have another student give copy of notes. Allow learner to tape record lecture. Speak more slowly. Teach and provide practice in identifying main ideas.
Completing Assignments	Allow more time if needed. Use cooperative work groups and accountability. Reduce large projects to small, manageable parts. Help learners create a plan for completing long-range assignments.
Following Directions	Provide written as well as verbal directions. Limit the number of directions given at any one time. Demonstrate the task for the learner. Have learners repeat directions before beginning assignment.
Short Attention Span	Vary the tasks (active, quiet, group, individual). Use high-interest, engaging activities. Make stimuli compelling (size, color). Use novelty and emotionality.
Organizational Skills	Have learners keep assignment books. Define lesson objectives before beginning instruction. Ask frequent questions to check for main ideas.
Focusing Attention	Gain attention before starting. Start with a provocative question or something else that stimulates thought. Set specific time limits for each task.
Reading Content Matter	Teach SQ3R (survey, question, read, recite, review). Record information on tape. Use high-interest, low-level reading materials. Teach new vocabulary words prior to reading text.
Memory	Encourage distributed practice. Encourage overlearning. Allow for open book tests.
Inappropriate Behavior	Allow students to devise classroom rules. Be consistent in enforcing rules. Develop behavior contracts. Use conferences with learners to reestablish expectations. Develop conflict resolution skills.
Written Expression	Allow for a variety of formats (such as oral reports and hands-on projects). Provide practice in written expression. Ask questions requiring short answers. Provide dictionaries and teach learners how to use them. Teach outlining and webbing.
Taking Tests	Select test formats that match students' abilities (objective, essay, oral, performance). Use alternative assessments such as projects and portfolios. Make assessments as authentic as possible to match the "real world."

especially on the use of information processing, social-cognitive, and contextualist (Vygotskian) theory. Then read A Voice from the Field and compare your responses to those of an experienced special education teacher.

> **?** *Why do you think the learners were puzzled as they left the room to go to lunch? Do you agree with Ms. Bailey's approach to discipline? Do you think Ms. Bailey individualized her lesson appropriately to accommodate her students' various physical and cognitive abilities? Do you think requiring the learners to complete the activity individually was a good idea?*

 # A VOICE FROM THE FIELD

Parts of Ms. Bailey's lesson were successful whereas other parts need improvement. I will analyze the lesson and offer suggestions to accommodate the special needs of the children. Vygotsky's ideas and information processing theory (IPT) will influence my analysis.

Ms. Bailey did not access the children's prior knowledge at the beginning of the lesson. She assumed that they knew what a quilt was, which may or may not have been the case. She may have asked children if any of them ever owned a favorite blanket as a child and explained that a quilt is a special kind of blanket. As a more powerful strategy, she could have asked the children to bring in a favorite blanket from home. She could have used a *think-pair-share* activity to have the children describe the blankets to each other and share their discoveries with the class. From the descriptions, Ms. Bailey could have used questioning techniques to lead the students to identify the concept of a pattern.

Remembering about a favorite blanket is an example of *episodic knowledge.* It is in long-term memory because the security of a favorite blanket is a powerful memory for the children. According to IPT, it is important to activate any background knowledge that students have. The knowledge is pulled from long-term memory into working memory. In this way, the *schema* the children have for blanket or quilt would be in working memory at the time of the lesson.

Ms. Bailey attempted to gain the children's attention by reading a short and interesting paragraph on the historical background of the postage stamp design. Although she did try to obtain the children's attention, she was not enthusiastic as she tried to do this. It was obvious that the children were not engaged or anxious to see what was coming next in the lesson. The paragraph reading could be considered auditory stimulation from the environment. This information would go to the sensory register for less than one-quarter of a second and then decay. Ms. Bailey could have enhanced the historical information she provided by bringing in a quilt or a picture of the quilt for the children to see and touch.

If the children had seen a real quilt or a picture of a quilt they may have shown more interest in the activity. This attention to the quilt and recognition of patterns would have ensured a more solid transfer of information from the sensory register to the working memory. According to IPT, pattern recognition and securing attention are vital for transferring information from the sensory register to the working memory.

Ms. Bailey did have an objective for developing declarative knowledge. This objective was for the students to describe a pattern and solve a problem related to patterns. Ms. Bailey could have introduced the lesson with a goal statement that enlisted the aid of the children in meeting a challenge. She also could have led the children to identify the objective. The statement could have included a description of what a pattern was. She could have then told the students she needed them to help make a quilt with a postage stamp design. The quilt had to contain 16 textiles: eight colors must be used and no one color could touch another textile of the same color on a side or a corner. Because of the students' varied physical and cognitive abilities, Ms. Bailey could have arranged them in heterogeneous groups (three to four students per group) to complete this task. She could have assigned the classroom teacher and the aide to work with two groups while she worked with the third group. In this way, the students could have helped each other while the adults facilitated. Ms. Bailey could have assigned each student in the group a specific job (materials collector, pattern arranger, and checker). Perhaps the most physically challenged child would use limited finger movement to push the textiles to the spots where they belonged. Most students in the class would only be able to complete the assigned job with the help of a more physically capable peer or adult. Vygotsky calls this principle the *zone of proximal development.*

Ms. Bailey could have also broken down or individualized the task to accommodate students that needed more help with the activity. She could have asked each group to begin by taking eight different colored textiles out of the bag and then taking eight more of the exact same colors out. She may have provided each group with a blank graph containing 16 spaces that they were to place the textiles on. In this way, the children would have developed a stronger idea of the pattern they were to create. Now the children would be ready to explore with the textiles and have a better chance of success with the task. For children who were still unable to solve the problem, Ms. Bailey may have provided miniature graphs of the colonial postage stamp design with either the first letters of the color belonging in the square or the squares themselves colored in. The children could then have matched the textiles to the correct squares. This adaptation would eliminate the refocusing problems children experienced when trying to copy the design from the poster board in front of the room. Vygotsky uses the term *scaffolding* to refer to the idea of supporting and adapting conditions for the child so they can complete a task as independently as possible.

On the other hand, not all groups may have needed the support and may have completed the task easily. In this case, Ms. Bailey could have had a more challenging problem prepared or could have used the children in this group to help the students who were having trouble. For example, she could have asked them to build the postage stamp design using four colors where no same colors could touch on a side or corner. They would then transfer this design to graph paper. If one group helped another group, Ms. Bailey would be free to observe all the students in the class and determine how the lesson could be adjusted. In this case, the responsibility for learning is in the hands of the students. This *responsibility taking* is one of the most important instructional implications of Vygotskys' theories.

Verbal praise and verbal reprimands were used throughout the lesson to encourage children to stay on-task and to redirect them when necessary. Ms. Bailey did not use the classroom behavior plan consistently at the time of her lesson. The behavior plan consisted of rewarding children with a star (each child had an index card taped to his or her desk for stars) for on-task and appropriate behavior and taking away a star for off-task or inappropriate behavior. This system is very effective because it prevents interruptions to the lesson. At this point in the year, children know why the teacher has given them a star or taken away a star. Following through with this plan could have saved Ms. Bailey the time used to address verbal interruptions. If necessary, she could have used time later in the day to explain to children why they received or lost a star. This explanation would add a *cognitive element* to the *behavioral* star system used in class.

Ms. Bailey used some elements of COVER while neglecting others in helping her students transfer declarative knowledge to LTM. Although Ms. Bailey did read the students the paragraph about the origin of the postage stamp design, she did not help the children connect this information to anything they had stored in LTM. She could have activated any background knowledge that children had which related to patterns, quilts, or blankets. The suggestion for eliciting background knowledge was mentioned earlier. Ms. Bailey's idea of transferring the postage stamp design to graph paper was an effective way for the children to *organize* the problem they were presented with. Unfortunately, time ran out before all of the students could successfully complete this activity. Ms. Bailey also could have begun the lesson with an advance organizer. The organizer may have contained the main objectives from the lesson, which were pattern recognition and problem solving. It also would have provided the children with a framework for the upcoming learning. Ms. Bailey's lesson also made partial use of visualization. She made a poster of how the completed design should look. However, her visualization technique may have been enhanced with a real quilt, a picture of a quilt, or a picture of colonial women weaving a quilt. Graphing of the postage stamp design was also an example of *elaboration.* The children would have to elaborate on their ideas of the postage stamp design in order to transfer it to graph paper. Ms. Bailey could have asked children to come up with a variation of the postage stamp design as a way to further elaborate on the idea of a pattern. She also could have asked the children to look around the room or at their clothes and to identify any patterns they saw. Ms. Bailey did not use *rehearsal* in her lesson. She could have included this aspect of COVER simply by asking children throughout the lesson what a pattern is. They would have answered in unison by the end of class that a pattern is a design that repeats itself over and over and over again. According to IPT, the more elements from COVER that are used, the better the chance of transferring information to LTM.

Misjudging the time needed to complete a lesson is a common problem, even for seasoned teachers. When Ms. Bailey realized she was going to run short of time, she should have made the decision to skip the grid paper activity and allow the children more time to struggle with the pattern creation problem. Allowing more time for trial and error could have led to a more powerful learning experience for the children.

Also related to the time problem was the lack of closure in the lesson. Because Ms. Bailey knew the children were going to have to leave for lunch, she could have asked them to stop and summarize what they had done up to that point. She needed to decide on the spot whether to continue the activity after lunch or to tell the learners how they would continue the next day. This activity could have helped the teacher establish closure to the lesson and the children organize the information they had just learned.

If the lesson had gone as expected and time did not run short, Ms. Bailey could have been ready with a practice activity when the children returned from lunch.

She could have done a learning log where the children answer questions related to patterns and how they were represented in colonial America. She could have had the children color in the blank graph paper to design their own quilts with a specified pattern. In each of these activities, the children would have a chance to use what they had learned. They would be solving a problem related to patterns with the information they now have in LTM. This practice activity would also allow the teacher to individually assess which students understood the concepts. The learners would then receive specific and timely feedback on their assessments so they would know what they were doing right or what they needed to rethink. IPT refers to applying knowledge to a new situation as *procedural knowledge*. This process is necessary to help make certain thoughts and behaviors automatic so working memory is freed up to give other matters conscious attention.

In conclusion, one does not doubt the hard work that Ms. Bailey put into executing this lesson. She did use an attention-getting activity and the task itself was interesting as well as fun for the students. However, to give students a better chance of learning or transferring knowledge to long-term memory, Ms. Bailey could have done certain things differently. She could have accessed the children's prior knowledge as well as their attention. Without these cues, the information would not have a chance of making it to the children's working memory, and they would not be able to think about the ideas from the lesson. She needed to improve her ability to break down the task into smaller parts to accommodate for physical and cognitive needs. Allowing children to work in groups also would have facilitated this strategy. Perhaps she could have taken the grid activity out of the initial lesson so the learners could have more time to solve the pattern problem.

Finally, Ms. Bailey could have ended her lesson with some type of summary statement and practice activity to assess whether children really learned what she was trying to teach them. In this way, she would have built individual accountability into a cooperative activity.

This is the voice of Genevieve Hill. Ms. Hill is a special education teacher and a mentor for student teachers. She also wrote the scenario for this chapter.

Answer to Think about it . . . SAT score: (page 215)

An SAT score of 300 would place your friend two standard deviations below the mean (−2 SD). We shall do more with this concept in Chapter 7.

PLANNING FOR INSTRUCTION

This chapter explored many issues related to teaching children with special needs. Today, many teachers in regular classrooms encounter students with a broader range of abilities because of inclusion. Using knowledge of cognitively based instructional strategies, developmental levels, individual differences, new management and discipline approaches, and best practices in special education, you will now adjust the strategies used in your lesson plans to accommodate special needs

> ◎ **CORE CONCEPT** Learners with special needs are *not* so different from other learners. Therefore, when instruction is properly adjusted, powerful techniques can and should be used with these learners.

learners. Remember, if we truly believe that it is our job not to teach, but to help students learn, then we need to look at indicators that help us better address students' individual needs. Are grade and age levels the best measures for designing instruction? Do labels such as *learning disabled, mentally retarded, attention deficit disorder,* and *gifted* really give us enough information to help meet students' learning needs? As you continue planning for instruction, it is important to keep in mind the academic diversity in today's classrooms. You must now plan to provide classroom instruction for low-, middle-, and high-achieving learners that sit side by side everyday in our classrooms. You can use the techniques of differentiated instruction to accomplish this.

For the purpose of illustration, we will adjust the lesson on thunderstorms using two (of the many) specific, differentiated instructional techniques (see pages 235 for compacting and 234 for tiered activities) to meet the needs of diverse students.

Consider

A few students in the class have not grasped the content and concepts from the learning packet. Therefore, they are not ready to share and teach information to other group members. We decided to implement *anchoring activities.*

Accommodation 1:   During the first 15 minutes of each class, and at other times students have completed assigned work, students will be engaged in *anchoring activities.* These activities provide opportunities to review, learn, or advance content knowledge and provide mechanisms for declarative knowledge (COVER) and procedural knowledge (practice and feedback). Because the students are at varying levels of cognitive abilities and mastery, using these anchoring activities will be helpful to all students. Specifically, many of the students have not grasped the following concepts: (1) process of water cycle, (2) relationship between air temperature and thunderstorms, and (3) amount and impact of electricity carried by thunderstorms. Those students who have mastered the content have expressed an interest in learning about weather instruments, specifically methods of recording weather.

During the 15 or so minutes (time is flexible) at the beginning of each lesson, students work independently or in small groups of two or three. Using learning packets, science books, and other resources, students choose a topic to focus on and work through the information. The teacher supplies visual organizers to help students organize information, develop relationships, and make connections. The teacher allows time to check student work and for students to check each others' work. During any other "down" time, students will return to the anchoring activity.

Consider

The jigsaw method and student groupings used during the thunderstorm lesson were not working well. The diversity of ability levels, including widely varied reading levels, affected the rate of learning for low, middle and high achievers. The use of *tiered activities* was now implemented.

Accommodation 2:   Provide the same essential ideas and skills for all students, but design entry to the information at various levels of complexity, abstractness, and based on students' prior knowledge and experience. All students participate in the unit activities with the following specific accommodations at the lesson level:

1. Design three versions of the thunderstorm lesson representing three levels of reading ability to provide for varying ability levels.

2. Note-taking strategies differ. Some students receive partially completed content organizers; others work with more complex thinking tools.

3. Questions/activities provided in learning packet are adjusted. For lower-ability groups, more lower-level questions and activities are offered. Quizzes and tests reflect cognitive levels.

4. The last activity in the lesson, creating a severe storms safety manual for the community, will be designed to adjust to the student's reading, writing, and thinking abilities as well as style preferences. All students respond to the essential ideas, content, concepts, and skills outlined in the lesson objectives. However, varying levels of performance will be required depending on students' ability. Lower-achieving students will design manuals with more pictures, graphs, and possibly audiotapes. Written criteria will demonstrate comprehension and application of the content. Middle-achieving students might be expected to conduct data analysis and interviewing, and to develop graphics/charts that show analysis of data collected. Relationships among water cycle, thunderstorms, air temperature, and environmental impact should be well developed. Content of community manual will demonstrate ability to apply and analyze information. High-ability students will respond to all questions and will be expected to conduct original research by designing an experiment and preparing a written document or other medium that demonstrates a synthesis of content and a plan of implementation.

Consider

What if the class has mostly special needs learners? Can the teacher provide rich content? What about designing units of instruction for sixth- and seventh-grade special needs students who have a wide range of disabilities including perceptual impairments, emotional disturbances, attention deficit/hyperactivity disorder, and minor forms of dyslexia with reading levels ranging from third to sixth grades? Can teachers design units that are meaningful and engaging, that challenge the students with significant content?

Your Turn

We ask you now to make accommodations to your lesson plan for special needs learners.

CHAPTER SUMMARY

In this chapter we address the field of special education from a growth, rather than a deficit, paradigm. We attempt to help you look beyond both disability and grade-level labels to provide powerful instruction and promote deep learning among *all* students with whom you work. The ideas in this chapter stem from the core belief that learners, adolescents, and adults who are disabled are not so different from their nondisabled peers. Likewise, they stem from the belief that nondisabled people are not nearly so alike as our schools seem to believe.

In the abstract it is certainly easy enough to agree with these beliefs. However, much of what transpires in our schools does not reflect these core beliefs. The history of special education shows a field that was, and continues to be, heavily influenced by the behavioral tradition and the view of learners with disabilities as "broken and needing to be fixed." Prior to the civil rights movement in the late 1960's and early 1970's, so many learners were identified as having learning problems, and referrals were so easy to make, that many regular education teachers seem to have lost their tolerance for increasingly minor deviations from some ideal norm. The civil rights movement instigated laws to protect learners from unfair placement into special education classes. It also encouraged the identification of those who rightly needed special education services. Eventually, mainstreaming and inclusion led to more and more learners receiving part or all of their education in regular classrooms with their nondisabled peers.

A common practice in our schools is to seek homogeneous groupings to facilitate teaching. The natural outgrowth of that practice in regular education is to place learners in grades according to their chronological ages. In special education it leads to grouping learners by disability labels. Both of these practices are based on an assumption that competes with this chapter's core concept. They view learners with disabilities as being very different from learners without disabilities; they also assume that nondisabled learners of the same chronological ages are very similar to one another. This discounts the importance of mental age, the cognitive age at which we function. In this chapter we tried to demonstrate, using mental age, that a range of levels is present even in a normally distributed regular education classroom.

Some helpful general information can be derived from knowing that learners are third graders or that they are mentally retarded. But the kinds of specific information on which we need to base our instruction can only be obtained as we work with learners and observe their learning and behavior patterns. We all differ from one another qualitatively. In the classroom, it is the quantitative differences that seem to command the most attention. That is, some are slower and some are faster than others at understanding concepts and skills. In addition, some are faster in some subjects and at some skills, and slower in others. All learners, however, should have a rich context and stimulating environment in which they can learn deeply. In that regard, the powerful principles and strategies that we address in earlier chapters of this book are just as applicable in special education classrooms as they are in regular education

For differing ability levels, flexible grouping and adjusting the cognitive level of questions enhances the potential for students' success (Courtesy of © Charles Gupton/Corbis Stock Market).

classrooms. Differentiated instruction gives us ideas for general strategies that can help us accommodate the needs of a wide variety of learners in both regular and special education classrooms.

Special education researchers believe that some learners with disabilities need very specific remedial programs to help them overcome their learning or behavior problems. These special programs tend to emphasize direct instruction, high levels of structure, and precise sequence. They tend to be skill oriented. Some learners might need these programs of instruction. But the number of such learners is small. Unfortunately, the practices in special education tend to be *drill and skill* oriented, and are based on the assumption that the number of learners needing such specialized educational programming is very large.

Even learners with specialized needs can benefit from powerful principles and strategies. These strategies can be used in self-contained special education classrooms, in regular education classrooms, and in inclusive classrooms. They are simply part of good teaching. By responding to the needs of individual learners, we often help other learners whose needs are not as compelling but who nevertheless benefit from whatever accommodations we have made. Teachers have a responsibility to all learners—not just those who happen to fit nicely into some idealized view of what a learner should be.

Getting to the Core

What Is the History of Special Education in America?

- With the dawning of the Industrial Age, classes and schools grew in size and, reflecting the factory model of efficiency, schools organized themselves for group rather than individual instruction. Children were placed into grades according to their chronological ages and as these groupings became more systematized, children who had been able to cling to the fringes of the system began to fall between the cracks. This gave way to special education classes for what were then called exceptional children. Because chronological groupings did not work as well for these children, assignments were made to special education classes based upon disability label as well as age.

- As federal and state money poured into local school district budgets to subsidize the education of children with disabilities, the number of children enrolled in special education classes grew rapidly. Children who otherwise would have remained in regular education were referred to special education, and it was relatively easy to refer children for special education services.

◎ CORE CONCEPT Learners with special needs are *not* so different from other learners. Therefore, when instruction is properly adjusted, powerful techniques can and should be used with these learners.

- In 1975, Public Law 94-142, also called the Education for All Handicapped Children Act, was passed. This law protected the due process rights of children so that they were not unfairly labeled as handicapped and segregated from other children by being placed in full-time special education classrooms. The law has been repeatedly revised. Today we know it as The Individuals with Disabilities Education Act (IDEA).

How Do We Group Children for Instruction in America's Schools?

- Children are placed in classrooms based on their chronological ages. For some children with serious learning or behavior problems, chronological age (CA) is not an adequate or appropriate way to group because of the wide variety of problems they display. These children are grouped by their disability label—mentally retarded (MR), emotionally disturbed (ED), learning disabled (LD), visually impaired (VI), hearing impaired (HI), crippled and other health impaired (COHI), speech and language disordered, severely multiply handicapped (SMH), or gifted.

How Homogeneous Are Our Classrooms?

- We all possess two "ages." One is our chronological age, determined at birth. The other is our mental age (MA), or the age at which we function on cognitive tasks similar to those required in school. By using MAs, CAs, IQ and the idea of a normal, bell-shaped curve, one can easily see that learners at the same CAs are not so similar to one another as one might think. The normal curve provides some statistical evidence for this assertion.

- On the surface, grouping children by either CA or by type of disability results in more homogeneous classrooms and allow teachers to make appropriate instructional decisions based on learners' needs. However, children of the same chronological age are not as similar to one another as we might assume, and disabled children are not so different from their chronological peers.

- In special education classrooms, disability labels have typically been used to group students. But learning problems can differ widely. Students with learning disabilities often have wide variations in abilities. They can be truly gifted in some areas and quite disabled in other areas.

- Often students with disabilities have social skills similar to those of their non-disabled peers.

- For small groups of students classified as severely and profoundly disabled, inclusion in mainstream activities is difficult.

How Should We Use General and Specific Information?

- Both elementary and special educators use labels to group and teach children. Too often these labels are used as if they yield the *specific* information that is needed to teach these students.

- General information provides some basic information about students—their chronological age, the curriculum they will be studying during the year, where they may be in terms of social and emotional development (based on their CAs), etc. Specific information is what you learn about individual children once they arrive in your classroom—their personality types or learning styles, their academic strengths and weaknesses, etc.

- Using general information as if it were specific information is a mistake in that it keeps classroom instruction from changing to accommodate the needs of children even in regular education and at every grade level. Grade-level groupings (and the general information they imply) simply do not provide sufficient or appropriate information to help us plan and carry out effective instruction.

- Developmental theory suggests that all people develop in essentially the same way, but at differing rates and with varying strengths and weaknesses. All learners share similar general characteristics by virtue of their being human, *but no two learners are exactly the same.* We all differ qualitatively from one another. The major difference between learners in special education and those in regular education is typically a *quantitative* one rather than a qualitative one. Some children develop more slowly cognitively or socially than others.

- Understanding this takes the mystery out of special education. Children with learning and behavior disabilities are not so different from all other children.

- However, some researchers suggest that a small portion of children may indeed be very different from others in some very specific ways and they may require very specialized instructional strategies. *Their numbers are small.* And even these children differ widely in the scope of their disabilities. So we must use caution against generalizing from a small population with very specific needs to the entire population of special needs learners.

How Do Powerful Principles Relate to Learners with Special Needs?

- General principles of learning hold true for special needs learners just as they do for all other learners.

- An individualized education plan (IEP) establishes an education program for students identified as having special learning needs. This includes academic and behavior goals and objectives for the child.

- Throughout American history, general education and, to a greater extent, special education have been greatly influenced by behavioral theory. Because IEPs are a mandated part of federal law, it appears that special education is locked into the behavioral tradition even as more contemporary research has suggested the use of powerful principles and strategies derived from the cognitive sciences.

- Teachers should use alternatives to behavioral theory, including social-cognitive, contextualist, and information-processing theories (IPT) to encourage learning. Using declarative and procedural knowledge, powerful principles represented by COVER and practice/feedback will help promote learning. Specific instructional strategies like questioning, problems, case method, projects, learning centers, and organizers should be utilized to vary instruction and accommodate individual differences.

- It is important to consider what is causing learners to have learning problems. We can use IPT to help us understand at least some of the possible reasons. Perhaps a few learners simply lack any prior knowledge upon which to build new knowledge. Because humans cannot learn anything new unless they already know something about a subject (no connections can be formed in long-term memory), no real learning can take place unless the teacher goes back to more fundamental concepts with which learners are already familiar. To ensure that learners process information deeply into LTM, the teacher encourages them to organize (O) and visualize (V) the information, and then engages in several forms of elaborative rehearsal (ER). Students self-assess their own work as the teacher assesses it (feedback), and then carry out another project in a different venue (practice). In addition to theory, specific powerful strategies that the teacher can employ include cooperative learning, project learning, higher-order questioning, and graphic organizers.

How Can We Teach Groups of Learners with Diverse Abilities and Needs?

- Today's classrooms represent a community of diverse learners that consist of students with different developmental levels, learning and personality styles, cognitive abilities, cultural differences, and motivational needs. Most elementary schools deal with learner differences by using *ability grouping;* high schools use *tracking.* Current research on ability grouping and tracking has caused schools to rethink how they organize the delivery of curriculum and instruction.

- Methods of *differentiating instruction* to meet the needs of slower, average, and gifted students in the same classroom are readily available for teachers. Instructional strategies that encourage differentiated instruction include flexible grouping, tiered activities, compacting, adjusting questions and entry points, among others.

What Are Some Specific Techniques to Use with Learners with Disabilities?

- The powerful cognitive strategies discussed in previous chapters can be used more frequently to promote deeper understanding with children with special needs.

- One example is a four-step process that includes (1) introducing and identifying key concepts, (2) presenting lessons in small, connected chunks of information that build upon one another and incorporate metacognitive strategies that help students transfer information into long-term memory, (3) participation that promotes group cohesion and group work to increase engagement, and (4) corrective feedback as part of the evaluation process that identifies what must be retaught. For at-risk learners, motivation is also an important factor. Peer tutoring, cooperative learning, and interage cooperation are critical motivators for special needs learners.

- Another sequence of strategies includes (1) focusing on big ideas and preteaching background knowledge; (2) integrating new knowledge with old knowledge; (3) using mediated scaffolding (personal guidance, assistance, and support); (4) teaching conspicuous strategies (specific steps that lead to solving complex problems); and (5) judicious review that requires students to frequently revisit and apply previously learned knowledge.

How Can Powerful Principles Accommodate Learners with Special Needs in Regular Classrooms?

- Learning strategies instruction focuses on making the student a more active learner by teaching students how to learn and how to effectively use what they have learned.

- Think about teaching in terms of units of instruction that are centered on big ideas and that bring in facts, skills, and concepts in the context of pursuing those big ideas. In the process of teaching these units, there will likely be adaptations that you can make to help included students as well as other learners in your classroom.

Changes Needed to Support Powerful Classroom Practices

CHAPTER **7**

From Tests to Authentic Performances

(Source: © 1998, Washington Post Writers Group. Reprinted with permission.)

 SCENARIO

Mr. Dalgleish is a very experienced teacher. Lately, however, he has confronted a dilemma that has him perplexed. Throughout his teaching career Mr. D (as the children call him) has used unit teaching as his predominant strategy. His units are typically thematic. He tries to help children develop an understanding that various disciplines can connect to one another. One example of a unit he planned and teaches focuses on measurement. The title of the unit is "How Do We Measure Up?" In this unit children read stories having to do with measurement. They calculate various lengths, distances, heights, and weights. They draw items to scale. They study the history of weights and measures and learn about how ancient cultures measured things. They learn about metric measurements by inventing something in their own "laboratories." Further, they predict where things would weigh more—on Earth, Mars, Venus, and so on, and then check the actual weights of objects on these planets. They even learn about the musical scale and measures. This unit of instruction takes almost four weeks to complete. It includes all of the basic academic subjects (reading, writing, arithmetic, history, and science) and then some.

During this unit of instruction, children work on the various tasks in small groups. Mr. D feels that this helps all the children because they provide support to one another as they work. It seems to be especially helpful for the two special needs children who are included in his classroom. Mr. D occasionally gives direct instruction on a specific piece of content that he wants the children to know, but more often than not the children share information with one another through demonstrations, discussions, and presentations. Mr. D requires the children to keep track of information by taking notes and keeping them in folders. The children keep journals in which they reflect and make connections between new knowledge and prior understandings.

Mr. D periodically checks both notes and journals to keep track of the children's progress through the unit. He makes notes of things he needs to help them clarify or correct. During each unit he gives several short quizzes that count very little but that help him uncover misunderstandings. At the conclusion of each unit, Mr. D gives a major unit test to all the students. This test counts heavily toward their marking period grade. It includes true/false, multiple-choice, and short-answer questions. Most children take almost an hour to complete the unit test.

Mr. D is very proud of his units of instruction. He believes that the children learn a great deal from these units. Yet their performances on the unit exams never fail to disappoint him. Although some children do quite well, many do not. Considering all of the integration of content and active learning that takes place during the unit, Mr. D expects that all the students should do very well on the exam. But they don't. Even the children are perplexed. They tell Mr. D that they understand the information and can use it—they just don't do well on tests.

Now back to Mr. D's dilemma. He wonders if he should continue with the units, or if he should better prepare the children

Getting to the Core

◎ CORE CONCEPT There lies, somewhere between rigid, standardized tests of trivia on the one hand and idiosyncratic, arbitrary teacher-made tests on the other, a way to develop standards of understanding performances and to judge them using authentic measures.

How Important Is Assessment?

What Are the Major Categories of Assessment?
- Norm- and Criterion-Referenced Standardized Tests
- A Closer Look at Standardized Tests
- Reliability and Validity of Standardized Tests
- The SAT as an Example
- Standardized Tests: The Pros and Cons
- In Pursuit of Trivia
- Standardized Tests and Social Bias
- Standardized Tests in Perspective

How Do Standardized Tests Relate to Classroom Assessment?

So What Is a Teacher to Do?
- Develop Valid Conventional Tests Using What We Know from Research
- Use Multiple Sources
- Do More Formative Assessment
- Assess While You Teach, Teach While You Assess
- Consider Balancing Traditional with Alternative Assessments

How Do We Get from Alternative Assessment to Evaluation?
- Develop and Use Rubrics
- Some Examples of Rubrics
- Porfolios in the Assessment Process

How Can We Use Assessment to Understand Student Learning?

How Can We Put All of This Together?

for the unit test by teaching more directly the major concepts and skills. After all, he reasons, the test results and the marking period grades are what the children and parents seem to care about the most.

> **?** *Do you think Mr. D's unit tests adequately measure what students are learning? Why or why not? Can you suggest some alternative ways for Mr. D. to assess what his students have learned at the end of a unit of instruction? Using your suggestions, do you think the results he sees will be better? A fairer representation of what the children have learned? Why?*

INTRODUCTION

The core concept for this chapter suggests that there is a continuum we can use to think about assessment and evaluation of student learning. That continuum ranges from standardized assessments to teacher-made assessments. Both of these, and the variations that range between them, are essential elements of the teaching and learning process. You have already learned the importance of providing learners with specific feedback on their performances. They improve by using that feedback. Feedback is especially helpful in developing procedural knowledge. It also helps learners identify their novice, naïve, or incorrect representations of declarative knowledge.

Feedback is equally important for teachers. When we assess students' work we are, in effect, assessing our own work as well. David Allen (1998) puts it aptly when he writes, "It often seems that in looking at students' work samples teachers are really looking—as in double exposure—at their own work" (3). By looking carefully at students' work, we receive feedback on our performances. We identify areas of knowledge that students need to address further, and we can determine when students are ready to move on, to build on something we now know they truly understand.

> "Not everything that counts can be counted, and not everything that can be counted counts."
>
> —**Albert Einstein**

How Important Is Assessment?

Perhaps no other area of education is as hotly debated as assessment. People are very divided on the issue of how best to measure learning outcomes. The call for teacher accountability has also exacerbated the emotionality and intensity of the great assessment debate. Assessment is as much a political issue as it is a pedagogical issue. Even real estate values are affected by assessment results. Houses located in school districts boasting above-average standardized test results are more highly valued than those in districts with lower profiles. The standards-based movement (which we addressed in Chapter 4) currently overtaking our country, in which minimum standards of achievement are set for all children at each grade level, has produced a spate of literature relating not only to assessment but also to accountability and reporting of data.

Parents and their school-age children seem to be much more concerned about assessments and the grades that are earned on them than they are concerned about what is actually *learned* in school! The quest for a good grade is so very strong that a recent article in a local newspaper addressed at least one of the unfortunate consequences of this quest—*cheating*. This article cited the following percentages based upon an informal survey of teens: 77 percent of girls and 79 percent of boys admitted to some form of cheating (Dougherty 2000). Of course, there are different forms of cheating. Copying homework, writing answers to test questions on one's arm, handing in someone else's work, and so forth, are all forms of academic dishonesty that influence assessment results. National studies substantiate what this local survey found—a large percentage of students cheat. Why? There are lots of specific reasons, but they all boil down to one general reason. Students feel tremendous pressure to get good grades. Given the importance that society puts on grades, this is understandable. But the importance of grades in our society raises the issue of whether or not grades measure anything of real significance, which in turn raises the broader question of the reliability and validity of assessments in general.

> **Think about it . . .**
>
> Have you ever cheated or been tempted to cheat? Why? What were the circumstances? What were the consequences?
>
> When you are a teacher, what are some things you might do to prevent students from feeling that they need to cheat?

What Are the Major Categories of Assessment?

First, let us be clear about what is meant by assessment. Huba and Freed (2000) define assessment in the following way:

> Assessment is the process of gathering and discussing information from multiple and diverse sources in order to develop a deep understanding of what students know, understand, and can do with their knowledge as a result of their educational experiences; the process culminates when assessment results are used to improve subsequent learning. (8)

There are two major kinds of assessments—standardized and teacher-made. Usually, these assessments are in the form of traditional tests. In traditional testing formats, students typically choose or select a response from among several choices. Other traditional testing formats include true-false, matching, or fill-in-the-blanks. The accompanying box gives a brief example of a traditional multiple-choice test. We'll call it the Test of Smart People. See how you do on it. The answers are on page 295.

This test could be an example of a standardized test. Such tests usually sample a wide variety of knowledge domains rather than just one (i.e., history, science, math). Standardized tests have a set of specific procedures that students must follow during their administration. The test administrator must control testing conditions so that they are similar for all people who take the test.

Norm- and Criterion-Referenced Standardized Tests

Standardized tests are either norm referenced or criterion referenced. Some are referenced both ways. If they are norm referenced, they compare the scores of any one student to a group of students who took the same test. More specifically, test questions are given to a large number of people called a norm group. Then the central tendency (usually the mean or arithmetic average) and the dispersion (standard deviation) are statistically derived. In other words, standardized test

Test of Smart People

1. Who was Don Quixote's squire?
   a. Pancho Villa   c. Sancho Panza
   b. Santa Ana   d. Miguel
                        Cervantes

2. How many miles are in 9 kilometers?
   a. 5.65 miles   c. 13.5 miles
   b. 6.5 miles   d. none of these

3. Who said, "It's not the size of the dog in the fight, it's the size of the fight in the dog"?
   a. George Patton   c. Teddy
   b. Abraham   Roosevelt
      Lincoln   d. Mark Twain

4. Which of the following bodies is not a star?
   a. nova   c. comet
   b. white dwarf d. pulsar

5. The statue of David was carved by which of the following artists?
   a. Michelangelo   c. Brunelleschi
   b. da Vinci   d. Raphael

Think about it . . .

What does the Test of Smart People reveal about what you know and can do?

What doesn't the Test of Smart People reveal about what you know and can do?

Why are these two questions important to ask about *any* test, standardized or teacher-made?

makers find the average score, and then how the scores deviate above and below the average. Then they can compare any one individual's score to the entire group's scores. For example, if the Test of Smart People was given to a large number of people and the mean score was 3 and the standard deviation was 0.5, then we know that a person with a score of 3.5 was one standard deviation *above the mean.* Likewise, a person with a score of 1.5 scored three standard deviations *below the mean.* The 3.5 score puts a person in the high-average range, whereas the 1.5 puts the person in the very low range.

The entire concept of norm referencing is based upon the normal curve and all of its related assumptions. The raw score (actual number of questions that a student answered correctly) is converted into other scores of some type to provide meaning to raw scores. Thus, various scores that represent performance are reported. The converted scores reported most often for standardized tests are percentiles. They are also the most easily misunderstood. Basically, a percentile tells how well a student did compared to other students. A student who scores at the 99th percentile has done as well as, or better than, 99 percent of the students in the norm group for that test. A student scoring in the 50th percentile performed as well as, or better than, 50 percent of those in the norm group. Note that, in the case of percentiles, 50th percentile is average. In the case of percentage, 50 percent (on a test) would be failing! Those unfamiliar with the idea of percentiles often confuse them with percentages.

There are several other converted scores with which you should be familiar. They are shown in Figure 7.1. Standard scores (like the z and T scores) use the mean and the standard deviation of the raw score distribution to give raw scores meaning. Rather than troubling you with the computations, which are always done by test publishers and given to you with the test scores, we suggest you just get a sense of what represents below-average, average, and above-average performance. Z scores are the most basic standard scores. They simply correspond to the standard deviations of the

FIGURE 7.1

Standard scores and the normal curve

(Source: Biehler, Robert F. and Jack Snowman, Psychology Applied to Teaching, *Sixth Edition. Copyright © 1986 by Houghton-Mifflin Company. Reprinted with permission.)*

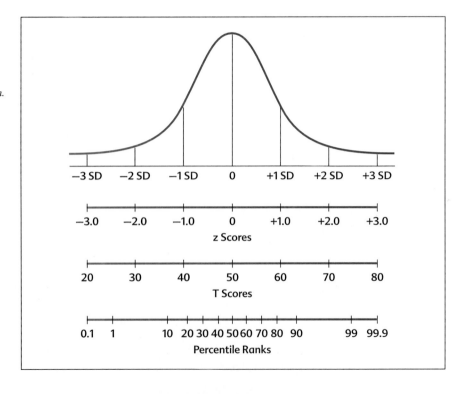

normal curve. A z score of 0 is set at the mean, a z score of +2 is two standard deviations above the mean, a z score of –2.5 is two and a half standard deviations below the mean, and so forth. T scores are similar to z scores, but in order to eliminate negative numbers and decimals a T score has an arbitrary mean of 50 and a standard deviation of 10. Therefore, a T score of 70 is +2 standard deviations above the mean, and a T score of 25 is two and a half standard deviations below the mean. If you know this much, you can interpret at least in a general way how well any given learners did on a standardized, norm-referenced test. The Individual Profile Report (see page 264) includes norm-referenced scores for a student (small insert, bottom right corner), including percentiles and standard (scale) scores.

Standardized tests can be both norm- *and* criterion-referenced. In criterion referencing, rather than comparing a student to other students, the student is compared to a set standard of performance. For example, if a test sets mastery of fourth-grade mathematics at 75 percent, and the student gets 75 percent or more of the questions testing these concepts correct, then the student has achieved high *mastery* and the score is reported that way. It matters not what others have scored. Theoretically, all the students taking the test can reach high mastery on it. That cannot happen on a norm-referenced test, because students are compared to one another and somebody must be higher, and somebody must be lower, than the average. Further, on criterion-referenced tests students scoring 70 percent on a given subtest of the larger test might receive a score of moderate mastery; those receiving a score below 50 percent might receive a low mastery score. (See the Terra Nova Individual Profile Report on p. 264.)

Standardized tests are used to make very important decisions for schools and students. The public and its representatives in politics judge the effectiveness of school districts by using the results of these tests. Federal and state money is sometimes apportioned based upon test results. Decisions about placing students into certain programs and classes, most notably special education, are based in part on the results of standardized tests. Therefore, they deserve closer scrutiny.

A Closer Look at Standardized Tests

There is, and has been for quite a long time, a great debate about the value of standardized tests. Suppose the results of the Test of Smart People heavily influenced some important educational decision made on your behalf. Perhaps it was which graduate schools you can and cannot be accepted to. How would you feel about this? Standardized tests have a long history of use in our country. You have taken many standardized tests during your school career. One example we are quite certain you are familiar with is the SAT. It is likely that the SAT was the most recent, high-stakes standardized test that you have taken. In a moment we will take a close look at the SAT because it represents a typical, standardized, norm-referenced assessment.

Reliability and Validity of Standardized Tests

To begin our close look at standardized tests, we need to discuss two concepts from basic statistics. Unfortunately, often these concepts are not well understood by the general public or by many teachers. The first of these is *reliabilty*. In the world of tests and measurements, reliability is the ability of a test to yield a stable score over time. That is, the test scores for an individual should not vary widely from one test administration to the next. Just think of a ruler. Suppose you measure the length of a line and get a measurement of 7 inches. Then suppose that you measure that line a second time, the same way, and with the same ruler. But this time you get a measurement of 9 inches. Yet a third measurement yields 10.5 inches. You certainly can't put much faith in those measurements. The ruler is simply not reliable.

The Individual Profile Report provides comprehensive information to help teachers and parents understand student test performance.

(Source: CTB/McGraw-Hill, Terra Nova Individual Profile Report, copyright © 1997 CTB/McGraw-Hill. Reproduced with permission of the McGraw-Hill Companies.)

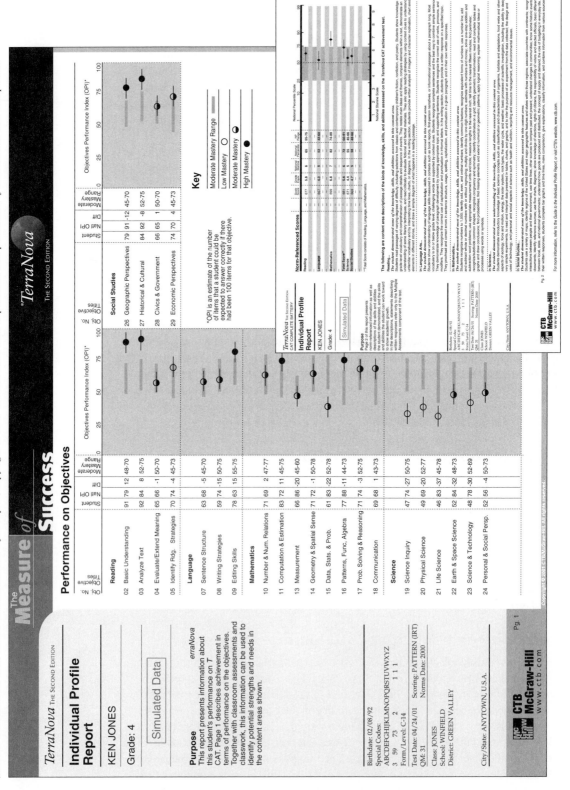

The same holds true for assessments. We cannot put much faith in the scores derived from tests that have poor reliability. If we give a reading test today and then a similar test tomorrow, and the scores for individual learners vary widely, then we cannot make educational decisions with reasonable confidence on the basis of these scores. To help us understand how reliable their tests are, publishers will usually disclose the reliability coefficients in their test manuals.

Test makers calculate these coefficients in a number of ways. One way, for example, is to administer a test twice, perhaps several weeks apart. It would be expected that the two sets of scores would correlate. That is, students scoring high on the first test administration would also score high on the second, and those scoring lower on the first would also score lower on the second. If that happens, it means we can predict one score if we know the other score. The *correlation coefficient* tells us the degree to which two sets of scores are related to one another.

Because we normally look for a positive relationship between test scores, at least in the context of test reliability, +1 is the highest reliability coefficient we can expect. But no test is perfect. Test experts disagree on what is acceptable reliability because so much depends on what the test is testing and how the results will be used. Trice (2000) asserts that correlations between +.30 and +.70 are moderate, and those between +.70 and +1.00 are high. Luftig (1989) contends that .70 is minimally acceptable, and that consumers should reject outright tests that possess reliabilities below .70.

Whereas reliability tells us about stability of scores over time, *validity* tells us whether a test measures what it purports to measure. To put it another way, validity is "the extent to which a test accomplishes a specific goal" (Trice 2000, 39). By way of a more concrete analogy, imagine that you use a cloth tape measure to find the length of a garment that are planning to buy. You measure it once, and you get 32 inches. You measure it again, and sure enough, it is 32 inches. Expecting a perfect fit you try the garment on. But alas, it is way too long! What happened? It turns out that over time the cloth measure has stretched. It is no longer measuring standard inches. Because it does not measure what it purports to measure, it no longer accomplishes the goal of telling us whether a garment will fit. Publishers, in their test manuals, also disclose information about validity.

There are several types of validity. We will discuss content validity later in the chapter when we discuss classroom assessments. The two kinds of validity most associated with standardized tests are criterion and construct validity. According to Trice (2000), criterion validity "measures the extent to which a test predicts another performance—the criterion" (44). Construct validity, on the other hand, helps us establish whether a test measures something not directly measurable (like IQ) by comparing it to a known and respected measure of that construct (in this case, intelligence). Validity is not always expressed as a coefficient. When it is, it should, like reliability, approach .70 in order to be considered sufficiently valid (Luftig 1989).

What is the relationship between reliability and validity? A test can be reliable but not valid. As in the example above, the tape measure gave the same measurement repeatedly, so it was reliable. It did not, however, measure what it was supposed to measure—inches. Therefore, even though it was reliable it was not valid. So too it is with tests and assessments; they can be reliable but not valid. However, a test cannot be valid if it is unreliable. Just think about it. How could a test measure a trait or ability if the scores are unstable? Scores that vary widely prevent a test from being a valid measurement.

> **Think about it . . .**
>
> Check in your school library to see if there is a test collection. If so, locate a test manual and peruse it. Can you find the reliability and validity of the test? What do these coefficients tell you about the usefulness of the test?

It is worth repeating that no test is perfect. Every test contains error. Test publishers try to minimize error by studying and reporting, and then improving, the reliability and validity of their tests. In any case, by knowing the reliability and validity coefficients we have some idea about the quality of the test.

The SAT as an Example

Adelman (1999) points out that we can't stop talking about the SAT. He notes that "the word 'SAT' is now shorthand for all standardized testing" (B4). It is because we think he is correct that we chose to examine standardized testing more closely by focusing on the SAT as an exemplar. We also chose it because most of you have taken the SAT not all that long ago. We hope that revisiting the test does not cause you the same sweaty palms it may have caused you a few years back!

According to the National Center for Fair and Open Testing (2000), the SAT is the nation's oldest and most widely used (and according to the center, misused) college entrance exam. It has a verbal and a math section each scored on a 200 to 800 point scale. The center points out that the 138 questions are "nearly exclusively multiple choice; ten math questions require students to 'grid in' the answer." The SAT, according to the center, "does not include advanced mathematics topics nor does it attempt to assess higher-order thinking or reasoning skills." Further, they point out that although "a verbal score is provided, test takers do not write a single word." They also point out that it is a timed test, with deadlines that prevent some students from finishing all sections. (Quotations from ***http://www.fairtest.org/facts/satfact.htm.***)

The characteristics of the group on whom the SATs were normed are well known and widely reported. In addition, Educational Testing Service (ETS, makers of the SAT under contract to The College Board) has reported validity and reliability data for the SAT tests. Here are the facts:

1. The SATs were first normed on 10,654 students. "Ninety-eight percent of them were white, 60 percent were male, and 40 percent were attending private, college preparatory high schools." (Bracey 1997, 44)

2. The average raw score was assigned a scaled score of 500. The standard deviation was 100. The scores could range from 200 (lowest) to 800 (highest) for each of the two sections (verbal and mathematics). (Bracey 1997, 45)

3. The reliability of the SAT verbal and mathematics sections range between 0.91 and 0.93. (***http://www.collegeboard.org/***)

4. Validity (as predictor of college freshman grade point average) is 0.56 for females, 0.60 for males.

It is important for you to recognize that one of the strengths of standardized tests is that the technical characteristics of their tests are *known*. As you will learn later, that is not the case with most classroom assessments constructed by teachers. You can see from the data reported above that the SAT was normed on a large group of college-bound students. The test reliability is high, so we can put faith in the accuracy of the scores and their stability over time. Regarding predictive validity (which is one type of criterion validity), it appears that the SAT scores (verbal and math combined) are, according to Trice (2000), in the moderate range. That is, the SAT is a moderately valid predictor of college freshman grades.

It might seem a bit unfair to critique the SAT, especially in view of the fact that publishers of this and all standardized tests provide us with the very data we need to do so. According to PBS's *Frontline* special on the secrets of the SAT, Americans put a great deal of emphasis on standardized test scores; indeed, SAT scores seem to have become a national obsession. As we pointed out earlier, many very important educational decisions are based on the results of standardized tests. So are political decisions that relate to the funding of educational programs and entities. In addition, testing is a big, lucrative, competitive business in our country. That makes it necessary for those who publish and sell tests to address the quality of their products.

Although the group on which the original SAT was normed is large, there was a question of its currency and whether or not it represented contemporary high schoolers. It was normed in 1941, over 50 years ago, on what Bracey (1997) called an "elite" population that no longer reflects the makeup of current SAT takers. Today, many more women, minority, public school, and less-affluent students take the SAT than were represented in the original normative group. In fact, many more students take the SAT, period! Although a score of 500 once represented an average score, the College Board (sponsors of the SAT) recognized that this was no longer accurate given today's typical test taker. So in 1995 the SATs were renormed (or in College Board jargon, recentered) so that 500 once again accurately reflected the average score of today's college-bound youth.

Test reliability is high. But some very serious questions have been raised related to the validity of the SATs. It is certainly not solely the test publisher's fault if its tests are misused. But publishers must share some responsibility for the ways their tests are used. The SAT, according to the National Center for Fair and Open Testing (2000), is validated only for the purpose of predicting first-year college grades. The College Board itself makes no claims to the contrary. The issue, then, is how well does it do this (i.e., exactly how good is "moderate" validity in the context of this test and its use?)?

According to the National Center for Fair and Open Testing, the SAT does not predict first-year grades very well. In addition, the center claims that SATs predict other outcomes, such as graduation rates, even more poorly. Adelman (1999) and Trice (2000) disagree with the first criticism. They seem to think that SATs do a decent job of predicting first-year college grades. The question is, so what? The point raised by Adelman, in agreement with the center, is that predicting first-year grades "has nothing to do with the principal goal of students at four-year colleges and their families: completing a bachelor's degree" (B4). That, according to Adelman, is best predicted by the successful completion of a high-quality, four-year high school curriculum. Further, the National Center points out that high school grade point average and class rank are better predictors of first-year grades. Sacks (2000) agrees. He points out that the SAT, when combined with high school grades, adds only modestly to the prediction of first-year college grades. He claims that SAT scores explain just 16 percent of the variation in freshman grades, leaving a full 84 percent of the variance unaccounted for. That is a large percentage of unknown variance.

There are many other concerns about the SATs. Some most likely contribute to the unaccounted variance mentioned above. Among them: The scores attained on the SAT are highly correlated to family income (Sacks 2000); SATs penalize women and minority students (Sacks 2000); only about 200 out of 1,800 four-year colleges place enough weight on these scores in the admissions process to affect students' lives (Adelman 1999). Perhaps Stedman (1994) levels the most biting critique when he characterizes the SAT as an irrelevant measure of educational quality. He notes that it fails to measure most of what is taught in high school, including science, foreign language, English literature, and U.S. history. You can see, then, that even a well-constructed, widely used standardized test has its strengths as well as its limitations.

Standardized Tests: The Pros and Cons

Most of the public, and many teachers, are not sufficiently familiar with concepts related to the technical quality of standardized tests to judge their appropriate use. Normative groups, reliability, and validity, and several other pertinent concepts (such as standard error of measurement, sources of error) that are beyond the scope of this book, should be well understood in order to judge the suitability of any given standardized test. The public often gives these tests far more credibility than they deserve. The SATs are appropriately renormed, possess high reliability, and have moderate predictive validity. Still, they are used in ways for which they are not validated. For example, they are used to predict success in college but are not validated for that purpose. They cost the public a great deal of money, yet there is considerable debate about whether or not all but a very few colleges need the scores to make their admissions decisions.

There are many standardized tests in use today. You might have already taken, or soon will take, one or more of the Praxis Series. These are a set of professional assessments for beginning teachers put out by Educational Testing Service (ETS). Many states require them for initial teacher licensure. The standardized tests that you are most likely to come across as a classroom teacher, however, are the following achievement tests: California Achievement Tests, Comprehensive Tests of Basic Skills, Iowa Tests of Basic Skills, Metropolitan Achievement Tests, and Stanford Achievement Tests (Popham 1999). We shall now take a closer look at these tests. We will leave the scrutiny of their technical qualities up to you rather than reiterate what we wrote above. We have already made the point that one of the positive attributes of standardized tests is that their technical qualities are known. It will be good practice for you to find, study, and discuss these qualities with others (see the Think about it box on p. 265). Instead, now we will examine a bit more generally the advantages and disadvantages of standardized assessments.

Popham (1999) tells us that what standardized test makers try to do is to "create assessment tools that permit someone to make a valid inference about the knowledge and/or skills that a given student possesses in a particular content area" (9). He goes on to say that, given the norm group for comparison, parents and educators can get an idea of a child's strengths and weaknesses relative to other children of the same age or in the same grade. Additionally, if teachers know how their students stack up to other children across the nation, Popham says that they can use that information to devise classroom instruction.

More specifically, Popham identifies two useful inferences that teachers and parents can make from standardized tests that possess acceptable technical characteristics:

1. The relative strengths and weaknesses of a child across subject areas (i.e., strong in math, weak in science).

2. How a child has grown over time in different subject areas (e.g., a child's percentile scores remain stable over three years in most subjects but drop over time in one subject).

However, Pophan is very firm in his conviction that standardized tests do not measure educational quality. His overarching reason for this conviction is that "any inference about educational quality made on the basis of students' standardized achievement test performances is apt to be invalid" (1999, 10). He likens using standardized achievement tests to measure educational quality to measuring temperature with a tablespoon. It is not the purpose of tablespoons to tell us how hot or cold something is; likewise, it is not the purpose of standardized tests to tell us how good or bad a school is. In fact, they really can't do that. They simply don't sample enough of any one domain, test questions are not aligned to what is taught in any given school, and questions that tap important concepts are systematically excluded from the test because too many children answer them correctly and they no longer spread out test scores. But perhaps the most compelling of Popham's arguments is that only one (the first identified below) of three factors that influence test results is linked to instructional quality. The three factors that he identifies as contributing to students' scores on standardized tests are: (1) what is taught in school, (2) a student's native intelligence, and (3) a student's out-of-school learning (12). Popham presents sample questions from standardized tests to make his point.

Sacks (2000) presents a much broader assault on standardized tests. Essentially, in addition to arguing that as a collective nation we are too enamored of tests, he claims:

- The ability of standardized tests to predict one's academic success is questionable.

- The correlation of standardized test scores with socioeconomic status is high.

- Standardized tests reward passive, superficial learning and drive instruction in undesirable directions like teaching to the tests.

In this last point he is in strong agreement with David Perkins, who wrote:

> . . . conventional multiple-choice, knowledge-oriented testing does not serve the cause of education well. Such testing drives teachers and students toward rote styles of instruction that may help with retention of knowledge but have little hope of building understanding or the active use of knowledge. (1992, 15)

In Pursuit of Trivia

The big problem alluded to in Sacks's last point, and supported by Perkins, is the propensity of standardized tests to measure knowledge of trivia. That is, many standardized tests fail to assess higher-order thinking skills (a criticism leveled at the SAT earlier in this chapter) and instead ask only for recall of facts and the production of routine procedures. This is lamentable, because the assumption that underlies such testing runs contrary to what we know about promoting deep and lasting knowledge through the use of powerful principles and strategies. The assumption is that learning is simply an accumulation of facts and procedures. This reductionist view is rooted firmly in behaviorism, and it grossly oversimplifies the teaching and learning process. We have inveighed against such a narrow view of human learning throughout this textbook.

Still, it is not entirely unexpected that standardized tests, though they need not do so, often test only recall of facts. Questions of fact are easier to develop in multiple-choice and true-false format than are questions that tap higher-order thinking. They are also more time efficient because the test taker need not take the time to reason through a complex problem. With facts, either you can or cannot recall the answer. So standardized test makers, already hard pressed to sample adequately a domain of knowledge in an acceptable time frame, willingly use such questions. Few people even question the test makers—after all, we have pointed out time and again that most people hold the same naïve conception about what it means to be smart. They believe that remembering facts is paramount. People who can remember facts do quite well, thank you. Think of the huge rewards offered by game shows like *Jeopardy* and *Who Wants to Be a Millionaire?* Hopefully we have addressed the issue of deep and lasting knowledge sufficiently in earlier chapters; we will not repeat our argument here.

SPOTLIGHT ON BEHAVIOR MANAGEMENT

"But will they behave?"

Assessing Students to Improve Behavior

If the "information age" has done only one thing for us, it has emphasized that the more information one has, the more powerful one is. This is especially true when assessing students' behavior. Information is critical as we try to interpret our thoughts and feelings and those of our students.

Recall how this helped the teacher you read about in previous Spotlights on Behavior Management. When she began to compile information about Juan and Eliza, a clearer picture began to form. Do you remember how, in Chapter 3, the teacher learned that Juan had been going through some tough times at home? She also used a variety of sources of information to learn that Juan didn't think very highly of himself. How did the teacher learn this? She asked several questions. She watched the way her students entered and exited the room, who they interacted with and how. She looked for clues in the way they completed (or didn't complete) their work. She listened for the way they spoke to one another and to her.

This is all very valuable information, but for assessment to be truly useful it has to be more systematic than this. We must collect and organize this information in meaningful ways so that later we can put the pieces together. There are many tools to help teachers collect and organize behavioral information. In this section we will briefly share two systems: journals and a more structured system called a functional behavior assessment.

◎ **CORE CONCEPT** There lies, somewhere between rigid, standardized tests of trivia on the one hand and idiosyncratic, arbitrary teacher-made tests on the other, a way to develop standards of understanding performances and to judge them using authentic measures.

A reflective journal can be a small notebook, loose-leaf binder, or computer file that you create to record your observations, questions, and reflections. If you set this up with your word processor, you can create files for individual students and record your observations according to which student you are observing and thinking about. Likewise, a binder or notebook can be sectioned into parts. In this journal you can keep a record of your observations, thoughts, questions, and hypotheses about your students and how to best meet their needs. If you have a large class, perhaps a few lines, every so often, is enough to keep a running record of most of your students.

We want to pause here to warn you of a common pitfall. Often, in the midst of their own feelings of counteraggression or because they are concentrating on other aspects of the classroom, we hear preservice teachers make statements about student behavior that are much too general to be useful. Be careful to avoid these unhelpful generalizations. Rather, as we emphasized in the last chapter, strive for specific observations upon which you can base hypotheses and ask further questions. For example, be specific about who the student is and what you saw him or her do. Identify the person(s) or thing at which the behavior was directed. Describe how long it lasted. Identify where the event took place. Describe the intensity of the behavior. It will also be useful to describe what helped the student calm down and return to productive involvement in the classroom.

You can follow your observations with specific questions they raise for you, a reflection, or a plan of action. Be sure to remain clear about what you actually saw and what you are hypothesizing about. Here are two brief examples that will illustrate what we mean. Journal Entry 1 is *not* helpful. Journal Entry 2 is much more useful.

Journal Entry 1 (not helpful)
Raheam had a bad day today. It was awful. I couldn't seem to keep him on-task. He just kept

yelling. I finally moved his desk to the corner to keep him from distracting the rest of the class.

Journal Entry 2 (more helpful)

Raheam came in today with an angry look on his face and immediately went to his desk and put his coat over his head. When I asked him to put his coat away he yelled, "Leave me alone!" He didn't interact with other students unless they initiated the interaction. When they did, he yelled, "Leave me alone!" This is unusual for Raheam. Although he is not the most outgoing student in the class, he does usually get along well with the others. I wonder if something happened on the way to school or at home. I will call his mom first.

Examining Journal Entry 1, it is easy to see how a busy and frustrated teacher might quickly jot this in a journal. It is also easy to see that it is much less helpful than the second entry.

Using the second entry, it is evident that this is unusual behavior for Raheam. Because of the way Raheam entered the room, we can eliminate the classroom as the source of his troubles. He has definitely carried something in with him. Can you make some inferences or develop some questions that you might be able to use to gain more information? Try before reading on!

The 1997 reauthorization of the Individuals with Disabilities Education Act (IDEA 1997) requires an even more specific form of behavioral assessment for any child who has an individualized education plan (IEP) and whose behavior may impede the learning of others. This specific plan is called a *functional behavior assessment (FBA)*. Additionally, any time that a student with an IEP is under consideration for a change in placement because of his or her behavior, an FBA must be completed.

FBAs are a form of assessment that allows the assessor to (1) provide a clear description of an undesirable behavior, (2) make predictions about when and where the behavior will occur, and (3) define the *functions* that that behavior serves for the student. If you have access to a school (via field placement, student teaching, or employment) ask for a blank copy of the FBA form. If you can't find an example locally, try searching the Internet. Here is one place you can look: **http://204.98.1.2/sped/functanal.html.**

FBAs begin with, but are meant to lead us beyond, observable behavior. They provide a clear and accurate description of the problem behavior *and* identify the

purpose it serves for the student (Fitzsimmons 1998). Say, for example, Raheam was putting his coat over his head daily in an effort to get our attention. It is not the function of his behavior (the reason behind it) that is the problem. It is the behavior itself. So, knowing why Raheam is behaving in this manner leads us to design an intervention that helps Raheam learn how to get the attention of adults in a more socially acceptable way.

FBAs take on many forms, as you will notice when you begin to look at various samples. However, Fitzsimmons (1998) identifies five steps that should be common among them:

1. Identify the seriousness of the problem. Try common management strategies first.

2. Specifically and clearly define the problem. Avoid generalizations.

3. Collect data on possible causes of the problem. Ask if it is linked to a skill deficit, or if something is interfering with the performance of a particular skill.

4. Analyze your data. Put the pieces of the puzzle together. Charting behaviors and events can be useful here.

5. Formulate and test a hypothesis.

The FBA is usually suggested and completed by members of the IEP team for a student who is receiving special education services. You may be part of that team. What if a student is not receiving special education services and his or her behavior is consistently troubling you? As you have been learning, you will need to begin with a close look at yourself and your teaching. Ask yourself if you have a strong relationship with the student. Examine (or have someone else observe) your teaching. Are you challenging this student? Is he or she appropriately engaged and active during your lessons? How do you react when his or her behavior becomes troubling? Are you acting on your counteraggressive feelings?

Once you have taken a close look at what *you* have control of, turn your attention to the student. Ask the many questions that are a result of your careful observation and thought. Perhaps a functional behavior assessment is the right tool for the job or maybe all you needed was to think clearly and carefully about the problem. In either case, these are authentic assessments that can provide you with the information that you need to respond to your students in a helpful manner.

Should standardized tests be used to make "high-stakes" decisions about students' futures (Courtesy of © Charles Gupton/Corbis Stock Market)?

Standardized Tests and Social Bias

According to MacMillan (2001, p. 70), test bias exists "if the assessment distorts performance because of the student's ethnicity, gender, race, religious background, and so on." Standardized tests are particularly prone to these biases. For example, if a test of intelligence actually measures a language difference that the learner brings to the testing session, the test score is misleading. This error is due to measurement bias. Of course, it also relates to reliability and validity for the test's use with a particular learner or group of learners. To the extent that the child's social categories are not represented, or poorly represented, in the group on which the test instrument was normed, the instrument is biased. In that case, the test is not a fair measure of what the child knows or can do.

This problem relates directly to the issue of disproportionate numbers of minority learners in special education classes that we wrote about in Chapter 6. Although by law tests cannot be the only criteria on which learners are placed in special education classes, standardized test scores are always a part (and usually large part) of the process of deciding on eligibility for special education services. It should not surprise us, then, that learners from minority groups are identified more often (proportionately) for special education and related services than other learners. Research has long documented that learners from minority groups are, under testing conditions, disadvantaged by their cultural differences (Aiken 1997; Gregory 1996; Kaplan and Saccuzzo 1993).

Test bias becomes an even more important issue as the stakes associated with performance on tests increase. In the past, many court cases have been focused on the issue of discriminatory practices related to possible test bias. We can expect the current high-stakes testing initiatives to exacerbate the problems related to test bias.

Standardized Tests in Perspective

Let us try to put the standardized test debate into perspective. Schmoker (2000) calls for us to move away from a debate over the value of standardized tests

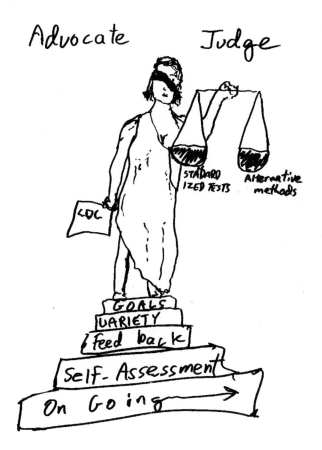

Advocate   Judge

FIGURE 7.2
An organizer developed by teachers showing how assessments should be balanced and justice should be blind. It also shows the two major roles teachers assume.

toward a synthesis of assessment models (See Figure 7.2). Schmoker acknowledges what he terms the "serious limitations" of standardized tests. He includes among these the limitations of the multiple-choice format to reveal a student's ability to "construct a proposal, build a case, analyze an issue in writing, or originally apply a host of mathematical processes" (62). On the other hand, he recognizes that standardized tests "provide data and results orientation that are essential to improvement" (62–63). Schmoker reiterates Popham's points about the potential contributions of standardized tests, and goes beyond them to point out that these tests provide focus and guidance as schools try to improve student learning.

Schmoker's most important point, in our view, is his call for us to go beyond standardized tests. He suggests that we create local, criterion-referenced assessments of the performances we expect of our students. He urges us to develop "our own end-of-course and formative assessments, whose substance captures but goes beyond standardized tests" and then to gradually supplement these objective assessments with "summative projects, essential questions, and scientific experiments and proposals that reinforce and build on essential knowledge and concepts" (65).

To pull all of this together, perhaps we need to consider that it is not so much the standardized tests themselves, but

When Teachers Are Cheaters

As we wrote this chapter, Kantrowitz and McGinn had just written a piece in *Newsweek* (June 19, 2000, 48–49) with the title that we used for this box. In an ironic twist, it was teachers who were caught cheating by coaching their students on standardized tests. Teachers and school administrators are feeling the pressure to improve test scores, which policymakers and the general public use to measure students' success. This is very unfortunate not only because of the reprehensible behavior being modeled, but also because placing so much importance on standardized test scores cheats students out of a rich academic curriculum and makes it less likely that powerful principles will be used to promote the deep learning typically not measured by such tests.

the manner in which we view and use them, that is the real problem. After all, it is people who put so much stock in the results of tests. It is educators who put these tests to use. If we keep standardized test results in their proper perspective, and if we understand what they can and cannot do in our service and in the service of our students, we will have reached a balance that will ultimately serve well our students, their parents, and society in general.

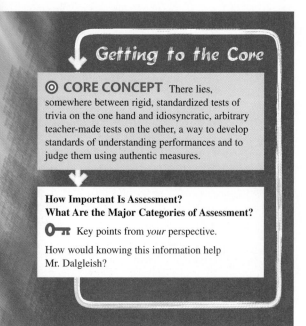

Getting to the Core

◎ **CORE CONCEPT** There lies, somewhere between rigid, standardized tests of trivia on the one hand and idiosyncratic, arbitrary teacher-made tests on the other, a way to develop standards of understanding performances and to judge them using authentic measures.

How Important Is Assessment?
What Are the Major Categories of Assessment?

Key points from *your* perspective.

How would knowing this information help Mr. Dalgleish?

How Do Standardized Tests Relate to Classroom Assessment?

Popham (1999) ended his article on standardized tests by writing:

> Educators should definitely be held accountable. . . . But to evaluate educational quality by using the wrong assessment instruments is a subversion of good sense. Although educators need to produce valid evidence regarding their effectiveness, standardized achievement tests are the wrong tools for the task. (1999, 15)

That, of course, raises the question of what the right tools are for measuring educational quality. In reality, standardized tests do not play a big role in classroom assessment. Burke (1999) points out that it is classroom teachers who give students grades. These grades are based upon the work that students do in the classroom. Teacher-made tests are supposed to be designed to measure what students have learned in a particular class. They are usually criterion, rather than norm, referenced. The criteria are derived from what the teacher expected students to know as a result of classroom learning activities. If, for example, you just finished a unit on the American Constitution, your test would ask questions about the Constitution rather than a wide range of questions more typical of standardized tests.

Perhaps not surprisingly, teacher-made tests can be criticized for sharing some of the very same faults that typify standardized tests. Actually, one problem peculiar to teacher-made tests is that they have, more often than not, unknown technical qualities. We simply do not know the reliability and validity of our tests with the precision that we know those qualities of standardized tests. Nor do teachers use normative groups as a basis of comparison for their students. Of course, teacher-made tests are not usually norm referenced, so it can be argued that these qualities are not so important. But at least one technical quality is critically important. We ought to know if our tests are valid measures of what we expect students to learn. If they are not, then what is the point of giving them? And what would be the meaning of any letter grade derived from a test lacking validity?

Trice (2000) says that *content validity* "measures the outcomes of the instructional objectives in the assessment" and singles it out as the technical quality that should be a primary concern of teachers. He feels that "all too often tests used by teachers do not measure the objectives very well" (40). Our experience suggests that he is quite correct. There are ways to increase the content validity of teacher-made tests. Teachers should know them, and put them to work.

In addition, teacher-made tests also tend to be, at least for the most part, very conventional. This was a criticism of standardized tests as well. What typically happens in classroom assessment? Chances are good that we need not tell *you*. You already know! Following instruction, you either get a quiz or a test. More often than not, the quiz or test will be "objective" and will consist of true or false, multiple-choice, and matching questions. The word *objective* in relation to testing, according to Woolfolk (2001), means *not open to many interpretations* (559). These tests, as Huba and Freed (2000) point out, are used extensively by many teachers because they are easily scored, information can be collected efficiently, and the interpretation of the test scores seems relatively straightforward. This makes them understandably attractive to classroom teachers who face increasingly large class sizes and whose judgments are more often called into question when they use *subjective* measures to grade student performance. Huba and Freed go on to note that even though it is possible to construct objective test items that tap higher-order thinking skills, few teachers have the training and experience to do so. Therefore, most objective tests assess only recall of factual information.

Teachers who do develop tests using other than multiple-choice formats face charges that they are too subjective in their grading. This can actually be related to the issue of reliability. Suppose you are a fourth-grade teacher and have just completed a math unit with your fourth graders. Now you are going to test them on what they should have learned. You devise a test that will allow them to show their work. The test includes 10 problems. Each problem is worth a maximum of 10 points.

One of the test questions appears below, followed by the child's answer. Evaluate this answer and award it anywhere from 0 (lowest) to 10 (highest) points. When you have finished scoring it, turn to the Math Test section on page 295 at the end of the chapter.

A Person Who Helped Create Change . . .

Kay Burke is an experienced teacher and administrator who works with educators throughout the United States, Canada, and Australia. Her hands-on presentations, training programs, and books on positive discipline, authentic assessment, student portfolios, and professional portfolios are popular with educators who teach at all levels from kindergarten through college. Kay has authored, co-authored, and edited a number of books published by SkyLight Professional Development, including *How to Assess Authentic Learning, What to Do With the Kid Who . . . : Developing Cooperation, Self-Discipline and Responsibility in the Classroom, Designing Professional Portfolios for Change, The Portfolio Connection: Student Work Linked to Standards,* and *The Mentoring Guidebook: Mapping the Journey.*

Photo courtesy of Kay Burke and SkyLight Professional Development (www.skylightedu.com).
Source: IRI Skylight, back cover of How to Assess Authentic Learning.

Question:
If apples are being sold at three for 27¢, how much will Johnny have to spend for seven apples? (Show your work.)

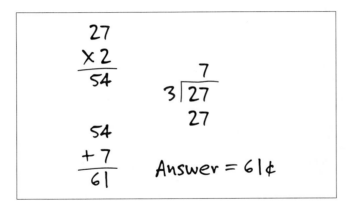

Teacher-made tests generally report scores as the percentage of correct answers. Often this percentage is, in turn, converted to a letter grade and then averaged with other grades to produce a quarter, semester, and final grade. Schools have varying scales for what the percentage cutoffs are for As, Bs, Cs, and so on. In one school an A might be 90 to 100 percent. In another school the range might be 93 to 100 percent. Some schools report percentages on the report card rather than grades. As we pointed out earlier, grading in this manner is a form of criterion referencing. The criterion is the level of mastery of the material. It could, however, turn out to be only a measure of retention of facts. There is a big difference! This assumes that the teacher is not grading on a curve. If that is the case, then a form of norm referencing is being used. Because norm referencing assumes a normal curve and distribution, and because that assumption rarely holds in classrooms that are, by and large, homogeneously grouped, grading on a curve is difficult to justify.

It seems, then, that on the one hand we have standardized assessments that have known technical qualities but that tend to be rigidly formal and emphasize mostly factual knowledge. They permit comparisons across large groups and between individuals and groups of people, but the comparisons are not always clear. On the other hand we have teacher-made tests that tend to be rather arbitrary. They have unknown technical qualities. If they lack content validity then they render the grades that derive from them meaningless. Teacher-made tests are very idiosyncratic; what appears in them is not always consistent from teacher to teacher. Two different versions of the same test developed by the same teacher may also vary significantly. We usually have no way of knowing. Subjective grading raises the question of reliability because teachers' judgments reflect assumptions they make about teaching and learning.

So What Is a Teacher to Do?

We have examined the continuum from standardized tests to teacher-made tests. As it turns out, if we look at actual testing practices the continuum is only along the dimension of known technical qualities (standardized tests) to unknown technical qualities (teacher-made tests). In many other ways both types of tests are similar in that they tend to be conventional and very important. Both forms of testing have a huge impact on the lives of children and adolescents (and, of course, their families). How can we change our classroom assessment practices so that we encourage valid performances of student understanding that can be reliably measured? Let us revisit for a moment the definition of assessment that we presented earlier:

> Assessment is the process of gathering and discussing information from multiple and diverse sources in order to develop a deep understanding of what students know,

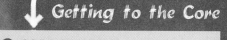

Getting to the Core

◎ **CORE CONCEPT** There lies, somewhere between rigid, standardized tests of trivia on the one hand and idiosyncratic, arbitrary teacher-made tests on the other, a way to develop standards of understanding performances and to judge them using authentic measures.

How Important Is Assessment?

What Are the Major Categories of Assessment?

How Do Standardized Tests Relate to Classroom Assessment?

O─π Key points from *your* perspective.

How would knowing this information help Mr. Dalgleish?

understand, and can do with their knowledge as a result of their educational experiences; the process culminates when assessment results are used to improve subsequent learning. (Huba and Freed 2000, 8)

Note carefully in the definition the following ideas—*multiple sources, know, understand,* and *can do* with knowledge; used to *improve learning.* These elements are all too often excluded from assessment programs and procedures that actually take place in classrooms.

One way to make the daunting task of assessing student learning manageable is to focus on three *fundamental questions* that you should ask yourself when developing a lesson, a unit, or even an entire curriculum: They are:

1. What do I want my students to know?

2. What do I want my students to be able to do?

3. What evidence will I accept to verify that learning?

No doubt you now recognize the first question as focusing on the declarative knowledge that you want your students to retain and understand. You should also recognize the second question as relating to the procedural knowledge that you want them to be able to use. The third question, of course, gets to the heart of our current discussion—assessment.

Develop Valid Conventional Tests Using What We Know from Research

We need to use caution at this point. It would be awfully easy to suggest that you never use conventional tests in light of all that we have presented so far in this chapter. It is possible, though, that you will need to use some conventional tests for a variety of reasons. You might decide that the evidence you will accept could be appropriately gathered by a conventional, objective test that you design. In fact, Trice (2000) asserts that traditional tests are often the most authentic way to measure certain objectives. He also points out that school districts sometimes require traditional testing of students. This is especially true of districts where, either because of state mandates or local agreement, standards for student learning have been developed and implemented. Such standards, according to Burke (1999), help provide teachers with a way to focus on clear expectations for their students to reach agreed-upon objectives. Assessments must be aligned with these standards, or else students and teachers will become confused. In any case, traditional tests can certainly play a role in a balanced program of classroom and schoolwide assessment. What, then, can you do to design good, fair, traditional tests?

It is certainly beyond the scope of this general methods book to go into great detail about the way to construct good, traditional tests. We can, however, address the one critically important quality that teacher-made tests must possess. You may remember that earlier we called this quality *construct validity.* Tombari and Borich (1999) tell us that "an assessment has construct validity when it produces learner behaviors that bear a direct link to the cognitive activity that you want

> **Examples of Student Performance Standards from a School District**
>
> **Students will be able to** *apply simple concepts of negative numbers in counting and temperature.* **(fifth grade—mathematics)**
>
> **Students will be able to** *write a persuasive essay with a stated opinion and supporting detail.* **(eighth grade—writing)**
>
> **Students will be able to** *analyze and criticize the effectiveness of elements of novels of recognized literary merit and create an informed personal reaction.* **(eleventh grade—reading)**
>
> *(Source: Centennial (PA) School District,* Student Performance Standards. *Public Draft, April, 1999.)*

Tips for Constructing Test Questions

True-False Items
- Avoid absolute words like "all," "never," and "always."
- Make sure items are clearly true or false rather than ambiguous.
- Limit true-false questions to ten.
- Consider asking students to make false questions true to encourage higher-order thinking.

Matching Items
- Limit list to between five and ten items.
- Use homogeneous lists. (Don't mix names with dates.)
- Give clear instructions. (Write letter, number, etc.)
- Give more choices than there are questions.

Multiple-Choice Items
- State main idea in the core or stem of the question.
- Use reasonable incorrect choices. (Avoid ridiculous choices.)
- Make options the same length (nothing very long or very short).
- Include multiple correct answers (a and b, all of the above).

Completion Items
- Structure for a brief, specific answer for each item.
- Avoid passages lifted directly from text (emphasis on memorization).
- Use blanks of equal length.
- Avoid multiple blanks that sometimes make a sentence too confusing.

Essay Items
- Avoid all-encompassing questions ("Discuss" is ambiguous . . . tell all you know about a subject).
- Define criteria for evaluation.
- Give point value.
- Use some higher-order thinking verbs like "predict" or "compare and contrast" rather than all recall verbs like "list" and "name."

(Source: From The Mindful School: How to Assess Authentic Learning, *Third Edition, by Kay Burke. © 1999, 1994, 1993 SkyLight Training and Publishing, Inc. Reprinted with permission of SkyLight Professional Development, a Pearson Education Company.)*

to assess" (53). They acknowledge that construct validity is no easy thing to accomplish. To enhance the likelihood of good construct validity, Tombari and Borich suggest that we take the following steps (53–56):

1. **Specify the construct domain.** That is, you need to be clear about exactly what cognitive activity you want to assess. We described Bloom's taxonomy in Chapter 4. We also presented a "cueing bookmark" with examples of questions at these various levels on page 88 in Chapter 3. These tools can help you select levels of cognitive activity and even develop questions that require their use. For example, you might want students to *analyze* a case study. Or you might want them to just *recall* a fact.

2. **Choose as many indicators of the domain as possible.** Identify as many of the pertinent cognitive activities as you can. Using Bloom's taxonomy as a guide, you might decide to include *comprehension, analysis, synthesis, and evaluation* when having the students critique the case study. This increases the validity of the assessment.

3. **Design the assessment task so that it requires only the cognitive skills relevant to the construct you wish to assess.** If you are testing the ability to solve mathematical problems, you might want to assess how students represent the information, set up the algorithm, and compute the answer. But if you write word problems that a student cannot read because they are too far above the student's reading level, you are now measuring reading ability. Validity of the test will suffer.

4. **Write task directions that require the thought processes that you intend to assess.** If you are asking students to answer questions about a case study, be clear about what you want them to do. For example, rather than write "analyze the case," you might write "use the 5-point process outlined in the textbook to decide how well Company X is meeting the challenges of the new economy."

It is especially challenging to develop an objective-type (multiple-choice, true-false) test that meets these requirements. Writing valid objective test items that tap the higher levels of cognitive ability is no easy task. That is probably why one of the major criticisms of both standardized and teacher-made tests is that they tend to measure mostly low-level thinking—the recognition and recall of facts. To combat this problem, teachers also use questions that require short answers or longer essays.

There is a fair amount of research on assessment practice. Actually, people usually speak of assessment and *evaluation.* What's the difference? Burke (1999) makes the contrast clear when she writes that assessment involves an ongoing process of gathering and analyzing evidence of student learning, whereas evaluation is the process of interpreting and making judgments based on this evidence.

Use Multiple Sources

Zemelman, Daniels, and Hyde (1998), in addressing best practice, suggest among other things that teachers *triangulate* their assessments. That is, they should use a number of different assessments on which to evaluate student learning. Burke (1999) presents a wide range of assessment approaches. Among these she includes the teacher-made tests we have already discussed; in addition she suggests portfolios, performance tasks, learning logs and journals, metacognitive reflection (as in self-assessment), projects, graphic organizers, observation checklists, and interviews and conferences. Her book, *How to Assess Authentic Learning,* is an excellent compilation of very practical strategies and suggestions for teachers. It is a great resource to help you develop a balanced assessment program that goes well beyond just traditional tests in order to make sound evaluations.

Do More Formative Assessment

Research suggests that we do far too much summative, and not enough formative, assessment. The two are not at all the same.

	Formative	**Summative**
Purpose	Monitor student progress and guide the teaching process during a unit of instruction.	Judge what has been learned at the completion of a unit of instruction.
Tools	Informal observation, quizzes, homework, questions students ask.	Formal tests, final exams, major projects, term papers.
Use of Information	Shape the teaching and learning process while it is taking place.	Give a grade, promote a child, place a child in an educational setting.

Black and Wiliam (1998) cite evidence gleaned from numerous research studies that clearly supports more formative assessment in order to raise standards. Their own review of the research led them to conclude that "strengthening the practice of formative assessment produces significant and often substantial learning gains" (140). More important, they point out, these same studies indicate that "improved formative assessment helps low achievers more than other students and so reduces the range of achievement while raising achievement overall" (141). In the context of their discussion of formative assessment, they highlight that improved formative assessment means that (1) new ways to enhance feedback given to students will require changes in typical classroom practice; (2) students must be actively involved in their learning; and (3) the results of formative assessment have to be used, sometimes even on the fly, to adjust instruction.

Unfortunately, as Black and Wiliam point out and our own experience affirms, there is lots of room for improvement in our current classroom assessment practices. They suggest:

- Providing specific feedback to learners about the particular qualities of their work and advice for how to improve it without comparing them to other learners.
- Having learners engage in self-assessment so that they understand the main purposes of their learning.
- Viewing instruction and formative assessment as indivisible. (142–143)

You might recognize the implicit connection between these suggestions and our claim in Chapter 1 that things have not changed much in education over the years. We know that all too often nonspecific feedback is provided to students. Phrases such as "Excellent work," "You did a fair job on this," "You made some valid points," and "Your thesis is unclear" do not provide the specificity necessary for students to improve upon their work. We know from information processing theory the importance of specific feedback. Teachers do not always provide specific feedback to their students.

Offering specific feedback should be accompanied by allowing students multiple opportunities to improve their work. If the bulk of our assessments are summative, then students have no way to show how they have benefited from feedback and improved their understanding or performance. The pressure put on teachers and parents to affix grades to every piece of work that a child produces only worsens this problem. One of the most frequent questions students ask—What did I get?—illustrates the overriding concern not for learning, but rather for the final evaluation of that learning. Yet another frequent question—What did *you* get?—further illustrates the competitive nature of the assessment system.

Students often hear from teachers and other educators that it is okay to make mistakes. Indeed, they say, we can learn a great deal from these mistakes. But students are not buying this. All too often, given the preponderance of summative assessment, mistakes prove costly for students when their work is evaluated, and they do not have the opportunity to revisit it and learn from their mistakes. So what should we do? We encourage you to do lots of informal assessment. For example, before beginning a unit or topic of study, ascertain students' prior knowledge. Ask them questions or have them prepare an organizer or chart. In some way, assess their entry knowledge. Then, as you proceed through the lessons of the unit, consider giving quizzes that do not count very much toward the final grade, but that will give you the information you need to adjust your instruction, and their learning activities, if necessary. Require students to formulate questions, generate responses, construct concept maps, organize their notes, do homework, and anything else that they do not do for a grade but that gives you valuable information.

Angelo and Cross (1993) offer a number of simple, quick assessment techniques that yield lots of information for teachers to use to adjust their instruction. These suggestions are directed at college-level teachers; however, our experience is that they are suitable for high school and middle school teachers. Elementary school teachers can use some of their suggestions if they modify the assessments to make them developmentally appropriate.

To assess prior knowledge, recall, and understanding, one of the techniques Angelo and Cross suggest is the "minute paper." This technique entails using the last few minutes of a class period to ask students to respond briefly to two questions

"Human beings learn and progress by making—and correcting—mistakes. Why, then, do schools teach students to avoid and fear them?"

—Neal Postman, 1995

such as: What was the most important thing you learned today? What important question do you still have? Another technique, the "muddiest point," asks students to jot down a response to the question: "What was the muddiest point in _____?" (1993, 154).

To assess analysis and critical thinking, Angelo and Cross offer the defining features matrix as an example. Using this matrix, students categorize concepts according to the presence or absence of some important, defining features. In this way the teacher can get a sense of whether or not students can engage in analysis of concepts.

It behooves all teachers to get feedback on how their students are reacting to instruction. Just as students cannot improve their learning without frequent and specific feedback, teachers cannot improve their instruction without feedback. In most cases students can provide this feedback. It can be provided on a teacher-constructed form during interviews with children or groups of children, or during whole-class discussions. One thing is certain—getting feedback only at the end of a semester or year, or even at the end of a unit of instruction, will not allow you to adjust your instruction to benefit learners. It will be too late for these learners, even though their feedback might benefit the next group of learners. But why wait?

Assess While You Teach, Teach While You Assess

Too often the classroom cycle is TEACH–ASSESS–EVALUATE–GRADE–TEACH NEW TOPIC. Because evaluation is usually done to determine a grade, and assessment is done in order to evaluate understanding, they are really one chunk of the cycle. So a more concise depiction is TEACH–ASSESS–TEACH–ASSESS, and so on. This leads to the very problem we have been discussing to this point. That is, in this cycle, where teaching and assessment are seen and treated as separate processes, the tendency is to do more, rather than less, summative assessment.

Bondy and Kendall (in Blythe and Associates, 1998) liken ongoing assessment to coaching. Basketball coaches, to use their example, ask players to concentrate on a few skills or plays. Then during practice they watch carefully and analyze the players' performances. They offer suggestions during practice, and in the locker room after practice where more sustained feedback can be given. On the basis of the coach's assessment of their performances, the players may be given new skills or plays. Finally, a "real" game is played against an opponent. It concludes not only with a score, but also with debriefing in the locker room and follow-up sessions during which game tapes might be analyzed. All of this is done to determine what went well and what needs to be improved for the next game.

Notice in this example how instruction and feedback are seamless. Bondy and Kendall write, "Ongoing assessment is the process of providing students with clear responses to their performances of understanding in a way that will help them improve the next performance" (1998, 72). Now it is important for you to realize that implicit in this example and definition is that the students are *actively involved* in the learning process. To the extent to which this is not the case, a teacher has no way to *really* assess student learning during the teaching process. To return to the coaching example, if the players only sit and listen to the coach tell them how to play, the coach cannot give them feedback on how well they are doing—because they are not doing much of anything! On game day the coach can determine whether or not the players listened and learned—but then it is too late. We argue early on and often in this book that learners must be actively engaged in their learning. For ongoing assessment to be effective this must be the case. Think about these points:

- Assessments should be rich sources of information for both teachers and students.

- If needed, high-quality instruction should be provided to correct student misunderstandings.

- Teachers should give students a second (or even third) chance to show improvement.

- Students should be given a chance to add their input, and to evaluate their own performances.

Students benefit the most from assessment that is ongoing rather than that which is done only at the end of a unit of instruction, and from specific feedback rather than just a traditional grade.

Consider Balancing Traditional with Alternative Assessments

You have probably already deduced that most of the examples used above require students to actually *do* something. In that sense, they illustrate the active nature of learning and the idea that what we know is not, and should not be, isolated from what we can do. Remember that previously we talked about declarative and procedural knowledge. They interact with one another so that *by knowing we can do, and by doing we come to know.*

In assessment lingo, *alternative* usually refers to doing something other than traditional, objective-type testing (see table). On conventional tests students typically choose a response (as with multiple-choice and true-false questions) or make very simple, one- or two-word responses (as in completion questions). A clear alternative is to require students to actually generate their own responses to questions. This could be in the form of writing an essay, analyzing a case, or solving a problem for which no answers are offered as possible choices.

Key Assessment Terminology

Alternative	Requires students to generate rather than choose or select a response
Performance	Requires students to actively accomplish complex and significant tasks
Authentic	Requires students to complete a realistic lifelike task
Portfolio	Requires students to assemble a purposeful collection of their work

An alternative to conventional tests, even those that include some student-generated responses, is the performance assessment. *Performance assessments* require students to actively demonstrate their ability to apply what they have learned by accomplishing complex and significant tasks. For example, Neill (1997) points out that in order to develop competence as an effective writer, students need to actually write something and then to receive feedback on their writing. He argues that the appropriate assessment of writing cannot be reduced to multiple-choice tests. His argument holds for much, if not most, significant learning.

Some of you might be thinking about attending graduate school. In order to be admitted, you will most likely be required to take the Graduate Record Exam (GRE). Williams (1997) suggests an alternative to this exam. Admitting that other major areas of studies would require a different test, in the area of social sciences she suggests that candidates for admission be given some basics by way of background information and general rules for completing tasks. This levels the playing field, so to speak, by taking the advantage away from those who have direct experience in a field and instead emphasizing the ability to think in ways important for graduate-level education. Then, candidates might be asked to review a flawed article, given several attributes of a review that experts in the field agree are important. Further, she describes a few other abilities that could be assessed: among them, an applicant's ability to pose and defend a research question, to prepare a plan for an introductory lecture, and to interpret sensibly a confusing set of research findings. These are much different from the typical, multiple-choice questions that appear on the GRE.

In basic education, teachers are beginning to realize the value of alternative assessments as a way to balance out conventional assessment procedures. They are devising clever, effective, and engaging assessment activities that are consistent with the powerful principles and strategies that we presented in earlier chapters of this textbook. Rogers (1989, 716) shares some sample assessment procedures used by teachers in schools in Connecticut and Vermont. Among them are:

> At the conclusion of a unit on Native Americans, a FIFTH-GRADE teacher
> showed individual children two pictures: one, of an Indian in full ceremonial
> dress; the other, of an Indian in jeans and a T-shirt. In both cases the child was
> asked, "Who is this person? What can you tell me about him? What does he do?
> Where does he live? Would you like to know him? Why?"

> A HIGH SCHOOL teacher conducted a unit on sex-role stereotyping. Later, the
> teacher showed individual students pictures and cartoons that depicted some
> form of stereotyping and asked the students to "tell me about what you see."

The more the assessment approaches a real-life task, the more it is said to be *authentic*. For example, if you are preparing to be a teacher you know that you will be developing, presenting, and evaluating many lessons. Therefore, because that is what you will actually be spending a lot of time doing, part of the assessment of your performance (at least in some classes) should be based on your ability to do exactly that. In fact, we could argue that the Praxis Series that we mentioned earlier falls short in this very area. Because of this shortcoming, an increasing number of school districts require candidates for teaching positions to teach a short lesson as part of the interview process.

What might an authentic assessment look like in basic education? First of all, authentic assessment must be based upon active and authentic learning. Few if any of us actually make a living by taking traditional tests, although we concede that the ability to score well on such tests allows us access to more potential ways to make our living. In Chapter 4 we presented a specific technique called problem-based learning. Stepien and Gallagher (1993) claim that problem-based learning is about as authentic as you can get. In their article they refer to a problem-based unit in a high school American studies course. In their role as directors of the Virginia colony students explain to the king what they intend to do about the fact that Virginia has not produced revenue for the last three years (27). The students craft a problem statement and then work on solutions to the problem. Assessment takes place in this unit, as it does in most problem-based learning units, through the use of problem logs in which students are presented with various exercises (e.g., questions such as What do you think the problem is now? or Based on X, what do you think about Y?) that are used as formative assessments. The summative assessment of this unit consists of the evaluation of a solution package submitted by each student. In addition, a meeting between the king (played by another teacher) and three of the directors, chosen by lot and representing all the students, is reviewed and evaluated. No conventional test is given to the students involved in this unit.

You need not restrict your use of authentic assessment to problem-based learning strategies. In science classes, students can develop projects for a science fair that are based on the ideas they are learning about and ways to use these ideas to

Think about it . . .

Can you link authentic assessments to standards? One standard from a local school district that we listed earlier was:

> Students will be able to write a persuasive essay with a stated opinion and supporting detail. (eighth grade—writing)

Design an authentic assessment that you can use to determine how well a student has met this standard.

Having students make presentations is an excellent way to assess their learning (Courtesy of Will Hart/Photo Edit).

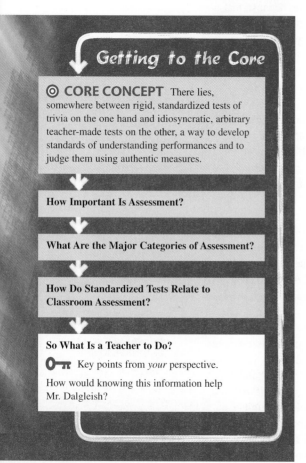

Getting to the Core

◎ **CORE CONCEPT** There lies, somewhere between rigid, standardized tests of trivia on the one hand and idiosyncratic, arbitrary teacher-made tests on the other, a way to develop standards of understanding performances and to judge them using authentic measures.

How Important Is Assessment?

What Are the Major Categories of Assessment?

How Do Standardized Tests Relate to Classroom Assessment?

So What Is a Teacher to Do?

⚷ Key points from *your* perspective.

How would knowing this information help Mr. Dalgleish?

better understand phenomena or solve problems. The teacher, peers, other knowledgeable experts, and the student can then evaluate the quality of these projects. Elementary-age children can write purposeful letters to a specified audience, such as a political representative. Middle school children might plan and conduct a schoolwide assembly for their peers, teachers, and parents about something they have been studying (i.e., the benefits of exercise). An entire school might have a theme on which many teachers focus their lessons. One possibility is "Think Globally, Act Locally," in which students learn about and design resource conserving practices for use in the school and in the community.

How Do We Get from Alternative Assessment to Evaluation?

Earlier we distinguished assessment from evaluation. You may recall that while assessment involves gathering data, evaluation involves making judgments based on these data. Reliability and validity are no less important to alternative assessment and evaluation than they are to traditional assessment. The quality of the data that we gather and the accuracy of the judgments we make will be negatively influenced if the assessments we use are unreliable and invalid. It is especially important to be vigilant about the technical qualities of the performance assessments that we develop and use. In that regard, Airasian (1996, 139) presents four essential qualities that should characterize every performance assessment. According to him, performance assessments should:

- Have clear purposes.
- Identify observable aspects of the performance/product to be judged.
- Provide appropriate settings in which to elicit or judge performances.
- Have predetermined criteria for scoring or rating performances.

Following these basic guidelines will certainly enhance the likelihood that performance assessments will be reliable and valid.

Develop and Use Rubrics

The key to successful alternative assessments is to clearly identify the criteria for assessing the performances that they require. The development and use of *rubrics* is, in our view, absolutely essential to the entire process of evaluating student performance. Rubrics are really "markers" or criteria that describe levels of understanding and performance. They make fully explicit the criteria that are often tacit. They are criterion rather than norm referenced. They identify the factors that will "count" in the evaluation of a performance and the scoring of an assessment, and then they build a scale for determining the score. If you develop them properly, rubrics communicate to students exactly what is expected of them and where they are at any point in relation to where they need to be. They also increase the reliability of the assessment by specifying the criteria on which a student is assessed. Finally, they provide a check on construct validity by making explicit and open to examination the understandings and performances that relate to the goals and objectives that students are expected to accomplish.

To construct rubrics:

1. Specify the learning objective(s) and how you would measure their attainment.
2. List the criteria for a piece of work or a performance.
3. Articulate gradations of quality from excellent to poor.
4. Determine the relative weight of each of the criteria.

As you go about constructing these rubrics you should be careful to keep the language clear and positive. You might also consider involving the students in the process of developing the criteria. By thinking about what makes an excellent performance, students are involved in a very important metacognitive process that is also engaging and motivating.

Learning and Teaching in the Age of Technology

Harris (1998, 119) reminds us that there are four basic types of alternative assessments to evaluate student learning:

- Performance-based assessment in which teachers observe and evaluate student performances on the basis of criteria in a rubric scale.

- Authentic/project assessment that evaluates real-life problem solving and task activities.
- Portfolio assessment, which is a purposeful, orderly collection and display of the artifacts of student effort and achievements.

⊙ **CORE CONCEPT** There lies, somewhere between rigid, standardized tests of trivia on the one hand and idiosyncratic, arbitrary teacher-made tests on the other, a way to develop standards of understanding performances and to judge them using authentic measures.

- Journal assessment in which the teacher reviews students' written reflections on their work and progress.

Clearly, all the multimedia formats we have enumerated can be viewed and evaluated through these lenses. Computer presentations of skills, or procedural knowledge, can demonstrate student performance in science, mathematics, art, and music, and virtually every other area of the curriculum.

David Niguidula (1998) shows how to apply the latest technology to create "digital portfolios" for and by students. The model he describes is based on three critical design decisions: (1) The portfolio should be a lens for looking at students' work; (2) student work itself must be prominent; (3) student work must be presented in context including student self-evaluation of their work (185). He describes a senior in high school whose opening digital page includes three buttons:

1. Who am I as communicator?
2. Who am I as researcher?
3. Who am I as problem solver?

These questions are based on the school's overall goals and vision for its graduates. The student then includes examples of the three fundamental visions of student competency in all areas of his work.

Assessment can be structured around student work in teams to solve real-world, messy problems using guidelines suggested by Fogarty (1997). Multimedia or hypermedia projects can be thought of as electronic portfolios that display the products of student research. Increasingly, the ability to gather and record multimedia resources on student produced CD-ROM or DVD disks will add to student and teacher ability to create portfolios over time, giving learners a sense of their own growth over months and years. Two important clearing houses for technologically based alternative assessments are ERIC Clearinghouse on Assessment and Evaluation and the National Center for Research on Evaluation, Standards, and Student Testing.

Teaching Tips

1. Give students a research question or problem assignment to be completed individually or in small groups. As they proceed in the assignment have them e-mail you questions they might have. By responding to questions, you are informally assessing for understanding. Common issues and concerns can be posted on the class website for all to access.

2. Allow students to develop electronic portfolios (collection of choice pieces of written work, scanned images, photos, video clips and sound bites) to represent learning outcomes. These pieces can easily be combined with some written material as well.

3. Have students design rubrics to evaluate projects, papers, and classroom activities based on stated criteria. Compare with your ideas and design a new rubric representing student input.

Suggested Websites

http://www.miamisci.org/ph/lpdefine.html
Forms of alternative assessment including portfolio, project, and other alternative assessment models with practical examples.

http://ericae.net/
Eric Clearing House: balanced information concerning educational assessment, evaluation, and research methodology.

http://www.cresst96.cse.ucla.edu/index.htm
National Center for Research on Evaluation, Standards, and Student Testing: conducts research on important topics related to K–12 educational testing.

http://www.ets.org
The Educational Testing Network.

http://www.ncrel.org/sdrs/areas/as0cont.htm
Critical Issues in Assessment.

Some Examples of Rubrics

Here is an example of one rubric (that would appear with several others) that can be used to judge a student presentation:

Expresses Ideas Clearly

4 Clearly and effectively communicates the main idea and provides rich, vivid, and powerful detail to support that idea.

3 Clearly communicates the main idea and provides acceptable support.

2 Communicates important information but the main idea is not clearly evident.

1 Communicates information in isolated and random fashion. (adapted from Marzano, Pickering, and McTighe 1993)

Note that one of the important criteria for the oral presentation is that the person can express ideas clearly. Then, gradations of that criterion are articulated so that they can be scored.

A high school biology teacher with whom we worked required her students to complete an observation log. She explained to her students, "In this project you will take on the responsibilities and actions of modern-day scientists. You will examine everyday biology taking place, and document what you see, as well as provide hypotheses that might explain the things that you observe." The table on page 288 presents the rubric that she developed to assess her students' observation logs.

If you have difficulty differentiating levels of quality, you might begin by looking at a model of excellence. If you have given an assignment on a previous occasion, select an example of a performance that was excellent. Ask yourself what made it excellent. List its qualities and then use these qualities as the exemplars for the highest level of performance. You can then work backward and build your scale and descriptors. If you need to, you may also look at an example of unsatisfactory work and work up to the exemplar.

Rubrics can be used at all levels of education, from primary grades to college level. Burke (1999) offers examples for each of these levels in Figure 7.3 (see p. 289).

Portfolios in the Assessment Process

A popular assessment tool among teachers and students alike is the *portfolio*. Essentially, a portfolio is a collection of a student's work that has been completed over a specific period of time. Students and teachers might collect samples (often called artifacts) of work and include them in student portfolios. Often both student and teacher contribute to the compilation of portfolio materials.

It is customary for students to comment on, and assess, the artifacts that they include in their portfolios. Usually they link the various artifacts through prose in order to make connections among and between them. In this manner students tell the "story" of what they have learned. Students may be asked to synthesize all that they have presented into a comprehensive summary of what they have accomplished and what it has meant to them. They may highlight their new understandings and skills. The portfolio is usually assembled as formative activities and assessments take place, and then finalized and commented upon as part of a summative assessment activity. Teachers develop rubrics for portfolios, often with

Think about it . . .

Try your hand at developing a rubric. Specify an objective, and then follow the steps listed in this chapter. If you need further help, visit About.com Rubrics at http://search.about.com/ fullsearch.htm?terms= rubrics&PM=59_0100_s.

Observation Log Project

	Excellent, 30 Points	Satisfactory, 20 Points	Borderline, 10 Points	Unsatisfactory, 0 Points
Observation Log Book	Entries contain data and time; observations of appearances or behaviors neatly written in blue or black ink; sketches or photographs included; documentation of experiments conducted or experts consulted.	Entries contain three of the four things listed.	Entries contain two of the four things listed.	Entries contain one or none of the four things listed.
Length of Written Observation	Written observation is a total of five complete sentences or more.	Written observation is a total of four complete sentences or more.	Written observation is a total of three complete sentences or more.	Written observation is two complete sentences or less.
Frequency of Entries	Entries are completed five times a week.	Entries are completed four times a week.	Entries are completed three times a week.	Entries are completed two times a week or less.
Observation Log Book Date of Completion (Date of Presentation)	Observation log book completed and handed in on June 1.	Observation log book completed and handed in on May 3.	Observation log book completed and handed in on March 31.	Observation log book completed and handed in before March 31 or not at all.
Presentation	The subject is addressed clearly for eight or more minutes; speech is easy to understand; appropriate eye contact; visual aids (three or more posters, charts, or graphs).	The subject is addressed well for five to eight minutes, but is confusing at times; appropriate volume and eye contact; use of visual aids (two posters, charts, or graphs).	The subject is addressed adequately for three to five minutes; speech is erratic; eye contact is erratic (reads notes); visual aids (one poster, chart, or graph).	The subject needs more explanation or is not addressed; presentation time is less than three minutes; speech is difficult to understand; eye contact is lacking; no visual aids.

Source: Reprinted by permission of Staci Horne and Teresa Perlowski, Biology teachers, Phillipsburg High School, New Jersey.

student input. Portfolios may take the place of a final exam or some other form of more traditional assessment.

Portfolios are very popular because they allow for purposeful selection and presentation of student work. They are one form of alternative assessment that more and more teachers are using in their classrooms. Some school districts have begun to adopt portfolios as a kind of capstone assessment at the end of one's high school career. Further, more and more schools are requiring teachers, as part of their professional evaluations, to assemble portfolios of their own to document their professional activities and growth.

EXAMPLES

PRIMARY

RUBRIC FOR ORAL READING
FIRST GRADE

Student: _____

Book: _____

Performance Task: _____

Book 1 — Knows only beginning sounds of words and a few words

Book 2 — Knows how to read some words in text with help

Book 3 — Knows how to read most words with minimal help

Book 4 — Knows how to read entire book independently

Score	Date
____	September _____
____	January _____
____	June _____

Signed: _____
(Teacher)

MIDDLE SCHOOL

WEIGHTED COMPUTER LITERACY SCALE

Name: _____ Date: _____
Topic: Hypercard
Type of Assessment: ☐ Self ☐ Group ☐ Teacher
Score   1   2   3   4   5
(1–5)   Low   High
Directions: Circle the score for each indicator.

Terminology   Score: ____ x 1 = ____ (25)
- Understands Key Functions   1 2 3 4 5
- Relates One Function to Others 1 2 3 4 5
- Used to Solve Problems   1 2 3 4 5
- Correct Spelling   1 2 3 4 5
- Appropriate to Level   1 2 3 4 5

Organization   Score: ____ x 2 = ____ (50)
- Easy to Complex   1 2 3 4 5
- Each Card Complete   1 2 3 4 5
- Uses Graphics   1 2 3 4 5
- Key Ideas Covered   1 2 3 4 5
- Supportive Data Included   1 2 3 4 5

Creativity   Score: ____ x 1 = ____ (25)
- Color   1 2 3 4 5
- Style   1 2 3 4 5
- Pattern   1 2 3 4 5
- Appropriate Use of Language   1 2 3 4 5
- Multiple Uses   1 2 3 4 5

Scale: 93–100 = A   78–86 = C   **Total Score:** ____ (100)
         87–92 = B   70–77 = D
Comments:

(Courtesy of Kathy Bartley and Jeanne Lipman, Gabbard Institute, 1994)

HIGH SCHOOL

ORAL PRESENTATION RUBRIC

Name: _____   Date: _____
Subject: _____   Final Grade: _____

5
The subject is addressed clearly
Speech is loud enough and easy to understand
Good eye contact
Visual aid is used effectively
Well-organized

4
Subject is addressed adequately
Speech has appropriate volume
Eye contact is intermittent
Visual aid helps presentations
Good organization

3
Subject is addressed adequately
Speech volume is erratic
Student reads notes—erratic eye contact
Visual aid does not enhance speech
Speech gets "off track" in places

2
Speech needs more explanation
Speech is difficult to understand at times
Lack of adequate eye contact
Poor visual aid
Lack of organization

1
Speech does not address topic
Speech cannot be heard
Very little eye contact
No visual aid
No organization

Scale: 5 = A; 4 = B; 3 = C; 2 = D; 1 = Not Yet
General Comments:

COLLEGE

WEIGHTED WRITING RUBRIC

Name: _____   Date: _____
Piece of Writing: _____

Score   Score: 1   2   3   4   5
(1–5)   Low   High

CONTENT   Score _ x 7 = ____ (35)
- evidence of reason
- key ideas covered
- appropriate quotes
- supportive statistics
- topic addressed

ORGANIZATION   Score _ x 6 = ____ (30)
- creative introduction
- thesis statement
- appropriate support statements
- effective transition

USAGE   Score _ x 5 = ____ (25)
- correct subject-verb agreement
- no run-ons, fragments, or comma splices
- correct verb tense
- mix of simple and complex sentences

MECHANICS   Score _ x 2 = ____ (10)
- few or no misspellings
- correct use of punctuation
- correct use of capitalization

                                     TOTAL SCORE: ____ (100)
Scale: 93–100=A, 87–92=B, 78–86=C

Comments:

©1999 SkyLight Training and Publishing, Inc.

FIGURE 7.3

Examples of rubrics.

Source: From The Mindful School: How to Assess Authentic Learning, *Third Edition, by Kay Burke.* © *1999, 1994, 1993 SkyLight Training and Publishing, Inc. Reprinted with permission of SkyLight Professional Development, a Pearson Education Company.*

How Can We Use Assessment to Understand Student Learning?

In the spirit of all that we have written in this textbook, we encourage you to examine student work very carefully and try to use it to help you understand student learning. In that way you can reflect deeply on your teaching and you can think about additional strategies you might use to help your students learn. You can engage in this process alone, or you can do it in collaboration with others.

Langer and Colton (1997) share ways to analyze student work. They suggest that we:

1. Select an assignment and identify the learning objectives.

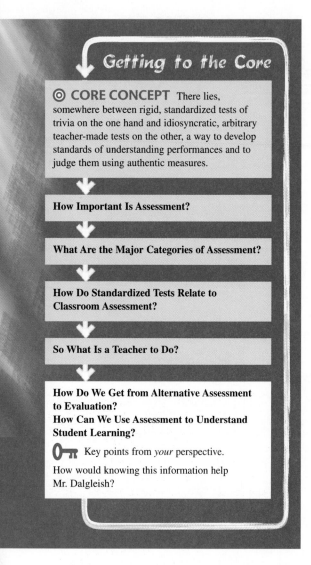

Getting to the Core

◎ **CORE CONCEPT** There lies, somewhere between rigid, standardized tests of trivia on the one hand and idiosyncratic, arbitrary teacher-made tests on the other, a way to develop standards of understanding performances and to judge them using authentic measures.

How Important Is Assessment?

What Are the Major Categories of Assessment?

How Do Standardized Tests Relate to Classroom Assessment?

So What Is a Teacher to Do?

How Do We Get from Alternative Assessment to Evaluation?
How Can We Use Assessment to Understand Student Learning?

⦿┳   Key points from *your* perspective.

How would knowing this information help Mr. Dalgleish?

2. Review a student's work on an assignment by asking: Given the objectives, what specifically did I want this student to achieve?

3. Analyze the relationship between what you did as a teacher and the student's performance on the assignment. Ask such questions as: Why did I select this sample? Why did the student perform this way? What instructional approaches should I use next with this student?

Suppose you look at the writing sample titled "the BIG?" that appears in Figure 7.4. It was taken from a second-grade student as a response to an activity that involved taking a ride in a makeshift space ship as part of a unit on space travel. The objective required the children to describe in writing the experience they had on the imaginary ride. After you study the sample, imagine that you are the child's teacher for language arts. Why did the student perform this way? What might you do next to help her?

There are increasing calls for teachers to examine student work in a collaborative manner. Using a process that mirrors the best of cognitive science, Blythe, Allen, and Powell (1999) suggest ways that teachers can cooperate in order to examine student work. They suggest that teachers look at the ways they currently examine student work, establish goals and frame questions, choose a process for looking at the work collaboratively, and then implement the process. At the end of a cycle, they suggest that teachers reflect on and, if need be, refine the process. The process they suggest is not too different from a similar process physicians use to review treatment protocols and outcomes for their patients.

It is important to remember that the end process of assessment includes using the data to improve learning. That is a far cry from simply using the process to give a student a letter grade. We encourage you to use assessment as a lens through which to view your own teaching.

How Can We Put All of This Together?

One very practical way to use the information from this chapter is to think of assessment in three ways: informal, traditional, and alternative. You can then use a three-pronged approach that might involve the following:

- Use *informal* assessment frequently during a unit or segment of instruction. Use it in a formative fashion to assess students' prior knowledge of the concept or topic, and use it frequently during and at the end of lessons to keep tabs on student understanding.

- Use *traditional* assessment, such as quizzes and tests (including standardized tests), to fill in gaps that need more systematic data at various critical points of instruction.

- Use *alternative* assessment in a summative way to judge final performances that end a unit or segment of instruction. Use them in place of final exams. Encourage students to demonstrate both declarative and procedural knowledge in these final performances.

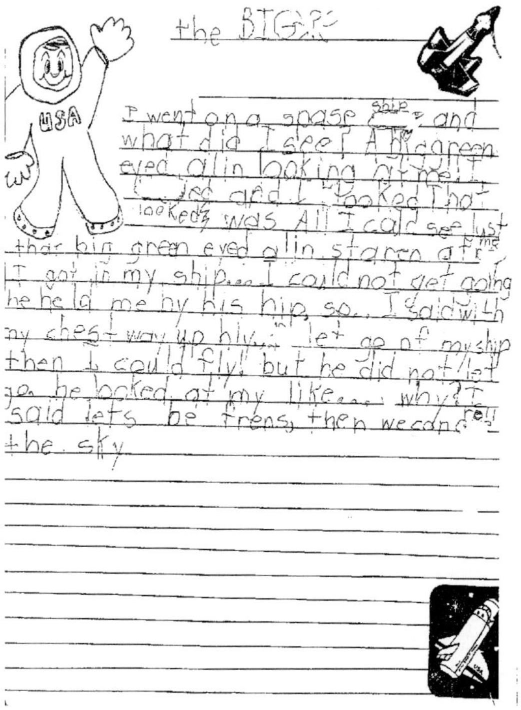

FIGURE 7.4
Writing sample.

If you think back to previous chapters in this textbook, you will realize that alternative assessments are very consistent with the social nature of learning that we wrote about in Chapter 2. Performances can be very public, and students can do group and cooperative projects as final performances (providing, of course, that there is some measure of individual accountability). The more complex the performance needed to do well on the alternative assessment, the more a student will need to elaborate and be actively involved in the assessment. Alternative assessments are more likely than traditional assessments to include both declarative and procedural knowledge. The more authentic the assessment, the more consistent it is with the natural learning cycle and the more motivating it is for students. This is all consistent with the powerful principles presented in Chapter 3.

The idea of including a variety of teaching strategies strongly suggests that you will also need a variety of assessment strategies. Many of the very strategies we shared with you in Chapter 4 can also be used as assessment strategies. For example, graphic organizers are a teaching tool and, when used to assess the connections that students have made between and among ideas, also an assessment tool. If you use a variety of assessment strategies, you are more likely to be fair to all of your students. Chapter 5 explains the nature of individual differences and provides information about styles and preferences. These hold true no less for assessment than they do for instruction.

Assessment and the 4MAT System

The 4MAT system that we wrote about in Chapters 3 and 5 requires that we teach "around the circle." That means we must also assess "around the circle." In general, quadrant 1 through quadrant 2 RM emphasizes self-reflection and observations. Quadrant 2 LM and quadrant 3 LM emphasize assessment of mastery of factual information. Quadrant 3 RM through quadrant 4 emphasizes performance assessment. Here are a few specific assessment strategies that show the way a variety of strategies can be used during a unit of instruction.

Quadrant 1: Assess quality of journal entries, personal reflections, relational thinking, participation in group activities, self-assessment.

Quadrant 2: Assess using essays, spatial representations, outlines, diagrams, oral exams, objective tests, research.

Quadrant 3: Assess field and lab work, demonstrations, worksheets, chapter questions.

Quadrant 4: Assess quality of exhibitions, publications, synthesizing performances, taking a position, self-assessment.

(Source: After the work of Bernice McCarthy, 1997, 4MAT and Assessment, Wauconda, IL: About Learning, Inc.)

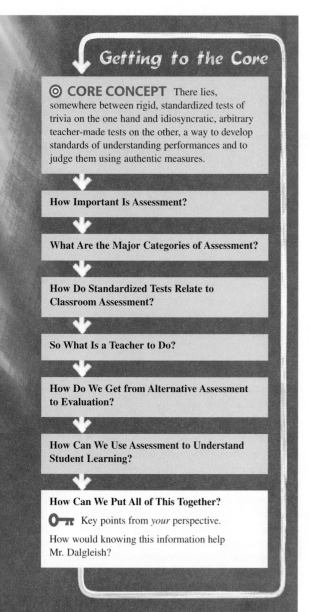

Getting to the Core

◎ CORE CONCEPT There lies, somewhere between rigid, standardized tests of trivia on the one hand and idiosyncratic, arbitrary teacher-made tests on the other, a way to develop standards of understanding performances and to judge them using authentic measures.

How Important Is Assessment?

What Are the Major Categories of Assessment?

How Do Standardized Tests Relate to Classroom Assessment?

So What Is a Teacher to Do?

How Do We Get from Alternative Assessment to Evaluation?

How Can We Use Assessment to Understand Student Learning?

How Can We Put All of This Together?

⊙━ Key points from *your* perspective.

How would knowing this information help Mr. Dalgleish?

When assessments are varied and less rigidly formalized than conventional tests, accommodations can be made more easily for students with various special needs. Alternative assessments, by virtue of being criterion referenced, have the potential to be much more valid and reliable indicators of the accomplishments of students with disabilities.

 SCENARIO REVISITED

We now ask that you revisit the scenario that we presented at the beginning of this chapter. Answer the questions yet again, using what you have learned from reading this and previous chapters. Then read A Voice from the Field and compare your responses to those of an experienced teacher.

> **?** *Do you think Mr. D's unit tests adequately measure what students are learning? Why or why not? Can you suggest some alternative ways for Mr. D. to assess what his students have learned at the end of a unit of instruction? Using your suggestions, do you think the results he sees will be better? A fairer representation of what the children have learned? Why?*

 A VOICE FROM THE FIELD

Mr. Dagliesh is doing so many things right, yet he is filled with self-doubt about his effectiveness based on student performance on a single end of unit test! Are Mr. D's criterion-referenced objective tests even valid? Do they adequately measure what he's trying to measure? He certainly proceeds under the assumption that they do, yet they do not jive with what he is seeing every day as the children engage in his wonderful activities. He feels compelled to introduce "objective" measures by which to assess and evaluate. After all, it is what students, parents, and administrators need and demand: documentation and quantifiable data that show how much Susie did or did not learn in this unit. Seemingly subjective measures, where the teacher must rely heavily on his own judgment, certainly cannot be valid measures of student learning. So which one should he use? He should not use only one. He should use as many different forms of assessment as he can.

Mr. D missed many, many opportunities to gather information and use the results to improve his students' learning. Perhaps he was aware of these opportunities but did not think that they were as "valid" as an end of unit test. In order for assessment to be valid, it must be accurately aligned with the instructional objectives and activities developed by the teacher. Let's take a look at Mr. D's instruction.

Mr. D is to be commended for designing instruction which promotes conceptual understanding. He teaches thematically, integrating content areas to deepen understanding. He taps all four quadrants of McCarthy's 4MAT wheel and addresses a variety of learning styles. He includes direct and indirect instruction; has children work cooperatively and collaboratively in small groups; encourages the children to support one another in their work; and teaches the students to be responsible for their own learning by having them learn from each other through demonstrations, discussions, and presentations. Students develop organizational skills through the unit notebook, and the journal provides an opportunity for them to establish a personal connection to the material, as well as to apply writing skills. Mr. D is truly promoting higher-order thinking through all of his instructional activities; yet what he is assessing is his students' recall of factual information, as if each of his students developed understanding in the same way.

For a teacher to go to such lengths to ensure student understanding and still feel the need to give an end of unit objective test is confirmation of the pressure felt by teachers everywhere to present a "grade" to students, parents, and administrators as evidence of learning. Why do we feel a need to separate ourselves from our students' learning when it is "time to assess"? Why do so many teachers not trust their powers of observation and their ability to remain objective even when using other methods of assessment? Perhaps Mr. D knows the importance of documentation and record keeping, but lacks a system by which he can in fact document and even quantify the observations he makes each day during instruction. Could this be the answer for him as he approaches the end of a unit and feels his self-confidence wane? Mr. D. could really use some rubrics.

Journals, portfolios, cooperative learning groups, student demonstrations, discussions, and presentations all lend themselves to evaluation through a rubric. Journal entries can be assessed on the basis of organization and content and portfolios can be developed on the basis of a student-designed rubric with a rationale during class or small-group discussions. Mr. D can assess his students' listening and speaking skills, their ability to incorporate the ideas of others, and how well they make connections.

Mr. D is already an advocate of students working together in small groups, and knows the value of students supporting each other. Here, too, lie wonderful opportunities for assessment. Mr. D's instructional objectives for cooperative lessons should include appropriate academic and social goals for each group. He needs to be sure to include and adjust for his special needs students. Jobs for each student in the group should be established. The development of a rubric will help him communicate his expectations clearly to all the children. In fact, developing the rubric *with* the class increases the students' ownership of the content. He should insist on accountability from each member of the group as well as from the group as a whole, and allow them to assess themselves as individuals and as a group. Mr. D must continue to monitor the groups as they work, but now with a checklist linked directly to the rubric.

A sample rubric for a group project in Mr. D's measurement unit might look like this:

Academic

4 Content: includes, compares and contrasts information about two or more ancient cultures; connections to current culture made; clearly organized.

Presentation: thorough, creative, and interactive; rich visual media.

3 Content: two cultures; some comparisons and connections made.

Presentation: opportunities for interaction; some visual media.

2 Content: one ancient culture; not clearly organized according to outline provided; some connections to present.

Presentation: largely lecture; little interaction.

1 Content: sparse content; no discernible organization; few or no connections made.

Presentation: lecture, no interaction among group members or with audience; no visual media.

0 No attempt made.

Social

4 Consistent active listening; sharing of materials; peaceful resolution of conflict; involvement of all group members; validation and constructive criticism.

3 Some active listening; sharing of materials; peaceful resolution of conflict; involvement of all group members; validation and constructive criticism of ideas.

2 Little active listening; peaceful resolution of conflict; involvement of all group members; validation and constructive criticism.

1 Arguing, interrupting; no validation of each other as group members or of ideas; some group members off-task or not included.

What does Mr. D do with his rubric scores? He can weight them as he sees fit, just as he has done with his traditional assessments. He can even keep his quizzes and tests, and weight them according to how they align with his instruction. He will have a variety of documentation to share with parents during conference time and be able to truly address each student's individual achievement over time. As a parent, I value information about my child that is obtained through multiple sources, rather than a single test grade.

Certainly, Mr. D is going to see results, and they will not be limited only to students' grades. He will likely see, as I have in my classroom, an increase in motivation in students who traditionally work for "the grade." More significantly, he will see the spark of motivation in those students who previously had no chance of achieving "the grade"—his special needs students, who will be included not only in instruction, but also now in assessment. Mr. D will gain insight into his students' achievements, as well as their strengths, interests, and learning styles. Finally, Mr. D himself will be validated for his wonderful instructional activities. Here is a man who was going to do less of what children need to help them learn; and use that time and energy to prepare them to take their unit test. Mr. D scraps the unit test and uses that energy to prepare students and their parents for an assessment that looks like instruction from a teacher who already knows how— and how well—his students learn.

This is the voice of Ruth Desiderio. Ms. Desiderio is certified as an elementary and special education teacher. She currently teaches students with special needs.

Answers to Test of Smart People

1. c   2. a   3. d   4. c   5. a

Answers to Math Test

Here are the grades given to this child by a group of teachers during a workshop held in February 2000. Each teacher graded the answer independently. Were they surprised by the distribution! (Score given on left, number of teachers giving that score on the right.)

10—0	5—6	0—1
9—2	4—0	
8—3	3—2	
7—4	2—1	
6—1	1—0	

PLANNING FOR INSTRUCTION

We ask you now to make accommodations to your lesson plan for special needs learners. You are now ready to design assessments that match your instruction. There are two major kinds of assessments—standardized and teacher-made. Because standardized tests are mainly used for districtwide and statewide achievement and aptitude testing, we will focus on teacher-made assessments. As discussed in Chapter 7, teachers use far more summative (formal tests, final exams, projects, and term papers) than formative (observations, quizzes, homework, organizers, and student questions) assess-

> ◎ **CORE CONCEPT** There lies, somewhere between rigid, standardized tests of trivia on the one hand and idiosyncratic, arbitrary teacher-made tests on the other, a way to develop standards of understanding performances and to judge them using authentic measures.

ment with their learners. Formative assessments used throughout the instructional process provide the teacher and student with an ongoing opportunity to check for understanding. Traditional assessments such as tests, term papers, and projects have a definite role in the classroom; however, the use of nontraditional assessments such as performance, authentic, and portfolio assessments are often underused despite the rich information they yield, both for the learner and the teacher. Using frequent, informal assessment techniques such as your own observations, quizzes to check content acquisition, visual tools that show how learners organize and analyze content, structured student-to-student questioning strategies, and rubrics that specify criteria for measuring quality of performance, all encourage and promote student learning.

Now we encourage you to revisit two important questions: (1) What do I want my students to know and be able to do? and (2) What evidence would I accept to verify that learning? You will now have the opportunity to design alternative assessments for your unit or lesson plan and vary your assessments in the same ways, and for the same reasons, that you vary your instructional strategies. These assessments answer question 2.

In this section of Planning for Instruction we will revisit *our* unit on weather and *our* lesson plan on thunderstorms. We will provide examples of specific assessment strategies that check student understanding along with examples of alternative, performance, authentic, and portfolio assessments.

Consider

How do I know if the students really comprehended the information on thunderstorms? What questions are still unanswered in their minds? Have I given enough opportunity for all students to ask questions?

Let's go back to your lesson plan that develops the advance organizer into a detailed graphic organizer. The teacher-led discussion using questioning strategies helped develop a content-rich graphic organizer. We will now add another component to better assess what students learned. Grouped by two or three, students will develop a list of factual, *skinny* questions (questions that can be answered with a yes or no). Next, students will develop a list of *juicy* questions (complex, open-ended, no one clear answer, and thought provoking). Give the students 10 to 15 minutes to complete this task and make sure they are prepared to ask these questions of the teacher.

Do you think they will have more skinny or juicy questions? Most likely, the students will answer the skinny questions themselves because they are factual and the information is readily available. Most of the juicy questions, those that take more thought and are more complex, will remain unanswered. Hopefully, the students will be able to answer a few of them given additional time. Areas of confusion or vagueness will surface and provide the teacher with the opportunity to assist students in answering their own questions—additional information and examples can then be provided (scaffolding).

The questions are student driven, so there is built-in motivation. Students work in small groups to allow for conversations and the opportunity to hear answers to questions from another student's perspective. Additionally, the more introverted and shy student who rarely asks and answers questions in large groups will feel more comfortable in this setting. This instructional strategy provides both an assess/teach and teach/assess opportunity.

Consider

What are some other quick assessments I can use to check understanding? To assess learning?

Using a Venn diagram (below) or a compare/contrast chart, you can assist students in identifying similarities and differences among different ideas and concepts. For example, in our lesson, students using a Venn diagram can list what is unique to thunder on one side and what is unique to lightning on the other. In the middle, they can identify common characteristics.

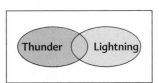

Using a sequential thinking map, students can demonstrate the *formation of a thunderstorm* by completing a teacher-made organizer or designing one of their own. Using sequential visuals helps concretize the process and demonstrates to student and teacher an understanding of the content.

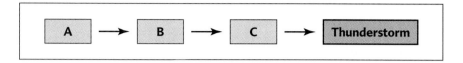

Consider

I want to make sure my assessments are addressing multiple intelligences to encourage maximum engagement. Try the following options.

Assign one paragraph or a seven-line outline research brief to be presented to groups or to class (verbal/linguistic).

Design a mural, bulletin board, or three-dimensional model of the water cycle or thunderstorm (visual/spatial).

Write an imaginary story about a person surviving a severe storm or how severe weather has changed family vacation plans or school events (intrapersonal).

Consider

I want my students to be critical of what they learned and demonstrate the ability to self-evaluate. After the completion of the last step of the unit, allow the students to work individually or in groups to evaluate content learned and how they learned it by using the PMI strategy. Using a three-column chart students will respond to the following:

1. What was positive (P) about what you learned and how you learned it?

2. What were some minuses (M) or negatives about what you learned and how you learned it?

3. What was most intriguing (I) about what you learned and how you learned it?

This strategy challenges students to look at what they have learned from three different perspectives. Looking at minuses, they are encouraged to examine negative aspects of learned material. For example, students might identify that severe storms are scary, people get hurt, property is damaged, and fires start. This is important because it provides an opportunity to explore both sides of an issue. It might lead to deeper understanding of how to better plan for and protect yourself during severe weather conditions. Encouraging students to list what intrigues them can lead to creative new ways of thinking about and interpreting the content.

Consider

How do I measure/assess student understanding? Can I actually grade a journal? How do I help students know what they are expected to demonstrate?

During the unit on severe weather, all students will keep a daily journal that uses a triple-entry (column) approach. Students complete each column with:

- Specific content learned.

- Examples of content in everyday life.

- Questions they wanted to ask the teacher.

To encourage seriousness in journal writing, it counts for 15 percent of the unit grade. First, the teacher models a few journal entries that explicitly illustrate the three criteria. In addition, the teacher shares a rubric with the students that provides the specific criteria and assessment procedures. This prompts students to respond to the specific criteria and to help the teacher look for the criteria in the journal. For example, each of the criteria (in columns) can be assessed individually by deciding what you want students to demonstrate. The column for *specific content learned* can be evaluated from *very descriptive,* to *descriptive,* to *not descriptive.* The column *asking for examples* can be evaluated on a continuum from *excellent connection,* to *good connection,* to *vague connection.* The column *questions to ask teacher* can be evaluated on a continuum from *very thoughtful,* to *thoughtful,* to *not thoughtful.*

In addition, you can include a summative assessment for this journal assignment that includes writing a two-page summary that synthesizes all the entries. This could be assessed using criteria similar to those stated above.

Consider

Can I assess a student-produced safety manual, graphic organizer, or videotape production? Design a rubric that specifically states what needs to be included (core idea, content, examples, relationships among content variables, demonstration of skills, creativity, etc.). Also, describe each criterion to be assessed on a continuum based on level of performance. For example, in our unit we expect connections to be made among thunderstorms, tornadoes, hurricanes, and snowstorms. So, one line of the rubric will say *clear connections and relationships were made among thunderstorms, tornadoes, hurricanes, and snowstorms.* The criterion will be *excellent connection, good connection, vague connection, and no connection.* This procedure can be followed with modifications for all the criteria.

Your Turn

We ask you now to add assessments to your lesson plan. Keep in mind the need to balance traditional with alternative assessments.

CHAPTER SUMMARY

In this chapter we address a very "hot" topic in American education—*assessment.* Just how important is assessment? Given our national obsession with scores, ranks, SATs, and the like, it is *very* important. Assessment is so important that many students cheat rather than risk low scores.

We presented the two major categories of assessments. Some tests are norm referenced and others are criterion referenced, and some are referenced both ways. The tendency is for standardized tests to be norm referenced, and teacher-made tests to be criterion referenced. Norm-referenced tests compare students to one another or to a group on whom any given test was standardized. Criterion-referenced tests compare a student's performance to set criteria, usually the learning objectives initially established by the teacher.

Standardized tests are published commercially by large companies. Their technical qualities are known and disseminated. That is, consumers can know their reliability and validity. Despite this, standardized tests are very controversial. One of the most controversial is the SAT, which we used as an example to help you gain a deeper understanding of standardized tests in general. Standardized tests can play an important role in a balanced assessment program. Unfortunately, people put more faith in those tests results than they do in more valid measures of performance.

Standardized tests play a minor role in classroom assessment. That is because it is teachers that construct classroom tests and other classroom assessments and then use them as a basis to give students their grades. Therefore, it is very important that teachers' tests be both reliable and valid. Yet most teachers do not have data about the technical qualities of the assessments that they construct; nor do most teachers have the expertise to ascertain these qualities. That makes it very important to develop tests that have good construct validity. It also means that teachers need to use what the research tells us about best assessment practices.

Teachers should use multiple sources to assess students' knowledge and skills. They should also do more formative assessment than summative assessment in order to refine lessons to promote student learning. They do not have to throw out all conventional testing that they presently conduct; they need only balance it with alternative assessments.

To address the issues of validity and reliability, teachers are well advised to learn how to develop and use rubrics in the classroom assessment process. Rubrics spell out the criteria to which teacher-made assessments are referenced. They make explicit and public the criteria upon which student performance will be assessed. This increases both the reliability and the validity of the assessment itself. Rubrics can be applied to portfolio assessment as well. Student portfolios are purposeful collections of work assembled over a specified period of time. They are an excellent form of summative evaluation and can replace traditional final exams.

Beyond assessment, we should try to understand student learning and then adjust our instruction accordingly. Assessment samples can engage us in a process of self-reflection about our teaching as we view our own work through our students' work. When we reflect on student work in a collaborative fashion, the process becomes a source of renewal for our own professional growth.

To put all of this information together, we discussed a three-pronged approach to assessment that used informal, traditional, and alternative assessments. In addition, we made connections to previous chapters in the textbook. It behooves us to vary our assessments in the same ways, and for the same reasons, that we vary our instructional strategies.

Getting to the Core

How Important Is Assessment?

- Real estate values are affected by school districts' assessment results. Parents and students seem to be much more concerned about assessments and the grades students earn on them than they are concerned with what students actually learn in school. This pressure for good grades can encourage students to resort to cheating.

What Are the Major Categories of Assessment?

- There are two major categories of assessment: standardized and teacher-made. Standardized tests

◎ CORE CONCEPT There lies, somewhere between rigid, standardized tests of trivia on the one hand and idiosyncratic, arbitrary teacher-made tests on the other, a way to develop standards of understanding performances and to judge them using authentic measures.

sample a wide variety of knowledge domains rather than just one and have a set of specific procedures to follow.

- Standardized tests are either norm referenced or criterion referenced. Norm-referenced tests compare the scores of any one student to a group of students who took the same test. Test makers find the average score and then determine how the scores deviated above and below the average of the group on whom the test was normed. They can then compare any one individual score to the scores of the entire group. Among scores reported on standardized tests are percentiles. Percentiles tell how well a student did compared to other students. Criterion-referenced standardized tests compare a student not to other students, but to a set standard of performance.

- Standardized tests have a long history of use in our country and the results of standardized tests influence educational decisions.

- Reliability is the ability of a test to yield a reliable score over time. Standardized test makers usually disclose reliability coefficients in test manuals.

- Validity tells us whether a test measures what it purports to measure—does the test accomplish a specific goal? Standardized test publishers also disclose information about test validity.

- There are three types of validity: content validity, criterion validity, and construct validity.

- One of the strengths of a standardized test is that its technical characteristics are known.

- The public often gives these tests far too much credibility and far too little scrutiny. There are concerns about standardized tests being used in ways for which they are not validated.

- Standardized tests can be useful for inferring (1) students' relative strengths and weaknesses across subject areas and (2) how a student has grown over time in different subject areas.

- Standardized tests do not measure educational quality. Additionally, the ability of standardized tests to predict one's academic success is questionable.

- The biggest problem of standardized tests is their propensity to measure knowledge of trivia. Many fail to assess higher-order thinking skills and instead only ask for recall of basic facts and routine procedures.

- Any forms of assessment, especially standardized tests, are considered biased if they "project only predominant values and attitudes and do not reflect the linguistic and cultural experiences of minority groups."

- Minority groups are, under testing conditions, disadvantaged by their cultural differences.

- Standardized tests can provide data and results that are essential to student improvement. These tests can provide focus and guidance as schools try to improve student learning. We need to consider how to better use these standardized tests scores to help us improve classroom teaching and learning.

How Do Standardized Tests Relate to Classroom Assessment?

- In reality, standardized tests do not play a large role in classroom assessment. Teacher-made tests do. Teacher-made tests are usually criterion referenced, rather than norm referenced. They often have unknown technical qualities. Content validity measures the outcomes of the instructional objectives in the assessment. This type of validity is what should be of primary concern to teachers. More often than not, quizzes or tests will be objective, or not open to many interpretations. True/false, multiple-choice, and matching questions are used by many teachers because they are easily scored, information can be efficiently gathered, and their interpretation is rather straightforward.

So What Is a Teacher to Do?

- Assessment programs and procedures should include multiple sources and be designed so that students can demonstrate that they know, understand, and can do something with their knowledge. Results should be used to improve learning. When developing assessments, focus on three essential questions: (1) What do I want my students to know? (2) What do I want my students to be able to do? and (3) What evidence will I accept to verify that learning?

- To enhance the likelihood of good construct validity a teacher must (1) specify the construct domain, (2) choose as many indicators of the domain as possible, (3) design the assessment task so that it requires only the cognitive skills relevant to the construct being assessed, and (4) write task directions that require the thought processes being assessed.

- Teachers should try to triangulate their assessments or use a number of different assessments to evaluate student learning such as, teacher-made tests, portfolios, performance tasks, learning logs and journals, and so on.

- The purpose of formative assessment is to monitor student progress and guide the teaching process during a unit of instruction. Formative assessments can be done using tools such as informal observations, quizzes, homework, and student questions. This information can help shape the teaching and learning process while it is taking place. The purpose of summative assessments, on the other hand, is to judge what has been learned at the completion of a unit of instruction. Summative assessments typically include formal tests, final exams, major projects, and term papers. This information is used to give a grade, promote a student, or place a student in an educational setting.

- We know from information processing theory the importance of specific feedback. In addition, specific feedback should also be accompanied by allowing students multiple opportunities to improve their work.

- Teaching and assessment are often treated as separate processes using more summative assessments. Instead, classroom assessments should operate much like coaching—with seamless instruction and feedback.

- Alternative assessment usually refers to something other than traditional, objective-type testing. Performance assessments require students to actively accomplish complex and significant tasks. Authentic assessments require students to complete realistic, lifelike tasks. Portfolios require students to assemble purposeful collections of their work.

How Do We Get from Alternative Assessment to Evaluation?

- Reliability and validity are no less important to alternative assessments and evaluation than they are to traditional assessment. Performance assessments should (1) have a clear purpose, (2) identify observable aspects of the performance/product to be judged, (3) provide appropriate settings in which to elicit or judge performances, and (4) have predetermined criteria for scoring or rating performances.

- Rubrics are essential to the process of evaluating student performance. To construct rubrics, you need to (1) specify the learning objective(s) and how you would measure their attainment, (2) list the criteria for a piece of work or performance, (3) articulate gradations of quality from excellent to poor, and (4) determine the relative weight of each of the criteria.

- A portfolio is a collection of a student's work that has been completed over a specified period of time. It is customary for students to comment on and assess the artifacts that they include in their portfolios.

How Can We Use Assessment to Understand Student Learning?

- We encourage you to examine student work very carefully and try to use it to help you understand student learning. Examine student work in collaboration with other students.

- It is important to remember that the end process for assessment includes using the data to improve learning.

How Can We Put All of This Together?

- Assessment can be thought of in three ways: informal, traditional, and alternative. Each of these can be used as a three-pronged approach to assessment in your classrooms. Alternative assessments are very consistent with the social nature of learning. Alternative assessments are also more likely than traditional assessments to include both declarative and procedural knowledge.

CHAPTER 8

Core Concepts, Generative Topics, Essential Questions, and Integrated Themes

(*Source:* It's a Teacher's Life *by David Sipress, copyright © 1993 by David Sipress. Used by permission of Dutton Signet, a division of Penguin Putnam, Inc.*)

 SCENARIO

Vicky has been teaching high school social studies for nearly 12 years. She also teaches the geography course for the social studies department and finds it increasingly more difficult to cover all of the material set by the curriculum by the end of the term. She has worked diligently to prioritize the content she wants to cover and has sequenced the subject matter as the textbook describes. No matter what she tries semester after semester she seems to lose the battle to cover all of the content. She employs many effective instructional strategies that include organizers, cooperative learning, questioning strategies, experiments, and field trips. She incorporates a variety of alternative assessments to allow students with learning differences to demonstrate better what they have learned. All this takes time and in many ways slows down coverage of the subject matter. She has set an ambitious agenda for students and for herself, and she feels compelled to cover the intended curriculum set by the school district. By midterm she usually finds herself attempting to catch up and begins to rush through major ideas. This results in confusion and frustration among her students.

In an effort to help her deal with this issue of curriculum coverage and to better understand what is expected of high school students in geography from a national perspective, she consults a reference book called *Content Knowledge: A Compendium of Standards and Benchmarks for K–12 Education* written by John S. Kendall and Robert J. Marzano (1996). She finds a summary of standards in geography that include 18 specific objectives (i.e., the student will understand the characteristics and use of maps, globes, and other geographic tools and technologies). These 18 objectives are organized into six categories including the world in spatial terms, places and regions, physical systems, human systems, environment and society, and uses of geography (Kendall and Marzano 1996, 363). Although this information is interesting and gives her many new ideas about teaching geography, she is still frustrated because now she has even more content to cover than before. Vicky does not know what to do next. She is concerned that if she covers too much content students will get overwhelmed.

? *What should Vicky do? Is there just too much content to cover in a term? Is she approaching the problem of coverage in the wrong manner? Are there options and alternatives? How would her students respond to this question? Is there anything we learned in previous chapters that would help us better address the challenge of content coverage?*

INTRODUCTION

The cartoon on the previous page and the above scenario capture the main idea presented in this chapter. In our attempts to "cover" information, we wage a losing battle with

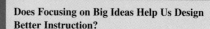
Getting to the Core

◎ **CORE CONCEPT** Less is more.

Does Focusing on Big Ideas Help Us Design Better Instruction?

What Are Core Concepts?
- Generating Core Concepts
- Using Core Concepts: Some Examples

What Are Generative Topics?
- Examples of Generative Topics

What Are Essential Questions?
- Characteristics of Essential Questions
- Essential Questions in the Classroom

What Is Meant by Integrated Themes?
- Examples of an Integrated Thematic Unit
- The Way We Learn, Naturally

How Are Big Ideas, Essential Questions, and Themes Related to Standards-Based Education?

the knowledge explosion. Most teachers recognize this as a major issue. They get little assistance from textbook publishers, who seem to simply add new concepts rather than reorganize content to effectively integrate new ideas with older ideas (Schmidt, McKnight, and Raizen 1997). Dempster (1993) identified three core beliefs upon which contemporary curriculum is based:

1. More is better.

2. Merely exposing students to information contains minimal risk.

3. Most students learn quickly, and once such learning has been demonstrated, further practice is not necessary.

He goes on to present research that shows each of these fundamental beliefs to be false. He cites research on elaboration, interference, and practice that strongly suggests we have an overcrowded curriculum that impedes the deep learning that has been championed in previous chapters of this book. For example, we discussed the power of elaboration in Chapter 3. There is minimal opportunity to elaborate if more time is spent hurrying through the curriculum than thinking about key ideas and concepts. Further, in your basic educational psychology class you learned about interference learning and distributed practice. Interference learning means that new information that you learn can interfere with information you already know, and vice versa. Mere exposure to information can actually interfere with deep learning. Finally, distributed practice (over time) helps develop procedural knowledge and is essential for being able to actually use what we learn. A crowded curriculum makes distributed practice unlikely. Teachers must reevaluate *what* they are teaching and attempting to cover. Deciding what is most essential to the learner and how to best organize this information is critical to student success. This leads us to the core concept of this chapter—*less is more.* To that we would also add, *deeper is better.*

Does Focusing on Big Ideas Help Us Design Better Instruction?

You learned in Chapter 3 that recent advances in psychology demonstrate that learners can only remember 7 ± 2 chunks of information. Additionally, they can process only about one new idea or concept every 10 seconds. Teachers routinely expect more than this—even though research suggests that more is simply not humanly possible. There are four major ideas that are central to reducing the sheer bulk of material that teachers try valiantly to "cover" and students try, often in vain, to retain, understand, and use. *Core concepts* can assist teachers in separating the wheat from the chaff in curriculum and instruction. *Generative topics* are closely related to core concepts, and can help teachers define big ideas. We will help you connect the use of *essential questions* to the ideas of core concepts and generative topics. They are powerful and centering questions that engage students in exploring the central issue(s) of a topic. Finally, *integrated themes* can be used in conjunction with core concepts, generative topics, and essential questions as a way to help teachers change classroom practice in view of what cognitive science has taught us about how students learn.

What Are Core Concepts?

Core concepts are the declarative knowledge that you want your learners to remember, understand, and be able to use long after they have forgotten unessential or peripheral information. They should be made quite clear to learners, as we have done in each chapter of this textbook.

According to Day (in Cashin 1987), core concepts:

- Are central to a domain of knowledge.

- Not everyone agrees with them, but they are widely used.

- Are likely to stand the test of time.

Generating Core Concepts

If you have difficulty imagining how to generate core concepts, you might want to think of umbrellas. This is an approach that we learned from McCarthy and Morris (1999). Think of a small umbrella under a medium-sized umbrella, which in turn is under a large umbrella. Begin with a concept embedded in a chapter of a text, say, for example, the Civil War. Next, ask yourself what the purpose of studying this war might be. The typical reason is that it comes next in the book. The next level of justification is that students must come to command certain facts to be considered culturally literate. Although there is nothing wrong with these justifications, limitations on time in school and human memory preclude deep processing of endless facts. This much we know for sure. Further, life is not a game of trivial pursuit; that is why professional teachers must identify core concepts that help learners make generalizations about wars.

> **Think about it . . .** Peruse a chapter in a textbook that you are currently using or find one that attempts to be very comprehensive. Alternatively, locate a school district curriculum guide used by a school district and look at any given subject area that teachers are expected to cover. Now, having reviewed the chapter or curriculum guide, decide which one or two major ideas students must absolutely master. Relegate all other ideas to a supporting role.
>
> Read on for more help with selecting core concepts.

This fourth-grade class is exploring the core concept "The Power of Light."

Back to the umbrellas. The U.S. Civil War is the textbook-imposed topic, and it becomes the fabric of the smallest umbrella. Now ask yourself what the next level of generality is. We suggest that one strong possibility is *war*. War is the fabric for the medium-sized umbrella. Finally, ask what the next level of generality might be. We suggest either *controversy* or *conflict* (or both). Conflict occurs when one course of action impedes another; controversy occurs only when people have freedom to give voice to their conflicts. These concepts become the fabric of the largest umbrella that encompasses the other two umbrellas.

Viewed this way, learning about the Civil War becomes a way of learning about the core concepts of controversy and conflict and how they can lead to war. This helps students understand why wars start and how they might be avoided. It also gives them a way of analyzing past wars and potential future wars. Of course, conflict and controversy are part of everyday life. They are, in a sense, miniwars or battles. In that regard, focusing on such concepts and analyzing them can lead to personal insights that serve us a lifetime. In short, zeroing in on core concepts transcends triviality. It empowers learners and helps them understand ideas at higher cognitive and sometimes very personal levels.

You can also think about core concepts in terms of what you learned earlier about information processing theory (IPT). We know from theory that human beings have limited space in working memory (5 to 9 chunks of information at one time). Organizing the information in working memory for retention and later use is extremely important. Connecting new information to prior knowledge leads to retention and understanding of facts, ideas, and concepts, and helps the learner put them to use at the appropriate time. In the above example, if the learner has been provided with a rich experience to connect to prior knowledge (i.e., connecting conflict to difficulties in friendships and with family members), understanding the Civil War and retaining facts about it might be much easier to do. Additionally, the core concept of conflict now transcends war and can be associated with family relationships and personal relationships with peers and, with careful articulation, analogies can be drawn to mathematical and scientific conflicts. Even conflicts depicted in literature and the arts can be understood better in the broader context of conflict.

In this example, learners have connected new information to previous and current experiences in an organized manner. This approach does not ignore factual learning; rather, it gives the learner some way to organize, retain, and use the facts that are important to understanding substantial ideas.

The table on the following page illustrates some examples of how factual information and topics progress to core concepts (big ideas). Let's once again use an umbrella as a symbolic representation of this core concept process. Think of just one umbrella. The handle represents the facts, the stem is the topics, and the opened-up umbrella spreading over all the information represents the core concept. Try to use the umbrella as a metaphor to better understand the table.

Using Core Concepts: Some Examples

Let's revisit the U.S. Civil War example and look at how one teacher used this approach to plan her instruction. To begin, she constructed a unit of instruction on conflict around three conflicts involving American troops: The Revolutionary War, The Civil War, and World War II. She asked students to compare and contrast these wars. While learning facts from the textbook, one another, and the teacher,

Facts	Topics	Core Concepts
Dates of battles, names of generals, etc.	Civil War	Conflict
Names, temperatures, etc.	Planets	Systems
Magellan, Columbus, dates, places	Explorers	Discovery
Christmas, Hanukkah, Thanksgiving	Holidays	Celebration
Quadratic, 2 + 2 = 4	Equations	Balance

Source: This table is a synthesis of the work of Heidi Hayes Jacobs (1997) and Brooks and Brooks (1993).

the students also constructed a broader understanding of conflict. For example, one interpretation was that the Revolutionary War and the Civil War were fought to achieve freedom, whereas World War II was fought to protect it (Brooks and Brooks 1993, 7). Thus, students got a deeper understanding of conflict; in this case, students got a deeper understanding of what might cause it.

Here is another example. It relates back to the scenario at the start of this chapter. How can Vicky use the core concept strategy in her geography class to help solve her problem of not being able to cover all of the material required by the curriculum? Are there ways to reorganize the content to look at bigger ideas? Let's give Vicky a core concept such as the following: *All precipitation is caused by atmospheric chilling.* That is certainly a broad idea and raises many questions. Let's add some factual information that is important to understanding the core concept: *cold air can hold less water vapor than warm air.* Now, let's look at three ways air can be chilled, thus causing precipitation (snow, rain, sleet, and hail). They are:

1. **Convectional lifting:** Helps create tropical rain forests

2. **Mountain barriers:** Helps create precipitation on the windward side of mountains as the air rises over them

3. **Frontal mass of cool air:** Helps determine rainy or clear weather; causes storms when warmer air is forced to rise over it

Using these three topics filtered through the lens of the core concept that *all precipitation is caused by atmospheric chilling,* students would learn a concept central to a domain of knowledge. Through powerful instructional strategies such as questioning, cooperative learning, and the use of effective instructional materials, students would be able to understand what causes deserts, which side of a mountain is dryer, and how rain forests are created. They might also be able to explain how those counter-level freezers in supermarkets keep food frozen—given that there is no top on them! Therefore, if students truly understand that *all precipitation is caused by atmospheric chilling,* then they understand a core concept and can use it to explain other phenomena such as the one mentioned above.

One reason that teachers do not use core concepts is because they need to or are required to use textbooks. Many of these teachers feel the same frustration articulated by the teacher in the cartoon at the beginning of this chapter. They just cannot get through all the material in the book, try as they might. We have developed a flowchart to help you stay true to the idea of core concepts as you reduce the bulk of information that is covered in textbooks you might use (see Fig. 8.1).

Think about it . . .

Consider the core concept, *all precipitation is caused by atmospheric chilling.*

Does it meet Day's (see p. 305) three criteria for a core concept?

Does it provide the learner with a way to learn even more information?

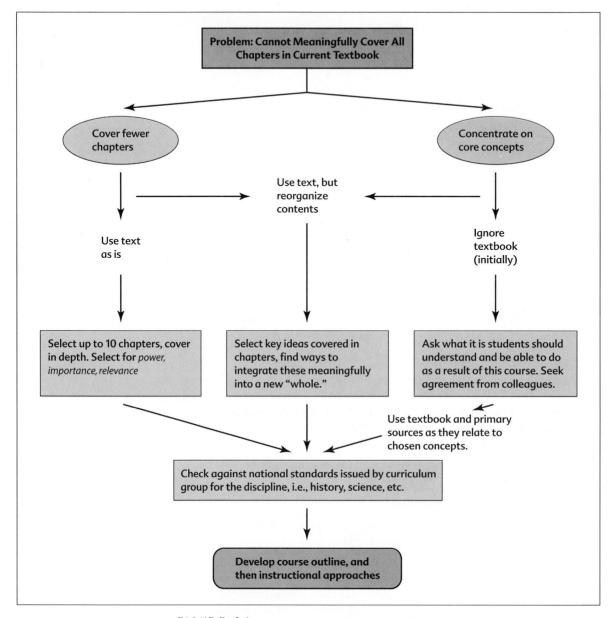

FIGURE 8.1

Flowchart to reduce information in textbook that is used in class.

We are so convinced of the power of core concepts that we use them ourselves. In this book! Since Chapter 1! Every chapter presents a core concept, or big idea, to which everything else in the chapter is related. That keeps us from violating the very premise of *less is more.* Unlike some other methods textbooks, we eschew the tendency to cover lots of topics in a superficial manner. We would rather help you understand a few ideas in some depth, and provide you with opportunites to practice them. Once understood, these very ideas will help you *generate your own knowledge* about other ideas, concepts, and methods that we did not introduce in this book. Which, by the way, leads us to our next major idea.

What Are Generative Topics?

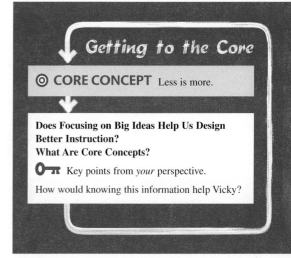

Another way of looking at *big ideas* is through *generative topics.* Generative topics and core concepts are sometimes referred to interchangeably. However, we have decided to write a separate section for generative topics to encourage you to broaden your perspective on how to use big ideas and to become acquainted with the terms that appear in professional literature.

In this context the word *generative* means that the topics provide the opportunity to generate new information from what you have just learned. Perkins (1992) writes:

> Many of the topics taught in the conventional treatment of the subject matters do not appear to be very generative. They are not chosen for their outreach, their import, and their connectability. A pedagogy of understanding invites reorganizing the curriculum around generative topics that provoke and support a variety of understanding performances. (92–93)

Blythe and Associates (1998) define generative topics as "issues, themes, concepts, ideas, and so on that provide enough depth, significance, connections, and variety of perspective to support students' development of powerful understandings." (25) They have identified the key features of generative topics:

- **Central to one or more disciplines.** They allow students to gain necessary skills and understanding to proceed to more sophisticated work in the domain or discipline.

- **Interesting to students.** The generativity of a topic for a particular group of students varies with the students' age, social and cultural contexts, personal interests, and intellectual experiences.

- **Interesting to the teacher.** Their teacher's passion for and curiosity about a particular issue or question will serve as the best model for students who are just learning how to explore the unfamiliar and complex territory of questions that do not have simple, straightforward answers.

- **Accessible.** Age-appropriate resources must be available to help students investigate the topic or topics to be addressed through a variety of teaching strategies and activities.

- **Providing opportunities for multiple connections.** Students should have the chance to make connections to previous experiences, both in and out of school. Generative topics should have an inexhaustible quality that allows for deep exploration. (29–30)

As you can see, the criteria for generative topics are similar to the criteria we listed earlier for core concepts. They both take into consideration the use of *big ideas* and they are both aimed at helping learners make connections among substantial, disciplinary-specific concepts.

Examples of Generative Topics

Blythe and Associates (1998) offer the following as examples of generative topics:

- **In biology:** the definition of life, rain forests, dinosaurs, endangered species, global warming

- **In mathematics:** the concept of zero, patterns, equality, representations in signs and symbols, size and scale
- **In history:** maritime disasters, survival, revolution, conflict, power
- **In literature:** interpreting texts, folktales, humor, multiple perspectives (30)

Gardner (1999) insists that if generative topics are to be powerful, they need to be carefully planned and presented to the students. The generative topic must be central to the subject matter and engage the learner in relevant and meaningful activities. So is there really a difference between generative topics and core concepts? Some researchers emphasize the core or centrality of the big idea. Hence, they refer to core concepts. Other researchers (Blythe and Associates, 1998; Gardner 1999; Perkins, 1992) emphasize the generative quality of big ideas; that is, the ability of big ideas to help us generate our own new knowledge. Either way, you are still encouraged to think BIG!

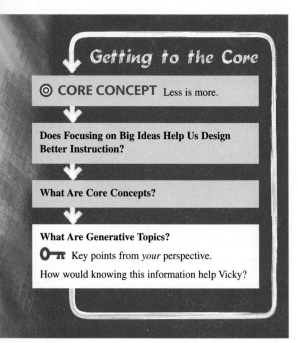

What Are Essential Questions?

The third way to understand and use big ideas in your teaching is through *essential questions.* As you learned in Chapter 4, there are questions and then there are *questions.* If we want to encourage critical thinking among students, then we must present them with challenging and substantial questions. Questions should be interesting for the students, if not compelling. When we explored questioning strategies in Chapter 4, we focused on methods that encourage both lower- and higher-order thinking and specific techniques such as prompting, probing, wait-time, and reinforcement. We now expand our view and use the *question as a mechanism to find the central issue or issues of the topic being taught.* An essential question will engage the learner and provide a structure to get to the core of the topic or the curriculum. Some examples of essential questions, offered by Wiggins and McTighe (1998, 28) are:

- Is there enough to go around (e.g., food, clothes, water)?
- Does art reflect culture or shape it?
- Are mathematical ideas inventions or discoveries?
- What do we fear?
- Who owns what and why?

Questions such as these cause us to really *think* deeply and critically. They prevent students from coming up with quick, poorly thought-out responses. None of these questions has simple answers. Rather, the answers are complex and require deliberate and thoughtful responses. In order to effectively respond to an essential question, the learner needs to have both a good understanding of the content and the ability to make connections between familiar and unfamiliar information.

SPOTLIGHT ON BEHAVIOR MANAGEMENT

But will they behave?

Getting to the Core of Behavior Management

Throughout this behavior management strand we have been looking in on a few students and their teacher. Now we would like to take you on a journey through this teacher's mind as she sits down late one summer to reflect on her classroom management plan for the upcoming school year. She has recently learned many of the concepts you have been reading about in this book. As we travel along with her thoughts, we will highlight core concepts from the "But will they behave?" strand in boldface. When you read the bold type, consider how the statement can be applied to you and your field experience.

Our teacher finds a quiet place in the park on a warm, sunny day. In the shade of a large tree, she pours herself an iced tea and pulls a yellow legal pad and her favorite pen from a backpack. She closes her eyes and thinks about her classroom. Immediately a situation from last year between her and Juan comes to mind. It always seemed to be Juan who got under her skin. "This year will be different," she thinks as she recalls some new ideas she learned at a recent conference.

She takes the cap off her pen and at the top of the first page of her pad writes: **look at behavioral issues as opportunities to learn more about students and to provide them with skills they need to solve their own problems.** Reflecting on her past actions, this teacher realizes that she was reacting to student conflict. Rather than looking for the opportunity inherent in crises, she feared conflict in her classroom. In light of this, she realizes that her own behavior was quite irrational!

⊙ **CORE CONCEPT** Less is more.

She remembers the **conflict cycle paradigm** and its explanation of how **students recreate their feelings in staff.** This leads her to think about the times that she entered into power struggles with Juan. They often resulted in him being sent to the office and her being extremely frustrated and angry. However, she notes, his behavior never really seemed to change. What really began to hit home was how frustrated she and her student got during these times. She thought of the importance of **developing insight into her own thoughts and actions and into the thoughts and actions of her students.**

She considers how her students create their feelings in her—how Juan draws out her counteraggression—how the withdrawn Eliza makes her feel helpless. She realizes that she will really have to gain an understanding of each student's individual needs and how these students recreate their feelings in her. She decides that she will need to remain calm and rational as she interacts with her students. She will have clearly communicated expectations, but it will be just fine to tell students that she needs time and space to think about an appropriate response.

In order to gain this kind of insight she must **build more significant relationships with her students.** Writing this on her pad, she reminds herself that these **personal connections are necessary to create a sense of belonging.** She also plans to get a head start on reading the files of the new students that she will be working with this year. She has heard other teachers say that they wait to read school files so that they do not develop preconceived notions about students. However, this seems like faulty logic. She knows she is competent enough, particularly with her knowledge of the conflict cycle paradigm, counteraggression, and the importance of developing positive relationships, to use the documented information in order to make better professional decisions.

Sitting there in the cool shade, she realizes that this is easier said than done because it must begin with a change in her own perspective and some critical thought about how *she* behaves in the classroom. As her thinking returns to the conflict cycle paradigm, she considers how she **often escalated behavioral problems by reacting counteraggressively rather than acting thoughtfully and rationally.**

During this reflective period, our teacher has the opportunity to **shift her thinking from the "what" of behavior to the "why" of behavior.** She realizes that in the heat of the moment she becomes overwhelmed with her own need to be in control of escalating behavioral situations in the classroom. She often reacts to these situations counteraggressively. This personal need to have a classroom that looks like it is well mannered (particularly to other adults who might pass her door) clouds her rational thought. So, when behavioral events occur, she focuses on the behavior itself and tries short-term, control-oriented fixes in an attempt to stop the misbehavior. These attempts result in her own frustration and an escalation of the situation. On the next line of her pad she writes: **managing your own counteraggression is critical to responding in a helpful manner.**

Now, with some distance and reflection, she can see that she really has to carefully consider her students' needs. Why do they behave the way they do? Which of their basic needs are not being met? How can she meet those needs? What are their irrational beliefs? How can she help them change those beliefs? With this kind of reflection, slowly and with a lot of practice, our teacher is sure she will be able to adjust her own thinking and acting *during* events in the classroom.

Sitting there in the park, feeling a sense of accomplishment about this difficult reflection, she writes: **Managing the classroom environment in a manner that serves to minimize conflict and maximize problem solving will help me maintain momentum and better manage instructional time.** This directs her attention to what students do in her classroom. She learned that students are better behaved if they are engaged. Students are more likely to remain productively engaged if they feel that they belong and that the activity is meaningful. Considering the kinds of educational experiences that she had planned for students, she recalls that when students were involved in **highly motivating and engaging activities the potential for behavioral problems was dramatically reduced.** In fact, she recalls the time when the whole class was involved in building a Native American long house during a social studies unit. She didn't even have to address behavior. The students were so involved that even Juan and Eliza were working side by side. She promises herself that she will use far fewer worksheets and drill and practice activities. Instead she will construct authentic experiences that allow students to work with concepts at deeper levels. On the next page of her pad she brainstorms several activities that she can use to get her students excited and involved.

Several students in her class have special education needs. Our teacher begins to wonder if their "labels" have somehow clouded her perspective. Have her expectations been somehow altered? Do the labels "emotionally disturbed" and "learning disabled" explain their behavior? Our teacher remembers reading somewhere that **diagnostic labels do not explain behavior or lead us to treatment.** So she decides to take a new approach during this upcoming year. In large print she writes: **all students need to experience caring and belonging in the classroom.** She vows to **look for the individual and unique needs of these students** and figure out how she can help them meet those needs. In fact, she thinks, maybe there is a way to use the concepts of caring, belonging, and individual needs as a theme that runs through her classroom activities.

Replacing the cap on her pen and draining the last of her iced tea, the teacher closes her eyes and visualizes her classroom. More important, she imagines her interactions with her students. Smiling, she packs her things and plans to implement her new knowledge. Tomorrow she will go to school and read her new students' files. She realizes that change will be slow and that she will sometimes fall back into her old ways. This "new" approach will be hard work. However, it feels right.

Managing student behavior is a constant process of questioning and seeking the answers to your questions as you assess your thoughts and actions and the thoughts and actions of your students. It is far from an exact science, yet there are elements of the scientific method involved. One is confronted with a problem, a hypothesis is formed, it is tested, and adjustments are made. New questions are asked. It is based on an understanding of the principles of human behavior and a willingness to reflect and examine this behavior. It takes practice and a keen sense of observation.

We hope that this strand has been useful as you reflect on how you will interact with your students. Incorporating these core concepts into your repertoire will allow you to have more meaningful relationships with your students. In the final chapter, we will provide you with a plan of action to help you implement these core concepts.

Characteristics of Essential Questions

Wiggins and McTighe (1998, 29–30) characterize essential questions as questions that do the following:

1. **Go to the heart of a discipline.** These are questions that are important as well as controversial.

2. **Recur naturally throughout one's learning and in the history of a field.** These are important questions that we keep on asking over time and that are a result of an increasing depth of understanding of the topic. Our questions become more and more sophisticated as our understanding of the topic becomes more substantial.

3. **Raise other important questions.** They invariably open up the complexities of a subject or topic. This causes the learner to understand the need for further research to avoid shallow and ambiguous answers.

4. **Provide subject- and topic-specific doorways to essential questions.** Focus and uncover essential questions through the lens of particular topics and subjects. An example would be, Is science fiction great literature?

5. **Have no one obvious "right" answer.** Answers to these questions are not self-evidently true. Their purpose is to provide opportunities for discussion and to look at the many sides of an issue or question.

6. **Are deliberately framed to provoke and sustain student interest.** These thought-provoking questions invite students to think counterintuitively and to be engaged in spirited debate. These questions are designed to encourage creativity and to appeal to students with a variety of interests and diverse learning styles.

Essential questions are designed to create genuine interest, arouse curiosity, raise issues, encourage thinking outside the box, and help develop conversations between teacher and student as well as among students. Just think about what might happen if you asked the following kinds of questions: What makes things fly? Do humans need each other to survive? In this very book we raise a question that is essential for teachers: How do humans learn? Do these questions meet the six criteria stated above?

Wiggins and McTighe (1998) further comment on the distinctions between essential and unit questions. They say it is not important to state clearly whether a question is an essential or unit question, but rather to focus on its larger purposes. This allows the teacher to better facilitate the learning process and guide the exploration of critical ideas. The table on the next page illustrates sample essential and unit questions.

To highlight the connection between essential questions and curriculum coverage, Heidi Jacobs (1997) writes:

A Person Who Helped Create Change . . .

Heidi Hayes Jacobs, president of Curriculum Designers, Inc., has served as an educational consultant to over 1,000 schools nationally and internationally. She has been an adjunct associate professor in the Department of Curriculum and Teaching at Teachers College, Columbia University since 1981. She works with schools and districts, K–12, on issues and practices pertaining to curriculum reform, instructional strategies to encourage critical thinking, and strategic planning. Her book, *Interdisciplinary Curriculum: Design and Implementation,* published by ASCD, has been a best-seller. In the spring of 1997, her book, *Mapping the Big Picture: Integrating Curriculum and Assessment K–12,* was released by ASCD. She has published numerous articles in professional journals. She completed her doctoral work at Columbia University's Teachers College in 1981 where she studied under a national Graduate Leadership Fellowship from the United States Office of Education.

Photo: Courtesy of Curriculum Designers, Inc. (www.curriculumdesigners.com).

The essential question is conceptual commitment. When a teacher or group of teachers selects a question to frame and guide curricular design, it is a decision of intent. In a sense you are saying, "This is our focus of learning. I will put my teaching skills into helping my students examine the key concept implicit in the essential question." *Given the limited time you have with your students, curriculum design has become more and more an issue of deciding what you won't teach as well as what you will teach. You cannot do it all. As a designer, you must choose the essential.*" (Jacobs 1997, 27)

As we discussed earlier in Chapter 4, both teacher and student questions are powerful instructional tools. Young children naturally ask questions as they begin to explore their world. As they get older, they still have questions, but are not always encouraged to ask them. Through thoughtful facilitation, teachers can encourage learners to ask good questions, maybe even essential ones!

> **Think about it . . .**
>
> How do you think essential questions would help you as a learner?
>
> Can you think of an example of an essential question that intrigues you?

Essential Question	Unit Question
Must a story have a moral, heroes, and villains?	What is the moral of the story of the Holocaust? Is Huck Finn a hero?
How does an organism's structure enable it to survive in its environment?	How do the structures of amphibians and reptiles support their survival?
Who is a friend?	Are Frog and Toad true friends? Has it been true in recent U.S. history and foreign affairs that "the enemy of my enemy is my friend"?
What is light?	How do cats see in the dark? Is light a particle or a wave?
Do we always mean what we say and say what we mean?	What are sarcasm, irony, and satire? How do these genres allow us to communicate *without* saying what we mean?
Is U.S. history a history of progress?	Is the gap between rich and poor any better now than it was 100 years ago? Do new technologies always lead to progress?

Source: From Understanding by Design *by Grant Wiggins and Jay McTighe, Alexandria, VA: Association for Supervision and Curriculum Development, p. 31. Copyright © 1998 ASCD. Reprinted by permission. All rights reserved.*

Essential Questions in the Classroom

Let's now look at an example of how Kathleen DiTanna, a ninth-grade high school English teacher in an inner-city school, uses an essential question to engage her students. The following description includes a variety of planning elements for a unit on the question, "What is a hero?"

Topic:
Everyday heroes

Essential Question:
What is a hero?

After just completing an introductory unit on Greek mythology with a focus on literary analysis (plot, setting, character, conflict, theme, irony, foreshadowing, flashback, protagonist and antagonist) it was the appropriate time to begin to ask the question, What is a hero? The unit began with comparing the heroic deeds of the Greeks to the heroic deeds of famous Americans. The discussion continued with the question, Do heroes always have to be famous and do great deeds? After writing ideas in their journals, students responded by saying a hero is someone who helps others. Heroes could be parents, brothers, sisters, teachers, or friends. Many students revealed heroic deeds they have done. So the discussion led to the topic, "everyday heroes."

In order to create a high level of interest, the unit was designed around the essential question, What is a hero? The teacher, with the students' help, constructed an advance organizer to help visualize the big ideas to be explored. The elements of a hero we examined consisted of (1) characteristics of a hero, (2) acts of heroes, (3) types of heroes, and (4) challenges of heroes.

Students worked in small groups, analyzing the four elements of their assigned heroes. The teacher distributed questions to each group that focused them on higher-level thinking skills. The most powerful element of the lesson centered on the essential question, What is a hero? This is a complex question with no simple answer. It also raised many other issues. The teacher used the following questions to help learners attempt to answer the essential question, or get the big idea.

- What obstacles did your hero have to overcome? How?
- Retell in your own words the story you read.
- What is the main idea of this story?
- What do you think about a certain character?
- What might have happened to your character if he/she had chosen another path?
- Predict what might have happened to this "hero" if he/she had made different choices.
- What do all the characters have in common?
- Can you compare/contrast the experiences of your character with your life, or the life of someone you know who has overcome adversity?
- Reflect on being a hero. Do you think you can become a hero? How?
- *What is a hero?*

The teacher extended this unit on everyday heroes to other lessons. Using the same characteristics of heroes when the students read *The Diary of Anne Frank,* the essential question remained the same. Students were quick to see the universal theme running through literature and they quickly made connections to other works. Essential questions in literature help guide students' understanding of core ideas and allow students to connect universal themes to their own experiences.

One of us developed a unit for high school learners that was then adapted for middle and elementary school students. It is one that we hope you can relate to very personally. You can probably recall studying about epic literature or poems in high school. An epic is, in a very real sense, an encyclopedia of an ancient culture. The oldest known epic is that of *Gilgamesh.* We are confident that you have learned about epics. An organizer may help bring back the core concept: An ancient culture can often be understood through its epic literature.

The Iliad and *The Odyssey* are Homeric epics. Maybe you have read one or both of them. If your teacher used some of the ideas we have presented in this book, you

FIGURE 8.2
Elements of epics.

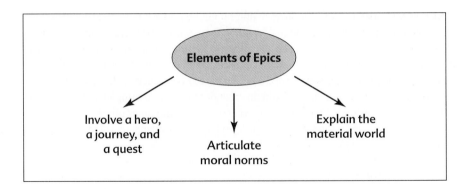

saw these epics as stories about unforgettable characters who fought shattering wars, went on fantastic voyages, and acted out awesome passions for glory, love, and vengeance (see Fig. 8.2). If the teacher used some of the ideas from this chapter, she helped you see the timeless issues that each epic raises. Why, for example, does Odysseus long so powerfully to return home? That raises many big, essential questions. One such question might be: Why do we love our own so strongly? Another might be: What does it mean to be alive? These questions can lead learners into deep reflection about important ideas. They can bring their knowledge to bear on these questions and, in so doing, generate even more knowledge for themselves. In the process, *The Odyssey* comes to life and is remembered not as some poem written long ago that is irrelevant to those of us alive today, but as a piece of literature written in a tradition that gives us insight into cultures and important issues that we face even now.

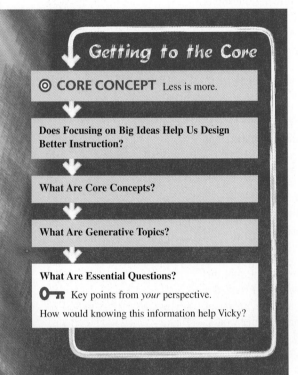

What Is Meant by Integrated Themes?

We have closely examined core concepts, generative topics, and essential questions as tools that encourage both the teacher and the student to use BIG ideas. Now we will discuss one last idea that will help us put these tools to use. Integrated themes focus on ideas, concepts, and attitudes common to many disciplines. They encourage learners to see how various disciplines are interrelated.

We are beginning to realize, as we understand more about how humans learn, that teaching subjects in isolation from one another leaves learners with a disconnected view of content. Traditionally, our schools have been organized to teach subjects independently of one another and, at least for the most part, to ignore the relationships among subjects. This is true even in elementary school, where time for reading, math, social studies, and science is set aside in separate blocks. Yet the relationships among, for example, mathematics, science, and history are so plentiful, it is hard to truly understand one without understanding the other. The relationships among art, music, literature, and history are also significant, yet we tend to require students to study them in isolation.

When we go to an art museum to see a special collection of impressionist paintings, we examine these paintings from a broad perspective. In order to truly appreciate a work of art, we need a perspective on a particular period of history, knowledge of how the artist uses light (science) and of the methods employed to convey the images such as proportions, shape, and size (math). Look at the painting below (Paul Cezanne: *Woman with Coffee Pot,* circa 1890–1895) and examine the many ways it can be approached. Consider the learner examining the painting from the perspectives of a time period (history), the use of shapes, angles, and perspective (math), the concept of light (science), and the artist's theme (the story of art).

When we go food shopping at a supermarket, we need a thorough knowledge of nutrition facts to understand food labels. We are expected to understand what is meant by calories, calories from fat, protein, sugar content, and cholesterol (science); percentages, serving size, measurements, prices, quantity discounts, and pricing (math); and we need the ability to critically read questionable advertising to better navigate ourselves through the shopping experience. This all requires knowledge and skills in many areas.

> Think about it . . .
>
> Look at the Cezanne painting below.
>
> What was it like to live during this time period?
>
> How does the artist use space?
>
> Are shapes of objects important to the message?
>
> How does the artist use foreground and background?

The Way We Learn, Naturally

As we reflect on life, we realize that its elements are not compartmentalized; rather, they are integrated in a very natural way. Our schools and curriculum should reflect this natural way of behaving, and learning. As we broaden our view beyond big ideas to examine the ways that they are interconnected, we begin to see relationships among individual subjects. We can then use the power of big ideas (interdependence, survival, patterns, sound, light, etc.) to develop enriching units of study that involve multiple disciplines. In order to help our learners investigate connected knowledge, we must demand that they interpret, analyze, synthesize, and evaluate information (think critically). The ability to process information by seeing critical relationships and connections among content areas will serve the learner well in the complex world in which he or she will live. Should this not be one of the teacher's roles? Piaget (cited in Post et al. 1997, 23) states:

Paul Cezanne: *Woman with Coffee Pot.* Circa 1890–1895. (Courtesy of © Archivo Iconografico, S.A./CORBIS.)

> To understand is to discover. . . . A student who achieves a certain knowledge through free investigation and spontaneous effort will later be able to retain it. He will have acquired a methodology that will serve him for the rest of his life, which will stimulate his curiosity without the risk of exhausting it. At the very least, instead of having his memory take priority over his reasoning power . . . he will learn to make his reason function by himself and learn to build his own ideas freely. The goal of intellectual education is not to know how to repeat or retain ready-made truths. It is in learning to master the truth by oneself at the risk of losing a lot of time in going through all the roundabout ways that are inherent in real activity.

Many of the powerful instructional strategies discussed earlier in this book are excellent tools to facilitate the process of integrating learning. The use of project learning, cooperative learning, multisensory approaches (multiple intelligences), and other powerful strategies enable learners to construct, deeper meaning about what they are learning.

However, this does not mean that we do not teach specific subjects. In order for a person to effectively integrate content, it is critical that content first be learned. We must have a foundation from which to work. Beane (1995) supports the notion that in order to integrate subject matter, you must truly understand it. He writes:

> Notice that, in order to define curriculum integration, there must be reference to knowledge. How could there not be? If we are to broaden and deepen understandings about ourselves and our world, we must come to know "stuff" and to do that we must be skilled in ways of knowing and understanding. As it turns out, the disciplines of knowledge include much (but not all) of what we know about ourselves and our world and about ways of making and communicating meaning. Thus authentic curriculum integration, involving as it does the search for self and social meaning, must take the disciplines of knowledge seriously—though again, more is involved than just the correlation of knowledge from various disciplines. (100)

So, we are searching for a balance in the way we learn information. To best develop relationships and connections among the elements of the content that we study, we must stop and recognize that we do not learn information in isolation. Neither do our students.

In his book *Disciplined Mind: What All Students Should Understand* (1999), Howard Gardner clearly advocates a thematic approach to helping students learn. This book examines education's ultimate goal, and approaches this examination through three recurring themes: *truth (and falsity), beauty (and ugliness), and goodness (and evil).* Gardner deliberately chooses these three themes to illustrate the nature of truth, beauty, and goodness, and he explores these powerful themes through the theory of evolution, the music of Mozart (*The Marriage of Figaro*), and

Learning and Teaching in the Age of Technology

Determining what specific content to teach can be one of the most daunting and frustrating tasks a teacher faces. In this age of technology, new knowledge grows exponentially. Teachers need to help students master increasingly more complex information in the same amount of time that they had before this information explosion. How do we make decisions about what to focus on? What knowledge is going to be most the most beneficial and most necessary for them to master? In this chapter you are exploring strategies such as core concepts, generative topics, essential questions, and thematic units that help students "uncover" information. These strategies, if used properly, help teachers help students to see "big ideas." The teacher's goal is to help students retain essential ideas, concepts, and facts. With the help of dynamic technology, teachers can better design instruction using visual organizers, project-based learning, learning centers, and so on, to encourage the understanding of complex concepts and problems. The following website, **http://www.ncrel.org/tandl/plan3.htm**, explains how to use technology to design instruction that is consistent with integrated themes.

◎ **CORE CONCEPT** Less is more.

the Holocaust. Using these recurring themes to study the three events, Gardner creates three powerful generative topics or concept (big) ideas. Identifying these big ideas through the three events exemplifies a powerful use of thematic units.

Students studying wars during various time periods in history through the core concept of conflict are still required to learn specific information about each war, such as dates, times, and places, but they also learn such things as the nature and causes of conflicts, how conflicts are or might be resolved, and so forth. Studying core concepts through the use of essential questions will help the students to seek answers that are personally meaningful. For example, conflict occurs in students' lives, and being able to analyze and resolve these conflicts has personal relevance.

We do not want you to forget what you learned about information processing theory (IPT). That model helps us understand how humans learn and the importance of the interaction between the environment and the learner. As students engage in an interactive process that encourages them to see patterns and connections, IPT also helps them better understand the new content. This helps them make personal connections to their lives, thereby leading to better retention. Through the effective use of strategies such as questioning (lower and higher order), cooperative learning, advance and graphic organizers, direct instruction, inquiry, discovery, and others, teachers will more likely be successful in making the learning personally meaningful for their students.

Example of an Integrated Thematic Unit

Now we invite you to take a careful look at a classroom example of an integrated unit designed by experienced teachers. Pay special attention to how this example addresses powerful instructional strategies, individual differences, special needs, and time use. Taking these ideas and making them work in our classrooms is, without a doubt, challenging. Let's peek into a middle school and see how a team of teachers suspended classes for a week and engaged 51 eighth graders in an

Teaching Tips

1. Using *Inspiration* or other electronic mapping programs, have students design visual organizers of text chapters, video programs, novels, and short stories that best represent their major components. Use these organizers to illustrate different ways students can demonstrate understanding of content. They are also good tools to informally assess individual and group understanding of learned material.

2. Given a classroom management problem (being disrespectful to others) ask students to think about how being disrespected makes them feel. Give students Post-its and ask them to write down as many of these feelings, using one Post-it per feeling, as they can. Then arrange students in groups of five and ask them to come up with five common feelings of the group and write them on

an overhead transparency. Design a final transparency that represents the collected opinion of the class. Show it using overhead projector, and discuss.

3. Using the websites below, ask students to conduct research to learn about essential questions, and then ask them to design an essential question of their own for their research projects.

Suggested Websites

http://www.biopoint.com/ibr/askquestion.html

http://wwwgen.bham.wednet.edu/essenque.htm

http://edweb.sdsu.edu/webquest/

http://www.exploratorium.edu/IFI/index.html

http://www.sdcoe.k12.ca.us/score/actbank/torganiz.htm

http://www.graphic.org/goindex.html

integrated unit on the twentieth century. They called it "Century Week." Note carefully how the teachers used *time* to meet the project's instructional goals. The teachers first established the core concept/generative topic, essential question, and specific topics.

Core concept/generative topic: Forces.

Essential question: What forces shaped the twentieth century?

Topics (forces): Popular culture; mass media; science and the environment; medicine, health and nutrition; politics, government and economics; war and peace; transportation; communication; arts; and family and society.

Century Week was a seven-day project created for eighth graders that focused on the *forces* of the twentieth century. Given that the school has been working on best practices, core concept development, and alternative scheduling, it seemed like an intriguing idea for this middle school to take the opportunity to design an integrated unit of study that would better use time and allow for more diverse instructional strategies. The *forces* to be studied are the 10 listed in the adjacent box and are integrated through art, music, technology, health, and physical education.

The first task was to confirm the choice of forces. The 51 students were divided into 10 groups by selected *force.* Each of the five students in the group was assigned a 20-year time period and a specific *force* to study. The cooperative groups jigsawed into groups of 10 to plan and make a presentation of the forces that guided each of the 20-year periods of the century.

Each team of teachers wrote guiding questions for each force using the core concept and essential question as their guide. Teachers designed assignments to help facilitate the learning process and a variety of authentic assessments were implemented.

Students were asked to rate the *forces* they preferred to study and to name a few students with whom they would like to work. Then the teachers assigned students to groups and created booklets for the students that included general schedule, group roster, guiding questions, assignments, and assessment rubric. The seven-day schedule began on days 1 and 2 with a PBS film introducing the twentieth century and a keynote speaker, a graduate of the school and the inventor of the first computerized spreadsheet, who described the birth pains of the computer industry from personal experience.

On days 3 and 4, the groups researched their forces using a wide variety of school resources. From their research, each student chose two milestones, or important events, people, movements, or ideas that fit into his/her force and 20-year span. Students were asked to justify their choices and write up a description of their milestones. On days 5 and 6, the groups jigsawed to form 20-year span groups. Students taught each other what they learned about each force during that period of time. Then students began to plan a presentation. The gym was set up for presentations with each double-decade group assigned a position on the stage. They were given time to rehearse their presentations. On day 7 the groups made presentation to their peers, students in other grades, teachers, and parents.

In addition to the research and group presentations, each student was asked to write a paper justifying the choice of the two milestones, to complete a self-evaluation, and to complete a group evaluation. Also, students were asked to write journals that evaluated the entire week. On the basis of all these data, students were given three grades, one each for the work on the milestones, the research, and the presentation, and an overall average grade which appeared on the student's core progress report for the quarter.

The group cohesion was strong and constructive, and the students worked well independently. There were no breaches of discipline, though students were often allowed to move from room to room or go off with a partner to accomplish various tasks. The new groupings of students, and the variety within the project, provided a number of benefits. Teachers observed students working in the new settings and saw new—usually better—behavior and many teachers began to appreciate the diversity of learning and personality styles among the students. Students had the opportunity to form new connections with teachers and each other; they saw teachers out of their typical disciplinary settings. Students with differing talents developed new appreciation for one another. The lead teachers worked with other students in the grade with whom they had not worked previously, forming new relationships. New student leaders emerged as tasks changed, and some of the most "difficult" students in the grade began to motivate others to do the work! These students earned new respect from teachers and peers. This demonstrated the power of collaborative learning.

The variety of activities and the relatively unstructured settings allowed students who learn through different modalities to use their preferences. The kinesthetically inclined were not forced to sit in chairs and the visual learners had many opportunities to learn (and teach) to their strengths. The learning was completely integrated. Students understood how technology had an impact on all of the forces discussed, rather than viewing it as a separate force. The connectedness of the forces, both across time and within a time period, was apparent. Students came away with a conceptual view of history that would prepare them well for the ninth-grade curriculum. They were able to understand the twentieth century through the lens of the core concept and essential question. The arts, often given short shrift in our overscheduled days, were highlighted in both content and process. There were no tardies or absences all week and students were self-motivated—they went to work without being prompted to do so. The students' own video and still photos enhanced the project and were good records of the activities. The bulletin board of photos increased interest in school and the video included students' and adults' comments.

The advantages of using a flexible scheduling model (discussed in Chapter 4) were also evident. Alternative activities that allow for student differences in the amount of time they need to do research, whether because of learning style differences or the nature of the milestone chosen, were more easily accommodated in a longer block of class time. (Contributed by Linda Schaffzin and Leslie Pugach, both middle school teachers.)

This example of an integrated unit clearly demonstrates how you can take a large body of information and not only develop a core concept and essential question, but also integrate many different topics usually taught in isolation from one another. Additionally, the use of an alternative schedule helped meet the teaching and learning needs of the initiative.

Thematic units of instruction are challenging for both the teacher and the student. They provide opportunities for students to make connections and see relationships among different areas of content rather then seeing them in isolation. The use of powerful instructional strategies such as cooperative learning, effective questioning, webbing, and graphic organizers, and the availability of rich resources including technology, are critical to the success of thematic units. So if you want to challenge your learners' many intelligences and provide experiences that best represent the real world in which they live, then you must look at the opportunities that thematic, integrated units offer.

Think about it . . .   How can you develop lessons and units based on integrated themes and interdisciplinary approaches to the curriculum?

Check these out:

Mapping the Big Picture: Integrating Curriculum and Assessment K–12 by Heidi Hayes Jacobs (1997)

Interdisciplinary High School Teaching: Strategies for Integrated Learning by John Clark and Russell Agne (1997)

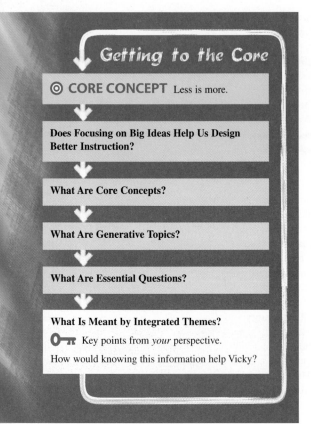

Getting to the Core

◎ **CORE CONCEPT** Less is more.

Does Focusing on Big Ideas Help Us Design Better Instruction?

What Are Core Concepts?

What Are Generative Topics?

What Are Essential Questions?

What Is Meant by Integrated Themes?

⊙━ᴛ Key points from *your* perspective.

How would knowing this information help Vicky?

How Are Big Ideas, Essential Questions, and Themes Related to Standards-Based Education?

We made the point in Chapter 4 that although standards are becoming increasingly important in determining *what* we teach, *how* we teach is still within the purview of professional teachers. The main idea presented in this chapter, that we need to focus on big, enabling concepts, important questions, and the connected nature of subject matter, holds exciting promise for helping students meet high standards. This assumes, of course, that the standards are, indeed, set high. Standards that require students to think critically, solve complex problems, reason logically, and engage in other understanding performances are high standards. Standards that set as their goal the equivalent of remembering trivia are, in our estimation, not high. There currently rages a debate about standards, how they should be written, what kinds of knowledge they should require, and what kinds of performances they should encourage. On the one hand, education writer E. D. Hirsch has produced lists of what every student should know and be able to do at each grade level. You may have seen his Core Knowledge series. On the other hand, education professor Ted Sizer has, through his Coalition of Essential Schools, led a school reform movement that emphasizes habits of mind. In this view, student interest should dictate topics, and depth should be encouraged. Hirsch represents a very conservative or traditionalist agenda, and Sizer represents a much more progressive one.

We certainly hope that, when all is said and done, standards will emerge that blend both content knowledge and habits of mind. That is, the standards will require students to know subject matter and to be able to use it to create deeper understandings and solve tomorrow's problems, many of which we cannot know today. We also hope that the standards will reflect the core concept for this chapter—less is more. Too many standards will exacerbate the "coverage" dilemma about which we have already written. In the meantime, teachers can address the standards now in place by using the big ideas addressed above. For example, a standard from a school district's curriculum guide reads:

> Students will know that the components of a standard essay include an introduction, body, and conclusion.

What is the big idea here? It seems to us that a least one possible core concept that relates to this standard is *communication*. That leaves open more than just writing essays. It can be broadened to include other forms of written communication (i.e., poems), oral communication (speaking), and nonverbal communication. In the context of this large concept of communication, we can help our students meet the explicit standards and, in all likelihood, even exceed them. Further, if we want to really push the connections, we can ask students to examine ways that people communicated in the past (history), telecommunications (present), the ways animals communicate (science), and the communicative power of data (math). Some students might be interested in the ways we communicate through art and music. Of course, these are but examples of the possibilities for using core concepts, generative topics, and themes to help students master standards. We might even decide to have them explore an essential question, perhaps one similar to one that Wiggins and McTighe included in their chart (1998, 456): "Do we always say what we mean and mean what we say?" By helping students discern big ideas, important questions, and interrelationships among concepts, we do indeed help them master the highest of academic standards.

 ## SCENARIO REVISITED

Now we would like you to review once again the scenario that was presented at the beginning of this chapter. Answer the questions, this time using what you have learned from reading the chapter. Then see how what you write compares to the response of an experienced teacher.

> **?** *What should Vicky do? Is there just too much content*
> *to cover in a term? Is she approaching the problem*
> *of coverage in the wrong manner? Are there options and*
> *alternatives? How would her students respond to this question?*
> *Is there anything we learned in previous chapters that would*
> *help us better address the challenge of content coverage?*

A VOICE FROM THE FIELD

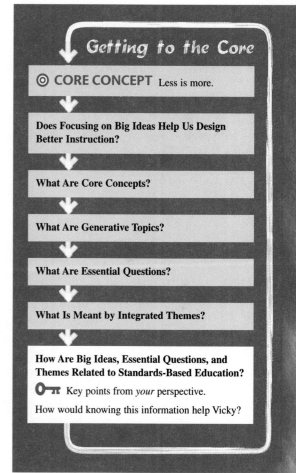

Getting to the Core

◎ **CORE CONCEPT** Less is more.

⬇

Does Focusing on Big Ideas Help Us Design Better Instruction?

⬇

What Are Core Concepts?

⬇

What Are Generative Topics?

⬇

What Are Essential Questions?

⬇

What Is Meant by Integrated Themes?

⬇

How Are Big Ideas, Essential Questions, and Themes Related to Standards-Based Education?

🔑 Key points from *your* perspective.

How would knowing this information help Vicky?

Vicky's situation reminds me of an apocryphal story I love about a general in battle. The general's army is in an increasingly desperate position. A scouting report comes in: "The enemy is amassing troops all along our rear." A few minutes later, another report: "They're on our right flank! They're on our left flank!" Five minutes after that: "They're charging us from the front!" At this, the general looks around at his aides and roars, "Excellent—they'll never get away from us this time!"

Like this general, Vicky has a "problem" which is also an opportunity: no matter which way she goes with her curriculum, she is bound to run into big, important ideas from which her students will benefit. Now all Vicky has to do is pick a direction and charge!

Let's look at Vicky's scenario first through the lens of core concepts. I have brainstormed four possible core concepts that lend themselves to deep, meaningful exploration of geography and its relation to the other aspects of social studies:

1. Maps are always subjective, and are constantly subject to change.

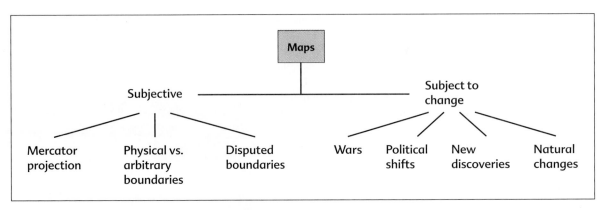

FIGURE 8.3

Advance organizer for maps.

2. Major cities should be located next to at least one body of water.

3. Culture is always responsive to environment.

4. You can't separate history from geography.

How would these core concepts play out in the classroom? Let's look at the first one: **Maps are always subjective, and are constantly subject to change.** If Vicky were to base a unit on this concept, she might start with an advance organizer like the one in Figure 8.3.

Perhaps Vicky would assign case studies to cooperative groups of students to illustrate and explore each subheading so that, for example, one group might investigate map changes in Europe caused by this century's world wars. Another group might look into map changes caused by nature, focusing on the ongoing creation of volcanic islands in the Pacific Rim's "ring of fire." Yet a third group could hone in on the subjectivity of our maps through an inquiry into the history of the Mercator projection.

Just as Vicky could streamline her curriculum through the use of core concepts, she could also align it to any number of geography-intensive generative topics, such as (1) quests, (2) great migrations, and (3) the Seven Wonders of the ancient world. Again, these would easily be adaptable to classroom use. Looking at the first topic, quests, we could create an advance organizer like the one in Figure 8.4. The second topic, great migrations, might lead to the framework in Figure 8.5.

Working with any one of these generative topics, learners would almost unavoidably be forced to work with maps and globes. Further, and more important, the learners would be doing this work within a meaningful, schematized frame of reference—which could logically be expected to lead to greater retention and deeper processing.

Now let's take a quick look at how Vicky could use *essential questions* to guide her students' learning. Here are four possibilities:

1. What role does geography play in human conflicts?

2. Does geography dictate culture?

3. Is it possible for humans to conquer their environment?

4. (honors level): Can we ever get out of Socrates' cave? (in Plato's *Republic*, Socrates proposes that humans see only a dim, distorted reflection of reality; Socrates likened this to cavemen interpreting events outside their cave by

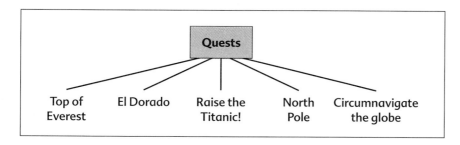

FIGURE 8.4
Advance organizer for quests.

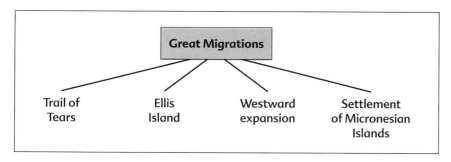

FIGURE 8.5
Advance organizer for great migrations.

looking at the shadows cast on the rear wall of their cave. Further, Socrates said, the cavemen do not realize that they are seeing shadows; they THINK they are actually viewing reality directly!)

Expanding on the first question, we might come up with Figure 8.6. Looking at even one subheading of this organizer, we can see how skills-intensive this unit would be. For example, to examine the effects of Russian winter on Napoleon's army, learners would need to be able to work with and understand:

1. Various types of maps (topographical, political, weather).
2. Map scale (to measure the vast distances involved in a march across Russia).
3. Microenvironments (tundra, taiga, steppe).
4. Latitude and longitude (to discuss troop locations, etc.).

Of course, this is in addition to the historical background the students would need to internalize!

Finally, Vicky could enlist her students' other subject area teachers in the planning and implementation of an integrated thematic unit. Some possibilities: (1) humans make sense of their world, (2) culture and environment, (3) explorations, and (4) dealing with disaster.

Let's say that the other teachers eagerly jump aboard, and that Vicky's students do become immersed for some extended time period in this theme. Perhaps at the end of the unit, the learners will not only learn the various lower-level skills of each subject, but also synthesize some higher-level idea, like "Human systems of knowledge are often created in direct response to the environment." Which brings us back, full circle, to core concepts.

Now that we have seen some of the curricular possibilities inherent in Vicky's situation, I hope you will agree with me that, returning to the metaphor of the general, Vicky shouldn't see herself as being surrounded; rather, she is centrally located!

This is the voice of Jordan Sonnenblick. Mr. Sonnenblick is a middle school English teacher.

FIGURE 8.6

Advance organizer for role of geography in human conflicts.

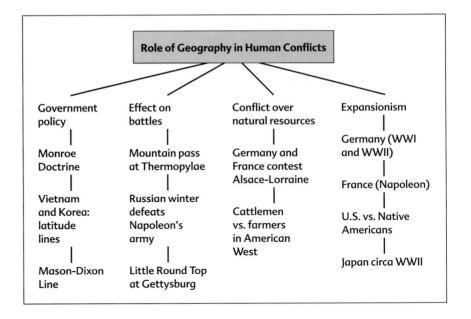

PLANNING FOR INSTRUCTION

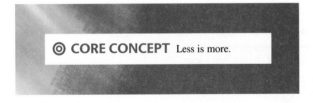

In this chapter we have addressed one of the major problems facing teachers, that of *content coverage.* How do we manage our instructional time and cover required content while considering such challenges as the information explosion; rapidly changing curriculum; proliferation of local, state, and national standards; and the myriad of social issues faced by members of our society? All of these issues abound while teachers try to implement powerful but time-consuming instructional strategies. Teachers must reevaluate what they are teaching and attempting to cover. Deciding what is most *essential* to the learner and how to best organize this information is critical to student success. In Chapter 8 we have examined core concepts, generative topics, essential questions, and thematic units that help us cover (or, better yet, help our learners *uncover*) big ideas that harbor important information. Now that we have thoroughly examined these ideas and offered examples, it is time to integrate this new information into your unit of study. Again, we will give you specific examples based on our weather unit. Keep in mind the core concept of this chapter, *less is more.* To that we would add, *deeper is better.*

Consider

How do we decide on a core concept for our unit on weather? Is there a good process? We need to think big, really BIG. Here is our thinking using the umbrella approach discussed in Chapter 8. Go back to the goal of the unit that states that students will explore types of severe weather conditions, specifically severe storms, and the impact they have on people's lives and on the environment.

1. Identify the specific topics to be covered: tornadoes, thunderstorms, hurricanes and snowstorms; water cycle; weather instruments; geographic location; and impact of storms on people and the environment (advance organizer).

2. Consider that core concepts are central to a domain of knowledge, are widely used but not everybody agrees with them, and are likely to stand the test of time.

3. Ask the *purpose* of studying severe weather.

4. Begin to make generalizations about severe weather—for example, how it affects what we wear, what we do inside and outside, places we take vacations, where we live, what food we eat, the kinds of tires we buy for our car, how many days of school we have, our moods, and so on.

5. Link these questions and generalizations to prior knowledge and experiences—for example, how the topic of severe weather and severe storms connect to bigger ideas and concepts.

The following core concepts emerge from this process:

Interdependency: Specific topics of weather depend on each other. (This can be broadened to include dependency of living organisms on weather, etc.)

Relationships: Specific topics of weather relate to each other. (This can be broadened to cause/effect, etc.)

Systems: A big idea in science, and in life, involves thinking about systems.

We now have more powerful ideas that meet the criteria for core concepts. They easily help learners connect now to their prior knowledge and in the future to new experiences. These core concepts are big ideas that can be associated with other units and lessons. For example, interdependency can be a core concept when studying nutrition, poverty, wars, stock markets, or literature. Systems is another powerful concept because it could relate to farming, health, animal life, and recreation, to name a few things. Once students have a firm understanding of these "big ideas," they are better able to connect newly learned materials to the same core concept, and even to generate new knowledge based upon the core concept.

Consider

How can questions help me look at big ideas? Can a question be a big idea? Can questions help structure the unit?

For our unit on severe weather, we want to create genuine interest, arouse curiosity, raise important issues, encourage conversation, and nurture creativity. The following are a few essential questions we could use in our unit:

1. Are natural catastrophes *really* catastrophes?

2. Is weather our friend or our foe?

3. Would we still have storms if the sun disappeared?

4. If my parents build a house on the beach, will it still be standing in 2050?

5. Why does it rain?

6. Is all precipitation caused by atmospheric chilling? (Refer back to unit on cycles in this chapter.)

In order to effectively respond to these questions, the student needs to have a good understanding of the content and the ability to make connections and develop relationships among familiar and unfamiliar information.

Consider

Can I use core concepts, generative topics, and essential questions to help me design units that integrate different subjects? The following are some examples of how our unit on weather can be integrated with other subjects using core concepts, generative topics, and essential questions.

Essential question: *Does the role of severe weather impact human conflicts?* Using this question, the students will:

Examine severe weather conditions (science).

Determine how wars and battles have been affected by severe weather (social studies).

Use weather forecasting models and weather instruments to determine timing (day and hours) of attacks on enemies or planned movements of men, tanks, ships, and planes (mathematics).

Listen to music and view art/photographs that depict severe weather conditions and that depict conflict from various time periods (music and art).

Read historical novels that demonstrate the interdependency and relationships (core concepts) of the above elements (social studies and English).

Your Turn

Now, consider using a core concept, generative topic, or essential question to decide about the "big idea" of the unit. Use the above information to think through the process.

CHAPTER SUMMARY

This chapter on core concepts, generative topics, essential questions, and thematic units examines covering, or uncovering, information in alternative ways. It presents us with ways, as teachers, to reduce the sheer bulk of an ever-expanding curriculum. It also provides an opportunity to bring order to curricula that are now somewhat disjointed. Departing from our typical chapter summary, we will conclude this chapter with a brief exercise that summarizes the core concept of the chapter, *less is more.*

This unique summary comes from a recent experience one of us had while attending a concert. But wait—let's get *you* involved in this. We want you to think about a musical instrument. Think about a violin. Try to visualize its shape, its various components, the musician playing it, and the sound that emanates from this wooden structure. Try to capture in your mind's eye the power this instrument has when it is played by itself. Now, do the same for several other instruments: the viola, cello, flute, oboe, clarinet, bassoon, harp, piano, tuba, horn, trumpet, and drums. Pick just a few with which you are most familiar. Hopefully, you have managed to imagine the sound of each of these instruments when played individually. Each instrument has a distinct sound, very unlike the others. The sound reflects the musician's practice and dedication as much as it does the instrument's structure.

Now imagine what it is like just prior to the beginning of the concert, when all the musicians are warming up and the sounds are quite indistinguishable and confusing. That is because all of these instruments are being played at the same time and nobody is coordinating their interactions. This is not unlike the way we *play* our different subjects for our students—all in isolation, with little or no coordination. However, the orchestra has a solution to the problem. It has a *conductor.* The conductor waives his wand and, as if by some magical power, all of the instruments come together and make a collective sound. Not just any sound, of course, but a beautiful sound that we call music.

Using this as a metaphor, we can think about music in relationship to core concepts, generative topics, essential questions, and thematic units. Subject areas can be seen as instruments (of learning, naturally); each is an entity unto itself. However, when combined with other subjects, any one subject takes on a new life. Art and history, math and science, foreign languages and music, all become more powerful when they are linked with one another. An orchestra is much more than any of its single instruments. The sum is much greater than the parts. So it is with learning as we have championed it in the chapters of this book.

Core concepts and their cousins (generative topics and essential questions) are the music that emanates from the subject/instruments. When working in harmony, there is a clear thematic unity not unlike that discernible in any great piece of classical music. Rather than seeing hundreds of individual instruments and hearing isolated sounds from them, all of the instruments come together under the skilled guidance of the conductor. Likewise, rather than seeing hundreds of isolated facts, ideas, and concepts, core concepts and thematic units bring them all together under the skilled guidance of a teacher.

Getting to the Core

◎ CORE CONCEPT Less is more.

Does Focusing on Big Ideas Help Us Design Better Instruction?

- Teachers do not have enough time to teach the amount of material they are usually asked to cover. We are waging a losing battle with the knowledge explosion. Research states that we have an overcrowded curriculum that impedes the deep learning that is essential to student understanding. In light of this, teachers need to reevaluate what they are teaching and attempting to cover. Using big ideas, like core concepts, generative topics, essential questions, and integrated units, can help teachers create learning situations where less is more and deeper is better.

What Are Core Concepts?

- Core concepts are the declarative knowledge that learners should remember and be able to use. They are central to a domain of knowledge, not everyone agrees with them, but they are widely used, and are likely to stand the test of time.

- Core concepts help students connect new information to prior knowledge in an efficient and organized way. They help teachers organize content in a way that presents a few big ideas in great depth.

What Are Generative Topics?

- Generative topics are issues, themes, concepts, and ideas that support students' development of powerful understandings by providing for depth, connectivity, and a variety of perspectives on content.

- Generative topics are those topics that have staying power, are diverse in nature, relate and connect to other things, and provide the opportunity to generate new information from what was learned. They are central to one or more disciplines, interesting to students, interesting to the teacher, accessible, and provide opportunities for multiple connections.

- Generative topics focus on the ability of big ideas to help us generate our own knowledge.

What Are Essential Questions?

- Essential questions can be used to help learners find the central issue or issues of the topic being taught. They engage the learner and provide a structure to get to the core of the topic or curriculum.

- Essential questions cause us to really think deeply and critically. They go to the heart of the problem. They also raise other important questions and have no one obvious right answer. They help teachers focus student learning on key concepts or issues.

What Is Meant by Integrated Themes?

- Integrated themes focus on ideas, concepts, and attitudes common to many disciplines.
- The relationships and connections between subjects as they occur in the real world are very important to learning and understanding. As we broaden our view beyond big ideas to examine ways that they are interrelated, we begin to see relationships and connections among the individual subjects. We can then use the power of big ideas to develop enriching units of study that involve multiple subjects.

How Are Big Ideas, Essential Questions, and Themes Related to Standards-Based Education?

- Standards should reflect both content knowledge (knowledge of subject matter) and habits of mind (create deeper understanding of knowledge to solve problems and think critically).
- Standards that require students to think critically, solve complex problems, and reason logically using subject matter (content) knowledge are high standards.
- Big ideas, essential questions, and themes all help to keep standards-based education from focusing too narrowly on only small pieces of content. They help provide a broader context for what is learned, and they help learners use what they learned in new situations.

Putting It All Together

CHAPTER 9

A Blueprint for Change

(Source: From It's a Teacher's Life *by David Sipress, copyright © 1993 by David Sipress. Used by permission of Dutton Signet, a division of Penguin Putnam, Inc. Also reprinted by permission of International Creative Management, Inc.)*

 SCENARIO

Chris Romano was *really* excited. She was about to begin her student teaching experience. Finally, after more than three years of diligent work in her university classes, she would be able to put to use what she had learned from her professors and her peers. Of course, she had worked with children in part-time arrangements throughout her teacher preparation program, but she had never had the opportunity to teach all day long, day in and day out, for a whole semester.

332

Armed with her notes and lots of great ideas, Chris arrived early on her first day of student teaching. She gazed around the room to which she was assigned. It was large and contained all of the basics that one would expect—desks, chairs, bulletin boards, chalkboards, books, and a computer. Chris had visited the classroom on one previous occasion, a week earlier, to meet her cooperating teacher and the children. That visit lasted only an hour, but she got a good feel for the classroom environment.

As Chris was imagining what it would be like to teach these children, her cooperating teacher, Mr. Bullock, whisked in and gave Chris a hearty, enthusiastic greeting. They chatted for a while, and then the children arrived. The plan was for Chris to observe for a day or two, and then begin assisting the children who needed extra help. As she felt more comfortable, Chris would be given increased responsibilities. By the midpoint of her student teaching semester, Chris would take over "full control," which meant that she would be responsible for planning and carrying out instruction for the entire day. Mr. Bullock would reverse roles with her; he would become her assistant. Awesome, Chris thought.

Chris began her observations and noticed that Mr. Bullock did a lot of teacher-centered instruction. Typically, he would teach a lesson to the entire group. He would follow this lesson by assigning independent work for the children to complete. When they finished, children placed the work in their individual work folders and then chose projects from a number of supplemental activities available in the classroom to do until the next large-group lesson. The typical day consisted, roughly, of reading instruction and activities for two hours, math instruction and activities for 45 minutes, lunch, and then afternoon activities that included specials (such as art and music) and alternating days of science and social studies.

It slowly dawned on Chris that Mr. Bullock reminded her of so many of the teachers she had when she was in school. Even in high school most of the teachers taught in pretty much the same manner in which her own mother and father had been taught years earlier. But in her teacher preparation program, Chris had been taught to use more varied strategies that encourage children to become truly active in their learning. She had been taught to use the richness of the diversity of the group to encourage children to support and learn from one another during cooperative learning activities. She had been taught to help the children make connections between what they were learning and what they already knew. She knew that the children would learn best not from what she told them, but rather from what they themselves did.

Chris also knew how powerful visuals, organizers, and similar cognitive tools could be for promoting lasting learning among her students. She had learned specific strategies for employing these tools. She had become fairly comfortable with

Getting to the Core

◎ CORE CONCEPT Everything changes. Society has changed, children have changed, and what we know about how people learn has changed. For the most part schools have not changed. NOW IS THE TIME FOR SCHOOLS TO CHANGE.

Can Teaching Change?

What Is the Feden-Vogel Model?
- Core Concepts upon Which Our Model Is Based
- The Planning Organizer
- The Planning Template: Five Steps to Planning a Unit
- The Lesson Plan Form
- Components of the Lesson Plan Form
- A Caveat

It's All Very Interesting, but How Can These Tools Really Be Used?

What Are Some Examples of Putting These Tools to Use?
- Example 1: The Deer Problem in Pennsylvania
- Example 2: Area of Irregular Polygons
- Real Plans for Real Learners
- A Word about Multidisciplinary Units

project-based learning and with facilitating discussions, even among young learners. She had worked with special needs learners for a semester, and was anxious to practice adapting some of the techniques she knew how to use for learners who had some specific difficulties. She was prepared to use alternative assessment strategies to provide her, and her students, with feedback on how they were progressing toward attaining the objectives of the units she had already begun to plan. She was also aware that typical textbooks expose learners to too many ideas, too quickly. She had looked over the science and social studies texts in her assigned classroom and made some decisions about the key ideas she wanted students to know and use, and the subordinate ideas that she would not emphasize.

But alas, Chris was watching Mr. Bullock closely and she did not see him using very many of the ideas she had been taught. His classroom was, she thought, very traditional. That the children seemed happy and respectful did not surprise Chris— Mr. Bullock was a very kind man, but he was also firm and had a very natural rapport with the children.

As Chris watched, she began to worry about what was in store for her. How was she going to use what see had learned in her college classes? Her university supervisor would, of course, expect her to demonstrate her ability to apply what she has learned with the children in this classroom. Yet she was a guest in Mr. Bullock's classroom. And things were going well in that classroom, at least on the surface, despite the fact that he used little of what Chris learned in her college courses.

> **?** *How would you suggest Chris negotiate her way through this dilemma? First, restate the problem. Next, think about several specific changes Chris might make that would be the least intrusive. Then suggest a way for her to approach Mr. Bullock about using some of her approaches. Finally, think about what she means by "things were going well in that classroom." What do you think that means, and does not mean?*

INTRODUCTION

"And the end of all our exploring
Will be to arrive where we started
And know the place for the first time."

—T. S. Eliot

We have, throughout this book, been telling the story of change. Our point is that what goes on in classrooms has *not* changed very much; this, despite all that we now know and understand about how people learn, and how we can help them do so. The point is so fundamentally important to the story that we tell that we believe it is worth reiterating. Oakes and Lipton (1999) describe what it would be like if you were teaching in a city school in the early 1800s, and then a century later in the early 1900s. Following these two descriptions, they write:

> As archaic as these pictures of past classrooms strike us, there is also something disturbingly familiar about them. Tables and chairs may have replaced bolted desks, and desks in U shapes or groups of four may have replaced rows. However, individual teachers still instruct large groups of students, and students work mostly alone. Teachers transmit knowledge to students in an orderly sequence of steps, often prescribed by school policy and watched for in observations by superiors. Students drill and memorize and recite answers, and the mind-as-muscle metaphor still holds sway. End-of-unit tests assess whether learning took

place. Mastery is rewarded, mistakes are corrected, and unlearned material is retaught. Then everyone moves on to the next topic or skill. (191–192)

Then they ask, "Why, in the face of cognitive and sociocultural research that has made such strides unraveling the mystery of learning, are conventional classroom practices so hard to change?" (194). We assume that they ask the question rhetorically, because they already know many of the reasons why things change slowly, if at all. In answer to their own question, Oakes and Lipton posit the two main reasons traditional teaching practices remain—they are *familiar* to, and *comfortable* for, most all of us. Oakes and Lipton point out that "entrenched conventions" are powerful and difficult to displace (194). Remember Chapter 1 and the fourth graders depicted in the story by Watson and Konicek (1990)? Many of these children held onto their beliefs about their clothes producing heat even after compelling evidence to the contrary. Humans tend to hold firm to the beliefs that they perceive have served them well, even if these beliefs are naïve or uninformed by newer information. That is the conceptual equivalent to the power of socially entrenched conventions.

Can Teaching Change?

Our story has been one that tells how to create change, at least in the classroom. We tell the story of instructional change. It is time now to put all the things you have learned in this book together. The intent is to help you use the core concepts, featured in each chapter, in your own teaching. In that way you will be joining the other teachers who are changing the ways they teach in order to promote better learning among their students. These changes will be consistent with ideas that have emerged, and continue to emerge, from cognitive science. The ideas promoted by cognitive science lead to powerful learning principles that in turn lead to powerful instructional strategies. Beyond that, these ideas also lead to better ways to understand assessment and technology.

To accomplish instruction that promotes deep learning, you will need a solid plan of action. In this chapter we shall lay out a detailed plan for change that, if you master it, can serve as a guide for your action. We will include examples from elementary, middle, and high school levels. We will include an example from special education. All the chapters in the text have led up to this plan, so you will be building on your prior knowledge as you encounter its elements.

Of course, there are always dangers in presenting what some might view as a *recipe* that suggests one size fits all. So we encourage you to think about what we present as a set of lenses through which to view planning, teaching, and evaluation, rather than a formalized set of rigid rules to be mindlessly applied in the classroom. You also need to bear in mind one more very important point—as a teacher, you must know your content! This book is about teaching *methods*. A basic assumption is that you know your *content*. The best teaching in the world will do little good in the hands of teachers who lacks knowledge of the subject or subjects they teach.

What Is the Feden-Vogel Model?

We have worked with preservice teachers at both the undergraduate and graduate levels for many, many years now. We have also worked with practicing teachers as they attempt to learn new strategies they can use to promote better student learning.

During all this work we have come to understand what excellent teachers do in their classrooms. Further, we have combined these strategies with ideas from cognitive science to develop a model that we will share with you. This model has been continually modified as practicing teachers critique it.

In order to change existing practices, it is necessary to look at what we now know about teaching and learning that we did not know, or did not know so well, a few years ago. Research from cognitive science has yielded lots of promising information that is backed by empirical data. One of the most useful of the models that has emerged from cognitive science is information processing theory (IPT). That is why we wrote about it extensively in Chapter 2, and again in Chapter 3. IPT is not a single model. Rather, it represents a number of models. We chose the memory model because it has great intuitive appeal to teachers. Also, it is not so much of a stretch from what teachers already do in their classrooms. The most fundamental point of IPT is that the learner must *actively process* information for that information to reach long-term memory.

IPT, coupled with theories that speak to the sociocultural nature of learning, helps us understand that this active processing leads to the construction of knowledge that takes place in an environment that includes other people. Indeed, those other people can exert a mighty influence on what we learn, and how well we learn it. These theories have been well studied over the recent past. Research studies document their value to human learners. We insisted that our own model, which we shall share with you in this chapter, must be grounded in theory that has an empirical base.

Yet anything that will really help teachers also needs to have a "system" or structure that helps make the theories practical. That is what led us to the 4MAT system we wrote about in Chapters 3 and 5. Although it is based upon learning styles, it is just as easily conceived of as a practical embodiment of the essential elements of IPT. Depending upon the manner in which a unit of instruction is constructed, 4MAT can also include the social aspects of cognitive theory. In fact, social learning is an integral part of the 4MAT system. Therefore, the 4MAT system helps teachers incorporate powerful theory into good practice.

Because active processing takes time, and using the 4MAT system for planning instruction requires that more time be spent on any given topic, concept, or theme, we needed to address the dilemma of content coverage in order to further our thinking about our model. That is to say, when teachers liked the idea of using sound educational theory and a system like 4MAT, we had to be able to answer the question that invariably arose. That question is: But how can we do all of this and still get the kids to learn what they need to learn? That is what led us to the literature on core concepts, essential questions, and generative topics that we wrote about in Chapter 8. As we worked with teachers on developing these concepts, questions, and topics, it became clear to us that learners would actually learn more, rather than less, if instruction focused on big ideas. Why? Because all the smaller ideas, facts, and concepts would finally have places to exist in a coherent "whole." Usually, these smaller ideas are isolated from other ideas. That makes them easy to forget. Now there would be a place for them to "hang," they could be retained and used.

Finally, the specific methods that teachers use to help learners learn must, at least in our view, actively engage these learners in meaningful, motivating, and cooperative activity. Without those, the notion of active processing would be empty. So we incorporate into our model informal strategies such as interactive direct instruction, discussion and sharing of ideas, and even very formal strategies such as problem-based and project-based learning, among others.

The "model" that we conceptualized led us to develop three items, or *conceptual tools*. These tools include a planning organizer, a planning template, and a lesson plan form. Deliberately, we have kept these tools simple. This allows maximum autonomy for the teacher and keeps the tools from becoming recipes that tempt one to follow them in mindless fashion. Besides, all too many systems available to teachers have become way too complicated for these teachers to use in an efficient manner. We present a number of practical examples that teachers have used with students in their classrooms. These examples come from elementary classrooms, middle school classrooms, high school classrooms, and even university-level classrooms. The examples are linked to the core concepts that serve as the focus of each chapter.

Core Concepts upon Which Our Model Is Based

In this book, we contend that what transpires in classrooms, at least instructionally, has not changed in well over 100 years! The classrooms in which you spent your lives are essentially the same as those in which your parents, your grandparents, and your great-grandparents spent theirs. That led to the *first core concept:*

1. Change is inevitable. Society has changed, kids have changed, and what we know about how humans learn has changed. But schools and the way teachers teach have not changed substantially in modern times. And surprisingly, there is compelling evidence that learners themselves can proceed successfully through formal education *without* changing very much, at least conceptually!

What do we know about human learning? We know what the *second core concept* clearly states:

2. Human beings learn best in cooperation with other human beings by actively processing information that they find personally meaningful.

In practical terms, how can we put the major ideas from the second core concept into practice? Humans actively process at least two types of knowledge, declarative (facts and ideas) and procedural (the use of facts and ideas). The *third core concept* addresses general principles of how humans do this processing:

3. The ability to retain and understand *declarative* knowledge is greatly enhanced when human learners make connections to what they already know by organizing, visualizing, and elaborating upon facts, ideas, and concepts. The ability to correctly use *procedural* knowledge is enhanced by practice and specific feedback.

Classroom teachers can use very specific instructional methods to help their students *really* learn by deeply processing declarative and procedural knowledge. The *fourth core concept* presents this idea:

4. Deep (rather than surface) processing of information promotes retention, understanding, and the ability to use knowledge. The use of powerful instructional strategies encourages deep processing of information. Both deep processing and the use of powerful instructional strategies take time.

It might seem that, because there are some general principles of learning and strategies for instruction, all learners are the same. But this is not the case at all. Our *fifth core concept* addresses this very point:

5. There are differences among learners and teachers in classroom settings that are significant and that must be understood and exploited if optimal learning environments are to be established.

Paradoxically, the differences among children that we focus on can become too rigidly defined. In fact, we have produced an entire track in our educational system for "special education" students. The labels (learning disabled, mentally retarded, etc.) that children must bear in order to get special education services can make them seem very different from other children. As our *sixth core concept* states:

6. Learners with special needs are *not* so different from other learners. Therefore, when instruction is properly adjusted, powerful techniques can and should be used with these learners.

Teaching and assessment go hand in hand. The best assessments help learners improve their understanding and their performances. Although standardized tests have their place in education, the tests that help teachers and learners the most in their day-to-day work with one another are the very assessments that teachers develop and use. To be helpful, these assessments must be reliable and valid. Using rubrics, or standards, can improve the reliability of teacher-made assessments. In addition, the more performance based and authentic the assessment, the more valid it will be. The *seventh core concept* makes clear that:

7. There lies, somewhere between rigid, standardized tests of trivia on the one hand and idiosyncratic, arbitrary teacher-made tests on the other, a way to develop standards of understanding performances and to judge them using authentic measures.

With all the emphasis on active learning, deep reflection, and collaboration, it is very clear that learning takes time and that the techniques that encourage these things are incompatible with coverage of the increasing amount of information that confronts students and teachers in today's classrooms. Therefore, it is imperative that we abandon the attempt to transmit all the knowledge that every constituent of public education deems vitally important for learners to know. Research, and plain old common sense, tell us that this attempt is futile. Rather than buckle to all of the interest groups and political agendas, teachers and experts in various fields must determine what essential ideas and skills are necessary for twenty-first century learners to be effective participants in a democratic society. To this end, we offer the *eighth core concept* as simply:

8. Less is more.

Which brings us full circle to where we started. Our *ninth core concept* notes that:

9. Everything changes. Society has changed, children have changed, and what we know about how people learn has changed. For the most part schools have not changed. NOW IS THE TIME FOR SCHOOLS TO CHANGE.

To provide you with a practical way to align your own teaching with the core concepts that we suggest will lead to change in American classrooms, we offer the following tools for you to use as you think about teaching and learning.

The Planning Organizer

The organizer that we present in Figure 9.1 is a tool for sketching out a unit of instruction around a core concept, an essential question, or a generative topic. Putting the core concept in the center of the organizer will help you stay focused on that concept as you plan the major activities in which your learners will engage. To help you understand each step, we have also developed a planning template (see Fig. 9.2). This template will lead you through the process of thinking about your units of instruction. It incorporates elements of some of the core concepts that we have presented in this book.

The Planning Template: Five Steps to Planning a Unit

Step 2:

When you *teach,* you always begin with Step 1—activating prior knowledge. But when you *plan* you begin with Step 2, the declarative knowledge that you want the learners to learn. This is usually defined in the school's curriculum guide. This guide is often in line with state learning standards. Not typically in the curriculum guides are the core concepts, essential questions, or generative topics that provide coherence to the facts, concepts, and ideas that you want learners to master. These are very important for the reasons we have mentioned many times in this text.

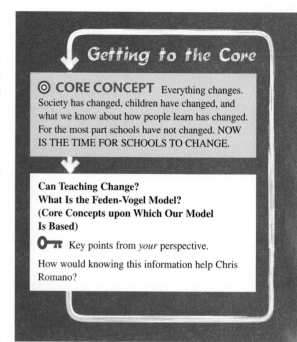

In planning and eventually carrying out this step, we encourage you to make ample use of organizers, visuals, visualizations, imagery, and elaborative rehearsal strategies. You should plan to help learners make connections to other things that they know and that they have found meaningful. In this way you put to use powerful general principles. Of course, in addition to modeling these principles by using them in your teaching, you might want to help your learners make use of them as they go about learning declarative knowledge. Thus, they will learn not only facts, ideas, and concepts, but also processes that will help them learn new information on their own.

To explain further what we mean by this last sentence, we will use as an example a 1992 movie titled *Lorenzo's Oil.* It is a true story about a boy who is diagnosed with a rare, inherited genetic disorder called adrenoleukodystrophy (ALD) and whose health begins to rapidly deteriorate. Unable to get help from the medical profession, Lorenzo's parents become experts in biochemistry and lipid metabolism even though they have no formal training in these areas. At the end of the movie, Lorenzo's father is awarded an honorary Ph.D. for discovering a treatment for ALD. In one scene, he uses the metaphor of a large sink with two faucets to represent the metabolic disorder in order to try to understand the interrelationship between two variables; in another scene, he uses paper clips to form a chain. In both cases he is using powerful representations to figure out a problem for which there is no known or readily apparent solution. He has learned how to learn, and he is using that ability to great advantage.

It is also important to think about the use of groups in Step 2. It is often helpful to learners to work with one another as they unlock the essence of new declarative knowledge. In fact, at one point in the story *Lorenzo's Oil,* Lorenzo's father convenes

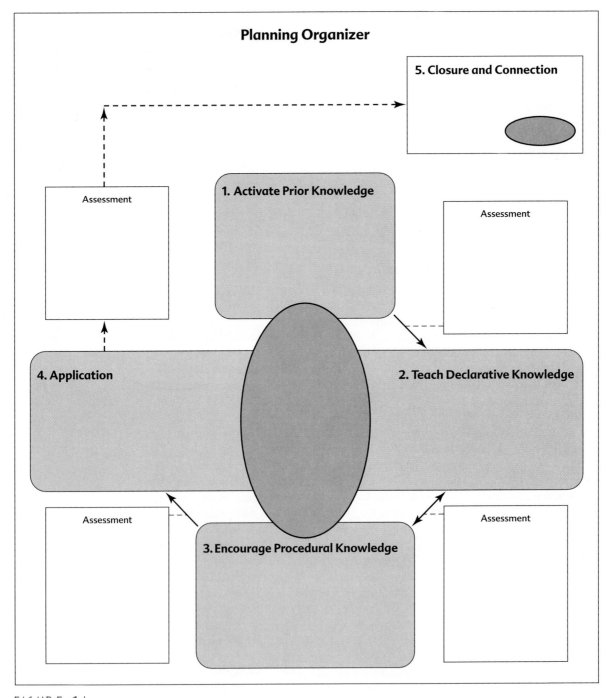

FIGURE 9.1

Planning Organizer.

(© 1997 by Preston D. Feden and Robert M. Vogel. All Rights Reserved.)

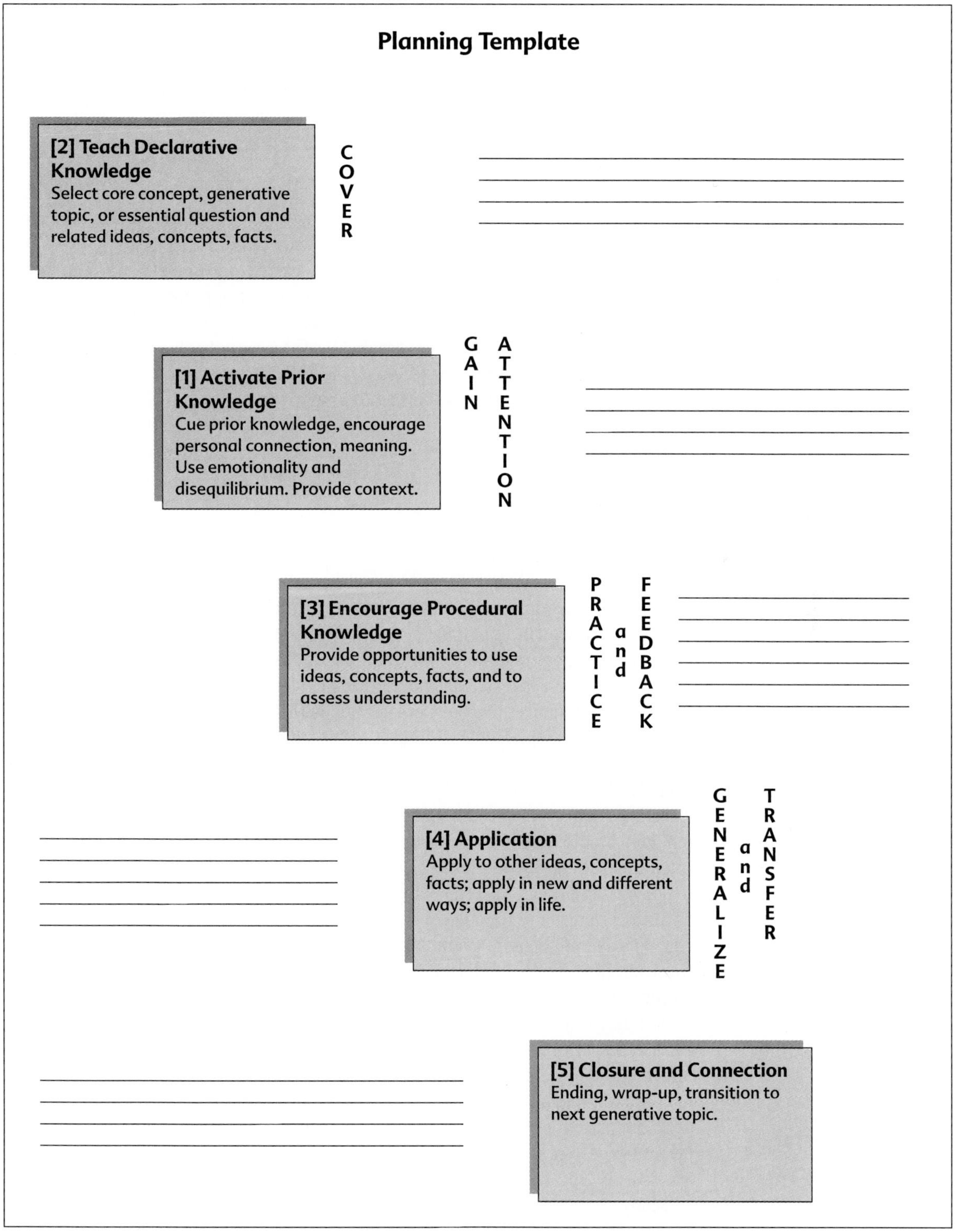

Planning Template

[2] Teach Declarative Knowledge
Select core concept, generative topic, or essential question and related ideas, concepts, facts.

C O V E R

_____
_____
_____
_____

[1] Activate Prior Knowledge
Cue prior knowledge, encourage personal connection, meaning. Use emotionality and disequilibrium. Provide context.

GAIN ATTENTION

_____
_____
_____

[3] Encourage Procedural Knowledge
Provide opportunities to use ideas, concepts, facts, and to assess understanding.

PRACTICE and FEEDBACK

_____
_____
_____
_____
_____

_____
_____
_____
_____
_____

[4] Application
Apply to other ideas, concepts, facts; apply in new and different ways; apply in life.

GENERALIZE and TRANSFER

_____
_____
_____
_____

[5] Closure and Connection
Ending, wrap-up, transition to next generative topic.

FIGURE 9.2

Planning Template.

a group of experts on ALD at a conference. He has been concerned that many researchers are looking at ALD in isolation from one another. The conference is very productive because it provides opportunities for researchers to share their studies and results, and to gain new insights that others have to offer. Learning declarative knowledge happens the same way in our classrooms.

Step 1:

This step comes second in planning, but first in the teaching/learning process. It is important to gain learners' attention in order to focus them on the topic, and to motivate them, *really* motivate them, to want to learn about it. *Intrigue* is a powerful motivator, and as such is useful as a tool for developing strategies for Step 1. The more compelling the activity, the better. This is a very appropriate place to engage learners in some type of a common experience. In that way each learner can make a personal connection with the material. All of this activity should help the learner activate prior knowledge—that is, what she or he already knows about the topic. From an IPT perspective, this is critically important so that learners are prepared to connect information that is new to them with information that they already know and have stored in their long-term memories. In that regard, Step 1 should always be more general, and possibly more abstract, than the specific declarative knowledge you want learners to master. For example, if as part of a language arts unit you want students to learn to write various types of letters to another person, Step 1 might engage students in a communication experience. Perhaps with their backs to one another, one student will give the other verbal directions that involve drawing shapes, such as "draw a diamond, now draw a circle touching its top point . . ." which illustrate the importance of clear communication. Communication is a broader concept than is letter writing, but the two are very much related to one another. It is likely that students have prior knowledge of, and experience with, some forms of communication, but perhaps not with the *particular* form you need to teach. In this example, letter writing is a particular form of written communication.

Step 3:

This step requires that you help learners develop procedural knowledge by allowing them ample time to use, or practice, the information they learned in Step 2. Too often this step is skipped because there is not enough time and we must move on to "cover" additional material. That is a mistake. Without practice, learners do not have the opportunity to apply what they are learning to situations in which those concepts and ideas are relevant. Nor do they have opportunities to receive feedback from teachers, peers, and others more knowledgeable than they are in order to correct any misunderstandings they may have. These opportunities are vitally important for learners to refine their conceptual knowledge base. Watching learners use the information that they have been learning yields valuable assessment information as well. Teachers who realize that learners have not fully grasped an idea or concept can develop a plan to assist these learners. This plan can be based upon the pattern of errors or misconceptions that the learners exhibit through their performances on procedural tasks. Feedback, to be of maximum use to the learners, must be specific.

Many teachers tell us that, in practice, they often go back and forth between Steps 2 and 3 several times before finally arriving with their learners at Step 4. That is, they teach some facts, concepts, ideas, and then they have the learners practice them, and then they teach a few more facts, concepts, and ideas, and have the learners practice them, and so on, until they feel that the learners are ready for Step 4. Note, then, the two-way arrow between Steps 2 and 3 on the organizer (Fig. 9.1) that indicates this common practice. But we also want to caution against going too long without having the learners apply what they are learning to new and different contexts. That application is important to help them transfer and generalize knowledge to situations other than those in which it was initially learned and practiced. It combats the fragile knowledge (Perkins, 1992) that we wrote about in Chapter 1.

Step 4:

Here you ask learners to apply information in new and different ways. That is, facts, ideas, concepts, and skills should be applied in ways other than those in which the teacher originally helped the learners learn them. Applying knowledge and skills in this way helps learners generalize and transfer what they have learned in the classroom to the real world. Although it takes additional time, Step 4 encourages learners to develop deeper understandings and more finely honed skills.

Step 5:

Finally, in this step teachers bring closure to the unit of instruction and make a transition to the next unit. Now the teacher or learners can suggest possible connections between ideas, concepts, and skills in the newly completed unit and the next unit. Bringing closure and exploring connections both help learners focus on the interrelated nature of knowledge and fight their tendency (and ours) to compartmentalize everything that we learn (or teach) into neat, discrete entities that lack real-world counterparts.

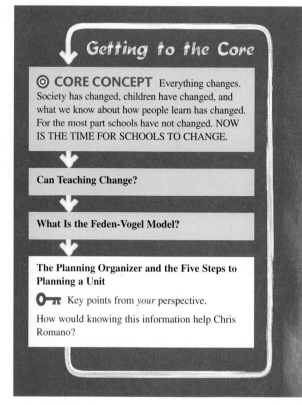

Getting to the Core

◎ **CORE CONCEPT** Everything changes. Society has changed, children have changed, and what we know about how people learn has changed. For the most part schools have not changed. NOW IS THE TIME FOR SCHOOLS TO CHANGE.

Can Teaching Change?

What Is the Feden-Vogel Model?

The Planning Organizer and the Five Steps to Planning a Unit

⚷ Key points from *your* perspective.

How would knowing this information help Chris Romano?

The Lesson Plan Form

We encourage you to plan units of instruction in order to keep the big ideas and their connections in mind as you help students learn. These units might last for one or two weeks, or even longer. But in order to conduct daily lessons you will need to prepare plans each day.

Truth be told, experienced teachers normally keep a lesson planning book that has a very general outline of what will be done every day for a given week. Our students always ask why *they* must plan in so much detail when their cooperating teachers do not.

Of course, our answer to such questions is that their cooperating teachers are more expert, and they are able to think through the details of plans without having to write everything down. However, some experienced teachers that we know still plan out their lessons in great detail, even after years of teaching experience. Planning your lessons in detail will help you think them through, teach them smoothly, evaluate them after they are completed, and revise them for future plans as you see fit. These detailed plans also allow more expert teachers to examine your plans and ask you questions about them. They are a reflection of your thinking about teaching, and they permit others to give you feedback before you actually teach your lesson to learners.

The lesson plan form in Figure 9.3 derives from the organizer and template in Figures 9.1 and 9.2. The big idea is this:

- Use the Organizer as your overall unit plan that highlights the critical activities in which you will engage learners. It is the cover sheet for your unit of instruction. It *communicates* the overall unit plan.
- Use the Template as your thinking tool. It helps you *think* about your unit activities as you construct the unit.
- Use the Lesson Plan Form as your *implementation guide.* That is, it is the lessons that you plan, and then lead learners through, to attain the overall goals and objectives of the unit. As such, these plans follow the cover sheet and become the pages of your unit.

Components of the Lesson Plan Form

The components of the lesson plan form are pretty much self-explanatory. They are meant to build on, or from, our organizer and template, which are in turn derived from the ideas that we present in this book. It never hurts to restate the core concept of your unit on each plan, just as a reminder to yourself of the big idea. The topic of the lesson, which is a bit narrower than the core concept, along with the specific outcomes you expect (in terms of learner knowledge and performance) should be explicit from the outset.

Every plan that you construct should help learners connect what they already know, understand, and can do to the new learning that you want to bring about. A well-thought-out plan will address this explicitly. The planning form we offer includes a place to put down, in writing, how you will help learners make these connections. Remember, connecting new knowledge to prior knowledge maximizes the chances that learners will be able to encode information, in an organized and meaningful way, in their long-term memories. Any of learners' developmental characteristics that relate to readiness to learn, and that are especially relevant to this lesson and the subject matter it addresses, should be noted.

Perhaps the most essential aspects of lesson planning are the instructional strategies and procedures that you will use to help learners master both declarative and procedural knowledge. We have written extensively about strategies in Chapters 3, 4, and 5. The procedures that you follow during each lesson should include a logical and organized sequence. This sequence usually includes an introduction to the lesson, a presentation of content (which does *not* mean that you must present it in a traditional fashion, but rather that the lesson should be focused on substantial subject matter content), and a closure.

Finally, each lesson should include some type of formative assessment, even if only a very informal one. Noting student reaction to the lesson and any modifications you would make can help you plan lessons in the future. These last three elements of a plan are the only ones completed *after* the lesson is implemented with students.

A Caveat

The organizer and template that we describe above are meant to help you think through your planning to promote student learning through powerful instruction. As such, they are merely tools—we do not suggest that you use them in recipe-like fashion as a replacement for the thinking that only you can do. Every school is different, every classroom is different, every teacher is different, and every learner is different.

Lesson Plan Form

Core Concept:
Lesson Topic:

Objectives (s) / Outcome (s)

Connecting prior knowledge and experience to new learning.

Developmental Characteristics (cognitive, social, and emotional)

REFER BACK TO UNIT PLAN WRITTEN EARLIER. INCLUDE HERE ONLY THOSE CHARACTERISTICS
THAT ARE DIRECTLY RELEVANT TO THIS LESSON.

Instructional Strategies (cross-reference to instructional procedures)

| Advance Organizer (big idea) | Graphic Organizers |

| Questioning Strategies | Cooperative Learning/group activities |

| Variations for learning styles and personality types | Other strategies |

Instructional Procedures   → | 1 | 2 | 3 | 4 | 5 |
(Check box to designate step of Organizer)

Include a separate procedure section for each step of the Organizer. Each step should include an introduction,
body of presentation, closure, and assessment strategy.

Complete instructional procedure section on reverse side.

FIGURE 9.3
Lesson Plan Form.

Instructional Procedures ⟶ | 1 | 2 | 3 | 4 | **5** |
(Check box to designate step of Organizer)

Include a separate procedure section for each step of the Organizer. Each step should include an introduction, body of presentation, closure, and assessment strategy.

Student Reaction	**Modification for the future**

FIGURE 9.3
Lesson Plan Form (continued).

One size does not, indeed *cannot,* fit all. Teachers with whom we work modify these tools so that they work for them. That is what we hope you will do.

It's All Very Interesting, but How Can These Tools Really Be Used?

It might seem a bit confusing—having so many tools that relate so closely with one another (see Fig. 9.4). But wait—you have already used these very tools, or at least the thinking that goes into them! Look back at all the Planning for Instruction sections that appear in each chapter. They ask you to do various activities that, now, you can simply put together in the way we just described. If you have been diligent and faithful about completing these activities, you have pretty much worked through a unit plan and at least one specific lesson plan in the manner we suggest. Your plans, and the teaching and learning that spring forth from them, will be consistent with cognitively oriented, powerful strategies that make it more likely that your learners will deeply process new information. You have already "walked the talk," so to speak.

Go ahead. Take the time to put what you planned in conjunction with previous chapters into the various templates we offer you. If you have not completed the Planning for Instruction sections of each chapter, then this will be an opportunity for you to use our planning tools to develop a unit and a lesson plan or two from scratch. The next section will help you see how experienced teachers planned lessons using these tools. In addition, we will connect examples of what these teachers planned to some of the core concepts and major ideas that we champion in this book.

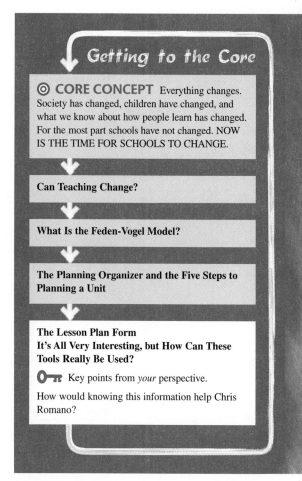

Getting to the Core

◎ **CORE CONCEPT** Everything changes. Society has changed, children have changed, and what we know about how people learn has changed. For the most part schools have not changed. NOW IS THE TIME FOR SCHOOLS TO CHANGE.

Can Teaching Change?

What Is the Feden-Vogel Model?

The Planning Organizer and the Five Steps to Planning a Unit

The Lesson Plan Form
It's All Very Interesting, but How Can These Tools Really Be Used?

⊶ Key points from *your* perspective.

How would knowing this information help Chris Romano?

What Are Some Examples of Putting These Tools to Use?

We have dozens of lessons that can serve as excellent examples of how teachers have put to use the powerful principles and strategies that change the way we do business in our classrooms. But the best units and lessons for your learners are the ones that *you* will create specifically for *them.* All classrooms are different, and each group of learners forms a community unlike any other that you have taught in the past, or that you are likely to teach in the future. The best we can do is to offer an example or two to illustrate some of the concepts and strategies that form the heart of this book. These are authentic examples of the work of practicing classroom teachers.

Example 1: The Deer Problem in Pennsylvania

Suppose you want to teach your learners a problem-solving strategy. Helping students solve problems that they encounter can be a very worthwhile endeavor. Here we present a unit that focuses on problem solving. Elementary-age learners take the

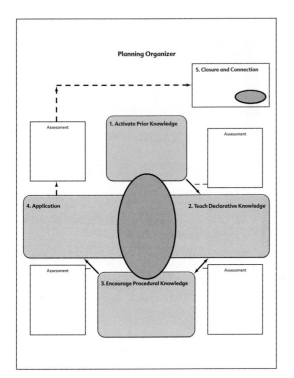

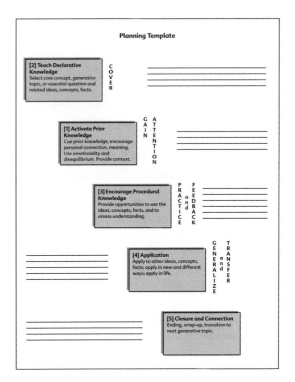

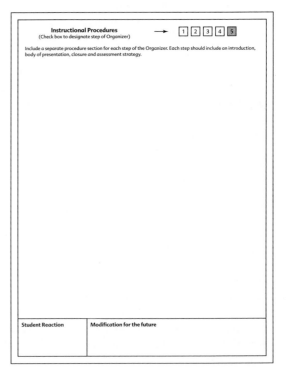

FIGURE 9.4

Tools to help work through a unit plan.

perspectives of different stakeholders in the context of a real-life problem (see Fig. 9.5). This class included learners with a wide range of abilities and social skills. To understand the characteristics of this class and its students, let us turn to the classroom teacher's statement of developmental characteristics.

Developmental Characteristics

Cognitive Characteristics: The elementary school child is beginning to deal with abstraction but needs concrete experience to aid learning. This child tends to be eager to learn. For this reason, my lesson provided a concrete context (John Street needs you to help solve the deer kill problem) but also pushed the students to understand multiple points of view (perspective-taking activity). Perspective taking is an abstract sort of task. I also provided other concrete (writing on poster board, filling out charts) and abstract kinds of activities (creating solutions, judging the best solution) to accommodate and challenge the students.

The cognitive abilities of my students differ greatly. There are some children who cannot read but can understand and discuss concepts. There are others who can read but have difficulty understanding higher cognitive level questions. Still others can read and excel with higher-order thinking. The best strategy I have found to deal with various abilities is to group students heterogeneously for many activities. Grouping allows me to individualize the components of a lesson to meet the various needs of the students in my class.

Socioemotional Characteristics: The most poignant socioemotional characteristic to consider for the deer lesson was the development of interpersonal reasoning. At the age of 10, children are becoming capable of taking a third-person point of view. They are just beginning to understand new situations from more than one perspective. Perspective taking was integral for the deer kill lesson. I knew some children would have an easier time doing this than others. For this reason, I placed children with varying socioemotional levels (based on my judgment) into the same group. I also had an adult with each group to ask questions to help the learners stay focused. Finally, I began the lesson with a reference to a "point of view" scenario—homework not done. When doing this activity, I said, "put yourself in their shoes" to help children understand that they had to think about how each person involved in the situation felt. This provided a concrete reference point to those struggling with perspective taking.

Physical Characteristics: The research on physical levels of development addresses the common growth spurt in girls, onset of puberty, and fine motor coordination. Because my students all face a physical challenge, fine motor coordination in terms of writing, was the biggest concern in my class. When filling out the problem/solution frame, I had some children trace words, others circle words, and others write independently. I had to group children so that at least one child in each group could write. I had to adapt by tracing and offering a multiple-choice component so that each child could participate independently in the lesson to the best of his or her ability. This grouping addressed multiple levels of physical competence.

When planning my lesson for children with physical challenges, I had to consider whether children could sit on a regular chair or if they had a wheelchair. This information was necessary to ensure that all children could fit at the table and see what the others were doing. Last, the varying physical levels were important when assigning roles to the students. I gave each child a job that he or she could do as independently as possible.

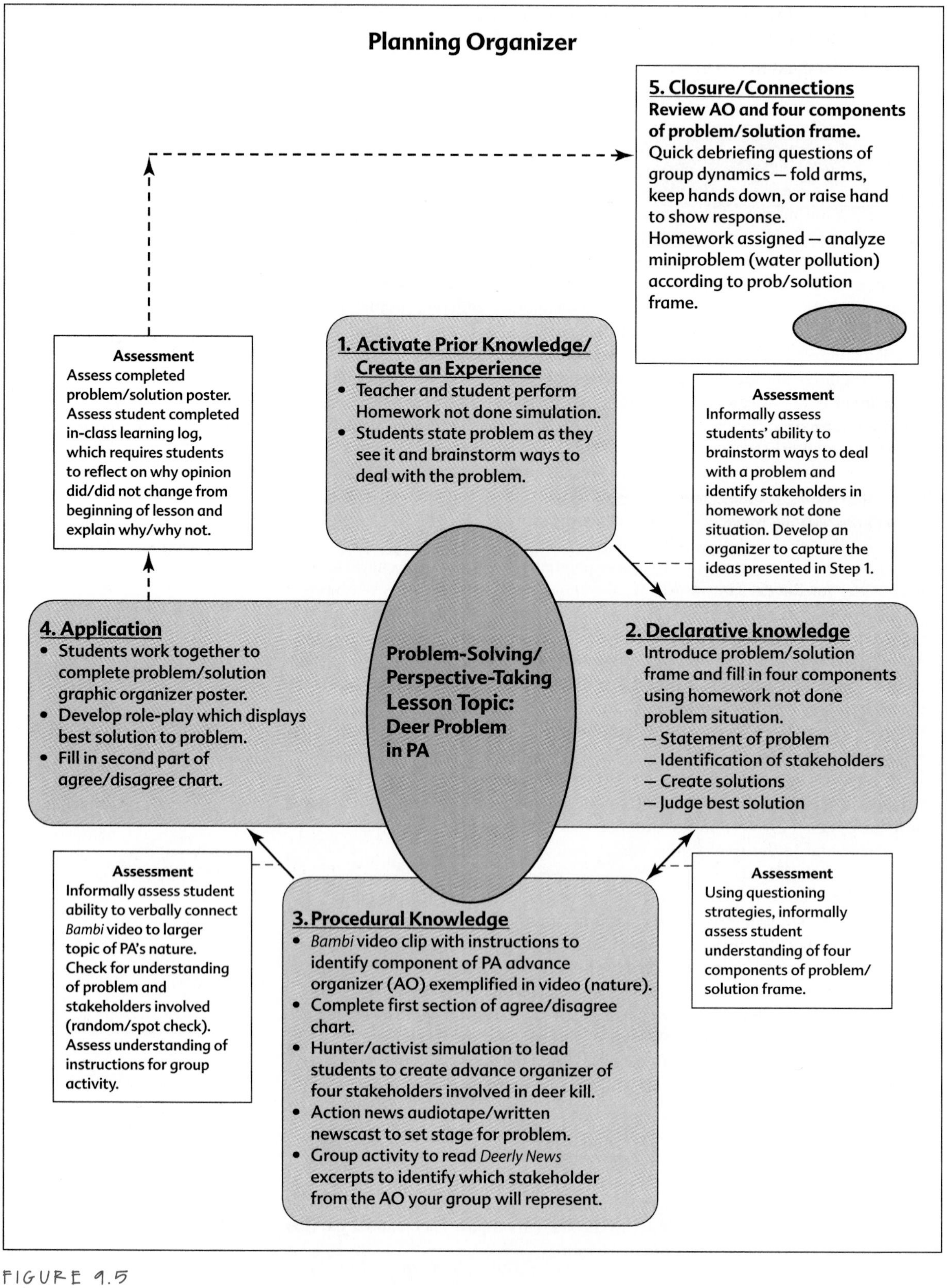

Planning Organizer

5. Closure/Connections
Review AO and four components of problem/solution frame.
Quick debriefing questions of group dynamics — fold arms, keep hands down, or raise hand to show response.
Homework assigned — analyze miniproblem (water pollution) according to prob/solution frame.

Assessment
Assess completed problem/solution poster. Assess student completed in-class learning log, which requires students to reflect on why opinion did/did not change from beginning of lesson and explain why/why not.

1. Activate Prior Knowledge/Create an Experience
- Teacher and student perform Homework not done simulation.
- Students state problem as they see it and brainstorm ways to deal with the problem.

Assessment
Informally assess students' ability to brainstorm ways to deal with a problem and identify stakeholders in homework not done situation. Develop an organizer to capture the ideas presented in Step 1.

4. Application
- Students work together to complete problem/solution graphic organizer poster.
- Develop role-play which displays best solution to problem.
- Fill in second part of agree/disagree chart.

Problem-Solving/Perspective-Taking Lesson Topic: Deer Problem in PA

2. Declarative knowledge
- Introduce problem/solution frame and fill in four components using homework not done problem situation.
  — Statement of problem
  — Identification of stakeholders
  — Create solutions
  — Judge best solution

Assessment
Informally assess student ability to verbally connect *Bambi* video to larger topic of PA's nature. Check for understanding of problem and stakeholders involved (random/spot check). Assess understanding of instructions for group activity.

3. Procedural Knowledge
- *Bambi* video clip with instructions to identify component of PA advance organizer (AO) exemplified in video (nature).
- Complete first section of agree/disagree chart.
- Hunter/activist simulation to lead students to create advance organizer of four stakeholders involved in deer kill.
- Action news audiotape/written newscast to set stage for problem.
- Group activity to read *Deerly News* excerpts to identify which stakeholder from the AO your group will represent.

Assessment
Using questioning strategies, informally assess student understanding of four components of problem/solution frame.

FIGURE 9.5
Problem-solving unit of instruction.
Lesson reprinted by permission of Allison Kane and Genevieve Hill.

SPOTLIGHT ON BEHAVIOR MANAGEMENT

"But will they behave?"

Putting Together a Plan for Behavior Management

In the final chapter of Charles's (1999) *Building Classroom Discipline,* the author helps teachers prepare for the "three faces of discipline" (Charles 1999, 261). These are "preventative discipline," "supportive discipline," and "corrective discipline." Another way of looking at this might be what you do *before, during, and after* disruptive behavioral events occur in the classroom. In this final spotlight section we would like to help you plan for these three faces of discipline using the core concepts that we have provided. What follows is a list of important ideas to consider. Our space here is limited, so as a follow-up activity, try putting your head together with a colleague to brainstorm further ideas for each section.

Preventive or Before Inappropriate Behavior Occurs

Gain an understanding of the conflict cycle paradigm.

Realize the effects of counteraggression.

Spend time reflecting on your own behavior.

Plan to create an atmosphere of caring and belonging in your classroom.

Learn as much about your students as possible.

Observe.

◎ CORE CONCEPT Everything changes. Society has changed, children have changed, and what we know about how people learn has changed. For the most part schools have not changed. NOW IS THE TIME FOR SCHOOLS TO CHANGE.

Create educational experiences that are engaging and enjoyable.

Construct a classroom environment that meets students' basic needs.

Develop meaningful relationships with each student.

Have clear expectations.

Continue to emphasize that your classroom and school comprise a community.

Find meaningful ways to demonstrate community daily.

Leave your bad moods and personal issues at home.

Look for students' behavioral patterns.

Supportive or When Inappropriate Behavior Occurs

Use the three-step statement (Chapter 4, p. 130) to redirect students.

Use your proximity and communication skills to redirect students who are drifting toward problem behavior.

Do not ignore seemingly insignificant misbehavior.

Intervene early to keep an issue from becoming overblown.

Avoid acting counteraggressively.

Think.

Remove the fuel that escalates the conflict—go to neutral corners.

Deescalate the situation by using I statements and calm body language.

Use crises as opportunities to learn more about a student's thought processes.

Look for the "why" of the behavior rather than the "what."

Have realistic expectations of each student.

Be sure students and adults are calm and thinking rationally before moving on to any corrective feedback or problem solving.

Corrective or After Inappropriate Behavior Occurs

Allow the student to explain the situation.

Listen.

Let the needs of the student rather than diagnostic labels drive your intervention.

Help students see crisis as an opportunity by supporting them in solving problems.

Be consistent in your approach.

Be mindful of meeting your students' needs.

Create hypotheses, reflect, ask further questions—think.

Keep records, notes, or complete an FBA for your most challenging students.

Teach students the skills they need to be successful both academically and socially.

Provide students the opportunity to practice these new skills.

These are just some of the ideas that we raised in the Spotlight on Behavior Management strand in this book. We have asked you to change your perspective and focus heavily on your own thoughts, feelings, and actions. As professional educators we are in the business of interpersonal relationships. Unless there is a strong and meaningful bond between teacher and student, the process of education breaks down. This relationship begins with you and your genuine interest in how your own actions impact your classroom.

The conflict cycle paradigm demonstrates how the thoughts and feelings of individuals interact, sometimes to the detriment of the relationship. We believe that it is extremely important for you to recognize this process and reflect on how you think and act when confronted with others, particularly in situations of conflict.

We want you to realize the importance of curriculum and educational experiences in the management of student behavior. The more thought and energy you put into creating engaging and meaningful educational experiences for your students, the less energy you will have to put into managing their behavior. This book is full of ways for you to do that.

Additionally, you should consider the use of technology, especially the Internet, as a great tool to support your work with students, particularly those students whose behavior is challenging. You can search for information on the Internet. You can also search for people who are in similar circumstances or people who have expertise and are available for consultation and support, both in a formal and informal way. You can "talk" to individual people in chat rooms or newsgroups.

The following are some of our favorite websites:

http://www.reclaiming.com/
The Reclaiming Youth Network provides information and support for youth empowerment called the Circle of Courage.

http://www.at-risk.com/
The Bureau for At-Risk Youth is an educational publisher and distributor of products for teachers and other youth service workers.

http://www.disciplineassociates.com/
Products for managing student behavior.

http://www.nrcys.ou.edu/
The National Resources Center for Youth Services provides training, technical assistance, and publications for children and youth.

www.empowerkids.org
Strength-Based Services International is an organization providing strength-based practices for family and child care practitioners.

http://www.kidspeace.org/
Kids Peace: The National Center for Kids Overcoming Crisis provides mental health treatment, crisis intervention, and public information.

Finally, we want to acknowledge what you are probably thinking by now. This is very hard work! You will sometimes make mistakes or slip into patterns of behavior that you later note were not very helpful. As long as you have a process for examining your own behavior, you will learn from mistakes and not repeat them. Use a journal, a group of colleagues, or even an Internet chat group to discuss and reflect on your own behavior. The more meaningfully you think about your own professional response, the more progress your students will make.

The learners in this classroom were all physically challenged. Most of them needed a "concrete context" because they were not developmentally ready to process abstractions. Hence, the teacher presented a real-world problem (the deer kill problem) yet by having them take multiple perspectives, the teacher also involved them with some abstractions. Because of the wide developmental range, the teacher used heterogeneous groupings so that she could meet the needs of students even as they helped one another to learn and practice the information.

This teacher carefully considered the learners' developmental characteristics as she selected the core concept and topic of the unit. She judged that they were ready to tackle the declarative and procedural knowledge that she planned to teach. Here she used the idea of zone of proximal development that we addressed in Chapter 2. She was already thinking about various grouping strategies that she would employ during instruction. She understood the power of having students work together to learn information, and she also knew that groupings must be made judiciously to enrich the experience of all the learners in the group.

To get a clearer picture of the activities that this teacher put into the organizer, and to see how she used some of the powerful principles and strategies that are likely to produce real conceptual change among her students, we shall now examine the template that she completed and that further details her instructional strategies (see Fig. 9.6).

To activate students' prior knowledge and also gain their attention (Step 1), the teacher employed simulation and brainstorming strategies. The box at right presents her description of her procedures. She also took the opportunity to assess what they might already know about solving problems. Notice how carefully she thought about a way to draw learners into the content to maximize both motivation and the likelihood that they would be able to connect the content to what they already know.

A look at what she wanted them to know (Step 2) indicates that a step-by-step process of problem solving was the major objective and the basis for the declarative knowledge. Specifically, the teacher wanted learners to use a type of organizer called a "problem/solution frame" that required them to (1) restate the problem, (2) identify who cares (stakeholders), (3) create three possible solutions to the problem, and (4) judge the best solution. She referred back to Step 1 as they progressed through Step 2.

The template shows how she used COVER strategies with her learners. The "strategies" box provides an excerpt from her plan that tells how she used several other powerful strategies during Step 2 of this lesson.

Note the level of the questions that she asked the learners. Using Bloom's taxonomy (discussed in Chapter 4), note that the questions go well beyond the knowledge level. In fact, they include the higher levels of application, analysis, and evaluation. Note, too, that this teacher used a specific form of cooperative learning, think-pair-share, to encourage the learners to work with one another. By using a number of different strategies, she increased her chances of meeting the needs of more learners, and their chances of learning the material. For example, extroverted learners enjoy working with others, and concrete sequential learners like the steps involved in the problem-solving process.

1. Teacher and student act out a short scene where student is in trouble for not doing her homework. Students are questioned about what they just saw. The idea of the problem is elicited. Students brainstorm ways they normally handle problems. The problem/solution frame is displayed on chart paper in front of room while simulation and questioning is taking place.

2. Teacher randomly assesses student understanding of stakeholders.

Strategies

Organizers: graphic organizer (problem-solving model).

Questioning: examples of questions used— "After developing three solutions to the problem, how did you choose the best one?" "What makes that solution better than the others?" "Will that solution satisfy both the teacher and the student (both stakeholders) and if so, how?"

Cooperative/group activities: think-pair-share.

Variations for styles: cooperative activity, graphic organizer, problem-solving activity.

Planning Template

Connect: *Bambi* video clip to corresponding component of PA advance organizer (AO), homework not done problem to deer kill in PA problem. **Organize:** Use of advance and graphic organizers, problem/solution frame. **Visualize:** Use of video clip, homework not done and hunter/activist simulations. **Elaboration:** Students elaborate on problems to complete problem/solution frame, role-play activity, second section of agree/disagree chart and in-class learning log. **Rehearsal:** Review of problem/solution frame, use of problem/solution frame to complete homework miniproblem.

C O V E R

[2] Teach Declarative Knowledge
Select core concept, generative topic, or essential question and related ideas, concepts, facts.

G A I N   **A T T E N T I O N**

[1] Activate Prior Knowledge
Cue prior knowledge, encourage personal connection, meaning. Use emotionality and disequilibrium. Provide context.

Teacher/student homework not done simulation. Brainstorming to find ways to deal with problems.

P R A C T I C E   **and**   **F E E D B A C K**

[3] Encourage Procedural Knowledge
Provide opportunities to use ideas, concepts, facts, and assess understanding.

Practice: Group completion of problem/solution frame for hunter/activist problem situation. **Feedback:** Provided by adult and students working within the small groups.

Complete problem/solution frame poster. Develop and complete role-play. Use problem/solution frame introduced during homework not done simulation to solve hunter/activist problem. Complete agree/disagree learning log; compare opinions from start to end of hunter/activist problem.

G E N E R A L I Z E   **and**   **T R A N S F E R**

[4] Application
Apply to other ideas, concepts, facts; apply in new and different ways; apply in life.

Review of AO and problem/solution frame. Debriefing of cooperative learning groups. Homework miniproblem about water pollution situation in Schuykill River.

[5] Closure and Connection
Ending, wrap-up, transition to next generative topic.

FIGURE 9.6

Template completed by teacher detailing instructional strategies.

In order for learners to practice the algorithm for solving a problem (Step 3), the teacher had them create solutions for a problem that recently aired on local television news. Again, note that the children worked together on a real problem by applying the problem-solving strategy they were taught in Step 2 of this lesson.

In this particular lesson plan, the teacher made excellent use of cooperative learning strategies and the principles of connect, organize, and elaborate. She made adjustments to accommodate the wide variety of developmental levels and learning needs of these elementary-age learners. In particular, this teacher used powerful strategies with learners who are physically challenged—a point we stressed in Chapter 6. She adhered to the idea of *less is more* by focusing an entire unit on one substantial concept. Finally, at the end of the unit, the teacher had students apply what they learned about problem solving to a problem involving water pollution that they had not seen earlier. A look back at the planning organizer (Fig. 9.5) shows that she used a variety of informal assessment techniques during each step of the unit, rather than doing only the summative assessment that followed the completion of the entire unit. In this unit and in each of its lessons, we see evidence of the use of many of the core concepts that are included in this textbook.

3. The children are told that they will work together to create solutions to the deer kill problem and will have help when they need it. They are given the following oral directions:

- Once in groups, they will read two letters to the editor in the *Philadelphia Deerly News*. Each letter contains an opposing view related to the deer kill problem. (Review concerned parties from the advance organizer.)

- Students fill in the blank sections on a poster-size problem/solution frame (the frame is color coded by section).

- They will identify and restate the problem between the two concerned parties.

- They will then generate possible compromises/solutions to the problem.

- They will discuss their solutions and pick the best one. They will prepare to role-play their solution for the other group.

Example 2: Area of Irregular Polygons

This example features a high school math teacher. She has developed a unit of instruction with the overall objective of having the learners "develop steps needed to determine the area of any irregular polygon." She explains the developmental characteristics of this group of learners as follows:

Developmental Characteristics (Cognitive, Social, and Emotional)

I teach at Saint Hubert High School for Girls. So first, let me explain the social characteristics of my students. These characteristics are very closely tied to their physical characteristics. All the students look alike. Fortunately, they wear uniforms, so they don't have to worry about their clothes. However, they all seem to wear their hair the same way, which is pulled back in a ponytail. One day I was examining my classes and 95% of my students had their hair in ponytails. The remaining students had short hair. Many times they ask for their peers' opinions on how they should get their hair done. For example, they ask if they should dye their hair, cut it, highlight it, and so on. They are seeking acceptance from their peers before they change their hairstyle.

Because I deal with girls all day, I often see the social conflicts these girls have with one another because of envy or anxiety. These emotions are more common with females than with males. I have witnessed many conflicts where hurt feelings were very deep and the students shouted at each other and cried. I have to be the mediator during these conflicts and I try to help them work through the problems. Girls form very close friendships with one another and when their trust is broken it is very devastating for them.

Regarding emotional characteristics, I have one student at the present who is suffering from severe panic attacks and depression. She is out several weeks at a time and has spent some time at Friends Hospital. She gets physically sick during these emotional attacks. I have also had students with eating disorders. It is very distressing to see such young girls dealing with so much anxiety and stress that they are suffering from these "disorders." It not only affects them emotionally, but it is often accompanied by physical ailments.

Girls at this age are also eager to gain the approval of their teachers. I am very conscious of trying to compliment them when they do well on a test or when they are trying to understand a concept that has been very confusing for them. Many of my students say that they are stupid when they do not do well on a test. I tell them that they are not stupid and I ask them to come and see me so I can help them with what they had problems with on the test. Often, they realize that something was just not clear and once I explain it they understand what they did wrong.

Finally, I will discuss the cognitive characteristics of adolescents. In high school, the students are starting to move into higher-order thinking and are developing problem-solving skills. Teachers can begin to ask them to think more abstractly. I often try to ask my students open-ended questions to get them to think about things in real life and see how math applies to these things.

Furthermore, teachers need to be aware of how self-conscious girls are at this age. When I have students go to the blackboard, I will always call on many students to go up to the board at the same time so they are not alone. I let them volunteer to go up, because several of them are very uncomfortable going to the board in front of their peers. I will call on them randomly to answer questions verbally in class, but I will not force them to go to the blackboard.

Source: Lesson reprinted by permission of Kristie McGovern.

Building from these characteristics and the content standards that she must help the students meet, this teacher sketched out the unit of instruction (see Fig. 9.7).

A quick look at the structure of the unit in Figure 9.7 shows that a fairly significant amount of time will be spent on one major concept; a concept, by the way, that might typically be "covered" during a single-period lecture. This teacher is going to make use of an advance organizer to help students remember what they already know about area and polygons, and she will use a real-life problem to make this concept practical and meaningful for the learners. She has a clear focus on what declarative knowledge she wants them to know, and rather than tell them what it is, she will actively involve them in constructing that information under her guidance. Then she will have her learners apply what they have learned to another, similar problem, and finally to a real-life problem of their own making.

One of the strategies this teacher employs involves using a problem to actively engage the learners at the outset of the lesson. Her instructional procedures for Step 1 illustrate this technique (see Fig. 9.8).

Her instructional procedures in Step 2 indicate her determination to lead her learners to deduce meaning, rather than just telling them what to do and having them repeat it (see Fig. 9.9). Through the use of cooperative group work and skillful questioning strategies, the teacher provides scaffolding to support learners' efforts as they work through the problem of finding the area of an irregular polygon. She also plans to carefully assess their progress as they do their work.

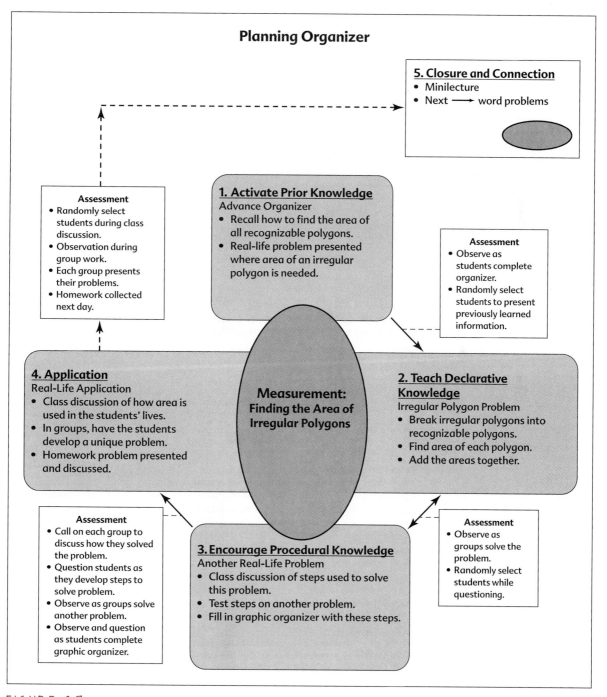

FIGURE 9.7

Measurement unit of instruction.

(Source: Lesson written by Kristie A. McGovern.)

In Step 3, the students articulate the steps they used to arrive at an answer for the problem they confronted (see Fig. 9.10). Then they use these steps to solve a different, authentic problem. Finally, they complete a graphic organizer in order to help them put together what they deduced in a connected fashion.

Instructional Procedures — STEP 1
(Check box to designate step of Organizer)

This lesson follows the indirect model of instruction. First, hand out the advance organizer, Form A. (Form B is the completed advance organizer.) To recall the students' prior knowledge question them regarding the shapes shown and the area formulas they have learned for each of these shapes (type 1—convergent). This will get them ready to learn the next topic, the area of irregular polygons.

The deductive method is used for this lesson. Therefore, the next step will be to present the overall topic for the lesson. At this point, introduce students to the real-life problem related to this topic. Move the desks into a circle around the center of the room. Have a very large cutout of an irregular shape that will be placed on the floor (see figure below). Tell the students that you want to design a rug for under the teacher's desk in this shape. You need to know how much material you should buy to make this rug. Question the students here so they can tell you how you can find the total material needed (type 2—divergent). This will relate the problem to the topic presented to them. To help them solve this problem, have all different sizes of carpet remnants in the shape of circles, ovals, rectangles, triangles, squares, and parallelograms so they can try to find a way to design this carpet. Show the students all the remnants they are able to use.

ASSESSMENT:
• Teacher observation as students complete the advance organizer.
• Teacher randomly selects students to give previously learned information for the organizer.

FIGURE 9.8

Teacher's instructional procedures, Step 1.

Instructional Procedures — STEP 2
(Check box to designate step of Organizer)

First, the students work together in small groups of three or four to come up with a plan to solve this problem. Once they develop a plan, they can get to work trying to piece together the irregular shape using the remnants. Let them play around with these remnants until they come up with the shape of the cutout. By including all different shapes, there are both examples and nonexamples of carpeting that will help form these irregular shapes. For example, the circles and ovals will never be used because all polygons are formed by line segments. You will never have a curved polygon. The students will need to try all different combinations until they find the one that will form this shape, which is a rectangle with a triangle on either end.

After they have pieced together this shape, ask them questions regarding how they found these pieces (divergent). Ask them if they tried to use a circle or oval and make sure they know why those shapes will not be used. Next, try to steer them in the direction of determining the total area of this newly designed shape. They know how to measure objects, so use questioning to get them to measure the necessary items of each shape. For example, they need to measure the base and height of the triangle and the length and width of the rectangle. More questioning will lead them to finding the area of each separate polygon and adding them all together to find the total area. (The questions will involve a series of convergent and divergent questions.) Throughout this whole process, the students will be evaluating their own work and the work of others to help guide one another to find the area. They will need to work together to try to solve this problem. Because the carpet remnants and cutout figure are large, they will need to help each other find the needed areas.

ASSESSMENT:
• Teacher observation as groups solve the real-life problem.
• Teacher randomly selects students while questioning them.

FIGURE 9.9

Teacher's instructional procedures, Step 2.

Instructional Procedures — STEP 3
(Check box to designate step of Organizer)

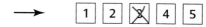

At this point again use questions to try to get them to develop the three steps they used to arrive at their answer. Do not write these on the organizer yet. Have them *test* their "new" steps on another real-life project. This project involves planting a garden in the shape given below. Have another large cutout and ask them if their steps can help find the area to plant this garden, because you need to buy soil on the way home from school. At this point they are again using the carpet remnants and helping one another with the answer. They are testing their proposed steps to solving the problem. Use questioning if they are having problems in any area of this new situation.

After evaluating their proposed steps, the class will then be able to fill in the bottom of their organizer (graphic organizer). The class started out with the overall topic and through experimentation broke it down into three steps that can be used to help with any area problem.

ASSESSMENT:
• Teacher calls on each group to discuss how they solved the real-life problem.
• Teacher questioning while students develop formal steps to solve the problem.
• Teacher observation as the groups solve another problem.
• Teacher questioning and observation as students fill in the organizer.

FIGURE 9.10

Teacher's instructional procedures, Step 3.

Her unit concludes with a discussion of ways that what students have learned relates to problems they may confront in the "real world," and the assignment to design a project that involves finding the area of an irregular polygon (see Fig. 9.11). Because so much of this unit requires group work, the procedures in Step 4 specify a substantial homework assignment that will be used to assess each learner's mastery of the concept of area and ability to find the area of an irregular polygon.

Rather than teach this concept and the related skill directly in the usual fashion, this math teacher plans to employ indirect instruction and a number of powerful principles and strategies to help her learners see the concepts that underlie finding the area (in this case, of irregular polygons). She will use authentic problems and lots of formative assessment. She is cognizant of the need to hold individual learners accountable for learning the information. She will take lots of time to allow the learners to deeply process the information that she wants them to understand.

Real Plans for Real Learners

Please remember that these plans are authentic and not scripted. That is, real teachers plan to use them with real learners, in real classrooms. We use them to illustrate some, but not all, of the core concepts and powerful principles and strategies that we address in this book. No teacher will use *every* concept or strategy in lesson planning or in teaching. Adhering to the spirit of the core concepts is just as important as adhering to the exact words of each one.

These two teachers, and many others that we know, understand that traditional instruction has some limitations, and that we must change what we do in our classrooms in light of new research on teaching and learning. So they plan accordingly.

Instructional Procedures — STEP 4 $\longrightarrow$
(Check box to designate step of Organizer)

The next segment of the lesson is to ask the class as a large group to discuss any experience they have had where they need to find the area of any polygons. During this group discussion, they can share any experiences they have had with their classmates. Use questioning to help them (divergent). For example, ask them if they were ever involved in painting or wallpapering a room, or if they ever helped a relative sew clothing. Then the class can discuss how area is used in each of these projects.

Then tell them to work in smaller groups and design their own unique project that will require the class to find the area of an irregular polygon. Help the groups develop these projects. Make sure each group is ready to discuss their work with the whole class. When all the groups are ready, again have the whole room get together to discuss their unique projects.

For homework, give them an activity that can be used to assess their learning and to cover individual accountability. Have them pick one irregularly shaped object in their house that fits the definition of a polygon. Ask them to describe it and draw a sketch of the object. Then ask them to give all the necessary dimensions of the object needed to find the area. As they compute the area of the whole shape using their three steps, ask them to explain each step and show their work. After explaining this homework project to the class, the students should make sure they understand the topic and the steps involved and discuss with their groups what they are going to do for homework. Tell them to make sure everyone in the group is prepared to accomplish the homework assignment.

ASSESSMENT:
• Teacher calls on each group to discuss how they solved the real-life problem.
• Teacher questioning while students develop formal steps to solve the problem.
• Teacher observation as the groups solve another problem.
• Teacher questioning and observation as students fill in the organizer.

FIGURE 9.11

Teacher's instructional procedures, Step 4.

- They allow their learners to work together to learn new information and practice new skills.

- They strive to use examples and problems that their learners will find meaningful and to which the learners can make very personal connections.

- They encourage their learners to think about what they already know about the topic and content, and they help the learners organize, visualize, and elaborate upon information as it is being learned.

- They allow the learners to practice using the new ideas, concepts, and facts that they are learning, and they provide ample, specific feedback to their learners.

- They take the time necessary to help their learners deeply process information. That means that their units focus on less material, and attempt to help the learners generalize and transfer what they learn to new contexts.

- They base their plans and their instructional strategies on their learners' developmental characteristics so that modeling and scaffolding techniques can move the learners to higher conceptual levels.

- They provide sufficiently varied learning activities to enhance the likelihood that learners with different learning styles will be able to benefit from the lessons, and they adjust activities as necessary on the basis of formative assessment.

- They employ fewer traditional tests, and many more performance and authentic assessments, to judge how well their learners have mastered the objectives of the units and lessons.

The illustration on the next page presents four more examples of unit organizers from various levels of basic education. They will give you an overview of the activities that have been planned by each teacher.

Learning and Teaching in the Age of Technology

Roblyer, Edwards, and Havriluk (1997) highlight our feelings of intimidation at the breakneck speed of change and the responsibility we feel as educators to bring the most powerful tools to our students: "Many teachers feel threatened by this challenge, for one reason, because it represents a journey into the unknown. Technology's well-recognized pattern of rapid change complicates this problem; just when you get used to one machine or software option, it changes and you have to learn another one" (47–48). There is hope that interfaces will continue to get easier and more user friendly, more software will be available in interactive easily accessible CD-ROM formats, and computers will not continue to be outdated when you buy them. The only constant is change, and that is the world awaiting our students. On the other hand, the kind of healthy structuring of positive, nonthreatening learning climates that promote collaboration, flexibility, openness, high expectations and standards, will serve us all well in the face of such perplexing change.

Though all the research isn't conclusive, we have enough experience with technology in education to see that it helps gain learner attention; engages learners through productive work; increases learners' perception of control; links them to information sources, helping them visualize problems and solutions; tracks learner progress, linking learners to learning tools; supports and stimulates cooperative learning and shared intelligence; and helps scaffold problem-solving and higher-level skills. All of this frees teachers to work with students on production tasks rather than record keeping, provides more accurate information to teachers more quickly, and allows teachers to produce better-looking, more student-friendly materials more quickly (Roblyer, Edwards, and Havriluk 1997, 29).

Walker (1999) summarizes most of what we have tried to convey in Teaching and Learning in the Age of Technology by suggesting that future generations will value the ability to use information technology as highly as we value the abilities to read and write today. She succinctly outlines the expectations of the next generation of educated Americans as people who will use several symbol systems, apply knowledge to life, think strategically, manage information, and learn, think, and create as part of a team (18–19). It is our task to help our students meet these well-articulated expectations.

◎ **CORE CONCEPT** Everything changes. Society has changed, children have changed, and what we know about how people learn has changed. For the most part schools have not changed. NOW IS THE TIME FOR SCHOOLS TO CHANGE.

SAMPLE ORGANIZERS

Elementary School Unit

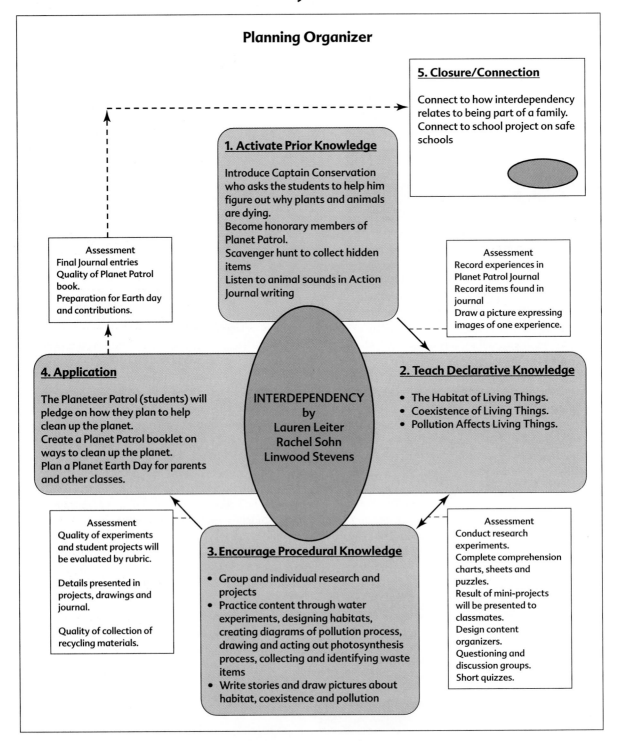

Planning Organizer

5. Closure/Connection

Connect to how interdependency relates to being part of a family. Connect to school project on safe schools

1. Activate Prior Knowledge

Introduce Captain Conservation who asks the students to help him figure out why plants and animals are dying.
Become honorary members of Planet Patrol.
Scavenger hunt to collect hidden items
Listen to animal sounds in Action Journal writing

Assessment
Final Journal entries
Quality of Planet Patrol book.
Preparation for Earth day and contributions.

Assessment
Record experiences in Planet Patrol Journal
Record items found in journal
Draw a picture expressing images of one experience.

4. Application

The Planeteer Patrol (students) will pledge on how they plan to help clean up the planet.
Create a Planet Patrol booklet on ways to clean up the planet.
Plan a Planet Earth Day for parents and other classes.

INTERDEPENDENCY
by
Lauren Leiter
Rachel Sohn
Linwood Stevens

2. Teach Declarative Knowledge

- The Habitat of Living Things.
- Coexistence of Living Things.
- Pollution Affects Living Things.

Assessment
Quality of experiments and student projects will be evaluated by rubric.

Details presented in projects, drawings and journal.

Quality of collection of recycling materials.

3. Encourage Procedural Knowledge

- Group and individual research and projects
- Practice content through water experiments, designing habitats, creating diagrams of pollution process, drawing and acting out photosynthesis process, collecting and identifying waste items
- Write stories and draw pictures about habitat, coexistence and pollution

Assessment
Conduct research experiments.
Complete comprehension charts, sheets and puzzles.
Result of mini-projects will be presented to classmates.
Design content organizers.
Questioning and discussion groups.
Short quizzes.

(Source: Reprinted by permission of Lauren Leiter, Rachel Sohn, and Linwood Stevens.)

Middle School Unit

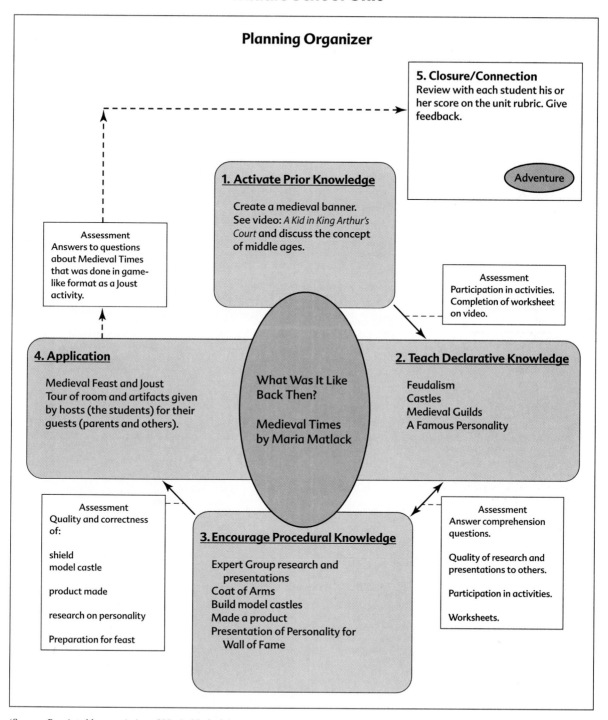

Planning Organizer

5. Closure/Connection
Review with each student his or her score on the unit rubric. Give feedback.

Adventure

1. Activate Prior Knowledge

Create a medieval banner. See video: *A Kid in King Arthur's Court* and discuss the concept of middle ages.

Assessment
Answers to questions about Medieval Times that was done in game-like format as a Joust activity.

Assessment
Participation in activities. Completion of worksheet on video.

4. Application

Medieval Feast and Joust Tour of room and artifacts given by hosts (the students) for their guests (parents and others).

What Was It Like Back Then?

Medieval Times by Maria Matlack

2. Teach Declarative Knowledge

Feudalism
Castles
Medieval Guilds
A Famous Personality

Assessment
Quality and correctness of:

shield
model castle

product made

research on personality

Preparation for feast

3. Encourage Procedural Knowledge

Expert Group research and
    presentations
Coat of Arms
Build model castles
Made a product
Presentation of Personality for
    Wall of Fame

Assessment
Answer comprehension questions.

Quality of research and presentations to others.

Participation in activities.

Worksheets.

(Source: Reprinted by permission of Maria Matlack.)

High School Unit

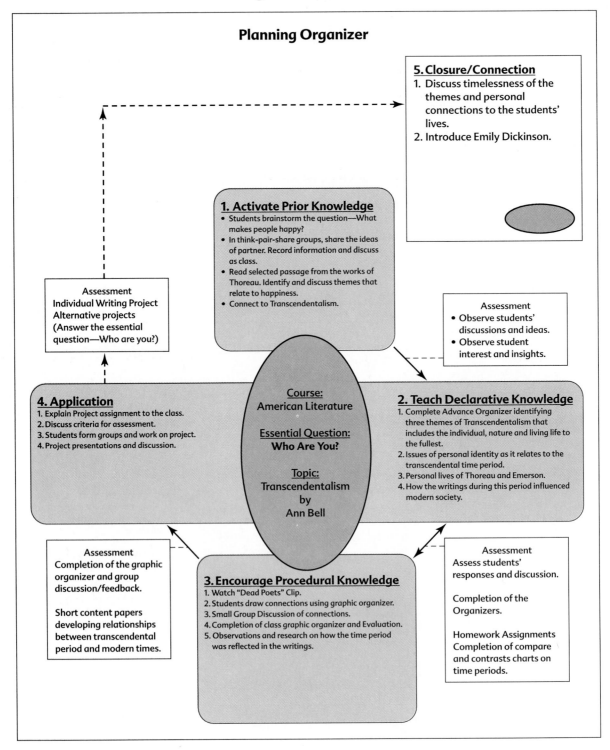

Planning Organizer

5. Closure/Connection
1. Discuss timelessness of the themes and personal connections to the students' lives.
2. Introduce Emily Dickinson.

1. Activate Prior Knowledge
- Students brainstorm the question—What makes people happy?
- In think-pair-share groups, share the ideas of partner. Record information and discuss as class.
- Read selected passage from the works of Thoreau. Identify and discuss themes that relate to happiness.
- Connect to Transcendentalism.

Assessment
Individual Writing Project
Alternative projects
(Answer the essential question—Who are you?)

Assessment
- Observe students' discussions and ideas.
- Observe student interest and insights.

Course:
American Literature

Essential Question:
Who Are You?

Topic:
Transcendentalism
by
Ann Bell

4. Application
1. Explain Project assignment to the class.
2. Discuss criteria for assessment.
3. Students form groups and work on project.
4. Project presentations and discussion.

2. Teach Declarative Knowledge
1. Complete Advance Organizer identifying three themes of Transcendentalism that includes the individual, nature and living life to the fullest.
2. Issues of personal identity as it relates to the transcendental time period.
3. Personal lives of Thoreau and Emerson.
4. How the writings during this period influenced modern society.

Assessment
Completion of the graphic organizer and group discussion/feedback.

Short content papers developing relationships between transcendental period and modern times.

3. Encourage Procedural Knowledge
1. Watch "Dead Poets" Clip.
2. Students draw connections using graphic organizer.
3. Small Group Discussion of connections.
4. Completion of class graphic organizer and Evaluation.
5. Observations and research on how the time period was reflected in the writings.

Assessment
Assess students' responses and discussion.

Completion of the Organizers.

Homework Assignments
Completion of compare and contrasts charts on time periods.

(Source: Reprinted by permission of Ann Bell.)

Special Education Unit

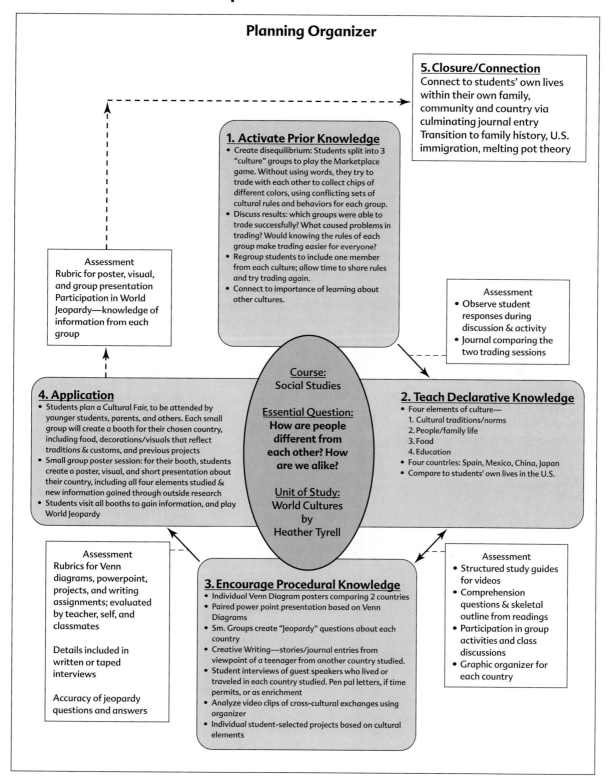

Planning Organizer

5. Closure/Connection
Connect to students' own lives within their own family, community and country via culminating journal entry Transition to family history, U.S. immigration, melting pot theory

1. Activate Prior Knowledge
- Create disequilibrium: Students split into 3 "culture" groups to play the Marketplace game. Without using words, they try to trade with each other to collect chips of different colors, using conflicting sets of cultural rules and behaviors for each group.
- Discuss results: which groups were able to trade successfully? What caused problems in trading? Would knowing the rules of each group make trading easier for everyone?
- Regroup students to include one member from each culture; allow time to share rules and try trading again.
- Connect to importance of learning about other cultures.

Assessment
Rubric for poster, visual, and group presentation Participation in World Jeopardy—knowledge of information from each group

Assessment
- Observe student responses during discussion & activity
- Journal comparing the two trading sessions

Course:
Social Studies

Essential Question:
How are people different from each other? How are we alike?

Unit of Study:
World Cultures
by
Heather Tyrell

4. Application
- Students plan a Cultural Fair, to be attended by younger students, parents, and others. Each small group will create a booth for their chosen country, including food, decorations/visuals that reflect traditions & customs, and previous projects
- Small group poster session: for their booth, students create a poster, visual, and short presentation about their country, including all four elements studied & new information gained through outside research
- Students visit all booths to gain information, and play World Jeopardy

2. Teach Declarative Knowledge
- Four elements of culture—
  1. Cultural traditions/norms
  2. People/family life
  3. Food
  4. Education
- Four countries: Spain, Mexico, China, Japan
- Compare to students' own lives in the U.S.

Assessment
Rubrics for Venn diagrams, powerpoint, projects, and writing assignments; evaluated by teacher, self, and classmates

Details included in written or taped interviews

Accuracy of jeopardy questions and answers

3. Encourage Procedural Knowledge
- Individual Venn Diagram posters comparing 2 countries
- Paired power point presentation based on Venn Diagrams
- Sm. Groups create "Jeopardy" questions about each country
- Creative Writing—stories/journal entries from viewpoint of a teenager from another country studied.
- Student interviews of guest speakers who lived or traveled in each country studied. Pen pal letters, if time permits, or as enrichment
- Analyze video clips of cross-cultural exchanges using organizer
- Individual student-selected projects based on cultural elements

Assessment
- Structured study guides for videos
- Comprehension questions & skeletal outline from readings
- Participation in group activities and class discussions
- Graphic organizer for each country

(Source: Reprinted by permission of Heather Terrell.)

A Word about Interdisciplinary Units

We have not written much in this chapter about interdisciplinary units of instruction. Such units would cut across subject and skill areas to help learners see more clearly the interconnectedness of knowledge. For example, even though it is not readily apparent from the organizer because of space limitations, the "medieval times" unit titled *What Was It Like Back Then* combines social studies, math, language arts, art, and music. Students must figure out averages in a jousting activity, and they must read stories and demonstrate comprehension skills. They examine art forms and listen to music. To the extent such planning is feasible, interdisciplinary units take maximum advantage of the natural tendency of human learners to make connections among the ideas, concepts, and skills with which they are confronted. At the elementary level, a teacher in her own classroom can often implement interdisciplinary units. She need simply use a theme (such as the one in the medieval times example) and connect all the other subjects to one another through the thematic strand. In high school classrooms, interdisciplinary units will take a bit more team planning. Teachers from various disciplines will have to co-plan lessons and units to provide learners with opportunities to make connections among the ideas and skills from the different subjects. Wonderful things happen when an art teacher and a math teacher combine their plans and focus on trigonometric functions. Or when a music teacher and a social studies teacher get together and plan a unit on "unlocking culture through music." We have witnessed the very positive results on learner motivation and achievement when teachers approach their units across disciplines.

This is what teachers do if they want to promote, *really promote,* conceptual change among their learners. Learners have changed conceptually *not* when they can parrot back the words of the teacher, or pass a test that requires only recognition or recall of facts. They have changed conceptually when they understand major ideas, facts, and concepts that underlie a body of knowledge, and demonstrate this understanding by engaging in performances such as solving problems or doing any number of higher-order tasks. When we change conceptually, we change forever. We look at problems and opportunities in ways that we were not able to look at them before. We read and write and calculate in substantially different, more expert, ways than we did before that change. The plans that these teachers have constructed are much more likely to bring about conceptual change than are plans that emphasize lecture, limited discussion, and traditional tests.

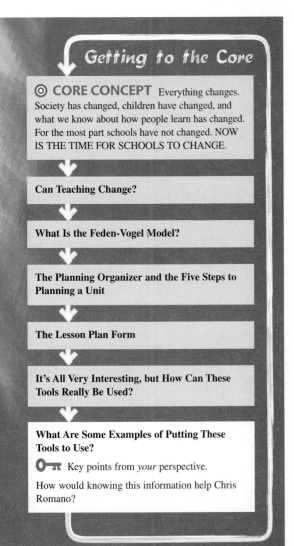

Getting to the Core

◉ **CORE CONCEPT** Everything changes. Society has changed, children have changed, and what we know about how people learn has changed. For the most part schools have not changed. NOW IS THE TIME FOR SCHOOLS TO CHANGE.

Can Teaching Change?

What Is the Feden-Vogel Model?

The Planning Organizer and the Five Steps to Planning a Unit

The Lesson Plan Form

It's All Very Interesting, but How Can These Tools Really Be Used?

What Are Some Examples of Putting These Tools to Use?

⊶ Key points from *your* perspective.

How would knowing this information help Chris Romano?

  ѕСЕΝΑRΙΟ REVISITED

We now ask that you revisit the scenario that we presented at the beginning of this chapter. Answer the questions yet again, using what you have learned from reading this and previous chapters. You might encounter this scenario during student teaching, especially if you use the ideas that you encountered in this textbook. So read A Voice from the Field very carefully.

? *How would you suggest Chris negotiate her way through this dilemma? First,*
restate the problem. Next, think about several specific changes Chris might
make that would be the least intrusive. Then suggest a way for her to approach
Mr. Bullock about using some of her approaches. Finally, think about what she
means by "things were going well in that classroom." What do you think that
means, and does not mean?

 # A VOICE FROM THE FIELD

Chris's dilemma is not unlike the situations that many student teachers face in
their classrooms. From their university coursework and coordinating experiences
with children, they have an ideal image of education. Chris sees herself applying
her knowledge and skills and helping students learn in a "real" school. Unfortunately, much of what she has learned is not yet being practiced in America's
schools. Chris finds herself in an environment in which the students and teachers
are unaccustomed to the variety of instructional strategies and activities that
she plans to implement.

Although Mr. Bullock has made his classroom and his students available to
Chris to practice and develop her teaching skills, she is a guest in his classroom.
She expects that he will be inclined to work with her and encourage her to apply
what she has learned in her teacher education program. However, Mr. Bullock
has a very different teaching style, he has not been exposed to the recent theories about how children learn, and he is under pressure to cover the district's curriculum. His methods seem to be working for him on the surface, so he may resist
supporting Chris's new approach to teaching.

The key element to a successful student teaching experience is open communication between the student teacher, cooperating teacher, and university
supervisor. Many cooperating teachers are very welcoming and offer the student teacher freedom in planning lessons, borrowing resources, and managing
students' behaviors. However, because she is a new teacher in his classroom,
Chris should talk to Mr. Bullock about his expectations for her so they reach an
understanding about her responsibilities as his student teacher, her access to
his supplies and materials, and how much input he will have in her lessons.
Chris should ask specific questions about the classroom management plan that
is in place, including rules, consequences, rewards, and acceptable and unacceptable behaviors. Chris also needs to inquire about the structure of the
school day and how flexible it can be, as well as the content material for each
subject area.

At the same time, Chris should make Mr. Bullock aware of her course requirements. For example, she can give him a copy of her syllabus so he understands
that she is expected to use cooperative learning and to adjust her lessons to
meet individual needs. Chris can also explain how she sees her role in the classroom to give him an idea of the teaching methods and strategies that will pervade her lessons. The two should work together to devise a clear action plan, or
schedule, of the sequence in which Chris will assume teaching responsibilities in
the classroom.

Most important, Chris needs to get to know her students. Through her own observations and interactions with the children and through frequent discussions with Mr. Bullock, it is essential for Chris to find out what interests and motivates the students as well as their individual needs and abilities.

A clear and consistent line of communication between Mr. Bullock and Chris will promote an optimal learning environment for the children. Providing Mr. Bullock with a copy of her lesson plans each week will allow him to offer advice and ask questions. With the same plan in mind, they can work as a team.

By suggesting that "things were going well in that classroom," Chris probably meant that she observed few disruptions. Perhaps the children follow classroom rules and teacher directions and seem to complete their assignments. Mr. Bullock is a kind and enthusiastic man whom the students respect, yet he is firm and enforces a strict classroom discipline plan so the students rarely act out. They know he means what he says.

On the other hand, an orderly classroom environment does not ensure that the students are learning. Although the students appear to be working quietly, worksheets that provide drill and practice and require only recall of facts do not help the students make connections to the new information. Also, Chris should closely observe what the students are working on during independent seat work time. It is not uncommon for them to complete homework assignments for other subjects or to look at unrelated reading materials or activities if the teacher does not monitor their progress.

Research affirms that children learn best in cooperation with others by actively processing information that they find personally meaningful. Because Mr. Bullock uses primarily lecture and independent reading and writing activities, it is unlikely that he is reaching many of his students. In fact, very few children are able to learn through solely independent, paper and pencil tasks. "Things in the classroom," in terms of students' gaining new knowledge, are not necessarily going well.

Although Chris recognizes the problem in Mr. Bullock's classroom and has plans to improve it, she cannot introduce a variety of new instructional strategies and tools all at once. After all, changes in education do not occur overnight and inflicting too many changes in the children's routines would be ineffective and overwhelming for them. Chris must plan to lead the students through each new strategy and activity in clear, step-by-step demonstrations.

Chris is on the right track in exploring the textbooks and curriculum guides and choosing key ideas or core concepts around which to plan her units of instruction. Thematic units are valuable instructional tools that will permit Chris to lead her students to deeper understanding of the facts and ideas within the context of an interesting, central question. Using the 4MAT system, incorporating visual aids and organizers, asking more thought-provoking questions, and posing problems that are personally relevant to students are smooth ways for Chris to transition the class into methods of instruction that differ from Mr. Bullock's. Slowly, Chris will transfer ownership of learning to the students.

In order for students to achieve greater understanding of the concepts explored in class and to apply these concepts to the world outside of school, Chris can improve the quality of in-class and at-home assignments. Rather than calculating answers, memorizing notes, and writing words in isolation, students could be challenged to practice and to demonstrate their knowledge in meaningful ways. Chris can make these changes without significantly altering the structure of the classroom.

As Chris introduces each new instructional strategy to the students, she also needs to teach them the skills necessary to effectively use the strategy. For instance, she cannot assume that students know how to participate in discussions, find main ideas, make comparisons, use research materials, and so forth.

Once Chris establishes herself in the classroom and earns the students' respect and the students begin to feel comfortable taking more control of their learning, Chris can create meaningful real-life experiences for them and utilize powerful tools such as cooperative learning and project-based learning. Again, it is vital for Chris to teach directly the skills needed to work cooperatively, to utilize a variety of resources, and to organize information. Students should have an opportunity to practice the new skills with specific feedback before applying them on their own. Prior to rearranging desks and furniture and making additional resources available to students, Chris should consult with Mr. Bullock and provide him with a copy of her plans. By providing the students with a multitude of opportunities to explain, generalize, find evidence and examples, apply, analogize, and represent the information in new ways, Chris will help all her learners succeed.

While sharing her lesson plans and unit organizers with Mr. Bullock, Chris will give him an explicit, thorough and written explanation of the students' goals and objectives for understanding. He can also survey the skills and activities that she uses to foster understanding and appreciation of key concepts. Furthermore, he will observe the effectiveness of her methods in class by watching the students' level of engagement and motivation increase as they participate in hands-on, cooperative activities. Mr. Bullock is used to a structured classroom setting, so if Chris wants him to consider her style she must carefully organize and develop a specific classroom management plan for each lesson. He will not be open to incorporating teaching strategies that compromise order in the room.

To give Mr. Bullock concrete evidence of students' learning, Chris can involve him in assessing students' work. Chris has learned to design activities and projects, or "performances of understanding," as authentic assessments of students' understanding. By showing Mr. Bullock descriptions of the assignments given to the students and explaining to him the rubrics used to evaluate the students' work, Chris will demonstrate how the students not only remember the information, but also can use it in new ways. Hopefully, Mr. Bullock will recognize that leading students to develop problem-solving and critical thinking skills is far more valuable to them than teaching them to recall isolated facts.

Student teaching will be both a challenging and fulfilling experience for Chris. Despite the obstacles that she may encounter, Chris needs to stay focused on her goal—to teach for understanding. At times she may be tempted to succumb to the traditional, teacher-centered methods of her cooperating teacher which require much less preparation. However, Chris has the knowledge and the skills to help children grow and learn and to inspire change in education.

This is the voice of Erin McVan. Erin is a recent graduate of La Salle University. She distinguished herself as a student teacher for two semesters, one in a special education classroom and one in a regular elementary education classroom. She was the recipient of the La Salle University Department of Education Award for academic excellence.

PLANNING FOR INSTRUCTION

> ⊚ **CORE CONCEPT** Everything changes.
> Society has changed, children have changed, and
> what we know about how people learn has changed.
> For the most part schools have not changed. NOW
> IS THE TIME FOR SCHOOLS TO CHANGE.

Well, you've done it! You have planned for instruction. If you worked through all the chapters in this book, you ended up in this chapter simply filling in the blanks on the thinking tools we have provided. Armed with the big ideas (expressed as core concepts) presented in this book, and plenty of practice thinking about and using them, you are poised to change the way traditional classrooms operate.

We leave you with full-size copies of the organizer, template, and lesson plan form. Along with our *tools* goes our permission for you to copy them freely and use them as you go about *applying cognitive science to promote student learning*. That is, after all, what this book is all about.

Best wishes for a successful teaching career!

CHAPTER SUMMARY

In this, our final chapter, we have encouraged you to put all the ideas presented in earlier chapters together into a coherent "whole." This is important in order to understand and be able to use these ideas. Figure 9.12 is a rendering of the way a group of teachers with whom we recently worked put some of the concepts together for themselves.

Can teaching change? You bet it can! To help you think about newer ideas about teaching, we offer some "thinking tools" for your consideration, along with our permission for you to copy and use them in your planning and teaching. These tools include an organizer, a template, and a plan form. We caution you not to use them in recipe-like fashion; instead, we encourage you to use them as tools to help you to incorporate the powerful principles and strategies that are derived from cognitive science into your teaching. The tools help you keep your plans and your lessons consistent with the core concepts, or big ideas, about what we now know and understand about teaching and learning.

> `Think about it . . .` In the teachers'
> rendering above,
> can you:
> - Explain what connections they made among the concepts that they chose to depict?
> - Interpret the picture (much as you might one that hangs in an art gallery)? What does it "say" to the onlooker?
>
> What picture might you draw? Why?

As it turns out, well before you arrived at this chapter you had already laid out the plans for a unit and a lesson that are consistent with the tools we now share. In the Planning for Instruction sections of each chapter, you carefully and deliberately built an instructional sequence that could simply be plugged into these tools. So you have already proceeded through all the thinking that goes into promoting student learning through powerful instruction.

Nevertheless, we did want to show you some examples of teacher's plans that adhere to the principles and strategies that we call *powerful*. We chose an elementary-level and a secondary-level example for you to review, and we provided some guidance and interpretation so that you could discern more easily the major ideas being used by each teacher. These plans are meant to provide models for you and to make concrete what can sometimes seem rather abstract—notions such as scaffolding, COVER, zone of proximal development, and so forth.

FIGURE 9.12
Teaching & Learning: A Synthesis

We truly hope that this chapter has, indeed, helped you put together the core concepts, ideas, and practices that will help you effect change in American classrooms. And just in case you are still unsure about what change is necessary—*classrooms need to change from places where teachers tell students what they want them to know,* and then students tell the information back to the teachers, *to places where teachers guide students to deep understandings by actively engaging them in substantial, authentic learning activities.*

Getting to the Core

Can Teaching Change?

- Yes. Change is possible if teachers employ the ideas, techniques, and practices featured throughout this book, ideas that are consistent with and continue to emerge from cognitive science.

- To accomplish instruction that promotes deep learning, you will need a solid plan of action that will help you conceptualize your ideas, plan your instruction, and evaluate how effectively it worked to promote learning among your students.

> ◎ **CORE CONCEPT** Everything changes. Society has changed, children have changed, and what we know about how people learn has changed. For the most part schools have not changed. NOW IS THE TIME FOR SCHOOLS TO CHANGE.

What Is the Feden-Vogel Model? (Core Concepts upon Which Our Model Is Based)

- The Feden-Vogel Model is a set of tools that can help you plan for, teach, and assess conceptual change among the learners with whom you work. It is based on successful practices of excellent teachers and on powerful principles from cognitive science such as IPT, social learning theory, and the 4MAT system.

- The model is also based on each of the nine core concepts presented throughout each chapter of this book.

- The model is comprised of three different pieces or tools: (1) the Planning Organizer, (2) the Planning Template, and (3) the Lesson Plan Form.

The Planning Organizer and the Five Steps to Planning a Unit

- This organizer is designed to help you plan for a unit of instruction that is based around a core idea, essential question, or generative topic.

Step 2: Teach Knowledge

- Begin planning with Step 2—the declarative knowledge that you want your learners to know and learn. This includes not only the content, but also the core concepts, generative topics, and/or essential questions. It is important to use COVER strategies such as organizers, visuals, visualizations, imagery, elaborative rehearsal and personal connections, and cooperative learning.

Step 1: Activate Knowledge

- This step gains learners' attention in order to focus them on the topic, and motivate them, *really* motivate them, to want to learn about it. All of this activity should help learners activate their prior knowledge.

- Activating prior knowledge is critically important so learners are prepared to connect information that is new to them with information that they already know and have stored in their long-term memories.

Step 3: Encourage Knowledge

- Step 3 calls for the development of procedural knowledge by allowing learners ample time to use, or practice, the information that they learned in Step 2. Without practice, learners do not have the opportunity to apply what they are learning to relevant situations nor do they have opportunities to receive feedback from teachers and peers.

This step also provides tremendous assessment information for teachers and gives them a chance to refine their lessons or plans to assist learners who have not fully grasped an idea or concept. In practice, many teachers often go back and forth between Steps 2 and 3.

Step 4: Application

- This step is designed to help you plan for learners to use and apply in new and different ways the new information that they have just learned and practiced. Applying knowledge and skills in these new ways helps learners generalize and transfer what they have learned in the classroom to the real world.

Step 5: Closure

- Step 5 helps you bring the unit of instruction to a close and provides an opportunity for transition into the next unit. Bringing closure and exploring connections help learners focus on the interrelated nature of knowledge and fight their tendency (and ours) to compartmentalize everything that we learn (or teach) into neat, discrete entities that lack real-world counterparts.

The Lesson Plan Form

- The Lesson Plan Form is a guide to implementing lessons. The components of the form include: the core concept and lesson topic, the objectives and/or outcomes, the connections to prior knowledge, the students' developmental characteristics, a summary of instructional strategies used throughout the lesson, and the instructional procedures. It is also important to include some type of formative assessment as well.

It's All Very Interesting, but How Can These Tools Really Be Used?

- Look back over the Planning for Instruction sections you have completed throughout this book. You now have a unit plan!

What Are Some Examples of Putting These Tools to Use?

- See Example 1 (The Deer Problem, p. 347) and Example 2 (Area of Irregular Polygons, p. 355) as well as the additional four examples at the end of this chapter for specific examples of these tools in use.

Real Plans for Real Learners

We know that traditional instruction has some limitations, and that we must change what we do in our classrooms in light of new research on teaching and learning. Therefore, when developing our lessons and plans, we can:

- Allow learners to work together, use examples and problems that learners will find meaningful, make personal connections and encourage learners to think about what they already know about the topic and content, and then help the learners organize, visuallize, and elaborate upon information as it is being learned.

- Allow the learners to practice using the new ideas, concepts, and facts, and provide ample, specific feedback to learners.

- Base plans and instructional strategies on developmental characteristics so that modeling and scaffolding techniques can move the learners to higher conceptual levels.

- Provide sufficiently varied learning activities to enhance the likelihood that learners with different learning styles will be able to benefit from the lessons, and adjust activities as necessary on the basis of formative assessment.

- Employ fewer traditional tests and use performance and authentic assessments to judge mastery of content.

Planning Organizer

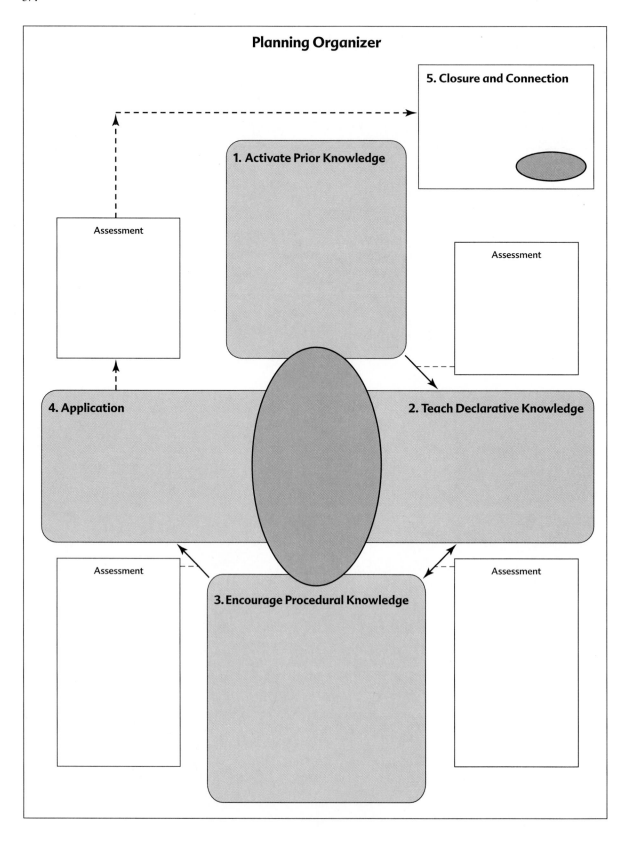

5. Closure and Connection

1. Activate Prior Knowledge

Assessment

Assessment

4. Application

2. Teach Declarative Knowledge

Assessment

Assessment

3. Encourage Procedural Knowledge

Planning Template

[2] Teach Declarative Knowledge
Select core concept, generative topic, or essential question and related ideas, concepts, facts.

C O V E R

_____
_____
_____
_____

[1] Activate Prior Knowledge
Cue prior knowledge, encourage personal connection, meaning. Use emotionality and disequilibrium. Provide context.

G A I N   A T T E N T I O N

_____
_____
_____
_____

[3] Encourage Procedural Knowledge
Provide opportunities to use ideas, concepts, facts, and to assess understanding.

P R A C T I C E   a n d   F E E D B A C K

_____
_____
_____
_____
_____

_____
_____
_____
_____
_____

[4] Application
Apply to other ideas, concepts, facts; apply in new and different ways; apply in life.

G E N E R A L I Z E   a n d   T R A N S F E R

_____
_____
_____
_____
_____

[5] Closure and Connection
Ending, wrap-up, transition to next generative topic.

Lesson Plan Form

Core Concept:
Lesson Topic:

Objectives (s) / Outcome (s)

Connecting prior knowledge and experience to new learning.

Developmental Characteristics (cognitive, social, and emotional)

REFER BACK TO UNIT PLAN WRITTEN EARLIER. INCLUDE HERE ONLY THOSE CHARACTERISTICS THAT ARE DIRECTLY RELEVANT TO THIS LESSON.

Instructional Strategies (cross-reference to instructional procedures)

Advance Organizer (big idea)   **Graphic Organizers**

Questioning Strategies   **Cooperative Learning/group activities**

Variations for learning styles and personality types   **Other strategies**

Instructional Procedures
(Check box to designate step of Organizer)   → | 1 | 2 | 3 | 4 | 5 |

Include a separate procedure section for each step of the Organizer. Each step should include an introduction, body of presentation, closure, and assessment strategy.

Complete instructional procedure section on reverse side.

Instructional Procedures
(Check box to designate step of Organizer) $\longrightarrow$ | 1 | 2 | 3 | 4 | **5** |

Include a separate procedure section for each step of the Organizer. Each step should include an introduction, body of presentation, closure, and assessment strategy.

Student Reaction	Modification for the future

References

Adelman, C. (1999 Nov. 5). Why can't we stop talking about the SAT? *The Chronicle of Higher Education, 66* (11), B4–B5.

Aiken, L. R. (1997). *Psychological testing and assessment* (9th ed.). Boston: Allyn and Bacon.

Airasian, P. (1996). *Assessment in the classroom.* New York: McGraw-Hill.

Alexander, K. L., Entwisle, D. R., and Dauber, S. L. (1994). *On the success of failure: A reassessment of the effects of retention in primary grades.* New York: Cambridge University Press.

Allen, D. (Ed.). (1998). *Assessing student learning: From grading to understanding.* New York: Teachers College Press.

Angelo, T., and Cross, K. P. (1993). *Classroom assessment techniques: A handbook for college teachers* (2nd ed.). San Francisco: Jossey-Bass.

Arends, R. I. (1998). *Learning to teach* (4th ed.). Boston: McGraw-Hill.

Armstrong, T. (1994). *Multiple intelligences in the classroom.* Alexandria, VA: ASCD.

Aronson, E., Stephan, C., Sikes, J., Blaney, N., and Snapp, M. (1978). *The jigsaw classroom.* Beverly Hills, CA: Sage.

Aspy, D., Aspy, C., and Quinby, P. (1993). What doctors can teach teachers about problem-based learning. *Educational Leadership, 50* (7), 22–24.

Ault, K. (1986). *Improving college teaching through adapting learning styles theory and practice.* (ERIC Document Reproduction Service No. ED 272 494).

Ausubel, D. P. (1963). *The psychology of meaningful verbal learning.* New York: Grune and Stratton.

Ball, W. (1996). Socratic seminars. In R. Canady and M. Rettig (Eds.), *Teaching in the block: Strategies for engaging learners.* Larchmont, NY: Eye on Education.

Bandura, A. (1978). The self system in reciprocal determination. *American Psychologist, 33,* 344–358.

Bandura, A. (1982). The self and mechansims of agency. In J. Suls (Ed.), *Psychological perspectives on the self:* Vol. 1. (pp. 3–39) Hillsdale, NJ: Lawrence Erlbaum Associates.

Bandura, A. (1986). *Social foundations of thought and action: A social cognitive theory.* Englewood Cliffs, NJ: Prentice Hall.

Bandura, A. (1989). Human agency in social cognitive theory. *American Psychologist, 44,* 1175–1184.

Barr, R., and Tagg, J. (1995). From teaching to learning—a new paradigm for undergraduate education. *Change, 27,* 13–25.

Bauer, A., and Shea, T. (2000). *Learners with emotional and behavioral disorders: An introduction,* Upper Saddle River, NJ: Merrill.

Beane, J. A. (1995, April). Curriculum integration and the disciplines of knowledge. *Phi Delta Kappan, 76* (8), 612–622.

Becker, H. (1999) Internet use by teachers. *Teaching, Learning, and Computing, 1998: A National Survey of Schools and Teachers* (rev. ed.).

Bellanca, J., and Fogarty, R. (1991). *Blueprints for thinking in the cooperative classroom.* Arlington Heights, IL: Skylight Professional Development.

Berliner, D., and Biddle, B. (1995). *The manufactured crisis: Myths, fraud, and the attack on America's public schools.* Reading, MA: Addison-Wesley.

Bigge. M. L., and Shermis, S. S. (1999). *Learning theories for teachers* (6th ed.). New York: Longman.

Black, P., and Wiliam, D. (1998). Inside the black box: Raising standards through classroom assessment. *Phi Delta Kappan, 80* (2), 139–148.

Blackburn, R. T., Pellino, G., Boberg, A., and O'Connell, C. (1980). Are instructional improvement programs off target? *Current Issues in Higher Education 1,* 32–48.

Blatt, B., and Kaplan, F. (1974). *Christmas in purgatory: A photographic essay on mental retardation.* Syracuse, NY: Human Policy Press.

Bloom, Benjamin. Biography. *http://www.funderunderstanding.com/messages/1137.htlm.*

Bloom, B. S. (Ed.) (1984). *Taxonomy of educational objectives. Handbook 1: Cognitive domain.* New York: Longman. (Originally published in 1956: renewed in 1984.)

Blum, H., and Yocom, D. (1996). A fun alternative: Using instructional games to foster student learning. *Teaching Exceptional Children, 29* (2), 60–63.

Blythe, T., Allen, D., and Powell, B. S. (1999). *Looking together at student work: A companion guide to assessing student learning.* New York: Teachers College Press.

Blythe, T., and Associates. (1998). *The teaching for understanding guide.* San Francisco: Jossey-Bass.

Bondy, C. E., and Kendall, B. (1998). Ongoing assessment. In T. Blythe and associates. *The teaching for understanding guide.* San Francisco: Jossey-Bass.

Borich, G. D. (2000). *Effective teaching methods* (4th ed.). Upper Saddle River, NJ: Merrill.

Bracey, G. W. (1995). *Final exam: A study of the perpetual scrutiny of American education.* Bloomington, IN: TECHNOS Press of the Agency for Instructional Technology.

Bracey, G. W. (1997). *Setting the record straight: Responses to misconceptions about public education in the United States.* Alexandria, VA: ASCD.

Brendtro, L., Brokenleg, M., and Van Bockern, S. (1990). *Reclaiming youth at risk: Our hope for the future.* Bloomington, IN: National Educational Service.

Brooks, J. G., and Brooks, M. G. (1993). *In search of understanding: The case for constructivist classrooms.* Alexandria, VA: ASCD

Bruer, J. T. (1993). The mind's journey from novice to expert. *American Educator, 17,* 7–8.

Bruer, J. (1998). Brain science, brain fiction. *Educational Leadership, 56* (3), 14–18.

Bruner, J. S. (1978). The role of dialogue in language acquisition. In A. Sinclair, R. J. Jarvella, and W. J. M. Levelt (Eds.), *The child's conception of language.* New York: Springer-Verlag.

Burke, K. (1999). *How to assess authentic learning.* (3rd ed.). Arlington Heights, IL: Skylight Professional Development.

Burke, M. D., Hagan, S. L., and Grossen, B. (1998). What curricular designs and strategies accommodate diverse learners? *Teaching Exceptional Children, 31*(1), 34–38.

Burtch, J. A. (1999, February). Technology is for everyone. *Educational Leadership, 56* (7), 33–34.

Butler, Kathleen A. (1993). *Learning styles and performance assessment: A model teaching guide.* Columbia, CT. The Learner's Dimension.

Butler, Kathleen, A. (1987). *Learning and teaching style: In theory and practice.* Columbia, CT: The Learner's Dimension. (Originally published in 1984; revised in 1986 and 1987.)

Butler, Kathleen, A. (1996). *Learning style: Personal exploration and practical applications.* Columbia, CT: The Learner's Dimension.

Caine, R. N., and Caine, G. (1991). *Making connections: Teaching and the human brain.* Alexandria, VA: ASCD.

Campbell, B. (1994). *The multiple intelligences handbook.* Stanwood, WA: Campbell and Associates.

Carnevale, D. (1999, Nov. 5). Web services help professors detect plagiarism. *The Chronicle of Higher Education,* A47–A49.

Carson, C., Huelskamp, R., and Woodall, T. (1993). Perspectives on education in America: An annotated briefing. *The Journal of Educational Research, 86,* 259.

Cashin, W. D. (Ed.). (1987). *National Issues in Higher Education, 26,* 25–36.

CBS News. (2000). Secret service studies school shootings (Online). Available: cbsnews.cbs.com/now/story/0,1597,171898-412,00.shtml.

Chapman, C., and Freeman, L. (1996). *Multiple intelligences centers and projects.* Arlington Heights, IL: Skylight Training and Publishing.

Charles, C. M. (1999). *Building classroom discipline* (6th ed.). New York: Longman.

Chodzinski, R. T., and Burke, F. (1998). Bullying: A conflict management issue for teachers, parents and child caregivers. *Mosaic, 5* (3), 1–12.

Clark, J. H. & Agne, R. M. (1997). *Interdisciplinary high school teaching: Strategies for integrated learning.* Boston: Allyn and Bacon.

Collopy, R., and Green, T. (1995). Using motivational theory with at-risk children. *Educational Leadership, 53* (1), 37–40.

Coloroso, B. (1994). *Kids are worth it! Giving your child the gift of inner discipline.* New York: Morrow.

Cooper, J. L. (1990, May). Cooperative learning and college teaching: Tips from the trenches. *The Teaching Professor,* pp. 1–2.

Cooper, J. L., Robinson, P., and McKinney, M. (1994). Cooperative learning in the classroom. In D. Halpern and associates, *Changing college classrooms: New teaching and learning strategies for an increasingly complex world.* San Francisco, CA: Jossey-Bass.

Cooper, J. M. (1999). *Classroom teaching skills* (6th ed.). New York: Houghton Mifflin.

Corey, S. (1940). The teachers out-talk the pupils. In G. D. Borich. (2000). *Effective teaching methods* (4th ed.). Upper Saddle River, NJ: Merrill.

Cotton, K., and Savard, W. (1981). *Instructional grouping: Ability grouping.* Portland, OR: Northwest Regional Laboratory.

Couch, R. (1993). *Synectics and imagery: Developing creative thinking through images.* Selected readings from the Annual Conference of the International Visual Literacy Association, Pittsburgh, PA. (ERIC Document Reproduction Service No. ED 363 330)

Cuban, L. (1993). *How teachers taught: Constancy and change in American classrooms* (2nd ed.). New York: Teacher's College Press.

Cullum, A. (1971). *The geranium on the window sill just died but teacher you went right on.* London: Harlin Quist.

Cunningham, P. M., Hall, D. P., and Sigmon, C. M. (1999) *The teacher's guide to the four blocks: A multimethod, multilevel framework for grades 1–3.* Greensboro, NC: Carson-Dellosa Publishing.

Danforth, S., and Boyle, J. R. (2000). *Cases in behavior management.* Upper Saddle River, NJ: Merrill.

Darling-Hammond, L. (1997). *The right to learn: A blueprint for creating schools that work.* San Francisco: Jossey-Bass.

Datnow, A., Hubbard, L., and Conchas, G. (1999). *How context mediates policy: The implementation of single gender public schooling in California.* Paper presented at the annual meeting of the American Educational Research Association, Montreal.

Davidson, T., Fountain, P., Grogan, R., Short, V., and Steely, J. (1976). *Learning center book: Integrated approach.* Pacific Palisades, CA: Goodyear Publishing.

Day, V., and Hackett, G. (1996). LEARN to succeed. *Teaching Exceptional Children, 29* (2), 70–71.

Dempster, F. (1993). Exposing our students to less should help them learn more. *Phi Delta Kappan, 74* (6), 433–437.

Dexter, S. L., Anderson, R. E., and Becker, H. J. (1999). Teachers' views of computers as catalysts for changes in their teaching practice. *ISTE-JRCE, 3,* (3).

Dillon, J. T. (1982). Do your questions promote or prevent thinking? *Learning, 11,* 56–59.

DiTiberio, J. (1996). Education, learning styles, and cognitive styles. In Hammer, A. (ed.), *MBTI applications: A decade of research on the Myers-Briggs type indicator.* Palo Alto, CA: Consulting Psychologists Press.

Dougherty, M. (February 7, 2000). Cheating 101. *Bucks County Courier Times.* IE

Dowd, S. B. (1996). Deep or surface learning? *The Teaching Professor, 10* (1), 5.

Drew, C. J., Hardman, M. L., and Logan, D. R. (1996). *Mental retardation: A life cycle approach* (6th ed.). Englewood Cliffs, NJ: Merrill/Prentice Hall.

Dunn, L. (1968). Special education for the mildly retarded— is much of it justifiable? *Exceptional Children, 35,* 5–22.

Eccles, J. S., and Jacobs, J. E. (1986). Social forces shape math attitudes and performance. *Signs: Journal of Women in Culture and Society, 11,* 367–380.

Eggen, P., and Kauchak, D. (2001). *Educational psychology: Windows on classrooms.* (5th ed.) Upper Saddle River, NJ: Merrill, Prentice Hall.

Eisenberg, N., Martin, C. L., and Fabes, R. A. (1996). Gender development and gender effects. In J. E. Ormrod, *Educational psychology: Developing learners* (3rd ed.). Upper Saddle River, NJ: Merrill/Prentice Hall.

Erikson, E. (1968). *Identity: Youth and Crisis.* New York: Norton.

Fagot, B. I., Hagan, R., Leinbach, M. D., and Kronsberg, S. (1985). Differential reactions to assertive and communicative acts of toddler boys and girls. *Child Development, 56,* 1499–1505.

Feden, P. D. (1994). About instruction: Powerful new strategies worth knowing. *Educational Horizons, 73* (1), 18–24.

Feden, P. D., and Clabaugh, G. (1986). The new breed educator: A rationale and program for combining elementary and special education teacher preparation. *Teacher Education and Special Education, 9* (4), 180–189.

Feden, P. D., Vogel, R. M., and Clabaugh, G. K. (1992). Preparing expert teachers: Transcending the school-as-factory. *Educational Horizons, 70* (3), 130–134.

Fitzsimmons, M. K. (1998). Functional behavior assessment and behavior intervention plans. Reston, VA: ERIC Clearinghouse on Disabilities and Gifted Education. (ERIC Document Reproduction Service No. ED 429 420)

Fogarty, R. (1997). *Problem-based learning and curriculum for the multiple intelligences classroom.* Arlington Heights, IL: Skylight Professional Development.

Fogarty, R., and Bellanca, J. (1989). *Patterns for thinking: Patterns for transfer.* Arlington Heights, IL: Skylight Professional Development.

Fosnot, C. T. (Ed.). (1996). *Constructivism: Theory, perspectives, and practice.* New York: Teachers College Press.

Fransen, R. (1999). Between the eyes. *Reclaiming Children and Youth, 8* (3), 132.

Froschl, M., and Gropper, N. (1999). Fostering friendships, curbing bullying. *Educational Leadership, 56* (8), 72–75.

Gage, N. L. (1963). *Handbook of research on teaching.* Chicago: Rand McNally.

Gagne, E. D., Yekovich, C. W., and Yekovich, F. R. (1993). *The cognitive psychology of school learning* (2nd ed.). New York: HarperCollins.

Gardner, H. (1983). *Frames of mind: The theory of multiple intelligences.* New York: Basic Books.

Gardner, H. (1991). *The unschooled mind: How children think and how schools should teach.* New York: Basic Books.

Gardner, H. (1993). *Multiple intelligences: The theory in practice.* New York: Basic Books.

Gardner, H. (1999). *The disciplined mind: What all students should understand.* New York: Basic Books.

Gardner, H. (2000). *The disciplined mind: Beyond facts and standardized tests, the K–12 education every child deserves.* New York: Penguin Books.

Gibbs, G. (1992). *Improving the quality of student learning.* Bristol, Australia: Technical and Educational Services.

Goldman, S., Williams, S., Sherwood, R., and Hasselbring, T., and The Cognition and Technology Group at Vanderbilt. (1999). *Technology for teaching and learning with understanding: A primer.* New York: Houghton Mifflin.

Good, T., and Brophy, J. (1997). *Looking in classrooms* (7th ed.). New York: Harper Collins.

Goodlad, J. (1983). A study of schooling: Some findings and hypotheses. *Phi Delta Kappan, 64,* 467.

Gordon, P., Rogers, A., Comfort, M., Gavula, N., and McGee, B. (2001). A taste of problem-based learning increases achievement of urban minority middle school students. *Educational Horizons, 79* (4), 171–175.

Grant, L., and Rothenberg, J. (1986). The social enhancement of ability differences: Teacher-student interactions in first- and second-grade reading groups. *Elementary School Journal* (87), 29–49.

Gregorc, A. (1982). *An adult's guide to styles.* Maynard, MA: Gabriel Systems.

Gregorc, A. (1985). *The Gregorc style delineator.* Maynard, MA: Gabriel Systems.

Gregory, R. J. (1996). *Psychological testing: History, principles, and applications* (2nd ed.). Boston: Allyn and Bacon.

Grossen, B., and Carnine, D. (1996). Considerate instruction helps students with disabilities achieve world class standards. *Teaching Exceptional Children, 28* (4), 77–81.

Gunter, M. A., Estes, T. H., and Schwab, J. (1995). *Instruction: A models approach* (2nd ed.). Needham Heights, MA: Allyn and Bacon.

Guskin, A. (1994). Restructuring the role of faculty. *Change, 26,* 16–25.

Hallinan, M. (1984). *Summary and Implications.* In P. Peterson, L. Wilkinson, and M. Hallinan. (Eds.). *The social context of instruction: Group organization and group processes* (pp. 229–240). San Diego: Academic Press.

Hamilton, R., and Ghatala, E. (1994). *Learning and instruction.* Boston: McGraw-Hill.

Hancock, L. (1996, February 19). Why do schools flunk biology? *Newsweek,* p. 58.

Hardman, M. L., Drew, C. J., and Egan, M. W. (1999). *Human exceptionality: Society, school, and family* (6th ed.). Boston: Allyn and Bacon.

Harris, J. (1998). *Virtual architecture: Designing and directing curriculum-based telecomputing.* Eugene, OR: International Society for Technology in Education (ISTE).

Hayden, T. L. (1980). *One child.* New York: Putnam Publishing Group.

Heaton, S., and O'Shea, D. (1995). Using mnemonics to make mnemonics. *Teaching Exceptional Children, 27* (1), 34–36.

Herbert, C. (1974). *I see a child.* New York: Anchor Books.

Hewitt, M. B. (1998). Helping students feel like they belong. *Reclaiming Children and Youth, 7* (3), 155–159.

Hirsch, E. D., Jr. (1996). *The schools we need: And why we don't have them.* New York: Doubleday.

Hirschberg, C. (1999, September). How good are our schools? *Life Magazine,* pp. 40–42.

Huba, M., and Freed, J. (2000). *Learner-centered assessment on college campuses.* Boston: Allyn and Bacon.

Hunter, M. (1981). *Improved instruction.* El Segundo, CA: TIP Publications.

Hyerle, D. (1996). *Visual tools for constructing knowledge.* Alexandria, VA: Association for Supervision and Development.

Hynd, G. W., and Semrud-Clikeman, M. (1989). Dyslexia and neurodevelopmental pathology: Relationships to cognition, intelligence, and reading acquisition. *Journal of Learning Disabilities, 22,* 204–216.

Inspiration. (2001). Portland, OR: Inspiration Software. (www.inspiration.com).

Jacobs, H. H. (1997). *Mapping the big picture: Integrating curriculum and assessment K–12.* Alexandria, VA: ASCD.

Jennings, J. F. (1996). *The good—and the not so good—news about American schools.* Washington, DC: National Center for Education Policy.

Johnson, D. W., Johnson, R. T., and Smith, K. A. (1991). *Cooperative learning: Increasing college faculty instructional productivity.* Washington, DC: ASHE-ERIC Higher Education Report No. 4.

Johnson, P. E., and Johnson, R. E. (1996). The role of concrete-abstract thinking levels in teachers' multiethnic beliefs. *Journal of Research and Development in Education, 29* (3), 134–140.

Johnson, R. T., and Johnson, D. W. (1994). An overview of cooperative learning. In J. S. Thousand, R. A. Villa, and A. I. Nevin (Eds.), *Creativity and collaborative learning: A practical guide to empowering students and teachers* (pp. 31–44). Baltimore, MD: Brookes.

Johnson, R. T., and Johnson, D. W., and Smith, K. A. (1991). *Active learning: Cooperation in the college classroom.* Edina, MN: Interaction.

Joyce, B., Showers, B., and Rolheiser-Bennett, C. (1987). Staff development and student learning: A synthesis of research on models of teaching. *Educational Leadership, 45* (2), 11–23.

Jung, C. G. (1971). *Psychological types.* Princeton, NJ: Princeton University Press. (Original work published in 1921.)

Kagan, S. (1992). *Cooperative learning.* San Juan Capistrano, CA: Resources for Teachers.

Kagan, S., and Kagan, M. (1998). *Multiple intelligences: The complete MI handbook.* San Clemente, CA: Kagan Cooperative Learning.

Kantrowitz and McGinn (2000, June 19). *Newsweek,* 48–49.

Kaplan, R. M., and Saccuzzo, D. T. (1993). *Psychological testing.* Pacific Grove, CA: Brooks/Cole.

Kendall, J. S., and Marzano, R. J. (1996). *Content Knowledge: A compendium of standards and benchmarks for K–12 education.* Aurora, CO: Mid-continent Regional Educational Laboratory.

Kirk, S., and Gallagher, J. (1986). *Educating exceptional children* (5th ed.). Boston, MA: Houghton Mifflin.

Klingner, J. K., and Vaughn, S. (1999). Students' perceptions of instruction in inclusive classrooms: Implications for students with learning disabilities. *Exceptional Children, 66* (1), 23–37.

Kohlberg, L. (1984). *The psychology of moral development: The nature and validity of moral stages.* San Francisco: Harper and Row.

Kohn, A. (1993). *Punished by rewards: The trouble with gold stars, incentive plans, As, praise, and other bribes.* Boston: Houghton Mifflin.

Kolb, D. (1976). *Learning style inventory.* Boston: McBer.

Kowalski, T., Weaver, R., and Henson, K. (1990). *Case studies on teaching.* New York: Longman.

Labaree, David F. (1999, January/February). Too easy a target: The trouble with ed schools and the implications for the university. *Academe, 85* (1), 34–39.

Lafond, S. (1999, Fall). Teaching and learning with presentation software. *Curriculum/Technology Quarterly, 9* (1), 1–4.

Langer, G., and Colton, A. (1997, Winter). How to analyze student work. *ASCD Professional Development Newsletter,* p. 3.

Lankford, H., and Wyckoff, J. (1995). Where has the money gone? An analysis of school district spending in New York. *Educational Evaluation and Policy Analysis, 17* (2), 195–218.

Lawrence, G. (1993). *People types and tiger stripes: A practical guide to learning styles* (3rd ed.). Gainesville, FL: Center for Applications of Psychological Type.

Lenz, B. K., Alley, G., and Schumaker, J. (1987). Activating the inactive learner: Advance organizers in the secondary content classroom. *Learning Disability Quarterly, 10* (1), 53–67.

Lewin, K. (1951). *Field theory in social science: Selected research papers.* D. Cartwright (editor). New York: Harper and Row.

Long, N. J. (1979). The conflict cycle. *The Pointer, 24* (1), 6–11.

Long, N. J. (1986). The nine psychoeducational stages of helping emotionally disturbed students through the reeducation process. *The Pointer, 30,* 5–20.

Long, N. J. (1996). The conflict cycle paradigm on how troubled students get teachers out of control. In N. Long and W. Morse (Eds.), *Conflict in the classroom: The education of at-risk and troubled students* (5th ed.). Austin, TX: Pro-Ed.

Long, N. J., Fecser, F. A., and Brendtro, L. K. (1998). Life space crisis intervention: New skills for reclaiming students showing patterns of self-defeating behavior. *Healing, 3* (2), 2–2.

Luftig, R. (1989). *Assessment of learners with special needs.* Boston: Allyn and Bacon.

Lyon, G. R. (1995). Research initiatives in learning disabilities: Contributions from scientists supported by the National Institute of Child Health and Human Development. *Journal of Child Neurology, 10,* 120–126.

Macionis, J. (1997). *Sociology* (5th ed.). Upper Saddle River, NJ: Prentice Hall.

MacMillan, J. (2001). *Classroom assessment: Principles and practice for effective instruction* (2nd ed.). Boston: Allyn and Bacon.

Mamchur, C. (1996). *A teacher's guide to cognitive type theory and learning style.* Alexandria, VA: ASCD.

Martin, C. L. (1989). Children's use of gender-related information in making social judgements. *Developmental Psychology, 25,* 80–88.

Marzano, R. J., Gaddy, B. B., and Dean, C. (2000). *What works in classroom instruction.* Aurora, CO: Midcontinent Research for Education and Learning.

Marzano, R., Pickering, D., and McTighe, J. (1993). *Assessing student outcomes: Performance assessment using the dimensions of learning model.* Alexandria, VA: ASCD.

Massachusetts Governor's Commission on Gay and Lesbian Youth. (February 25, 1993). *Making schools safe for gay and lesbian youth: Breaking the silence in schools and in families. Report of the Massachusetts governor's commission on gay and lesbian youth.*

Matson, J., Benavidez, D., Compton, L., Paclwaskyj, T., and Baglio, C. (1996). Behavioral treatment of autistic persons: A review of research from 1980 to the present. *Research in Developmental Disabilities, 17,* 433–465.

McCarthy, B. (1987). *The 4MAT system: Teaching to learning styles with right/left mode techniques.* Wauconda, IL: Excel.

McCarthy, B. (1996). *About learning.* Wauconda, IL: Excel.

McCarthy, B., and Morris, S. (1994, 1999, 2000). *4MAT 2.0 II.* Wauconda, IL: *About Learning.*

McCaulley, M. (1976). *The Myers-Briggs type indicator and the teaching-learning process.* Gainesville, FL: Center for Applications of Psychological Type.

McCoy, K. (1995). *Teaching special learners in the general education classroom: Methods and techniques.* Denver, CO: Love Publishing.

McFarling, U., and Boyd, R. (1999, October 18). Entering the age of biogenetics. The gene blueprint is nearly done. The impact is expected to be great. *Philadelphia Inquirer,* p. C01.

McKenzie, J. (1999, Summer). Reaching the reluctant teacher. *From now on (FNO). (http://www.fno.org/ sum99/reluctant.html).*

McLoyd, V. C. (1998). Socioeconomic disadvantage and child development. *American Psychologist, 53,* 185–204.

McTighe, J., and Lyman, F., Jr. (1988). Cueing thinking in the classroom: The promise of theory-embedded tools. *Educational Leadership, 45,* 18–24.

Melear, C. T., and Alcock, M. W. (1998). *Learning styles and personality types of African-American children: Implications for science education.* Paper presented at the annual meeting of the National Association for Research in Science Teaching, San Diego, CA. (ERIC Document Reproduction Service Number ED 418 874)

Mendler, A. (1992). *What do I do when? . . . How to achieve discipline with dignity in the classroom.* Bloomington, IN: National Educational Service.

Middendorf, J. M., and Kalish, A. (1996). The "change-up" in lectures. *The National Teaching and Learning FORUM, 5* (2), 1–4.

Miles, K. H. (1995, Winter). Freeing resources for improving schools: A case study of teacher allocation in Boston Public Schools. *Educational Evaluation and Policy Analysis, 17,* 476–493.

Miller, L. S. (1995). *An American imperative: Accelerating minority educational advancement.* New Haven, CT. Yale University Press.

Miller, P. H. (1993). *Theories of developmental psychology* (3rd ed.). New York: Freeman.

Millis, B. J. (1995). Introducing faculty to cooperative learning. In W. A.Wright and associates, *Teaching improvement practices: Successful strategies for higher education.* Bolton: Anker.

Millis, B. J., and Cottell, P. G. (1998). *Cooperative learning for higher education faculty.* American Council on Education (Series on Higher Education). Phoenix, AZ: Oryx Press.

Morris, S., and McCarthy, B. (1999). *4MAT in action* (4th ed.). Barrington, IL: Excel.

Muscott, H. S. (1995). Techniques for avoiding counteraggressive responses when teaching youth with aggressive behaviors. *Journal of Emotional and Behavioral Problems, 4* (1), 41–44.

Myers, I. B. (1980). Taking type into account in education. In M. H. McCaulley and F. L. Natter, *Psychological (Myers-Briggs) type differences in education* (2nd ed.). Gainesville, FL: Center for Applications of Psychological Type.

Myers, I. B. (1990). *Gifts differing* (2nd ed.). Palo Alto, CA: Consulting Psychologists Press.

Myers, I. B., and Briggs, K. C. (1976). *Myers-Briggs type indicator.* Palo Alto, CA: Consulting Psychologists Press. (Original work published in 1943.)

Myers, I. B., and McCaulley, M. H. (1985). *A guide to the development and use of the Myers-Briggs type indicator.* Palo Alto, CA: Consulting Psychologists Press.

National Center for Children in Poverty. (1999, June). *Young children in poverty: A statistical update.*

National Center for Fair & Open Testing. (2000). *http://www.fairtest.org/facts/satfact.htm.*

Neill, D. M. (1997). Transforming student assessment. *Phi Delta Kappan, 79* (1), 34–58.

Niguidula, D. (1998). A richer picture of student work: The digital portfolio. In Allen, D. *Assessing student learning: From grading to understanding* (pp. 183–198). New York: Teachers College Press, Columbia University.

Nolan, J., and Francis, P. (1992). Changing perspectives in curriculum and instruction. In C. Glickman (Ed.), *Supervision in transition: The 1992 yearbook of the association for supervision and curriculum development.* VA: ASCD.

Oakes, J. (1990). *Multiplying inequalities: The effects of race, social class and tracking on opportunities to learn mathematics and science.* Santa Monica, CA: RAND.

Oakes, J. (1985). *Keeping track: How schools structure inequality.* Birmingham, NY: Vail-Ballou Press.

Oakes, J. (1992). Can tracking research inform practice? *Educational Researcher, 21* (4), 12–21.

Oakes, J., and Lipton, M. (1999). *Teaching to change the world.* Boston: McGraw-Hill.

Olweus, D. (1993). *Bullying at school: What we know and what we can do.* Oxford, England: Blackwell.

O'Neil, J. (August, 1992). What is problem-based learning? *ASCD Update, 34,* 4.

Organelle Project (1999). *www.vetigers.stier.org/library/cellscience.htm*

Orlich, D., Harder, R., Callahan, R., and Gibson, H. (2001). *Teaching strategies: A guide to better instruction* (6th ed.). Boston: Houghton Mifflin.

Ormrod, J. E. (2000). *Educational psychology: Developing learners* (3rd ed.). Upper Saddle River, NJ: Merrill/Prentice Hall.

Ormrod, J. E. (1999). *Human learning.* (3rd ed.). New Jersey: Prentice Hall.

O'Sullivan, C. E., Reese, C. M., and Mazzeo, J. (1997). *NAEP 1996 science report card for the nation and the states.* Washington, DC: National Center for Educational Statistics.

Palincsar, A. S. (1986). The role of dialogue in providing scaffolding instruction. *Educational Psychologist, 21,* 73–98.

Palincsar, A. S., and Brown, D. (1987). Enhancing instructional time through attention to metacognition. *Journal of Learning Disabilities, 20* (2), 66–75.

Park, C. S. (1997). Learning style preferences of Korean, Mexican, Armenian-American, and Anglo students in secondary schools. *NASSP Bulletin, 81* (585), 103–111.

Paul, J. L., and Epanchin, B. C. (1991). *Educating emotionally disturbed children and youth: Theories and practices for teachers.* Englewood Cliffs, NJ: Prentice Hall.

Perkins, D. (1992). *Smart schools: Better thinking and learning for every child.* New York: Free Press.

Perkins, D. (1995). *Outsmarting IQ: The emerging science of learnable intelligence.* New York: Free Press.

Picou, A., Gatlin-Watts, R., and Packer, J. (1998). A test for learning style differences for the U.S. border population. *Texas papers in Foreign Language Education, 3* (2), 105–116. (ERIC Document Reproduction Service No. ED 423 678)

Popham, W. J. (1999). Why standardized tests don't measure educational quality. *Educational Leadership, 56* (6), 8–15.

Post, T. A., Humphreys, A. H., Ellis, A. K., and Buggey, L. J. (1997). *Interdisciplinary approaches to curriculum: Themes for teaching.* Upper Saddle River, NJ: Merrill/Prentice Hall.

Postman, N. (1995). The error of our ways. *Teacher Magazine, 6* (9), 32–37.

Raffini, J. P. (1996). *150 ways to increase intrinsic motivation in the classroom.* Boston: Allyn and Bacon.

Redl, F. (1966a). This is what children stir up in us. Talk presented at the 1966 New England Kindergarten Conference, Lesley College, Cambridge, MA (Online). Available: *www.lesley.edu/faculty/mmindess/onlncourse/What_Children_Stir_Up.html*

Redl, F. (1996b). *When we deal with children.* New York: Free Press.

Redl, F., and Weinman, D. (1951). *Children who hate: The disorganization and breakdown of behavior controls.* New York: Free Press.

Redl, F., and Weinman, D. (1952). *Controls from within: Techniques for the treatment of the aggressive child.* New York: Free Press.

Reese, C. M., Miller, K. E., and Doose, J. A. (1997). *NAEP 1996 mathematics report card for the nation and the states.* Washington, DC: National Center for Educational Statistics.

Reid, D. K. (1988). *Teaching the learning disabled: A cognitive developmental approach.* Boston: Allyn and Bacon.

Research Connections in Special Education. (1998, Fall). No. 3.

Rhem, J. (1995). Deep/surface approaches to learning and instruction. *The National Teaching and Learning FORUM, 5*(1), 1–4.

Risner, G., Skeel, D., and Nicholson, J. (1992). A closer look at textbooks. In Orlich, D., Harder, R., Callahan, R., and Gibson, H. (2001). *Teaching strategies: A guide to better instruction* (6th ed.). Boston: Houghton Mifflin.

Roblyer, M. D., Edwards, J., Havriluk, M. A. (1997). *Integrating educational technology into teaching.* Upper Saddle River, NJ: Prentice Hall.

Rogers, J. (1993, May). The inclusion revolution *(The Research Bulletin No. 11).* Bloomington, IN: Phi Delta Kappa Center for Evaluation, Development, and Research.

Rogers, V. (1989). Assessing the curriculum experienced by children. *Phi Delta Kappan, 70* (9), 714–717.

Rop, C. (1998). Breaking the gender barrier in the physical sciences. *Educational Leadership, 53*(4), 58–60.

Rosenshine, B. V. (1987). Explicit teaching. In D. C. Berliner and B. V. Rosenshine (Eds.), *Talks to teachers* (pp. 75–92). New York: Random House.

Sacks, P. (2000). *Standardized minds: The high price of America's testing culture and what we can do to change it.* Cambridge, MA: Perseus Books.

Sadker, M. P., and Sadker, D. (1985). Sexism in the schoolroom of the 80s. *Psychology Today, 19,* 54–57.

Sadker, M. P., and Sadker, D. (1994). *Failing at fairness: How our schools cheat girls.* New York: Touchstone.

Sandia National Laboratories. (1993). Perspectives on education in America. *Journal of Educational Research, 86,* 259–310.

Savoie, J., and Hughes, A. (1994). Problem-based learning as classroom solution. *Educational Leadership, 52* (3), 54–57.

Schlechty, P. C. (1997). *Inventing better schools: An action plan for educational reform.* San Francisco, CA: Jossey-Bass.

Schmidt, W., McKnight, C., and Raizen, S. (1996). *Splintered vision: An investigation of U.S. science and mathematics education: Executive summary.* Lansing,

MI: U.S. National Research Center for the Third International Mathematics and Science Study, Michigan State University.

Schmidt, W., McKnight, C., and Raizen, S. (1997). *A splintered vision: An investigation of U.S. science and mathematics education.* New York: Kluwer Academic Publishers.

Schmoker, M., and Marzano, R. (1999). Realizing the promise of standards-based education. *Educational Leadership, 56*(6), 17–21.

Schmoker, M. (2000). The results we want. *Educational Leadership, 57* (5), 62–65.

Schneider, J., and Houston, P. (1993). *Exploding the myths: Another round in the education debate.* Arlington, VA.: American Association of School Administrators.

Schraer, W. D., and Stoltze, H. J. (1993). *Biology: The study of life.* Needham, MA: Prentice Hall.

Scott, H. V. (1994). *A serious look at the 4MAT model.* (ERIC DOCUMENT REPRODUCTION NO. ED 383 654).

Sikorski, M., Niemiec, R., and Wahlberg, H. (1996). A classroom checkup: Best teaching practices in special education. *Teaching Exceptional Children, 29* (1), 27–29.

Sizer, T. (1996). *Horace's hope: What works for the American high school.* Boston: Houghton Mifflin.

Slavin, R. E. (1989–1990). Research in cooperative learning: Consensus and controversy. *Educational Leadership, 47* (4), 52–55.

Smith, P., and Ragan, T. (1999). *Instructional design* (2nd ed.). Upper Saddle River, NJ: Merrill/Prentice Hall.

Stedman, L. C. (1994). The sandia report and U.S. achievement: An assessment. *The Journal of Educatinal Research, 87* (3), 133–146.

Stepien, W., and Gallagher, S. (1993). Problem-based learning: As authentic as it gets. *Educational Leadership, 50* (7), 25–28.

Stratton, J. (1995). *How students have changed: A call to action for our children's future.* Arlington, VA: American Association of School Administrators.

Streitmatter, J. (1997). An exploratory study of risk-taking and attitudes in a girls only middle school math class. *Elementary School Journal, 98* (1), 15–26.

Tapscott, D. (1999, February). Educating the Net generation. *Educational Leadership, 56* (5), 6–11.

T.H.E. Journal Technological Horizons in Education. http://www.thejournal.com.

Thielens, W., Jr. (1987, April). *The disciplines and undergraduate lecturing.* Paper presented at an annual meeting of the American Educational Research Association, Washington, DC. (ERIC DOCUMENT REPRODUCTION NO. ED 286 436.)

Thoman, E. (1999, February). Skills and strategies for media education. *Educational Leadership, 56* (5), 50–54.

Thomas, R. (1996, July 28). Samuel A. Kirk, 92, pioneer of special education field. *The New York Times,* 32.

Tombari, M., and Borich, G. (1999). *Authentic assessment in the classroom: Applications and practice.* Upper Saddle River, NJ: Merrill/Prentice Hall.

Tomlinson, C. A. (1999). *The differentiated classroom: Responding to the needs of all learners.* Alexandria, VA: ASCD.

Tomlinson, C. A. (1999, September). Mapping a route toward differentiated instruction. *Educational Leadership, 57* (1), 12–16.

Torgeson, J., Wagner, R., and Rashotte, C. (1997). Prevention and remediation of severe reading disabilities: Keeping the end in mind. *Scientific Studies of Reading, 1,* 217–234.

Torp, L. and Sage, S. (1998). *Problems as possibilities.* Alexandria, VA: ASCD.

Trice, A. (2000). *A handbook of classroom assessment.* New York: Longman.

U.S. Bureau of the Census. (1996). *Statistics.* Washington, DC: U.S. Government Printing Office.

U.S. Bureau of the Census. (1997). *Statistical abstract of the United States.* Washington, DC: U.S. Government Printing Office.

University of Kansas, Center for Research on Learning. (1997–1999). *http://www.ku-crl.org/htmlfiles/lscurriculum/ls.html*

VanTassell-Baska, J., Patton, J., and Prillaman, D. (1991). *Gifted youth at risk: A report of a national study.* Reston, VA: Council for Exceptional Children.

Vygotsky, L. S. (1978). *Mind in society: The development of higher psychological processes.* Cambridge, MA: Harvard University Press.

Walker, D. (1999, October). Technology and literacy: Raising the bar. *Educational Leadership, 57U* (2), 18–21.

Watson, B., and Konicek, R. (1990). Teaching for conceptual change: Confronting children's experience. *Phi Delta Kappan, 71* (9), 680–685.

Werts, M., Wolery, M., Gast, D., and Holcombe, A. (1996). Sneak in some extra learning by using instructive feedback. *Teaching Exceptional Children, 28* (3), 70–71.

Wertsch, J. V., and Rogoff, B. (1984). Editor's notes. In B. Rogoff and J.V. Wertsch (Eds.), *Children's learning in the zone of proximal development.* San Francisco: Jossey-Bass.

Wiggins, G., McTighe, J. (1998). *Understanding by design.* Alexandria, VA: ASCD.

Wilen, W. W. (1991). *Questioning strategies for teachers.* Washington, DC: National Education Association.

Williams, W. (1997). Reliance on test scores is a conspiracy of lethargy. *The Chronicle of Higher Education, 64* (7), A60.

Willingham, W., and Cole, N. (1997). *Gender and fair assessment.* Mahweh, NJ: Erlbaum.

Willis, S. (1999, Summer). Crossing discipline lines. *Curriculum/Technology Quarterly, 8* (4), A–D.

Wood, D., Bruner, J. S., and Ross, G. (1976). The role of tutoring in problem solving. *Journal of Child Psychology and Psychiatry, 17,* 89–100.

Wood, M., and Long, N. J. (1991). *Life space crisis intervention: Talking with children and youth in crisis.* Austin, TX: Pro-Ed.

Woolfolk, A. (2001). *Educational psychology* (8th ed.). Boston: Allyn and Bacon.

Young, B., and Smith, T. (1999). *The condition of education, 1996: Issues in focus: The social context of education.* Washington, DC: U.S. Department of Education (online). *http://NCES.ed.gov/pubs/ce/c9700.html.*

Zajonic, R. B. (1980). Feeling and thinking: Preferences need no inferences. *American Psychologist, 35,* 151–175.

Zemelman, S., Daniels, H., and Hyde, A. (1998). *Best practice: New standards for teaching and learning in America's schools* (2nd ed.). Portsmouth, NH: Heinemann.

Name Index

Subject Index